Seventh Edition

The World to 1500:
A Global History

L. S. Stavrianos

PRENTICE HALL
Upper Saddle River, New Jersey 07458

Library of Congress Cataloging-in-Publication Data

STAVRIANOS, LEFTEN STAVROS.
    The world to 1500: a global history / L.S. STAVRIANOS.—7th ed.
        p.   cm.
    Includes bibliographical references (p.   ) and index.
    ISBN 0-13-923905-7 (alk. paper)
    1. History, Ancient.   2. Middle Ages—History.   I. Title.
    D57.S73   1999
    930—dc21   98-42417

Editorial director: *Charlyce Jones Owen*
Acquisitions editor: *Todd Armstrong*
Production editor: *Edie Riker*
Buyer: *Lynn Pearlman*
Marketing manager: *Sheryl Adams*
Photo editor: *Lorinda Morris-Nantz*
Photo researcher: *Beth Boyd*
Photo permissions: *Tony Arabia*
Cover director: *Jayne Conte*
Cover art: *Mappamondo Catalano (Catalan World Map).*
        Biblioteca Estense, Modena, Italy. Art Resource, New York
Editorial assistant: *Holly Jo Brown*

This book was set in 10/12 Stone Serif by East End Publishing Services
and was printed and bound by Courier Companies, Inc. The cover was
printed by The Lehigh Press, Inc.

 © 1999, 1995, 1991, 1988, 1982, 1975, 1970 by Prentice-Hall, Inc.
Simon & Schuster / A Viacom Company
Upper Saddle River, New Jersey 07458

Printed in the United States of America

10   9   8   7   6   5   4   3   2   1

ISBN   0-13-923905-7

Prentice-Hall International (UK) Limited, *London*
Prentice-Hall of Australia Pty. Limited, *Sydney*
Prentice-Hall Canada Inc., *Toronto*
Prentice-Hall Hispanoamericana, S.A., *Mexico*
Prentice-Hall of India Private Limited, *New Delhi*
Prentice-Hall of Japan, Inc., *Tokyo*
Simon & Schuster Asia Pte. Ltd., *Singapore*
Editora Prentice-Hall do Brasil, Ltda., *Rio de Janeiro*

Dedicated to Agustina Franco Serrano
with appreciation for her contribution
to the preparation of this edition

Contents

List of Maps

Photo Credits

From the Author to the Reader

Ours is a time of problems, of gigantic problems. Everything is being transformed under the magic influence of science and technology. And every day, if we want to live with open eyes, we have a problem to study, to resolve.

Pope Pius VI, May 18, 1969

WHY A TWENTY-FIRST CENTURY GLOBAL HISTORY?

Each age writes its own history. Not because the earlier history is wrong, but because each age faces new problems, asks new questions, and seeks new answers. This precept is self-evident today when the tempo of change is increasing exponentially, creating a correspondingly urgent need for new history posing new questions and offering new answers.

Our own generation, for example, was brought up on West-oriented history, and naturally so, in a West-dominated world. The nineteenth and early twentieth centuries were an era of Western hegemony in politics, in economics, and in culture. But the two World Wars and the ensuing colonial revolutions quickly ended that hegemony, as evidenced by the disappearance of the great European empires from the maps of the world. The names and the colors on those maps changed radically, reflecting the new world that had emerged by the mid-twentieth century.

Slowly and reluctantly we recognized that our traditional West-oriented history was irrelevant and misleading in this world. A new global perspective was needed to make sense of the altered circumstances. The transition from the old to the new was achieved, albeit with much soul searching and acrimony. By the 1960s the reality of the shift was evident in the emergence of the World History Association, in the appearance of the *Journal of World History*, and in the publication of the first edition of this text.

This brings us back to our original question: Why publish a new edition for the twenty-first century, only a few decades after the first edition? The answer is the same as the answer given to justify the first edition: Namely, a new world requires a correspondingly new historical approach. The postcolonial world of the 1960s necessitated a new global history. Today the equally new world of the 1990s, and of the twenty-first century, requires an equally new historical approach. The new world of the 1960s was in large part the product of the colonial revolutions. The new world of the 1990s, as Pope Pius VI noted, is the product of the "magic influence of science and technology." The pervasiveness of this influence is evident in the "gigantic problems" it has created in all aspects of our lives. For example, students of the late twentieth century doubtless remember their daily prostration under their wooden desks, probaby wondering what protection those flimsy structures could offer against nuclear bombs.

That generation of students had to face up to not only new dangers to human life, but also to unprecedented peril to the mother Earth which had given birth to that life. Oceanographer Jacques Cousteau has warned: "Mankind has probably done more damage to the Earth in the twentieth century than in all previous human history."[1] Likewise the environmental organization Worldwatch Institute concluded in 1989: "By the end of the next decade the die will pretty well be cast. As the world enters the twenty-first century, the community of nations either will have rallied and turned back the threatening trends, or environmental deterioration and social disintegration will be feeding on each other."[2]

This dismal prospect of species and planet destruction has prompted the publication of a stream of books with titles such as *End of the American Century*, *End of the World*, *End of the Future*, and *End of History*. These gloomy titles seem to be justified if we view ourselves as but one link in a long species chain. Approximately 40 million different species of plants and animals now exist on planet Earth. Beyond that, somewhere between 5 and 40 billion species have existed at one time or another. Thus only one in a thousand species is still alive, making the survival record of Earth species a 99.9 percent failure. This record seems to provide statistical support for the current popularity of "end of" books.

The statistics are misleading, however, because of a fundamental difference between the human species and all those extinct species. The latter became extinct primarily because they proved incapable of adapting to changes in their environment, as occurred, for example, during the Ice Age. *Homo sapiens*, by contrast, being endowed with superior intelligence, was able to adapt environment to its needs by mastering fire, fashioning clothes, constructing shelters, and so forth. Thus *Homo sapiens* stands out as a unique species capable of adapting environment to its needs and thereby becoming the master rather than the creature of its destiny.

The crucial difference between master and creature is currently being dramatically illustrated by the changing relationship between humans and the smallpox virus, the most universally feared of all diseases. Appearing first in the Far East at least two thousand years ago, it reached Europe in the eighth century C.E. and then spread to the Americas after Columbus. With the European dispersal over other continents, the virus decimated overseas populations lacking immunity. Hence the genocidal disaster suffered by Amerindians, Australian aborigines, and island populations in Polynesia and the Caribbean. The virus also persisted in Europe, reaching plague proportions, and ultimately carrying off one-third of the continent's population.

The taming of the virus began in 1796 when the English physician Edward Jenner discovered that a person inoculated and infected with cowpox was protected against smallpox. Today the smallpox-Homo sapiens relationship is completely reversed with a few stocks of the virus isolated in American and Russian laboratories. The last known case of smallpox was recorded in Somalia in 1977, and in 1980 the virus was declared eradicated in the wild.

Scientists have been recommending that the remaining stocks of the virus be destroyed lest it escape from storage, but a final decision has been deferred because of concern that the virus might be needed for future research. This concern has abated because scientists have been producing harmless clones of DNA fragments of smallpox and believe they now have the full genetic blueprint that will enable them to conduct research tests even if the virus itself were eliminated. In January 1996 the executive board of the United Nations World Health Organization agreed to set June 30, 1999 as the destruction date for all remaining stocks. So the killer virus, which for so long has tormented the human species, is now under lock and key, awaiting execution (and extinction) on a date set by its erstwhile victims. Thus *Homo sapiens* reigns supreme in both the animate and inanimate worlds.

"For the first time in the course of history," concludes physicist Werner Heisenberg, "man on earth faces only himself; he finds no longer any other partner or foe." The great irony of our era is that this primacy is a root cause of our current global malaise and apprehension. Having eliminated all possible rivals, we humans no longer confront any foes. We confront only ourselves.

This new confrontation with our inner self rather than with the outside world is a formidable undertaking. It requires not merely the acquisition of more knowledge and technology, an enterprise in which we have proven unequaled. It requires also the crowning of that knowledge with an ethical compass to provide it with direction and purpose. In the seventeenth century, when the scientific revolution was emerging, the English philosopher Francis Bacon noted its potentiality and warned against its perils. He enthusiastically endorsed the pursuit of "knowledge and skill" through science, but he added that the pursuit should be conducted with "humility and charity," and not "for the pleasure of mind, or for contention, or for superiority to others, or for profit or fame, or power, or any of these inferior things; but for the benefit and use of life."[3]

The degree to which we have ignored Bacon's warning against "inferior things" is painfully registered in what we see daily on our TV screens, and also in Fordham University's annual report, *The Index of Social Health*. This monitors the well-being of American society on the basis of Census Bureau statistics regarding teenage suicide, unemployment, drug abuse, high school drop-out rate, and the availability of affordable housing. The *Index* recorded a drop from 75 in 1970 to 36 in 1991, which the director of the annual report labeled "awful."

The "awful" deterioration in social health is not limited to the United States. Oceanographer Jacques Cousteau recognized this in the course of a one-day walk in Paris from 7 A.M. to 7 P.M. During his walk he had a counter, which he clicked "every time I was solicited by any kind of advertising for something I didn't need. I clicked it 183 times in all by the end of the day."

This experience is scarcely unique. It is the norm, regardless of whether one is walking in Paris or Athens or Los Angeles or Mexico City. But Cousteau, being the thoughtful scientist that he was, set out to probe the social significance of his personal experience. "It is the job of society, not of the individual person," he concluded from his probing, "to control this destructive consumerism. I am not for some kind of ecological statism. No. But when you are driving in the street and see a red light, you stop. You don't think the red light is an attempt to curb your freedom. On the contrary, you know it is there to protect you. Why not have the same thing in economics? . . . Responsibility lies with the institutions of society, not in the virtues of the individual."[4]

This conclusion, set forth in Cousteau's article entitled "Consumer Society Is the Enemy," is significant because throughout the world, consumer societies are becoming the norm. In China, for example, when Mao began his rule in 1949, the popular clamor was for the "big four" (bicycle, radio, watch, and sewing machine). Since then, consumer expectations have escalated to the "big eight," adding items such as color TV, refrigerator, and motorcycle. The list continues to lengthen, an outstanding recent addition being the automobile, which is becoming a status symbol among the billions of "have-nots" in the Third World. Between 1990 and 2000 the number of automobiles will increase in Indonesia from 272,524 to an estimated 675,000; in India from 354,393 to 1,100,000; and in China from 420,670 to 2,210,000.[5]

Environmentalists are concerned about the impact of millions of additional automobiles on the global atmosphere. Norway's former prime minister Gro Harlem Brundtland notes, however, that Western Europeans who initiated the industrial revolution and the ensuing atmospheric pollution, cannot now condemn "have-nots" to the status of "never-will-haves."[6]

These developments raise profound issues for individuals and for societies, today and in the forseeable future. So we now find ourselves at a point where we can no longer avoid facing up to fundamentals. What is the meaning of life? What is the purpose of human existence? Francis Bacon confronted this head-on when he urged that the newly emerging discipline of science be employed for the "benefit and use of life" and not for "inferior things" such as "profit, or fame, or power." Thus Bacon posed the issue squarely: must *Homo sapiens* end up as *Homo economicus*, dedicated to achieving a bloated stomach and a bloated bank account?

The first objective of every society must be to satisfy basic human needs—food, shelter, health, education—so priority must be given to improving economic efficiency until those needs are satisfied. But once they are met, should economic productivity continue to receive priority regardless of individual, social, and ecological costs? This basic question has not received the consideration it warrants, so that by default, a mindless consumerism and materialism have spread over the planet, as Cousteau discovered during his walk in Paris.

Such equivocation cannot be sustained indefinitely. Consequently *Homo sapiens* now is engaged willy-nilly in a search for an alternative to *Homo economicus*, or more precisely, for an ethical compass to direct our rampant technology. This represents a great challenge to the human species—

the greatest in its meteoric career. Hitherto it has used its superior intelligence to master its environment, leading to its current primacy on planet Earth. But with this primacy achieved, and crumbling quickly into the current worldwide social and environmental degradation, humanity is confronted now with the novel challenge of achieving transcendence from the intelligent *Homo sapiens* to the wise *Homo humanus*—in short, from intelligence to wisdom.

In the forthcoming chapters we shall see that humans are facing up to the challenges of today, as they have repeatedly and triumphantly to those of the past. Consequently the world on the eve of the twenty-first century is undergoing unprecedented social experimentation and innovation. Their extent and significance are evidenced by the recent transformations throughout the globe. In China, for example, hardened revolutionaries are groping for "a communism with a Chinese face;" in the former USSR the economist Nikolai Shmelev advises his fellow countrymen not to fear losing their "ideological virginity"[7]: and even in the dominant market economies, capitalism itself is emerging in alternative forms. These include the American variety emphasizing untrammeled free enterprise; the German and Scandinavian varieties stressing the welfare state and worker participation in decision making; and the proliferating Asian melange with varying combinations of national economic planning, huge interlinked conglomerates, lifetime jobs in large companies, and government aid to export-oriented domestic industries.

Such effervescence suggests a twenty-first century of great potentiality as well as great peril. Lacking a crystal ball, historians cannot predict the outcome with any certainty. But they can predict with reasonable assurance a twenty-first century that is neither utopian nor dystopian, but a century of possibilities. Which of these will actually be realized will be determined by the readers of these lines who will be making fateful actions and decisions in forthcoming decades.

Given these circumstances, this is not a time for self-deluding utopian fantasies, nor is it a time for gloomy foreboding. Rather it is a time for hard-headed reappraisal of existing practices and institutions, retaining what works and discarding what does not—which is precisely what is going on now throughout the world. This new edition of the text has been prepared with the hope of facilitating the reappraising process and thereby contributing to Francis Bacon's espousal of that which "benefits" life, and also to his rejection of "inferior things."

NOTES

1. *New Perspectives Quarterly* (Summer 1996), pp. 48, 49.
2. *Worldwatch Institute Reports, State of the World 1987, 1989* (W.W. Norton, 1987–1989), pp. 194, 213.
3. Cited in A. Pacey, *The Culture of Technology* (MIT Press, 1983), pp. 114–15, 178–79.
4. J. Cousteau, "Consumer Society Is the Enemy," *New Perspectives Quarterly* (Summer 1996) pp. 48, 49.
5. *New York Times*, June 6, 1996.
6. *New Perspectives Quarterly* (Spring 1989) pp. 4–8.
7. *New York Times*, June 25, 1987.

Acknowledgments

Grateful acknowledgment is made to the following authors and publishers for permission for quotation of the chapter opening epigraphs. Chapter 1, Clyde Kluckholn, *Mirror for Man* (New York: McGraw-Hill, 1949), p. 11. Chapter 2, R. J. Braidwood, "Near Eastern Prehistory," *Science* vol. 127 (June 20, 1958), 1419–30. Chapter 8, Robert Lopez, *The Birth of Europe*, © 1962 by Max Leclerc et Cie, Prop. of Librairie Armand Colin and © 1966 trans. by J. M. Dent & Sons, Ltd., and published in 1967 by M. Evans and Co., Inc., New York, by arrangement with J. M. Dent & Sons, Ltd. Chapter 9, Lynn White, Jr., "Tibet, India, and Malaya as Sources of Western Medieval Technology," *American Historical Review* XLV (April 1960), 515, 526. Chapter 12, W. C. Bark, *Origins of the Medieval World* (Stanford: Stanford University Press, 1958), p. 66. Chapter 14, Lynn White, Jr., "Technology and Invention in the Middle Ages," *Speculum*, XV (1940), 156. Chapter 17, A. J. Toynbee, *Civilization on Trial*, © 1948 by Oxford University Press, Inc. Chapter 21, Lynn White, Jr., "Technology and Invention in the Middle Ages," *Speculum*, XV (1940), 156.

PART I

Before Civilization

P art I is concerned with the 4 million years before human civilization. The other parts of this book are devoted to history since humans became civilized, less than 6,000 years ago. Thus, by far the longest phase of human evolution will receive by far the briefest consideration. The reason for the disproportionate emphasis on the story of civilized people is the constantly accelerating tempo of human history. Geologic time is measured in billions of years, and human prehistory in thousands, but since the advent of civilization, the time unit has shrunk progressively to centuries and to decades, until fateful events now daily crowd us, unceasingly and inexorably. Indeed the pace of change has reached such proportions that it is a very real question whether the human species is capable of adjusting quickly enough to avoid obsolescence, or even extinction.

The disparity in the pace of events, and the corresponding disparity in emphasis in this study, should not lead us, however, to minimize the significance of what happened during prehistory. During those millennia, two developments provided the bedrock foundation for all later history. One was the gradual transition from hominid to Homo sapiens, or thinking human being. The other was the transformation of the human newcomer from a food gatherer who was dependent on the bounty of nature to a food producer who became increasingly independent of nature—the master of its own destiny. These two epochal events—the appearance of human beings and their invention of agriculture—are the subjects of the two chapters of Part I.

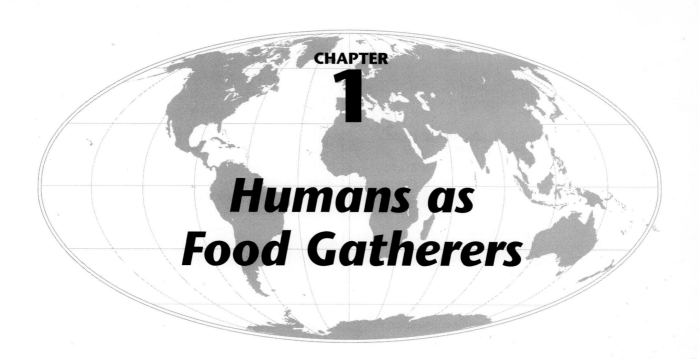

CHAPTER 1

Humans as Food Gatherers

Anthropology holds up a great mirror to man and lets him look at himself in his infinite variety.

Clyde Kluckhohn

One of the outstanding achievements of modern peoples is their study and reconstruction of the past. The ancients had little understanding of what had happened before them. Thucydides, the most objective of Greek historians, began his study of the Peloponnesian War by stating that nothing of great importance had happened before his time. His ignorance of history prevented him from recognizing the unique glory and contribution of Athens. By contrast, our age is more history-minded than any other. We know more about the early history of the Egyptians, the Greeks, or the Chinese than they themselves knew. Furthermore, knowledge of our early human ancestors is being increased every year by the findings of scientists in various fields such as geology, archeology, anthropology, paleontology, and biology. To this list of fields should be added

space technology, which is being used to survey the surface and even the subsurface of the earth from satellites, space shuttles, and airplanes. These are equipped with sensors that can measure subtle variations in temperatures on the ground. Because sand, cultivated soil, vegetation, and different types of rocks have distinctive temperatures and emit heat at different rates, the sensors can identify loose soils that had been prehistoric agricultural fields or were covering ancient caravan routes or architectural ruins. Thus radar imaging systems have been used to map the ancient intercontinental Silk Road traversing Central Asia, as well as Maya causeways in the Guatemalan jungle and footpaths along the shore of Lake Arenal in Costa Rica.

A spectacular recent example of technology enabling us to recover lost chapters of our human past is the discovery of obliterated sections of the Great Wall of China. Segments of the Great Wall have been lost for centuries under layers of shifting desert sand. These segments were brought to light by radar images taken from the space shuttle *Endeavor* in April 1994. The images disclosed a 47-mile stretch of the wall in a remote section of China 430 miles west of the capital, Beijing. In Beijing's environs, the Wall was carefully preserved through the centuries, providing photo opportunities, showing, for example, President Nixon and Chairman Mao striding atop the Wall. By contrast, the Wall was allowed to crumble in remote areas. There the Wall was not constructed with stones. Mud and branches were often substituted. Thus long segments deteriorated and disappeared from view until the recent uncovering by the wizardry of modern technology.[1]

This type of investigation and research has extended our knowledge back before the beginning of civilization, even before there were written records. This is very important, for it was only about 5,000 years ago that humans learned to write, whereas their hominid beginnings have been traced back over 4 million years. We shall consider these long prehistoric millennia when people became human. They existed, as did the other animals, by collecting food wherever it was to be found, rather than by growing it as their agriculturist descendants would learn to do.

I. FROM HOMINIDS TO HUMANS

Our globe revolves around the sun, which is one of 10 billion stars in our galaxy. This in turn is one of millions of galaxies that make up the universe. The enormity of this scale should be kept in mind while we trace through our human experiences and human concerns in the following pages. It is well to remember that in the context of the universe our planet earth is literally like a speck of dust on the Pacific Ocean.

Earth took form about 5 billion years ago, and the first life appeared on it about 4 billion years ago in the form of single-celled creatures. Although such primitive life traditionally has been viewed as qualitatively different from nonlife, scientists no longer accept this assumed dichotomy between organic and inorganic.

Rather they think of living matter as having evolved naturally from nonliving matter. They classify all matter into a hierarchy of states of organization. At a certain level in this hierarchy the transition occurs from inorganic to organic. More specifically, electrons, protons, and neutrons combine to form atoms, and the atoms form molecules. The molecules become more or less well organized aggregates, and one class of these is living matter.

Organic matter in turn went through a comparable hierarchical evolution: from the original microorganisms to primitive plants such as seaweeds, to animals without backbones (invertebrates) such as jellyfish and worms, and ultimately to animals having backbones (vertebrates). These vertebrates, with some of their invertebrate and plant cousins, began their successful adaptation to life on land about 300 million years ago. First came the amphibians, followed by the great army of prehistoric reptiles, then the birds, and finally the mammals. For the past 60 million years, mammals have been the dominant form of life on earth.

Almost all scientists accept the proposition that humans belong to the animal kingdom—more specifically to the order of Primata, which they share with the tree shrews, lemurs, tarsiers, monkeys, and apes. Evidence from several fields of study supports this conclusion. Anatomists have found basic similarities between humans and the other higher animals in the general plan of their skeletal, muscular, and organic structures. Embryologists have noted that the human embryo displays, at different stages of its development, characteristics of some of the lower forms of life, such as gill arches at the end of one month and a rudimentary tail at two months. Anthropologists have shown that human fossil remains show a consistent trend away from the general anthropoid type, or hominids, toward Homo sapiens. Other scientists have discovered many similar indications of our ties to the other animals, including close resemblance between the chemical composition of the blood of apes and of humans, possession of common parasites, and similarities in their ways of learning.

The differentiation of the human stock occurred during the Pleistocene epoch, with its six or seven glacial and five or six interglacial periods. These drastic environmental changes compelled all animals to adapt and readapt themselves continually to new conditions. Success in this crucial matter depended not on brute strength nor on the ability to resist cold but rather on the continuous growth of intelligence and the use of that intelligence to work out satisfactory adaptations. This, of course, is the secret of the unchallenged primacy of human beings on earth. Humans have been, first and foremost, generalists. They never adapted exclusively to one type of environment, as the gibbon did to the forest with its long lithe arms, or the polar bear to the arctic with its heavy white fur. Rather humans relied on their brains, not their bodies, to adapt to any environment.

The human species is the product of natural selection from a succession of humanlike ancestors, or hominids, some of which were capable of using simple stone tools and weapons. The earliest of these hominids was Australopithecus, believed to have appeared first in the savannas of eastern and southern Africa over 4 million years ago. The pelvis and leg of this hominid were strikingly similar to those of modern humans, but the cranial capacity was only about one-third that of a human, or hardly larger than that of living apes. Thus a humanlike system of walking erect on two legs rather than on all fours was combined with an apelike brain.

The African savannas were ideal for primates at that level of development. The climate was warm enough to make the lack of clothing bearable, and the open grasslands, in contrast to dense forests and deserts, afforded both water and animal foods. Thus, despite their simple tools, the Australopithecines subsisted on an adequate diet, including eggs, crabs, tortoises, birds, rodents, and young antelopes. The last were easy prey because they "freeze" in the grass when faced with danger.

Australopithecus roamed the African plains for over 2 million years, during which time several species of this hominid appeared, flourished, and disappeared. Anthropologists are not agreed on details because many new finds are made each year, and theories change with these finds. For example, recent fossil discoveries in Java challenge the traditional "out-of-Africa" theory that earliest humans originated in Africa and fanned out from there to Asia, Europe, the Americas, and Australia. The Java fossils are of such surprising antiquity that they strengthen the position of the multiregionalists who believe that early humans originated and evolved independently in many parts of the world.[2] Doubtless many more discoveries will be made in the years to come, and many more new theories about human origins will be formulated to take into account the new fossil findings.

Regardless of the exact date and exact location, human beings or Homo sapiens (thinking humans) eventually did appear, certainly by 40,000 years ago, though recent excavations indicate a much earlier date. Viewed in the broadest perspective, this development represents the second major turning point in the course of events on this planet. The first occurred when life originated out of inorganic matter. After that momentous step, all living forms evolved by adapting to their environments through mutation and natural selection. That is, the genes adapted to the environment, as was evident during the climatic upheavals of the Pleistocene. But with the appearance of humans, the evolutionary process was reversed. No longer did genes adapt to environment; instead, humans adapted by changing the environment to suit their genes. Today, a third epochal turning point appears imminent as humans' growing knowledge of the structure and function of genes may soon enable them to modify their genes as well as their environment.

Humans, and only humans, have been able to create a made-to-order environment, or culture, as it is called. The reason is that only humans can symbolize, or envision, things and concepts divorced from here-and-now reality. Only humans laugh, and only they know that they will die. Only they have wondered about the universe and its origins, about their place in it and in the hereafter.

With these unique and revolutionizing abilities, humans have been able to cope with their environment without mutations. Human culture became the new, nonbiological way of having fur in the arctic, water storage in the desert, and fins in the water. More concretely, culture consists of tools, clothing, ornaments, institutions, language, art forms, and religious beliefs and practices. All these have served to adapt humans to their physical environment and to their fellow humans. Indeed, the story of humanity as related in the following chapters is simply the story of a succession of cultures that we have created, from our Paleolithic origins to the present day.

When humans used their superior brains to change their environment to suit their genes rather than the opposite, as had been the prevailing pattern in the past, they made a quantum leap ahead of all other species on this planet. This explains why humans today are the dominant species after a modest beginning in Africa's savanna. But this raises a puzzling question. Why are humans today seemingly incapable of controlling their environment, which they themselves have created? Why are they discovering that their own homemade environment is becoming less and less fit for habitation?

The answer seems to lie in the basic difference between genetic and cultural evolution. Genetic evolution functions via gene mutations which, if favored by selection, become dominant in a population in the biologically brief period of a few thousand years. This was the evolutionary path that led through a succession of hominids from Australopithecus to Homo sapiens.

By contrast, cultural evolution, occurring through the introduction of new tools or ideas or institutions, can change and has changed societies almost overnight. Witness how steam power affected the entire globe in the nineteenth century, how the internal combustion engine did likewise in the twentieth, and how nuclear power and computers are transforming our environment today—so much so that Albert Einstein warned us that humanity now faces either new "ways of thinking" or "unparalleled catastrophe."

The key problem appears to be the time lag between technological change and the social change it necessitates. The reason for the lag is that technological change usually is welcomed and quickly adopted because it improves productivity and living standards, whereas social change is commonly resisted because it requires self-appraisal and adaptation, which are threatening and uncomfortable. This explains today's paradox of humans' acquiring more and more knowledge, and being more and more able to

Venus of Willendorf, a stone figure dating between 15,000 and 10,000 B.C.E. Because of the proportions of this figure, it can be considered a manifestation of early fertility cults.

great statement

change their environment as they wish, yet their not being able to change their environment to make it more livable. In short, our problem as a species is to balance our ever-expanding knowledge with wisdom in how we use that knowledge. We shall see in the following chapters that learning how to balance knowledge and wisdom is becoming so urgent that, as Einstein has warned us, our future as a species depends on the outcome.

We shall see that this problem of balance has risen repeatedly throughout human history and is rising today more frequently and urgently as our knowledge is growing with ever-increasing speed, and our wisdom failing to keep up.

II. LIFE OF THE FOOD GATHERERS

Homo sapiens with their superior intelligence developed the so-called "blade technique." They used the long, sharp flakes, or "blades," struck off the core of a stone to fashion a variety of new tools as well as "tools to make tools." Some of the new tools were composites of different materials, such as spears with hafted heads of bone, antler, or flint, and flint blades set in bone or wooden handles. Another departure was the construction of projectiles such as the bola, sling, spear thrower, and bow and arrow. The latter must have been relatively inefficient at first, but it was gradually improved until it became the most formidable weapon prior to modern firearms. Other inventions of the upper Paleolithic included bone and ivory bodkins, bone needles with eyes, belt fasteners, and even buttons—all of which indicate that Magdalenian hunters wore sewn skin garments with fitted sleeves and trousers.

Although this late Paleolithic technology was advanced compared to that of the early Paleolithic a million years before, it still was primitive in the sense that productivity was low. Food gatherers had no formal political structure with full-time political leaders. Rather they formed autonomous bands that usually numbered twenty to fifty persons. Larger groups were possible, and some did exist in areas that yielded plentiful food supplies, such as the American Northwest, with its inexhaustible salmon runs, and the Dordogne valley in southern France, with its great reindeer herds in Magdalenian times. Judging from contemporary hunting societies, authority in Paleolithic times was rigidly limited and lacked an established and recognized power to control people. Leaders arose naturally for specific purposes; an old man might be the accepted planner of ceremonies because of his ritual knowledge, whereas a young person with proven skill in the chase might take the lead in hunting parties. But the important point is that all such leaders were persons of influence rather than authority since there were no institutions for imposing one's will upon others.

Social organization necessarily was as simple as political organization, if indeed the two can be distinguished at this stage. The basic unit was the family, consisting of the parents and their immature and unmarried children. Extra wives usually were permitted, but in practice polygamy was rare. Relations between the sexes were more equal during the Paleolithic millennia than at any time since. The chief reason seems to have been that women contributed to the food supply of the band as much as did the men, if not more so. Consequently for most of human history there was none of the dependence and inferior status that is commonly associated today with the "weaker" female sex.

From a study of ninety food-gathering bands surviving to the present, anthropologists have found that the men hunt animals and provide meat, whereas the women gather everything they can find around their camp—roots, berries, nuts, fruits, vegetables, insects, lizards, snakes, rodents, shellfish, and so forth. Although the meat the men bring in is highly prized, the fact is that what the women collect is the main part of the diet. The women usually gather twice as much food as the men are able to hunt and kill and bring back to the camp. Thus the sexes have different tasks, but these tasks are equally important. Food-gathering women not only bear the children and rear them but also provide most of the food.

It is true that the men were responsible for the defense of the band and had control over the weapons, but they did not use the weapons against the women to intimidate and subjugate them. In fact, when Europeans first came into contact with food-hunting peoples in overseas lands, they usually were surprised and shocked by the equality that food-gathering women enjoyed compared to European women. The Jesuit missionary Paul le Jeune spent the winter of 1633–1634 with a band of Montagnais-Naskapi Indians on the Labrador Peninsula of eastern Canada. "The women have great power here," le Jeune reported, and he urged the Indian men to assert themselves. "I told him that he was the master, and that in France women do not rule their husbands." Another Jesuit father reported, "The choice of plans, of undertakings, of journeys, of winterings, lies in nearly every instance in the hands of the housewife." It is significant that anthropologist Eleanor Leacock

A Stone Age Saharan rock painting, the Fresco of Tassili n'Ajjer, Algeria. One scholar believes this strikingly beautiful painting represents women gathering grain (represented by the dots, presumably). If so, it would have likely been wild grain unless cereal crops were cultivated very early here—something for which we have no evidence. Whether gathering grain or engaged in graceful dance, the figures here remind us of the ancient human presence in the once-green Saharan regions.

found the same quality in sex relations among the Montagnais-Naskapi when she studied them in 1950–1951. "It was beautiful to see the sense of group responsibility . . . and the sense of easy autonomy in relationships unburdened by centuries of training in deferential behavior by sex and status."[3]

Not only was there sex equality among the food gatherers but there were also strong kinship ties. Each person had duties toward the other tribal members and in turn enjoyed rights and privileges. All helped each other in the quest for food and in providing shelter from the elements and defense from their enemies. Some fighting between tribal groups arose from personal feuds and from competition for hunting and fishing grounds. But Paleolithic society lacked both the manpower and the resources essential for large-scale warfare, which did not become possible until the rise of agriculture, with its greatly increased productivity and correspondingly increased population. In short, the essence of Paleolithic social organization was cooperation. Families and bands were primarily mutual-aid societies working together in the harsh struggle for existence.

After observing the daily life of food gatherers in various parts of the world, anthropolo-

Detail from American Museum of Natural History representation of a Neolithic village in Denmark, about 2700 B.C.E. Note the variety of occupations: hunter, wood-gatherer, fire tender, grain-grinder, potter, and weaver.

gist R. B. Lee concludes: "A truly communal life is often dismissed as a utopian ideal, to be endorsed in theory but unattainable in practice. But the evidence for foraging peoples tells us otherwise. A sharing way of life is not only possible but has actually existed in many parts of the world and over long periods of time."[4]

Anthropologists recently have focused on the diets as well as the social institutions of our prehistoric ancestors, especially because what they ate seems to hold lessons for us today. What people ate thousands of years ago can be determined in two ways. One is by examining coprolites, or fossilized feces. They reveal many things, such as pollen, plant crystals, feathers, bones, hair, and eggshells, so a coprolite provides a capsule record of what passed through a person's digestive tract millennia ago. The other way to determine the diets of our food-gathering ancestors is to observe what present-day food gatherers eat, whether they be the aborigines of Australia or the !Kung of South Africa's Kalahari

desert. Such observation has revealed that present-day food gatherers have a surprisingly abundant and reliable food supply, even though they are living on undesirable lands that nobody else wanted. One reason for the plentiful food is that the food gatherers have an extraordinary knowledge of their home territory and all its plant and animal life. They cannot read or write, but they can learn and remember. The !Kung, for example, remember so much that they are now using some 500 different types of plants and animals as food and for medical, cosmetic, toxic, and other purposes. Among the insects they eat and enjoy are beetle grubs, caterpillars, bee larvae, termites, ants, and cicadas. Because of our customs, we do not consider most of these as food, yet they are nutritious. Termites, for example, are 45 percent protein, an even higher proportion than in dried fish.

The great number of foods that the food gatherers are willing to eat provides a valuable life insurance for them. Depending on a multitude of different plants and animals for their food supply, they are better off in this regard than agriculturists who grow only a few crops, and who are in danger of starvation if those crops fail because of drought, flood, frost, or pests. The food gatherers run no such danger; if they find some plants or animals in short supply, they are certain to make up the lack with the hundreds of others that they know they can find. For example, anthropologists who were studying the !Kung in the summer of 1964 noted that a serious drought that summer was hurting the neighboring Bantu farmers. Their crops had failed and their families were starving. So the Bantu women joined the !Kung women when they started out on their daily expeditions in search of roots, greens, berries, nuts, birds, eggs, and so forth. There was no shortage of these hundreds of different foodstuffs, so the Bantu as well as the !Kung families survived easily despite the drought.

The food supply of !Kung and other gatherers is not only abundant but also healthy. It is low in salt, saturated fats, and carbohydrates, and high in polyunsaturated oils, roughage, vitamins, and minerals. This diet, together with the active life they lead as nomads, explains why few food gatherers suffer from the diseases common in industrialized societies—medical problems such as high blood pressure, obesity, varicose veins, ulcers, and colitis. On the other hand, many !Kung die from accidental injuries that cannot be treated because of the lack of doctors and hospitals. So scientists find that about one-tenth of the !Kung population is over sixty years of age, which is roughly the same percentage as in industrialized countries where doctors and hospitals are readily available.

The above conclusions about prehistoric diet have been tested by the anthropologist Vaughn M. Bryant, Jr., of Texas A&M University. While doing fieldwork in an archeological dig in southwest Texas, he switched his diet to that of the prehistoric people of that region—a diet that he knew well from his coprolite research. Pleased with the results of the new diet, he continued it after returning to his campus. He also added exercise to his daily routine in order to approximate the rigors of prehistoric life. He rode his bike to school, climbed stairs instead of taking elevators, and walked across the campus instead of driving. Since changing to his new way of life, he reports:

I've felt much better, both physically and mentally. I just have more energy than I used to. . . . I haven't had a serious illness in the past four years. I haven't missed a day of work. . . . In three months or so, I lost 30 pounds . . . without counting calories and without having to go hungry. . . . Those fruits and vegetables are so low in calories. . . . I think snacking helped, too. It seems when you snack all day you eat less than if you sit down and gorge yourself at three meals. . . . When you think about it, there's nothing weird about this diet. I think we were designed by nature to eat foods similar to what primates—the great apes—generally eat: fruits and other plant foods, a little meat, a lot of complex carbohydrates and fiber, and not very much fat. Until just a few thousand years ago, everyone probably ate the way I do.[5]

Turning our discussion from social institutions and practices to general beliefs, we find that primitive humans were basically ahistorical and nonevolutionary in their attitudes toward themselves and their society. They assumed that the future would be identical to the present, as the present was to the past. Consequently there was no notion of change, and hence no inclination to criticize or to tamper with existing institutions and practices. To their way of thinking, everything, including themselves, their culture, and their habitat, had appeared with the creation and was destined to continue unaltered into the future. The creation myths of hunting peoples are strikingly similar, involving heroes who fashioned the landscape, stocked it with game, brought forth the people, and taught them the arts and their customs.

The following origin myth of the Andaman islanders is fairly typical:

The first man was Jutpu. He was born inside the joint of a big bamboo, just like a bird in an egg. The bamboo split and he came out. He was a little child. When it rained he made a small hut for himself and lived in it. He made little bows and arrows. One day he found a lump of quartz and with it he sacrificed himself. Jutpu was lonely, living all by himself. He took some clay (kot) from a nest of the white ants and moulded it into the shape of a woman. She became alive and became his wife. She was called Kot. They lived together at Teraut-buliu. Afterwards Jutpu made other people out of clay. These were the ancestors. Jutpu taught them how to make canoes and bows and arrows, and how to hunt and fish. His wife taught the women how to make baskets and nets and mats and belts, and how to use clay for making patterns on the body.[6]

Primitive humans were very knowledgeable concerning nature. They had to be, for their very existence depended on it. Their knowledge was passed on orally from generation to generation, and much of it is only now being recognized and utilized. An example is the manifold uses of India's neem tree, a fast-growing evergreen. For millenia it has been prominent in village culture and in ancient texts. Its bark, leaves, flowers, seeds, and fruit were used to treat diseases ranging from diabetes to ulcers and constipation. Neem twigs were used as an antiseptic toothbrush, and its oil is now used in the preparation of toothpaste and soap. Neem extract also is a potent insecticide, effective against two hundred insects, including locusts, mosquito larvae, and boll weevils.

Despite their abundant first-hand contact with and knowledge of nature, early humans had little explanatory knowledge; they could give no naturalistic explanation if floods or droughts came or if the hunting or fishing was poor. Not knowing how to cope with nature by naturalistic means, they had to resort to the supernatural. They turned to magic and spent much time in efforts to persuade or fool nature into yielding a greater abundance. By making each useful animal or plant the totem of a particular group, and by using images, symbols, and imitative dances, primitive people believed that the animal or food could be encouraged to flourish and multiply. As long as the rules of the totems were strictly observed, the reproduction of the group and of its food supply could be assured.

All group members seem to have participated at first in the ritual ceremonies, but toward the end of the Paleolithic, part-time specialists in the form of medicine men or shamans seem to have appeared. These people were thought to have peculiar relations with the forces that were supposed to control those parts of the universe or environment that mattered—primarily food and fertility but also health and personal luck. More and more, as they were relieved from the full-time work of food and tool production, they used their magical arts for the common good. Shamans are still found today in nearly every surviving food-gathering culture, including those of the Bushmen, the Eskimos, and the Australian aborigines. The earliest pictorial representation of these shamans is the "Sorcerer" of the cave of Trois-Frères in France. This "terrible masterpiece," as it has been called, is a Paleolithic painting of a man clad in a deerskin, with the horns of a stag, the face of an owl, the ears of a wolf, the arms of a bear, and the tail of a horse. Other nearby paintings suggest that the cave was a meeting place where a sorcerer invoked animal spirits for success in the hunt and worked up his audience to the emotional pitch necessary to face danger.

Paleolithic technology, however, was not productive enough to support anything approaching a hierarchy of priests, so no cohesive theology could be developed. Conceptions of gods and spirits were hazy, and much emphasis was placed on individual visions. Religion was not used as a method of social control. Benefits did not depend on the morality of the individual. People begged or bargained with the supernatural, as we can see from the following statement made by an Eskimo to the Arctic explorer Knud Rasmussen:

We believe our Angakut, our magicians, and we believe them because we wish to live long, and because we do not want to expose ourselves to the danger of famine and starvation. We believe, in order to make our lives and food secure. If we do not believe the magicians, the animals we hunt would make themselves invisible to us; if we did not follow their advice, we should fall ill and die.[7]

Fear of what couldn't be understood and the desire to bring the supernatural under human control were expressed in art as well as religion. By far the outstanding example of Paleolithic art consists of its extraordinary cave paintings, the best of which are located in southern France and northwestern Spain. The

Two prehistoric cave paintings from France.

subjects of the drawings are usually the larger game: bison, bear, horse, woolly rhinoceros, mammoth, and wild boar. The best of the drawings are in full color, remarkably alive, and charged with energy. Despite their extraordinary artistic quality, the cave drawings apparently were designed for utilitarian reasons. They were drawn in the darkest and most dangerous parts of the caves, although the people lived only in or near the cave entrances. The artists also commonly painted one picture over another, with no apparent desire to preserve their works. Hence it appears that the reason these Paleolithic artists made their way to the depths of the earth and created the most realistic reproductions possible of the animals they hunted was the belief that they thereby gained some sort of magic power over their game.

In conclusion, the recent findings of scientists in various fields have led us to recognize and appreciate the achievements of our prehistoric ancestors as constituting a major and decisive element in our total human heritage. Even in the realm of technology, where we consider ourselves today to be especially successful, the hunter-gatherers acquired a vast amount of data that is basic for us to the very present. They knew their habitats intimately, so they used those species of plants and animals that were beneficial and avoided those that were useless or injurious. They developed a great variety of tools including knives, axes, scrapers, hammers, awls, and needles. They also created an equal variety of weapons such as spears, harpoons, clubs, shields, armor, blowguns, and bows and arrows. Some of their inventions—such as the nonsubmersible kayak, the snowhouse, and the outrigger canoe—and the use of numerous poisons—such as hydrocyanic acid, which South American Indians learned to remove from a species of manioc which became a staple article of their diet, and other poisons such as curare, snake venoms, hemlock, and alkaloids that were used to kill game and human enemies—required considerable knowledge and skill. In preparing and preserving foods, our early ancestors used virtually all the techniques known to us today. They had earth ovens, they practiced stone boiling, they froze food in the arctic, they preserved it by drying, and they sealed foods airtight with tallow. Apart from recent inventions such as plastic containers and the harnessing of gas and electricity, Paleolithic cooks would have felt at home with modern kitchens and cuisines.

In coping with illnesses, prehistoric peoples were by no means wholly dependent on magic. They knew how to set broken bones with splints, to use tourniquets, to employ poultices and bandages, to use steam baths and massage, to practice bloodletting as therapy, and to administer enemas (which South American tribes did with rubber syringes). Preliterate peoples also had knowledge of heavenly bodies, distinguishing and naming constellations of stars. Finally, oceanic navigation was achieved in prehistoric times by the Polynesians, who made regular voyages between Hawaii and Tahiti, a distance of 2,350 miles. After reviewing these achievements in all phases of life, anthropologist Leslie A. White concludes: "The accumulated knowledge, skills, tools, machines, and techniques developed by primitive, preliterate peoples laid the basis for civilization and all the higher cultures. . . . It is indeed remarkable to see how close to the present day, primitive peoples have come at many points on the technological level."[8]

As impressive and significant as Paleolithic technology was the Paleolithic society. The everyday life of our prehistoric ancestors was in many ways very attractive. Its members were equal with one another. Warm bonds of kinship permeated and determined their social relationships. Paleolithic life offered everyone specific and accepted obligations and rewards. There was no problem of alienation or of anxiety in the face of an uncertain or unpredictable future. To the present day, an Australian aborigine can take a piece of broken glass, fashion it skillfully into an arrowhead or spear point, fit it to a spear thrower or to a bow that he has strung himself, set forth and kill his game, prepare his dinner with due attention to ceremony, and after dinner, round out the day with storytelling, sharing his adventures with the stay-at-homes. In this manner the Paleolithic hunter was a "complete man" to a degree that has not been approached since the agricultural revolution.

But the bonds that held Paleolithic society together were restricting as well as comforting. The individual was wholly subordinate to the band or tribe, which was viewed as a timeless procession of the dead, the living, and the unborn, attended by all the unseen powers of the spirit world. To this procession of life the individual was completely subject. Doubtless the overwhelming majority of individuals felt themselves to be participants rather than captives. Yet the fact remains that the result was stagnation along with security. Although the Paleolithic way of life was psychically satisfying, it was also a dead-end street. Sometimes deviance from tradition actually ended in death—for example, among the Arunta of Australia, whose elders arranged with the enemy to kill those individuals who had not been living in accordance with tribal tradition. It was this stultifying and constraining tradition that was the all-important other side of Paleolithic society.

Not only were some Paleolithic nonconformists killed, but so were the infants and the infirm in case of food shortage. The food gatherers had to move perpetually because sooner or later they exhausted the food supplies in the vicinity of their camp. This inescapable mobility forced them to prune ruthlessly their material

possessions. It also forced them on certain occasions to prune equally ruthlessly some of their band members—the infants, the aged, and the infirm. A food-gathering mother obviously could carry only one infant at a time. A second born before the first had been weaned had to be killed at birth, as were also all but one infant in cases of multiple birth. Only a few food gatherers could support themselves in a given area.

THE LIFE OF THE FOOD GATHERERS

We may assume that the style of human life during the Paleolithic millennia was basically the same as that of the food gatherers that fifteenth- and sixteenth-century Europeans discovered in the New World. The accounts left by the explorers, and by the settlers and missionaries who followed them, are valuable in giving us a glimpse into our common human past. The following report is by the Jesuit father Jacob Baegert, who lived between 1750 and 1767 among the Indians of California.* His description of the "Californians" gives us a picture of Paleolithic ancestors, and also challenges common assumptions about "human nature."

With all their poor diet and hardships, the Californians are seldom sick. They are in general strong, hardy, and much more healthier than the many thousands who live daily in abundance and on the choicest fare that the skill of Parisian cooks can prepare. . . .

For the small-pox the Californians are, like other Americans, indebted to Europeans, and this disease assumes a most pestilential character among them. A piece of cloth which a Spaniard, just recovered from the smallpox, had given to a Californian communicated, in the year 1763, the disease to a small mission, and in three months more than a hundred individuals died. . . .

From what I have already said of the Californians, it might be inferred that they are the most unhappy and pitiable of the children of Adam. Yet such a supposition would be utterly wrong, and I can assure the reader that . . . they live unquestionably much happier than the civilized inhabitants of

Europe. . . . Throughout the whole year nothing happens that causes a Californian trouble or vexation, nothing that renders his life cumbersome and death desirable. . . . Envy, jealousy, and slander embitter not his life, and he is not exposed to the fear of losing what he possesses, nor to the care of increasing it . . . the Californians do not know the meaning of meum [mine] and tuum [thine], those two ideas which, according to St. Gregory, fill the few days of our existence with bitterness and unaccountable evils.

Though the Californians seem to possess nothing, they have, nevertheless, all that they want, for they covet nothing beyond the productions of their poor, ill-favored country, and these are always within their reach. It is no wonder, then, that they always exhibit a joyful temper, and constantly indulge in merriment and laughter, showing thus their contentment, which, after all, is the real source of happiness.

*Smithsonian Institution, *Annual Report for 1863* (Washington, D.C., 1864), pp. 352–369.

Consequently they were easily swept aside when the agricultural revolution made possible the sustenance of relatively large numbers of food producers, or peasants, who spread irresistibly into the sparsely populated hunting grounds. This fact explains why food-gathering bands were inevitably doomed once the agricultural revolution got under way, and why today only a few such bands survive in out-of-the-way places where agriculture is not feasible for one reason or another.

We shall see that the agricultural revolution also set off a chain reaction of urbanization, class differentiation, and social cleavage that undermined the appealing equality of primitive society. But in doing so it also broke the restricting bonds of tribal traditionalism and thereby launched humanity, for good or ill, on the fateful course that was to lead from hunting ground to megalopolis, from human muscle to atomic power. Before turning to the agricultural revolution, however, it is necessary to consider the global spread of Paleolithic peoples and the ensuing repercussions this dispersal created, affecting us to the present day.

III. APPEARANCE OF RACES

It is commonly assumed that population explosion is a phenomenon peculiar to our times, but this is not so. Spectacular population spurts have occurred with each major technological breakthrough in history, and for the obvious reason that an advance in technology leads to increased productivity, which can support a larger number of people. By human standards of the time, the differential between early and late Paleolithic technology did represent a major advance. This in turn led to a population jump from an estimated 125,000 hominids in the early Paleolithic to 5.32 million Homo sapiens at the end of the Paleolithic 10,000 years ago, on the eve of the agricultural revolution. This increase of over forty-two times is thus comparable to the population explosions that, as we shall see, were to accompany each of the later technological revolutions.

Another demographic pattern set at this time and repeated in the future was the disproportionate increase of any population that took the lead in technological innovation, and hence the spread of that population over larger areas. This pattern has prevailed since the first appearance of life on earth, in accordance with the Law of Cultural Dominance propounded as follows by the anthropologists M. D. Sahlins and E. R. Service:

. . . that cultural system which more effectively exploits the energy resources of a given environment will tend to spread in that environment at the expense of less effective systems. . . . Higher forms characteristically exploit more different kinds of resources more effectively than lower; hence in most environments they are more effective than lower; thus their greater range.[9]

At all times, the best-adapted species, or that which is most efficiently exploiting the physical environment, is the species that has prevailed and extended its domain. Thus the Australopithecines, with their primitive pebble tools and lack of clothing, were unable to extend their range beyond the warm savanna lands. Homo sapiens, with more advanced technology and correspondingly more efficient adaptation, were able to push north into the Siberian tundra as well as south into the African and Southeast Asian tropical rain forests.

Part of the superior human technology was the construction of various devices for crossing bodies of water. Depending on local natural resources, these devices were of four basic types: skin boat, bark boat, raft, and dugout. With this variety of boats, early humans were able to cross rivers and lakes and even the wider expanses of water from Africa to Europe, from Southeast Asia to Australia, and from Siberia to North America. This spreading out was greatly helped by the Ice Age, which sucked the ocean waters up into the ice caps, thus lowering the level of the oceans and creating land bridges between continents. Under these circumstances, humans occupied all continents except Antarctica. They became, together with their inseparable dog, the most widespread animal in the world. (See map of Early Human Migrations, p. 16.)

Hand in hand with the dispersal of Homo sapiens went race differentiation. A variety of so-called races appeared, with distinguishing characteristics in skin color, hair texture, and facial

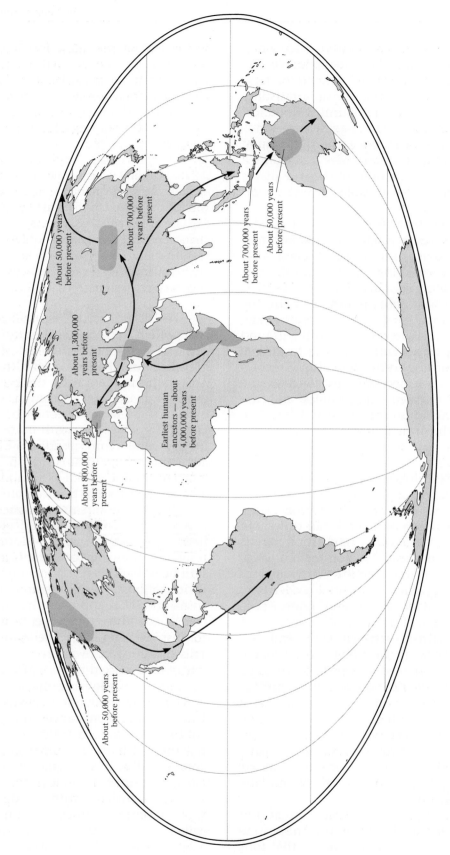

Early Human Migrations

About 50,000 years before present

About 700,000 years before present

About 1,300,000 years before present

About 800,000 years before present

Earliest human ancestors — about 4,000,000 years before present

About 700,000 years before present

About 50,000 years before present

About 50,000 years before present

structure. These races are believed to have emerged because of the relative isolation of the various human populations and their adaptation to differing local environments. The significant point concerning this differentiation within the human species is that it occurred so late—well after the emergence of Homo sapiens. All modern races, then, stem from a common stock, and after it had attained its full human development. This explains why the Europeans were able to interbreed with all the races in the lands they discovered. It also explains why, as virtually all anthropologists agree, there are no significant differences in innate mental capacity among all races. Representatives of late Paleolithic or of the contemporary Australian aborigines would stand as much chance of graduating from a university as would representatives of any other living races.

The details about how the races appeared in various regions are not known and probably never will be. Archeologists have long accepted the "out-of-Africa" theory about human origins, which holds that humans appeared first in Africa, whence they migrated to other continents. This theory, along with others, is being questioned because of discoveries being made virtually every year in new excavations throughout the world. For example, stone tools recently found in northern Australia indicate human settlements in that region as early as 176,000 years ago, which undermines past theories that dated earliest immigrations at 50,000 to 60,000 years ago. Equally disparate are past theories about the date of early migrations to Central Asia, compared to much older bones and stone tools recently found there in caves.

So great and numerous are the disparities disclosed by ongoing excavations that archeologists now are reassessing cherished past assumptions. Some are asking whether the original human birthplace was in Africa or in Asia. Others, known as multiregionalists, believe the cradle of the human race will never be found because a single source for all humans does not exist anywhere. Rather they find more plausible the theory of multiple origins for the human species at different places.

Despite the present uncertainty about human origins and evolution, we do know that by the end of the latest Ice Age, about 10,000 years ago, the global distribution of races was beginning to be the same as today. The Caucasoids occupied Europe, North and East Africa, and the Middle East, extending into India and central Asia. The Negroids were in the Sahara (better watered then) and a bit southward, whereas the Pygmies and Bushmen, in contrast to later times, occupied the remainder of Africa. Other Pygmies, the Negritos, lived in the forests of India and Southeast Asia, while in the open country of these regions and in Australia were the Australoids. Finally in East Asia and the Americas were the Mongoloids.

Although that racial pattern is vaguely similar to today's, the map of Global Race Distribution (p. 18) shows that basic changes had occurred by 1000 C.E. and still more by today. These changes, as we shall note later, came as a direct result of later technological revolutions. It was the failure to keep up with these revolutions that explains the virtual disappearance of the Bushmen and Pygmies and Australoids, as well as the swamping of the American Indians in most of the New World. Put in other words, it explains why 10,000 years ago blonds probably were no more numerous than Bushmen, whereas today there are 100,000 blonds for every living Bushman.

The very different experiences of the Bushmen, compared with those of the Caucasoids or other races, had nothing to do with differences in ability. We will return to this important point at the end of Part IV, "Races in History," where we shall consider the reasons for the varied racial experiences.

In conclusion, it is noteworthy that while humans were dividing into various races, they were also growing in height. Whereas our early ancestors reached an average height of four feet, six inches, today our average is five feet, ten inches. This growth is believed to be due to abundant and reliable food supplies, especially animal protein, and to immunization during childhood, which has curbed growth inhibiting diseases. The body growth has continued through modern times, as evident in the size of the body armor of medieval knights, into which most adult males today would be unable to squeeze.

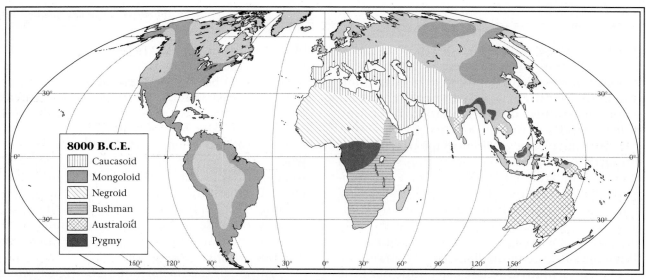

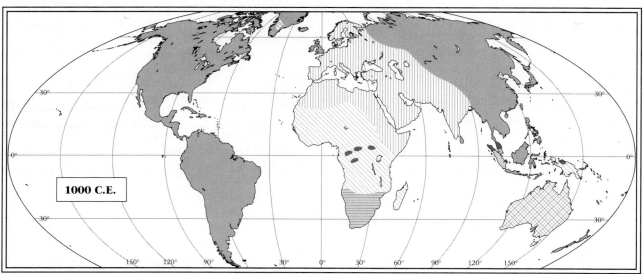

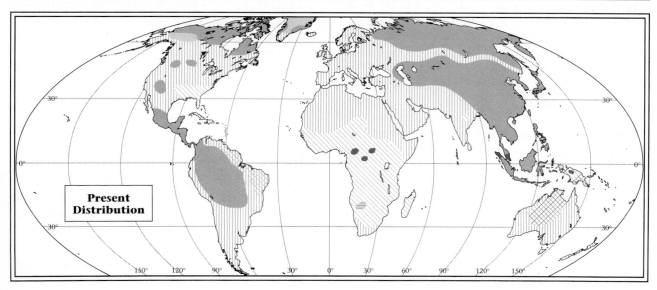

Global Race Distribution

SUGGESTED READINGS

Essential aids for the study of world history are G. Barraclough, *The Times Atlas of World History* (Times Books, 1991); W. L. Langer, *An Encyclopedia of World History* (Houghton Mifflin, 1972), and the superbly illustrated *National Geographic Atlas of World History* (Washington, 1997).

Important recent books on early human history are by J. E. Pfeiffer, *The Emergence of Man* (Harper & Row, 1985); R. Lewin, *In the Age of Mankind* (Smithsonian Book, 1988), presents current theories about prehistory and human prospects today; and M. Wolpoff and R. Caspari, *Race and Human Evolution* (Simon & Schuster, 1997), which deals with the Afrocentric-multicentric controversy. The most recent and colorful survey of human origins, with superb illustrations, is by R. Gore, "The Dawn of Humans," *National Geographic* (May 1977).

For the status of Paleolithic women, see M. Ehrenberg, *Women in Prehistory* (British Museum, 1989); R. R. Reiter, ed., *Toward an Anthropology of Women* (Monthly Review Press, 1975); M. K. Martin and B. Voorhies, *Female of the Species* (Columbia University, 1975); and R. Bridenthal and C. Koonz, eds., *Becoming Visible: Women in European History* (Houghton Mifflin, 1977).

NOTES

1. *New York Times*, April 23, 1996.
2. C. C. Swisher et al., "Latest Homo erectus of Java," *Science* (December 13, 1996): 1870–1874; *New York Times*, December 13, 1996.
3. Cited by E. Leacock, "Women in Egalitarian Societies," in R. Bridenthal and C. Koonz, eds., *Becoming Visible: Women in European History* (Houghton Mifflin, 1977), pp. 21, 22.
4. B. Spencer, *Native Tribes of the Northern Territory of Australia* (London, 1914), p. 36; and R. B. Lee, *The !Kung San* (Cambridge University, 1979), p. 246.
5. V. M. Bryant, Jr., "I Put Myself on a Caveman Diet Permanently," *Prevention*, Vol. 3 (September 1979), pp. 128–137. More details on this subject can be found in Bryant's articles in *Scientific American*, Vol. 232 (January 1975); and in *American Antiquity*, Vol. 39, No. 3 (1974).
6. A. R. Radcliffe-Brown, *The Andaman Islanders* (Free Press, 1948), p. 192.
7. K. Rasmussen, *People of the Polar North* (Lippincott, 1980), p. 124.
8. L. A. White, *The Evolution of Culture: The Development of Civilization to the Fall of Rome* (McGraw-Hill, 1959), pp. 271, 272.
9. M. D. Sahlins and E. R. Service, eds., *Evolution and Culture* (University of Michigan, 1960), pp. 75, 79.

2

Humans as Food Growers

It is probably very difficult for us now to conceptualize fully (or to exaggerate) the consequences of the first appearance of effective food production. The whole range of human existence, from the biological (including diet, demography, disease, and so on) through the cultural (social organization, politics, religion, esthetics, and so forth) bands of the spectrum took on completely new dimensions.

Robert J. Braidwood

During Paleolithic times humans became "human" by learning to speak, to make tools, and to use fire. These advances gave them an enormous advantage over the other animals about them, and yet in one fundamental respect humans remained akin to animals: They were still hunters among other hunters. They were still food gatherers, as were countless other species that were completely dependent on the bounty of nature. And being dependent on nature, humans were dominated by nature. They had to be constantly on the move in order to follow animals and to locate berry patches or fishing grounds. They had to live in small groups or bands because not many could find enough food to support themselves in a given area. It is estimated that even in fertile areas with mild winters only one or two food collectors could support themselves per square mile. And as much as twenty or even thirty square miles were needed for each individual in regions of cold climate, tropical jungle, or desert.

The shift from being food gatherers to being food producers changed every aspect of human life. Why the shift was made and what its results were are the subjects of this chapter.

I. ORIGINS OF AGRICULTURE

When humans became food producers a new world with limitless horizons opened before them. They left behind them the Paleolithic (old stone) age and entered the Neolithic (new stone) age.

Neolithic humans differed from their Paleolithic predecessors in two respects: They made stone tools by grinding and polishing rather than by chipping and fracturing; and, even more important, they obtained food wholly or primarily from agriculture and/or stock raising rather than from hunting animals or gathering plants. The new cutting tools made of ground stone were more durable than earlier tools and facilitated important inventions like the plow and the wheel, which appeared toward the end of the Neolithic period. But still, the trick of grinding a chipped or hewn axe to a smooth, polished edge was a rather trivial matter compared to the transformation of humans from food collectors to food producers.

This transformation was not the result of sudden inspiration. It was not a case of some prehistoric Archimedes shouting "Eureka!" as he suddenly realized how plants grow. People actually understood the mechanics of plant growth before the agricultural revolution, just as they knew before Columbus's voyage that the earth was round—and just as modern hunting societies that are wholly without agriculture are nevertheless thoroughly familiar with the nature and behavior of plants in their habitats. They know that plants sprout from seeds, that they usually need water and sunshine to flourish, and that they grow better in one type of soil than in another. Such knowledge is acquired naturally by modern primitives because their very existence depends on practical understanding of the surrounding flora and fauna. There is no reason for doubting, and plenty of evidence for believing, that prehistoric people acquired the same practical understanding when they were in similar circumstances.

If the basic principles of plant life were known to humans thousands of years before the agricultural revolution, why did they delay so long before putting them into practice? One reason is that there was no incentive to do so. Hunting peoples did not normally live on the brink of starvation. Nor did they increase rapidly in numbers and outstrip the available food supply. Being nomads, they were always on the move and, therefore, could not have large families. Mothers had to breast-feed each of their babies because they did not have farm animals to provide milk. If a new baby was born too soon after the previous birth, the mother had to let it die because she could not breast-feed and carry two infants at one time from camp to camp. Usually mothers were spared the tragedy of infanticide because breast-feeding tends to suppress ovulation, so mothers did not normally become pregnant during the several years they fed each baby. If this natural form of birth control failed, then our ancestors resorted to such practices as infanticide, abortion, and lactation taboos, which kept their numbers low enough to pull through the lean months of each year. Thus hunting societies continued to exist for millennia at a comfortable equilibrium and consequently lacked stimulus for radical change.

Not only did the hunters under normal circumstances have plenty to eat, but also they had a rich variety of food. The Bushmen of South Africa provide a modern example. Although these hunters live in an unfavorable desert environment, they nevertheless collect food from 85 edible plant species and 223 animal species. Thus their diet is much richer in vitamins, minerals, and protein than that of peasants who rely on the few types of grains or tubers they grow. Historically, hunters also had a more dependable supply of food because they could draw on such a large number of plants and animals. By contrast, peasants always faced the danger of starvation if bad weather spoiled their crops.

Not only did hunters have a better and more dependable food supply than food-growing peasants, but in addition they had to work less for their food. Again, adult Bushmen living in a harsh desert spend an average of only fifteen hours per week hunting or collecting food. This is little more than two hours a day. It is not surprising, then, that Bushmen are exceptionally healthy, with 10 percent of their adults being over sixty years of age. Aiding their good health is their nomadic way of life. Since they are always on the move, they avoid diseases that develop from unsanitary conditions, such as from the human excreta and garbage that collect in the villages where peasants spend their lives.

For all these reasons, hunters did not shift to agriculture until 10,000 years ago, even though they knew much earlier how to grow things. Another reason for the late beginning of agriculture was the scarcity of plants and animals suitable for domestication. Throughout history humans have been able to domesticate only a few hundred plants and a few dozen animals, ones that happen to possess certain essential characteristics. Plants must be potentially high-yielding and be adaptable to a variety of environments. If not, domesticating them will have little effect. This explains why, out of approximately 200,000 species of flowering plants, only about 3,000 have been used to any extent for food. Of these, fewer than 30 are of major importance. They include four grasses (wheat, rice, maize, and sugar), starchy staples (potato, yam, manioc, and banana), and legumes, which are the meat of the poor (lentils, peas, vetches, beans, peanuts, and soybeans).

Like plants, animals also must be domesticated. They must be capable of overcoming their instinctive fear of humans, of breeding in captivity, and of accepting the diet provided by humans. The peoples of the Old World were fortunate in having available a variety of such animals to provide them with meat, milk, wool, and beasts of burden. The progress of American Indians, by contrast, was retarded because they had nothing comparable; they had to make do with a group of half-domesticated Andean cameloids: the llama, alpaca, and vicuna.

As we can see from this discussion, no breakthrough to agriculture could be expected unless some change occurred to upset the comfortable equilibrium of the hunting societies, and even then agriculture could occur only in areas where domesticable plants or animals were available. This is precisely what happened.

During the comparatively short period between 10,000 and 2,000 years ago, the great majority of humans on this planet shifted to agriculture. Obviously this was a forced shift, for no hunter would voluntarily leave his easy and secure way of life for the never-ending work of the peasant tied to his fields and his cattle. What forced the change was population pressure. Over tens of thousands of years, the num-

ber of humans had increased slowly, causing the migrations in Africa, Asia, Europe, Australia, and the Americas. Finally all the continents, except Antarctica, were populated. As the number of humans continued to grow slowly but steadily, hunters were forced to supplement the food they gathered with food they grew. Undoubtedly they were unhappy about staying in one area to grow crops and raise cattle, but the fact is that many more people per square mile can be supported by agriculture than by food gathering.

Agriculture first became a full-time occupation in those few regions where there were plants and/or animals that could be domesticated. In the process of domestication the wild plants and animals became larger and provided more food. Thus the hunters spent more and more of their time as food producers rather than food gatherers, until they ended up as peasants living in villages. From the first few centers of this agricultural revolution, the new way of life gradually spread over most of the globe.

II. SPREAD OF AGRICULTURE

The process of transition from hunting to agriculture was gradual and took place independently in many parts of the world. Agriculture developed independently in the Middle East—the Nile Valley in Egypt and Sudan, the valley of the Tigris and Euphrates in Syria and Iraq, and the eastern coast of the Mediterranean in the areas of Turkey, Syria, Lebanon, and Israel—as well as in Mexico, northern China, and Peru. New discoveries being made yearly suggest that there were other independent centers in Southeast Asia, West Africa, and elsewhere. We know the most about the Middle East and Mesoamerica (roughly tropical America north of Panama), both of which had an especially large number of domesticable plants and/or animals.

In the Middle East, ancient peoples found the ancestors of modern wheat, oats, rye, and barley, as well as those of the modern goat, sheep, cattle, and pig. In Mesoamerica, the two small republics of Costa Rica and El Salvador, although comprising only 1 percent of the area of the United States, yield as many plant species as do both the United States and Canada. This extraordinary diversity is the result of the variety of climates created by the wide range of altitude, temperature, and rainfall within a small area. Consequently, dozens of plants were successfully domesticated in Mesoamerica. The most important ones were maize, beans, and squashes.

Over a period of many centuries the various plants were adapted by humans to a variety of environmental conditions and spread to other areas, thereby creating a regional complex of multiple-species agriculture. This advanced type of agriculture had two great advantages: a high level of productivity and subsistence security. If one crop failed for climatic reasons, another with different requirements could survive. So agriculture provided the dependable food supply essential for dense populations and for the civilizations they produced.

The transition from the earliest domestication to agricultural revolution, or full dependence on agriculture, was very gradual and prolonged. Known as the phase of incipient agriculture, in the Middle East it lasted from roughly 9500 to 7500 B.C.E. In the New World it lasted even longer. One of the earliest centers of domestication in the New World was the Mexican valley of Tehuacán, where incipient agriculture began in approximately 7000 B.C.E. It is estimated that 2,000 years later only 10 percent of the diet of the local Indians was derived from their domesticated plants, primarily maize. By 3000 B.C.E., still only a third of the food came from domesticated sources. It was not until about 1500 B.C.E. that maize and other plants were hybridized to the point where their yield was sufficiently high to provide most of the food, thus completing the transition from incipient agriculture to the agricultural revolution.

From these two original centers of full-fledged agriculture, from northern China, and from other centers that will be identified in the future, the new mode of living spread to all parts of the globe. The diffusion process was sparked by the inefficiency of early agriculture, which was an intermittent or shifting type of cultivation. The land was cleared and used for crop growing for a few years; then it was abandoned to natural growth for eight to ten or more years to allow the fertility to be restored. As a result, the ratio of abandoned or recuperating land to that under cultivation at any specific time was

between five and ten to one. This very land-wasteful agriculture, together with increasing population, required constant extension of the limits of the tilled land into new regions. There was a continual "budding-off" or "hiving-off" from the agricultural settlements into the less densely populated lands of the food-gathering peoples. In this way agriculture was diffused in all directions from the original centers. (See maps of Expansion of Agriculturists, p. 24, and Dispersal of Agriculture, p. 26.)

This doesn't mean that agriculture eventually spread all over the globe. A great variety of local conditions determined where agriculture was to appear early, where late, and where not at all. In the Afro-Asian desert belt and in the arctic regions, agriculture was impossible for obvious reasons. Agriculture was also absent in parts of Africa and the Americas, as well as in all of Australia, because of a combination of isolation and unfavorable physical environment. In other regions such as central and western Europe, agriculture was hampered because the heavy forests were an almost insurmountable obstacle until the Iron Age, when cheap and effective implements became available. When the iron axe replaced the stone, it was possible to increase the efficiency of forest clearing and thereby to allow larger plots to be cultivated in areas where agriculture was already practiced. Hence efficient cultivation extended from the Mediterranean coastlands to the European interior, from the Indus River valley to the Ganges, from the Yellow River valley to the Yangtze, and from Africa's savannas to the tropical rain forests.

Very little is known concerning the precise details of the spread of agriculture from region to region. From the Middle East it spread eastward to the Indus valley, northward to central Asia and eastern Europe, and westward to central and western Europe. In China, wheat and barley were introduced from the Middle East about 1300 B.C.E., but recent research shows that native plants had been domesticated and cultivated in that region 3,000 years earlier. These plants included rice and tea grown in south China and millets, sorghum, and soybeans grown in north China. Distinctively Chinese was the mulberry tree, whose leaves fed the silkworms, and the lacquer tree, which yielded its famous varnish or lacquer.

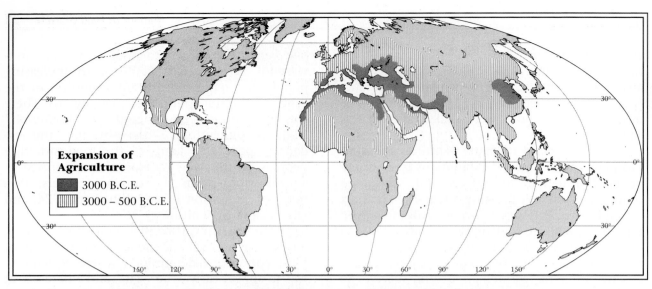

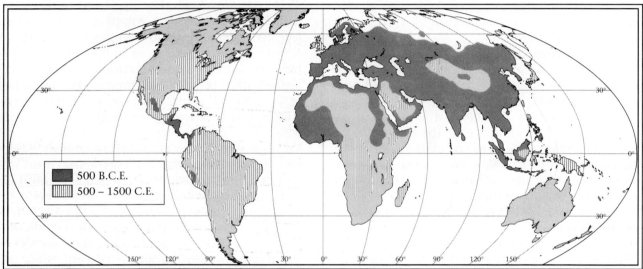

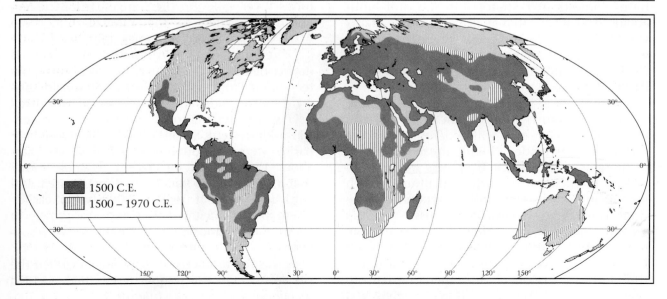

Expansion of Agriculturists

Women were the principal farmers in most Native American societies, growing corn, beans, and other crops that made up most of their food supply. This sixteenth-century French engraving shows Indian men preparing the soil for cultivation and Indian women sowing seeds in neat rows.

Agriculture in Africa developed independently about 5000 B.C.E. around the headwaters of the Niger and in the Nile valley about 4000 B.C.E. Whatever its origins, African agriculture for many centuries was confined to the open savanna lands and failed to penetrate southward into areas of tropical rain forest. This was partly because the millet and sorghum commonly grown in the savanna did not do well in the rain forest. But about the beginning of the Christian era this obstacle was overcome by two important developments. One was the appearance of iron working, which may have reached Africa from its place of origin in the Middle East. The other was the arrival, apparently from Southeast Asia, of bananas and Asian yams, which flourished under forest conditions. Thus two new crops along with iron tools brought about the rapid expansion of agriculture down to the southern part of the continent.

In modern times, with the partition of Africa among Western empires, African agriculture suffered a setback. European missionaries, officials, and scientists brought with them their familiar European cereals such as wheat and corn and assumed that the unfamiliar African cereals were inferior. With modern packaging

and advertising, European cereals were generally accepted as being truly superior. Today, however, it is gradually being realized that this assumption is unjustified. The U.S. National Academy of Sciences began publishing in 1996 a series of reports entitled *Lost Crops of Africa*. The reports state that Africa has more indigenous varieties of cereal than any other continent, including an African variety of rice (tef), an Ethiopian staple rich in protein and iron, and sorghum, which is used largely for animal feed in the United States but which yields a high quality flour. "Africa is called the hungry continent," concludes the National Academy report, "yet it is a cornucopia of food plants people are not taking advantage of."[1]

In the Americas agriculture arose independently in Mexico and Peru; we will focus our attention on maize in Mexico. The kernels of maize are clustered together on a corn cob, and unlike other grains (such as wheat), they do not fall to the ground and germinate. Thus the cultivation of maize requires human assistance, as evidenced by the presence of maize in archeological sites. Some kind of wild maize provided the base for modern domesticated maize, as seen in fossilized maize pollen discovered in the area

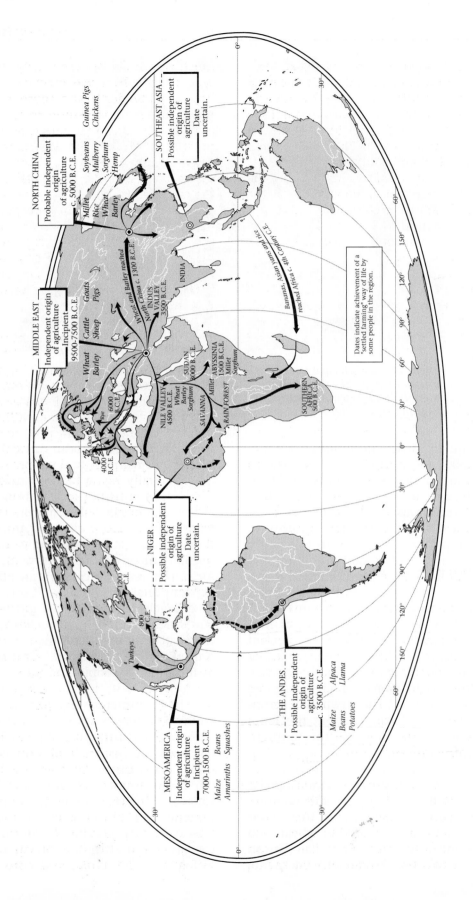

Dispersal of Agriculture

NORTH CHINA
Probable independent origin of agriculture c. 5000 B.C.E.

Millet   Soybeans   Guinea Pigs
Rice   Mulberry   Chickens
Wheat   Sorghum
Barley   Hemp

SOUTHEAST ASIA
Possible independent origin of agriculture
Date uncertain.

MIDDLE EAST
Independent origin of agriculture
Incipient
9500-7500 B.C.E.

Wheat   Cattle   Goats
Barley   Sheep   Pigs

Wheat and Barley reached
North China c. 1300 B.C.E.

INDUS
VALLEY
3500 B.C.E.

INDIA

Oats 2000 B.C.E.

6000
B.C.E.

4000
B.C.E.

Rye

NILE VALLEY
4500 B.C.E.

Wheat
Barley
Sorghum

SUDAN
4000 B.C.E.

Millet   ABYSSINIA
          1500 B.C.E.
          Millet
          Sorghum

SAVANNA

RAIN FOREST

SOUTHERN
AFRICA
500 B.C.E.

Bananas, Asian yams and rice
reached Africa c. 4th Century C.E.

Dates indicate achievement of a "settled farming" way of life by some people in the region.

NIGER
Possible independent origin of agriculture
Date uncertain.

1200
C.E.

800
C.E.

Turkeys

THE ANDES
Possible independent origin of agriculture
c. 3500 B.C.E.

Maize   Alpaca
Beans   Llama
Potatoes

MESOAMERICA
Independent origin of agriculture
Incipient
7000-1500 B.C.E.

Maize   Beans   Squashes
Amaranths

of Mexico City. Modern varieties of maize seem to be the result of a cross between this ancestral strain and wild teosinte grass. The hybrid was domesticated in the area of Mexico about 1500 B.C.E. Other domesticated crops in the Mexican region include squash (about 7000 B.C.E.) and beans (between 3000 and 5000 B.C.E.).

Many of the agricultural products in the area of Mexico were not domesticated at the same time. One must conclude that there was probably a long period of transition when the people of this area continued to forage for food while raising other crops.

Agriculture also seems to have become important in the mountains of Peru about 5600 B.C.E. Domesticated crops in this area include tomatoes, peanuts, lima beans, and potatoes. Also, maize different from the Mexican variety has been found there dating from between 4300 and 2000 B.C.E. From this original Mesoamerican center, agriculture spread both north and south. Maize arrived in the American Southwest about 3000 B.C.E. but did not have much effect until 750 C.E., when improvements over the first maize made its cultivation more productive than simple food collecting. Likewise, in eastern North America the Indians did not shift to dependence on agriculture until about 800 C.E., when they developed field cropping based on several varieties of maize, beans, and squash.

III. VARIETIES OF AGRICULTURE

The worldwide diffusion of agriculture led to the domestication of a variety of plants suitable to a variety of local conditions. In the Middle East wheat and barley had been the most common crops. But as the farmers moved northward they found that these crops did not do as well as rye, which originally had been a weed sown unintentionally with the wheat and barley. Hence there was a shift to rye in central Europe and, for the same reasons, another shift to oats further north.

Likewise, the extension of agriculture to sub-Saharan Africa led to the cultivation of native millets and of one type of rice, while around the shores of the Mediterranean the olive became one of the most important sources of edible oil. Across the Iranian plateau and in

northwest India an essentially Middle Eastern type of agriculture was practiced. But a dividing line running north and south through central India marks the transition to an entirely different climatic zone with correspondingly different plant life. This is the monsoon region, with heavy seasonal rainfall, constant heat, and dense jungles. Seed-bearing plants of the Middle Eastern variety, which require plenty of sun, cannot thrive here, so in their place we find the yam, taro, banana, and above all, rice. Finally, in the Americas the main crop everywhere was maize, supplemented by beans and squash in North America and by manioc and potatoes of both the sweet and "Irish" varieties in South America.

The net result of this agriculture diffusion was, very generally speaking, three great cereal areas: the rice area in East and Southeast Asia; the maize area in the Americas; and the wheat area in Europe, the Middle East, North Africa, and central Asia to the Indus and Yellow River valleys. During the several millennia between the agricultural and industrial revolutions these three cereals were as fundamental for human history as coal, iron, and copper were to become later. Recently wheat has been overtaking rice as the world's most important grain. The reason is that agricultural scientists have developed wheat varieties that are more resistant to heat, cold, drought, and pests. So wheat can be grown now in many more regions than in the past. Hence a global harvest of wheat in 1995 totaling 542 million tons.

Early farmers not only grew different crops in different regions of the world, but also they developed different types of agricultural techniques to raise those crops. One of the earliest is known as the "slash-and-burn" method. This slash-and-burn technique was carried on against forests because the land had to be cleared of trees and bushes so that the farmers could plant their seeds. But the clearing was a very hard job because the farmers had only stone tools in those early times. So they used fire to burn down the forests and thus clear the land for farming. Live trees, however, do not burn easily because they are full of sap. So the early farmers slashed a ring around the trunk of each tree, which stopped the flow of sap and caused the tree to die. The dead and dry trees were easy to burn, and the remaining ashes were a good fertilizer. So the farmers planted their seeds in the cleared and enriched land, watered and weeded the plants that sprouted, built fences to keep out wild animals such as rabbits or deer, and finally harvested the crop when it was ripe. This slash-and-burn technique made possible the extension of farming into large areas formerly covered by forests. It is a technique still practiced in many regions of the world.

Another technique still common on all continents is terrace agriculture. It remains the preferred method in mountainous areas where, in case of heavy rains, farmers face the danger of losing their crops to flash floods pouring down hillsides. To prevent such damage, farmers built stone walls on mountain slopes and then collected soil and piled it up behind the walls. Soil washed down the slopes and accumulated behind the walls as well. When enough soil piled up to fill the terraces, the farmers then had small level fields on which they could plant their crops without fear of losing them to floods. This is how potatoes are grown today in the Andean highlands of Peru, maize in the highlands of North China, and grapes in Mediterranean countries such as Spain, Italy, and Greece.

A third type of agriculture, vegetative root farming, is widely practiced in tropical regions. Live shoots of root plants such as taros, yams, and manioc are partly buried in moist ground where they grow into large tuberous roots that can be pulled up and fried, boiled, or baked into soup, paste, or cake. These are staple food crops that can be grown year round which provide a dietary mainstay when their starch is supplemented with fish (a common practice in East and Southeast Asia).

Finally, we should note raised field agriculture, which was developed about three thousand years ago in Peru's highlands. It was then dropped and has been forgotten for centuries. Scientists are very interested in this old technology because after discovering its secrets and using it to grow local Peruvian crops, they find it produces bigger crops than can be grown with the more expensive modern agricultural techniques with their chemicals and machinery.

The raised fields range from 13 to 33 feet wide, are 33 to 330 feet long, and are about 3 feet high. Crops are planted on those earthen platforms, which are separated from each other by canals of similar size. The platforms are constructed from earth that was shoveled out when the canals were dug. Growing crops on these individual raised fields rather than on the surrounding flat countryside gives the farmers several advantages, which are shown in the accompanying illustration.

- Crops are protected by the canal water heat against frost, which is common during the cold nights of the Andean highlands.
- Crops are protected against floods because surplus water flows into the canals.
- Crops are protected against drought by capillary action from the canals and by the ease of hand watering.
- Crops are fertilized with organic muck (green algae, cattle droppings, and dead plant matter), which is raised from the canal bottoms to the raised fields and provides fertilizer superior to the chemical varieties and costs nothing but the labor, which is plentiful in local villages.
- Fish raised in the canals improve substantially the diet of local farmers by increasing the protein in their diet.

Thanks to these advantages, experimental raised fields in Peru were yielding 30 tons of potatoes per acre in 1984, compared to 8 tons from surrounding fields cultivated in the usual manner with imported machinery and fertilizers. Because the raised field technology is a self-sustaining as well as a more productive system, it is being tried out in the United States and in Indonesia, as well as in several Latin American countries. Perhaps a type of agriculture developed originally in the Andean highlands, then forgotten for centuries and recently rediscovered and revived by scientists, may end up reappearing all over the world. The success of this ancient technology shows that lessons can be learned from our prehistoric successors, even in technological matters, despite all the marvels of modern "high technology."

In addition to these varieties of domesticated plants and of agricultural techniques, we should note that in those regions where there was too little rainfall for agriculture, the inhabitants turned to stock raising. They domesticated local animals rather than local plants. The first

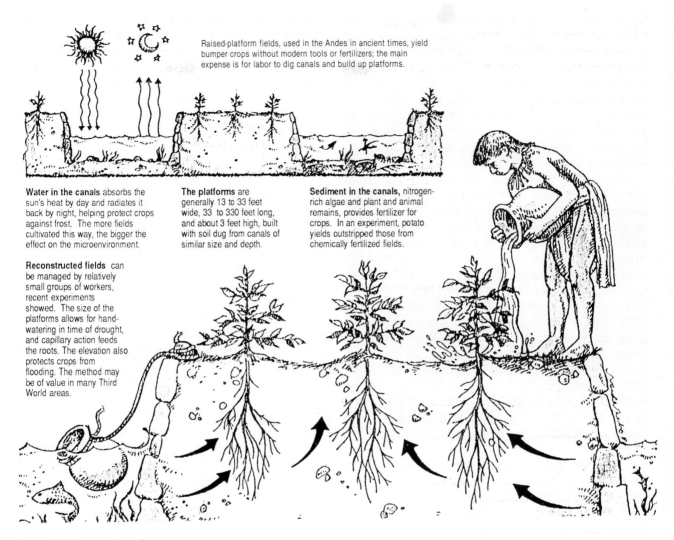

Raised-platform fields, used in the Andes in ancient times, yield bumper crops without modern tools or fertilizers; the main expense is for labor to dig canals and build up platforms.

Water in the canals absorbs the sun's heat by day and radiates it back by night, helping protect crops against frost. The more fields cultivated this way, the bigger the effect on the microenvironment.

The platforms are generally 13 to 33 feet wide, 33 to 330 feet long, and about 3 feet high, built with soil dug from canals of similar size and depth.

Sediment in the canals, nitrogen-rich algae and plant and animal remains, provides fertilizer for crops. In an experiment, potato yields outstripped those from chemically fertilized fields.

Reconstructed fields can be managed by relatively small groups of workers, recent experiments showed. The size of the platforms allows for hand-watering in time of drought, and capillary action feeds the roots. The elevation also protects crops from flooding. The method may be of value in many Third World areas.

Raised Field Agriculture

wild animal they domesticated was the dog. At first they killed and ate dogs, as they did other animals. Then they found that dogs were useful to keep in the camp because they frightened off wild animals by their barking and they also helped the hunters to find game. By 10,000 B.C.E., hunting bands on all continents had their packs of domesticated dogs.

Soon afterwards, humans domesticated other animals that were useful to them in one way or another. Thus those people became pastoral nomads, and many continue today to live in this way, roaming the vast steppes and desert lands from the Sahara to Manchuria and the broad savannas of sub-Saharan Africa. Pastoral nomadism was late in developing because it had to await the domestication of the horse and camel, which provided suitable transport in open country. But once pastoral nomadism got under way, between 1500 and 1000 B.C.E., a variety of forms developed. Some nomads depended on a single animal—camels in Arabia and cattle in East and South Africa—whereas others relied on a mix of livestock—herds of horses, cattle, camels, sheep, and goats in central Asia.

Yet regardless of the variety of animals, the pastoral nomads were poor compared to those who lived in the rich valleys of the Tigris-Euphrates, Nile, Indus, and Yellow rivers. In

This scene on an Attic jar from late in the sixth century B.C.E. shows how olives, one of Athens' most important crops, were harvested.

these valleys, a permanent type of irrigation agriculture was developed that was very productive and that in time supported great and wealthy civilizations. These valley civilizations were irresistible magnets to the comparatively poverty-stricken nomads of the central Eurasian steppes and of the Middle Eastern and North African deserts. Thus Eurasian history to modern times has been in large part the history of the rise and fall of great civilizations, with the pastoral nomads always ready to contribute to the fall of any civilization weakened by internal discord.

IV. LIFE OF THE FOOD GROWERS

The most obvious impact of the agricultural revolution was the new sedentary existence. Humans now had to settle down to care for their newly domesticated plants and animals. Thus the Paleolithic nomadic band gave way to the Neolithic village as the basic economic and cultural unit. Indeed the village remained the basis for a pattern of life that was to prevail until the late eighteenth century and that persists to the present day in the vast underdeveloped regions of the world.

Recent archeological excavations reveal that our early ancestors were not always restricted to a choice of nomadic hunting and gathering or sedentary farming. If local plant and animal food resources were unusually rich, it was possible for the local inhabitants to settle down in year-round villages, even though they depended entirely on hunting and gathering. This was the case in Abu Hureyre in northern Syria, where wild cereals, pulses, and legumes grew so densely that they yielded harvests as rich as though they were in planted gardens. Therefore it was possible for a large village of 300 to 400 gatherer-hunters to flourish in Abu Hureyre for several hundred years. Similar favorable conditions enabled food collectors to exist in permanent settlements in other regions such as the Pacific Northwest (Oregon, Washington, and British Columbia), where bountiful fish resources were available year-round. Likewise in the Southern Pacific, along the Peruvian coast, favorable sea currents nurtured marine life across the whole ecosystem, from phytoplankton to birds and sea mammals. So here also, food gatherers settled down in permanent villages, supported comfortably by the varieties of marine life swarming in the coastal waters. Yet such villages were the exception: Nomadism was the natural corollary of food gathering, just as a settled life was of food producing.

It is easy to romanticize Neolithic village life, but to do so would be grossly misleading. Everyone—men, women, and children—had to work, and work hard, to produce food and a few handicraft articles. Productivity was low since people learned slowly and painfully about soils, seeds, fertilizers, and crop rotation. Despite hard labor, famine was common; it often followed too much or too little rain or a plague of pests. Epidemics swept the villages repeatedly as sedentary life introduced the problem of the disposal of human excreta and other refuse. Although dogs helped with sanitation and personal modesty presumably caused people to deposit stools away from habitation, neither of these was sufficient to prevent the various diseases that follow the route from the bowel to the mouth. Furthermore, malnutrition was the rule because of inadequate food supply or unbalanced diet. Life expectancy under these circumstances was exceedingly low, but the high birthrate increased village populations everywhere until famine, epidemic, or emigration restored the balance between food supply and number of mouths to feed.

Yet Neolithic village life was not all misery and suffering. It was a time when people made technological progress at an infinitely more rapid rate than in the preceding Paleolithic period. Primarily, it was not because they had more leisure time than the hunters; we have seen that this was not so. Rather, the new sedentary life made a richer material existence physically possible. The living standards of the nomadic hunters were limited to what they could carry, whereas the Neolithic villagers could indulge in the building of substantial housing together with furnishings, utensils, implements, and assorted knickknacks. They learned to make pottery out of raw clay, at first imitating the baskets, gourds, and other containers of pre-agrarian times. Gradually they grasped the potential of pottery materials and techniques and began to fashion objects that no longer resembled the earlier containers. By the end of the Neolithic period, people in the Near East were building kilns, or ovens, that could fire pottery at a higher temperature and so allow for glazing. The glazed surface sealed the pottery and prevented seepage or evaporation. The agriculturist then had vessels that could be used not only for storing grain but also for cooking and for keeping liquids such as oil and beer.

Similar progress was made with textiles. Late Paleolithic peoples may have twisted or spun wild mountain sheep, goat, dog, or other animal fibers into coarse threads and woven them to make belts, headbands, or even rough blankets. Indeed they probably also modeled clay into crude containers. But it was during the Neolithic that people developed the textile art. They used fibers of the newly domesticated flax, cotton, and hemp plants and spun and wove the fibers on spindles and looms they had gradually

evolved. Neolithic villagers also learned to build dwellings that were relatively substantial and roomy. The materials varied with the locality. The Iroquois of northern New York were known as the people of the long house because they lived in huge bark and wood structures that accommodated ten or more families. In the Middle East adobe was used for the walls, whereas in Europe the most common material was split saplings plastered with clay and dung. The roofs were usually of thatch. Dwellings were furnished with fixed beds that might be covered with canopies. Also there were modern-looking dressers with at least two tiers of shelves and various wall cupboards. Light and warmth were provided by an open fire, generally placed near the center of the room. There was no chimney to let out the smoke—only a hole in the roof or a gap under the eaves.

Sedentary life also made possible a tribal political structure in place of the individual bands of the hunting peoples. Tribes were made up of the inhabitants of the villages of a given region, and they were identified and distinguished from others by distinctive characteristics of speech and custom. Some tribes, usually those with primitive economies, were so loosely organized that they were almost at the hunting-band level. Others boasted powerful chiefs and primitive nobilities distinct from the commoners, though the lines were blurred and never reached the exclusive class structures characteristic of the later civilizations.

The basic social unit of the Neolithic village customarily was the household consisting of two or more married couples and their children. This extended family was more common than the independent nuclear family because it was better suited for coping with the problems of everyday living. If an individual producer was temporarily or permanently out of commission, the extended family could absorb the loss. It could function more efficiently during intense work periods when many hands were needed for clearing forest, harvesting, or pasturing livestock. It could also exploit a large area effectively by sending members for long periods to care for distant gardens or grazing herds, while others tended nearby plots and did household chores.

The distinctive feature of the Neolithic village was social homogeneity. All families had the necessary skills and tools to produce what they needed, and, equally important, all had access to the basic natural resources essential for livelihood. Every family was automatically a component part of the village community, which owned the farmlands, pastures, and other resources of nature. Hence there was no division between landed proprietors and landless cultivators in tribal society. "Hunger and destitution," reports an American anthropologist, "could not exist at one end of the Indian village . . . while plenty prevailed elsewhere in the same village. . . ."[2]

Precisely because of this equality, tribal societies, whether of Neolithic times or of today, have a built-in brake on productivity. Output is geared to the limited traditional needs of the family, so there is no incentive to produce a surplus. This in turn means that labor is sporadic, diversified, and correspondingly limited. The daily grind—the eight-hour day, five-day week—is conspicuously absent. The typical tribe member worked fewer hours per year than a modern man or woman and, furthermore, worked at his or her pleasure. The basic reason was that a person then labored and produced in a specific social role—as a husband or father or brother, a wife or mother or sister, or a village member. Work was not a necessary evil tolerated for the sake of making a living; rather it was a concomitant of kin and community relations. One helped one's brother in the field because of kinship ties and not because one might be given a basket of yams. This tribal society was a comfortable egalitarian society. But for precisely that reason it was a low-productivity society, as can be seen from the work schedule of the Bemba tribe. (See p. 33.)

The equality in tribal social relations extended also to tribal gender relations. This equality was firmly grounded in the free access to land that tribal women enjoyed along with the men. An anthropologist who observed the Siang rice growers of central Borneo reported that widows continued to cultivate their own plots after losing their husbands. "On the whole, the women can swing an axe as effectively as the men." If the widow was encumbered by small children, "she is usually assisted by the others in the village, through gifts of rice and wild pig or by help in clearing her field, at least until such time as the children have become old enough to help her."[3]

Women had equal rights not only in agriculture but also in the new village crafts. Excavations at Catal Huyuk, a seventh-millennium-B.C.E. settlement in Asia Minor, reveal that women cultivated indigenous plants, baked bread in communal ovens, wove wool and cotton textiles, made mats and baskets out of the wheat straw, and fired pottery for cooking and storage. In this particular settlement, women appear to have enjoyed not merely equal status but a superior one. Pictorial representations, house furnishings, and burial remains all indicate that the family pecking order was first the mother, next the daughter, followed by the son, with the father in last place.

Turning finally to religion, the new life of the soil tillers gave rise to new beliefs and new gods. The spirits and the magic that had been used by the hunters were no longer appropriate. Now the agriculturists needed, and conceived, spirits who watched over their fields and flocks and hearths. Behind all these spirits stood a creator, usually vaguely defined. But most important, almost everywhere there was a goddess of the earth or of fertility—the earth mother. She was the source of productivity of plants and animals and of the fecundity of women. Life and well-being, the annual cycle of death and birth, ultimately depended on her, hence the creation of many fertility-goddess cults. Such cults were symbolized by the numerous clay figurines with exaggerated female characteristics—pendulous breasts and heavy thighs. They reflect the spread of agriculture from the Middle East and have been found throughout Europe and as far east as India.

V. DEMOGRAPHIC AND RACIAL RESULTS

We have seen that population increase was responsible for the agricultural revolution, but that revolution in turn caused still more population increase. Many more people can be supported per square mile by growing rather than gathering food. It is no surprise, therefore, that between 10,000 and 2,000 years ago the human population jumped from 5.32 million to 133 million, a twenty-five-fold increase within 8,000 years.

LOW PRODUCTIVITY OF TRIBAL SOCIETY

A Western observer kept the following record of the work of the Bemba tribe of Northern Rhodesia (now Zambia) during the month of September 1933. Admittedly this is a slack time of the year, when more beer is drunk than normally. Nevertheless the following selections from the record show that the Bemba tribe members do not have to cope with the "daily grind" of modern industrial society.*

September 1st, 1933. Two gourds of beer ready, one drunk by old men, one by young men. A new baby born. Women gather from other villages to congratulate, and spend two or three days in the village. Women's garden work postponed during this time.

2nd. Old men go out to clear the bush. Young men sit at home finishing the sour dregs of the beer. More visits of neighbouring women to see the new baby. Few women go out to do garden work.

3rd. Young men and women go to a church service conducted in a neighbouring village by a visiting Mission doctor. No garden work.

6th. Old and young men working by 6:30 A.M. and hard at it till 2 P.M. Two gourds of beer divided between old and young in the evening. Women working in their gardens normally.

7th. A buck shot by observer's party. Young men go out to fetch the meat. Women grind extra flour to eat with it. Two gourds of beer also made ready and drinking begins at 2 P.M. By 4 o'clock young men swaggering around the village, ready to quarrel, which they finally do. Dancing at night. Old women hilarious, and rebuked by their daughters for charging into a rough dance on the village square. Not enough beer for the younger women. They remain sober and express disapproval of the rest. No garden work done, except by old men.

8th. Every one off to their gardens in high spirits at 8 A.M. Back at 12 A.M. Young men sit in shelter and drink beer dregs for two hours, singing Scotch Mission hymns in sol-fa. Young girls go out on a miniature fish-poisoning expedition, but catch nothing.

15th. Three men begin digging dry-weather gardens by the river. Little boys go bird-snaring. Young women still away at the capital. Nobody to get relish. No proper meal cooked.

17th. Great heat. Young men sit about in shelter all day, comb each other's hair, shave, and delouse each other. No relish available. Women too tired to cook.

19th. Nine men clear bush. One woman hoeing. Three women piling branches. Young women go fish-poisoning and catch one fish (about 2 lb.).

22nd. Three men clear bush. One man hoes. Four young men go fishing with three of the wives. Three piling branches.

24th. Four gourds of beer divided between whole village. Sufficient for women as well as men. Beer-drinking lasts two days off and on.

25th. Two old men only able to tree-cut. Young men afraid to climb trees because of 'beer before the eyes.' They sit in their shelter and make baskets. One woman only does garden work. Young boys snare birds. Remains of beer drunk.

30th. More beer. Four men clear bush.

*A. I. Richards Land, *Labour and Diet in Northern Rhodesia* (Oxford University, 1939), pp. 162–164.

Not all the scattered peoples of the earth increased to the same degree. Those who switched to agriculture the earliest grew the fastest. We saw earlier that food-gathering women had few children because they breast-fed each baby for several years and they were less likely to become pregnant while they were breast-feeding. But with the agricultural revolution, mothers had cows, sheep, and goats that provided them with plenty of milk in addition to their own. So mothers now began using that milk to feed their babies and, therefore, they did not need to breast-feed each baby for several years. But they were more likely to become pregnant as soon as they stopped breast-feeding. So mothers living in villages with domesticated animals began having an average of six children, as compared to the average of four children they had had during the long centuries when they were nomadic food gatherers. That is why the population of the human race skyrocketed, as we have seen, between 10,000 and 2,000 years ago.

While agriculturists were increasing so rapidly and spreading all over the world, food gatherers were left far behind in numbers and were crowded out of the most fertile lands. Since early agriculture was not very productive, population pressure soon built up in the villages. The surplus population migrated to nearby fresh lands used by the food gatherers. Sometimes the outnumbered gatherers fled to other lands that were not suitable for farming. This happened in Africa to the Bushmen, who ended up in the Kalahari Desert, and to the Pygmies, who now live in dense jungles. (See map of Global Race Distribution, p. 18, and map of Recession of Hunters, p. 35.)

More commonly, the agricultural immigrants and the local food gatherers intermarried and produced a new hybrid people. Then as population pressure built up again, the new hybrid population would "bud-off" in turn to fresh lands, where further interbreeding would take place with native peoples. In this way agricultural techniques and crops were transmitted long distances, and the people who emerged at the end of the line were of an entirely different racial type from the originals. Thus the immigrants who brought wheat, cattle, the wheel, and the plow into north China were thoroughly Mongoloid, even though these materials originated in the Middle East.

The net result of these migrations that spread agriculture over the globe was that by 1500 B.C.E. the hunters, who in 8000 B.C.E. had comprised 100 percent of the human race, had shrunk to little more than 1 percent of the population. This occupational shift led in turn to a racial shift. Ten thousand years ago the race map of the globe showed a rough balance among six races—the Caucasoid, Mongoloid, Negroid, Bushman, Pygmy, and Australoid. (See map of Global Race Distribution, p. 18.) By 1000 C.E. this balance was drastically changed in favor of the agriculturist Mongoloids, Caucasoids, and Negroids, and against the Bushmen-Pygmies, who had remained food gatherers. The only reason the Australoids held their own was that their isolated island home had not yet been discovered by any agriculturists. This had to wait for the European explorers of the eighteenth century, and, when the discovery did take place belatedly, the consequences were all the more catastrophic for the hapless aborigines. Considering the globe as a whole, then, the racial effect of the agricultural revolution was to end the millennia-old racial equilibrium and to establish the Mongoloid-Caucasoid-Negroid predominance that persists to the present.

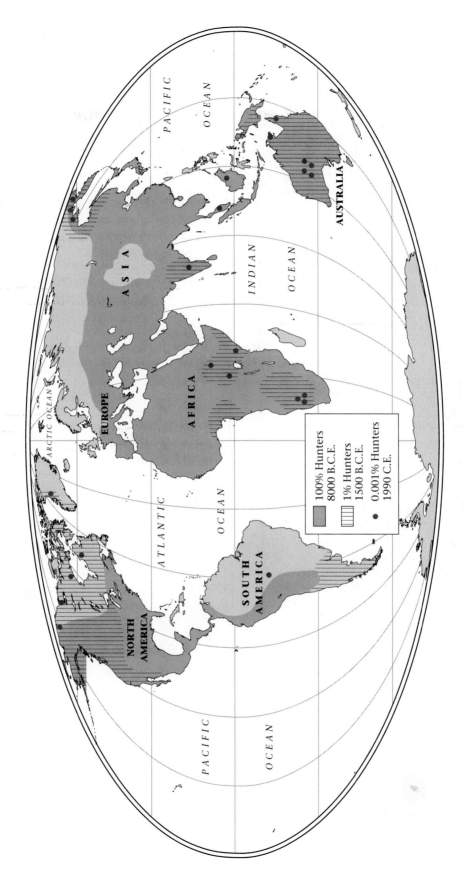

Recession of Hunters

SUGGESTED READINGS

Theories about the origins and nature of the agricultural revolution are constantly changing with new findings. The latest thinking is given in C. Wesley Cowan and Patty Jo Watson, *The Origins of Agriculture* (Smithsonian Institution Press, 1992); R. D. Hurt, *Indian Agriculture in America: Prehistory to the Present* (University Press of Kansas, 1987). See also M. N. Cohen, *The Food Crisis in Prehistory* (Yale University, 1977); S. Struever, ed., *Prehistoric Agriculture* (Natural History Press, 1971); L. R. Binford and S. R. Binford, eds., *New Perspectives in Archeology* (Aldine, 1968); and B. M. Fagan, ed., *Avenues to Antiquity* (W. H. Freeman, 1976). The independent origin of Chinese agriculture is described in Ping-ti Ho, *The Cradle of the East* (University of Chicago, 1975); and D. N. Keightly, ed., *The Origins of Chinese Civilization* (University of California, 1983). The cultural results of the spread of agriculture across Europe are analyzed in C. Renfrew, *Archeology and Language* (Cambridge University Press, 1988). The end result of the agricultural revolution for today's world is evident in J. Bertin, *Atlas of Food Crops* (Paris, 1971). The emergence of sedentism among food gatherers is analyzed in D. Price and J. A. Brown, *Prehistoric Food-Gatherers, the Emergence of Cultural Complexity* (Academic Press, 1985).

NOTES

1. Cited in *New York Times*, April 23, 1996.
2. L. H. Morgan, *Houses and House-Life of the American Aborigines* (New York, 1881), p. 45.
3. J. H. Provine, "Cooperative Ricefield Cultivation Among the Siang Dyaks of Central Borneo," *American Anthropologist*, Vol. 39, No. 1 (1937), pp. 80–91.

What It Means for Us Today

THE NATURE OF HUMAN NATURE

The world was surprised and excited in 1971 by the discovery of the Tasaday, a tribe of twenty-seven food-gathering people who had been living in complete isolation on Mindanao Island in the Philippines, where their tribal ancestors had lived similar lives for at least six centuries. The most striking and significant characteristic of this small band is their complete lack of aggressiveness. They have no words for weapon, hostility, anger, or war. Since contact with outsiders, they have eagerly adopted the long Filipino knife, the bolo, because it is superior to their stone tools for gathering food, chopping wood, and slashing through jungle brush. But they have turned down the spear and the bow and arrow because they cannot use them for food gathering. And all the food they collect (yams, fruit, berries, flowers, fish, crabs, frogs) they divide carefully and equally among all members of the band.

The validity of the Tasaday finding has been both questioned and defended. However, other small groups with similar social characteristics have been found all over the world, so the Tasaday remain significant as a common prehistoric type recognized by anthropologists. And the Tasaday are significant because they are food gatherers, as were all human beings before the agricultural revolution—in other words, for over 80 percent of human history. If, during all those tens of thousands of years, people everywhere were as peaceful as the Tasaday, then we cannot accept the common belief that Homo sapiens are innately aggressive.

Unfortunately, at the same time the world was learning about the Tasaday, another band of thirty people, the Fentou, were discovered in New Guinea. These tribesmen are fierce warriors, continually fighting with bows and arrows. Similar contradictions appeared historically among the American Indians. The Comanches and Apaches raised their children to be fighters, whereas the Hopis and Zunis raised theirs for peaceful living—and still do.

So where does this leave us regarding the nature of human nature? The record of history suggests that human beings are born neither peace-loving nor war-loving—neither cooperative nor aggressive. What determines how human beings act is not their genes but how their society teaches them to act. The psychologist Albert Bandura, who has specialized on this subject, has concluded that human nature is "a vast potentiality that can be fashioned by social influences into a variety of forms. . . . Aggression is not an inevitable or unchangeable aspect of man but a product of aggression-promoting conditions within a society."[1]

This question about human nature is of life-and-death significance for us all. With the development of technology, wars have become more deadly. They have also become more frequent. There were not many wars during the Paleolithic period, which covers most of human history, because the small food-gathering bands could use only so much territory. They had nothing to gain by trying to take over territory of a neighboring band. In fact, they had everything to lose because bloody wars might very well have destroyed the human race at a time when so few were scattered about the globe. Human young, after all, are wholly dependent not for one year like monkeys or three to four years like apes, but for six to eight years. The survival of the human young during their long years of dependence was best assured by a system of cooperative base camps that afforded the necessary food and protection. In short, cooperative kinship societies prevailed during the Paleolithic millennia precisely because they were so well suited to the survival of the species.

All this changed with the agricultural revolution. As agriculture became more productive, populations increased, villages grew into cities, and cities grew into empires with great palaces and temples and accumulated wealth. With so much now to fight over, wars became more and more frequent. They also became more and more destructive. Although relatively few people were killed by Roman soldiers with their short swords or by medieval knights in their heavy armor, by modern times the carnage had become general. During World War I, 8.4 million military and 1.3 million civilians were killed. During World War II, the score was 16.9 million military and 34.3 million civilians. A third world war would involve a far greater jump in casualties. The International Council of Scientific Unions, comprising scientists from thirty nations, reported in September 1985 that direct blast and radiation effects of nuclear attacks would take several hundred million lives, but from 1 billion to 4 billion of the world's 5 billion people would die of famine. This would result from a "nuclear winter," when huge clouds of sooty black smoke from nuclear blasts would envelop the earth and rob global crops of warmth and light from the sun.

The important lesson that history teaches us is that such wars are not inevitable. They have occurred not because of human nature but because of human societies. And human societies have been made by human beings and can be remade by human beings. This is the gist of the following conclusion by anthropologist Ashley Montagu concerning human nature: "Certainly we are born with genetically based capacities for many kinds of behavior, but the manner in which these capacities become abilities depends upon the training they receive, upon learning. . . . Our true inheritance lies in our ability to make and shape ourselves, not the creatures but the creators of destiny."[2]

SUGGESTED READINGS

The following authors argue that humans are by instinct aggressive creatures: R. Audrey, *African Genesis* (Atheneum, 1961), and his *Territorial Imperative* (Atheneum, 1966); also D. Norris, *The Naked Ape* (McGraw-Hill, 1967). The opposite view, that human conduct is molded by social environment, not heredity, is presented in the popular work by M. F. A. Montagu, *The Nature of Human Aggression* (Oxford University, 1976); in A. Bandura, *Aggression* (Prentice Hall, 1973); and in R. C. Lewontin, S. Rose, and L. J. Kamin, *Not in Our Genes* (Pantheon, 1984). The latest work on this subject is the provocative *War before Civilization* by L. H. Keeley (Oxford University, 1996).

NOTES

1. A. Bandura, *Agression* (Prentice Hall, 1973), pp. 113, 322.
2. *New York Times*, February 3, 1983 (Letters to the Editor).

PART II

Classical Civilizations of Eurasia, to 500 C.E.

We have seen in Part I that after hominids became humans, their first major achievement was the agricultural revolution. This revolution made it possible for the ancient river valley civilizations to develop in the Tigris-Euphrates, Nile, Indus, and Yellow river valleys. Beginning about 3500 B.C.E., the ancient civilizations lasted to the second millennium B.C.E., when they were uprooted by nomadic invaders from the steppes of central Asia and the deserts of the Middle East. Thus the ancient civilizations gave way to the new classical civilizations, which were different in several respects.

Whereas the ancient civilizations had been confined to river valleys, the classical civilizations expanded outward until they all had contact with one another. Civilization during the Classical Age, then, stretched without interruption across Eurasia, from the Atlantic Ocean to the Pacific. The classical civilizations were distinctive in content as well as in range. Like the ancient civilizations, each of the classical civilizations developed its own special style—its own social, religious, and philosophical systems—which persist to modern times. This creativity, it should be noted, was not limited to the Middle East, as it was at the time of the ancient civilizations. During the centuries of the Classical Age, all regions of Eurasia interacted as equals. All made their distinctive contributions, which still affect human beings throughout the globe to the present day.

3

First Eurasian Civilizations, 3500–1000 B.C.E.

The city came into being for the sake of life; it is for the sake of good life.

Aristotle

Every city is two cities, a city of the many poor and a city of the few rich; and these two cities are always at war.

Plato

The first light of civilization dawned on a desert plain scorched by the sun and nourished by two great rivers, the Tigris and the Euphrates. Although at one time it was believed that the Nile valley gave birth to civilization, it is now agreed that the earliest centers were in Sumer, the Old Testament's "land of Shinar." This area comprised the barren, wind-swept plains at the head of the Persian Gulf, in the southern part of what used to be known as Mesopotamia and is now the state of Iraq. About 3500 B.C.E. certain communities of agriculturists who had developed techniques for cultivating this arid wasteland successfully completed the transition from Neolithic tribalism to civilization.

The date given is an approximation, pinpointed merely for the sake of convenience. In fact, no one year, or decade or even century, can be specified. We have seen that the shift from food gathering to food growing did not suddenly occur when someone discovered the idea of agriculture. Likewise the transition to civilization did not happen at the moment that someone had the idea of developing urban centers and urban civilization. What happened, in short, was not an event but a process. The purpose of this chapter is to examine the nature and origins of this process.

I. HOW ANCIENT CIVILIZATIONS BEGAN

Precisely what do we mean by the term *civiliza-tion*? Anthropologists point to certain character-istics found in ancient civilizations that distin-guish them from the preceding tribal Neolithic cultures. They include such characteristics as urban centers, institutionalized political authori-ty in the form of the state, tribute or taxation, writing, social stratification into classes or hier-archies, monumental architecture, and special-ized arts and sciences. Not all civilizations have had all these characteristics. The Andean civi-lization, for example, developed without writ-ing, and the Egyptian and Mayan lacked cities as they are commonly defined. But this cluster of characteristics does serve as a general guide for defining the general nature of the civilizations that emerged at various times in various parts of the world.

The common characteristics of civilizations make clear that this new type of society was altogether different from the preceding egalitari-an tribal societies. How was the transition made from the simple Neolithic villages to the com-plex new civilizations? We can answer that ques-tion by tracing the transitional steps in the Mid-dle East, where the first civilizations emerged. In the hills above the Tigris-Euphrates humans had learned to domesticate plants and animals and so brought about the agricultural revolution. There also they now began the next great adven-ture when they moved down to the river valley and gradually developed a new and more pro-ductive irrigation agriculture and new social institutions. The interaction of the new technol-ogy and institutions set off a chain reaction that eventually ended in civilization.

The move to the lowlands presented the Neolithic agriculturists with new problems—inadequate rainfall, searing heat, periodic floods, and lack of stone for building. But there were advantages that more than compensated. There were date palms that provided plentiful food and abundant, though poor, wood. There were reedy marshes with wild fowl and game, fish that furnished valuable protein and fat for the diet, and above all, fabulously fertile valley bot-tom soil. The potential of this new environment

was very exciting, but there was one great obsta-cle. If rainfall was barely sufficient for growing crops in the hilly uplands, in the valleys below it rained even less. Irrigation was necessary to bring the rich alluvial soils under cultivation, so the pioneer farmers dug short canals leading from the river channels to their fields. The resul-tant crop yields were incredibly large compared to those they had previously wrested from the stony hillsides. Documents dating to 2500 B.C.E. indicate that the average yield on a field of bar-ley was eighty-six times the sowing! Food was now available as never before—more abundant, more varied, and thanks to irrigation, more assured. The increased food supply meant increased population, which in turn made it possible to create more irrigation canals, more new fields, and still more food.

While the technique of irrigation was being worked out, the new craft of metallurgy was also being mastered. It was particularly valuable for the valley settlements, where flint was unavail-able. At first the new native metals were treated just like tough and malleable stones, that is, worked cold by hammering and grinding. True metallurgy did not begin until people learned how to reduce metals from their ores by smelting. Copper seems to have been the first metal so treated, for it was discovered that when it was heated it became liquid and assumed the shape of any container or mold. As it cooled it hardened and could be given as good a cutting edge as stone. By 3000 B.C.E. it was widely known in the Middle East and India that a more durable alloy could be produced by adding small quantities of other metals to the copper. Finally they found the ideal combination of copper and tin. The result-ing bronze was decidedly superior to stone. Bronze was sought after for making weapons, since stone was too brittle to be dependable in battle. But being expensive because of the scarcity of both copper and tin, bronze wasn't available for general uses, like toolmaking.

Equally significant at this time was the invention of the plow. In the beginning a plow consisted simply of a sapling with one lopped and pointed branch left protruding two-thirds of the way down the trunk. A pair of oxen were yoked to the upper end of the trunk while the

This painting from a royal Egyptian tomb shows a noble family on a boat on a trip to hunt birds in the afterlife, just as they enjoyed doing in their lives on earth.

plowman steered by the lower end as the protruding branch was dragged through the earth. In the light soils of the semiarid Middle East this primitive contrivance was highly functional. By 3000 B.C.E. it was widely used in Mesopotamia and Egypt and was being introduced in India; by 1400 B.C.E. it had reached distant China. The ox-drawn plow is significant because it represents the first time people could use something besides their muscles for motive power. In this sense the plow was the precursor of the steam engine, the internal combustion engine, the electric generator, and the fission reactor.

By 3000 B.C.E. wind also was being har-nessed to supplement human muscles—in this case to furnish power for water transport. Clumsy square sails were used first in the Persian Gulf and then on the Nile River. They represented the first successful use of inorganic force to provide motive power. Crude though the early sailboats were, they offered a far more economic means for heavy transport than pack asses or oxcarts, so much of the commerce of the ancient civilizations was waterborne.

Another basic invention of this creative millennium was the wheel. In the earliest Mesopotamian models, the wheel and axle were fastened together solidly and the wheels were disks.

By 3000 B.C.E. the axle had been fixed to the cart with the wheel left separate, and shortly thereafter the spoked wheel appeared. Though these early carts were heavy and clumsy, they were preferable to what was available before—human shoulders and the pack animal, usually the ass. The wheel was also used for war chariots, which apparently were driven into the ranks of the enemy until they lost momentum. Then they were used as fighting platforms from which the crew could throw javelins and strike down at the enemy. Another, and more peaceful, use for this invention was the potter's wheel. In its simplest form the early potter's wheel was a pair of disk-shaped cart wheels with axle attached, the axle being set vertically. The operator spun the lower wheel by foot, while with the hands the operator spread and shaped the soft clay on the upper wheel. In this way pottery became the first technical product to be mass-produced.

Far-reaching institutional changes went hand in hand with the far-reaching technological advances. The increase in population enabled some of the villages to grow into towns dominated by a new elite of religious and, later, military and administrative leaders. The increased productivity of agriculture, with its food surpluses, could now support a growing new class of priests, soldiers, and bureaucrats. This development was not a sudden or simple one-way process—although there has been much debate on whether the technological change determined the institutional change or vice versa. This is similar to the debate about the early stages in human evolution: Did development of the human brain come first and then create human culture, including speech and toolmaking? Or did speech and toolmaking cause the brain to develop? It is now agreed that there was interaction back and forth, with speech and toolmaking being both the cause and the effect of brain development. Likewise it appears that technological and social change interacted reciprocally and eventually precipitated the urban revolution and civilization. The Neolithic cultivators did not at some given time agree—nor were they forced—to provide a surplus for a ruling elite and thus to shift over from the status of tribal people to that of peasants. Rather it was a gradual process in which cause and effect were functionally interrelated.

The beginning of the later class differentiation that distinguished civilization may be seen in the modest village shrines that were centers of socioreligious life. But there was not yet a full-time priesthood. When the villages grew to towns, the shrines likewise grew to temples with retinues of priests and attendants—the first persons ever to be freed from direct subsistence labor. We can see why the priests became the first elite group when we realize that they were the successors of the earlier tribal shamans. The shamans had been so influential because of the importance of group agricultural ceremonies, such as rainmaking, for Neolithic farmers. Now the new priesthood bore responsibility not only for the traditional supernatural phenomena but also for the growing managerial functions essential for an increasingly complex society.

The growth of technology and the increasing food surplus had made possible the emergence of the new priestly hierarchies, but the latter in turn contributed to both the technology and the economy. The earliest known examples of writing, which in itself was a priestly invention born of the need for keeping records, tell us that the priests supervised a multitude of economic as well as religious activities. They kept the records necessary for calculating the time of the annual floods. They assumed the vital managerial roles necessary for the proper functioning of the growing irrigation facilities, which included the rationing of water and the construction and maintenance of dams and canals. They also provided the main stimulus for crafts, which were designed mainly for the temples rather than for secular markets.

At this point the growing heterogeneity of society, to which the religious elite had contributed so vitally, began to undermine the position of that elite. The larger and more complex the towns grew, the more ineffective became purely religious sanctions. At the same time warfare was growing in scale and frequency, perhaps because population growth was outstripping agricultural resources, and, paradoxically, the wealth of the temples themselves may have contributed to the disorders by inviting raids. The outcome was a shift of power from the priesthood to a new secular elite.

Previously, the occasional threat of outside attack had been met by the community's adult

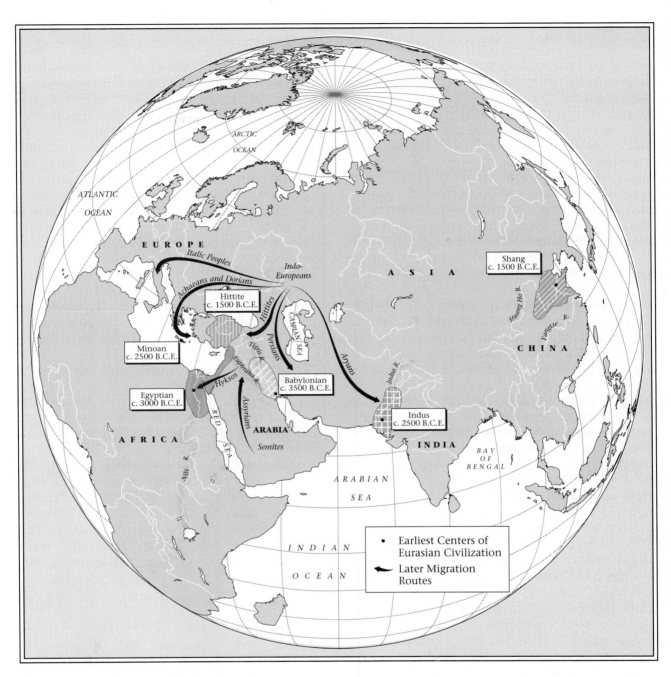

Ancient Civilizations of Eurasia, 3500–1500 B.C.E.

males, who assembled and selected a war leader for the duration. But as the intervals of peace became shorter, the tenure of these war leaders became longer, until finally they were ensconced as permanent military chiefs, and eventually as kings. Thus the palaces came to rival the temples, and in time, a working partnership necessarily evolved. The priests normally retained their great landholdings and continued

their sacred services, while the palace officials constructed walls around their cities and raised large armies, which they employed against neighboring cities and, eventually, for empire building.

One effect of this rise of secular states and empires was a great increase in the output of nonagricultural commodities. The mass production of pottery and metal utensils, and the hordes of assorted objects found in some of the more substantial houses, all suggest a new and significant middle-class market. Also, luxury commodities in great quantity were absorbed by the growing palace retinues. In addition, increasing militarization required armaments on an unprecedented scale. The armies needed not only metal weapons and armor but also more elaborate equipment such as chariots. All this was a far cry from the relatively limited production of earlier times when crafts were geared mainly to meeting temple needs.

Mass production had important implications for foreign affairs. Most of the crafts were dependent on raw materials brought from the outside, since the lowlands were almost totally devoid of minerals and quality timber. Copper, for example, came from Oman, south of the Persian Gulf; silver and lead from the Taurus Mountains in Asia Minor; and timber from the Zagros Mountains of Iran and from Lebanon on the Mediterranean coast. To pay for such imports, the various crafts had to expand production and provide exports in exchange. The alternative was to conquer the sources of the needed raw materials. That this option was not overlooked is evident from the career of Sargon, king of Akkad in the middle of the third millennium B.C.E. An epic poem, "The King of Battle," describes how Sargon led his army across unknown mountain passes into the heart of Asia Minor in support of Akkadian merchants who were being maltreated by the local ruler. Eventually Sargon's empire extended "from the Lower to the Upper Sea"—from the Persian Gulf to the Mediterranean—and he thereby controlled the crucial sources of metals, stone, and timber. Indeed, a slightly later source relates that Sargon "did not sleep" in his efforts to promote commerce: "Brisk activity dominates the wharf where the ships are docked; all lands live in peace, their inhabitants prosperous . . . without hindrance ships bring their merchandise to Sumer."[1]

The combined cost of the military and palace establishments was so expensive for the early city-states that it undermined the traditional assemblies. They balked against the onerous levies necessary to meet the rising expenditures. As a result, the assemblies were increasingly bypassed and replaced by permanent, hereditary royal authority.

The centralization of political power led to increased class differentiation, the growth of which we can see in the differences in grave offerings. During the early period the disparity was minimal, but the more time passed, the more pronounced it became. The great majority of the graves contained only a few pottery vessels or nothing at all, reflecting the poverty of the commoners. Those of the well-to-do exhibited "conspicuous consumption" in the form of copper vessels and beads of precious metal. The royal tombs, far outdoing the others, were luxuriously furnished with beautifully wrought weapons and precious ornaments and included large numbers of palace attendants—men-at-arms, harem ladies, musicians, charioteers, and general servants—who were sacrificed to accompany the royal occupant and attest to his or her power and wealth.

The royal tombs, whose lavish contents have been unearthed in many civilizations ranging from China to the Andes, point up the dramatic difference between these civilizations and the simple tribal societies they replaced. Our survey of what happened in the Middle East shows that the transition from tribalism to civilization was the end result of technological and social changes that interacted back and forth. Eventually they produced the first Eurasian civilizations that emerged on the banks of the Tigris-Euphrates, the Nile, and the Indus and Yellow rivers. (See map of Ancient Civilizations of Eurasia, 3500–1500 B.C.E. p. 47.)

II. HOW ANCIENT CIVILIZATIONS SPREAD

Once civilization took root in several regions of Eurasia and the New World, it spread out in all directions. Just as the agricultural revolution had replaced hunting societies with tribal ones, so now the tribal societies in turn were replaced by civilizations. They were replaced for precisely the same reason that the hunting bands had been replaced earlier. We noted in the preceding chapter that as the hunters increased in numbers, they had to shift to agriculture because farming was more productive. Many more farmers could live off a unit of land than could hunters. So it was now with the tribal cultivators—they were displaced because of their inferior productivity. The record of the Bemba work-days revealed how comfortable and easygoing life was in that tribe based on kinship relations. But productivity was low because there was no pressure to work more and produce more. Tribal members needed to work only enough to care for their families and for any kin in need.

When tribal populations increased, and the demand for food increased correspondingly, tribal societies could not compete with civilizations that were much more productive. They were more productive because they were class societies with a state structure that squeezed taxes and rents out of the peasants to support the kings, courtiers, bureaucrats, military leaders, ecclesiastics, and scribes. To pay the taxes and rents, the peasants of the civilizations had to work infinitely harder than did the tribal cultivators. Consider the contrast between the daily life of the Bemba and the wretchedness of Egyptian peasants and workers described in the following statement. It was uttered in the third millennium B.C.E. by an Egyptian father taking his son to school and trying to persuade him of the need to study hard by contrasting the misery of the many at the bottom with the blessings of the few at the top.

Put writing in your heart that you may protect yourself from hard labor of any kind and be a magistrate of high repute. The scribe is released from manual tasks; it is he who commands. . . . Do you not hold the scribe's palette? This is what makes the difference between you and the man who handles an oar.

I have seen the metal-worker at his task at the mouth of his furnace, with fingers like a crocodile's. He stank worse than fish-spawn. . . . The stonemason finds his work in every kind of hard stone. When he has finished his labors his arms are worn out, and he sleeps all doubled up until sunrise. His knees and spine are broken. . . . The barber shaves from morning till night; he never sits down except to meals. He hurries from house to house looking for business. He wears out his arms to fill his stomach, like bees eating their own honey. . . . The farmer wears the same clothes for all times. His voice is as raucous as a crow's. His fingers are always busy, his arms are dried up by the wind. He takes his rest—when he does get any rest—in the mud. If he's in good health he shares good health with the beasts; if he is ill his bed is the bare earth in the middle of his beasts. . . .

Apply your heart to learning. In truth there is nothing that can compare with it. If you have profited by a single day at school it is a gain for eternity.[2]

Early Egyptian painting, about 3000 B.C.E., portrays tribes of peasants immigrating to Egypt.

Obviously the Bemba tribal members enjoyed more comfortable and carefree lives than did the wretched farmers, masons, barbers, and metalworkers described by the Egyptian father. But precisely because the tribalists were better off, they were also doomed. They were far less productive than their Egyptian counterparts who were forced to work ever harder to meet the exactions of landlords and tax collectors. Thus, tribal societies were elbowed off the historical stage as inexorably as hunting bands had been shoved off earlier by tribal cultivators.

By the time tribalism had reached the outer fringes of Eurasia, it was being superseded in its core areas in the Middle East. The displacement process continued steadily as civilization spread out of the original river valleys and across adjacent uncivilized regions. By the time of Christ it extended with virtually no interruption from the English Channel to the China Sea. (Compare the map on p. 72–73 with the map on p. 47.)

If 3500 B.C.E. is accepted as the approximate date for the emergence of civilization in Mesopotamia, corresponding dates may be given for the other centers of civilization: in Egypt, about 3000 B.C.E.; in the Indus valley, about 2500 B.C.E.; in the Yellow River valley of China, about 1500 B.C.E.; and in Mesoamerica and Peru, about 500 B.C.E. These dates are rough estimates and are constantly being revised as new findings are made. Indeed radiocarbon dating, on which much prehistoric chronology has been based, has been found recently to be off by several centuries. Hence some scholars now question the traditional assumption that culture spread from the eastern Mediterranean to western Europe.

III. STYLES OF ANCIENT CIVILIZATIONS

We noted in the preceding chapter that the Neolithic cultures differed markedly according to the balance between farming and stockbreeding and the wide variety of plants cultivated and of animals bred. So now there were great differences among the scattered civilizations that emerged around the globe. Each of these civilizations had its distinctive style, which distinguished it from the others. These styles persist to the present day, so that anyone parachuted into the midst of a strange city would immediately recognize, from the architecture and costumes and foods and spoken language, whether the city was Chinese or Indian or Middle Eastern or western European.

Before considering the distinctive features of the various ancient civilizations, we should recognize certain common characteristics that they all shared. Perhaps the two most significant were the new inequity in social relations and the new inequity in gender relations.

The social inequity arose from the fact that all civilizations were based on tributary rather than kin relationships. Day-to-day life was determined not by the mutual aid and obligations of kin to kin but rather by the tribute collected in the form of taxes, rents, and labor services. Consequently the exploitation described by the Egyptian father was the rule rather than the exception. It may seem that the treatment of those peasants and masons and metalworkers on the banks of the Nile was unbelievably harsh, but many surviving accounts depict equally brutal exploitation in all other civilizations. An observer in Han China in the first century C.E. described a peasant with "legs like burnt stumps, back encrusted with salt, skin like leather that cannot be pierced by an awl, hobbling along on misshapen feet and painful legs."[3]

Such inequity persisted to modern times, as in tsarist Russia, where wealthy nobles customarily staffed each of their country estates with 300 to 800 servants. It was common practice for these nobles to sell, mortgage, or exchange their serfs, or "souls." They advertised their souls for sale together with household goods and other commodities. "To be sold: banquet tablecloths and also two trained girls and a peasant." "To be sold: girl of 16 of good behavior and a second-hand slightly used carriage."[4]

This inequity of past civilizations extended even to the dead. Archeologists find in the graves of commoners only a few pottery vessels or nothing at all, while in those of the well-to-do, they have found expensive furniture and jewelry, while royal tombs contain not only lavish personal adornments but also numerous personal attendants, including men-at-arms, harem ladies, eunuchs, musicians, and general servants—all sacrificed so that they might serve the royal personage in afterlife, as well as reflect his affluence and majesty here on earth. In one recently discovered tomb, the great unifying Chinese emperor Chin Shih Huang-ti surrounded himself with an army of 7,500 terra cotta warriors, each life-sized with individually modeled heads representative of the ethnic groups under the emperor's rule 2,000 years ago.

Even the skeletons in the graves reflect the harsh inequality of life in past civilizations. A study of skeletons at Tikal, Guatemala, in the first millennium C.E. disclosed that, while the average Mayan male was a mere five feet one inch in height, those few given elaborate burials had an average stature of five feet seven inches. Their bones also were substantially more robust and their life span clearly had been a longer one. Archeologists conclude that a "nutritional advantage" allowed the Mayan elite to realize their full potential in stature and life expectancy.[5] Such skeletal differentiation on the basis of class persists to the present day. Britain's Health Ministry reported in December 1984 that, "In almost every age group, people from households headed by a manual worker were shorter, on average, than people from non-worker households."[6]

The second common feature of ancient civilizations, in addition to social inequity, was gender inequity. We have seen that in Paleolithic times, women enjoyed equal status because as food gatherers they contributed even more to the food supply than did the male hunters. Likewise during the Neolithic age, when agriculture was simple, women cultivated the land surrounding their camps and continued to gather whatever food they could find. So they remained equal food providers with men and retained their equal status with men.

All this changed with the advent of the plow and of irrigation and of new crafts such as metallurgy. This advanced type of agriculture provided the economic foundations for civilization but at the same time undermined the economic independence of women, and consequently their social independence as well. Women found it difficult to participate in the new agriculture, which required the tending of draft animals, extraction of stumps, maintenance of irrigation ditches, and upkeep of plows and other equipment. This type of work was not suited to women, either because it was too heavy or because it kept them away from the children too long. So women gradually stopped being equal food producers with men. More and more they spent their time at home, taking care of their children and their husbands.

Men gradually dominated the new agriculture and crafts, while women became isolated and dependent. For the first time a distinction was made between the "inside" work of women and the "outside" work of men. Of course the "inside" work was essential for the family and

Diorama showing the city of Ur (Iraq) about 2000 B.C.E.

for society. But it was not generally seen to be as important as the work done by men. Since women were thought to be doing less important work, they were also thought to be the less important sex—the "second sex."

Furthermore, since women were tied down by the "inside" work, men gained a monopoly of not only the new agriculture and crafts but also the new positions in the state. They became the leaders in the assemblies, the courts, and the armies. Thus men ended up with a monopoly of economic power, political power, and military power. Women became dependent and submissive—the "weaker sex," as they came to be called. It was not accidental that when the Europeans began their overseas expansion in the fifteenth century, they discovered that women in food-gathering societies such as the Montagnais-Naskapi Indians of Labrador enjoyed a disconcerting degree of equality with men. But in the overseas civilizations, such as those of China, India, and the Middle East, they found women as restricted and submissive as they were in Europe—even more so.

Another reason why women had inferior status in the various civilizations was the new emphasis on inheritable private property. This caused men to go to great lengths to be certain that they were in fact the fathers of their heirs, who were to receive all their wealth. Consequently, the wealthy elite adopted strict regulations and elaborate precautions to control female (though not male) sexual activity. These included chastity belts, bookkeeping devices to record the exact dates of sexual encounters, the castration of men who served as harem guardians for their rulers, and the widespread practice of clitoridectomy (cutting the clitoris out of young girls) which, by decreasing or eliminating sexual pleasure, was believed to be an effective method of keeping women from "straying" with men other than their husbands.

It is well known that there were individual exceptions to this overall pattern of female subordination. Outstanding among them were the ambitious Egyptian Queen Cleopatra, who charmed both Julius Caesar and Mark Antony and sought to use them to restore real power to the Egyptian throne; Aspasia, who was known throughout Greece as the learned, witty, and beautiful mistress of Pericles; the masterful

Empress Irene who dethroned her son and became the first female ruler of the Byzantine Empire (797–802), although in deference to tradition she was referred to in official documents as "Irene, the faithful emperor"; and also Empress Wu Chao, who dethroned her son to become not only the first and only female ruler of China but also one of the most capable and enlightened. These illustrious personalities stand out prominently in the annals of history by virtue of their remarkable talents and achievements. Yet despite their fame, it cannot be said that their careers improved to any significant degree the daily lives of their less exalted sisters, just as in our time the careers of Evita Peron, Indira Gandhi, and Corazon Acquino have not appreciably improved the daily lives of the women of Argentina, India, or the Philippines.

Having surveyed the historic shift from equality to inequality in social and gender relations in all civilizations, we turn now to consider their individual distinctive styles.

Mesopotamia

The style of the pioneer civilization of Mesopotamia was urban. The first center was at Sumer, which by 3000 B.C.E. consisted of twelve separate city-states. The cities fought each other continually, so they were easily conquered by Indo-European invaders from the north and Semitic invaders from the south. Indeed the history of Mesopotamia was in large part a centuries-long struggle between the Indo-European and Semitic invaders for control of the fertile river valley.

The first great empire builder was the aforementioned Semite, Sargon the Great (c. 2276–2221 B.C.E.), whose conquests stretched from Akkad in the middle of the valley to the Persian Gulf in the south and the Mediterranean in the west. Another empire builder was also a Semite, Hammurabi (c. 1704–1662 B.C.E.), who, as we shall see, is most famous for his law code. This pattern of successive invasions continued to modern times, with Hammurabi followed by Hittites, Assyrians, Persians, Macedonians, Romans, Arabs, Mongols, Turks, and Westerners.

Despite the parade of empires, the cities remained the basic units of ancient Mesopotamia.

Most citizens earned their livelihood as farmers, craftmakers, merchants, fishermen, and cattle breeders. Each city had a section reserved for the craftmakers—the masons, smiths, carpenters, potters, and jewelers. They sold their handicrafts in a free town market and were paid in kind or in money that consisted of silver ingots or rings, which were weighed after each transaction.

Outside the city walls were the fields on which the urban inhabitants were dependent. Most of the land was held in the form of large estates that belonged to the king or the priests or other wealthy persons. The workers on these estates were allotted individual plots along with seed, implements, and draft animals. In return they provided the labor and, through a variety of arrangements, gave their surplus produce to the temple or palace or landowner. The basic crops were barley and wheat; the milk animals were goats and cows; sheep supplied the wool that was the chief textile fabric of Mesopotamia. The most common vegetables were beans, peas, garlic, leeks, onions, radishes, lettuce, and cucumbers; the fruits included melons, dates, pomegranates, figs, and apples.

The management of the estates required keeping careful accounts of many details: the rents received from the tenant farmers, the size of the herds, the amount of fodder needed for the animals and of seed for the next planting, and the intricate details regarding irrigation facilities and schedules. Management and accounting records were inscribed with a reed stylus on clay tablets that were then baked to preserve them. This earliest form of writing, known as cuneiform, was clearly invented as an instrument of administration, not for intellectual or literary purposes. As a distinguished scholar has put it, "Writing was not a deliberate invention, but the incidental by-product of a strong sense of private property, always a characteristic of classical Sumerian civilization."[7]

At first the cuneiform consisted of pictographs; the scribe drew simplified pictures of oxen, sheep, grain, fish, or whatever was being recorded. Soon the pictographs became conventionalized and were no longer left to the artistic fancy of each scribe. This ensured uniform writing and reading of records, but a basic problem remained: Pictographs could not be used to depict abstract concepts. Sumerian scribes met this difficulty by adding marks to the pictographs to denote new meanings, and more important, by selecting signs that represented sounds rather than objects or abstractions. This was the essence of the phonetic alphabet that was evolved centuries later, but the Sumerians failed to apply the phonetic principle systematically and comprehensively. They reduced their signs from an original number of about 2,000 to some 600 by 2900 B.C.E. Although that was a substantial improvement, cuneiform remained far more cumbersome than the alphabet developed later by the Phoenicians and the Greeks. Hence there was a need for those who had mastered the difficult art of writing; scribes alone had this skill and therefore enjoyed high status and privilege.

Although the origins of writing are to be found in the new circumstances arising from the production of economic surplus, it had other far-reaching and fateful effects. It stimulated intellectual development because factual data could now be collected, recorded, and passed along to successive generations. Equally significant, writing helped to define and consolidate individual cultures. It gave permanent written form to religious traditions, which thereby became sacred books; to social customs, which became law codes; and to oral myths and stories, which became classics. Thus writing became the chief means for the cultural integration of the civilizations of mankind.

The Sumerians developed sciences and mathematics, as well as writing, in response to the concrete needs of their increasingly complex society. Their earliest mathematical documents were accounts of flocks, measures of grain, and surveys of fields. Their chief contribution was the development of the first systems for measuring time, distance, area, and quantity. Also, as early as 3000 B.C.E., they were carefully studying and recording the movements of heavenly bodies, their motive again being utilitarian. They believed that the will of the gods determined celestial movements and that knowledge of those movements would enable man to know the divine will and act accordingly. Thus Mesopotamian astrologers over the course of many centuries accumulated an enormous amount of data that later was used to develop scientific astronomy.

Original pictograph	Pictograph in position of later cuneiform	Early Babylonian	Assyrian	Original or derived meaning
				bird
				fish
				donkey
				ox
				sun day
				grain
				orchard
				to plow to till
				boomerang to throw to throw down
				to stand to go

The origin and development of a few cuneiform characters.

The religious beliefs of the Sumerians and their successors were profoundly affected by their physical environment, and particularly by the annual flooding of the Tigris-Euphrates. The coincidence of heavy rains in the northern areas and deep snow in the Zagros and Taurus mountains frequently produced disastrous floods that devastated farmlands instead of filling irrigation canals. Ninurta, the Sumerian god of the flood, was viewed as a malevolent, not a benevolent, god. Sumerian literature is filled with lines like these:

The rampant flood which no man can oppose,

Which shakes the heavens and causes earth to tremble. . . .

And drowns the harvest in its time of ripeness.

Fear of the annual floods, together with the ever-present danger of outside invasion, left the Sumerians with a deep feeling of helplessness in a world of uncontrollable forces. "Mere man— his days are numbered," reads a Sumerian poem, "whatever he may do, he is but wind." The Mesopotamian view of life was tinged with an apprehension and pessimism reflecting the insecurity of the physical environment. Humans, it was felt, had been made only to serve the gods, whose will and acts were unpredictable. Hence a variety of techniques were employed to foresee the uncertain future. One was the interpretation of diverse omens, and especially dreams. Another was hepatoscopy, or divination by inspecting the livers of slaughtered animals. Still another was astrology, which, as already noted, involved the study of planets for their imagined influence

Sumerian statuettes from Tell Asmar. The group, dating from 3000–2500 B.C.E., was found buried beside the altar of a temple at a site near modern Baghdad. The tallest figure in this collection of gods, priests, and worshipers is the god Abu, the "lord of vegetation."

on or predictions about the destinies of men and women. Finally, each person had a personal god as a sort of private mentor. Through this personal god, the person's wishes and needs could be made known to the great gods, who were much too remote for direct communication.

Insecurity also prevailed between people, and the Mesopotamians sought to ease potential conflicts by compiling detailed codes of law. The most outstanding of these was that of Hammurabi, which tried to regulate all social relationships, clearly and for all time. The code sheds as much light on the society as it does on the legal system of ancient Babylon. The following presents some of its typical features:

1. The application of the principle of "an eye for an eye, a tooth for a tooth": "If a man has knocked out the eye of a patrician, his eye shall be knocked out. If he has broken the limb of a patrician, his limb shall be broken." (Laws 196, 197)

2. Class discrimination, so that the lower orders received less compensation: "If a man has smitten the privates of a patrician of his own rank, he shall pay one mina of silver. If the slave of anyone has smitten the privates of a freeborn man, his ear shall be cut off." (Laws 203, 205)

3. The strict requirement of a business society that property be safeguarded: "If a man has stolen goods from a temple, or house, he shall be put to death; and he that has received the stolen property from him shall be put to death." (Law 6)

4. The multitude of "welfare state" provisions, including annual price fixing for basic commodities, limitation of interest rate to 20 percent, minute regulation of family relationships, assurance of honest weights and measures, and responsibility of the city for indemnifying victims of unsolved robbery or murder: "If the highwayman has not been caught, the man that has been robbed shall state on oath what he has lost and the city or district governor in whose territory or district the robbery took place shall restore to him what he has lost." (Law 23)

5. A static view of the past, present, and future, typical of premodern peoples. Thus the code is presented as part of the divine order for the benefit of humankind under its justice, and any later ruler who dares alter the code is colorfully and explicitly cursed with "a reign of sighing, days few in number, years of famine, darkness without light, sudden death . . . the destruction of his city, the dispersion of his people, the transfer of his kingdom, the extinction of his name and memory from the land . . . his ghost [in the underworld] is to thirst for water." (Laws, Epilogue)

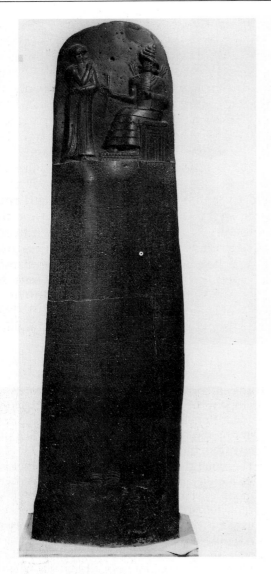

Stele with the Hammurabi Code, consisting of some 300 laws meant to regulate society.

Finally, the code of Hammurabi and all other Mesopotamian codes set forth in clear legal terms the superior status of men over women. Matrimony was chiefly a matter of utility—a substitute for nonexistent insurance against illness, disability, or old age. Consequently the choice was made not by the bride and groom, who might be blinded by love, but by the father, or after his death, by the mother or elder brothers. Following marriage, the husband was legally recognized as the undisputed head of the family. His wife and his children

had to show him due respect. As the head of the family, the husband was literally the owner of his wife and children. To honor a debt, he could pawn or sell them as though they were mere objects.

Adultery by the wife was mercilessly punished, usually by death for her and her paramour. For the husband, however, the concept of infidelity was irrelevant because he had the legal right to possess not only a principal wife but also a concubine and slaves "for his desires" and also to ensure descendants. Indeed a childless wife was duty bound to provide a concubine for her husband so that he might have children. Divorce for the husband was easy. He merely had to declare that his wife was barren or a spendthrift or had belittled him. For the wife to seek divorce, however, was a deadly gamble. The code provided that she submit to investigation. "If she has been discreet and has no vice, and her husband has gone out, and has greatly belittled her, she shall take her marriage portion [dowry] and go off to her father's house. . . . But if she has been found indiscreet and has gone out, ruined her house, belittled her husband, she shall be drowned."

Egypt

The style of Egypt's civilization, in contrast to Mesopotamia's, was imperial rather than urban. The main reason for its security and continuity was the geography of the country, a united river valley ruled by long-lasting dynasties. The Nile valley is well protected against foreign invasion by the Libyan Desert on the west, the Arabian Desert in the east, the Nubian Desert and the Nile's cataracts on the south, and the harborless coast of the Delta on the north. The Egyptian people were left free in their sheltered valley to pursue their own destiny without interference from the outside. There was not the constant rise and fall of empires, as there were in Mesopotamia because of foreign invaders. Also the Nile River provided a natural cohesion that held the entire valley together as a stable and functioning unit. Its slow but steady current carried northbound traffic effortlessly, and the prevailing north-to-northwest winds made the return trip almost as easy. Thus the Egyptians were provided with a priceless means for reliable communication and transportation that helped to unify the valley about 3100 B.C.E.

During the 2,500 years between its unification in 3100 B.C.E. and its conquest by the Persians in 525 B.C.E., only three empires ruled Egypt, and the intervening periods between empires were comparatively short. The civilization of Egypt therefore was stable and conservative. It was also a confident and optimistic civilization, partly because the Nile was gentle and predictable, compared to the Tigris-Euphrates with its devastating and unpredictable floods. Whereas the Mesopotamians regarded their flood god as harsh and merciless, the Egyptians viewed theirs as a god "whose coming brings joy to every human being."

A predominant feature of Egyptian religious belief concerned death and the physical preparations for the afterlife, especially that of the king. Since his death was not considered final, his body was embalmed and placed in a gigantic tomb, or pyramid, along with food and other necessities. The greatest of the pyramids was that of the Pharaoh Khufu, or Cheops. It covered thirteen acres, rose to a height of 481 feet, and contained some 2.3 million stone blocks, each weighing an average of 2.5 tons. And this was built with the simplest tools—ramps, rollers, and levers; no pulleys and no iron!

It has been said that the Egyptian peasants worked enthusiastically on these pyramids, believing that they were constructing the dwellings of a god on whom their collective well-being would depend. Whatever the justification for this statement—and it may be assumed that, enthusiastic or not, they had little choice in the matter—it does point up the supposed divinity of Egyptian kingship. From beginning to end the pharaoh was a god-king. No distinction was made between the sacred and the secular; indeed the notion was unthinkable. Thus there was an absence in Egypt of anything corresponding to the Mesopotamian law codes. All law was the expression of the divine authority of the god-king.

Royal authority was enforced by a bureaucracy headed by the vizier—"the steward of the whole land," "the eyes and ears of the king." Other officials included the royal sealbearer, who controlled the Nile traffic, the master of largesse, who was responsible for all livestock, and the head of the Exchequer, who maintained branch offices and storehouses throughout the kingdom for the collection of taxes. In bad years, the head of the Exchequer probably also took care of the distribution of seeds and livestock. There were governors, or nomarchs, to rule each province, or nome, and below them came the mayors of the towns and villages.

A final distinctive feature of Egyptian civilization was the overwhelming state domination of economic life. Individual property and enterprise were not unknown, but neither were they as common as in Mesopotamia. The state not only controlled most production, both agricultural and handicraft, but also directed distribution. Huge government warehouses and granaries were filled with taxes collected in kind—grains, animals, cloths, and metals. These were used for state expenses and also provided

Queen Nefertari guided by Isis.

Sphinx

reserves for years of scarcity. The king, it was said, was "he who presides over the food supplies of all." In addition to taxes, each community had to provide men for the corvée, or forced labor. The pyramids are the best-known examples of their work, but these laborers were also used for quarrying and mining and for maintaining the irrigation canals.

Egyptian craftmakers were universally recognized for their skills, particularly in luxury products. Their jewelry can scarcely be excelled today; their enamel work and ivory and pearl inlay were superb; they discovered how to make glass in many colors; they were the first to bark-tan leather in the manner still followed in most of the world; and their linen cloth was as fine as has ever been woven. Egyptian technology was very advanced in creating artificial beauty aids. Papyri were written to describe medical procedures for removing wrinkles and darkening gray hair. Among the substances used for cosmetic purposes were kohl for lengthening the eyebrows and lining the outer corners of the eyes; malachite and lead ore for green and gray eye shadow respectively; red ochre for rouge; henna for dyeing the nails, the palms of the hands, and the soles of the feet; and human hair for making wigs, over which melted beeswax was poured.

Crete

The style of the Minoan civilization of the island of Crete is summed up by the Greek word *thalassocracy*, or sea civilization. The prosperity of Crete depended on its trade, which included countries from one end of the Mediterranean to the other. The storms in the landlocked Mediterranean are not as fierce as in the open Atlantic, so Cretan merchants could sail, almost always in sight of land, to all the countries on the Mediterranean Sea. Moreover, the mountains of Crete were covered with forests, which provided timber for building the single-masted trading ships. In these ships, the Minoans carried back and forth the foodstuffs, ivory, and glass of Egypt; the horses and wood of Syria; the silver, pottery, and marble of the Aegean Isles; the copper of Cyprus; and their own olive oil and pottery.

This trade affected all aspects of the Minoan civilization. None of the cities was fortified because Minoan sea power was strong enough to protect the island. Cretan communities seem to have been socially and economically more egalitarian than their counterparts on the mainland. In place of a few great temples and palaces surrounded by relative slums, the pattern on Crete was the open village, with its outdoor shrine as the center for community life.

Minos Palace in Crete, Greece

Families as a rule lived in individual houses built of timber and stucco. Domestic slaves probably were held, though not in large numbers. Archeologists have found no buildings that appear to have been slave quarters, so Cretan galleys presumably were rowed by freemen.

Minoan artists did not try to impress by mere size, nor did they concern themselves with remote and awful deities or divine kings. Instead, on their household utensils, on the walls of their houses, and in their works of art, they reproduced the life about them. They found models everywhere: in natural objects such as birds, flowers, sea shells, and marine life of all types; and in scenes from their own everyday life, such as peasants returning from their fields, athletes wrestling with bulls, and women dancing in honor of the Great Goddess. In architecture the Minoans were more interested in personal comfort than outward appearance. The royal palace at Knossos was a sprawling complex that apparently had grown over several centuries. It included not only a throne room, reception chambers, and living quarters, but also storehouses and workshops that occupied most of the complex, as befitted a trading people. Outstanding was an elaborate plumbing and sanitation system that was not surpassed until modern times.

The freedom from wars and from large military and state establishments enabled the original Neolithic kin system to survive much more in Crete than on the Middle Eastern mainland. Consequently men were not able to gain the monopoly of economic, military, and political power in Crete that they did in Mesopotamia and Egypt. Frescoes, seals, and signet rings show that Cretan women continued to be active in "outside" work as well as "inside" work. They show women working in the fields, dancing in groves, crowding into bleachers at the bull arena, and actually participating in the bull wrestling. Some even took part in war, in contrast to their homebody counterparts in

Mesopotamia and Egypt. Cretan women could own property and could obtain divorce as easily as men. In this way the Cretan civilization stands out as the great exception among the ancient civilizations of Eurasia.

Indus

The style of the civilization in the Indus River valley was conservative, religious, and highly planned. We can see this in the cities, which were carefully built according to a common design. Each city at its height extended over six to seven square miles. Each was laid out on the grid pattern, with wide main streets encompassing large rectangular city blocks some 400 yards in length and 200 yards in width, far larger than the average city blocks of today. The buildings were constructed of bricks hardened in kilns, in contrast to the stone used in Egypt and the sun-dried bricks in Mesopotamia. The bricks everywhere were molded in two standard sizes (11 by 5.5 by 2.5 inches, and 9.2 by 4.5 by 2.2 inches), and weights and measures likewise were uniform

throughout the Indus lands. Such orderliness and organization seem to have been all-pervasive in this civilization. After it reached its maturity about 2500 B.C.E., it remained virtually static during the following millennium. Even when cities were destroyed by floods, the new cities were built to duplicate the old. Such undeviating continuity of tradition has had no equal, even in Egypt, and has given rise to the theory that the authority regulating this disciplined society may have been spiritual. This hypothesis is supported also by the absence of military equipment and fortifications.

Like all the other ancient civilizations, that of the Indus was predominantly agricultural. Wheat and barley were the staples, but field peas, melons, sesame, and dates were also grown, as well as cotton, which was first used for cloth making in this valley. There was also considerable trade with the outside world; the exported items included peacocks, apes, pearls, cotton textiles, copper, ivory, and ivory articles such as combs. Combs were fashioned in the same pattern as those still used in India today and are still indispensable for combing lice out

Indus stone stamp seals. Note the familiar humped bull of India.

of the hair. Most foreign trade was with Mesopotamia, and goods were transported with sailing boats that followed the coast to the Persian Gulf. If their ships were driven from sight of land, the sailors released crows that always flew toward the nearest point of coast. According to the Bible, this is precisely the method followed by Noah in the Ark, when he wished to find out where the land lay.

The causes and circumstances of the decline of the Indus civilization remain obscure. Hitherto it was widely believed that Aryan invaders, who came down from central Asia about 1500 B.C.E., were primarily responsible. But it has recently been suggested that the civilization may have been literally drowned in mud. Subterranean volcanic activity, according to this theory, caused a huge upwelling of mud, silt, and sand that dammed the Indus and formed a huge lake, swamping the capital, Mohenjo-daro. After several decades the dam was worn down, the water drained through, and the river resumed its normal course, but in the meantime the city had been ruined. Judging from the multiple layers of silt found in Mohenjo-daro, some such disaster occurred at least five times and perhaps more. The net result was irreparable damage to the heart of the Indus civilization, which left the outlying regions in the north too weak to resist assimilation by native cultures.

Much of this is guesswork and cannot be proven because the Indus script has not yet been deciphered. The script is pictographic and is read from left to right on one line and from right to left on the following line. This is the practice followed in early "Greek and is known as *boustrophedon*—"as the ox plows."

Shang

The style of the Shang civilization on the Yellow River in North China was the most different of all the Eurasian civilizations. To the present day, Chinese civilization remains distinctive and unique, and the main reason is the geographic isolation of the country. China is located at the eastern tip of Eurasia, separated from the rest of the continent by great mountains, deserts, and steppes. To the east China faces the vast Pacific Ocean, and to the north, the frozen Siberian steppes.

Although China was isolated, it was not completely cut off from outside influences. The early Shang civilization emerged north of the Yellow River precisely because that region was a cultural crossroads, influenced by nomadic sheepherding peoples to the northwest, by agricultural peoples to the east, and by forest dwellers to the south. Even the distant Middle East left its imprint on north China, contributing wheat cultivation and also the military technology of bronze weapons and of horse-drawn chariots, which were used by the invaders who established the Shang dynasty about 1500 B.C.E. These invaders became the masters of the scattered Neolithic communities of north China.

The same thing happened to the Shang as to the many other later invaders of China. Because of the great numbers of the Chinese people, the Shang were assimilated, and the general populace remained distinctively Chinese. Although China was enriched by elements from the Middle East such as barley, wheat, sheep, cattle, horses, bronze, and the wheel, these innovations did not change China fundamentally. Whereas the ancient Egyptian civilization has long since disappeared, and likewise those of Mesopotamia and the Indus, by contrast China's civilization has continued uninterrupted. Today China can boast the oldest continuous civilization in the world.

Not only the oldest, China's civilization is also the most unique. It was the first to raise silkworms and to weave their delicate fibers into fine silk cloth. It was the only major civilization that did not use animal milk and milk products for human consumption. Indeed the Chinese had the same reaction toward animal milk as Westerners did toward the eating of worms and ants. Also ancestor worship was a prominent and unique feature of Chinese religion from earliest times. Closely related was the importance attached to one's family name, which always preceded the personal name instead of following it, as in the West. This custom reflected the traditional primary role in Chinese society of the family, instead of the individual, the state, or the church. The familiar Chinese style of archi-

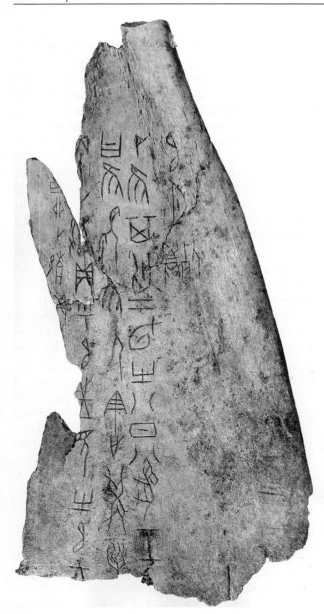

Shang oracle bone, animal bones engraved with written characters which were then heated until they cracked. The cracks were examined in relation to the writing. This practice was the foundation of the Chinese language. The characters are pictographs of classical Chinese.

tecture, with the ornate roof supported by rows of wooden pillars, also dates back to earliest times, as does the use of chopsticks rather than forks and spoons.

Most significant for the later history of China and all east Asia was the complex ideo-graphic script found in Shang remains. This is the direct ancestor of modern Chinese writing, illustrating again the continuity of Chinese civilization. Long ago the ancient hieroglyphics and cuneiform lost all intelligibility to the people of the Middle East, but the Shang script is still recognizable to modern Chinese. Most of the Shang writing surviving today is found on animal bones and turtle shells that were used for divination, another distinctive Chinese custom. Questions about sickness, dreams, hunting, the weather, or the harvest were inscribed on the bone or shell. Incisions were then made at various points and red-hot sticks pressed into them produce cracks. The shape, arrangement, and direction of these cracks were interpreted to yield a "Yes" or "No" answer by the diviner. These bones and shells were carefully buried, so many have survived and have revealed a good deal about Shang daily life, as well as about the Shang script.

As with the other Eurasian civilizations, the peasants were required to yield a portion of their crops to support the nobles, scribes, and officials gathered in the towns. Also they were obliged to serve under their lords in time of war as light-armed warriors. Only the ruling military class could afford the two-horse chariots and the bronze helmets and plate mail that they wore into battle. The elite's monopoly of bronze metallurgy enhanced the sharp class differentiation within Shang society. The gap is reflected in the elaborate palaces and royal tombs, on the one hand, and the crude pit dwellings of the common people, on the other. It shows also in the costly offerings that were placed in the tombs—bronze ritual vessels, fine silks, jades, marbles, musical instruments, and elaborate weapons.

As for relations between the sexes, the same inequity existed in Chinese civilization as in all others. The discrimination began at birth, for baby girls were more likely than baby boys to suffer from infanticide. During childhood, girls were subjected to the practice of footbinding, which left them crippled and kept them from venturing far beyond their households. With marriage, which was an arranged transaction, the trembling bride passed from the rule of her father to that of her husband's mother. In a well-to-do family she might have to accept second wives or concubines, particularly if she did not bear a male heir.

Chinese gender inequity was reflected in the distinctively Chinese view of the world as the product of two interacting, complementary elements, yin and yang. Yin was the attribute of all things female, dark, weak, passive. Yang was the attribute of all things male, bright, strong, and active. Although male and female were both necessary and complementary, one was by nature passive and subordinate. Starting with such philosophical premises, male moralists for thousands of years elaborated behavior patterns by which Chinese women were to be properly obedient and passive.

TRIBESPEOPLE AND PEASANTS

One of the costs of civilization was the division of people into rulers and ruled. This was discovered by Dutch officials in New Guinea. The Papuans there, who had never known civilization, refused to bow and scrape to the Dutch because they considered themselves to be free people. But the Indonesians, who had lived in a class society, were ready to accept the Dutch as masters. The following report by an American correspondent reveals how civilization can affect relations among human beings.*

A Dutch official walked into an office in Hollandia [New Guinea]. Seated at a table were an Indonesian official, still in the Netherlands' service, and two Papuan village headmen. The Indonesian jumped to his feet and stood still. The Papuans looked up, smiled and remained seated.

In the bar of a grimy Government hotel, about 9 o'clock one night, a Dutch official asked the Papuan bartender for a beer. The bartender, after five minutes, produced it. He also produced a pointed look at a wristwatch and asked the Dutchman how long he intended to stay.

A Dutch destroyer pulled into a south New Guinea coastal port. Local Dutch officials thought it would be a good idea to show some people from the jungles, still in the head-hunting stage, some real weapons.

Jungle people trekked down, wandered around the ship, and one of them gave the verdict:

"Yes, you have guns. But see these bows and arrows that we have? We think you are not able to use these fine bows and arrows. We can use them. . . ."

Netherlands officials, who have seen service in Indonesia, have had to do some considerable adjusting in New Guinea.

In Indonesia they came into a society that had its caste and class distinctions, its own ideas of authority and rights of rulers. They were masters and were treated as masters.

In New Guinea there are no masters and no slaves. Papuan life is a free sort of life. There are no village councils, no great lawgivers or authorities. A man's pretty much his own man, except for the influence on life of demons and spirits.

Between the Dutch and the Papuans there is no bowing and scraping. An Indonesian schoolteacher who tried to convince Papuans that the proper way to show respect was to walk hunched over in front of superiors was told:

"We are men, and men walk straight."

*New York Times, December 25, 1957. © 1957 by The New York Times Company. Reprinted by permission.

IV. NOMADS GAIN POWER

During the second millennium B.C.E., all the ancient civilizations collapsed, whether in the Middle East or India or far-off China. Was it internal rot or external force that was primarily responsible for that political and social demolition throughout Eurasia? Such a broad question is hard to answer with certainty and precision. But it is certain that both internal and external factors were important in determining the course of events.

Beginning with the internal weaknesses, there were first the scarcity and costliness of copper and bronze, which prevented their general use in making weapons and tools. Hence monarchs and their political and military allies had a virtual monopoly of armaments and so strengthened their privileged position at the top of the social pyramid. Further, only a small percentage of the total population was armed, a serious weakness when the old centers of civilization had to face the assault of nomads, who were all armed. The high cost of copper and bronze also deprived the peasantry of metal tools, forcing them to rely on stone axes and hoes and on flint knives and sickles. Since stone tools were less efficient and durable than metal, productivity was reduced.

Weakened by this rot inside, the ancient civilizations were easy targets for the nomads outside (for the origins of nomads, see Chapter 2, Section III). Three principal nomadic groups did the work of empire smashing: the Semitic tribespeople in the southern deserts, the Indo-Europeans in the Eurasian steppes to the west, and the Mongol-Turkish peoples to the east.

The Indo-Europeans, a cultural rather than a racial group, appear to have originated in the region of the Caspian Sea, where they tended their herds of cattle and did a little farming on the side. Primarily pastoralists, they were ever ready to pack their belongings into their great oxcarts and move on to more promising lands. Entire tribes participated in these migrations—women and children as well as the warriors. Thus they pushed westward to southern Russia and southeastern Europe and, by 2000 B.C.E., ranged in the broad belt from the Danubian plain to the Oxus and Jaxartes valleys. From this far-flung base they threatened more and more the centers of civilization that were geographically accessible to them—the Middle East, the Balkan peninsula, and the Indus valley.

The original dividing line between the Indo-European peoples in the western part of the steppes and the Mongol-Turkish in the eastern part consisted of the Altai and the Tien Shan mountains. To the east of this line the steppes are higher and drier and the climate generally harsher. The pastures here are not as rich as in the west and can support sheep, camels, and horses, but not cattle. The discrepancy between the relatively poor eastern and the richer western geographic areas created a persistent and powerful east-to-west gradient. The peoples of the eastern steppes were attracted to the west, both as refugees and as conquerors. A succession of tribes followed one after the other—Scythians migrated from the Altai to the Ukraine. Turkish tribes replaced them in central Asia but later followed them westward. Finally, the Mongols kept pushing from the rear until they erupted in the thirteenth century C.E. and overran most of Eurasia. These eastern nomads, because of their geographic location, had access not only to Europe, the Middle East, and India, but also to China, where they broke through periodically when the opportunity presented itself.

Because of the east-to-west gradient, the racial composition of the peoples of the western steppes gradually changed from predominantly Caucasoid to predominantly Mongoloid, at least as far west as the Caspian Sea. The racial shift began late in the first millennium B.C.E. and continued until the end of the medieval period. Then the tide was reversed by the Slavic Russians, who were armed with the weapons and transport of Western technology—muskets and cannon at first, and later machine guns and railroads.

Finally, the Semites occupied roughly the area from the Mediterranean to the Tigris and from the Taurus to Aden. Successive waves have appeared throughout history, emerging apparently from the deserts of Arabia. They used the donkey for transportation until about 1100 B.C.E., when the domestication of the camel transformed their culture as the domestication of the horse did that of the steppe nomads.

With the rise of civilization many Semitic tribes lived on the fringes of the cities, with the urban dwellers, but were always ready to seize any chance for raid and plunder.

The old centers of civilization on the periphery of Eurasia were irresistible magnets for the surrounding tribespeople. The abundant crops, the barns swollen with grain, and the dazzling luxuries of the cities all beckoned to the hungry nomads of steppes and deserts. Hence there were periodic raids and invasions, particularly of the Mesopotamian cities, which were more vulnerable than those of Crete, the Nile, or the Indus. Unsurprisingly, the settled peoples of all the civilizations regarded the nomads as an abomination. An Egyptian official wrote of the Semitic nomads, "Their name reeks more than the stink of bird droppings." At the other end of Eurasia a Chinese imperial secretary likewise reviled the Mongols: "In their breasts beat the hearts of beasts . . . from the most ancient times they have never been regarded as a part of humanity."

It was not until the second millennium B.C.E. that the balance of power throughout Eurasia shifted, and for the first time the nomads threatened the very existence of the great civilizations. The new military capabilities of the nomads rose from two fateful developments— the domestication of the horse and, later, the smelting of iron. As far as is known, the earliest domestication of animals took place in the Middle East, where people first learned to ride animals. Both these events occurred about 5000 B.C.E., but there was little riding then for the simple reason that the only animals available were the ox, which was too slow, and the onager, or wild ass, which was too small. The practice of animal domestication, however, spread northward to southern Russia, where both the onager and the wild horse were to be found. These two animals were domesticated there by 2500 B.C.E., and soon the horse became favored because it was larger, stronger, and faster. Furthermore, with selective breeding the horse gradually increased in size. A wild horse averages thirteen hands (a hand equals four inches), whereas a modern domestic horse averages fifteen to sixteen hands. When allowed to breed indiscriminately for a few generations, domestic horses

soon return to a smaller size, as illustrated by the mustang of the American West.

The first military use that the nomads made of their horse was to harness it to a light-bodied chariot with two spoked wheels, which they developed as an improvement on the clumsy Mesopotamian cart, with four solid wheels. The combination of the large horse and easily maneuvered chariot gave the nomads a formidable weapon—the war chariot. The first wave of nomadic invasions in the second millennium B.C.E. were invasions of charioteers. Riding hard into battle, one chariot warrior took charge of the horses while the others in the chariot shot arrows from their powerful compound bows. Few infantrymen could stand up for long to the volleys of arrows, let alone to the massed chariot charges that followed.

Toward the end of the second millennium the nomads further increased their military effectiveness by shifting from chariot to cavalry warfare. Their horses were now large enough and strong enough to bear the direct weight of the rider. The nomads also developed the bridle and bit, for guiding the horse, and the horned saddle and stirrup, which enabled them to ride with both hands free and to launch a shower of arrows at full gallop. Hence the Eurasian nomads, now with unprecedented mobility, were able to outride and outfight armies defending the urban centers. The technology of riding was the basis of nomadic military power throughout the classical and medieval ages, and it culminated in the extraordinary conquests of Genghis Khan in the thirteenth century. The centers of civilization were under constant threat of nomadic invasion until superior Western firearms were brought to bear.

The counterpart of the horse for the desert nomad was the camel. There were two varieties—the one-humped Arabian, which has adapted to hot desert conditions, and the two-humped Bactrian relative, which has adapted to cold desert conditions. Both can live off land where even the ass would starve, and both can go for weeks on fat stored in their humps and on water stored in their multiple stomachs. Where and when the camel was first tamed is not clear, but by 1000 B.C.E. transportation and communication across the deserts of central Asia and the Middle East were dependent on the "ship of the desert."

The discovery of the technique for smelting iron ore also enhanced nomadic military strength. The technique was developed in the middle of the second millennium B.C.E. in northeast Asia Minor. But not until the destruction of the Hittite Empire about 1200 B.C.E., when the local ironsmiths became scattered over wider areas, did their technique become generally known. Iron smelting appeared late because the process differs in basic ways from those used for working copper and its alloys.

In copper smelting, the molten metal collects in the bottom of the furnace, and the slag floats on top. In iron smelting, at least at the temperature possible with ancient furnaces, the iron is never completely liquefied. It forms instead a gray, spongy mass known technically as the bloom. The discovery that wrought iron could be produced by hammering the red-hot bloom was understandably slow in coming. Furthermore the new metal was no improvement over the copper and bronze already available. It was harder to work, required more fuel, and lost its cutting edge more easily. Later it was discovered that iron could be hardened by a process of repeated hammering, heating, plunging into cold water (quenching), and contacting the metal to the charcoal fuel. What had to be discovered, then, was not merely a new metal but a radically new technique of metallurgy, for the early smiths had no past experience to prepare them for the new methods.

Even the improved, harder type of iron was always liable to rust, but the fact that iron ore, in contrast to copper and tin, was very widespread and correspondingly cheap more than made up for rusting. Ordinary peasants could now afford iron tools. Agricultural productivity rose as fields were extended into heavily wooded areas that previously resisted the old stone axe. Equally significant was the effect of the cheap new metal on the Eurasian military balance. Previously the poverty-stricken nomads had not been able to afford as many of the expensive bronze weapons as could the rulers of the urban centers. But now iron ore was available in almost every region, and every village smith could forge new weapons that were both superior to and cheaper than the old. Thus nomadic warriors enjoyed not only superior mobility but also iron weapons that were as good and as plentiful as those of the soldiers guarding the civilized areas.

V. NOMADS DESTROY ANCIENT CIVILIZATIONS

With their horses and iron weapons, the nomads launched two great waves of invasion that overwhelmed the centers of civilization. During the first, between roughly 1700 and 1500 B.C.E., the invaders usually arrived with horse-drawn chariots and bronze weapons; by the second wave, from about 1200 to 1100 B.C.E., they commonly rode on horses and fought with iron weapons. These invasions were not vast incursions of foreign hordes that displaced native stock and completely changed ethnic patterns. Instead there were rather small numbers of invaders who used their superior military technology to establish themselves as military elites, ruling over subject peoples who far outnumbered them.

The end result was the uprooting of civilization everywhere except in the Middle East. Elsewhere empires rose and fell in rapid succession. Although because of its geographic accessibility the Middle East endured the largest number of invasions, civilization there survived, with its cities, palaces, temples, scribes, merchants, and government officials. One reason was that civilization had been established for a longer period and had sunk deeper roots in the Middle East. Moreover, such large expanses of the Middle East had become civilized by 1700 B.C.E. that not all could be overwhelmed and destroyed. Finally, invaders in the Middle East usually were not raw barbarians fresh from the steppes or desert. They were instead semicivilized barbarians who had settled earlier in surrounding lands and who, consequently, were already partially assimilated by the time of conquest.

Middle East

Considering first the Middle East, the invasions began about 2000 B.C.E. when the Indo-European Hittites filtered into Asia Minor. Together with the native peoples, the Hittites organized a large empire, including Asia Minor and much of Syria, though not Mesopotamia. The Hittites were followed by two other Indo-European invaders, the Kassites and the Hurrians. During this period even well-protected Egypt was overrun by a mixed, though mostly Semitic, group of invaders, the Hyksos. By 1500 B.C.E. the first wave of invasions ended, leaving the Middle East controlled by three major powers: the Hittites in the north, the Egyptians in the south, and the Semitic Assyrians in the east.

This triangular balance was upset by the second wave of invasions, which began about 1200 B.C.E. A long series of wars between the Hittites and Egyptians had weakened both empires. Three Semitic invaders moved to fill the vacuum: the Phoenicians into the Mediterranean coast; the Arameans into Syria, Palestine, and northern Mesopotamia; and the Hebrews into Palestine and Syria. About 1100 B.C.E. the powerful Second Assyrian Empire began to expand, with its iron weapons, disciplined army, efficient bureaucracy, and iron battering rams mounted on wheels. By the seventh century the Assyrian Empire, with its capital at Nineveh, included Mesopotamia, Asia Minor, Syria, Palestine, and Egypt. But overextension of the empire and the deep hostility of its subject peoples finally led to disaster. In 612 B.C.E. a coalition of enemies destroyed Nineveh and ended forever the role of the Assyrians in history.

The Assryians were followed by the Persians, who now organized the greatest empire to that date. Under their King Cyrus (550–529 B.C.E.), and using Assyrian military techniques, the Persians conquered all the lands from the Nile River in the west to the Indus River in the east. For the first time the entire Middle East was under one rule, and the barbarian invaders were firmly shut out.

Greece

In contrast to the Middle East, civilization in Greece, India, and China did not survive the barbarian invasions. In these peripheral areas, it lacked depth in time and space, and therefore civilization was plowed under. Thus it was in those regions that new classical civilizations

emerged, with new religious, social, and philosophical systems.

In Greece, the first invaders were the Indo-European Achaeans, who came in the twentieth century B.C.E. They were charioteers with bronze weapons, their general level of development far behind that of the Minoan Cretans. But by 1600 B.C.E. the newcomers had absorbed much of the Minoan culture, which had been transplanted to the mainland, and they had established a number of small kingdoms from Thessaly down to the southern tip of the Peloponnesus.

The most advanced settlements were those in the Peloponnesus, which was closest to Crete. Mycenae, the outstanding Achaean center there, gave its name to the emerging civilization. In contrast to the cities of Crete, all settlements in Mycenaean Greece were strongly fortified. Massive hilltop citadels were constructed, where the king and his retainers lived. The commoners

The Lion Gate at Mycenae, Greece.

built their dwellings outside the citadel but in time of danger sought refuge within its walls.

Unlike the other Indo-European invaders who had established themselves in the Middle East and the Indus valley, the Mycenaeans took to the sea after the fashion of the Minoans and developed a formidable maritime power. They raided or traded, as opportunities dictated, and they founded overseas colonies in Rhodes, Cyprus, and the west coast of Asia Minor. The Mycenaeans soon undermined the former economic hegemony of Crete in the Mediterranean, and by the fifteenth century B.C.E. they were raiding the great island itself. The unwalled cities, including the capital of Knossos, were taken and destroyed. These disasters, together with a series of devastating earthquakes, led to the virtual extinction of the formerly great Minoan civilization by 1150 B.C.E.

Meanwhile the Mycenaeans were experiencing a similar fate at the hands of new invaders, the Dorians. Appearing about 1200 B.C.E. and armed with superior iron weapons, the Dorians captured the Mycenaean citadels and towns one by one. Administrative systems disintegrated, rural populations scattered, foreign trade withered, and Greece reverted to an agrarian and pastoral economy. A Dark Age descended and obscured Greece until the rise of the city-states about 800 B.C.E.

The main Dorian settlements were again in the Peloponnesus. From there the invaders pushed on overseas to found colonies in Crete, in Rhodes, and on the adjacent coast of Asia Minor. Other Greeks, perhaps Mycenaean refugees, crossed from Athens to the Cyclades Islands and on to the central part of the west coast of Asia Minor. There they established settlements that became known as Ionia, which for a period was the most advanced region of the entire Greek world. Still further north, other bands speaking the Aeolic dialect sailed from Thessaly and central Greece to the island of Lesbos and thence to northern Asia Minor. These new Greek colonies in Asia Minor were never able to expand into the interior because of the resistance of the large local population. Although confined to the coastal areas, they prospered and were destined to play a major role in the general history of the Greek people.

Much more is known of this Dark Age in Greece than of the corresponding postinvasion period in India, largely because of the precious heritage of the four great poems left by the Greeks—Homer's *Iliad* and *Odyssey*, and Hesiod's *Works and Days* and *Birth of the Gods*. Homer wrote of war, adventure, and the life of nobles and kings, whereas Hesiod described the life and lore of the farmer and the genealogies of the gods. Between them they have left a vivid picture of the primitive agricultural and pastoral society of those centuries. Households were largely self-sufficient, growing their own food and making their own cloth with wool from their flocks of sheep. The only full-time traders were foreigners—Phoenicians or Cypriots—who appeared sporadically with trinkets for the commoners and more valuable goods for the nobles. The monotony of the farm work was broken by the occasional visit of a bard who sang of the glories of war and of the exploits of illustrious ancestors.

Each community consisted of the noble families, who governed and led in war, and the commoners, including freehold peasants, tenant farmers, and a few craftmakers, hired laborers, and slaves. At the top was the king, whose authority depended on his prowess in war and his ability to exercise leadership in the meetings of the council of nobles. Occasionally the king called a meeting of the assembly that included all adult males, but the purpose usually was to mobilize popular support for decisions already reached in conjunction with the nobles. These simple institutions, typical of the Indo-European tribes at this level of development, represented the embryo from which the Greek city-state was to develop its organs of government.

India

In India, the Indus valley civilization had the same fate as the Minoan civilization of Crete. About 1500 B.C.E., it was overrun by tribespeople who, with the military advantage of iron weapons and horsedrawn chariots, easily overwhelmed the copper weapons and oxdrawn carts of the natives. The invaders called themselves Aryans and the land in which they settled Aryavarta, or land of the Aryans. They were of the Indo-European family of peoples, of which the western branches had invaded Mesopotamia and Greece. Infiltrating in small groups, the Aryans easily overthrew the decaying Indus valley civilization, so a primitive new society emerged in the latter half of the second millennium B.C.E. Information concerning this society is scanty. Unlike the Indus civilization, which left a wealth of material remains but no decipherable written records, the Aryans left almost no remains, for they used wood or mud for their dwellings and had no large cities, but they did leave a wealth of literature in the form of Vedas. Thus material available for the reconstruction of Aryan life is the direct opposite of that for the Indus civilization.

The word *veda* means knowledge, and for the Hindus the Vedas are a primary source of religious belief, as the Bible is for Christians and the Koran for Muslims. There were originally four Vedas, but the most important is the oldest, the Rigveda. In the course of time other works were added to the four Vedas and acquired a similar sacred status. As Homer's epics are for Mycenaean Greece, the Rigveda is a primary source for study of the early Aryans. It is in essence a collection of 1,028 hymns arranged in ten books, making it as bulky as the *Iliad* and *Odyssey* combined.

The tall, blue-eyed, fair-skinned Aryans were very conscious of their physical features in contrast to those of the conquered indigenous people, who are referred to in the Vedas as short, black, noseless, and as dasas, or slaves. The image of the Aryans that emerges from the Vedic literature is that of a virile people, fond of war, drinking, chariot racing, and gambling. Their god of war, Indra, was the ideal Aryan warrior: He dashed into battle joyously, wore golden armor, and could consume the flesh of 300 buffaloes and drink three lakes of liquor at one time.

When they first arrived in India the Aryans were primarily pastoralists. Their economic life centered around their cattle, and wealth was judged on the basis of the size of the herds. As the newcomers settled in the fertile river valleys, they gradually shifted more to agriculture. They lived in villages consisting of a number of related families. Several villages comprised a clan, and several clans a tribe, at the head of which

was the king. As in Greece, the king's authority depended on his personal prowess and initiative; this authority was limited by the council of nobles and, in some tribes, by the freemen.

The outstanding characteristic of this early Aryan society was its basic difference from later Hinduism: Cows were worshiped but eaten. Intoxicating spirits were not forsaken but joyously consumed. There were classes but no castes, and the priests were subordinate to the nobles rather than dominating the social pyramid. In short, Aryan society resembled much more the other contemporary Indo-European societies than it did the classical Hinduism that was to develop in later centuries.

China

About 1500 B.C.E. charioteers with bronze weapons also invaded the distant valley of the Yellow River in north China. There they found the flourishing Neolithic culture of the Shang, to which they made contributions, but by which they were absorbed. As has always been true in China, these invasions did not create a complete break with the Chinese culture's past, as they did in Greece and India. Hence the distinctively Chinese civilization has continued uninterrupted from the early Shang period to the present, sometimes modified, but never destroyed or transformed.

The pattern of continuity is apparent in the transition from the Shang to the Zhou dynasty in 1027 B.C.E. The Zhou people had for long lived in the Wei valley on the fringes of civilization, so they shared the language and basic culture of the Shang but at the same time borrowed military techniques from the sheepherding "barbarians" to the north and west. Consequently when the Zhou overran north China, they did overthrow the Shang dynasty but did not interrupt the evolution of Chinese civilization. The writing system continued as before, as did ancestor worship, the methods of divination, and the division of society into aristocratic warriors and peasant masses. Political decentralization also persisted and, indeed, became more pronounced as the Zhou rulers assigned the conquered territories to vassal lords. The vassal lords journeyed periodically to the Zhou court for elaborate ceremonies of investiture, but gradually this practice lapsed. So eventually the lords, ensconced in their walled towns, ruled over the surrounding countryside with little control from the capital.

In 771 B.C.E. the Zhou capital was captured by new "barbarians" allied with rebellious lords. The Zhou dynasty resumed its rule from a center further to the east that was not so vulnerable to attacks from the borderlands. Thus the dynastic period before 771 B.C.E. is termed by the Chinese the Western Zhou, and the period thereafter, the Eastern Zhou. During the Eastern Zhou period the kings were rulers in name only. Although accorded certain religious functions and some ceremonial respect, their domains were smaller than those of their nominal vassals, and their power correspondingly weaker. Indeed they managed to survive until 256 B.C.E. only because they provided spiritual leadership. The dynasty was also a royal priesthood and, as such, was preserved as a symbol of national unity.

Although the Eastern Zhou was a period of political instability, it was also a period of cultural flowering. In this dynamic and creative age the great works of literature, philosophy, and social theory were written. This was the period when the classical Chinese civilization was taking form. It corresponded to the classical Greek and Indian civilizations roughly evolving at the same time. The origin and nature of these classical civilizations is the subject of the remaining chapters in Part II.

SUGGESTED READINGS

For the origins of civilizations, see J. Gowlett, *Ascent to Civilization* (Knopf, 1984); P. R. S. Moorey, ed., *The Origins of Civilization* (Clarendon, 1979); C. B. Heiser, Jr., *Seed to Civilization* (W. H. Freeman, 1973); J. E. Pfeiffer, *The Emergence of Society* (McGraw-Hill, 1977); and A. C. Renfrew, *Before Civilization* (Cape, 1973), which challenges the diffusionist theory of civilization.

Surveys of the various civilizations are given in K. C. Chang, *Shang Civilization* (Yale University, 1980);

O. R. Gurney, *The Hittites* (Penguin, 1980); C. Y. Hsu, *Western Chou Civilization* (Yale University, 1988); T. Jacobsen, *The Treasures of Darkness: A History of Mesopotamian Religion* (Yale University, 1976); N. Postgate, *The First Empires* (Elsevier, 1977); J. Hawkes and L. Woolley, "Prehistory and the Beginnings of Civilization," in *UNESCO History of Mankind*, Vol. 1 (Harper & Row, 1963); M. Hammond, *The City in the Ancient World* (Harvard University, 1972); J. G. Macqueen, *The Hittites and Their Contemporaries in Asia Minor* (Thames & Hudson, 1975); B. M. Fagan, ed., *Avenues to Antiquity* (W. H. Freeman, 1976); R. F. Willetts, *The Civilization of Ancient Crete* (University of California, 1977); and the lavishly illustrated *The Epic of Man* by the editors of Life (Time Incorporated, 1961), and *The Dawn of Civilization* (McGraw-Hill, 1961).

For the nomadic invaders, see E. D. Phillips, *The Royal Hordes: Nomad Peoples of the Steppes* (Thames & Hudson, 1965); O. Lattimore, *Studies in Frontier History* (Mouton, 1962), and *Inner Frontiers of China* (American Geographical Society, 1940); and A. Guha, ed., *Central Asia: Movement of Peoples and Ideas from Times Prehistoric to Modern* (Harper & Row, 1972). A survey of today's nomads is presented in the well-illustrated volume *Nomads of the World* (National Geographic Society, 1971).

NOTES

1. Cited by N. Bailkey, "Early Mesopotamian Constitutional Development," *American Historical Review* (July 1967), pp. 1, 225.
2. Adapted from J. Hawkes and L. Woolley, *UNESCO History of Mankind*, Vol. 1, *Prehistory and the Beginnings of Civilization* (Harper & Row, 1963), p. 467; and V. Gordon Childe, *Man Makes Himself* (Mentor Books, 1951), p. 149.
3. Cited by A. J. Wright, *Buddhism in Chinese History* (Sanford University, 1959), pp. 19–20.
4. Cited by G. Soloveytchik, *Potemkin* (Butterworth, 1938), p. 25.
5. W. A. Haviland, "Stature of Tikal," *American Antiquity* (July 1967), pp. 316–25.
6. *New York Times*, December 11, 1984.
7. E. A. Speiser, "The Beginnings of Civilization in Mesopotamia," *Supplement to the Journal of the American Oriental Society* (December 1939), p. 27.

4

Classical Civilizations Begin Eurasian Unification, 1000 B.C.E.–500 C.E.

Formerly the things which happened in the world had no connection among themselves. Each action interested only the locality where it happened. But since then all events are united in a common bundle.

Polybius

The most striking feature of the Classical Age was the beginning of the unification of Eurasia. A comparison of the map of Eurasia about 1500 B.C.E. with that of about 200 C.E. makes clear the extent of this unification. (See map on p. 47 and map of Early Eurasian Unification about 200 C.E., pp. 72–73.) The empires of the early period were almost entirely restricted to their respective river valleys and give the appearance of tiny islands in a vast sea of barbarism. By the first century C.E., however, the Roman, Parthian, Kushan, and Han empires spanned the breadth of Eurasia from the Scottish highlands to the China seas. This made possible a modest degree of interaction among empires.

Of course there had always been certain interregional contacts even at the time of the ancient civilizations, as evidenced by the nomadic invasions in all directions. But now in the Classical Age interregional contacts were substantially closer, more varied, and more sustained. And yet—even by the end of the classical period—the Roman and Chinese empires, at opposite ends of Eurasia, had not been able to establish direct, official contact and possessed no specific or reliable knowledge of each other. Thus Eurasian unity remained at the beginning stage throughout those centuries. The origins, nature, and significance of this first stage in the unification process are the subjects of this chapter.

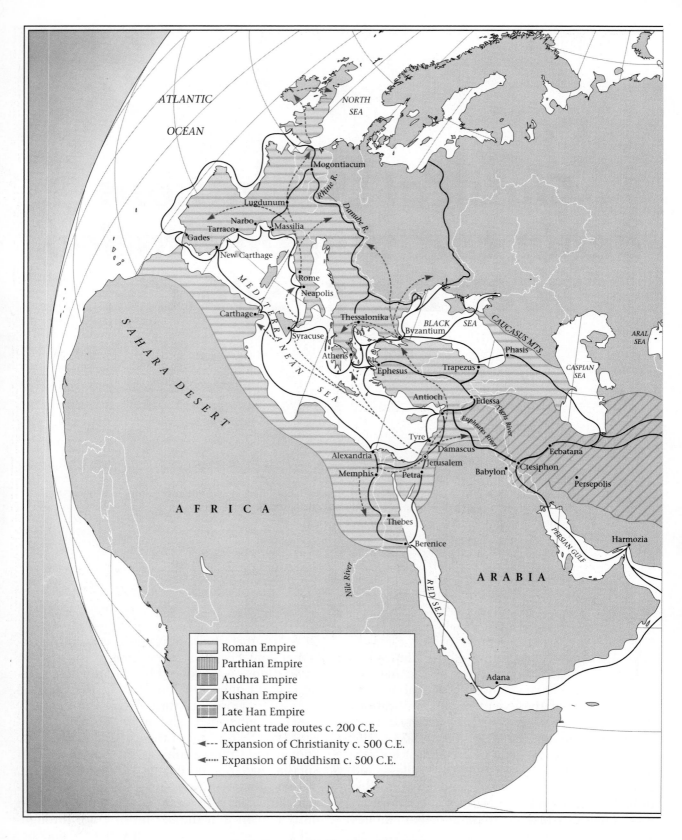

Early Eurasian Unification about 200 C.E.

Legend:

- Roman Empire
- Parthian Empire
- Andhra Empire
- Kushan Empire
- Late Han Empire
- Ancient trade routes c. 200 C.E.
- Expansion of Christianity c. 500 C.E.
- Expansion of Buddhism c. 500 C.E.

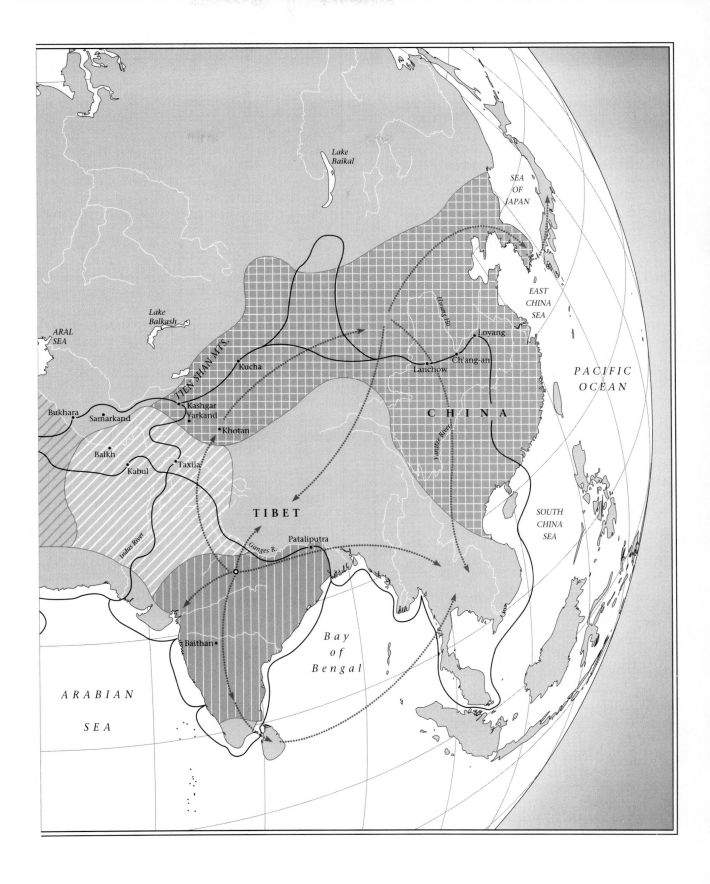

ARAL
SEA

Lake
Balkash

Lake
Baikal

SEA
OF
JAPAN

EAST
CHINA
SEA

PACIFIC
OCEAN

Bukhara

Samarkand

TIEN SHAN MTS.

Kucha

Kashgar
Yarkand

Khotan

Lanchow

Ch'ang-an

Loyang

Hwang Ho

C H I N A

Yangtze River

Balkh

Kabul

Taxila

T I B E T

SOUTH
CHINA
SEA

Indus River

Ganges R.

Pataliputra

Baithan

B a y
o f
B e n g a l

A R A B I A N

S E A

I. ROOTS OF UNIFICATION

Technological advance was at the root of the new Eurasian unity. This was not surprising, since from history's very beginning the territorial range of human activities had always depended on the level of technology. When people were at the food-gathering stage, the range of the individual band was its hunting ground. As people learned agriculture and metallurgy and shipbuilding, their range broadened to encompass, for example, the valley empires of Sargon and of the pharaohs. But now further technological advances allowed for a much greater extension of agriculture and civilization. Regional empires were organized and stretched contiguously across the breadth of Eurasia. The basic technological advance responsible was the discovery and ever more widespread use of iron.

Iron smelting was developed first in Asia Minor in the middle of the second millennium B.C.E., spreading from there after the destruction of the Hittite Empire about 1200 B.C.E. As we have seen, this discovery made possible the second wave of barbarian invasions at the end of the second millennium B.C.E. But some centuries passed before the new metal was available in sufficient quantities for everyday use. When hoes and axes and plows, as well as weapons, could be made of iron, then the economic, social, and political repercussions were immediate and far-reaching.

This stage was reached slowly—about 800 B.C.E. in India, 750 B.C.E. in central Europe, and 600 B.C.E. in China. In these and other regions the use of cheap iron led first and foremost to the cutting down of heavy forests hitherto invulnerable to stone-edged axes and wooden plows. Now farmers were able to use their strong, sharp iron axes and iron-shod plows to extend agriculture from the Middle East eastward across the Iranian plateau and westward across the Mediterranean lands and into central and northern Europe. Likewise in India the Aryan newcomers pushed eastward and cut down the forests of the Ganges valley. At the same time agriculturists in China were extending their operations from the Yellow River valley southward to the great Yangtze basin.

The expansion of the frontiers of agriculture made possible a corresponding expansion of the frontiers of civilization. They grew more in the half millennium from 1000 to 500 B.C.E. than in the preceding three millennia from 4000 to 1000 B.C.E. The basic reason for this was the tremendous increase in productivity that now took place. Not only was agriculture practiced in much larger areas, but also the combination of soils and climate in the newly opened lands of central Europe and of the Ganges and Yangtze monsoon basins was much more productive than were the comparatively arid Middle East, Indus, and Yellow River regions.

The jump in agricultural productivity meant that a surplus was now available for economic development and for state-building purposes. Trade increased in volume, especially along the rivers that constituted ready-made highways. Craftmakers appeared in growing numbers to provide the services needed in the new agricultural communities and the products demanded for the new trade. At first goods and services were exchanged by barter, with obvious inconvenience for both buyer and seller. Then media of exchange were developed, such as measures of grain or, more common, bars of metal. But with every transaction the weight and purity of the metal had to be checked against fraudulent clipping and debasing.

About 700 B.C.E., the Lydians of western Asia Minor began stamping pieces of metal and guaranteeing both their quality and their weight. Various Greek city-states soon improved on this technique by stamping flat, circular, two-sided coins. Thus gold and silver coins now helped large-scale wholesale or interregional trade. Additionally, copper coins enabled farmers to sell rather than barter their produce, and artisans to work for wages rather than foodstuffs. The net effect was a great boost in all kinds of commerce, a corresponding boost in manufacturing and agriculture, and an overall increase in efficiency and productivity. Now for the first time, the manufacturer of cheap goods had a mass market available. The small landholder could turn from subsistence agriculture to specialized farming, whether the specialty was the mulberry and silkworm in China or olive oil and wine in Greece.

The new iron tools also made it possible to build better and larger ships, which in turn led to longer voyages and to more trade and colonization. At the outset overseas expansion was hindered by piracy, which then was thought to be as normal an activity as brigandage on land. *The Odyssey*, which describes the half-piratical, half-commercial expeditions of Menelaus and Odysseus in the Aegean Sea, relates how all the voyagers as a matter of course asked those whom they met if they were pirates. But gradually maritime trade was developed on a regular large-scale basis, with great economic advantage. Transport by sea was many times cheaper than by land and remained so until the development of an efficient horse harness in the Middle Ages and the building of good roads in the eighteenth century.

By the end of the Classical Age, trade routes encircled all of Eurasia. (In contrast, local self-sufficiency was the rule in most regions following the invasions of the second millennium B.C.E.) In addition to the caravan routes across the interior of Eurasia, there were sea routes around its circumference—from the North Sea to the western Mediterranean, from the western Mediterranean to the Levant, from the Red Sea to India, and from India to Southeast Asia and, to a lesser degree, to China. This maritime commerce was accompanied by colonization, especially in the Mediterranean by the Phoenicians and Greeks, and later in Southeast Asia by the Indians.

Side by side with these economic developments came equally significant social and political changes. The military aristocracy, risen to prominence with the invasions of the second millennium B.C.E., was being undermined by the new class of merchants, craftmakers, and mariners. The old tribal society was being transformed by the use of money; personal services and allegiances were being replaced by the demands of the marketplace.

Equally disruptive was the political consolidation made possible by economic growth. Tribal chiefs and their advisory councils and assemblies were replaced by kingdoms and then by empires, whether in Italy, India, or China. Nor was it a one-way process of economic development stimulating political centralization. The reverse also operated, for the great new regional empires spanning the Eurasian land mass enforced order and security, making long-distance trade by land and sea possible. Regional

The Appian Way, "queen of roads," connecting Rome with southern Italy, is still in use today.

empires also were able to build and maintain regional road networks that facilitated commerce.

In the Persian Empire, for example, the so-called Royal Road ran 1,677 miles from Susa, located to the north of the Persian Gulf, westward to the Tigris, and thence across Syria and Asia Minor to Ephesus on the Aegean coast. The route was divided into 111 post stations, each with relays of fresh horses for the royal couriers. Caravans took ninety days to travel this road from end to end, whereas the royal couriers traversed it in a week. As the empire was enlarged, branch lines were constructed southwest to Egypt and southeast to the Indus valley. A few centuries later the Romans constructed their well-known system of roads; so well engineered were these that some, along with their bridges, are still in use.

At the other end of Eurasia, the Chinese built an elaborate network of both roads and canals, which enabled them to transport goods from present-day Canton to the Yangtze valley by an all-water route, thereby promoting their overseas trade. To the northwest they built roads that linked up with the long silk route, which, as will be noted in the following section, crossed the whole of central Asia to the Middle East. The main highways were lined with trees and provided with stations and guest houses. Road construction and maintenance was the responsibility of central and local officials who were punished if they did not carry out their duties properly. Likewise in India the Royal Highway ran from the Ganges delta to Taxila in the northwest, near the Khyber Pass, where it connected with the caravan routes west to the Middle East and north to central Asia.

All these developments involved profound changes in social relationships, in political organizations, and in ways of living and working. Such basic and all-inclusive disruption was unsettling and uncomfortable. It led to soul searching—to the posing of new questions and the seeking for new answers. Thinkers had to reconsider their respective traditions and to either abandon them or adapt them to the requirements of an age of transition. People speculated about such questions as the moral basis of ideal government, the functioning of the social order, and the origin and purpose of the universe and life.

About the sixth century B.C.E. such questions were being posed and discussed all over Eurasia. The answers made up the great philosophical, religious, and social systems of the Classical Age. It was not happenstance, then, that the spokespeople for these systems were all contemporaries—Confucius in China, Buddha in India, Zoroaster in Persia, and the rationalist philosophers in Greece. In all these regions the disruption and the challenge were the same, but the answers varied greatly, and the several Eurasian civilizations set off in decidedly different directions. Indeed, it was at this time that these civilizations developed their distinctive philosophical attitudes and social institutions, which have continued to distinguish them through the centuries to the present day.

The attitudes and institutions of each of the classical civilizations will be analyzed in the following chapters. The remainder of this chapter will be devoted to an examination of the interrelationships among these civilizations. Contemporary Eurasians were very much aware of these interrelationships. They were definitely aware that the historical stage was expanding—that life was becoming more complex and that many new domestic and external forces were pressing in on them. Thus the Greek historian Polybius, when starting his history of events from 220 to 145 B.C.E., observed that "during this period history becomes, so to speak, an organic whole. What happens in Italy and in Libya is bound up with what happened in Asia and in Greece, all events culminating in a single result."

Two aspects of this new "organic whole" were particularly clear, even to contemporaries. These were interregional commercial bonds and cultural bonds, the subject of the following two sections.

II. COMMERCIAL BONDS

The principal interregional bonds of a material nature were commercial in character, though not exclusively so. This was a time when not only goods but also people moved about from one region to another, taking with them their technological skills and their plants. We can see how wide-ranging this interchange was by the fact that cotton, sugar cane, and chickens, all first domesticated in India, spread to both China and western Eurasia during this period. Likewise the Chinese during these centuries obtained for the first time the grape vine, alfalfa, chive, cucumber, fig, sesame, pomegranate, and walnut. In return the Chinese gave to the rest of Eurasia the orange, peach, pear, peony, azalea, camellia, and chrysanthemum. There was a similar interchange of technology, as is evident in the case of that fundamental invention, the waterwheel. The first waterwheel to be found in western Asia was that of Mithridates, king of Pontus, and was erected on the south shore of the Black Sea about 65 B.C.E. The first waterwheel in China was built soon after, about 30 B.C.E. The difference between the two dates is much too small for direct diffusion from either source and thus strongly suggests diffusion in both directions from some unknown intermediate source. Such interaction between the various Eurasian regions was the result of a great increase in local and long-distance trade during the centuries of the Classical Age.

Trade was conducted both by land across central Eurasia and by sea around the coasts of the land mass. These two general routes were by

An Athenian silver four-drachma coin (tetradrachm) *from the fifth century B.C.E. (440–430 B.C.E.). On the front (left) is the profile of Athena and on the back (right) is her symbol of wisdom, the owl. The silver from which the coins were struck came chiefly from the state mines at Sunium in southern Attica.*

no means exclusive or independent of each other. A large proportion of the goods were moved along some combination of the two, usually by sea between Egypt and India and by one of several overland routes between India and China. Furthermore, the land and sea routes were competitive; excessively high charges or intolerable lack of security on one route normally shifted the trade to the other.

Maritime trade had first gotten under way at the time of the ancient civilizations. Egyptian traders ventured down the Red Sea to East Africa and along the Levant coast to Lebanon. Likewise, Sumerian merchants sailed down the Persian Gulf, along the Arabian peninsula, while their counterparts from the Indus valley worked their way westward until contact was established, perhaps at the Bahrain Islands in the Persian Gulf. But all these early seafarers were mere landlubbers compared to the Minoans of Crete. The great maritime traders of ancient times, they plied the Mediterranean from end to end as the unrivaled sailors of that inland sea.

With the invasions of the Achaeans and Dorians this far-flung commerce dried up, and the eastern Mediterranean people sank back to an agrarian and isolated existence. The first to resume the mercantile activities of the Cretans were the Phoenicians. A Semitic-speaking people who had settled along the narrow coastal plains of the eastern Mediterranean, they soon developed a flourishing trade as commercial middlemen. Caravans from the east brought in myrrh, spices, and the products of Mesopotamian craftsmanship. From lands overseas came assorted metals, hides, grains, olive oil, and slaves. The Phoenicians themselves manufactured fine furniture, jewelry, metalware, and especially textiles, made from the wool of their own sheep and colored by their famous purple dye obtained from shellfish found in large beds along the coast.

In developing this trade the Phoenicians evolved a type of ship rowed by tiers of oarsmen. It was fast and seaworthy for the long voyages that were made further and further to the west. In the eleventh century B.C.E. the Phoenicians began to spread out over the Aegean, and by the end of the ninth century they had entered the western Mediterranean. They founded trading posts and colonies on the northwest coast of Africa; the south coast of Spain; and on Sicily,

Malta, and the Balearic Islands. They even ventured beyond Gibraltar as far afield as Cornwall, England, where they traded for valuable tin.

From about 1100 B.C.E. until the late eighth century B.C.E. the sailors and merchants of Phoenicia controlled most of the maritime trade of the Mediterranean. Then the Greeks appeared as competitors, spurred on by the same pressure of overpopulation. First they established trading posts, which later developed into agricultural settlements wherever the land resources made this possible. Settlements were quite independent of the mother cities from whence they sprang, even though the colonists established the same institutions and copied the same religious practices they had left behind. So Greek colonization took the form of many independent city-states rather than one centrally controlled empire.

One principal area of Greek settlement was in Sicily and south Italy, where so many colonies were founded that the region came to be known as Magna Graecia, or Greater Greece. On the mainland the Greeks advanced as far north as Naples, where they established contact with Etruscans, who were themselves migrants from Asia Minor. In the western Mediterranean the Greeks established a firm base in northeastern Spain and southern France, where their chief colony was Massilia (Marseilles). Finally, the Greeks found a free field in the Black Sea region, where, at first discouraged by the cold and foggy climate, they eventually settled in large numbers because of the economic opportunities. The Black Sea itself provided the annual run of tunny fish, and the native Scythians, living in what is today southern Russia, exchanged their raw materials for Greek-manufactured goods. By the fifth century B.C.E. the entire Black Sea basin was ringed with flourishing Greek trading posts and settlements.

While the Greeks were prospering on the sea, the Persians were building an empire that eventually extended from the Nile valley to the Indus. Although Persians were a mountain people and had little maritime knowledge, they wanted nevertheless to open sea routes and so facilitate communications between their eastern and western provinces. For this purpose they made use of their subject peoples, the Phoenicians and Asia Minor Greeks, who were experienced seagoers. They appointed a Greek mariner, Scylax, to head an expedition that sailed about 510 B.C.E. from the Indus to Arsino at the head of the Red Sea. The Persians also had plans for cutting a canal from the Nile to the Red Sea and appear to have done considerable work toward that goal. Trade flourished and surpassed anything previously known in volume and in geographic range. Greek, Phoenician, Arab, and Indian mariners sailed back and forth among India, the Persian Gulf, Egypt, and the numerous ports of the Mediterranean.

The empire-builder Alexander and his successors continued the work of the Persians by sending more expeditions, which increased geographic knowledge. They also constructed a series of ports along the Red Sea, through which goods could be transported overland to the Nile and then shipped down the river to Alexandria. The Indian Ocean trade was carried on at this time in two stages. In the first, Indian and Arab traders sailed westward from Indian ports, hugging the coastline until they reached the Arabian peninsula and rounded it to their destination at Aden or Mocha. There they were met by Greco-Egyptian merchants who exchanged their wares for the eastern goods, which they transported via the Red Sea coastal ports to Alexandria.

All this was only the prelude to the great expansion of trade between East and West that blossomed shortly before the Christian era and lasted for about two centuries. One reason for this increase in trade was China's increasing influence in central Asia. The Chinese not only opened overland trade routes but also made it easier to obtain silk, the most important item in interregional commerce. The precise role of China will be considered shortly in the analysis of overland trade. The other main factor behind the trade boom was the consolidation of the Roman Empire, which encompassed the entire Mediterranean basin and much of central and northwestern Europe. The establishment of Pax Romana eliminated brigandage and piracy, which hitherto had hindered trade, and removed almost all tolls and exactions. The wealth of the empire also stimulated trade, particularly since the wealthy Roman ruling class had both the taste and the funds for exotic foreign products.

The Romans carried on a flourishing trade with all neighboring lands—with Scandinavia to the north, Germany across the Rhine, Dacia across the Danube, and Africa south of the Sahara. Most significant in its general Eurasian repercussions was commerce with the East. Eastern commerce was greatly expanded sometime in the first century B.C.E. when a Greek mariner discovered that the monsoon winds could be used to speed the voyage back and forth across the Indian Ocean. (This was more likely a rediscovery, since Arab sailors appear to have preceded the Greeks—monsoon is derived from the Arab word *Mauzim,* or season.) The northeast, or winter, monsoon blows from India toward East Africa from October to April, and the southwest, or summer, monsoon blows in the opposite direction from June to September. No longer was it necessary for the sailors to hug the coasts in a wide, time-consuming arc; now they could scud before the wind directly across the ocean. A merchant could journey from Rome to India in sixteen weeks, including the land stage through Egypt.

"Roman" merchants, mostly Greeks and Syrians, undertook such journeys and also a few settled permanently in Indian cities, as we know from Indian literary sources. They brought with them glass, copper, tin, linen and wool textiles, and, above all, gold coins. In return the Romans wanted pepper and other spices, cotton textiles, precious stones, and, most important, the Chinese silk brought to Indian ports via the overland Silk Road. A few of the more adventurous "Roman" traders made their way further east beyond India. In the second and third centuries C.E. they reached Burma, Malaya, Sumatra, and passed on through the Malacca Strait to Kattigara (Hanoi), from which they at last made direct contact with China.

As far as overland trade was concerned, much depended on the degree to which order and security could be maintained. When large sections of the land routes were under the firm control of some authority, trade could flourish; when anarchy prevailed, trade withered. This pattern is clearly apparent in surveying commercial trends through these centuries. A general upward trend is evident in the volume of trade, the result of the technological advances and the expansion of civilization and of empires. But within this overall trend there are dips and rises as a result of political conditions. For example,

the centuries of the Scythian Empire in western Eurasia, the Chinese empires in eastern Eurasia, and the Mongol Empire embracing most of the continental land mass were all centuries of safe trade routes and increasing commerce.

The Scythians, for example, carried on a lively trade with the Greek cities on the north shore of the Black Sea. They exchanged slaves, cattle, hides, furs, fish, timber, wax, and honey for Greek textiles, wine, olive oil, and various luxury goods. Likewise, the Chinese traded goods back and forth along the famous Silk Road from northwest China across central Asia to the Black Sea and Levant ports. The Chinese exported mostly silk, but they also brought cinnamon, rhubarb, and high-grade iron. In return they received furs, woolens, jade, and livestock from central Asia; amber from the Baltic; and—from the Roman provinces—glass, corals, pearls, linen and wool textiles, and, above all, gold.

This flourishing land trade declined gradually with the growing troubles and anarchy in the Roman and Chinese empires after the second century C.E. The great blow came when the Moslem Arabs conquered the entire Middle East in the seventh century and then pushed into central Asia. After the Arabs defeated the Chinese in the battle of Talas in 751, all central Asia was converted to Islam. The huge Moslem Empire now was a barrier rather than a bridge between China and the West or between China and India. Finally, the overland routes were closed and trade shifted to the surrounding seas, where the Arabs were becoming the leading mariners and merchants. It was not until the thirteenth century, when the Mongols conquered all of Eurasia from the Pacific Ocean to the Baltic and Black seas, that overland routes could be reopened, clearing the way for Marco Polo and his fellow merchants of medieval times.

Despite the various shifts in the direction of trade, one basic fact emerges from this survey—a huge increase occurred in both the range and the volume of commerce during the Classical Age as compared to the preceding ancient period. No longer was the scope of commerce confined to individual regions, whether in the Mediterranean Sea or the Arabian Sea or some segment of the Eurasian steppes. Instead trade now became interregional, with goods being carried from one end of Eurasia to the other by sea and by land.

III. CULTURAL BONDS

Commercial and cultural bonds were neither unconnected nor independent of each other. The Greek merchants who followed Alexander's armies spread their Hellenistic culture throughout the Orient. Likewise the spread of Buddhism from India to China can be traced along the well-known Silk Road. Cultural movements, however, had their own internal force and were by no means entirely caused by merchants and their trade routes. A fundamental factor affecting cultural developments in the classical world, exclusive of China, was the invention of a simple alphabetic script in the late second millennium B.C.E. Prior to that time only a handful of professional scribes had been able to read and write the complicated cuneiform script of Mesopotamia and the hieroglyphics of Egypt. The first alphabetic system was devised by Semitic traders in the Sinai peninsula who adapted the Egyptian signs, with which they had become familiar, to indicate consonantal sounds. But they continued to use many additional symbols for words and syllables and therefore failed to develop a strictly phonetic alphabet. The Phoenicians completed the transition in the thirteenth century B.C.E. by developing an alphabet of twenty-two signs denoting simple consonants. The Greeks improved the Phoenician alphabet by using some of its signs to indicate vowels. This Greek alphabet, with some modifications, was spread by the Romans westward and by the Byzantines eastward.

The alphabet is significant because it extended intelligent communication far beyond the narrow circle of the priests and officials of the old days. The scribes of Egypt and Mesopotamia naturally shunned the new style of writing, continuing to use their traditional scripts almost until the Christian era. Isolated China also maintained its usage of its combination phono-pictographic system, which has continued with modifications to the present day. But elsewhere in Eurasia the alphabet was adopted with slight adjustments to fit the different languages. Everywhere the effect was to reduce somewhat, though by no means entirely, the gap that had developed between urban ruling circles and peasant masses with the appearance of civilization. By challenging the monopoly of

The striding god from Artemisium is a bronze statue dating from about 460 B.C.E. It was found in the sea near Artemisium, the northern tip of the large Greek island of Euboea, and is now on display in the Athens archaeological museum. Exactly whom he represents is not known. Some have thought him to be Poseidon holding a trident; others believe that he is Zeus hurling a thunderbolt. In either case he is a splendid representative of the early classical period of Greek sculpture.

the privileged intellectual cliques who generally supported the status quo, the simplified scripts generated a certain ferment. And the ferment affected both politics and culture. India's famous statesman-historian, Jawaharlal Nehru, recognized the significance of this ferment when he wrote in his *Glimpses of World History,*[1] a series of letters to his teenage daughter, Indira Gandhi:

There must have been a wave of thought going through the world, a wave of discontent with existing conditions and of hope and aspiration for something better. For remember that the great founders of religions were always seeking something better and trying to change their people and improve them and lessen their misery. . . .

The overall cultural pattern noticeable among all Eurasian civilizations during these centuries of the Classical Age was the breakdown of local cultures, which were integrated into new regional civilizations with distinctive languages, religions, and social systems. It was much easier for these civilizations to exchange material goods than cultural traits. Textiles, spices, and luxury products were universally usable and desirable, whereas ancestor worship, the caste system, and the city-state were irrelevant and unacceptable outside their places of origin. Thus the commercial interregional bonds during this period of reorganization were generally more extensive and influential than the cultural.

Cultural bonds did develop, however, and in some cases were of prime historical significance. The first outstanding instance was the spread of Hellenism from the Greek world eastward to the Orient and westward to Europe. Toward the end of the classical period there also rose the great universal religions, especially Christianity and Buddhism, with their claims to the allegiance of all humanity rather than of any one group.

Let us first consider Hellenism, a term derived from the Greek word *Hellas*, meaning Greece. Its diffusion throughout the Middle East was made possible by Alexander's famous conquest eastward to central Asia and the Indus valley. As will be noted in the following chapter, this empire lasted for only a few years during Alexander's lifetime. At his death in 323 B.C.E. the empire was divided among his generals, and later it was partitioned between Rome in the West and the Parthians in the East. During this period of the fourth and third centuries B.C.E. the Greek military dominance paved the way for the hundreds of thousands of Greek merchants, administrators, and professionals who flocked to the numerous cities built by Alexander and his successors (and often named after the great general). From the first and most famous Alexandria in Egypt to the farthest Alexandria, Eschata (Kojand) in Afghanistan, these cities served as centers for the diffusion of Greek culture.

Although the majority of its inhabitants usually were non-Hellenic, the typical city was basically Greek, with elected magistrates, a council, and an assembly of the citizens. A new form of the Greek language, the Koine, or common tongue, was used widely throughout the Middle East. Many of the Greek emigrants married local women. Alexander himself set an example by taking a Persian noblewoman as wife. He then arranged for the mass marriage of 3,000 of his soldiers with Persian women after their return from the Indian campaign. He also enlisted Persian soldiers in his regiments and adopted the costume of the Persian King and the etiquette of his court.

Despite this impressive diffusion, Hellenism did not leave a permanent imprint on the Middle East. The basic reason was that its influence had been restricted to the cities where Greek settlers lived and where Greek dynasties had courts. Some of the native peoples were affected, but they were almost exclusively from the small upper classes. The great majority in the countryside, and even in many of the cities, continued to speak their own languages and worship their own gods. Thus Hellenism did not sink deep roots and was incapable of surviving permanently in its transplanted locales. When the Islamic conquerors appeared during the Middle Ages, they had little difficulty in overwhelming the little islands of Hellenistic culture, and today the Greek language and culture survive only in the Greek homeland on the southern tip of the Balkan peninsula.

Hellenism was slower to take root in the western Mediterranean because the indigenous populations had not yet reached a sufficiently affluent and sophisticated level of civilization. But for that very reason there was less competition from the local culture, and the long-run impact of Hellenism in that region was more durable.

As early as the sixth century B.C.E., the Romans were being influenced by the Greek colonies in southern Italy. But it was not until the third century onward, when the Romans conquered the heartland of Hellenism in the Balkans and the Levant, that they felt the full force of Greek culture. Roman soldiers and officials now came into direct contact with highly educated Greek rulers and administrators, and among the hostages and slaves brought to Rome were many Greeks who served in every capacity—from moral philosopher to acrobat, from laudatory poet to master chef. New intellectual horizons opened for upper-class Romans as they experienced the dazzling rhetoric and high-level discussions of their sophisticated Greek subjects.

Greeks served as tutors for leading Roman families, offering instruction in Greek language, rhetoric, philosophy, and literature. By the first century B.C.E. it was common for young Romans to be sent to Athens or Rhodes for training in the philosophical schools. In the field of literature, the Romans at first translated or imitated Greek originals, though gradually they turned to Roman themes.

Greek influence also was clear in the physical appearance of Rome and the other cities of the empire. All three Greek architectural forms were used—the Doric, Ionic, and Corinthian—though Roman buildings tended to be larger and more ornate. Thus towns and cities in Italy, as in the Middle East, began to take on a uniform physical appearance under the influence of Greek art and architecture. Indeed a basic contribution of the Romans to civilization was their appropriation and adaptation of Greek culture, which they then spread to diverse peoples who had never experienced direct contact with it— Gauls, Germans, Britons, and Iberians.

Much more durable than the impact of Hellenism was that of the two great universal religions, Christianity and Mahayana Buddhism. They began in the late classical period their expansion from their respective places of origin in the Middle East and India. During the course of the following centuries Christianity won over all Europe, and Buddhism, most of Asia. The reason for their success is to be found in certain characteristics that they had in common. One was their emphasis on salvation and the promise of an afterlife of eternal bliss. Another was their egalitarianism; their brotherhood was open to all who sought admittance—women as well as men, rich and poor alike, slave or free. Finally, both religions stressed a high code of ethics, the observance of which was essential for salvation. This requirement, together with efficient ecclesiastical organization, enabled these two religions to have an important influence on the daily lives of the faithful.

The features of these religions were particularly appealing in the later centuries of the Classical Age. These were times of social unrest and moral confusion, especially in the large cities, where the urban multitudes felt uprooted and

drifting. For such people, Christianity and Mahayana Buddhism offered solace, security, and guidance. When Pilate, voicing the despairing mood of the times, asked, "What is truth?" religion provided an answer. It was not accidental that the earliest converts to Christianity were the lowly and dispossessed. Likewise, the greatest triumph of Mahayana Buddhism was in China during the time of troubles following the collapse of the Han dynasty, when there seemed to be no solution to humankind's worldly problems.

Indeed, these satisfying characteristics of the two religions were evolved precisely in response to the needs of the times. They were present neither in the Judaism from which

Fasting Buddha. Before Gautama arrived at the "middle path," he practiced severe austerities for six years. According to a description in an ancient text: "My limbs became like some withered creepers with knotted joints; my buttocks like a buffalo's hoof . . . my ribs like rafters of a dilapidated shed; the pupils of my eyes appeared sunk deep in their sockets as water appears shining at the bottom of a deep well. . . ." This fourth–second century B.C.E. statue of the Buddha from Gandhara (in present-day Pakistan) reflects the Greek influence on early Buddhist sculpture.

Late Roman ivory plaque showing a scene from Christ's Passion—carrying the cross to the crucifixion.

Christianity had emerged nor in the original Buddhism from which developed the later Mahayana variant.

Judaism was the parochial faith of the Jewish people, who about the twelfth century B.C.E. adopted a national god, Jehovah. "I am Jehovah, thy God. . . . Thou shalt have no other gods before me." This first of Jehovah's Ten Commandments did not claim that Jehovah was the only god in the world but, rather, that he was the only god for the children of Israel. Moreover, the Judaistic faith was at this time more social and ethical than mystical and otherworldly. In the words of one Jewish prophet, Jehovah cared nothing for ritual and sacrifice; he cared only that men should "seek justice, relieve the oppressed, judge the fatherless, plead for the widow."

But from the sixth century B.C.E. onward, the Jews changed their religious ideas under the influence of the religious beliefs of the Persians and of their other rulers. They were also affected by the many Jews who lived outside Palestine, where, exposed to the tenets of Hellenism, they sought to interpret Judaism in terms of Greek philosophy. Thus the Jews gradually adopted a belief in the afterlife—obedience to God's will would bring eternal happiness in heaven, and disobedience would bring eternal punishment in hell.

Christianity's appeal to disparate and widespread groups was not immediate; Christianity was a Jewish cult during the lifetime and immediately after the crucifixion of Jesus. But it was universalized by Paul, a Hellenized Jew who lived in the city of Tarsus in Asia Minor. Paul boldly denied that Jesus was sent merely as the redeemer of the Jews. He announced that a loving Father had sent His only Son to atone for the sins of all mankind. Therefore, Christianity was not a sect of Judaism. It was a new church for Gentiles as well as for Jews. Paul's approach meant that Christianity henceforth could appeal not only to a handful of Jews but also to the millions of Gentiles throughout the Roman Empire.

The new religion grew despite steady persecution by Roman officials. Finally, in 313 C.E., Christianity received official toleration through Emperor Constantine's Edict of Milan, and in 399 it was made the official state religion of the Roman Empire. After the fall of the empire, Christian missionaries carried the faith to the English and German peoples between 600 and 800, and to the Scandinavian and Slavic peoples between 800 and 1100. With the expansion of Europe, both missionaries and emigrants spread Christianity to all parts of the globe.

The evolution of Buddhism was somewhat similar in that it began, as will be noted in Chapter 6, as a distinct Indian reaction against the injustice of the caste system and the exploitation by the Brahman priestly class. The founder, Siddhartha (c. 563–483 B.C.E.) of the Gautama clan, was of noble rank, but he became so distressed by the suffering he saw about him that he gave up his family and material comforts for the life of a wandering ascetic. Finally, in a moment of revelation, he achieved enlightenment and thenceforth was known as the Buddha, or the Enlightened One.

At the core of Buddhism are four great truths: (1) Life is sorrow; (2) the cause of sorrow is desire; (3) escape is possible only by stopping desire; and (4) the cessation of desire can only be achieved by the "eight-fold path," which is comprised of right belief, right ambition, right speech, right conduct, right living, right effort, right thoughts, and right pleasures. The objective of all this effort is Nirvana, literally meaning "emptiness," the "blowing out of the flame."

The Buddha had not intended to establish a new religion, but after his death his disciples preached his teachings and founded monastic communities that came to dominate Buddhism. The ideal of these communities was mental and physical discipline culminating in the mystic experience of Nirvana. Satisfying as this was for the monks, it ignored the needs of the everyday life of laypeople; hence the evolution of Mahayana, or the Greater Vehicle, as opposed to Hinayana, or the Lesser Vehicle. The Greater Vehicle was "greater" in the sense of its all-inclusiveness. It incorporated more of the concepts of pre-Buddhist Indian thought as well as the religious ideas of the people it converted. In doing so, it turned somewhat from its original contemplative bent and adopted precepts that were easier to comprehend and observe. Salvation now could be attained through faith, even an unthinking act of faith such as the mouthing of the name of Buddha. Also Nirvana changed—at least for the less-sophisticated believers—to mean an afterlife in Paradise, and Paradise was more attainable through good works that helped others.

This shift of emphasis from monasticism, asceticism, and contemplation to charity, faith, and salvation made Mahayana Buddhism more palatable to non-Indian peoples than the original religion had been, though both forms of the faith won foreign converts. Buddhism spread first to Ceylon and to northwest frontier regions of India in the third century B.C.E. Then in the first century B.C.E. it was carried into central Asia and China, first by traders, then by Indian missionaries, and most effectively by Chinese converts who studied in India and then returned to win over their fellow compatriots. So successful were they that by the late fourth century C.E., nine-tenths of the population of northwest China was said to have been converted, and by the sixth century south China had followed suit. From China, Buddhism spread still further: to Korea in the fourth century C.E., to Japan in the sixth century, and later to Tibet and Mongolia. Meanwhile Buddhism in both its Hinayana and Mahayana forms had been penetrating into Southeast Asia. This did not occur at any particular period; rather, it represented one aspect of the general Indianization of the region that took place over many centuries.

After these successes Buddhism declined in many countries. In China it reached its peak about 700 C.E. but thereafter suffered from internal decay and governmental hostility. Its great landholdings, its vast treasures, and the large numbers of monks and nuns it withdrew from the national economy all aroused official envy and displeasure and brought on persecution. Between 841 and 855, according to official accounts, 4,600 monasteries and 40,000 shrines were destroyed; 260,000 monks and nuns were defrocked and, together with their 150,000 slaves, returned to the tax registers. Buddhism never recovered from this blow, and thereafter it was merely one of "the three religions" (along with Taoism and Confucianism) in which the Chinese were interested. Likewise in India, Buddhism eventually gave way to a revival of Hinduism, so virtually no followers are to be found today in its own birthplace. In Ceylon and in many parts of Southeast Asia, however, Buddhism of the Hinayana variety remains predominant to the present.

Despite this relative decline after its period of greatness, Buddhism in late classical and early medieval times was the predominant religion of Asia. It prevailed in the whole continent except for Siberia and the Middle East, thus giving that vast area a degree of cultural unity unequaled

BUDDHISM IN INDIA AND CHINA

The unification of Eurasia began in classical times, and the bonds were partly commercial and partly cultural. Buddhism was one factor that played an important role in the cultural interaction. This is evident in the following experiences of a Chinese Buddhist monk, Hsüan-tsang, who spent the years from 629 to 645 C.E. visiting monasteries in India. While at the Nalanda monastery he announced his decision to return to China. The reaction of the monks is revealing.*

The monks of Nalanda [monastery], when they heard of it, begged him to remain, saying: "India is the land of Buddha's birth, and though he has left the world, there are still many traces of him. What greater happiness could there be than to visit them in turn, to adore him and chant his praises? Why then do you wish to leave, having come so far? Moreover China is a country of . . . unimportant barbarians, who despise the religious and the [Buddhist] Faith. That is why Buddha was not born there. The mind of the people is narrow, and their coarseness profound, hence neither sages nor saints go there. The climate is cold and the country rugged—you must think again."

The Master of the Law (the Chinese Buddhist) replied, "Buddha established his doctrine so that it might be diffused to all lands. Who would wish to enjoy it alone, and to forget those who are not enlightened? Besides, in my country the magistrates are clothed with dignity, and the laws are everywhere respected. The emperor is virtuous and the subjects loyal, parents are loving and sons obedient, humanity and justice are highly esteemed, and old men and sages are held in honour. Moreover, how deep and mysterious is their knowledge; their wisdom equals that of spirits. They have taken the Heavens as their model, and they know how to calculate the movements of the Seven Luminaries; they have invented all kinds of instruments, fixed the seasons of the year. . . . How then can you say that Buddha did not go to my country because of its insignificance?"

**J. Needham, *Science and Civilization in China* (Cambridge University, 1954), I, pp. 209–210.*

before or after. In doing so, it functioned as a great civilizing force in Asia, as Christianity did simultaneously in Europe. To many peoples Buddhism brought not only a religion and a set of ethics, but also a system of writing, a type of architecture, and all the other attributes of the great civilizations of India and China that the missionaries spread together with their religion. In the same way, at the other end of Eurasia, Christian missionaries were bringing to the barbaric Germanic and Slavic peoples the civilizations of Rome and of Constantinople, as well as the teachings of Christ. Such was the impact and historical significance of these powerful "cultural bonds" for the Eurasian peoples.

During the millennia of the ancient civilizations, the Middle East had been the center of initiative. It was the Middle East during that period that had made the fundamental contributions to humankind—contributions such as agriculture, metallurgy, urbanism, and imperial organization. But now in classical times this Middle Eastern predominance faded away, except in one area—that of religion. Not only Judaism but also Zoroastrianism have their roots in the Middle East. The latter religion, although observed today by only a handful of Parsis in India, had considerable influence in the Middle East when the Persian Empire was at its height.

Yet the fact remains that apart from these religions and other related sects, the Middle East no longer was the vital source of innovation during the Classical Age. The new ideas and institutions that took shape in classical times, and which have persisted in many cases to the present, were the products of what formerly had been the peripheral regions of Eurasia. Accordingly, the following three chapters are devoted to the civilizations of these regions: the Greco-Roman, the Indian, and the Chinese. Before considering those civilizations, we should note that the impact of the great Eurasian religions continues to be felt to the present day. Their teachings about war and peace, for example, remain very relevant for peoples of the twentieth and twenty-first centuries. Confucius stated that "Within the four seas, all men are brothers." Likewise, in the Old Testament there is the grand vision of the prophet Micah, which has been the motto of the United Nations: "And they shall beat their swords into plowshares and their spears into pruninghooks; nation shall not lift up a sword against nation, neither shall they learn war anymore." This common relevance of the great religions was strikingly illustrated on October 27, 1986, when their representatives joined Pope John Paul II in a "World Day of Prayer for Peace." The following are excerpts from their prayers, as well as those of other faiths:[2]

Buddhist

May all beings everywhere, plagued with sufferings of body and mind, obtain an ocean of happiness and joy.

Christian

I say to you that hear, love your enemies, do good to those who hate you, bless those who curse you, pray for those who abuse you. To him who strikes you on the cheek, offer the other also; and from him who takes away your cloak do not withhold your coat as well. Give to everyone who begs from you; and of him who takes away your goods do not ask them again. And as you wish that men would do to you, do so to them.

Jewish

Our God in heaven, the Lord of Peace will have compassion and mercy upon us and upon all the peoples of the earth who implore his mercy and his compassion, asking for peace, seeking peace.

African Animist

Almighty God, the Great Thumb we cannot evade to tie any knot, the Roaring Thunder that splits mighty trees, the All-Seeing Lord up on high who sees even the footprints of an antelope on a rock mass here on earth: You are the one who does not hesitate to respond to our call. You are the cornerstone of peace.

American Indian

In smoking the pipe, I invite my family to smoke with me and you, my friends, to pray with me in thanksgiving for this day and for world peace. I will pray that we all may commit ourselves to pray and to work for peace within our families, our tribes, and our nations. I pray for all our brothers and sisters walking our mother earth.

SUGGESTED READINGS

Interregional ties in Eurasia are clearly analyzed in the well-written study by G. F. Hudson, *Europe & China: A Survey of Their Relations from the Earliest Times to 1800* (Edward Arnold, 1931). See also the multivolume study by J. Needham, *Science and Civilization in China* (Cambridge University, 1954), the first volume of which provides an overall survey of China's interaction with the rest of Eurasia, including a theoretical analysis of culture diffusion. Various aspects of the commercial bonds of Eurasia are treated in A. Toussaint, *History of the Indian Ocean* (University of Chicago, 1966); S. Chandra, ed., *The Indian Ocean: Explorations in History, Commerce, and Politics* (Sage, 1987); D. Harden, *The Phoenicians* (Praeger, 1962); E. H. Warmington, *The Commerce Between the Roman Empire and India* (Cambridge University, 1928); Ying-shih Yu, *Trade and Expansion in Han China* (University of California, 1967); J. I. Miller, *The Spice Trade of the Roman Empire, 29 B.C.–A.D. 641* (Oxford University, 1969); C. G. F. Simkin, *The Traditional Trade of Asia* (Oxford University, 1969); and P. D. Curtin, *Cross Cultural Trade in World History* (Cambridge University, 1984).

For the cultural bonds of Eurasia, see H. G. Rawlinson, *Intercourse Between India and the Western World* (Cambridge University, 1916); E. Zürcher, *Buddhism: Its Origin and Spread* (St. Martin's, 1962); R. MacMullen, *Christianizing the Roman Empire, A.D. 100–400* (Yale University, 1984); and J. Pelikan, *Jesus through the Centuries* (Yale University, 1985).

NOTES

1. Jawaharlal Nehru, *Glimpses of World History* (Oxford University, 1982), p. 35.
2. *New York Times*, October 28, 1986.

Greco-Roman Civilization

The pupils of Athens have become teachers of others, and she has made the term Hellene no longer signify a race but a mental outlook.

Isocrates

Of the three chapters dealing with the three classical civilizations—the Greco-Roman, the Indian, and the Chinese—this on the Greco-Roman civilization is the longest. One reason is that two distinct, though related, civilizations are involved. The historical development of the West at this time was basically different from that of the unitary civilizations of India and China. All three civilizations spread out from restricted centers of origin to encompass entire surrounding regions—from the Greek peninsula to the western Mediterranean, from the Indus River valley to south India, and from the Yellow River valley to south China. As noted in Chapter 3, iron tools made this possible because they facilitated the extension of agriculture into forested regions and of commerce and colonization into new coastal areas. But here the common pattern ends. The newly civilized regions in India and China remained generally subservient to the original core areas, whereas in the West, Rome developed a military superiority that enabled it to conquer not only the Greek homeland in the Balkans but also the western portions of the ancient Middle East—Asia Minor, Palestine, Syria, and Egypt. In doing so, Rome began a new phase of history in the West, and launched a new, though related, Western civilization. The history and nature of these two sister civilizations, the Greek and the Roman, are the subjects of this chapter.

I. FORMATIVE AGE, 800–500 B.C.E.

With the Dorian invasions of the twelfth century B.C.E., Greece lapsed into a "Dark Age." (See Chapter 3, Section V.) The Greece of this period was tribal, aristocratic, agricultural, and confined to the Aegean basin. By the end of the sixth century B.C.E. all this had changed. The tribe had given way to the city-state; other social classes had risen to challenge the nobility; industry and commerce had come to play a considerable role; and Greek colonies were scattered on all the Mediterranean shores. These changes transformed the Greek world during its formative period and cleared the way for the Classical Age. (See map of Classical Age Empires in the Middle East and Europe, p. 89.)

A basic factor behind these developments was the geography of the Greek lands. Greece had no rich natural resources—no fertile river valleys or broad plains that, when properly developed and exploited, could support elaborate empires like those of the Middle East, India, and China. In Greece and on the Asia Minor coast there were successive mountain chains that restricted agricultural productivity and divided the countryside into compartments. Consequently, the Greeks had no natural geopolitical center to provide a basis for regional integration. Instead, after the invasions, they settled down in isolated villages, usually located near some easily defended hill or rise that provided both a refuge in time of danger and a location for a shrine to the gods. The settlement as a whole was called the polis and the place of refuge the acropolis—literally, "high town." If the polis was strategically situated near fertile lands or communication routes, it attracted more settlers and became the leading city of the region. In this manner dozens of small city-states emerged, relatively isolated and fiercely independent.

At the outset the city-states depended primarily on subsistence agriculture, herding, and fishing. But by the beginning of the eighth century B.C.E., economic self-sufficiency was undermined by population pressure. Land-hungry peasants were forced to take to the sea, becoming pirates or traders or colonists—or, as often happened, some combination of the three. By the fifth century the entire Mediterranean basin, including the Black Sea, was ringed with prosperous Greek colonies that were overseas replicas of the mother cities. (See Chapter 4, Section II.)

The founding of colonies set off a chain reaction that in the end transformed the Greek world. The colonies shipped raw materials, especially grain, to overpopulated Greece and in return received wine, olive oil, and manufactured goods, such as cloth and pottery. This trade pattern triggered an economic boom in the homeland. The Greek soil was better suited for olive orchards and vineyards than for wheat fields, and now that wheat could be imported, rocky hillsides could be planted with grape vines and olive trees. Hence the amount of land under cultivation increased substantially. The shift to commercial agriculture, therefore, made it possible to support a population three to four times larger than that under the former subsistence agriculture. Likewise manufactures increased, as we can see by the large quantities of Greek pottery unearthed not only around the Mediterranean but also far into the hinterland—into central Russia, southwest Germany, and northeast France. At the same time the Greek merchant marine prospered as it carried these goods back and forth. Indeed, this was the first time in history that bulky commodities, as distinct from luxury items, were traded and transported on such a large scale. All this economic activity was efficiently lubricated by the growing use of coin money, which the Greeks had pioneered.

The commercialization of agriculture meant debts as well as profits, especially for the small landholder. Formerly the nobles had collected rent in the form of a portion of the crop, so that in bad years the people pulled in their belts for the duration. But now the combination of foreign markets, the money economy, and new luxuries left the small farmers vulnerable to mortgages, foreclosures, and even loss of personal freedom. Inevitably this led to bitter class conflict and to popular clamor for debt cancellation and redistribution of land. Likewise in the cities new wealthy families emerged who wanted political recognition equal to their economic strength. They could count on the support of the urban poor, artisans, stevedores, and sailors. All these discontented elements, then, struck out against the traditional political system where all power lay in the hands of the land-owning aristocracy.

Change was greatly hastened in the seventh century when the aristocratic cavalryman, once the main figure on the battlefield, was replaced by the heavily armored infantryman,

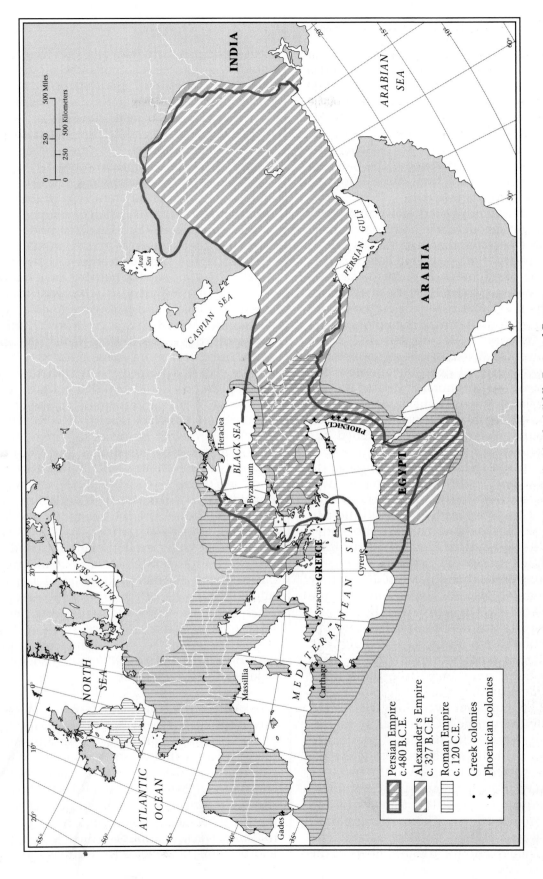

Classical Age Empires in the Middle East and Europe

the hoplite. Massed together in a solid block, or phalanx, with a shield in the left hand and a long spear in the right, the hoplites were trained to act in unison and could make bristling sweeps through the hitherto invincible horsemen. This innovation undermined the military basis of aristocratic political authority. At the same time it raised the status and influence of the independent farmer and artisan who could afford to equip himself for phalanx service.

The combination of economic and military change brought about corresponding political change. The city-states that had started out as monarchies in the Dark Age gradually changed to aristocratic oligarchies. Then, in the seventh century, they came under the rule of dictators, or tyrants as they were called. These ambitious leaders, usually of noble birth, championed popular demands, won mass support, and seized personal power. The word *tyrant* referred to one who ruled without legal right, but the term carried with it no sense of moral reproach. Indeed, tyrants commonly favored the interests of the common people against the privileged classes, and often, though not always, hastened the advent of democracy.

Sparta, in the southern Peloponnesus, was the classic example of the opposite trend—away from democracy. About 1000 B.C.E. the Dorian forefathers of the Spartans had overrun the rich valley of the Eurotas and reduced the native population to the status of helots, or serfs. Later in the eighth century the Spartans conquered the rich plains of neighboring Messenia, so they had no need for overseas expansion. But the price paid for their security was heavy and inevitable. Sparta was deprived of the economic and intellectual stimulus of foreign contacts and condemned to a static rule existence. In addition, the Spartans were forced to organize their state along strict military lines to keep down the large subject population. Everything was subordinated to military needs: Only healthy infants were allowed to live, with the sickly ones left to die of exposure in the wilderness. From the age of seven, boys lived and trained in the barracks. Until age sixty all men remained under military discipline. Private life was all but abolished and luxury was frowned upon. The morning plunge in the cold waters of the Eurotas, the scanty fare on the mess tables, and the rough timbers of the houses, shaped only with the axe, were famous throughout Greece. Life consisted almost exclusively of organized amusement, communal meals, public business, and military training and duties. This regimen made the Spartans the best infantrymen in all Greece. But it left them no time or inclination for writing plays, carving statues, or formulating philosophy.

Meanwhile the Athenians had been developing an altogether different type of society. Far from being a band of invaders camped amid a hostile population, the Athenians prided themselves on their status as native inhabitants of Attica. Like the Greeks of other city-states, they began with a monarchy, but that gave way to an oligarchy of nine archons who were the chief executive officers and who were invariably aristocrats. In contrast to Sparta, however, the evolution of Athens was toward increasing democracy. The burgeoning trade created a strong middle class that joined forces with the dispossessed peasantry and demanded political reform. In 594 B.C.E. all parties agreed on the appointment of Solon as chief magistrate with full powers for reform. His measures for the alleviation of social distress were simple and drastic. He restored to the debtors full title to their land, freed all citizens who had been enslaved for unpaid debts, and made such enslavement illegal in the future. In the realm of politics he admitted propertyless citizens to the Assembly for the first time, even though this body still possessed little power. He also made wealthy businessmen eligible to become archons and diluted the power of the aristocratic Areopagus, or chief judicial body, by establishing new and more popular courts of justice. In short, Solon's contribution was to create the constitutional base on which the famed Athenian democracy of later times would be built.

The three decades following Solon were filled with strife, for many problems remained unsolved. Enslavement was now illegal, but the poor still found it difficult to earn a living, and the aristocrats, though somewhat curbed, could still block popular legislation. Under these circumstances, Pisistratus established himself as the first tyrant of Athens about 560 B.C.E. During his thirty-year rule he divided the estates of the aristocrats, distributing them among landless peasants, and helped the urban poor with large-scale public works that beautified the city. Pisistratus was succeeded by his sons, but they proved incapable. More strife followed until Cleisthenes gained control about 506 B.C.E. He abolished the old tribes, setting up ten new ones that were based on territorial divisions rather than kinship. This change contributed much to undermining the political power of the aristocrats. Furthermore, he established a new Council of Five Hundred for which all male citizens over thirty years of age were eligible; it had authority to prepare measures for submission to the Assembly, as well as having supreme executive and administrative power. With these reforms of Cleisthenes, Athens by 500 B.C.E. had emerged a democracy, whereas Sparta remained a militarized and regimented society.

II. CLASSICAL AGE, 500–336 B.C.E.

In his famous funeral speech commemorating the Athenian soldiers who had fallen in battle against the Spartans in 431, Pericles declared, "Our city is open to the world. . . . Athens is the school of Hellas." This boast was fully justified. During the fifth century B.C.E. Athens overshadowed Sparta and all other Greek cities. This was the age of Periclean Athens—the Golden Age of classical Greece.

One reason for the dazzling preeminence of Athens was its leading role in the fateful defeat of the great Persian Empire. Shortly before the Persian Wars, the Athenians had the good fortune to discover the Laurium silver lodes. Deciding to use the treasure for naval construction, they built two hundred triremes of latest design. This fleet was decisive in the ensuing struggle.

The root of the war was the Persian conquest of the Greek city-states in Asia Minor during the mid-sixth century B.C.E. Heavy-handed Persian interference in their domestic affairs led the cities to revolt in 499. They appealed to the homeland cities for aid and received a positive response, partly because the Persian Empire at this time was expanding into southeastern Europe and menacing Greece from the north. Despite the naval assistance from across the Aegean, the Asia Minor cities were overwhelmed by 494. The Persian Emperor Darius resolved to

chastise the obstreperous Greeks and sent out an expedition that landed at Marathon, to the northwest of Athens, in 490. Although the Athenians fought almost alone, thanks to rivalries among the Greek cities, their phalanxes inflicted a stunning defeat on the invaders. The effect on Greek morale was enormous. "These were the first Greeks," wrote the historian Herodotus, "who had the courage to face up to Persian dress and the men who wore it, whereas up to that time the very name of the Persians brought terror to a Greek."

Ten years later the Persians came again with much larger forces, and this time by land through Thrace and Thessaly. A mixed force under Spartan command fought gallantly to the

The bronze helmut was dedicated to Zeus by Miltiades to commemorate the Athenian victory over the Persians in 490 B.C.E.

last man at the pass of Thermopylae. The Persians pressed on to Athens, which they sacked, but the Athenian fleet destroyed the Persians in nearby Salamis. An allied Greek fleet followed the retreating Persians across the Aegean and won another naval victory. Soon the Asia Minor cities were freed from Persian rule, and the Greeks emerged as the victors over the great empire that dominated the Middle East.

The repercussions of the Greek triumph were tremendous. First and foremost, it saved the Greeks from being engulfed in an oriental despotism, thereby allowing them to preserve their identity and to make their unique contribution to human civilization. The success of the Greeks, and especially of the Athenian fleet, also furthered the cause of democracy, for the rowers who drove the ships into battle were citizens who could not afford to equip themselves as hoplites. Thus the urban poor now assumed a military role even more important than that of the propertied hoplites. This naturally strengthened the movement for more democracy, which reached its height during the Age of Pericles (461–429 B.C.E.).

Although an aristocrat by birth, Pericles was an earnest democrat who completed the transference of power to the Assembly. All adult male citizens were members of this body, which was the sovereign power in the affairs of Athens. It held forty regular meetings a year and extraordinary sessions as required. It not only settled general questions of policy but also made detailed decisions in every sphere of government—foreign affairs, military operations, finance. Pericles also introduced pay for service in most public offices so that the poor could afford to assume such offices. In addition, he established an array of popular courts in which final decisions were rendered by juries chosen by lot; all citizens could serve on these juries. Pericles was quite justified, then, in his statement that "Athens is the school of Greece."

The prominent role of Athens in the Persian Wars led the city on a course that eventually ended in imperialism. Whereas Sparta was immobilized by its static economy and the constant threat of a helot revolt, Athens took the lead in organizing a confederacy of Asiatic Greeks and islanders. Known as the Delian Confederation because its headquarters was originally on the small island of Delos, its purpose was collective security against possible further Persian attacks. Although theoretically an alliance of equals—for the constitution provided each member with only one vote in the periodic meetings—from the start Athens provided the executive leadership. The generals were Athenians, and Athens also collected tribute from cities unable or unwilling to furnish ships. Step by step Athens tightened its hold: The treasury of the confederation was moved from Delos to Athens; Athenian coinage became the common medium of exchange; and members were denied the right of secession. Thus by 450 B.C.E. the confederation had become an empire, and the power of Athens extended, in the words of Euripides, from Ionia "to the outward Ocean of the West"—that is, to the Atlantic.

Almost inevitably, the sea power of Athens clashed with the land power of Sparta. The fighting dragged on indecisively for ten years. The Spartan armies raided Attica each year but could not penetrate the long walls that joined Athens to the sea and protected its supplies. The Athenians for their part were badly hurt by the great plague of 429 B.C.E., which killed off almost half the population, including Pericles. For a time they could only make random raids on the coast of the Peloponnesus. Then in 415 the fatal decision was made to send the Athenian fleet to capture Sicily and cut off Sparta's grain supply. "Fleet and army," wrote Thucydides, "perished from the face of the earth, nothing was saved." Athens' allies now revolted; the Spartans finally destroyed the long wall; and Athens was starved into capitulation in 404 B.C.E. Athens was left shorn of its fleets, its empire, and even its vaunted democracy, for the Spartan victors imposed a short-lived oligarchic regime.

This ruinous war left the Greek world exhausted and solved none of its problems. Spartan high-handedness caused Thebes and Athens to unite together in a new league for mutual protection. In 371 the Thebans inflicted on the Spartans their first major military defeat in two hundred years. For the next decade Thebes was supreme on the Greek mainland, but then intercity rivalries prevailed again, and the city-states once more were engulfed in a confused anarchy of shifting alliances and petty wars. The stage was set for a foreign power to

PERICLES'S FUNERAL ORATION

The Athenian leader Pericles has left the classic description of the culture of his city during its great Golden Age. He gave the following famous account during his funeral oration commemorating the Athenian soldiers who had fallen in battle against Sparta in 431 B.C.E.*

Our form of government does not enter into rivalry with the institutions of others. We do not copy our neighbours, but are an example to them. It is true that we are called a democracy, for the administration is in the hands of the many and not of the few. But while the law secures equal justice to all alike in their private disputes, the claim of excellence is also recognized, and when a citizen is in any way distinguished, he is preferred to the public service, not as a matter of privilege, but as the reward of merit. Neither is poverty a bar, but a man may benefit his country whatever be the obscurity of his condition. There is no exclusiveness in our public life, and in our private intercourse we are not suspicious of one another, nor angry with our neighbour if he does what he likes. . . . We are lovers of the beautiful, yet simple in our tastes, and we cultivate the mind without loss of manliness. Wealth we employ, not for talk and ostentation, but when there is a real use for it. To avow poverty with us is no disgrace; the true disgrace is in doing nothing to avoid it. An Athenian citizen does not neglect the state because he takes care of his own household; and even those of us who are engaged in business have a very fair idea of politics. We alone regard a man who takes no interest in public affairs, not as a harmless, but as a useless character; and if few of us are originators, we are all sound judges of policy. The great impediment to action is, in our opinion, not discussion, but the want of that knowledge which is gained by discussion preparatory to action. For we have a peculiar power of thinking before we act and of acting too. . . .

To sum up: I say that Athens is the school of Hellas. . . .

I have paid the required tribute, in obedience to the law, making use of such fitting words as I had. The tribute of deeds has been paid in part; for the dead have been honourably interred, and it remains only that their children should be maintained at the public charge until they are grown up: this is the solid prize with which, as with a garland, Athens crowns her sons living and dead, after a struggle like theirs.

*B. Jowett, trans., *The History of Thucydides* (Tandy-Thomas, 1909), book 2, pp. 35–46.

subjugate and forcibly unify Greece. In 338 B.C.E. Philip of Macedon smashed the combined armies of Thebes and Athens at Chaeronea. Philip deprived the Greek cities of most of their autonomy, but before he could proceed further he was assassinated in 336 B.C.E. His successor was his world-famous son, Alexander the Great.

The Classical Age was over; the Hellenistic Age was beginning. Before turning to the latter we shall pause to consider the civilization of the Classical Age, an age that is generally accepted as one of the great triumphs of the human mind and spirit.

III. CIVILIZATION OF THE CLASSICAL AGE

The "Golden Age of Pericles," "the Greek Miracle," "the Glory that was Greece"—these are some of the tributes commonly used in referring to the civilization of fifth-century Greece.

We shall see that this civilization had its shortcomings; nonetheless those extravagant praises are largely deserved. Why is this so? What was the basis of the Greek "genius"? First, it may be safely assumed that it was not literally a matter of genius—that the Indo-Europeans who migrated to the south Balkans did not happen to be genetically superior to those who migrated to the Middle East or India or western Europe. Instead, the answer must be sought through comparison of the historical development of the Greeks with that of the other Indo-Europeans who settled in other regions of Eurasia.

Such a comparison suggests two explanations for the extraordinary achievements of the Greeks. In the first place, they lived near enough to the earliest centers of civilization—Egypt and Mesopotamia—to profit from their pioneering accomplishments. But they were not so close that they lost their individuality. Indeed, the main significance of the outcome of the Persian Wars was precisely that it allowed the Greeks to have their cake and eat it too.

The second factor was the emergence and persistence of the Greek polis, which provided the essential institutional framework for the cultural blossoming. The polis, of course, was not a uniquely Greek institution. In India, for example, the Aryan immigrants in the earlier stage of their development also had what amounted to city-states in certain regions. But these were eventually absorbed by the territorial monarchies that came to dominate the Indian peninsula. It was the Greeks alone who were able to preserve their city-states for several centuries.

One reason for this longevity was the mountainous terrain, which did not afford a geopolitical base for a regional empire. (See Section I, this chapter.) Another was the direct access to the sea enjoyed by most of the Greek city-states, which gave them economic strength as well as intellectual stimulation. It is true that the Greeks paid a heavy price for their polis fragmentation in the form of continual wars. And war led eventually to unification imposed from without, first by Macedon and then by Rome. But in the meantime they enjoyed centuries of freedom within their respective states, and this freedom was a prerequisite for the great creative outburst of the fifth century.

The classical Greek civilization was not purely original. Like all civilizations, it borrowed heavily from what had gone before, in this case the Middle Eastern civilizations. But what the Greeks borrowed, whether art forms from Egypt or mathematics and astronomy from Mesopotamia, they stamped with the distinctive quality of their minds. And this distinctive stamp was, essentially, an open-mindedness, an intellectual curiosity, an eagerness to learn, and a commonsense approach. When the Greeks traveled abroad, as they did very often as traders, soldiers, colonists, and tourists, they did so with a critical eye and skeptical mind. They questioned everything and tested all issues at the bar of reason. In Plato's *Apology*, Socrates maintains that the individual must refuse, at all costs, to be coerced by human authority or by any tribunal to do anything, or think anything, which his own mind condemns as wrong— ". . .the life which is unexamined is not worth living. . . ." Socrates also pointed out the public value of free discussion, on which he based his defense in the famous trial for his own life.

And now, Athenians, I am not going to argue for my own sake, as you may think, but for yours. . . . For if you kill me you will not easily find another like me, who, if I may use such a ludicrous figure of speech, am a sort of gadfly . . . and all day long and in all places am always fastening upon you, arousing and persuading and reproaching you. . . . I would have you know that, if you kill such a one as I am, you will injure yourselves more than you will injure me.[1]

This sort of free thinking was uniquely Greek, at least in such a strong and pervasive form. Unique also was the secular view of life, the conviction that the chief business of existence was the complete expression of human personality here and now. This combination of rationalism and secularism enabled the Greeks to think freely and creatively about human problems and social issues. And they expressed their thoughts and emotions in their great literary, philosophical, and artistic creations, which are relevant and compelling to the present day.

These unique qualities of the Greeks are clearly reflected in their religious thought and practices. The Greeks viewed their gods as similar in nature to themselves, differing only in superior power, longevity, and beauty. By believing in such divinities the Greeks felt secure and at home in a world governed by familiar and comprehensible powers. The relationship between the people and their gods was essentially one of give and take. In return for prayers and sacrifices the gods were expected to demonstrate their good will. The religious tie consisted of "common shrines and sacrifices," as Herodotus stated, rather than of an organized church or a common faith. The Greek religion never formulated a unified body of doctrines or a sacred book, though Homer's *Iliad* and Hesiod's *Theogony* summed up prevailing religious concepts. The quality of Greek religion becomes evident when contrasted with that of the Mesopotamians. According to Mesopotamian explanations of the origins of things, the human race had been specifically created to build temples for the gods and to feed them with offerings. Such duties, in fact, were the whole reason for human existence. How different was the conception of the sixth-century Greek philosopher Xenophanes:

Mortals think that the gods are begotten, and wear clothes like their own, and have a voice and a form. If oxen or horses or lions had hands and could draw with them and make works of art as men do, horses would draw the shapes of gods like horses, oxen like oxen; each kind would represent their bodies just like their own forms. The Ethiopians say their gods are black and flat-nosed; the Thracians, that theirs are blue-eyed and red-haired.[2]

Religion in classical Greece was an integral part of polis life and accordingly affected every aspect of that life. Religion offered an interpretation of the natural world, a consecration of daily work and of social institutions, and was also one of the chief sources of inspiration for poets and artists. Every Greek temple was a focus of local and national culture. Many temples specialized, more or less accidentally, in the development of particular arts. A brotherhood of miracle workers, who grew up around the worship of the legendary Aesculapius on the island of Cos, evolved into the first scientific physicians. Outstanding was the renowned physician Hippocrates, whose medical treatises were resolutely clinical in tone. He diagnosed each case on the basis of objective observation, rejecting magical

causes or cures for disease. Regarding the "sacred" disease, epilepsy, he wrote:

It seems to me that the disease called sacred is no more divine than any other. It has a natural cause, just as other diseases have. Men think it divine because they do not understand it. . . . In Nature all things are alike in this, that they can all be traced to preceding causes.[3]

Likewise around the worship of Dionysus, the wine god, there grew a company of actors who evolved from dramatizing the ritual cult of the god to creating profound tragedy and uproarious comedy. This literature cannot be imagined apart from its setting in fifth-century Athens. Plays were produced before the assembled citizens at regularly held religious festivals organized and financed by the state. The close contact and empathy between author and audience were responsible for the balance and normality of Athenian drama. Aeschylus, in his *Persians*, presented a dramatized version of the victory at Salamis before the very citizens who had won that victory. Sophocles referred frequently to the gods in his tragedies yet was not interested primarily in religious problems. Rather he was chiefly concerned with human beings, noble and admirable, confronted with forces beyond their control, committing awful deeds, and suffering terrible retribution. For example, the qualities of heroism and suffering his King Oedipus shows in the face of overwhelming adversity are the essence of tragedy. Sophoclean tragedy expresses something of the meaning of human life and of the problems common to all humanity.

If Sophocles was only mildly interested in conventional religion, Euripides was positively skeptical. Writing plainly and without mincing words, he satirized those who deemed the gods superior to men. Generally critical and a dedicated fighter for unpopular causes, Euripides championed the rights of the slave and the foreigner, urged the emancipation of women, and attacked the glorification of war. The same is even more true of Aristophanes, whose comedies were filled with social satire. Himself a conservative who yearned for the good old days, he ridiculed democratic leaders and policies. In *The Lysistrata* he presented a group of women, who,

The Acropolis was both the religious and civic center of Athens. In its final form it is the work of Pericles and his successors in the late fifth century B.C.E. This photograph shows the Parthenon and to its left the Erechtheum.

appalled by the endless bloodshed, refuse to sleep with their husbands until they stop their wars. In *The Knights*, Aristophanes mocked democratic institutions with the story of a general who tries to persuade a sausage-seller to unseat Cleon, the democratic leader.[4]

Sausage-Seller	Tell me this, how can I, a sausage-seller, be a big man like that?
General	The easiest thing in the world. You've got all the qualifications: low birth, market-place training, insolence.
Sausage-Seller	I don't think I deserve it.
General	Not deserve it? It looks to me as if you've got too good a conscience. Was your father a gentleman?
Sausage-Seller	By the gods, no! My folks were scoundrels.
General	Lucky man! What a good start you've got for public life!
Sausage-Seller	But I can hardly read.
General	The only trouble is that you know anything. To be a leader of the people isn't for learned men, or honest men, but for the ignorant and vile. Don't miss this golden opportunity.

Greek art was another distinctive product of the polis-centered civilization. Art and architecture found their highest expression in the temples, the civic and religious core of polis culture. The temples were the revered dwelling places of the protecting gods and goddesses. A famous example is the Parthenon in Athens, which was built as a shrine to the protecting goddess Athena. Sculpture, the handmaiden of architecture, served to decorate the houses of the gods. Master sculptors, such as Phidias and Praxiteles, worked on temple walls and pediments and also carved statues for the interiors. All of Greek art embodied the basic Greek ideals of balance, harmony, and moderation. This is evident if we compare the Parthenon with an Egyptian pyramid or a Mesopotamian ziggurat or compare a Greek statue with the relatively crude and stilted sculptures of most Middle Eastern peoples of that time.

We find a similar contrast when we compare Greek philosophical speculation with that of other peoples. The sixth-century rationalist philosophers of Ionia on the Asia Minor coast were the first to challenge the traditional supernatural explanations of the nature of the world.

Socrates

They posed the basic question "What is the stuff of which the world is made?" The philosopher Thales speculated that everything originally was water, because this substance is found in liquid, solid, and vapor form. Heraclitus thought fire was the prime element because it was so active and could transform everything. Anaximenes believed it was air, arguing that air became fire when rarefied and became wind, cloud, water, earth, and stone when condensed. In the light of modern science these answers may appear naive, but what is important is that the question was asked and the answers were sought by the free use of reason, not by resorting to explanations based on the intervention of the gods.

As Greek society grew more complex, philosophers about the mid-fifth century B.C.E. turned their attention from the physical universe to human beings and their problems. Protagoras, the outstanding spokesperson of the Sophists, reflected this new interest. "Man is the measure of all things," he maintained, by which he meant that there are no absolute truths since everything is relative to the needs of man himself. The emphasis on man led the Sophists to condemn slavery and war and to espouse most popular causes. On the other hand many Greeks, especially those of conservative persuasion, feared that the relativism of the Sophists

endangered social order and morality. Typical was Socrates, who was profoundly disturbed by the political corruption of his day and by the absence of any unerring guide to correct living. Out of his never-ending conversations with his friends he evolved the science of dialectics. Provisional definitions were tested by questions and answers until universally recognized truths were reached. In this way, Socrates maintained, concepts of absolute truth or absolute good or absolute beauty could be discovered. These would provide enduring guides for personal conduct, in contrast to the relativism of the Sophists, which often provided rationalizations for private and public corruption.

Socrates's disciple Plato (427–347 B.C.E.) was an aristocrat who shared with his friends a great pride in Athens but also a distrust of the Athenian people. Distrust deepened into hatred when Athenian democracy condemned Socrates to death. Plato's goal became a society that preserved aristocratic privileges and yet was acceptable to the poorer classes. Accordingly he divided the citizens of his ideal Republic into four grades: guardians, philosophers, soldiers, and the masses who would do the work. This class differentiation was to be permanent, justified by

Plato

a myth, or "noble lie," that God had created men of four kinds: gold, silver, brass, and iron. Plato had hoped that the ruler of Syracuse would accept and apply his teachings, but when this did not happen he returned to Athens and for the next forty years instructed small groups of disciples.

The other great thinker of this period was Aristotle (384–322 B.C.E.), who began as Plato's disciple but who, following his master's death, founded the Lyceum. Aristotle was a classifier and rational thinker rather than a mystic, a logician and scientist rather than a philosopher. He took all knowledge for his province, so that he ranged more widely than anyone before or since. His outstanding contributions were in logic, physics, biology, and the humanities; indeed, he established these subjects as formal disciplines. As a great encyclopedist, he sought orderliness in every aspect of nature and of human life. Thus he balanced the classes of the human social world with corresponding orders in the natural world, beginning with minerals at the bottom, then vegetables, animals, and finally humans at the top. This gradation justified the division of human beings into born masters and born slaves:

. . . from the hour of their birth some are marked out for subjection, others for rule. . . . The art of war is a natural art of acquisition, for it includes hunting, an art which we ought to practice against wild beasts and against men who, though intended by nature to be governed, will not submit; for war of such a kind is naturally just.[5]

No account of classical Greece would be complete without reference to Herodotus and Thucydides, who related the stirring events of their times and in so doing created a new form of literature: history. Herodotus lived first among the Asia Minor Greeks, who had fallen under Persian rule, and then in Athens, where the Persians had suffered their great defeat. Herodotus wrote that the cause of the Persian defeat was the democratic constitution of the Athenians, making his *History* the first great tribute to democracy. The moral of his tale may be illustrated by the words he attributes to a Greek speaking of his countrymen to the Persian king:

For though they be free men, they are not in all respects free; Law is the master whom they own, and this master they fear more than your subjects fear you. Whatever it commands they do; and its commandment is always the same; it forbids them to flee in battle, whatever the number of their foes, and requires them to stand firm, and either to conquer or die.[6]

Thucydides's history was very different, being of the Peloponnesian War in which Athens, after twenty-seven years of bitter struggle, was finally beaten to its knees. Whereas Herodotus wrote about victory and glory, Thucydides analyzed defeat and suffering. His sympathies were unquestionably with Athens, whose armies he had led as a general. But he sternly suppressed his emotions and set himself the task of determining objectively the causes of the disaster. Although he did not use the phrase, he nevertheless said in effect that he was seeking to create a science of society.

Of the events of the war I have not ventured to speak from any chance information, nor according to any notion of my own; I have described nothing but what I either saw myself or learned from others of whom I made the most careful and particular enquiry. The task was a laborious one, because eye-witnesses of the same occurrences gave different accounts of them, as they remembered or were interested in the actions of one side or the other. And very likely the strictly historical character of my narrative may be disappointing to the ear. But if he who desires to have before his eyes a true picture of the events which had happened, and of the like events which may be expected to happen hereafter in the order of human things, shall pronounce what I have written to be useful, then I shall be satisfied. My history is an ever-lasting possession, not a prize composition which is heard and forgotten.[7]

Now that we have described the remarkable achievements of the Greeks in so many fields, we have also to point out certain failings. One was the presence of slaves, who together with the metics (resident aliens) were denied Athenian citizenship even though they made up the majority of the population. Women also had inferior status in Greece, as in other Mediterranean and Middle Eastern countries. In Athens (which had a worse record than some other city-states), women could not own property and had no political rights, including the right to vote or to serve on juries. Husbands had control of the children, which extended to the infanticide option that was subject exclusively to male decision. Professions such as law, medicine, and theater were all closed to women, as were also the Olympic games. Leading playwrights and philosophers wrote of the innate inferiority of women and warned of dire results if they were given too much authority. To safeguard their respectability, women were expected to remain secluded in their homes. Pericles advised widows that "the greatest glory of a woman is to be least talked about by men." Demosthenes best summed up the blatant gender inequity when he noted that there were three kinds of women in Athens: "We have mistresses [hetaerae] for our enjoyment, concubines or prostitutes to serve our person, and wives for bearing our legitimate offspring."[8]

In the Greek civilization, as in all others of ancient times, the strict rules about female seclusion applied only to upper-class females. Those who were not affluent could not afford to sit at home and hide themselves from the world. They had to get out and work to help support their families. Women from the wealthy families seldom were seen in the streets or in the markets. But working women were busy everywhere, earning wages in workshops or offering wares for sale in marketplaces or working in private houses as servants and nurses and female attendants. Aristotle noted that class determined the nature of women's lives when he wrote that since the poor had no slaves they had to allow their women to go out into the world.

Although these shortcomings were basic, classical Greece should be judged not by what it failed to do but by what it did. If this be the criterion, the contributions and their historical significance stand out clearly and overwhelmingly. The spirit of free inquiry, the theory and practice of democracy, the major forms of art and literature and philosophical thought, and the emphasis on individual freedom and individual responsibility—these are the splendid legacy of Greece to humanity.

IV. HELLENISTIC AGE, 336–31 B.C.E.

The Hellenistic Age derives its name from the new civilization that emerged as classical Greek culture spread throughout the Middle East in the wake of Alexander's conquests. (See Chapter 4, Section III.) On succeeding his father, Philip, in 336 B.C.E., Alexander first crushed a revolt in Thebes with such severity that the other Greek cities were persuaded to accept his rule. Then in 334 B.C.E., he led his Macedonian soldiers eastward against the Persians. Crossing the Hellespont, he overran first Asia Minor, then Syria, Egypt, Mesopotamia, and Persia itself, capturing Darius's capital, Persepolis, in 330 B.C.E. The following year the conqueror pushed on to the Hindu Kush and Bactria, and from there he marched on into India, penetrating as far as the Punjab. Only the refusal of his men to advance any further persuaded Alexander to return to Babylon, where he died of malarial fever in 323 at the age of thirty-three.

Rival generals now fought for control of the great empire until, by the beginning of the third century, three succession states emerged. One of these was Macedon, which now reverted

Alexander the Great

Darius I receiving tribute from a relief on the treasury at Persepolis. Note the incense burners before the king and the noble tribute bringer's gesture of respect. The scepter and lotus blossom held by Darius symbolize his kingship; his son and heir, Xerxes, stands behind him (491–486 B.C.E.)

to a modest, Hellenized, national kingdom. Macedon dominated, but did not directly rule, the Greek city-states to the south. A second was Egypt, ruled by the Ptolemies. It was the most viable of the succession states because of its natural riches and strong sea and desert defenses. The largest state, comprising the Asian provinces of the empire, fell to the Seleucids. Because of their vast holdings they fought a continual and losing battle against a host of surrounding enemies. First they ceded the Indus provinces to the Indian King Chandragupta, followed by Asia Minor to Celtic invaders and Persia and Mesopotamia to the Parthians. Finally in the first century B.C.E., Rome conquered the remaining provinces along the Mediterranean coast, along with Macedon and Egypt, thereby ending the Hellenistic Age and beginning the Roman.

Although Alexander's empire proved short-lived, the succession states survived more or less intact for three centuries, during which time the Middle East became Hellenized. Thousands of Greek merchants, administrators, teachers, professionals, and mercenary soldiers emigrated from their city-states to Egypt and the Asian provinces, attracted by the unprecedented opportunities afforded by those rich lands. Thus the foundations were laid for the new Hellenistic civilization, a hybrid creation that differed from the classical parent stock in virtually every respect.

The political framework changed radically because the polis was undermined and made sterile. The Greek city-states, trying to survive, experimented with federal union. The Achaean League included all the states of the Peloponnesus except Sparta, and the Aetolian Federation, nearly all of central Greece except Athens. Although often described as federal organizations, these leagues actually were confederacies that delegated little power to central authority. The leagues were both too weak and too late, and the city-states were dominated by one or another of the neighboring empires until the coming of the Roman legions.

As for the cities in the far-flung succession states, they never resembled the classical polis of mother Greece. They were divided internally by the distinctions between the Greek immigrants and the native people. Furthermore they were always completely subordinate to one or another imperial structure. If the citizens suffered from tyrannical or weak kings, they could do very little about it. The real decisions were made in the courts or on battlefields, not in meetings of popular assemblies. Thus the citizens understandably concentrated on accumulating wealth and enjoying life, leaving the poor and the slaves to shift for themselves as best they could. The civic spirit and social cohesion of the old polis gave way to self-centeredness and class strife.

Economic conditions and institutions also changed fundamentally. The Greek homeland suffered economic as well as political eclipse. It had depended on the export of wine, oil, and manufactured goods in return for foodstuffs and raw materials from the overseas colonies. But by the fourth century these colonies had taken root and developed their own industries and vineyards and olive orchards.

Although the Greek lands suffered economic decay, many Greeks got rich by emigrating to the Middle East, which was now open to them. They had much to contribute with their enterprising spirit and their advanced commercial and banking methods. They discovered and circulated the huge gold and silver hoard of the Persian dynasty. Also they introduced, or put to wider use, technological inventions such as the suction and piston pumps, the water mill, and the worm screw. The Greeks also directed large-scale public works and state enterprises, including irrigation systems, mines, quarries, salt pans, "royal lands," and workshops for luxury fabrics and ceramics. The net result was increased economic integration, which brought about a corresponding increase in regional commerce and productivity. The proceeds, however, were grossly maldistributed. Speculators took advantage of rising profits to reap great fortunes, while slaves increased in number and free workers declined in status. It was a period, in short, of greater productivity but also of greater economic inequality and social strife.

The average person during the Hellenistic Age was buffeted not only economically but also psychologically. A man—or a woman—felt lost in the large new cities with their teeming multitudes uprooted from their traditional environment. In the old polis, life had been relatively simple. Law, morality, religion, and duties were all clearly defined and generally accepted. Now all this was gone and citizens found themselves in a formless world. Furthermore, the Hellenistic cities frequently were torn by racial and cultural as well as class divisions. The rulers tried to cultivate a mystique of personal loyalty, adopting titles such as "Savior" and "Benefactor." But such expedients offered no lasting solution. Each person remained confronted with the question of how to conduct himself or herself in face of the impersonal and overwhelming forces of the time.

The response of intellectuals tended to be withdrawal from worldly affairs and a turn from reason to mysticism. Their withdrawal was reflected in the vogue for romantic adventure and utopian literature. When authors depicted an ideal society, they described not a city-state on the rocky soil of Hellas but a rainbow-tinted fairyland at the world's end. Especially popular in contemporary fiction were utopian island communities located in the Indian Ocean, blessed with natural riches that satisfied all material needs and inhabited by people who lived "simply and temperately . . . without jealousy and strife." This escapist tendency was reflected also in the philosophies of the day—Cynicism, Skepticism, Epicureanism, and Stoicism—which, though very different in many respects, were generally concerned with the pursuit of personal happiness rather than of social welfare.

Philosophy may have been the religion of the cultivated upper classes, but the religion of the lower classes was very different. They turned to cults of oriental origin—Mithraism, Gnosticism, the Egyptian mother-goddess Isis, and the astral religion of the Chaldeans. All these promised salvation in afterlife. All satisfied the emotional needs of the harried masses with comforting assurances of a paradise to come. Thus the secularism and rationalism of classical Greece now gave way to mysticism and otherworldliness.

In view of these antirational trends in philosophy and religion, it is surprising that more progress was achieved in science in the Hellenistic Age than in any other period prior to the seventeenth century. This gain was due in part to the economic opportunities afforded by Alexander's conquests. The greatly expanded markets provided the incentive to improve technology, which would increase output and thus profit. Also, the continual wars among the succession states, or between them and outside powers, created a demand for more complex war engines. Equally stimulating was the direct contact between Greek science and that of the Middle East—not only of Mesopotamia and Egypt but also, to a certain extent, of India. Finally, the Macedonian rulers of the Hellenistic states, raised as youths to value the prestige of Greek learning, generously supported scientific research, particularly in Egypt, where the Alexandria

This is a Roman copy of one of the masterpieces of Hellenistic sculpture, the Laocoon. *According to legend, Laocoon was a priest who warned the Trojans not to take the Greek's wooden horse within their city. This sculpture depicts his punishment. Great serpents sent by the goddess Athena, who was on the side of the Greeks, devoured Laocoon and his sons before the horrified people of Troy.*

Museum and Library was, in effect, the first state-supported research institute in history. It included astronomical observatories, laboratories and dissecting rooms, botanical and zoological gardens, and a library of from 500,000 to 700,000 volumes. From all over the Mediterranean world, in an early version of the "brain drain," came philosophers, mathematicians, physicians, botanists, zoologists, astronomers, philologists, geographers, artists, and poets—all attracted by the congenial and stimulating atmosphere, by the superb facilities, and by the free meals and lodgings and high salaries.

In mathematics the outstanding name was Euclid, with his *Elements of Geometry*. In astronomy, Hipparchus invented most of the instruments used until modern times and compiled the first star catalog. Ptolemy's compilation of

Hellenistic astronomical knowledge is the best-known work and remained the standard text until the Renaissance. Most original was Aristarchus, who was the first to grasp the enormous size of the universe and to place the sun and not the earth at its center. His views received little support, for they were considered impious as well as contrary to everyday experience. Thus Ptolemy's geocentric system remained generally accepted throughout medieval times. The progress in astronomy facilitated advances in scientific geography. Eratosthenes, the director of the Alexandria Museum, calculated the earth's circumference at 24,700 miles. Only 250 miles off, his calculations were not improved upon until the eighteenth century. He also drew a map of the inhabited world with a grid of latitudes and concluded, from the ebb and flow of tides in the Atlantic and Indian oceans, that the seas were one and that Europe, Asia, and Africa constituted a huge island.

Perhaps the outstanding contributions of Hellenistic science were in medicine and mechanics. The museum encouraged anatomical research, so that physicians now understood for the first time the role of the heart in blood circulation, the significance of the pulse, the functions of sensory and motor nerves, and the convolutions of the brain. Much of this knowledge was passed on by the great encyclopedist of medicine Galen, whose writings were so impressive that doctors dared not question him or strike out in new directions until modern times. In mechanics the outstanding figure was Archimedes, the founder of hydrostatics—the laws of floating bodies—which were used thereafter for testing the purity of metals. He also devised ingenious war machines and formulated the principles of the screw, the pulley, and the lever. It was in connection with the lever that he is supposed to have said, "Give me a place to stand, and I will move the world."

In conclusion, the historical significance of the Hellenistic Age is that it brought the East and West together, breaking the separate molds that had been formed through history. People now for the first time thought of the entire civilized world as a unit. At first the Greeks and Macedonians went to the East as conquerors and rulers and imposed a pattern of Hellenization.

But in the process they themselves were changed, so that the resulting Hellenistic civilization was a blend rather than a transplantation. And in the long run the religions of the East made their way west and contributed substantially to the transformation of the Roman Empire and medieval Europe.

V. EARLY REPUBLIC, TO 264 B.C.E.

Meanwhile the city-states in Greece continued to fight each other as they had in the past. They organized unions such as the Achaean League and the Aetolian Federation, but none proved lasting and effective. Despite many warnings, the divided Greeks ignored the rising power of the Romans. After destroying the Carthaginians, their great rivals in the western Mediterranean, the Romans turned eastward. First they conquered Macedon and the divided Greek cities, and then they overran the entire Hellenistic East.

Why were the Romans able to become the masters of the entire Mediterranean, and eventually of all Europe? Actually there were many similarities between the early histories of the Greeks and the Romans. Both were of the same ethnic stock, for just as the Indo-European Achaeans and Dorians filtered down the Balkan peninsula to Greece, so the Indo-European Latins filtered down the Italian peninsula to the south bank of the Tiber River. Among the Latin

Much of what we know of the Etruscans comes from their funerary art. This sculpture of an Etruscan couple is part of a sarcophagus.

communities formed at the time was Rome, which was located on the Tiber at the lowest point that could be conveniently crossed and at the highest to which small ships could go. This strategic position, similar to that of London on the Thames, made Rome from the very beginning both more mercantile and more open to foreign influences than other Latin settlements.

The chief foreign influences came from two civilized peoples who had come from overseas to settle in Italy—the Etruscans and the Greeks. The Etruscans, who arrived about 800 B.C.E., probably from Asia Minor, settled to the north of the Tiber and then conquered the Latins to the south. Before their rule was overthrown they passed on to the Romans some of their gods and goddesses, a knowledge of the arch and the vault, and the typically Eastern practice of forecasting the future by examining animal entrails. The Greeks, who appeared shortly after the Etruscans, established colonies in southern Italy and Sicily, including Tarentum, Syracuse, and Naples. Among their contributions to the Latins were the alphabet, some art and mythology, and certain religious concepts and practices, including the Greek-borrowed identities of Roman gods. The Greek's Zeus, Hermes, and Artemis became the Roman's Jupiter, Mercury, and Diana.

About 500 B.C.E. Rome expelled its last Etruscan king and began its career as an independent city-state. Within a few years it had conquered the surrounding peoples and controlled the entire Latin plain from the Apennine mountains to the sea coast. Roman institutions during this formative period were similar to those of the early Greek cities. The king originally held the imperium, or sovereign power. He was restrained only by an advisory council of aristocrats and a popular assembly that had power only to approve or disapprove legislation. Then, as in Greece, the monarchy was abolished, and the patricians became the dominant element in society. The sovereign power formerly held by the king was now delegated to two consuls, who were elected for one-year periods and who were always patricians. The Senate, which was the principal legislative body, was also an aristocratic institution and remained so even after a few commoners, or plebeians, were admitted.

Rome's development diverged from that of the Greek city-states when it accomplished what was beyond the capacity of the Greek cities—the conquest and unification of the entire peninsula. Why was it that Rome could master the Italian peninsula whereas no Greek city was able to unify even the Greek lands, let alone the whole of the Balkan peninsula? One reason was the marked difference in terrain. The Balkans are a jumble of mountains; indeed the name Balkan is derived from the Turkish word for mountain. The crisscrossing of ranges is very prevalent in Greece. In Italy, by contrast, there are only the Apennines, which are not as difficult to cross and which run north and south without transverse ranges. Consequently the Italian peninsula, not being so compartmentalized, is easier to unite and keep united. Furthermore, there was never a Balkan counterpart to the system of Roman roads that knitted Italy into one unit. For example, the famous Appian Way stretched all the way from Rome to Brindisium on the heel of the Italian boot. This road is still extant and was used by the British and American troops that landed in southern Italy in 1943.

Another reason for the success of the Romans was their enlightened treatment of the other Italian peoples. Upon its fellow Greeks Athens had levied tribute, and it never extended them citizenship. Rome granted full citizenship to about a fourth of the population of the peninsula. The rest were granted Latin citizenship, which carried substantial but not complete privileges. Autonomy was enjoyed by all. The only restrictions were the loss of control over foreign relations and a compulsory manpower levy for military service. This policy saved Rome, for her Italian allies remained loyal during the critical years when Hannibal was rampaging up and down the length of the peninsula.

Finally, the Romans prevailed because of the superior military force and strategy that they developed. In fighting their neighbors they learned that the traditional phalanx of 8,000 men was too large and unwieldy, especially in mountainous terrain. So they organized their soldiers into "maniples," or "handfuls," of 120 soldiers. Thirty of these, or 3,600 men, constituted a legion, which also had cavalry to protect its flanks. In addition to the traditional helmet, shield, lance, and sword, the Romans equipped the legion with an effective assault weapon—the iron-tipped javelin, which was flung at the enemy from a distance. Then the legionnaires attacked on the run, maneuvering skillfully to take advantage of any breaks in the opposing ranks.

By 295 B.C.E. the Romans had won central Italy and pushed south against Tarentum, the prosperous Greek city in the "instep" of the peninsula. The Tarentines called in the help of the Greek king, Pyrrhus of Epirus, ranked by Hannibal as second only to Alexander in generalship. Pyrrhus won two "Pyrrhic victories." But he could not afford his heavy losses, whereas the Romans, though they lost even more, could draw from a pool of 750,000 Italian fighting men. So Pyrrhus withdrew in 272 B.C.E. with the prophetic observation "What a battleground I am leaving for Rome and Carthage!" Only eight years later, in 264, Rome and Carthage were at war in Sicily.

Before considering the Punic Wars—so named after the Latin word *punicus* for Phoenician—it is necessary to note a certain democratization of Roman institutions. Since the plebeians had provided the manpower for the victorious legions, they were in a position to demand political concessions. When their demands were denied, they resorted to the novel but effective device of a walkout (secessio) and literally withdrew en masse from the city until their demands were met. One of the first gains won in this fashion by the plebeians was the right to choose officials known as tribunes to defend their interests. The tribunes were elected by the new Plebeian Assembly, which also cared for other matters of concern to the masses. Other concessions included the writing down of the laws so that they would be known to all and limitation of the amount of land that could be owned by any one individual.

Thus by 265 B.C.E. Rome, the mistress of Italy, was undergoing a process of democratization. Conceivably this could have culminated in the first democratic national state in the history of the world. But if this were in fact a possibility, it was effectively eliminated by the series of overseas wars in which Rome was now involved. The wars transformed Rome into a great empire, but they also transformed as profoundly its domestic institutions, and one of the many casualties was the trend toward democratization.

VI. LATE REPUBLIC, 265–27 B.C.E.

The transformation of Rome from an Italian republic to a great empire was sudden and spectacular, rather like the conquests of Alexander. Indeed certain common basic factors help to explain the explosive expansions of both Macedon and Rome. Each had evolved superior military instruments and techniques. Each enjoyed the vital advantage of social vigor and cohesion in contrast to the social decrepitude and fragmentation of the Persian Empire and the Hellenistic succession states.

Rome's great rival, Carthage, had started as a Phoenician colony about 850 B.C.E. Thanks to its near monopoly of the transit trade in the western Mediterranean, Carthage had become rich and powerful. With its wide-ranging fleets and mercenary troops, Carthage dominated northwestern Africa, southern Spain, Sardinia, Corsica, and western Sicily. At first there was no direct conflict between Rome and Carthage for the simple reason that one was a land power and the other a sea power. But they finally did clash when the Romans conquered southern Italy. The Romans feared Carthage's growing influence in Sicily, which was all too close to their newly won possessions.

The First Punic War (264–241 B.C.E.) forced the Romans for the first time to turn to the sea. They built a fleet, and by turning naval battles into boarding operations, they doggedly wore down the Carthaginians and conquered Sicily. The struggle to the death between the two great powers was now inevitable. Rome spent the next twenty years subduing the Celtic tribes in the Po Valley, thereby increasing its reserve of peasant soldiers. Carthage, to compensate for the loss of Sicily, consolidated its hold on Spain. From this base the great Carthaginian strategist, Hannibal, launched his daring invasion of Italy, crossing the Alps in 218 and thus beginning the Second Punic War (218–201). He defeated the Romans in battle after battle, particularly in his great triumph of Cannae (216). But the loyalty of Rome's allies robbed him of victory. When a Roman army landed near Carthage, Hannibal, undefeated in Italy, was recalled only to be defeated on his own ground. Once again Rome had exhausted an opponent, and in 201 Carthage was forced to accept a peace leaving it only its small home territory, its walls, and ten ships—enough to chase off pirates. Despite this catastrophic defeat, the Carthaginians made a remarkable economic recovery. But this alarmed the Romans so that they ruthlessly provoked the Third Punic War (149–146). Carthage itself was captured, the city completely destroyed, and the populace enslaved.

With these Punic Wars, Rome was caught in a chain reaction of conquest leading to further conquest. One reason was its overwhelming strength; with Carthage out of the way Rome was now the foremost power in the Mediterranean. Also conquest was manifestly profitable, as booty, slaves, and tribute poured in from each new province. Finally, there were the inevitable commitments and challenges associated with far-flung imperial frontiers. For example, since Philip V of Macedon had aided Hannibal during the Second Punic War, Rome—after having disposed of Carthage—turned on Macedon. The ensuing war proved to be the first of a series in which the Romans skillfully played off against each other the several Middle Eastern powers—Macedon, Seleucid Syria, Ptolemaic Egypt, and the rival Aetolian and Achaean leagues of Greek city-states.

Thus the Romans overran and annexed in quick succession Macedon; Greece; the Asia Minor states of Pergamum, Bithynia, and Cilicia; then Seleucid Syria; and finally Egypt in 31

B.C.E. In this manner the Romans took over the Hellenistic succession states of the East. In Asia though, they acquired only the provinces along the Mediterranean coast. All the interior had fallen to Parthia, which henceforth was to be Rome's chief rival in the East. Meanwhile Julius Caesar had gained fame by conquering (58–49 B.C.E.) all of Gaul between the English Channel and the Mediterranean. Finally the permanent occupation of Britain was begun in the first century of our era and was consolidated with the construction of a line of fortifications between the firths of Clyde and Forth. This marked the limits of Roman rule in northern Europe.

Rome did not treat its newly acquired provinces as generously as it had its earlier Italian allies. The Senate appointed governors who were given a free hand as long as they kept sending home an adequate flow of tribute, taxes, grain, and slaves. The result was shameless exploitation and extortion. The maladministration of Governor Gaius Verres in Sicily (73–71 B.C.E.), described in the following indictment by Cicero, was neither exceptional nor atypical:

Countless sums of money, under a new and unprincipled regulation, were wrung from the purses of the farmers; our most loyal allies were treated as if they were national enemies; Roman citizens were tortured and executed like slaves; the guiltiest criminals bought their legal acquittal, while the most honour-

Busts of a Roman couple from the period of the Republic. Although some people have identified the individuals as Cato the Younger and his daughter Porcia, no solid evidence confirms this claim.

able and honest men would be . . . condemned and banished unheard; strongly fortified harbours, mighty and well-defended cities were left open to the assaults of pirates and buccaneers. Sicilian soldiers and sailors, our allies and our friends, were starved to death; fine fleets, splendidly equipped, were to the great disgrace of our nation destroyed and lost to us. Famous and ancient works of art, some of them the gifts of wealthy kings . . . —this same governor stripped and despoiled every one of them. Nor was it only the civic statues and works of art he treated thus; he also pillaged the holiest and most venerated sanctuaries; in fact, he has not left the people of Sicily a single god whose workmanship he thought at all above the average of antiquity of artistic merit.[9]

These polices affected the Roman homeland almost as adversely as Rome affected the subject territories. Many of the small farmers in Italy had been ruined by the ravages of Hannibal's campaigns and by the long years of overseas service during the following wars. Then came the influx of cheap grain and of droves of slaves from the conquered provinces. The peasants were forced to sell out to the new class of the very rich, who were especially eager to accumulate large estates because agriculture was still considered the only respectable calling for gentlemen. Thus the second century B.C.E. saw the growth in Italy of large plantations (*latifundia*) worked by slaves and owned by absentee landlords. The dispossessed peasantry drifted to the towns, where they lived in squalid tenements and once again had to compete with slaves for such work as was available. The authorities took care to provide them with "bread and circuses" (*panis et circenses*) to keep them quiet. Despite the insecurity and rootlessness, city life at least was exciting and alluring. Poets were loud in their praise of rustic virtues, but the peasants themselves thought otherwise and continued to flock to Rome—the "common cesspool," as the contemporary historian Sallust termed it.

The political fruits of empire were as bitter as the economic. The earlier trend toward democratization was reversed because the Senate had directed the victorious overseas campaigns and gained greatly in prestige and power. Also the new urban mobs offered no basis for popular government since they were always ready to sell their votes or to support any demagogue who promised relief from their troubles. Equally disruptive was the changing character of the armed forces. Imperial obligations required a large standing army. It no longer sufficed to call up property owners for short-term militia service. So the ranks were opened to volunteers, and dispossessed peasants enlisted for long periods. Rome's legions accordingly changed from a citizen army to a professional one. The soldiers' first loyalty now was not to the state but to their commanders, to whom they looked for a share of the booty and of any land that might be available for distribution. The generals increasingly came to regard the legions entrusted to them as their own armies and used them to advance their personal fortunes.

Imperial expansion also disrupted Roman culture. The traditional Roman virtues had been those of poor, hard-working peasants. But when wealth began to pour into the capital, the ancient values of thrift, abstinence, and industry were soon forgotten. The last days of the republic were marked by a wild scramble for money, the sort of ostentatious waste to be expected from the newly rich, and a callous indifference to all human values. "Rome," grumbled a contemporary, "has become a city where paramours fetch a better price than plowlands, and pots of pickled fish than plowmen."

In light of the above, it is understandable that the period from the end of the Punic Wars in 146 B.C.E. to the end of the republic in 27 B.C.E. was one of crisis—of class war, slave revolts, and increasing military intervention in politics. A gallant reform effort was made at the outset by Tiberius Gracchus and his brother Gaius. They sought to use their elective positions as tribunes to push through a moderate program of land distribution. But the oligarchs would have none of it and resorted to violence to gain their ends. Tiberius was murdered in 133 B.C.E. along with three hundred of his followers. Twelve years later Gaius was driven to suicide, and the senatorial class resumed its sway.

The fate of the Gracchi brothers made clear the impossibility of orderly reform. The empire now was torn by generals competing for power at the top and by slave revolts from below. The most serious of the revolts was that of Spartacus, which broke out in 73 B.C.E. For a while the entire imperial system tottered, but in the end

Spartacus was defeated, and the roads to Rome were lined with his crucified followers.

The final victor was Julius Caesar, the conqueror of Gaul, who had built up a powerful and devoted army. In 49 B.C.E. he crossed the river Rubicon, which separated Gaul from Italy, and in a series of brilliant campaigns defeated the forces of the Senate under his rival Pompey. Caesar was now the undisputed master of the empire. Precisely what he would have done with his mastery cannot be known, for he was murdered in 44 B.C.E. by representatives of the old oligarchy.

His death was followed by another thirteen years of political jockeying and armed strife between his adopted son and heir Octavian and the political adventurer Mark Antony. With his naval victory over Antony and Cleopatra at Actium (31 B.C.E.), Octavian was supreme. He was only thirty-three years old at the time, the age at which the great Alexander had died. But Octavian had forty-four years of life ahead of him, during which he laid the foundations for two golden centuries of imperial peace and stability.

VII. EARLY EMPIRE, 27 B.C.E.–284 C.E.

In 27 B.C.E. the Senate conferred upon Octavian the titles of Augustus and Imperator, symbolizing the transformation of Rome from republic to empire. Octavian professed to prefer the republican title of First Citizen (Princeps). But in practice he acted like an emperor and grasped full powers, at the expense of both the Senate and the people. He created a centralized system of courts under his own supervision and assumed direct control over provincial governors, punishing them severely for graft and extortion. He standardized taxes and made their collection a state function rather than a private business operated by greedy tax farmers. He kept close check on the army and saw to it that the soldiers were well provided for and swore allegiance directly to him. He also created a permanent navy that suppressed piracy and safeguarded the transportation of both commodities and troops to all parts of the empire.

By these measures Augustus, as he came to be known, created an efficient administrative system that ensured the Pax Romana that was to prevail for two centuries. The four emperors following Augustus—Tiberius (14–37 C.E.), Caligula (37–41), Claudius (41–54), and Nero (54–68)—were unworthy of their high office. But the empire weathered their misrule and then blossomed under a succession of "five good emperors"—Nerva (96–98 C.E.), Trajan (98–117), Hadrian (117–138), Antoninus Pius (138–161), and Marcus Aurelius (161–180). During these reigns the Roman Empire reached its height, both in geographic extent and in the quality of its civilization.

In the extreme north, the imperial frontier was set by the fortifications built from the Forth to the Clyde. In the northeast, the Rhine and the Danube provided a natural frontier, which further east curved north of the Danube to include Dacia (modern Rumania). Both Asia Minor and Egypt were Roman possessions, but

An example of one of the greatest achievements of the Roman empire, this granite aqueduct was constructed in the time of Trajan and is still in use today.

between the two the frontier ran close to the Mediterranean coast, leaving the interior to the Parthians and, after 224 C.E., to the Sassanians. Likewise in North Africa the Romans controlled the coastal territories between Egypt and the Atlantic, with the Sahara as their southern limit.

This huge area, with its strong natural frontiers, constituted a prosperous and virtually self-sufficient economic unit. Various factors contributed to the flourishing imperial economy during these centuries—honest and efficient administration, monetary stability, large-scale public works, and extensive trade, both within and without the empire. Internal free trade ensured unhindered distribution of wheat, papyrus, and glassware from Egypt; linens, woolens, and fruits from Syria; wool, timber, and rugs from Asia Minor; wine, oil, and manufactured goods from Italy; grains, meats, and wool from Gaul; and a variety of minerals from Spain and Britain. The Romans also imported certain goods from the outside: amber, furs, and slaves from the Baltic Sea area; ivory, gold, and slaves from sub-Saharan Africa; and most important, various luxury items from Asia, including perfumes, precious stones, spices, and, above all, silk. (See Chapter 4, Section II.) Thanks to this thriving domestic and foreign trade, staples and luxuries poured into the capital from as near as Gaul and as far as China—enough staples to feed and clothe over a million people, and enough luxuries to satisfy the extravagances of the rulers of the Western world.

In the cultural field, a basic achievement of the Romans was the extension into central and western Europe of urban civilization, with all that that entailed. In this respect their role in the West was similar to that of the Greeks in the Middle East. In the third century B.C.E., after Alexander, the Greeks founded dozens of cities from which Hellenistic culture spread as far as India and Central Asia. So now the Romans founded cities such as London and Colchester in Britain, Autun and Vaison in Gaul, and Trier and Cologne in Germany. These cities, varying from 20 to 500 acres in size, were a distinct improvement on the relatively squalid hilltop forts and villages of the Celts and Germans. Even the slaves' quarters in these cities were more hygienic than the hovels of the contemporary native villagers. Furthermore the cities possessed public bathhouses for the comfort of the body and public theaters for the pleasures of the mind, as well as residential blocks and public markets and shops. These cities were the basic cells of the imperial culture as well as of the imperial political system.

The great city of the empire, of course, was Rome. It sprawled over 5,000 acres, and its population during the second century C.E. is estimated at a little over 1 million. A visitor would find a complete absence of sanitation facilities in the crowded tenements of the poor but would note that, instead, there were elaborate public latrines with seats of marble and decorated with statues of gods or heroes. An inevitable byproduct of this arrangement was the emptying of chamber pots into the streets—not a rare occurrence as we can see from the many references to this practice in Roman law. Noteworthy also was the total lack of street lighting, so that on moonless nights the capital was plunged in impenetrable darkness. Everyone locked doors and stayed at home; no one dared venture out except for the wealthy with their escort of slaves who carried torches and protected them against robbers. In daytime the streets teemed with life and reverberated with noise. Hawkers bawled their wares, money changers rang their coins, tinkers pounded their hammers, snake charmers played their flutes, and beggars rehearsed their misfortunes to passersby. Night provided no relief. Transport carts were banned from the streets in daytime, so immediately after sunset there appeared a great procession of carts, beasts of burden, and their drivers. This night traffic condemned Romans to perpetual insomnia unless they were wealthy enough to live in isolated villas.

Life under such conditions was made tolerable by the mass entertainment provided by the state. Most popular were the chariot races and gladiatorial contests. A better use of leisure was provided by the sumptuous public baths of Rome. These were so elaborate that those of Diocletian covered thirty-two acres; Caracalla's spread over twenty-seven acres. Such establishments were, of course, much more than simple bathing pools. In addition to hot, tepid, and cold baths, they provided exercise facilities, lounging halls, gardens, and libraries. They were, in short, "athletic clubs" on a grand scale,

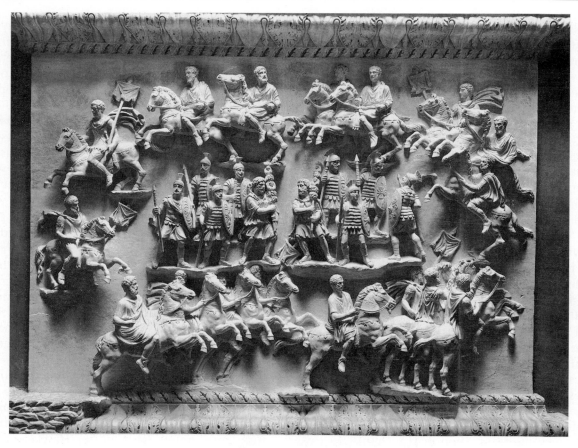

A relief from the column of Antonius Pius showing Roman foot soldiers surrounded by cavalry.

and they admirably promoted the ideal of "a healthy mind in a healthy body."

Finally the Rome of these centuries was also the center of imperial culture. This culture, as noted earlier, was essentially Greek-derived, particularly in such fields as literature, art, and philosophy. But in engineering and law, the Romans, with their bent for practicality, had important contributions of their own to make. Typically, the Romans achieved little in abstract science but excelled in the construction of aqueducts, sewer systems, bridges, and roads. The roads were superbly built, with a bottom layer of large stones set in firm soil, a middle layer of gravel, and a top layer of large slabs of stone. They were carefully cambered so that the surface water drained off into the ditches on each side. These famous roads, together with their bridges, were so well engineered that they continued to be used through the Middle Ages, and in some cases even to the present day. Likewise, Roman architecture,

in contrast to the Greek, was concerned primarily with secular structures such as baths, amphitheaters, stadiums, and triumphal arches. And new Roman building materials—concrete, brick, and mortar—made possible vaulting on a grand scale for their large buildings.

Perhaps the most important single intellectual contribution of the Romans was their body of law based on reason rather than custom. Their original laws, as set down in the Twelve Tablets about 450 B.C.E., were simple and conservative, typical of a peasant people. With the growth of commerce and of empire, life became more complicated, and these laws no longer sufficed. Typical was the problem of an alien in Rome who might be arrested and his property seized. What law would be applicable in such a case, particularly in view of the contemporary concept that a people carried their law with them wherever they went? The Romans established a special court to try such cases, and as a result of its operations they realized that among foreign peoples there were many legal systems but only a few almost universal legal principles. Hence the formulation of a new body of law—the *jus gentium*, or law of the people—which they accepted and applied both to themselves and to others.

The Twelve Tablets also defined the subordinate status of the Roman woman, who was subject to the authority of the eldest male ascendant in the family, the pater familias. The legal system included the principle of patriapostestas, by which the husband was the legal head of the household. As such he enjoyed absolute power, including the right of life and death and the right to sell into slavery all the members of his family. But Roman women, unlike the Athenian, did have the right to inherit and acquire real property and could dispose of it without the consent of their guardians. Also Roman women were not so rigidly confined to residential quarters as were their Athenian sisters. Generalizations are risky because of changes during the transition from republic to empire. Yet it is safe to conclude that the women of Rome were better off than those of Athens, though still definitely subordinate to men.

VIII. LATE EMPIRE, 284–476 C.E.

The great days of Rome came to an end with the death of Marcus Aurelius in 180 C.E. For some time his predecessors had passed on the succession to adopted sons of proven talent, a system that had made possible a string of unusually capable rulers. But Marcus Aurelius allowed his true son, Commodus, to succeed him. The results were disastrous. Commodus avoided his duties as head of the empire and spent most of his time at chariot races and gladiatorial contests. After his assassination in 193 he was followed by rulers who were for the most part equally incompetent. The Praetorian Guard, a highly trained and well-paid body created by Augustus to protect the security of the capital, now got out of control. An emperor could remain in power only while he had the support of this body. During the period from 235 to 284 there were almost two dozen emperors, and only one of them died a natural death. Such disintegration at the center inevitably weakened the frontier defenses. Outlying provinces were overrun by the German tribes in the West and by the revived Persian Empire of the Sassanians in the East.

The imperial decay of the third century was checked with the advent of the strong and capable emperors Diocletian (284–305) and Constantine (312–317). Among the policies they adopted to hold the empire together was a rigid regimentation imposed step by step in response to specific urgent needs. Because agricultural lands were left untilled, villages were required to pay a collective tax on abandoned lands. Because inflation was mounting, the famous Edict of Prices (301) set maximum prices for thousands of commodities and services, with specified variations according to quality. Interest rates were soaring, so they were limited to between 6 and 12 percent, depending on the degree of risk. Shortages of certain products brought on export prohibitions, as in the case of foodstuffs and "strategic products" such as iron, bronze, weapons, army equipment, and horses. These controls were extended to the point where they virtually became a caste system. Constantine required every soldier's son to be a soldier unless unfit for service. Similarly, agricultural

Bust of the Emperor Constantine (306–377 C.E.)

laborers were tied to the land on a permanent and hereditary basis. The tendency was to extend this requirement to all crafts and professions that were deemed indispensable or that had recruitment difficulties.

Another policy during this time of troubles was decentralization, which became necessary as the imperial economy deteriorated. Diocletian divided his realm in two, keeping the eastern half for his own administration and appointing a coemperor for the western. This division was hardened when Constantine built a new capital on the site of the old Greek colony of Byzantium on the Bosphorus. The choice was inspired, for Constantinople, as the new city soon came to be called, was easily defended because of the narrows at each end of the straits. The city also provided ready access to both the vital Danube and Euphrates frontiers. Thus Constantinople became one of the great cities of the world and served as the proud capital of the Eastern Roman, or Byzantine, Empire for centuries after Rome and the Western Empire had passed away.

Another policy of these later centuries that was to affect the future profoundly dealt with relations between Christianity and the imperial government. Constantine made the fateful decision to seek stability and cohesion through cooperation with Christianity rather than its suppression. This was the end of a centuries-old trend in religious attitudes and practices. The hardships of daily life during this later imperial phase caused increasing numbers to turn for solace to salvation religions, as had happened earlier in the Hellenistic East. (See Section IV, this chapter.) Spiritual needs no longer were satisfied by the cult of emperor and the official polytheism. Brotherhoods that celebrated the mysteries of oriental gods now provided satisfying explanations of the world, rules of conduct, and release from evil and from death.

The most successful of the new religions was Christianity. It offered the doctrine of one God, the Father Omnipotent, in place of the polytheism of the Greco-Roman gods and the monotheism of the oriental cults. It brought the solace of a Redeemer, Jesus, who was not an ambiguous figure in a mythological labyrinth but who miraculously lived an earthly life, even though he was the Son of God. "I bring you tidings of great joy which shall be to all people." Christianity also guaranteed salvation to the believer, but instead of a starry eternity, it restored him to life through a personal resurrection foreshadowed by the Resurrection of Christ himself. Perhaps most important of all, Christianity provided fellowship when times were disjointed and common people felt uprooted and

The Arch of Constantine, constructed between 312 and 315 C.E. to honor Constantine as sole emperor of Rome.

forsaken. All Christians were brothers, and their meetings were often called agape, meaning "love" in Greek. They assisted one another, and by their devotion and self-denial they set an aspiring and contagious example. Thus at a time when the laws and philosophy of the old order were becoming irrelevant and unviable, Christianity offered relevance and hope for the meek and the humble.

By the time of the great fire of 64 C.E., the Christians had become so numerous that Nero thought it wise to blame them for the disaster and to begin the first of numerous persecutions. But this merely hallowed the memory of the martyrs and spurred the proselytizing efforts. After a final major persecution early in the fourth century, Emperor Constantine issued the Edict of Milan (313) excusing Christians from pagan rituals and granting their religion the same tolerance accorded to all others. Finally, Emperor Theodosius (379–395) made Christianity in effect the state church. The old Roman aristocracy and the apostate Emperor Julian (361–363) fought a stubborn rearguard action to preserve pagan practices, but by the end of the fourth century Christianity reigned supreme.

Just as the emperors adopted Christianity with the aim of furthering social cohesion, so they adopted the pomp and circumstance of oriental court etiquette. In contrast to Augustus, who had dubbed himself "First Citizen," Diocletian took the name of Jovian, the earthly representative of Jupiter, and Constantine, after his conversion to Christianity, assumed sacred status. The power of the emperor henceforth was considered to be derived from the gods rather than delegated by citizens. Accordingly, court ritual now made the emperor remote and unapproachable. Bedecked in a jeweled diadem and a robe of purple silk interwoven with gold, the emperor forced all subjects to prostrate themselves. Only a privileged few were allowed to kiss the border of the emperor's robe. High imperial officials were correspondingly beatified—the treasurer became "count of the sacred largesses," and the imperial council was known as the "sacred consistory."

With these measures the emperors of the third and fourth centuries strove valiantly to halt the imperial decline. If resolve and effort alone were needed, they would have been spec-

This ivory relief, carved a little after 395 C.E., shows a Vandal warrior, Stilicho, who rose to prominence in the Roman army. From the third century onward, the Roman army was composed increasingly of foreign mercenaries.

tacularly successful. In fact they did stabilize the situation somewhat, but only temporarily. The net effect of their herculean endeavors was to postpone rather than to avert the end. Beginning in 406 the West Roman emperors were powerless to prevent permanent large-scale invasions of Franks, Burgundians, Visigoths, and Vandals in Gaul, Spain, and Africa. Nor could they prevent the ultimate indignity of the sack of Rome by barbarians in 410 and again in 455.

Finally, in 476 Romulus Augustulus, the last of the West Roman emperors, was forced to abdicate by Odoacer, the German, or Hunnic, leader of a band of mercenary soldiers.

Though this incident is generally taken to mark the end of the West Roman Empire, it attracted little attention at the time, for it was merely the culmination of a process of disintegration that had extended over two centuries. To understand the reason for the "fall of Rome," if this traditional cataclysmic phrase may be used, it is necessary to determine the dynamics of the prolonged but inexorable descent to oblivion.

The instrument responsible for the "fall" was, of course, the German barbarians. Thus a French historian has concluded, "Roman civilization did not die a natural death. It was murdered."[10] There is some justification for this verdict, yet it was not a case of irresistible hordes sweeping everything aside by sheer weight of numbers. Historians estimate that only about 100,000 Ostrogoths invaded Italy, and an equal number of Visigoths subjugated Spain and southern France. The Vandal force that crossed the Straits of Gibraltar to North Africa totaled about 80,000 men, or 1 percent of the native population of that province.

So the question still remains—why the "fall"? An American historian has stated that "though war was the apparent cause of death . . . the organic disease of the Empire was economic."[11] In fact, this "organic disease" is discernible not only in the Roman Empire but also in the Hellenistic states, in classical Greece, and even in the earlier ancient civilizations. All were afflicted by the same basic problem of low productivity. It stemmed from the failure to advance technology significantly after the Neolithic age, which had produced such core inventions as metallurgy, the plow, the wheel, the sail, and the solar calendar.

The underlying cause for the technological retardation appears to have been the institution of slavery, which was an integral and universally accepted part of all these civilizations. Even in classical Greece, where slavery never was as rampant as in Rome, Aristotle (as noted earlier) asserted that some men were born to rule and some to be ruled, and if the latter refused to accept their preordained fate, it was "naturally just" that they should be hunted down as though they were "wild beasts."

The repercussions of the institution of slavery were manifold and pernicious. The institution deprived the slave of any incentive to improve on the traditional operations of his or her craft. It also deprived the master of any incentive for technological innovation as long as plenty of slave labor was available. Thus during the reign of Vespasian when an obelisk was to be erected in the present-day Piazza San Pietro in Rome, an inventor of the time suggested an engineering technique that would have made the operation much easier. But the emperor preferred manual slave labor so as not to leave the slaves unemployed. Likewise the water mill, though known in the eastern provinces of the empire as early as the first century B.C.E., was not adopted in Rome until the fourth century, when the supply of slaves had shrunk.

Equally harmful was the natural tendency of a slave-owning society to associate manual labor with slaves and hence to regard such labor as beneath the dignity of free persons. Thus the Greek essayist Plutarch stated that the great Archimedes

. . . did not think the inventing of military engines an object worthy of his serious studies, but only reckoned them among the amusements of geometry. Nor had he gone so far, but at the pressing instances of Hiero of Syracuse, who entreated him to turn his art from abstracted motions to matters of sense, and to make his reasonings more intelligible to the generality of mankind, applying them to the use of common life.

The first to turn their thoughts to mechanics, a branch of knowledge which came afterwards to be so much admired, were Eudoxus and Archytas, who confirmed certain problems, not then soluble on theoretical grounds, by sensible experiments and the use of instruments. But Plato inveighed against them, with great indignation, as corrupting and debasing the excellence of geometry, by making her descend from incorporeal and intellectual, to corporeal and sensible things, and obliging her to make use of matter, which requires much manual labor, and is the object of servile trades. Mechanics were in consequence separated from geometry, and were for a long time despised by philosophers.[12]

In these various ways, then, the institution of slavery tended to inhibit technological innovation during the millennia following the egalitarian Neolithic age. Slavery also depressed the internal economic market because domestic purchasing power was restricted since slaves obviously could not purchase the fruits of their labor.

For some time these basic structural weaknesses were masked by imperial expansion, with the resulting flood of booty, tribute, foodstuffs, and slaves. But there were limits to the expansion of empires at that level of technological development—limits set by logistical and communications requirements. Thus Rome, like China, was able to advance just so far and no further. When that point was reached, the imperial frontiers became fixed, or even began shrinking, and the hitherto hidden structural defects came to light.

The army, which previously had been a profitable source of slaves and material wealth, now became a heavy but inescapable burden. Likewise, the bureaucracy had become swollen during the period of expansion and was impossible to support in a period of contraction. The excessive expenditures led to inflation that eventually reached runaway proportions. In Egypt, for example, a measure of wheat that cost 6 drachmai in the first century C.E. rose to 200 drachmai in 276, 9,000 in 314, 78,000 in 334, and to more than 2 million soon after that. With such inflation, coinage became worthless, and there was some reversion to barter. This trend was hastened by the growing diffusion of industry to the countryside and the provinces. The diffusion occurred for a number of reasons such as the deterioration of imperial communication facilities and the drop in the supply of slaves, which made it necessary to tap new labor pools. The shift of industry from the cities to villages and large country estates meant the agrarianization of the empire. The large estates became increasingly self-sufficient, boasting craftmakers of every kind as well as agricultural laborers. And the more self-sufficient they became, the more the imperial economy disintegrated into autarchic units.

Economic decentralization inevitably was accompanied by political decentralization. With the decline of trade and the shrinkage of state revenues, the imperial edifice no longer could be supported and slowly began to crumble. Diocletian and Constantine made desperate efforts to buttress the structure by imperial fiat. But the disease was "organic" rather than superficial, so all the regimentation, with its propping and bracing, was of no avail in the long run. Regimentation, however, was not the cause of imperial decay but an ineffective remedy that was tried to halt the decay. "Crisis preceded regimentation," as an economic historian has pointed out.[13]

It follows that a major reason why the West Roman Empire "fell" and the East did not was precisely because the economy of the West was less advanced and weaker. Italian agriculture was never as productive as that in the rich river valleys of the Middle East. The grain harvest in Italy was on average no more than four times the sowing. The rich soils of central and northern Europe had to await medieval technological advances for effective exploitation. Likewise industry in the West was of relatively recent origin and generally lagged behind that in the East. Thus although the whole Roman Empire was wracked by "organic disease," the Western part, being the less robust, was the first to succumb. The Eastern part survived to live on for another millennium.

Despite its demise, the West Roman Empire did leave a rich legacy. Most apparent are the material remains—the amphitheaters, arenas, temples, aqueducts, roads, and bridges. Equally obvious is the linguistic bequest in the form of the Romance (or Romanized) languages of Europe. Roman law, as noted before, is very much alive in the legal systems of numerous countries in Europe and the Americas. The organization and ritual of the Catholic church owe much to Roman imperial structure and religious traditions. Finally, the Pax Romana, which had brought two centuries of relative peace and prosperity, left a tradition of imperial unity in place of the city-state particularism of the Greeks. It was this tradition during the following centuries that fired the imagination and ambition of barbarian princes throughout Europe to become imperator or basileus or tsar.

SUGGESTED READINGS

The most recent survey of both Greece and Rome is *The Oxford History of the Classical World*, edited by J. Boardman, J. Griffin, and O. Murray (Oxford University, 1987). For Greece alone, see M. Grant, *The Rise of the Greeks* (Scribner's, 1988); R. Sealey, *A History of the Greek City-States* (University of California, 1977); and R. Meiggs, *The Athenian Empire* (Oxford University, 1972). On specific aspects of Greek history and civilization there are A. R. Burn, *Persia and the Greeks: The Defense of the West* (Edward Arnold, 1963); J. Boardman, *The Greeks Overseas: Their Early Colonies and Trade* (Thames & Hudson, 1982); C. Kerenyi, *The Gods of the Greeks* (Thames & Hudson, 1979); and R. Flacelière, *Daily Life in Greece at the Time of Pericles* (Macmillan, 1965).

For the Hellenistic world, see the standard history by W. W. Tarn and G. T. Griffith, *Hellenistic Civilization* (Edward Arnold, 1952); the brief survey by M. Grant, *From Alexander to Cleopatra* (Scribner's, 1982); the scholarly biography by N. G. L. Hammond, *Alexander the Great: King, Commander and Statesman* (Chatto & Windus, 1980); and the detailed analysis by M. Rostovzeff, *Social and Economic History of the Hellenistic World*, 3 vols. (Clarendon, 1941).

There are several good one-volume studies of Rome, including A. E. R. Boak and W. G. Sinnigen, *A History of Rome to 565 A.D.*, 5th ed. (Macmillan, 1965); and M. Grant, *History of Rome* (Scribner's, 1978). See M. P. Charlesworth, *The Roman Empire*, (Oxford University, 1951), for the first three centuries; for the later period, see A. H. M. Jones, *The Decline of the Ancient World* (Longmans, 1966). Special topics are treated in J. Carcopino, *Daily Life in Ancient Rome* (Yale University, 1940); R. MacMullen, *Christianizing the Roman Empire, A.D. 100–400* (Yale University, 1984); and M. I. Finley, ed., *Slavery in Classical Antiquity* (Heffer, 1960).

The status of women during the Greco-Roman period is best analyzed in S. B. Pomeroy, *Goddesses, Whores, Wives and Slaves* (Schocken, 1975); in V. Zinserling, *Women in Greece and Rome* (Schram, 1973); in the useful collection of source materials in M. R. Lefkowitz and M. B. Fant, *Women's Life in Greece and Rome* (Johns Hopkins University, 1982); and in the survey by M. W. Bingham and S. H. Gross, *Women in European History and Culture*, Vol. I, *Ancient Greece and Rome* (Glenhurst, 1983).

Finally, the problem of why Rome "fell" is analyzed in the following two convenient collections of readings, which also provide excellent bibliographies on the subject: S. N. Eisenstadt, ed., *The Decline of Empires* (Prentice Hall, 1967); and D. Kagan, ed., *Decline and Fall of the Roman Empire* (D. C. Heath, 1962).

NOTES

1. Plato, *Apology*, trans. B. Jowatt in *Dialogues of Plato*.
2. Cited by F. M. Cornford, *Greek Religious Thought...* (Dent, 1923), p. 85.
3. Cited by C. J. Singer, *A History of Biology* (Schuman, 1950), p. 4.
4. From *The Greek Mind* by W. R. Agard. © 1957 by Litton Educational Publishing Inc. Reprinted by permission of D. Van Nostrand Company.
5. Aristotle, *Politics*, I, 5, 2.
6. Herodotus, *The Persian Wars*, trans. G. Rawlinson, Book VII, Chap. 104.
7. Thucydides, *The Peloponnesian War*, trans. B. Jowatt, Book I, Chap. 22.
8. Cited by S. Pomeroy, *Women in Classical Antiquity* (Schocken, 1976), p. 8.
9. Cicero, *First Part of the Speech Against Gaius Verres at the First Hearing* (New York, 1928), Chap. 5.
10. A. Piganiol, *L'Empire Chrétien* (Presses Universitaires de France, 1947), p. 422.
11. R. S. Lopez, *The Birth of Europe* (M. Evans, 1967), p. 23.
12. *Life of Marcellus*, from *Plutarch's Lives*, Vol. 3, trans. J. and W. Langhorne (London, 1821), pp. 119ff.
13. J. Lévy, *The Economic Life of the Ancient World*, ed. J. G. Birain (University of Chicago, 1967), p. 99.

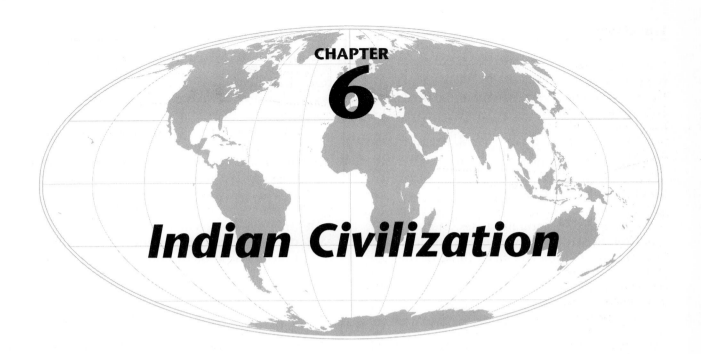

CHAPTER 6

Indian Civilization

Government is the science of punishment.

Kautilya

I consider that my duty is the good of the whole world.

Ashoka

Turning from Greece and Rome to India, we enter an altogether different world. The differences are not simply those that might naturally emerge from contrasting physical environments—differences in occupations, diet, habitation, dress, and the like. The differences were much more far-reaching and fundamental. There were nothing in the West remotely resembling basic Indian concepts and institutions such as caste, ahimsa (nonviolence), reincarnation, and karma (the law of moral consequences). These were not just eccentric or abstract ideas. They constituted the bedrock of Indian civilization, molding the thought and daily lives of all Indians. The pattern that resulted was so distinctive and so enduring that Indian civilization to the present day has distin-guishing characteristics that mark it off from all other Eurasian civilizations.

Distinctiveness also characterizes the civilization of China, as will be noted in the following chapter, but this is natural because of the unparalleled geographic and historical isolation of that country. In India, by contrast, the beginnings appeared to be basically similar to those of the other regions to the west where Aryan invaders had settled—the Iranian plateau and the Balkan and Italian peninsulas. As noted earlier (Chapter 3, Section V), the Aryan tribes that descended on India about 1500 B.C.E. possessed the same physical features, the same pastoral economy, the same social institutions, the same gods, and the same epics as did, for example, the Achaeans and the Dorians. Furthermore, the

Indo-Aryans were not isolated in their subcontinent to anywhere near the degree that the Chinese were on the eastern extremity of Eurasia. The mountain ranges of northwest India are not impassable; armies and merchants and pilgrims crossed back and forth through the centuries. In fact, during much of the time there was more interaction between northern India and the Middle East and central Asia than between north India and the southern part of the peninsula.

The question naturally arises, then, why the Indo-Aryans should have developed a civilization so basically different from those of their kin to the west. The scanty evidence available does not allow for a specific or definitive answer, but the most simple and likely explanation is that the Indo-Aryans were Indianized. In contrast to the Achaeans or Dorians or Latins, who settled in relatively uncivilized areas, the Indo-Aryans encountered in the Indus valley a highly developed civilization with large urban centers and a dense population. (See map of Classical Age Empires in India, p. 119.) The native population, although subjugated and despised, was too numerous and too advanced to be exterminated or pushed aside or assimilated, leaving few traces of the original culture. Instead, as the Aryan pastoralists settled down and took up agriculture, they perforce lived in close proximity with the prior inhabitants of their new land. After some centuries of such coexistence and intermarriage, the inevitable result was a cultural synthesis. The circumstances, nature, and consequences of this synthesis are the subject of this chapter.

I. ARYAN IMPACT

Following their penetration into the Indus valley, the Aryans concentrated in the more rainy parts of the Punjab where the pasture was adequate for their herds. Gradually they began to spread into the heavily forested basin of the Ganges. Their expansion was slow at first, since only stone, bronze, and copper axes were available. But iron was introduced about 800 B.C.E., and the expansion pace quickened. The main occupation shifted from pastoralism to agriculture. The monsoon climate of the Ganges valley was ideal for rice cultivation, which was more productive than the wheat and barley grown in the Punjab. As a

result the center of population density shifted from the northwest to the east, which then became the seat of the first powerful kingdoms.

The shift to agriculture stimulated various crafts necessary for the new villages, including carpentry, metallurgy, weaving, and tanning. Agriculture also promoted trade, with the river serving as the natural highway for transporting surplus food. Barter was common practice at first, and the cow was the unit of value in large-scale transactions. When coins appeared, the earliest weight standards, significantly enough, were exactly those of the pre-Aryan Indus civilization. Towns grew out of villages that were strategically located for trade or that had specialized in particular crafts.

This economic growth in turn facilitated political consolidation. Originally, the Indo-Aryans, like their relatives in the West, were organized under tribal chiefs assisted by councils of elders and general assemblies. With economic development the tribes gave way to kingdoms in the Ganges plain and to republics in the Punjab and in the foothills of the Himalayas. Of these early states the kingdom of Magadha in the lower Ganges soon rose to preeminence because of its location on two main trade routes and its control over rich iron-ore deposits. With these advantages Magadha was to serve as the base for the formation of both the Maurya and Gupta empires.

The Nanda dynasty in the fourth century B.C.E. was the first to exploit systematically the resources of Magadha for state-building purposes. They built canals, organized irrigation projects, and established an efficient administrative system for the collection of taxes. The Nandas have been described as the earliest empire builders of India. In fact, they laid the foundations of an empire but were not destined actually to fashion the first imperial structure. This was to be the historic role of Chandragupta Maurya, the young adventurer who usurped the Nanda throne in 321 B.C.E. and went on to build the famous empire named after him.

Economic and political developments were paralleled by fateful changes in social structure. Originally the Indo-Aryans, like other Aryans, were divided into three classes: the warrior nobles, the priests, and the common people. They had none of the restrictions associated with caste,

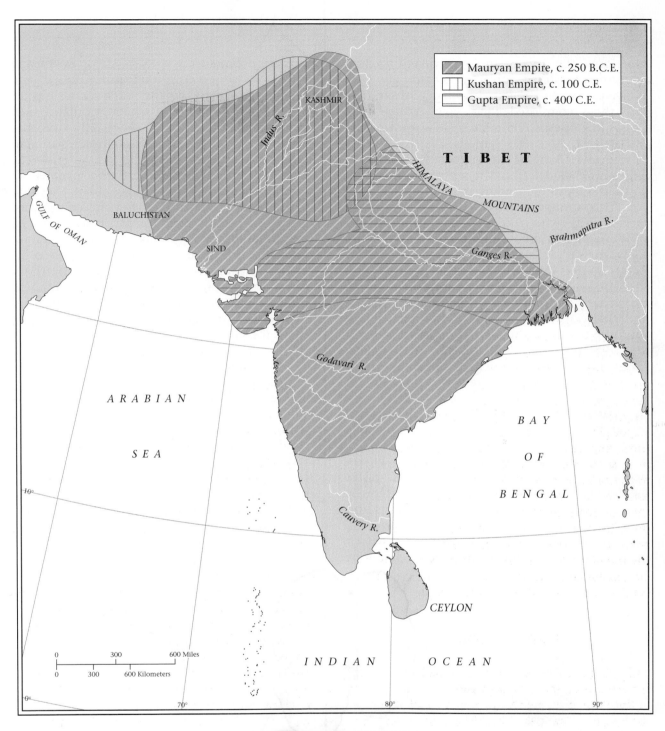

Classical Age Empires in India

such as hereditary professions, rules limiting marriages to people of the same caste, and taboos about dining companions. But by 500 B.C.E. the caste system was functioning with all its essential features. Although many theories have been advanced concerning its origins, it is generally

agreed that color was a basic factor. Indeed the Sanskrit word for caste, varna, means color.

The Aryan newcomers were very conscious of the difference in complexion between themselves and the dark natives, and dubbed them Dasas, or slaves. With their strong sense of racial superiority, the Aryans strove to prevent mixture with their despised subjects. Accordingly they evolved a system of four hereditary castes. The first three comprised their own occupational classes, the priests (Brahmans), the warrior nobles (Kshatriyas), and the farmers (Vaishyas). The fourth caste (Shudras) was reserved for the Dasas, who were excluded from the religious ceremonies and social rights enjoyed by their conquerors.

This arrangement ceased to correspond to racial reality with the passage of time. Aryan tribes frequently made alliances with Dasa tribes to wage war against other Aryan tribes. Also Aryan settlers mingled with the natives, who then adopted Aryan speech and customs. In such cases the Dasas' priests became Brahmans, and their chiefs, Kshatriyas. Thus today black southern Indian Brahmans are no less aristocratic by reason of their dark skin, nor are the light-skinned, grey-eyed untouchables of some northern Indian regions any more elevated because of their pale complexion. In response to these realities, traders and some landowners were classified as Vaishyas, and cultivators and general laborers became Shudras.

A bewildering variety of castes have grown up within these four broad divisions. The castes have four basic features in common. One is characteristic employment, so that bankers and merchants often belong to the Vaishya caste. Another feature of caste is the hereditary principle, expressed in complex marriage regulations and restrictions. Caste also involves further restrictions concerning food, water, touch, and ceremonial purity. Finally, each caste has its dharma, or moral code, which stipulates such duties as maintenance of the family unit and performance of prescribed ceremonies at marriage, birth, and death.

Outside this system are the pariahs, or untouchables, comprising today about a seventh of the Indian population. They are condemned to trades or crafts regarded as unclean because their function involves some ritual defilement or the taking of human or animal life. These occupations include hunters, fishermen, butchers, executioners, gravediggers, undertakers, tanners, leather workers, sweepers, and scavengers. Involvement in these occupations has led in turn to social segregation. Untouchables live in isolated villages or in quarters outside town limits and are required to use their own temples and wells. They have to be most careful to avoid polluting members of the castes by any kind of physical contact or, in extreme cases, by even coming within their sight. For this reason, until recent decades they never moved outside their quarters or villages without striking a pair of clappers together to warn others of their approach.

The untouchables are further subjected to psychological disabilities that are as crippling and degrading as the physical. The doctrine of karma holds that one's status in present life has been determined by the deeds of previous lives.

A Brahman, of India's priestly caste, preaches to the faithful.

The untouchables therefore deserve their low position because of past sins, and their only hope for improved status in future lives is the dutiful performance of their present duties.

This combination of social and religious sanctions has enabled caste to function to the present day. Of course, with its manifold provisions for mutual aid, caste does provide security as long as one follows its rules. So it continues to serve as the steel framework of Hindu society. And although it has been attacked by reformers and undermined by the pressures of modern industrial society, caste nevertheless still operates in rural India, where three-fourths of the total population continues to live.

II. REFORMATION AND COUNTER-REFORMATION

Caste, with its basic tenets of dharma, karma, and reincarnation, is part and parcel of the Hindu religious system. Originally the Aryans had typical tribal gods personifying natural forces, such as Indra, god of thunder and war; Agni, god of fire; and Soma, god of their sacred intoxicant of the same name. Gods of this nature were appropriate for pastoralists, but as the Aryans settled down to agriculture they perforce turned to new deities. Hence the advent of the "great gods" of Hinduism—Brahma, the Creator; Vishnu, the gracious Preserver; and Shiva, the Mighty and the Destroyer. It is not accidental that these new gods, particularly Shiva, bear striking resemblance to finds in the Indus valley sites. At this time, the Aryans naturally appropriated native religious ideas and practices that had evolved through the millennia in the ancient agriculture-based civilization.

With the new gods there came also a growing concentration of power in the hands of the priestly class, or Brahmans. This also was probably derived from pre-Aryan religious tradition. The Brahmans, who in some regions were in contact with native religious leaders, presumably learned of the magical claims and practices of their counterparts in the Indus civilization. Whatever the historic prototypes in the distant past, the Brahmans effectively exploited their mastery of the Vedas, or hymns, that were recited aloud during rituals and sacrifices. These were transmitted orally through the generations and were considered so sacred that they were memorized word for word, sound for sound. As the custodians and transmitters of this precious heritage, the Brahmans were able to assert and enforce their claims as the leaders of Hindu society, superior to the Kshatriya, or secular heads.

The Brahmans enjoyed numerous prerogatives and exemptions because of the sacred nature of their functions. Donors of gifts were assured definite reward in this, as well as in subsequent, lives. A "gift of land" was rated most highly, for it "liberated from all sin." Thus the Brahmans acquired vast estates, including entire villages. Additionally they were exempt from all taxes, since they were deemed to have discharged such debts through "acts of piety." And being sacrosanct, the Brahmans could not be sentenced to death or to any type of corporal punishment. Finally, the doctrines of karma, reincarnation, and dharma provided virtually irresistible means for Brahman control of the mind. There was little chance for individuals to assert themselves when a person's station in life was the inescapable result of one's own past actions, and when hope for a better life in the future depended entirely on one's faithful observance of specific caste duties, regardless of how onerous or degrading they might be.

The Brahman pretensions and exactions were one factor in the religious reformation in India in the sixth and fifth centuries B.C.E. Another was the economic growth previously noted, which created a wealthy merchant, or Vaishya, caste that resented the special privileges enjoyed by the two upper castes. Finally there was the tension between the Brahmans and the non-Aryans who had been admitted to the Hindu fold but who resented the priestly domination. Thus the Shakya tribes in the Nepal hills from which the Buddha came are thought to have been of Mongolian stock. This combination of factors lay behind the ferment in Indian religious and intellectual circles during these centuries. The demand arose for moksha, or freedom—for something more meaningful and satisfying than prescribed rituals and rigid doctrines.

One manifestation of the unrest was a trend toward asceticism. Some of the most active minds, alienated by the society about them, concentrated on pure introspection. They developed techniques for disciplining or "yoking" (yoga) the senses to an inward focus, ending in a state of trance or ecstasy, which mystics describe as "enlightenment" and skeptics call "self-hypnotism." Out of this inward searching and speculating came many reform movements, of which the most important was Buddhism. The new religion had no place for caste or for Brahmans. It required that the scriptures be understood by all believers and not merely by a few at the top. Buddhism also banned all magic, sacrifices, and obscure writings.

Buddhism became a powerful force not only in India but also in central Asia and East and Southeast Asia. After 600 C.E., however, it lost ground within India. Eventually it existed in only a few localities in the land of its birth. One reason for the decline of Buddhism at home was that it failed to provide for the usual crises of life. It offered no ceremonies for birth, marriage, death, and other critical turns in the lives of the laity. By contrast the Brahmans were ready with their rites, and their survival was assured despite the attacks of the reformers. More important, the Brahmans themselves embraced reform. In their philosophical texts, the Upanishads, they set forth their own paths to moksha—to freedom and release.

They taught that the supreme spirit permeating the universe was Brahman, a being capable of all knowledge and feeling. He was the universal soul and the all-pervading breath; all else was illusion. The individual soul—Atman—was a spark of the supreme being. By transmigration it passed from state to state until it attained release by reabsorption into Brahman, the Soul of the universe. This identification of the individual soul and the Soul of the universe was the ultimate goal that holy men sought to reach by discipline, meditation, and withdrawal from the world of the senses. Seekers after truth could now abandon the world and rest within the fold of Hinduism. Although Buddhism as a practicing faith disappeared in India, it has survived to the present because its basic tenets have been incorporated in the Hindu counter-reformation.

III. MAURYAN EMPIRE

Turning from religious movements to political developments, the outstanding political event was the emergence of India's first imperial structure, the Mauryan Empire. As noted earlier in this chapter, the migration of the Aryans to the Ganges valley had shifted the center of gravity to that region, and particularly to the kingdom of Magadha. Meanwhile the northwest provinces had been going their own way, isolated from the rest of India because of their close ties with Persian civilization. In fact, Emperor Darius crossed the Hindu Kush mountains about 518 B.C.E. and made the western Punjab the twentieth province of his empire. Two centuries later, in 327 B.C.E., Alexander the Great also invaded India from the northwest. But he stayed only two years, and soon after he left, Greek rule in the Punjab ended. Despite his short stay, Alexander did have considerable influence on India.

A magnificent South Indian bronze of Shiva, one of India's most important Hindu deities. The fluid, balanced image depicts the so-called "dancing Shiva" engaged in his dance of simultaneous destruction and creation of the universe, an artistic-mythical rendering of the eternal flux of all worldly existence (13th century; bronze; 33.5 x 24.8 cm).

One effect was the growth of the east-west trade from northwest India through Afghanistan and Iran to Asia Minor and Levant ports. The Greek colonies planted throughout the Middle East by Alexander doubtless contributed much to this trade, and the Hellenistic states that followed Alexander promoted it for two centuries.

Most important for Indian history was Alexander's role in creating a political vacuum in northwest India by overthrowing several local kingdoms and republics. Chandragupta Maurya promptly filled the void and founded the empire named after him. In 322 B.C.E., three years after Alexander's departure, Chandragupta, then an ambitious young general, unseated the Nanda dynasty of Magadha and founded his own. In the following years he extended his rule steadily northwestward until his empire extended from the Ganges to the Indus, including the deltas of both rivers. At the same time he organized a powerful army and an efficient administration to sustain his realm. Thus when Seleucus became king of the Middle East as one of the successors to Alexander and attempted to recover Alexander's Indian provinces, Chandragupta easily repelled the Greek forces.

Chandragupta's son conquered the Deccan region in the south, and his grandson, the famous Ashoka (273–232 B.C.E.), conquered Kalinga, or eastern India. Thus the Maurya Empire under Ashoka included the whole Indian peninsula except for the southern tip.

India under the Mauryas was wealthy and well governed, like the Roman Empire at its height. Numerous highways were crowded with merchants, soldiers, and royal messengers. The conquest of Kalinga on the east coast stimulated trade, and an admiralty department maintained waterways and harbors. The capital, Pataliputra, known as the "city of flowers," was famous for its parks, public buildings, and river frontage of over nine miles. Its educational institutions were crowded with students from all parts of the empire and from abroad.

All this was supported by "the king's sixth" of the harvest, which in practice was more commonly raised to a fourth, leaving the peasants with barely enough for existence. Law was severe, and order ruthlessly maintained. The army reputedly numbered 700,000 men, with 9,000 elephants and 10,000 chariots. Spies were

Lion capital from Ashoka column in Sarnath. This work on display in the New Delhi Museum dates from the reign of Ashoka (273–232 B.C.E.) and is one of the many monuments that this ruler of the Maurya Empire ordered erected in honor of the memory of Buddha.

efficient and numerous, sending in a stream of reports to the capital by messenger and carrier pigeon. Torture was frequently used as a means of punishment and to extort confessions. All in all, it was an efficient, harsh, bureaucratic society, based on the principle that "Government is the science of punishment."

Ashoka's reign differed radically from this traditional type of imperial rule. Having conquered the kingdom of Kalinga in a particularly bloody campaign, Ashoka underwent a spiritual experience. He himself described how over 100,000 prisoners were killed and how he felt "profound sorrow and regret." From then on, Ashoka tried to apply the gentle teachings of Buddha. He issued edicts based on Buddhist principles: simplicity, compassion, mutual tolerance, and respect for all forms of life. He ordered many public works that benefited his people rather than his government, including hospitals and medical care at state expense, orchards and resting places on highways, alms that were distributed to all sects, and Buddhist missions to several foreign countries.

Ashoka did not make Buddhism the state faith, nor did he persecute the other sects. To the contrary, he helped the worthy of whatever denomination. It was not a change of religion, then, but of general attitude. He laid most stress on tolerance and nonviolence, not only because they were morally desirable but also because they would promote harmony in his huge and diverse empire. This attitude proved successful during his reign, for Ashoka ruled with great popularity for forty-one years. But within half a century after his death his dynasty was overthrown and his empire destroyed.

This has been the pattern of Indian history to modern times. In contrast to China, where imperial unity was interspersed with short intervals of fragmentation, in India it was precisely the opposite—brief unity and prolonged fragmentation. This is not to say that India had no unity. It did, but it was cultural rather than political. And this culture emphasized loyalty to the social order rather than to the state, as we see by the fact that higher status was accorded to caste than to any political institution. Thus the culture that enhanced unity in one sphere undermined it in another.

IV. INVADERS, TRADERS, AND MISSIONARIES

With the end of the Maurya Empire early in the second century B.C.E. there followed five hundred years of confusion and obscurity. But one constant factor is clear throughout this period. That was the increasing interaction between India and the outside world, with manifold repercussions in all areas—political, economic, and cultural.

First there were the numerous invaders. Beginning with Alexander and his Greeks, there followed the Parthians, the Scythians, and the Kushans, to mention only the most important. The empires of all these peoples were based at least as much in Central Asia or the Middle East as in India. Their linking of India with foreign lands stimulated trade overland and overseas. Roman traders went to southern and western India, whereas Indian traders settled in large numbers in Southeast Asia. Just as the Greeks traded and colonized all through the Mediterranean, so did the Indians all through Southeast Asia.

In the realm of culture, Indian Buddhist missionaries during these centuries were carrying their message to all the surrounding countries. The begging priest could move among hostile or disordered peoples with safety since he was too poor to be worth robbing and also was respected as a man of religion. There was little incentive for robbing or injuring such a man, since the only return was the possibility of retribution from above. Hence there was diffusion of Buddhism and Brahmanism from India to the surrounding countries, with all the culture that went along with such transfer of religions. Nor was the culture flow exclusively one-sided. The succession of invaders from the north brought with them a variety of Greek, Persian, and central Asian influences. And by sea there came to India in the first century C.E. a new religion—Christianity. According to legend, St. Thomas arrived about 52 C.E. on the Malabar coast of southwest India, where he established a number of churches. Thence he traveled overland to the east coast. His preaching, however, was strongly opposed, and he was killed in 68 C.E. near Madras. His work in the Malabar region, however, bore fruit, for considerable Christian communities exist there to the present day.

V. GUPTA CLASSICAL AGE

In the fourth century C.E. the great Gupta Age began—a time when the invaders of the preceding centuries were assimilated and when various cultural trends reached fruition. This was the classical period of Indian civilization, comparable to the Early Empire or Augustan Age in the West. The Gupta Empire, like the Maurya, had as its base the Magadha state in the Ganges valley. This state had managed to preserve its independence following the Maurya collapse, and then, with the end of the Kushans, it began to expand once more into the resulting vacuum.

The Gupta era began with the accession of Chandragupta I, about 320, and reached its height under his grandson, Chandragupta II, who reigned from 375 to 415. He expanded his empire until it stretched from the Indus to the Bay of Bengal, and from the northern mountains to the Narbada River. The Gupta Empire was a north Indian empire and did not include the entire peninsula. Indeed south India at this time was in many ways a world apart, with the Vindhya range still an effective barrier dividing the peninsula in two. The peoples of the south spoke Dravidian or pre-Aryan languages—Tamil, Telugu, and Kanarese—in contrast to the Indo-Aryan speech of the north. On the other hand, the south had accepted the Hindu and Buddhist religions and social customs and used Sanskrit as its language of scripture and learning. Thus a single civilization bound together the diverse peoples despite their disparate ethnic and linguistic backgrounds and the existence in the south of several independent kingdoms.

The Gupta Empire enjoyed much prosperity, especially after Chandragupta II introduced standard gold and silver coins. The volume of trade reached new heights, both within the peninsula and with outside countries. The degree of security under Gupta rule is reflected in the drop of interest rates on loans for overseas trade from 240 percent during the Maurya period to 20 percent at this time. One of the chief industries was textiles—silk, muslin, calico, linen, wool, and cotton—which was produced in large quantities for both domestic and foreign markets. Other important crafts included metallurgy, pottery, carving, and the cutting and polishing of precious stones.

Judging from the reports of Chinese Buddhist pilgrims, Gupta rule was milder than that of the Maurya. Fa-hien, who spent the years 401 to 410 in India, traveling from monastery to mon-

Brahman relief dating from about 600–700 B.C.E.

astery, was impressed by the state services and by the general prosperity. Although the dynasty was Hindu, he found no discrimination against Buddhists. The countryside was peaceful and prosperous, and not overrun by police and spies as under the Maurya. Fa-hien also noted that

The people are numerous and happy; they have not to register their households, or attend to any magistrates and their rules; only those who cultivate the royal land have to pay (a portion of) the gain from it. If they want to go, they go; if they want to stay on, they stay. The king governs without decapitation or

A CHINESE VIEW OF INDIA

Chinese Buddhist pilgrims have left valuable descriptions of India in the Classical Age. The most famous was Hsüan-tsang, who visited all parts of the country between 629 and 645 C.E., and left the following vivid picture.*

The towns and villages have inner gates; the walls are wide and high; the streets and lanes are tortuous, and the roads winding. The thoroughfares are dirty and the stalls arranged on both sides of the road with appropriate signs. Butchers, fishers, dancers, executioners, and scavengers, and so on, have their abodes without the city. In coming and going these persons are bound to keep on the left side of the road till they arrive at their homes. Their houses are surrounded by low walls, and form the suburbs. The earth being soft and muddy, the walls of the towns are mostly built of brick or tiles. The towers on the walls are constructed of wood or bamboo; the houses have balconies and belvederes, which are made of wood, with a coating of lime or mortar, and covered with tiles. The different buildings have the same form as those in China: rushes, or dry branches, or tiles, or boards are used for covering them. The walls are covered with lime and mud, mixed with cow's dung for purity. At different seasons they scatter flowers about. Such are some of their different customs. . . .

They are very particular in their personal cleanliness, and allow no remissness in this particular. All wash themselves before eating; they never use that which has been left over [from a former meal]; they do not pass the dishes. Wooden and stone vessels, when used, must be destroyed; vessels of gold, silver, copper, or iron after each meal must be rubbed and polished. After eating they cleanse their teeth with a willow stick, and wash their hands and mouth.

Until these ablutions are finished they do not touch one another. Every time they perform the functions of nature they wash their bodies and use perfumes of sandal-wood or turmeric.

The most usual food is milk, butter, cream, soft sugar, sugar-candy, the oil of the mustard-seed, and all sorts of cakes made of corn are used as food. Fish, mutton, gazelle, and deer they eat generally fresh, sometimes salted; they are forbidden to eat the flesh of the ox, the ass, the elephant, the horse, the pig, the dog, the fox, the wolf, the lion, the monkey, and all the hairy kind. . . .

There is no lack of suitable things for household use. Although they have saucepans and stewpans, yet they do not know the steamer used for cooking rice. They have many vessels made of dried clay; they seldom use red copper vessels: they eat from one vessel, mixing all sorts of condiments together, which they take up with their fingers. They have no spoons or cups, and in short no sort of chopstick.

---

*Si-Yu-Ki, *Buddhist Records of the Western World*, trans. S. Beal (Kegan Paul, 1884), I. pp. 70–89. Reprinted by Paragon Reprint Corp., New York (1968).

(other) corporal punishments. Criminals are simply fined, lightly or heavily, according to the circumstances. Even in cases of repeated attempts at wicked rebellion, they only have their right hand cut off. The king's body-guards and attendants all have salaries . . . in the markets there are no butchers' shops and no dealers in intoxicating drink.[1]

In linguistics and literature, this was the period of the triumph of Sanskrit. Hitherto the learned and rather archaic language of the Brahmans, Sanskrit now staged a comeback and spread to administration and to secular literature. Poetry and prose flourished with the stimulus of lavish royal patronage. Outstanding were the works of Kalidasa, "the Indian Shakespeare," who rendered ancient legends and popular tales into both dramas and lyrics. His *Sakuntala* was translated into English in the late eighteenth century and has since been widely acclaimed and presented on foreign stages. Perhaps the greatest cultural achievement of the Gupta era was the reduction into final form of the two great national epics, the Mahabharata and the Ramayana. Dating back to many centuries before Christ, the early versions of these works have been entirely lost. Today they are known only in the form left by Gupta writers, in which they have remained the classics of Hindu literature and the repositories of Hindu tradition. Their heroes and heroines are a part of the life of the people; their mine of stories has been used by generations of writers, and their philosophical poem, the *Bhagavad Gita*, is the supreme scripture of the Hindus.

In the field of science the Gupta period was outstanding. Contact with Greeks resulted in mutually beneficial exchanges of ideas. Aryabhata, born in 476 C.E. at Pataliputra, is one of the greatest figures in the history of astronomy. He taught that the earth is a sphere, that it rotates on its own axis, that lunar eclipses are caused by the shadow of the earth falling on the moon, and that the length of the solar year is 365.3586805 days—a calculation with a remarkably slight margin of error.

The greatest achievement doubtless was the formulation of the theory of zero and the consequent evolution of the decimal system. The base could have been any number; the Hindus probably chose ten because they counted on their fin-

gers. With this system, individual numbers were needed only for 0, 1, 2 . . . 9. By contrast, for the ancient Greeks each 8 in 888 was different. And for the Romans, 888 was DCCCLXXXVIII. The difficulty of division and multiplication with these systems is apparent. The simple Hindu numerals were carried westward by Arab merchants and scholars, and so became known as "Arabic numerals." Despite their obvious advantage they were long scorned as pagan and as too vulnerable to forgery; one stroke could turn 0 into 6 or 9. It was not until the late fifteenth century that Hindu-Arabic numerals prevailed in the West and the door was opened to modern mathematics and science. In retrospect, this Indian contribution stands out as comparable to the invention of the wheel, the lever, or the alphabet.

SUGGESTED READINGS

The most useful collections of source materials are by W. T. deBary et al., *Sources of Indian Tradition* (Columbia University, 1958) and by A. T. Embree, ed., *The Hindu Tradition: Readings in Oriental Thought* (Vintage, 1972). An invaluable reference work is J. E. Schwartzberg, ed., *A Historical Atlas of South Asia* (University of Chicago, 1978).

A well-written general history of India is by S. Wolpert, *A New History of India* (Oxford University, 1977). See also P. Spear, *India: A Modern History* (University of Michigan, 1961); R. Thapar, *A History of India* (Penguin, 1961); D. D. Kosambi, *Ancient India: A History of Its Culture and Civilization* (Pantheon, 1965); and H. Kulke and D. Rothermund, *A History of India* (Croom Helm, 1986).

Sociological interpretations of India are given by D. G. Mandelbaum, *Society in India; Continuity and Change*, 2 vols. (University of California, 1970); and by B. S. Cohen, *India, The Social Anthropology of a Civilization* (Prentice Hall, 1971). Much interesting material is to be found in J. Auboyer, *Daily Life in Ancient India from Approximately 200 B.C. to A.D. 700* (Weidenfeld & Nicolson, 1961); and in M. Edwardes, *Everyday Life in Early India* (Batsford, 1969), a beautifully illustrated analysis of life in India between 300 B.C.E. and 700 C.E. Also, see K. W. Morgan, *Asian Religions: An Introduction to the Study of Hinduism, Buddhism, Islam, Confucianism, and Taoism* (Washington, 1964).

NOTE

1. Fa-hien, *A Record of Buddhist Kingdoms,* trans. J. Legge (Clarendon, 1886), pp. 42–43.

CHAPTER
7

Chinese Civilization

When the right men are available, government flourishes. When the right men are not available, government declines.

Confucius

As compared with the looseness and discontinuity of Indian civilization, Chinese civilization is characterized by cohesion and continuity. There has been no sharp break in China's evolution comparable to that caused in India by the appearance of the Aryans, the Moslems, or the British. There were, of course, numerous nomadic invasions of China, and even a few dynastic takeovers. But it was not the Chinese who were forced to adopt the language or the customs or the pastoralism of the invader. Rather, it was the invader who invariably became Chinese, quickly and completely.

One reason for this was the greater isolation of China, so that it was invaded only by the nomads of the northwest. It did not have to cope with the succession of peoples who invaded India and who, with their relatively sophisticated cultures, were able to retain in varying degrees their ethnic group and cultural identity. The Chinese were all Mongoloids to begin with, as were the nomadic invaders and the relatively primitive tribes that they assimilated in the course of their expansion eastward to the Pacific and southward to Vietnam. Thus the Chinese enjoyed racial and cultural homogeneity throughout their history. During the classical period this homogeneity was further cemented, as we shall see, by the standardization of the writing system, which enabled speakers of widely differing dialects to communicate with each other. In India, by contrast, there are today fourteen "national languages," one of which, English, serves, in Nehru's words, as "the link" among the other thirteen.

The remarkable political unity that has persisted through the ages in China has been as important as its cultural homogeneity. This unity results in large part from the unique secularism of Chinese civilization—the only great civilization that has at no time produced a priestly class. To be sure, the emperor was also a priest who made sacrifices to heaven on behalf of all his subjects, but his religious function was always secondary to the business of governing. Consequently, there was no place in China for the great division between religion and laity, between church and state, which existed in the other Eurasian civilizations. Nor was there any counterpart to India's epics, steeped in metaphysics and concerned with personal salvation. Rather, the Chinese classics emphasized the life of human beings in society, and particularly the relations between the members of a family and between a king and his subjects. This strong secular characteristic provided a firm underlying foundation for political organization and stability. This was further cemented during these centuries by a unique Chinese institution—a civil service recruited on the basis of public competitive examinations. It was 2,000 years before anything comparable appeared in the West, or anywhere else for that matter.

These, then, are some of the background factors that help explain the Chinese civilization and history to be analyzed in this chapter.

I. AGE OF TRANSITION

The period of the Eastern Zhou (771–256 B.C.E.) was on the surface inauspicious, with its powerless dynasty and its feudal lords constantly at war with one another. (See Chapter 3, Section V.) Yet it was also a period of basic socioeconomic change that determined the course of China's evolution decisively and permanently. The root cause for this change here, as in India, was the introduction of iron. Iron came late in China. It was not a significant factor until about 600 B.C.E. But by the fifth and fourth centuries B.C.E. it was making its mark on Chinese society and government.

The pattern of its impact was familiar. New and more efficient iron tools allowed agriculture to spread from the original Yellow River point of origin southward toward the heavily wooded

Yangtze basin (corresponding to the spread in India from the Indus to the Ganges). Iron tools also facilitated extensive drainage projects in the valleys, canal building for long-distance hauling of bulky commodities, and well digging for irrigation in the dry northwest lands.

All this meant a very substantial increase in productivity, which in turn stimulated trade and industry, and ended in the use of money in much of the economy. Money had been used earlier, usually in the form of cowrie shells. Now copper coins appeared, and their use grew in all branches of the economy. A new class of free and wealthy merchants and craftmakers were most involved in the increasing use of money. No longer dependent on feudal lords as they had been in the past, they now formed a new monetary aristocracy that soon challenged the leadership of the feudal lords.

With the use of money, land became a form of property that was bought and sold. Wealthy merchants purchased large estates, and nobles sought to increase their revenues by appointing agents to collect more rent. The agents collected the increased rent directly from the peasants instead of in the traditional way, from the village headman.

This economic change was accompanied by political change—by a fundamental shift from feudal decentralization to state centralization. The economic growth and use of money provided the rulers of the various feudal states with the financial resources needed for centralization. Since the newly reclaimed lands could be administered outside feudal relationships, rents were contributed directly to the princes' exchequers. Also the princes set up more and more profitable monopolies to produce and distribute iron and salt. The result was that the princes of the feudal states were able to change fiefs they had formerly parceled out to nobles into administrative units staffed by officials of their own central government. This was a gradual development, but where it did occur, it greatly increased the resources and power of the ruler and correspondingly weakened the Zhou dynasty in the capital. Indeed a basic reason for the success of the rulers of Ch'in in conquering all China was precisely that they pioneered in these measures and reaped the profits. We will discuss this topic in Section III of this chapter.

II. PHILOSOPHERS AND CLASSICS

The disruption and reorganization just described profoundly affected Chinese thinkers. It forced them to take a new look at their traditions and to either abandon them or adapt them to the requirements of a period of transition. Thus the Eastern Zhou period was a time of great intellectual ferment and creativity, reminiscent of the achievements under comparable circumstances of the rationalist philosophers in Greece and of the Buddha and other religious reformers in India.

Because of the secular, this-worldly nature of Chinese civilization, its outstanding thinkers tended to be practical politicians who were mainly interested in winning over to their views the rulers of the various states. In the course of their travels and teachings, they attracted disciples and gradually formed various schools of philosophy. So intense was this intellectual activity that the Chinese refer to this as the period of the "Hundred Schools." Here we shall consider a few of these schools that persisted through the centuries and had an important influence on the evolution of Chinese civilization.

Although the founders of the various schools often were bold innovators, almost all of them looked for inspiration to a supposedly golden age in the distant past. A similar tendency is found in most civilizations, but consciousness and veneration of the past were exceptionally strong among the Chinese. Hence they carefully preserved and studied the writings of earlier ages and considered them indispensable for the conduct of both private and public affairs.

The most important of these ancient works were the *Five Classics*, made up of poems, popular traditions, and historical documents. The *Classics* were studied and used by philosopher-teachers, of which the most outstanding by far was Confucius. His influence has been so overwhelming and lasting that the Chinese way of life during the past 2,000 years can be summarized with one word—Confucianism. Born in 551 B.C.E. to a poor family of the lower aristocracy, Confucius (the Latinized form of K'ung-fu-tzu, or Master Kung) had to make his own way in the world. And the world he faced was harsh. There was runaway feudal anarchy, with no higher power, spiritual or temporal, to attract national loyalty. Confucius was moved by this lack to wander from court to court, seeking a ruler who would adopt his ideas for successful government. He did hold a few minor posts, but his influence in the world of practical politics was slight. So he turned to educating young men who, he hoped, might be more effective in carrying out his ideas.

Confucius at last had found himself. He proved to be a teacher of rare enthusiasm and skill. Surviving records describe him as an attractive and magnetic person—sensible, kindhearted, distressed by the folly of his age, convinced that he could restore tranquility, and blessed with a saving sense of humor. Confucius's teachings were fundamentally conservative. He did not want to tamper with the existing social order: "Let the ruler be a ruler and the subject a subject; let the father be a father and the son a son." But while insisting on the right of the rulers to rule, he was equally insistent that they should do so on the basis of sound ethical principles. Like Plato, he wanted the kings to be sages, and this they could be if they possessed the five virtues of a gentleman—integrity, righteousness, loyalty, altruism, and love, or human-heartedness.

Confucius also was a rationalist in an age of gross superstition and fear of the supernatural. People firmly believed in the prophetic significance of dreams, in the arts of divination, and in the dread power of the spirits of the dead. But Confucius, though he recognized spirits and Heaven, largely ignored them in his teachings. "Recognize," he said, "that you know what you know, and that you are ignorant of what you do not know." And again, "If you do not know about the living, how can you know about the dead?"

Confucius's teachings were far from being generally accepted, let alone applied, during his lifetime. Yet in the end they prevailed and became the official creed of the nation. One reason was his basic conservatism, his acceptance of the status quo, which naturally appealed to those at the top. Another was his emphasis on ethical principles, which he insisted were essential for the proper exercise of authority. Finally, Confucius provided a philosophy for officialdom, for the bureaucrats who became indispensable with the establishment of imperial government 250 years after his death. As a famous

TEACHINGS OF CONFUCIUS

Confucianism was above all a practical moral system concerned with the problems of everyday life. The main emphasis was on propriety and social responsibility, as evident in the following sections.*

The Individual

It is by the rules of propriety that the character is established.

The rules of propriety serve as instruments to form men's characters. They remove from a man all perversity and increase what is beautiful in his nature. They make him correct, when employed in the ordering of himself; they ensure for him free course, when employed toward others.

The Family

The superior man while his parents are alive, reverently nourishes them; and when they are dead, reverently sacrifices to them. His chief thought is how, to the end of life, not to disgrace them.

There are three degrees of filial piety. The highest is being a credit to our parents; the next is not disgracing them; and the lowest is merely being able to support them.

The services of love and reverence to parents when alive, and those of grief and sorrow for them when dead—these completely discharge the duty of living men.

Government

Good government obtains when those who are near are made happy, and those who are far are attracted.

The people are the most important elements . . . the sovereign, least important.

If the people have plenty, their prince will not be left to want alone. If the people are in want, their prince will not be able to enjoy plenty alone.

When rulers love to observe the rules of propriety, these people respond readily to the calls upon them for service.

The ruler must first himself be possessed of the qualities which he requires of the people; and must be free from the qualities which he requires the people to abjure.

Education and Arts

In providing a system of education, one trouble is to secure proper respect for the teacher; when such is assured, what he teaches will also be regarded with respect; when that is done, the people will know how to respect learning.

A scholar should constantly pursue what is virtuous and find recreation in the arts.

Music produces pleasure which human nature cannot be without.

*M. M. Dawson, *The Ethics of Confucius* (Putnam's, 1915), pp. 2–5, 167–68, 255–57.

Confucianist reminded the founder of the Han dynasty: "You have won the empire on horseback but you cannot rule it from horseback."

In the second century B.C.E. Confucianism was declared the official dogma or faith of the empire. The *Classics* became the principal study of scholars and statesmen. Until the fall of the Manchu dynasty more than 2,000 years later, in 1911, the teachings of Confucius were unchallenged in China. Indeed they persisted even later, for Generalissimo Chiang Kai-shek urged dedication to the principles of Confucianism as the solution for the problems of the Republic. To the present day the Nationalist regime on Taiwan observes Confucius's birthday as Teachers' Day, a national holiday.

After Confucianism, the most influential Chinese philosophy was Taoism. This is understandable, for the two doctrines supplement each other neatly. Between them they satisfy both the intellectual and emotional needs of the Chinese people. Whereas Confucianism emphasized decorum, conformity, and social responsibility, Taoism stressed individual whim and fancy and conformity to the great pattern of nature. This pattern was defined as Tao (the "road" or "way"), and its disciples were known as Taoists. The key to conforming with Tao was abandonment of ambition, rejection of honors and responsibilities, and a meditative return to nature. The ideal subject had big bones, strong muscles, and an empty head, whereas the ideal ruler "keeps the people without knowledge and without desire . . . and fills their stomachs. . . . By non-action nothing is ungoverned."

Altogether different from Confucianism and Taoism were the doctrines of the Legalists. The Legalists were practicing statesmen, not philosophers, and were interested in reorganizing society to strengthen the princes they served and to enable them to wage war and unite the country by force. They viewed the nobility as useless hangovers from the past who could not be depended on by the princes, and who therefore should be replaced by state military forces. The Legalists also believed that the Chinese masses should be forced into productive work. They regarded merchants and scholars as nonessential and therefore not to be tolerated. All aspects of life were to be regulated in detail by laws designed to promote the economic and military power of the state. Rulers were to be guided not by the traditional virtues of humanity and righteousness extolled by the Confucianists but by their need for power and wealth.

These Legalist doctrines were used successfully by the Ch'in rulers to conquer other princes and to establish the first empire. They then extended their regimentation ruthlessly to the entire country, but the result, as we shall see, was a reaction that led to the overthrow of the empire a few years after the death of its founder. Legalism was discredited and Confucianism became the permanent official creed. Henceforth the Confucianists had a monopoly of social respectability and of governmental posts. And so the memory of other schools faded away, while Taoism, absorbing all sorts of popular superstitions and demon lore, became the religion of the uneducated masses and was tolerantly despised by the Confucian teachers and officials.

III. CH'IN EMPIRE

China's long history has been marked by three great revolutions that fundamentally changed its political and social structure. The first in 221 B.C.E. ended the feudal system and created a centralized empire; the second in 1911 C.E. ended the empire and established a republic; and the third in 1949 put the present Communist regime in power.

The first of these revolutions was the work of the leaders of the northwest state of Ch'in in the Wei River valley. This location contributed to the victory, for the valley is largely inaccessible and easy to defend. The Ch'in rulers were able to attack the other states to the east without fear of any enemy action in their rear. The frontier location also helped to keep the Ch'in military forces in fighting trim because of the constant wars against the barbarian nomads. In fact, the Ch'in were among the first Chinese to use iron weapons, in place of bronze, and cavalrymen in place of charioteers. Important also in the Ch'in triumph was the conquest in 318 B.C.E. of the great food-producing plain of Szechwan, which added greatly to the area and strength of Ch'in, placing it in somewhat the same relationship to the other Chinese states as Macedonia had been to the Greek cities. Finally, the Ch'in rulers were able and ambitious realists who pioneered in applying Legalist doctrines and in concentrating all power in their hands. (See map of Classical Age Empires in China, p. 134.)

With these advantages, the Ch'in leaders extended their possessions steadily, overcoming the surrounding states one by one. Contemporaries referred fearfully to the "wild beast of Ch'in" and compared its steady expansion to

The army of life-size terra-cotta soldiers found in the tomb of the first emperor of the Ch'in dynasty (246–210 B.C.E.).

that of a "silkworm devouring a mulberry leaf." By 221 B.C.E. the Ch'in ruler was master of all China, and he adopted the title of Shih Huangti, or "First Emperor." His successor would be "Second Emperor," and so on down the generations for "ten thousand years," meaning forever.

The new emperor applied to all China the Legalist doctrines that had succeeded so brilliantly in his home state. He abolished all feudal states and kingdoms. He reorganized his vast realm into administrative areas, or commanderies, each with a set of officials appointed by and responsible to the central government. Further, he disarmed all soldiers except his own, required the old aristocratic families to reside in his capital where they could be kept under watch, and planted Ch'in garrisons throughout the country. The new emperor also imposed economic centralization by standardizing weights, measures, and coinage.

In the light of future history, one of the most important innovations was the scrapping of the numerous ways of writing the Chinese characters that had been developed in the king-

doms. In their place a standardized script was substituted that was understandable from one end of China to the other. This proved to be a most effective and enduring bond of unity because of the nature of Chinese script. It is not based on a limited number of signs expressing the phonetic elements of a word. Rather, it consists of a large number of symbols or characters, each one of which denotes an object or an abstract concept. The system is precisely that used in the West for figures. All Westerners know what the symbol "5" means, even though they call it five, funf, cinque, or cinq. So it is with Chinese characters, or ideographs, which have meaning but no sound. They are ideas, like numerals, which every reader can sound according to his own dialect. Thus the new Ch'in standardized script, which has continued with modifications to the present, could be read and understood by all educated Chinese, even though they spoke dialects that often were mutually unintelligible. For the same reason, the script was equally comprehensible to foreign peoples, so that educated Japanese, Koreans, or

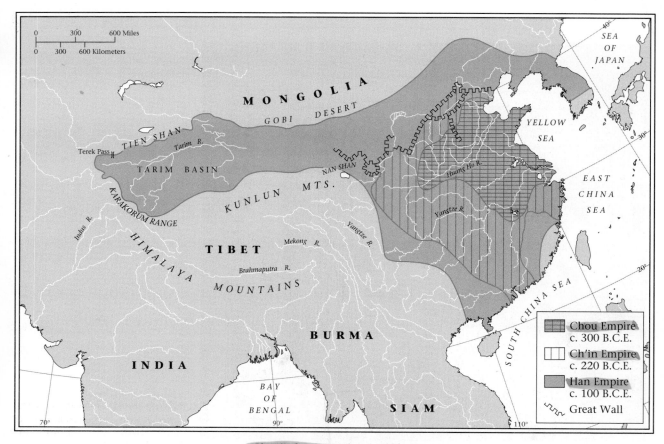

Classical Age Empires in China

Vietnamese can read Chinese without being able to speak a word of it. The significance of this for future Chinese national unity and for Chinese cultural influence throughout East Asia can well be imagined.

These changes made by the Ch'in dynasty hurt many vested interests and aroused passionate opposition. This was especially true of the scholars, who hated the Legalist doctrines and policies. The first emperor accordingly decided to deprive them of their intellectual props by ordering the "Burning of the Books." All the *Classics* were consigned to the flames, except those dealing with subjects of utilitarian value, such as medicine, agriculture, and divination. The plan failed, for scholars hid their books at great risk or else memorized entire texts before surrendering them. Later, after the fall of the dynasty, the greater part of the traditional literature was recovered from the hidden books and from the memories of old men. The persecution, however, effectively dampened the intellectual ferment that had characterized the Zhou period; the Golden Age of Chinese thought was over.

This intellectual loss should be balanced against the economic progress that was made through more efficient use of human and natural resources. The standardization of weights, measures, and coinage promoted economic growth. Also a network of trunk roads was built, radiating from the capital to the most distant frontiers. To make the roads as useful as possible, the emperor standardized the axle length of the two-wheeled Chinese carts—an essential measure because the wheels cut deep ruts in the sandy soil, so that every cart had to follow the existing ruts or be fitted with new axles. The emperor also used the new national unity and strength to expand the frontiers southward to present-day Vietnam. To the northwest the nomads were beaten back. To keep them out the famous Great Wall was built, running 1,400 miles from Inner Mongolia to the ocean. So great was the loss of life on this stupendous project that even today, more than 2,000 years later, people still speak of the fact that a million workers perished at this task and that every stone cost a human life. Just as the scholars cursed the emperor for the "Burning of

A section of the Great Wall of China, first built in the third century B.C.E. during the Ch'in Dynasty and later restored by the Ming Dynasty.

the Books," so the people cursed him for the building of the Great Wall.

It was this widespread resentment, together with the lack of a competent successor, that explains the popular revolt at the end of the dynasty in 207 B.C.E., only four years after the death of the first emperor. But although Ch'in rule was so short-lived, it left a deep and permanent imprint on China. The country had been transformed from a loose collection of feudal states into a centralized empire, which it remained until the twentieth century. It is only appropriate that the occidental name for China is derived from the Ch'in.

IV. HAN EMPIRE

The first emperor had abolished feudalism in one stroke, but the succeeding Han emperor, more practical and cautious, first restored feudalism a bit and then whittled it away to insignificance. At the outset, he granted fiefs to his sons and close relatives, but these holdings were all smaller than the former feudal states of the Zhou period. Furthermore, they were put under the direct rule of state officials. Then in 127 B.C.E. a decree was issued limiting the inheritance of the oldest son to one-half the fief, the remainder to be distributed among the other sons. Thus the fiefs shrank steadily in size and importance and became merely large estates. The imperial structure erected by the first emperor was gradually restored, though without the original terror and oppression. Thus the Han Empire flourished for four centuries, about the same length of time as the Roman Empire.

The Han Empire also resembled the Roman Empire in its vast size. During the first sixty years the Han rulers concentrated on national recuperation and dynastic consolidation. But under the "Martial Emperor," Wu Ti (141–87 B.C.E.), the imperial frontiers were greatly expanded in all directions. Tribal territories in the south were conquered, though several centuries of Chinese immigration and assimilation of the local peoples were necessary before this part of the empire became predominantly Chinese-speaking. The greatest expansion occurred to the west, where Chinese expeditions drove across central Asia, establishing contact with the Kushan Empire in northwest India and vastly increasing the volume of trade along the Silk Road. (See Chapter 4, Section II.)

The nomadic Hsiung-nu people had the advantage of superior cavalry forces, supported by a limitless supply of horses. In fact, the Chinese had to trade with the nomads for the horses needed by their own cavalry units. But the Chinese had a new weapon that was decisive—the crossbow, which they invented sometime late in the feudal wars. Fitted with a string drawn by a winding mechanism and released by a cocking piece, the crossbow had greater range and penetrating power than the ordinary bow. Because of this weapon and the resources of a great empire, China's frontiers during the Han period began to take on roughly modern lines.

The Han Empire was comparable to the Roman Empire in population as well as territorial extent. A census taken in the year 1 C.E., and believed to be reasonably accurate, showed the empire to have 12.2 million households with a total of 59.6 million people. By contrast the population of the Roman Empire at the time of Augustus (27 B.C.E.–14 C.E.) is estimated at 30 million to 50 million people in Europe, somewhat fewer in Asia, and not quite 20 million in Africa.

At the head of the Han realm stood the emperor, who had full political power and who was responsible for the physical well-being and prosperity of his subjects. The sanctity of the emperor's person was emphasized in his daily activities—in the long ceremonies of court or shrine over which he presided; in the prescribed robes for each occasion; in the army of officials, courtiers, eunuchs, and women who waited on him; in the elegant carriages in which he traveled; and finally in the majestic mausoleum prepared for the time when his mortal remains would be laid to rest with appropriate solemnity.

Below the emperor were two senior officials corresponding to a modern prime minister and a head of civil service. These men were in constant touch with the emperor and were responsible for the actual operation of government. Beneath them were nine ministries entrusted with the following functions: religious ceremonials, security of the palace, care of the imperial stables, punish-

A green glazed pottery model of a Later Han dynasty watchtower (87.6 x 35.6 x 38.1 cm). Note the resemblance to later Chinese Buddhist pagodas.

ment of criminals, receipt of homage and tribute from foreign leaders, maintenance of records of the imperial family, collection of state revenues, and management of the imperial exchequer.

In addition to the central government there was a provincial bureaucracy that administered, in descending order, commanderies, prefectures, districts, and wards. Officials at the grass-roots level were assigned such basic tasks as collection of tax in grain, textiles, or cash; arresting of criminals; maintenance of roads, canals, and granaries; and upkeep of the imperial post, with its horses and chain of stations.

In the first century B.C.E. this bureaucracy is said to have comprised some 130,000 officials, or only one for every 400 or 500 inhabitants. This small number in relation to the total population was typical throughout Chinese history and is to be explained by the restricted role of the imperial government. "Governing a country," according to a Chinese proverb, "is like cooking a small fish: neither should be overdone." Consequently Chinese governments did not assume responsibility for the social services taken for granted in the modern world, as is evident from the ministerial duties just listed. Rather, the main role of government was collection of revenue and defense of the country against external attack and of the dynasty against internal subversion.

The bureaucracy was a privileged, but not hereditary, elite. During the Han period, a unique system was originated for the selection of civil-service personnel by means of competitive public examinations. In 124 B.C.E. a sort of imperial university was established for students destined for government service. This was steadily expanded, so that the student body totaled 3,000 by the second half of the first century B.C.E., and 30,000 before the end of the Han era. In their later, fully developed form, the examinations were on three levels, and each led to the award of one of three degrees that roughly corresponded to those of bachelor, master, and doctor in Western universities. In principle the examinations were open to all, but such prolonged study was needed to become a candidate that only the sons of the well-to-do could qualify. On the other hand, poor boys were quite often given village, clan, or guild endowments so that they could study.

Since the examinations were based on the Confucian *Classics*, the empire in effect was run by Confucianists and according to Confucian principles. Each official was assigned to a post outside his home province to ensure that he would not use his position to build up local family power. The result was an administrative system that was far more efficient and responsive than any other until modern times. Indeed this civil service based on merit was a major factor in the continuity of the Chinese imperial system from the time of the first emperor to the twentieth century. There was another side, however, to this examination system. Since it was based on total acceptance of a single body of doctrine, it produced a rigid orthodoxy and an intellectual arrogance that was to hurt China

centuries later when Western merchants and gunboats appeared.

Although China was to suffer grievously in modern times because it lagged in science and industry, during the Han period it was a very different story. China then caught up technologically with the rest of Eurasia and, in many fields, took a lead that it was to maintain until recent centuries. Some of the more important Chinese inventions of these centuries were the water-powered mill, the shoulder collar for horses—which greatly increased their efficiency—and the techniques for casting iron, making paper, and glazing pottery. Rag paper, dating from about 100 C.E., soon replaced cumbersome wooden and bamboo slips for writing. But paper is not as durable as wood, and since it was developed by the Chinese long before printing, we must, oddly enough, blame the use of paper for the loss of certain books. Pottery glazes, however, which were eventually developed into porcelain, or china, were an undiluted blessing. They not only reached the level of true art, but they also represented a major advance in hygiene, since smooth porcelain was more sanitary than the rough pottery or wooden utensils hitherto available.

The outstanding Han contribution in literature was in the field of historical writing. This was to be expected from a people who looked to the past for guidance in dealing with the present. Their *Five Classics* already contained a good deal of assorted historical materials. But now in the first century B.C.E., a history appeared that was much more comprehensive and sophisticated than any to that date.

This was the *Shih chi*, or *Historical Records*, written by a father-son team, though authorship is commonly attributed to the son, Ssu-ma Ch'ien, who wrote the major part. As court astrologer, he had access to the imperial library and archives. He also had the advantage of extensive traveling throughout the empire, where he used the resources of local libraries. This history, he wrote, was not so much an original work as a compilation of all available historical materials. It was only when dealing with contemporary matters and personalities that he himself expressed personal judgments and wrote original history. As he explained modestly, "My narrative consists of no more than a systematization of the material that has been handed down to us. There is therefore no creation; only faithful representation."

This method had obvious disadvantages, especially the lack of dramatic quality and stylistic unity found in early historians such as Herodotus. On the other hand, it did assemble and preserve for posterity a tremendous quantity of historical material from contemporary books and archives. The *Historical Records* was in effect a universal history. It was equal to a work of approximately 1.5 million words. Its 130 chapters included chronological records and tables of the various dynasties; biographies of Han notables; and essays on varied topics such as rituals, music, astrology, astronomy, economic matters, and foreign peoples and lands. Future Chinese historians paid Ssu-ma Ch'ien the tribute of copying his method. As a result Chinese historiography has transmitted through the millennia a mass of data unequaled by that of any other country over so long a period.

All Chinese historians also shared a belief in the "Mandate of Heaven" concept. They held that a king ruled as the deputy of Heaven only as long as he possessed the virtues of justice, benevolence, and sincerity. When he no longer demonstrated these virtues and misruled his kingdom, he was automatically deprived of the Mandate of Heaven, and rebellion against him was then not a crime but a just punishment from Heaven through the medium of the rebels. Thus Chinese historians, although often aware of the social and economic factors behind dynastic decline, subordinated them to what they considered to be a more basic underlying consideration—the moral qualifications of the ruler. Chinese historiography, then, tended to be more a compilation of sources than the personal analyses of individual historians, and the organizational framework was based on the rise and fall of dynasties interpreted in accordance with the workings of the Mandate of Heaven.

V. IMPERIAL DECLINE

The traditional interpretation of Chinese history views it as a succession of dynastic cycles that repeated each other. But the cyclical facade obscures some fundamental changes. It is true,

Tomb figure of standing attendant from the Former Han dynasty, second century B.C.E.

of course, that dynasties did rise and fall. The founder of a line naturally was a man of ability, drive, and action. But his descendants, after a few generations of living in a court atmosphere, were likely to become effete and debauched.

Sometimes a strong ruler or a capable and devoted minister managed to halt the deterioration. But the overall trend was downhill, until successful revolt removed the dynasty and started the familiar cycle again.

More fundamental than the dynastic cycle, however, was what might be termed the economic-administrative cycle. This began with the security and prosperity common at the outset of every major dynasty. The restoration of peace led to population increase, greater production, correspondingly greater revenues, and full government coffers. But a combination of personal ambitions, family influences, and institutional pressures inevitably led the emperors sooner or later to overextend themselves. They squandered their human and financial resources on roads, canals, fortifications, palaces, court extravagances, and frontier wars. Thus each dynasty began to experience financial difficulties about a century after its founding.

To meet the deficits the government raised taxes. And taxes bore most heavily on the small peasant proprietors who were the backbone of Chinese society. At the beginning of each dynasty small proprietors constituted the majority of the peasantry. But as taxes increased, more and more of them lost their plots to the large landowners and became tenants. The landowners, who had political influence commensurate with their wealth, paid negligible taxes. So the more their holdings increased, the more the government revenues declined, and the more the taxes rose for the diminishing number of small peasants. Thus a vicious circle was set in motion—rising taxes, falling revenues, neglected roads and dikes, and declining productivity. Eventually this development resulted in famines, banditry, and full-scale peasant uprisings. Meanwhile frontier defenses were likely to be neglected, inviting raids across the borders by nomads. Often it was the combination of internal revolt and external invasion that brought down the tottering dynasty and cleared the way for a new beginning.

This was essentially the pattern of the Earlier Han dynasty. The "Martial Emperor," Wu Ti (141–87 B.C.E.), had won great victories and extended China's frontiers deep into central Asia. But in doing so he overstrained the imperial resources. He resorted to a variety of measures to cope with the crisis, including currency debasement; sale of ranks; and reinstitution of government monopolies on salt, iron, and liquor. Although he managed to remain solvent for the duration of his reign, his successors sank deeper into trouble as the number of taxpaying small peasants declined. Large-scale revolts broke out, and even at the court various omens were interpreted as portents from Heaven that the end of the dynasty was drawing near.

In fact the dynasty was briefly ousted (9–25 C.E.) by Wang Mang, a powerful minister who had already dominated the court for some three decades. He boldly tackled the basic economic problem by nationalizing the great private estates and distributing them among the taxpaying peasants. This and other reforms alienated the wealthy families, who opposed the usurper bitterly. At the same time a disastrous change in the lower course of the Yellow River made millions homeless and drove the uprooted peasants into banditry and rebellion. The nomads took advantage of the disorders to invade the country and sack the capital, where Wang Mang died at their hands in 23 C.E. He was succeeded on the throne by a distant cousin of the former Han emperor.

The history of the Later Han (25–222 C.E.) was basically the same as that of its predecessor. During the lengthy wars many of the old aristocrats and landowners had been wiped out. Tax returns, therefore, were adequate at the beginning of the revived dynasty. But again the taxpaying peasantry began to be squeezed out, and the downward spiral once more was under way. Great rebellions broke out, and the situation resembled that of the last days of Rome. The decimation of the small peasants had also destroyed the original peasant draft army. This was replaced by professional troops, whose first loyalty was to their generals. The generals, therefore, could ignore the central government. Great landowners also defied the government by evading taxes and enlarging their holdings by various legal and extralegal means. Helpless peasants, fleeing the barbarian invaders or government tax collectors, became the virtual serfs of these landowners in return for economic and physical security. The great families converted their manors into fortresses, virtually taking over the functions of government in their respective localities. Their estates were largely self-sufficient, so that trade declined and cities shrank correspondingly. Thus in 222 C.E. the Han dynasty disappeared from the stage of history, in a swirl of peasant revolts, warlord coups, and nomadic raids. China then entered a prolonged period of disunity and disorder similar to that in the West following the collapse of the Roman Empire.

SUGGESTED READINGS

The best general histories are by E. O. Reischauer and J. K. Fairbank, *East Asia: The Great Tradition* (Houghton Mifflin, 1978); C. O. Hucker, *China's Imperial Past: An Introduction to Chinese History and Culture* (Stanford University, 1975); and W. Rodzinsi, *The Walled Kingdom: A History of China from Antiquity to the Present* (Free Press, 1985). For more detail, see the ongoing ten-volume *Cambridge History of China* (Cambridge University, 1978).

For a collection of primary materials regarding Chinese intellectual and religious development, see W. T. de Bary et al., *Sources of Chinese Tradition* (Columbia University, 1960). Concerning the greatest figure in Chinese culture, there is H. G. Creel, *Confucius, the Man and the Myth* (John Day, 1949); and A. Waley, *The Analects of Confucius* (Allen & Unwin, 1938). For daily life in premodern China, see M. Loewe, *Everyday Life in Early Imperial China* (Putnam, 1968); and J. Gernet, *Daily Life in China on the Eve of the Mongol Invasion 1250–1276* (Stanford University, 1970). Finally, there is the delightful book by J. Spence, *Emperor of China: Self-Portrait of K'ang-hsi* (Knopf, 1974), consisting of translations from the writings of the emperor of China from 1661 onward.

8
End of Classical Civilizations

All in all, the invasions gave the coup de gráce to a culture which had come to a standstill after reaching its apogee and seemed doomed to wither away. We are reminded of the cruel bombings in our own day which destroyed ramshackle old buildings and so made possible the reconstruction of towns on more modern lines.

Robert Lopez

The great civilizations of Greece, Rome, India, and China dominated Eurasia in classical times. Yet in the end, the nomads and pastoralists of the frontier regions overran these civilizations and fundamentally altered the course of global history. Beneath the seeming invulnerability of the empires lay roots of decline that brought on decay and eventual disintegration. Because technology was at a standstill, productivity was low. Together these factors made the classical civilizations vulnerable to the barbarian attacks from the third to the sixth centuries.

The effect of the nomadic invasions varied from region to region. Northern China and northern India were overrun but retained their distinctive civilizations. Southern China and southern India escaped invasion because of their distance from the lands of the nomads. Byzantium and Persia proved powerful enough to repel the invaders. The West, however, suffered repeated attacks by Germans, Huns, Moslems, Magyars, and Vikings, so that the old order was uprooted to a degree unequaled anywhere else in Eurasia. Ironically, however, this destruction was a principal reason for the primacy of the West in modern times. A new civilization was able to emerge out of the ashes of the old, a civilization better adapted to the demands of a changing world. The purpose of this chapter is to analyze why the classical civilizations declined, and why the West would be the exception as it started out on a new road leading distantly to world domination.

I. DECLINE OF CLASSICAL CIVILIZATIONS

The basic reason for the decline of the classical civilizations, as just noted, was their relatively stagnant technology, which therefore kept their productivity low. John Maynard Keynes described the technological slowdown:

The absence of important technological inventions between the prehistoric age and comparatively modern times is truly remarkable. Almost everything which really matters and which the world possessed at the commencement of the modern age was already known to man at the dawn of history. . . . At some epoch before the dawn of history . . . there must have been an era of progress and invention comparable to that in which we live today. But through the greater part of recorded history there was nothing of the kind.[1]

Keynes's observation is fully justified. The Neolithic Age preceding civilization had been, in fact, remarkable for its technological progress. It was then that humankind invented the wheeled cart, the sailboat, and the plow; discovered the chemical processes involved in metallurgy; worked out an accurate solar calendar; and learned how to harness the power of animals and of the wind. After the urban revolution, this headlong advance was arrested. During the following millennia only three discoveries were made that compared in significance with those of the earlier period. These were iron, the alphabet, and coinage. All three, significantly enough, were discovered not in the old centers of civilization along the Nile and Tigris-Euphrates, but rather in peripheral and less restricting environs—the Caucasus frontier regions and the Aegean commercial cities.

Apart from these three great inventions, the advances made at this time were based on the earlier discoveries, merely refining the skill with which they were used or applying them on a much larger scale. In many cases even such modest gains were not made, even though they would have yielded rich returns. For example, the ancient harness developed for use with oxen was applied to the horse in such a way that the animal could not pull without choking. As a result at least two-thirds of the power of the horse was wasted. A sensibly functioning harness had to wait for the Middle Ages. Until then horses could pull only the lighter loads. Heavy loads were pulled by human beings. We can see this in the carvings showing thousands of workers engaged in pulling and hauling during the construction of the pyramids and the ziggurats. Another example was the water mill, which made its appearance in Asia Minor and in China in the first century B.C.E. This invention was potentially a great labor saver and could have eliminated many hours of tedious work by women and slaves in grinding corn. Yet water mills were not built in Rome until the fourth century, and even then they were comparatively rare.

Significantly enough, it was only war that could arouse the classical civilizations from their technological lethargy. The Greeks invented ingenious ratchet-equipped catapults and wheeled assault towers pulled by block and tackle. Another first was their so-called "Greek fire" (eighth century C.E.), a petroleum-based incendiary that set fire to enemy ships and siege machinery. But these innovations obviously did not produce wealth nor could they solve the basic economic problem of the old civilizations.

Since labor productivity was not increased by new inventions, wealth could be increased only by bringing new areas under cultivation or by conquest and exploitation. But virgin lands were not limitless. Instead, extensive fertile regions throughout the Mediterranean basin were now being eliminated as food sources because of large-scale erosion, which was becoming a serious problem. Likewise empires could not expand indefinitely; there were strict limits beyond which they stalled because of the level of their military technology. Thus there had to be a point of diminishing returns at which the pressure of military and bureaucratic establishments became too much for productive capacities. A vicious circle then set in, as previously noted. Two good examples on which we have more information are the falls of the Han and Roman empires. Rising taxes and increasing poverty caused uprisings in the cities and countryside, inviting nomadic incursions and ultimately leading to successful internal revolt or invasion from the outside, or a combination of the two, hence the cyclical nature of imperial history in premodern times. One historian, concluding an analysis of the decline of the Roman Empire, emphasized technological backwardness:

The Roman Empire, we must not forget, was technically more backward than the Middle Ages. In agriculture a two-field system of alternate crops and fallow was usually followed, and the potentially richest soils were little exploited. The horse collar had not been invented, so that oxen had to be employed for plowing and for carting. Water mills existed, but seem to have been relatively rare, and corn was generally ground by animals or by human labor in hand querns. Yet with this primitive technique, agriculture had to carry an ambitious superstructure far heavier than that of any medieval state. No medieval kingdom attempted, as did the Roman Empire, to support, as well as a landed aristocracy and the church, a professional standing army, and a salaried bureaucracy.[2]

In retrospect it is clear that the cycle could have been broken only by technological advances that would have provided the economic support necessary for the expensive imperial organizations. But technology was stagnant, and the basic reason was that the ruling establishments everywhere knew how to expropriate existing wealth but did not know how to create more wealth. They were capable of siphoning off astonishingly large surpluses from their peasant subjects, as evident in the stupendous amounts of capital and labor invested in pyramids, ziggurats, cathedrals, and palaces. But technological innovation required something more than efficient organization and coercion, and all the agricultural civilizations failed to achieve this something more—which was why they remained agricultural.

The widespread presence of slavery was one reason for the technological standstill. It was usually simpler and cheaper to put slaves to work than to design and construct new machines. Thus the inventors of the time usually produced gadgets intended not to save labor but to amuse or to carry on religious ritual. Hero of Alexandria in the first century C.E. used his knowledge of steam power to construct a machine that opened temple doors. Likewise, in the same century, Emperor Vespasian in Rome forbade the use of a machine that would erect

A page from an early manuscript of a codification of Roman law made by the Visigothic king Alaric II. This page shows a barbarian king, a bishop, a count, and a duke. Codifications such as this one contributed to the preservation of the principles of Roman law.

columns inexpensively, commenting, "Let me provide food for the common folk." Laudable though this sentiment might be, the fact remains that it made the cities of the classical empires parasites of the countryside rather than centers of productive industry.

Slavery also inhibited technology by fostering a negative attitude toward work. Since labor was the lot of the slaves, it came to be regarded as beneath the dignity of any free citizen. Even in civilizations where slavery was not so widespread, this attitude toward labor existed; witness the cult of the long fingernail in China. Division into sharply distinct social classes promoted upper-class contempt for work and workers, and slavery accentuated this attitude. As Aristotle wrote in his *Politics*, "in the best-governed polis . . . the citizens may not lead either the life of craftsmen or of traders, for such a life is devoid of nobility and hostile to perfection of character." Likewise the Roman philosopher Seneca, in a letter to Lucilius in 65 C.E., expressed the same scorn for manual labor, which, he said, should be proffered with "bowed body and lowered eyes":

Some things we know to have appeared only within our own memory; the use, for example, of glass windows which let in the full brilliance of day through a transparent pane, or the substructure of our baths and the pipes let into their walls to distribute heat and preserve an equal warmth above and below. . . . Or the shorthand which catches even the quickest speech, the hand keeping pace with the tongue. All these are the inventions of the meanest slaves. Philosophy sits more loftily enthroned: she doesn't train the hand, but is instructress of the spirit. . . . No, she's not, I say, an artisan producing tools for the mere everyday necessities.[3]

It was the isolation of the philosopher from the artisan that blocked the technological growth of the Eurasian civilizations. And it was the interaction between the two—the ordered speculation of the philosopher and the practical experience and traditional lore of the artisan—that enabled the West to achieve its great scientific and industrial revolutions in modern times, and thereby make its unique contribution to human development. Such interaction was impossible in the classical civilizations because of the sharp social cleavages and the resulting social attitudes. The lofty intellectual lacked interest, and the lowly artisan lacked incentive.

Technological stagnation explains the cyclical nature of Eurasian imperial history during the premodern millennia. Empires rose and fell in a basically similar pattern. None was able to break through to a new level of development; hence the repetitive cycles that contrast sharply with the dynamism of modern industrialized societies. W. W. Rostow has described this common feature of agricultural civilizations that was pervasive in the times before Britain erupted in its epochal and pioneering industrial revolution:

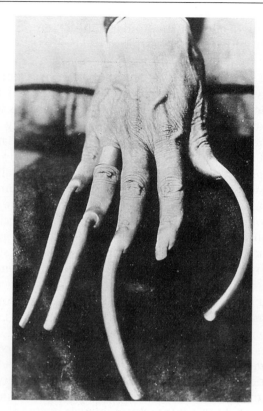

The fingernails of a Chinese aristocrat, who allows them to grow in order to prove that he is not a manual worker.

. . . limitations of technology decreed a ceiling beyond which they could not penetrate. They did not lack inventiveness and innovations, some of high productivity. But they did lack a systematic understanding of their physical environment capable of making invention a more or less regular current flow, rather than a stock of ad hoc achievements inherited from the past. . . .

It followed from this productivity ceiling that food production absorbed 75 percent or more of the working force and that a high proportion of income above minimum consumption levels was spent in non-productive or low-productive outlays: religious and other monuments, wars, high living for those who controlled land rents; and for poorer folks there was beggar-thy-neighbor struggle for land or the dissipation of the occasional surplus in an expensive wedding or funeral. Social values were geared to the limited horizons which men could perceive to be open to them; and social structures tended to hierarchy. . . .[4]

II. BARBARIAN INVASIONS

The period from the third to the sixth centuries was one of Eurasia-wide invasions comparable to the bronze and iron invasions of the second millennium B.C.E. And just as the earlier invasions were responsible for the transition from the ancient to the classical civilizations, so these later invasions ended the classical civilizations and cleared the way for the medieval. (See map of Barbarian Invasions in Eurasia, Fourth and Fifth Centuries C.E., p. 146.)

The general direction of nomadic movement was from east to west because of the geographic steppe gradient—the lure that the better-watered and more fertile lands of the western steppes held for the nomads of the east. (See Chapter 4, Section IV.) The main invasion routes followed the corridor of grassland that stretched across central Eurasia, beginning near Peking and ending in the Hungarian plains of central Europe. This is why so many of these nomadic peoples ended their wanderings in present-day Hungary, which became their base for raids into the surrounding European countries.

A basic factor behind the invasions was the constantly increasing interaction between the centers of civilization and the surrounding nomads. In many of the centers, nomads were used as slaves or mercenary soldiers, a practice that was often the initial wedge either for a military coup in the imperial capital or for an invasion by fellow-tribespeople of the barbarian mercenaries. Another factor was the gradual settling down of nomadic peoples, often in regions adjacent to imperial frontiers. This shift from nomadism to agriculture normally led to population growth and to greater economic and military strength. And if imperial weakness was great enough to hold out the promise of success, the new military strength was used. Invasions also were often the end result of a series of shock waves. A defeat before the Great Wall of China or a stumbling block such as the formation of an aggressive tribal confederacy in Mongolia frequently turned the nomads westward. A series of invasions, like a train of shocks moving ever further west, ended finally in nomadic incursions across the Oxus or Danube or Rhine rivers.

Because of the Eurasia-wide scope of the invasions, a great variety of peoples were involved. Han China, Gupta India, and Sassanian Iran usually were assaulted by Turco-Mongols, often referred to as Huns. But the Roman Empire, being at the western end of the invasion route, was the object of attack, at one time or another, of all the peoples along that route, as well as of surrounding barbarians. The procession included assorted Germanic tribes, Iranians, Balto-Slavs, and Vikings, as well as the Turco-Mongols.

The outcome of the invasions varied as much as their personnel. In China, the Han Empire finally succumbed to Turco-Mongol invaders in 222 C.E. Three separate kingdoms emerged: Wei, north of the Yangtze; Wu, in the south; and Shu, in the west. After decades of warfare, Wei defeated its rivals and established in 265 a new dynasty, the Ch'in. This dynasty ruled all China until 316, when a new wave of invaders overran the entire northern half of the country. The Ch'in court fled south to Nanking, whence it ruled the Yangtze valley and those regions of the south settled by the Chinese. China remained divided in two in this manner until finally reunited by the Sui dynasty in 589. It is easy to understand why the Chinese historians called these centuries the "Age of Confusion."

We shall see later that the West Roman Empire, under similar circumstances, was completely changed in its politics, culture, and race. But north China was spared such a complete transformation, primarily because the native Chinese population greatly outnumbered the nomadic invaders. The north at that time was still by far the most populous part of the country and, therefore, was able to absorb the nomads without undergoing radical change. In fact large numbers of Chinese migrated from north to south during these troubled centuries to escape the barbarians, so that not only did the north remain Chinese but also the south became more Chinese. Consequently, the partial barbarization of the north was counterbalanced by the southward expansion of Chinese culture, providing an enormous depth to China from north to south. Thus with reunification of the entire country by the Sui dynasty in 589, China resumed its normal course, as distinctively Chinese as during the Han period.

Turning to India, the invasions there occurred much later, for the Gupta Empire was at its height when China already was beset with

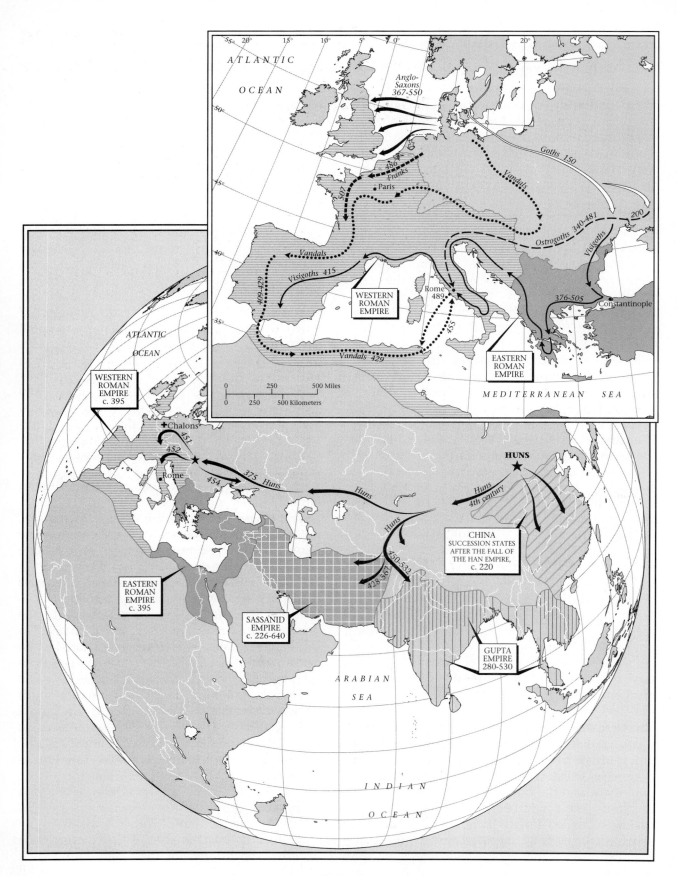

Barbarian Invasions in Eurasia, Fourth and Fifth Centuries C.E.

THE HSIUNG-NU BARBARIANS

Between the third and sixth centuries C.E. the classical civilizations of Eurasia were overthrown by barbarian invaders. The following selection from the Chinese historian Pan Ku describes the Hsiung-nu nomads that overwhelmed the Han Empire. *

The Hsiung-nu live in the north and are a nomadic people. They raise a variety of animals, most of which are horses, cattle, and sheep. Other animals such as camels and donkeys are comparatively small in number. They move constantly to seek water and grass; they have no cities, houses, or crop fields. Land, however, is divided among different tribal groups.

The Hsiung-nu do not have any written language; consequently all agreements or promises are made in oral form. Small children are taught to ride sheep and shoot birds and squirrels. When they grow older, they begin to shoot foxes and rabbits. Meat, instead of grain, is their staple food. All able-bodied men are expert archers and are members of the cavalry in their respective tribes.

Under normal circumstances when life is comparatively easy, the Hsiung-nu earn their livelihood by tending their herds and augment it by hunting. When life becomes difficult, all men are taught the art of warfare, preparing ardently for the launching of attacks. This, you might say, is the nature of the Hsiung-nu. They rely on bows and arrows if the enemy is at a distance and switch to knives and spears in close combat. They attack when they are certain of victory, but are not ashamed to run away from the battlefield if they think that the odds are heavily against them. They go wherever there are profits to be realized; they do not know of such things as righteousness and propriety. . . .

From the king down, all the Hsiung-nu people eat animals' meat, wear their skins, and convert their furs into garments. The young and the strong have priority to the best food; the elderly have to be sat-

isfied with the leftovers. They highly value youth and strength, and look down upon the old and the weak. After the death of his father, a man will marry his step-mother. Likewise he takes his brother's wife as his own when and if his brother dies. . . .

The khan [ruler] worships the rising sun early in the morning and the moon in the evening. In seating arrangement the person who sits on the left and faces the north is the most honored among the group. The dead are buried in coffins, accompanied with gold, silver, and clothing. But the graves are not marked with trees, nor do the mourners wear mourning clothes. Upon the death of a khan approximately one hundred of his favorite ministers and concubines will be put to death so that their spirits will be able to follow his.

During a military campaign the Hsiung-nu watch closely the size of the moon. They attack when the moon is large and bright and withdraw when it becomes small and dim. A Hsiung-nu soldier who kills an enemy will be awarded one goblet of wine plus whatever material goods he has taken from his victim. If he captures a man or woman alive, the latter becomes his slave. Thus on the battlefield all Hsiung-nu soldiers fight valiantly for their own material ends, upon which they converge like hungry vultures. Upon a setback, however, they disintegrate quickly and disperse like flying clouds. Their favorite strategy is to entice their enemy to a pre-arranged place and then encircle him. After a battle, the warrior who brings home the body of a dead comrade will inherit all of the latter's worldly possessions.

*From Dun J. Li, *The Essence of Chinese Civilization* (D. Van Nostrand, 1967), pp. 211–13. By permission of the author.

its "Age of Confusion." During the fifth century, however, the eastern branch of the Huns, or the "White Huns" as they are called, crossed the Oxus River and drove south to India, while the western branch advanced over the Russian steppes to Europe. Under the impact of the Hun onslaught the Gupta Empire disintegrated during the first half of the sixth century. Very little is known of events during the following centuries, except that the periodic invasions continued. In addition, there were migrations into India on a large enough scale to form new cultural and social groups. An outstanding example is that of the Rajputs, a sturdy and brave people who gave their name to the area known as Rajputana in northwest India. They were a military aristocracy who were soon absorbed into the Hindu caste of Kshatriyas, or warriors. They became intensely proud of their Hinduism and for some time dominated north and central India. In fact they were still prominent in the nineteenth century, and to some extent even to the present day.

The Rajput experience is significant because it helps explain why India, despite the long centuries of turmoil and invasions, was not fundamentally changed. The newcomers were assimilated into the prevailing caste system. It was much more a case of their adapting to India's civilization than the other way around. Thus India, like China, emerged from its time of troubles with the civilization it had evolved during classical times modified but not transformed.

III. GERMANS AND HUNS IN THE WEST

In Europe, however, the pattern of events was precisely the opposite; there it was transformation rather than modification. The most numerous invaders were the Germans, who occupied the central and east European lands from the Baltic to the Danube and from the Rhine to the Russian plains. Organized in tribes, the more important were the Franks, Vandals, Lombards, and Ostrogoths and Visigoths. All shared the same general religious beliefs and institutions, and all spoke closely related dialects, so that they could understand each other. Fortunately for the Romans, however, they were not united.

They were as ready to fight against each other as against their common foe, thus allowing the Roman Empire to survive as long as it did.

We must pay special attention to the institutions and customs of these Germanic peoples, for they became a basic element in the new civilization that emerged in the West after the fall of Rome. The contemporary Roman historian Tacitus described the Germans as a cattle people who rated their wealth by the number of their animals. Cattle rustling, in fact, was a major cause for strife among them. The social organization of the Germans consisted of three main elements. At the top were the nobles, whose status was usually hereditary and who were the large landholders. Most Germans were freemen who customarily owned their own plots of land. Those who did not were obliged to work for the nobles as sharecroppers. At the bottom was a class of people neither free nor slave. They were bound to the land but could not be sold apart from it. This form of bondage, similar to that of the Roman colonus, was the basis for the institution of serfdom that prevailed in western Europe in medieval times.

The main source of authority in these tribes was the assembly of freemen. It selected the king, if there was one, and also the military leader for each campaign. Tacitus noted that the Germans usually chose their kings on the basis of inheritance. But their war chiefs were selected for their valor and ability on the battlefield. The chief weapon was a long, straight, double-edged sword with a broad point, used for slashing rather than thrusting. Young men were given the right to carry a sword after solemn rites that were the origin of the later medieval ceremony by which a squire was raised to knighthood. Each outstanding warrior leader had a retinue of young followers, or comitatus, who fought beside him in battle and owed him loyalty and obedience. In return the chief provided arms and subsistence as well as a share of the war booty. This institution contributed to the later system of feudalism, which was based on the loyalty of knights to their feudal lords.

Tacitus described the Germans as great eaters, heavy drinkers, and confirmed gamblers. On the other hand he praised their high moral standards, which he held up as a model for his fellow Romans. He also stressed their hospitality as universal and unstinted. During the winter season groups would go from house to house, staying at each until the owner's supplies were exhausted. This is reminiscent of the later medieval arrangement by which a king or noble was entitled, as a part of his feudal dues, to so many days of entertainment for himself and his entourage.

The position of women in the German tribes was much more favorable than that of their sisters in the Roman Empire. Tacitus noted that they inherited and controlled property and took their place beside their husbands both in peace and in war. "Tradition says that [German] armies already wavering and giving way have been rallied by women." Tacitus also noted that German women were active in tribal affairs. "They even believe that the female sex has a certain sanctity and ability to foretell the future and they do not despise their [women's] counsels, or make light of their answers."[5] Thus German tribal women were better off than their Roman contemporaries, who were restricted to their households, and better off also than their medieval successors, who, in accord with Christian doctrine, were required to be pious and submissive.

Such were the people who began to press upon the imperial frontiers as early as the first century B.C.E. At that time the Roman legions were strong enough to hold the line with little difficulty. But with the decline of the empire the army also became weaker, and the Romans were hard pressed to keep control. They resorted to diplomacy, playing off one tribe against another. Also, since they had no choice, they allowed whole bands of German warriors to settle on the Roman side of the border in return for their aid against the tribes on the other side. This policy worked as long as the Romans were able to keep their allies in check. But by the fourth century C.E. they could no longer do so and the floodgates burst.

The onslaught was triggered by dread new invaders that the Europeans had never seen before—the Huns. Their appearance and their deliberate policy of frightfulness terrorized both the Romans and the Germans. The contemporary Roman historian Ammianus Marcellinus described them as "almost glued to their horses" and "so monstrously ugly and misshapen that you might suppose they were two legged animals. . . ."

Terracotta mounted figure from central Asia dating from the Hunnic period. This statue, from a private collection in Paris, possibly represents the Hunnic leader Attila himself.

When provoked they fight, entering battle in wedges and uttering various savage yells. As they are agile and quick they purposely scatter in an irregular line and deal terrible slaughter as they dart about. . . . None has fixed dwelling: without home or law or stable livelihood, they roam about like refugees with the wagons in which they live. . . . None of them can tell you his origin, for he was conceived in one place, born far from there, and brought up still farther away.[6]

Apparently displaced from their original pasture lands in central Asia by other nomads, the Huns headed westward and crossed the Volga in 372 C.E. There on the Russian steppes they quickly defeated the easternmost German tribe, the Ostrogoths, and then terrorized the neighboring Visigoths into seeking refuge across the Danube River on Roman territory. The Visigoths under Alaric marched to Italy and sacked Rome in 410, an event that shocked the imperial world at the time but that soon was to be repeated.

Eventually the Visigoths settled in southern Gaul and northern Spain, where they founded the first German kingdom on Roman territory. Behind the Visigoths came the Huns, who established their base on the Hungarian plains whence they raided both the eastern and western provinces of the empire. Under their feared leader, Attila, they appeared in 452 before the undefended gates of Rome, where, according to an implausible tradition, Pope Leo I persuaded the Hun chieftain to spare the capital. In any case, Attila turned northward without sacking the capital, and a year later he was found dead one morning, of a burst artery, lying beside his new bride, a German princess whom he had married the day before. His empire collapsed with his death, and the Huns disappeared from European history.

The Hunnic devastations, however, shattered Roman control over the western provinces, and German tribes now migrated across the frontiers virtually at will. The Vandals crossed the Rhine, pushed their way through Gaul and Spain, and crossed the Straits of Gibraltar to North Africa, where they established a kingdom. From their new base they turned to sea raiding, and in 455 one of their expeditions sacked Rome. Mean-while the Burgundians were occupying the Rhone Valley; the Franks were spreading out and sinking deep roots in northern Gaul; and the Angles, Saxons, and Jutes promptly invaded England when the last Roman soldiers departed in 407. The local Celtic population fled to the mountains of Scotland and Wales, so that Anglo-Saxon stock now became the dominant ethnic strain in England. Thus it was that the West Roman Empire passed under the control of new German succession kingdoms, a passing symbolized by the deposing of the last emperor, Romulus Augustulus, by the German Odoacer, in 476.

To this point the course of events in Europe was familiar. The West Roman Empire had succumbed to the barbarians as had the Han and Gupta empires in China and India. Furthermore it appeared in the sixth century that the aftermath of imperial disintegration in the West would be the same as that in China. Just as the Sui dynasty had finally united China in 589, so Europe at about the same time seemed to be on the road to reunification by the Frankish kings and the East Roman emperors.

The Franks had originated in the lower Rhine valley, whence they had emigrated in the fifth century to northern Gaul. There they

One of the reasons the Byzantyines were able to repulse the Arab attack on Constantinople in 717–718 was a secret weapon: Greek fire, a highly flammable mixture of petroleum, sulphur, and pitch that would burn even on water. In this fourteenth-century manuscript, the Byzantine navy is spraying Greek fire from a copper tube onto an enemy vessel.

A sixth-century ivory panel depicting the Byzantine emperor Justinian as the champion of the Christian faith. From 500 to 1100, the Byzantine Empire was the center of Christian civilization.

played a modest role in the turbulent history of the times until, under the leadership of the Merovingian kings, they became the most powerful people in the West. The most outstanding of the Merovingians was Clovis (481–511), who united the Frankish tribes; defeated the Romans, Byzantines, and Visigoths; and organized a kingdom stretching from the Pyrenees across Gaul and well into Germany. A principal reason for Clovis's success was his conversion to Catholicism, which won him the support not only of the pope but also of the local Gallo-Roman population. It appeared that the Merovingians might be able to re-create the West Roman

Empire, enlarged by the addition of the Frankish lands on the eastern bank of the Rhine.

This imperial ambition was shared by the rulers at Constantinople. While the West Roman Empire had been falling apart, the East Roman Empire remained intact, thanks to its naval power, its superior financial resources, and the natural strength of its capital located on the straits between Europe and Asia. Thus Constantinople survived the barbarian invasions that overwhelmed Rome, and, in fact, endured another millennium before falling to the Turks in 1453. During those centuries the empire developed a distinctive civilization, a mixture of

Greek, Roman, Christian, and Eastern elements. To emphasize this distinctiveness, the empire is commonly referred to as the Byzantine Empire, so named after the original Greek colony on the site of Constantinople.

After the western provinces had become German kingdoms, the rule of the Byzantine emperors was restricted to the eastern half of the original empire—that is, to the Balkan peninsula, Asia Minor, Syria, and Egypt. This contraction was unacceptable to Justinian the Great (527–565), who was an Illyrian by birth and a westerner at heart. He spoke and thought in Latin and was determined to recover the western lands and to restore the original Roman Empire. One of his generals, Belisarius, with a small number of heavily armed troops, conquered the Vandal kingdoms in North Africa in one year. Southeast Spain also was recovered from the Visigoths, but eighteen years of bitter fighting was needed to subdue the Ostrogoths in Italy. Thus within two decades almost all the Mediterranean had become once more a Roman lake, and Justinian expressed the hope "that God will grant us the remainder of the empire that the Romans lost through indolence."

IV. CONTINUED INVASIONS IN THE WEST

But this was not to be. The West did not follow the path of China. Instead a new wave of invasions smashed the fragile new imperial structures of the Franks and the Byzantines, and it left the West once more in confusion and disunity. Again it was turmoil in Mongolia that pushed hordes of refugees westward along the invasion route to Europe. Like their Hunnic predecessors, these Avars, as they came to be known in the West, used the Hungarian plains as a base from which they launched raids in all directions. They forced the Germanic Lombards into Italy (568), where the Lombards in turn drove out the Byzantines from most of the peninsula, thus blasting Justinian's hopes for an imperial restoration. The Avars also pushed Slavic tribes southward into the Balkan peninsula, where they occupied a broad band from the Adriatic to the Black seas.

In the eighth century hopes were rearoused for Western imperial unity by the spectacular successes of the Carolingian dynasty, which had replaced the Merovingians. The successors of Clovis were weak rulers, being known as "do-nothing kings." The kingdom was held together, however, by the strong-willed ministers who held the office of "mayor of the palace." The most outstanding of these was Charles Martel, the Hammer, who was the power behind the throne from 714 to 741. His greatest achievement was the defeat at the Battle of Tours (732) of the Moslems who had overrun North Africa and Spain and had advanced into southern France.

Martel's son, Pepin the Short, was not content to remain the minister of "do-nothing" kings and in 751 deposed the last Merovingian and established what came to be known as the Carolingian dynasty. The name is derived from Charlemagne, the son of Pepin, and the most famous of the line. During his long reign from 768 to 814, Charlemagne campaigned ceaselessly

Charlemagne: King of the Franks (768–814) and emperor of the West (800–814).

to extend his frontiers. He conquered the Saxons in northwest Germany, dispersed the Avars in Hungary, annexed the Lombard kingdom in Italy, and forced the Moslems back over the Pyrenees. By the end of the eighth century he was the undisputed master of the West, his empire extending from the North Sea to the Pyrenees and from the Atlantic Ocean to the Slavic lands in eastern Europe. In recognition of his supremacy, Pope Leo III crowned him emperor on Christmas Day in the year 800. And the assembled multitude, according to Charlemagne's secretary and biographer, shouted, "To Charles Augustus, crowned of God the great and pacific Emperor of the Romans, life and victory!"

The scene shows that the dream of imperial unity had not yet died. But it was destined to remain a dream, for soon after Charlemagne's death Europe was swamped by new waves of attacks from the south, the east, and the north. In the south, Moslem pirates and adventurers conquered the islands of Crete and Sicily and also raided all the Mediterranean coasts with devastating effect on maritime trade. In the east, still another nomadic force from central Asia, the Magyars, reached the Hungarian plains in 895 and followed the example of the preceding Huns and Avars in raiding the surrounding lands.

Most wide-ranging were the raids of the Norsemen, or Vikings. They were the equivalent on sea of the nomads on land. In place of horses they built fast ships with shallow draught that gave them unrivaled speed and mobility. The Vikings from Norway sailed westward to Iceland, Greenland, and North America. With their comrades from Denmark they raided the British Isles and the west coast of Europe and even forced their way through the Straits of Gibraltar to ravage both shores of the Mediterranean. Since Sweden faces eastward, the Vikings from that country crossed the Baltic Sea to Russian rivers and followed them to their outlets in the Caspian and Black seas.

Thus the whole of Europe was overrun by these daring raiders. At first, in the late eighth and ninth centuries, they were interested only in plunder, and they destroyed countless monasteries and towns. Few regions were safe, for the Norsemen with their shallow-draught ships were able to penetrate the rivers far into the interior. In the churches of the time was heard the prayer,

The Oseberg longship, excavated in 1904, is the best-preserved Viking ship in the world and is on display in the Viking Ship Museum in Oslo, Norway.

"From the wrath of the Northmen, O Lord, deliver us." In the tenth and eleventh centuries the Vikings began to settle in the overseas territories, thus occupying and ruling large parts of northern France and the British Isles. But wherever they settled they were eventually absorbed into the existing Christian state. The king of France, for example, in the hope of forestalling further depredations by the Vikings, recognized their leader in 911 and gave him the title of duke of what came to be known as Normandy, a name derived from the Norsemen who settled there. One of the descendants of this Duke Rollo of Normandy was William the Conqueror, who successfully invaded England in 1066.

The triple assault of Moslems, Magyars, and Vikings destroyed the Carolingian Empire. Western Europe once more was in a shambles. The

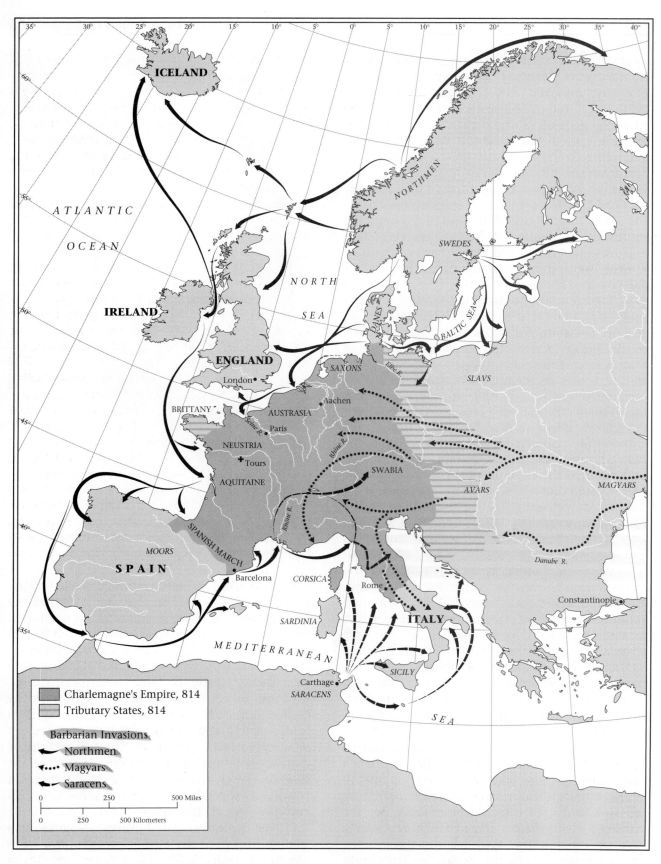

Legend (inset):

Charlemagne's Empire, 814
Tributary States, 814

Barbarian Invasions
Northmen
Magyars
Saracens

0   250   500 Miles

0   250   500 Kilometers

Map labels:

ICELAND

ATLANTIC OCEAN

NORTHMEN

SWEDES

IRELAND

NORTH SEA

BALTIC SEA

SLAVS

ENGLAND
London

SAXONS

DANES
Elbe R.

BRITTANY

AUSTRASIA
Aachen

Seine R.
Paris

Rhine R.

NEUSTRIA
+ Tours

AQUITAINE

SWABIA

AVARS

MAGYARS

Rhône R.

MOORS

SPANISH MARCH

SPAIN

Barcelona

CORSICA

Danube R.

SARDINIA

Rome

ITALY

Constantinople

MEDITERRANEAN

SICILY

Carthage
SARACENS

SEA

Continued Barbarian Invasions in the West, Ninth and Tenth Centuries lowest point was reached in the tenth century. At no time since the end of the Roman Empire did the present seem so wretched and the future so bleak. (See map of Continued Barbarian Invasions in the West, Ninth and Tenth Centuries, p. 154.)

V. THE GREAT WESTERN EXCEPTION

From this survey of the invasions marking the transition from the classical to the medieval eras, it is apparent that the various regions of Eurasia were affected quite differently. South China and south India were unscathed because they were geographically too remote to be reached by the invaders. Through the centuries, the Byzantine Empire, with its resourceful diplomacy and its financial and naval strength, successfully repelled a long succession of assailants—Germans, Huns, Avars, Slavs, Persians, and Arabs. Persia was equally successful under its Sassanian dynasty, which replaced the Parthian in 226 C.E. The Sassanians united the country by appealing to Persian pride, by reviving Zoroastrianism as a state religion, and by organizing a force of heavily armored cavalrymen. Thus Persia was able to repel waves of nomads along the Oxus River while fighting Byzantium to an exhausting standstill that left both empires easy prey for the oncoming Moslem Arabs.

China and India, as noted earlier, did not fare so well in their northern regions. Both were overrun by barbarians, yet both were able to preserve the distinctive civilizations that they had developed during the Classical Age. Thus the Chinese of the first-century-B.C.E. Han period would have felt quite at home had they been resurrected in the early eighth century C.E. They would have found the contemporary T'ang dynasty essentially the same as the Han, and they would have noted the same language, the same Confucianism and ancestor worship and imperial administration, and so forth.

This points up the uniqueness of the historical experience of the West. If the Romans of the first century B.C.E. had been resurrected in the Europe of 1000 or 1500 or 1800, they would have been astonished by the German peoples in many parts of the old empire and by the strange new ways of life. They would have found the Latin language replaced by several new Germanic and Romance languages; the Roman togas replaced by blouses and trousers; the ancient Roman gods cast aside for the new Christianity; the Roman imperial structure superseded by a conglomeration of new nation-states; and the old ways of earning a living rivaled by new agricultural techniques, by commerce with hitherto unknown parts of the globe, and by new crafts with strange machines that saved labor and that ran without the traditional human or animal power.

The explanation, of course, is that only in the West was a classical civilization permanently submerged and succeeded by something fundamentally new. Everywhere else in Eurasia the various regional civilizations escaped the invaders (south China and south India), repelled them (Byzantium and Persia), or endured and survived them (north China and north India). Only in the West was the classical civilization shattered beyond recall despite repeated attempts at restoration over several centuries.

Since it was precisely this uniqueness that made it possible for the West to attain worldwide supremacy in modern times, we must pay special attention to its origins. As noted in Section I of this chapter, technological stagnation was a basic structural weakness of the classical civilizations. But since this was true of all of them, why did only the west European civilization founder?

A comparison of the west European institutions and experiences with those of the rest of Eurasia leads to certain conclusions. In the first place western Europe was not as productive in classical times as, for example, China. The monsoon winds provide most of east Asia with plentiful rainfall during the summer growing months, in contrast to Europe where most of the rain comes in the sterile winter months. This, together with the greater solar heat in the lower latitudes, allows more intensive and prolonged cultivation in east Asia, including two crops per year in many localities. Furthermore, rice, the principal crop of east Asia, produces a much larger yield per acre than wheat, rye, and the other cereals grown in the West. According to one estimate, rice on a given plot of land yields caloric value that is five times as great as that of wheat on the same land. The net result was a far greater productivity in China than in the West, which led to the correspondingly denser population found in China from the beginnings of agriculture to modern times. This superiority in productivity and in population in turn made China more capable of supporting its empire's bureaucratic and military establishments and of resisting, or, if necessary, absorbing, barbarian invaders.

Another was the absence in the West of anything comparable to the Chinese writing system, which provided lasting cultural homogeneity, and to the Chinese examination system, which provided administrative efficiency and stability. Finally, the Roman Empire had to cope with more formidable enemies on its frontiers. Being located on the western receiving end of the steppe invasion route, Europe bore the brunt of attacks by virtually all the nomadic peoples. Furthermore, the Roman Empire's Germanic neighbors were more numerous than the nomads on China's northwestern frontier. Also the neighboring Persians and Arabs were more advanced, and a more serious and lasting military threat, than were China's nomadic neighbors. For all these reasons the invasions in the West dragged on centuries longer than in the rest of Eurasia. Hence the unique denouement in the West—the absolute and final dissolution of the Roman imperial structure and of its classical civilization.

This outcome is of such significance that it can fairly be described as a major turning point in world history. It was so fateful because the wholesale destruction cleared the way for innovation that was long overdue. One historian has presented the following conclusion concerning the end of the Roman Empire:

All in all, the invasions gave the coup de gráce to a culture which had come to a standstill after reaching its apogee and seemed doomed to wither away. We are reminded of the cruel bombings in our own day which destroyed ramshackle old buildings and so made possible the reconstruction of towns on more modern lines.[7]

But this "culture" was no different from all the others of Eurasia that were also at a "standstill." Those others, however, managed to survive the invasions and to gain a new lease on life. But it was the old life that was prolonged, whereas the West, with the death of the Roman Empire, was able to start a new life—to make a new beginning.

The significance of this new beginning becomes clear if it is recalled that during the ancient period the Middle East had been the center of initiative from which had diffused the fundamental innovations of those millennia. But during the classical period it was Europe, India, and China that generated most of the innovations, while the Middle East lagged

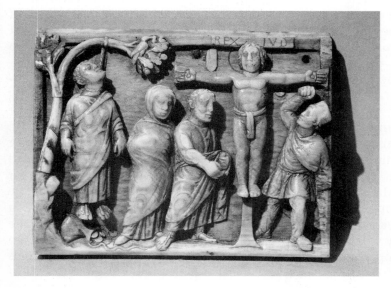

This late-Roman ivory plaque shows a scene from Christ's Passion. The art of the late empire was transitional between the classical past and the medieval future.

behind. And the reason was precisely that the ancient civilization of the Middle East had survived the invasions of the second millennium B.C.E., whereas the ancient civilizations of the peripheral regions had gone under, leaving the way clear for a fresh start—for the emergence of the new classical civilizations.

So it was during the transition from the classical to the medieval civilizations. But this time the existing classical civilizations survived everywhere except in the West. For this reason the West alone was free to strike out in new directions and to evolve, during the Medieval Age, a new technology, new institutions, and new ideas—in short, a new civilization. And in modern times this new civilization proved its superiority over the "standstill" civilizations of the rest of Eurasia—indeed of the entire world—as inevitably and completely as the agricultural civilizations had triumphed over tribal cultures at an earlier time.

SUGGESTED READINGS

The problem of the rise and fall of empires is considered in the following collection of readings: S. W. Eisentadt, ed., *The Decline of Empires* (Prentice Hall, 1967); and C. M. Cipolla, ed., *The Economic Decline of Empires* (Methuen, 1979). Various viewpoints regarding the decline of Rome are presented by P. Brown, *The World of Late Antiquity* (Harcourt, 1971); S. Magzarino, *The End of the Ancient World* (Faber and Faber, 1966); and F. W. Walbank, *The Awful Revolution* (University of Liverpool, 1969).

The invaders of the Roman Empire are considered by R. MacMullen, *Enemies of the Roman Order* (Oxford University, 1967); E. A. Thompson, *A History of Attila and the Huns* (Clarendon, 1948); O. J. Maenchen-Helfen, *The World of the Huns* (University of California, 1973); T. S. Burns, *A History of the Ostrogoths* (Indiana University, 1984); and G. Jones, *A History of the Vikings* (Oxford University, 1968). The developments following the invasions are analyzed in J. D. Randers-Pherson, *Barbarians and Romans: The Birth and Struggle of Europe, A.D. 400–700* (University of Oklahoma, 1983); in W. C. Bark, *Origins of the Medieval World* (Stanford University, 1958), which stresses the creativity of the early Middle Ages in the West; and in R. S. Hoyt, ed., *Life and Thought in Early Middle Ages* (University of Minnesota, 1967), which also interprets this period as one of transition and transformation. This thesis has been presented more recently by M. Grant, *Dawn of the Middle Ages* (McGraw-Hill, 1981).

NOTES

1. J. M. Keynes, *Essays in Persuasion* (Harcourt, 1932), pp. 360–361.
2. A. H. M. Jones, "The Decline and Fall of the Roman Empire," *History*, XL (October 1955), p. 220.
3. Cited by F. Klemm, *A History of Western Technology* (Allen & Unwin, 1959), p. 23.
4. W. W. Rostow, *The Process of Economic Growth*, 2nd ed. (Norton, 1962), pp. 311–312.
5. Cited by S. H. Gross and M. W. Bingham, *Women in Medieval-Renaissance Europe* (Glenhurst, 1983), p. 11.
6. Cited by M. Hadas, *A History of Rome* (Doubleday, 1956), pp. 204–205.
7. R. Lopez, *The Birth of Europe* (M. Evans, 1967), p. 58.

What It Means for Us Today

CIVILIZATION: CURSE OR BLESSING?

In all civilizations there have been poets and thinkers who have looked to the past with longing. They have regarded the prehistoric human as the "noble savage," untainted by the corrupting influence of civilization. Long ago, "in the beginning," during that wonderful first chapter of human existence, there was paradise on earth. In the Hindu epics there are passages extolling an idyllic past in which castes were absent and humans could enjoy life in freedom and security. Likewise Hesiod, an eighth-century-B.C.E. Greek poet, described a Golden Age of long ago and then traced humanity's declining fortunes through the Silver and Iron ages to the deplorable present in which the author lived.

This concept of original bliss had some basis in historical fact. As far as economic and social relationships were concerned, the tribal peoples before the advent of civilization had enjoyed free and equal access to the natural resources necessary for livelihood. Economic equality and social homogeneity had been the hallmark of their Neolithic villages. But when the tribal peoples became peasants they no longer had free access to land and they no longer enjoyed the full product of their labor. Their specific obligations varied from region to region, but the result everywhere was the same. After making the payments required by the state, the church, the landlord, and the money-lender, the peasants were left with half or less of what they produced. They were left with only enough for sheer existence. Historians estimate that in the civilizations around the world, the ruling elites comprised only 1 to 2 percent of the total population. Yet everywhere they extorted half to two-thirds of the entire national income. This fact explains why a peasant uprising occurred almost every year during the millennia of China's history, and why tsarist Russia was wracked by 1,467 revolts between 1801 and 1861, when the serfs at last were emancipated.

The coming of civilization brought drastic change in political as well as economic relationships. The Neolithic villagers had been subject to only a few controls, whether internal or external. But tribal chiefs and elders now were replaced by a king or emperor and by an ever-present bureaucracy, including palace functionaries, provincial and district officials, judges, clerks, and accountants. Working closely with this imperial administration was the ecclesiastical hierarchy that was also an essential feature of civilization. In place of the former shaman, who had been a "leisure-time specialist," there was the priest, a "full-time specialist." Now it was possible to develop an official theology and a priestly hierarchy. Both the theology and the hierarchy served to buttress the existing social order. They gave political institutions and leaders divine sanction and attributes. For example, the Egyptian pharaoh was not only the ruler of his country but also the "living god." This coupling of divine and secular authority provided most powerful support for the status quo. It was a rare individual who dared risk both swift punishment in this life and everlasting punishment in the afterlife.

The transformation of culture wrought by civilization was fundamental and enduring. The culture of a Neolithic village had been autonomous and homogeneous. All members had shared common knowledge, customs, and attitudes and had not depended on outside sources for the maintenance of their way of life. But with civilization, a new and more complex society emerged. In addition to the traditional culture of village agricultural people, there was now the new culture of the scribes, who knew the mysterious art of writing; of the priests, who knew the secrets of the heavens; of the artists, who knew how to paint and carve; and of the merchants, who exchanged goods with lands beyond deserts and seas. So there was no longer a single culture. Instead there developed what has been called high culture and low culture. The high culture was to be found in the schools, temples, and palaces of the cities; the low culture was in the villages. The high culture was passed on in writing by philosophers, theologians, and literary people; the low culture was passed on by word of mouth among illiterate peasants.

The high and low cultures of the various civilizations differed in details but were all similar in essentials. They were all based on "sacred books," such as the Indian Vedas, the Buddhist Canon, the Chinese Classics, and the Christian Old and New Testaments. Since these texts were the basis of knowledge, they dominated education. Anyone who wished to get ahead had to memorize large portions of them. The sacred books also were used to enforce loyalty and obedience. Repudiation of official teachings or challenge to the social order were branded as crimes punishable in this world and in the next. The "hells" that were so prominent in all high cultures were eternal concentration camps for those who dared resist their secular or religious leaders.

The low cultures of all civilizations also were essentially the same. Peasants everywhere had a considerable body of factual information concerning the care of animals and plants. They all regarded hard work as a virtue and looked down on town people as weaklings who tired easily. All peasants also had a common passion to own a plot of land, a few animals, and the simple tools of field and shop. These meant independence and security, and to attain them all peasantries stubbornly resisted, and still resist, intervention, whether by a landlord or by today's government-run collective. The "rugged individualism" of the peasant was balanced, however, by the communal life and relationships of the village. The good neighbor was always ready to offer aid and sympathy when needed, as well as to participate in house-raisings, housewarmings, harvest festivals, and other community affairs.

Relations between the high and low cultures usually were strained. On the one hand, the peasants felt superior, regarding country life and agricultural work as morally "good," in contrast to urban life and professions. On the other hand, the peasants were economically and politically subject to the city. The landlords, the tax collectors, the church officials, and the soldiers all came from the city. Their arrogance and arbitrariness made it crystal clear who were the rulers and who the ruled. Whereas the elite viewed their rich life as the product of their own superior mental and moral qualities, their good life was actually made possible by the exploitation of the peasantry. Inevitably, in the course of millennia, the peasants internalized the attitudes of the elite toward them and became servile and obsequious.

It is clear that the coming of civilization was a setback for equality among human beings. Yet civilization also brought great gains and achievements. Viewed in the light of historical perspective, it was a major step forward despite all the injustice and exploitation. In this respect it resembled the industrial revolution, which at first caused painful social disruption and human suffering, but which in the long run decisively advanced human productivity and well-being. So it was with the coming of civilization. The average Neolithic tribal member probably led a more rounded and satisfying life than the average peasant or urban worker. But precisely because tribal culture was comfortable and tension-free, it was also relatively unproductive. The demands of the tax collector, the priest, and the landowner were harsh, but they were also effective in stimulating output. Positive proof of this enhanced productivity can be seen in the enormous population increase in the agrarian river valleys. Living standards also rose along with population figures. Certainly the monarchs and the top officials, both secular and ecclesiastical, enjoyed a variety of food and drink, along with richness in clothing and housing, that no tribal chieftain could ever have imagined. The new middle classes—merchants, scribes, lower officials, and clergy—also were able to lead lives that probably were as pleasant and refined as those enjoyed by their counterparts today. Even the masses may in some cases have been better off in the material sense, if not the psychosocial.

Civilization, with the new art of writing, made it possible to accumulate more and more knowledge and transmit it to successive generations. Various sciences, including mathematics, astronomy, and medicine, were able to take root and to flourish. Also the appearance of wealthy upper classes gave opportunities for the creativity of architects, sculptors, painters, musicians, and poets. The results of this creativity we can see today in masterpieces such as the Parthenon, the Taj Mahal, and Notre Dame Cathedral.

These precious gains benefited the few much more than the many, who in the final analysis bore the costs of the high culture. But the important point insofar as the whole history of humanity is concerned is that the advances were made. And it was these advances, accumulating through the millennia, that finally allowed us to gain such mastery over nature and to attain such productivity through science and technology which today benefit the many along with the few.

It is true that many millions of people are still illiterate, diseased, and hungry. But that condition is very different from the mid-fourteenth century, when a third to a half of Europe's total population was wiped out by the Black Death. It is different also from 1846, when a million Irish died of hunger because of the potato blight, and from 1876, when 5 million Indians starved to death when their crops failed. These victims of plague and famine could not possibly have been saved because the people of those times lacked the necessary knowledge.

Today we have that knowledge, and therefore we have the potential to free ourselves from millennia-old scourges. It is tragic that the potential has not yet been realized, but the fact remains that it does exist. And it exists because of the advances made possible in the past by the different civilizations of the human race. Therefore, to answer the question, has civilization been a curse or a blessing?—in the past it has been both. What it will be in the future depends on whether the knowledge accumulated from past civilizations is used for destructive or constructive purposes.

SUGGESTED READINGS

Archeologists and anthropologists have written thought-provoking books on the relative merits of civilization: Chang Kwang-Chih, *Early Chinese Civilization: Anthropological Perspectives* (Harvard University, 1972); V. Gordon Childe, *Man Makes Himself* (Mentor, 1951); R. Redfield, *Peasant Society and Culture: An Anthropological View to Civilization* (University of Chicago, 1956); L. A. White, *The Evolution of Culture; The Development of Civilization to the Fall of Rome* (McGraw-Hill, 1959); and W. Goldschmidt, *Man's Way* (Holt, 1959). Also noteworthy are the views of the distinguished philosopher K. Jaspers in his *The Origin and Goal of History* (Yale University, 1953), and *Man in the Modern Age* (Doubleday Anchor, 1957). Other viewpoints are presented by W. W. Wagar, *Building the City of Man* (Grossman, 1971); and H. Baudet, *Paradise on Earth: Some Thoughts on European Images of Non-European Man* (Yale University, 1965).

PART III

Medieval Civilizations of Eurasia, 500–1500

Like the Classical Age, the Medieval Age was heralded by invasions—by the Dorians, Aryans, and Zhou in the first case, and by the Germans, Huns, and Turks in the second. There the parallel ends, however, for the medieval centuries, unlike the classical, suffered continued invasions that affected virtually all regions of Eurasia. Beginning in the seventh century there were the invasions of the Islamic warriors, who overran not only the entire Middle East, where they originated, but eventually North Africa, Spain, the Balkans, India, Southeast Asia, and much of central Asia. Even more extensive were the conquests of the Turks and the Mongols during the half-millennium between 1000 and 1500. They encompassed the great bulk of the Eurasian landmass from the Baltic Sea to the Pacific Ocean.

Despite their fury and range, these great conquests did not uproot civilization in most of Eurasia as did the earlier incursions of the Dorians, Aryans, and Zhou. By medieval times most civilizations had sunk roots too deep to be pulled up so easily. Thus the traditional civilizations everywhere survived. In China, for example, the native Ming dynasty replaced the Mongol Yüan, and the country returned with a vengeance to age-old ways. In the sprawling Moslem world the indigenous Greco-Roman, Iranian, Semitic, and Egyptian traditions were not wiped out but rather were fused into the civilization of Islam. Likewise the East Roman Empire continued without interruption for a full millennium as the Byzantine Empire, so that its inhabitants referred to themselves in modern times as "Romaioi," or Romans.

The one exception to this general pattern, as noted in the preceding chapter, was in the West. There, and there alone, the prevailing classical civilization was torn up root and branch. Only in the West, therefore, was the ground sufficiently cleared for a new civilization to emerge. In contrast to the traditional civilizations of the rest of Eurasia, the new civilization was free to develop along fresh lines.

It was this unique feature of the West that enabled it to develop the economic vigor, the technological skills, and the social dynamism to expand overseas and to gain control of the sea routes of the world. With this fateful development the Medieval Age came to an end. But it should be noted that it ended not with land invasions by Eurasian nomads, as did the ancient and classical periods, but rather with the maritime enterprise of the West. The overseas activities of Western explorers, merchants, missionaries, and settlers marked the transition from medieval to modern times, and from the Eurasian to the global phase of world history.

Medieval Civilizations Complete Eurasian Unification

> What has emerged is a sense of the remarkable complexity of the interplay between the Occident and East Asia from Roman and Han times onward. This involved a two-way traffic, in many items, along many routes, and of varying density in different periods. . . . Despite difficult communication, mankind in the Old World at least has long lived in a more unified realm of discourse than we have been prepared to admit.
>
> *Lynn White, Jr.*

Just as an emerging Eurasian unity differentiated the Classical Age from the Ancient Age, so now a full-fledged Eurasian unity differentiated the Medieval Age from the Classical Age. The early stage had been attained as a result of improved technology, particularly the large-scale production of iron, with its manifold repercussions in all aspects of life. (See Chapter 4.) Likewise full unity was now made possible by further technological advances, especially in shipbuilding and navigation. But more significant during these centuries was a political consideration—the existence for the first time of tremendous empires. These empires did not comprise merely river valleys as in the Ancient Age, nor did they encompass merely regions as

in the Classical Age. Now they reached across several regions at once to embrace a large proportion of the entire Eurasian landmass.

As we have seen, the great Alexander knew nothing of the Ganges valley or of China. And virtually no direct relations existed between the later Roman and Han empires at the opposite ends of Eurasia. Alexander's empire was primarily confined to the Middle East, and the Roman and Han empires were for all practical purposes restricted to the western and eastern tips of Eurasia. In striking contrast, during the medieval period the Islamic Empire by the mid-eighth century stretched from the Pyrenees to the Indian Ocean, and from Morocco to the borders of China. In later centuries Islam expanded much further into central Asia, Southeast Asia, and Africa's interior. Even more impressive was the thirteenth-century Mongol Empire that included Korea, China, all of central Asia, Russia, and most of the Middle East—the greatest empire of all time.

Empires of such unprecedented size eliminated the age-old regional isolation. Direct contact and interaction among the various parts of the landmass were now possible. This chapter will consider the nature of the resulting new bonds—commercial, technological, religious, and intellectual.

I. COMMERCIAL BONDS

In classical times, the existence of the large Roman and Han empires at the opposite ends of the Eurasian trade routes stimulated commerce at all points between them. Conversely, the disintegration of these empires undermined and reduced this commerce. It revived, however, and reached new heights during medieval times with the appearance of the Islamic and later the Mongol empires.

The Moslem conquests unified the entire Middle East, through which ran all the trans-Eurasian trade routes—both the land routes that terminated at various Black Sea and Syrian ports, and the sea routes that ran through the Red Sea and the Persian Gulf. Particularly flourishing was the trade across the Arabian Sea with the Malabar coast of southwest India. Sizable settlements of Moslem merchants, mostly Arabs and Persians, grew up in the ports of India and Ceylon. Horses; silver; wrought-iron objects; and linen, cotton, and woolen fabrics were shipped from west to east, where they were exchanged for silks, precious stones, teak, and assorted spices.

Moslem merchants went on from India and Ceylon to Kalah Bar (Kedah) on the Malay coast. From there, some sailed on to Sumatra and Java, and others went through the Malacca Straits and then north to Kanfu (Canton) in south China. The customary schedule was to leave the Persian Gulf in September or October, sail with the northeast monsoon to India and Malaya, and arrive in the China Sea in time for the southern monsoon to Canton. There the Moslem merchants spent the summer, and then they returned

learned weather patterns

with the northeast monsoon to the Malacca Straits and across the Bay of Bengal, arriving back in the Persian Gulf in the early summer—making a round trip of a year and a half.

After the first Moslem reached Canton in 671, considerable numbers settled there as they had in the various Indian Ocean ports. Granted autonomy by the local authorities, they selected their own headman, who was responsible for maintaining order in their section of the city. The descendants of some of these Moslem families later entered the Chinese civil service, as Marco Polo was also to do. By 758 the Moslems were numerous enough to attack Canton, and as a result the Chinese closed the port to foreign trade. Reopened in 792, Canton continued to be a center for Moslem traders until 878, when they were massacred by rebellious Chinese bands. Thereafter Moslem and Chinese merchants met at Kalah Bar in Malaya to exchange their commodities. *got around wars to trade*

With the advent of the Sung dynasty (960–1127), the Chinese ports again were reopened to foreigners. During the Sung period the Chinese made considerable progress in shipbuilding and navigation. By the end of the twelfth century they were replacing the Moslems in the waters of east and Southeast Asia. When the Mongols conquered China and founded the Yüan dynasty (1279–1368), Chinese ships were the largest and best-equipped, and Chinese merchants were settling in various ports in Southeast Asia and India. Marco Polo, who in 1291 accompanied a Mongol princess around Southeast Asia to Iran, witnessed and described the vigor of Chinese maritime enterprise. So did the Arab traveler Ibn Battuta, who fifty years later chose to make his way from India to China on a Chinese junk. Noteworthy also is the nature of China's imports and exports, which reflected its leading position in the world's economy during this period. Apart from fine cotton textiles, the imports were raw materials such as hides and horses from central Asia, and fine woods, gems, spices, and ivory from south Asia. Conversely, Chinese exports, apart from some minerals, were manufactured goods such as books, paintings, and especially porcelains and silks.

During the Ming dynasty (1368–1644), Chinese maritime activity reached its height,

Seventeeth-century leather wall hanging of bustling seaports during the Sung dynasty.

Chinas expeditions were far more remarkable than Portugese

ending in a remarkable but short-lived naval domination of the Pacific and Indian oceans in the early fifteenth century. For example, a series of seven expeditions was sent out between 1405 and 1433 under the superintendency of the chief court eunuch, a certain Cheng Ho. These expeditions were unprecedented in their magnitude and in their achievements. The first, made up of sixty-two ships and 28,000 men, sailed as far as Java, Ceylon, and Calicut. On the return a flotilla of Sumatran pirates tried to block the way, but they were completely annihilated. The later expeditions pressed on further, reaching as far as the east coast of Africa and the entrances to the Persian Gulf and the Red Sea. More than thirty ports in the Indian Ocean were visited by the Chinese, and everywhere they persuaded or compelled the local rulers to recognize the suzerainty of the Ming emperor. And all this at a time when the Portuguese were just beginning to feel their way down the coast of Africa, where they did not reach Cape Verde until 1455! (See map of Early Fifteenth-Century Chinese and Portuguese Voyages, p. 168.)

These extraordinary Chinese expeditions were suddenly halted by imperial order in 1433. The reasons for their beginning as well as for their ending remain a mystery. It is believed that the expeditions may have been launched to compensate for the loss of foreign trade over the land routes when the Mongol Empire disintegrated. Or they may have been sent to enhance the prestige of the imperial court or to find the emperor's predecessor, who had disappeared underground as a Buddhist monk. Some think that the expeditions may have been halted because of their excessive cost or because of the traditional rivalry between court eunuchs and

Early Fifteenth-Century Chinese and Portuguese Voyages

Legend:
- ....▸ Portuguese routes, 1418-1460
- —▸ Chinese routes (Cheng Ho), 1405-1433

Confucian bureaucrats. In any case, the withdrawal of the Chinese left a power vacuum in the waters of east and south Asia. Japanese pirates harried the coasts of China, and in the Indian Ocean the Moslem Arabs regained their former primacy. But adept though they were as merchants, the Arabs lacked the unity and the resources to develop naval power as had the Chinese. Thus when the Portuguese sailed around Africa into the Indian Ocean in 1498, they encountered no effective resistance and proceeded to establish their domination.

Meanwhile a great revolution in land trade had occurred with the rise of the Mongol Empire. For the first and only time in history one political authority extended across the breadth of Eurasia—from the Baltic Sea to the Pacific, and from Siberia to the Persian Gulf. A mid-fourteenth-century Italian handbook summarized the commercial significance of this Pax Mongolica in describing a trade route running across central Asia from its beginning point at Tana at the mouth of the Don River:

The road you travel from Tana to Cathay [China] is perfectly safe, whether by day or by night, according to what the merchants say who have used it. . . . You may reckon that from Tana to Sarai [on the Volga] the road is less safe than on any other part of the journey; and yet even when this part of the road is at its worst, if you are some sixty men in the company you will go as safely as if you were in your own house.[1]

When Kublai Khan in 1264 moved his capital from Karakorum in Mongolia to Peking, China was automatically opened to the European merchants trading along the trans-Eurasian routes. The first Europeans to arrive at Kublai's new court were not diplomatic emissaries but two Venetian merchants, Nicolo and Maffeo Polo. Of greater economic importance than access to China was access for the first time to the source of spices in India and the East Indies. Hitherto spices had reached Europe via two routes: through the Red Sea and Egypt, or to the Persian Gulf and then by caravan routes to ports on the Black Sea or the eastern Mediterranean. The first route was controlled by Arabs, who shipped the spices to Egypt, and by the Venetians, who loaded cargoes at Alexandria for distribution in Europe. The second route was dominated by the Mongol ruler (Ilkhanate) of Persia and Mesopotamia, and by the Genoese who awaited the spices at the port terminals.

The Genoese, however, were not content to sail only the Black Sea. They ascended the Don River from the Azov Sea in small, light vessels, which they transported, probably on ox-wagons, across the narrow neck of land to the Volga and thence to the Caspian Sea and to Persia. Thus the Genoese were able to reach the Persian Gulf and to go directly to India and the East Indies, where they discovered how cheap the spices were in their places of origin and what fabulous profits had been made during the past centuries by the

*Marco Polo in the court
of Kublai Khan.*

succession of middlemen between the producers in Southeast Asia and the consumers in Europe.

This revival of overland trade during the Pax Mongolica proved short-lived. One reason was the expulsion of the Mongols from China in 1368 and the general disintegration of the Mongol Empire, which led to fragmentation in central Asia and hence to the disruption of trans-Eurasian trade. More important was the conversion of Ilkhan Ghazan (1295–1304) to Islam, which automatically barred to European merchants the transit route to the spice islands. Almost all spices henceforth were shipped along the Red Sea–Nile route, with golden profits for the Arab and Venetian middlemen. But other Europeans were unwilling to continue paying exorbitant prices, particularly since they now knew from where the spices came and at what cost; hence the search for a new sea route around the Moslem barrier—a search that was to end with da Gama's great voyage around Africa.

II. TECHNOLOGICAL BONDS

The great Moslem and Mongol empires quickened not only the flow of trade within Eurasia but also the diffusion of technology. An outstanding example is the lateen sail, a tall, triangular, fore-and-aft sail that has always been used on Arab craft. In the Mediterranean, by contrast, the Egyptians, Phoenicians, Greeks, and Romans had used a square sail, which is easier to handle in bad weather. But the Arab sail is much more maneuverable, being able to keep closer to the wind and to tack on rivers and narrow waters. For this reason it soon replaced the square sail in the Levant, and by the eleventh century it had become the normal rig throughout the Mediterranean. Today this triangular sail is known as the "Latin," or "lateen," sail, though it was the Arabs who, with the Moslem invasions, introduced it into the Mediterranean. And from there it spread to the Atlantic, where, during the fifteenth century, Portuguese and Spanish ship designers combined the square sail on the foremast with the lateen on the main and mizzen. The resulting hybrid three-masters were capable of sailing in all reasonable weathers and thus made possible the long ocean voyages of Columbus and da Gama.

The English philosopher Francis Bacon wrote in 1620:

It is well to observe the force and virtue and consequences of discoveries. These are to be seen nowhere more conspicuously than in those three which were unknown to the ancients, and of which the origin, though recent, is obscure and inglorious; namely, printing, gunpowder, and the magnet. For these three have changed the whole face and state of things throughout the world, the first in literature, the second in warfare, the third in navigation; whence have followed innumerable changes; insomuch that no empire, no sect, no star, seems to have exerted greater power and influence in human affairs than these mechanical discoveries.[2]

All three of these inventions, whose historical significance Bacon correctly noted, were of Chinese origin. The oldest existing example of block printing—printing in which a single block of wood is engraved for each page printed—is a Chinese Buddhist sacred text from the year 868. The first invention of separate movable type also is Chinese, the work of a simple artisan who between 1041 and 1049 made movable type of baked clay. In later centuries the Chinese substituted wood and various metals for the clay. The diffusion of these inventions has been traced from China to the Middle East and thence to Europe, where the first example of block printing dates back to 1423, followed in 1456 by the first book printed with movable type—Gutenberg's Bible.

Gunpowder was used in China for fireworks as early as the T'ang dynasty (618–906). By 1120 the Chinese had evolved a weapon known as the "firelance" comprising a stout bamboo tube filled with gunpowder. This was almost certainly the precursor of the metal-barrel gun, which appeared about 1280, though it is not known whether it was first constructed by Chinese or Arabs or Europeans.

The earliest definite reference to magnetism is found in a Chinese book of about 240 B.C.E., but for centuries thereafter the compass was used only for magical purposes. By 1125, however, it was used in navigation, and apparently the Arab merchants who came to China learned of this instrument and introduced it into Europe.

Pattern of Chinese → Arab → Europe

In addition to these three basic inventions, the Chinese gave much more to their Eurasian neighbors. In 105 C.E. they invented paper, the prerequisite for printing. Chinese prisoners of war who were taken to Samarkand in 751 introduced the paper-making process to the Arabs, who in turn spread it to Syria, Egypt, Morocco, and, in 1150, to Spain. From there it passed on to France and the rest of Europe, displacing parchment as it went. Its value is evident in the fact that to produce one copy of the Bible on parchment, the skins of no fewer than three hundred sheep would be required.

Other Chinese inventions that spread throughout Eurasia with profound repercussions were the stern-post rudder, which appeared in Europe about 1180 at the same time as the compass; the foot-stirrup, which made possible the heavily armored feudal knights of medieval Europe; and the breast-strap harness, which rests on the horse's shoulders and allows it to pull with full force without choking as had been the case with the old throat harness. Finally the Chinese domesticated numerous fruits and plants, which were spread throughout Eurasia, usually by the Arabs. These include the chrysanthemum, the camellia, the azalea, the tea rose, the Chinese aster, the lemon, and the orange. The orange is still called "Chinese apple" in Holland and Germany.

III. RELIGIOUS BONDS

The medieval period was characterized not only by an unprecedented trans-Eurasian exchange of goods and technologies, but also by an unprecedented diffusion of religious creeds. In the case of Christianity and Buddhism, this began toward the end of the classical period and continued during the medieval. (See Chapter 4, Section III.) But by all odds the outstanding religious change during the medieval centuries was the appearance of Islam. Apart from its teachings, which will be noted in the following chapter, the new religion profoundly affected extensive regions of Eurasia and Africa as it burst out from the Arabian peninsula following the death of Mohammed in 632 C.E.

The spread of Islam (the details of which will be noted later) occurred in two stages. During the first, from 632 to 750, it flooded over the Middle East and then west to the Pyrenees and east to central Asia. The net effect was the virtual transformation of the Mediterranean into a Moslem lake. But the second stage of expansion between 1000 and 1500 made the Indian Ocean also a Moslem preserve, for during these centuries Islam expanded much further—into India, Southeast Asia, and Africa.

The vast extension of the domains of Islam naturally alarmed the rulers of Christendom,

Movable Chinese wood types: Four types carved with characters representing words and syllables.

who were now isolated on the western tip of Eurasia. This explains their ambivalent reaction to the appearance of the Mongols in the thirteenth century. They were terrified by the slaughter inflicted by the Mongol horsemen. But the picture was not all black, because the Mongols also crushed the Moslems in Persia and Mesopotamia. The Christian rulers therefore hoped they might be able to convert the pagan Mongols to Christianity, as they had earlier converted the pagan Magyars and Vikings.

The pope sent two missions to the court of the grand khan in Karakorum in northern Mongolia. They tried to persuade the khan to adopt Christianity and to join the pope in a crusade against the Moslems. But the traditional magicians or shamans were very influential at the

Fifteenth-century Arab manuscript from the collection of the National Library, Paris, showing Mohammed and his daughter Fatima.

court, and the missions failed to win any converts. They were successful, however, in gathering the first reliable information about Mongol customs and military tactics. They also learned that twenty days' journey east from Karakorum was the mysterious land of Cathay, or China. It was known to be not only wealthy but also non-Islamic and, therefore, a possible ally against the Moslems.

Since China was a part of the great Mongol Empire, Kublai Khan moved his capital in 1264 from Karakorum to Cambaluc, or modern Peking. The first Europeans to arrive in the capital were the two aforementioned Venetian merchants, Nicolo and Maffeo Polo. Kublai welcomed them warmly, questioned them about Europe, and gave them letters to deliver to the pope. In these letters he asked for a hundred missionary-scholars to come to his court to instruct his people and to dispute with representatives of other religions.

In making this request it is doubtful that Kublai was motivated by zeal for Christianity. More likely he wanted trained men for his bureaucracy, since he had only recently conquered China and did not wish to risk the appointment of too many Chinese to higher offices. In fact he did employ large numbers of foreigners in his service, and he was careful to maintain a balance among the various elements in order to safeguard his authority.

IV. EXPANDING HORIZONS

The great breakthrough in European knowledge of the world came with the Mongol Empire. Its existence brought about the transition from a Mediterranean to a Eurasian perspective, just as the voyages of Columbus and da Gama later brought about a transition from a Eurasian to a global perspective. The travels of merchants, missionaries, and prisoners of war revealed the existence of a great empire in the Far East that not only equaled but surpassed Europe in population, wealth, and level of civilization. Nor was this a one-way process, for the East now became aware of the West as well. Marco Polo, who opened the eyes of the West to Cathay, had his counterparts in China and the Middle East.

MARCO POLO'S NEW WORLD

Medieval Eurasia was united primarily by merchants who traveled back and forth from the Mediterranean Sea to China and Southeast Asia. The following excerpts from Marco Polo's great travel account make clear how much the horizons of the medieval world were opening up.*

As regards the size of this city [Cambaluc, or modern Beijing], you must know that it has a compass of 24 miles, for each side of it hath a length of 6 miles. . . . There are 12 gates, and over each gate there is a great and handsome palace. . . . The streets are so straight and wide that you can see right along them from end to end and from one gate to the other. And up and down the city there are beautiful palaces, and many great and fine hostelries, and fine houses in great numbers. . . .

And first let us speak of the [Chinese] ships in which merchants go to and fro amongst the Isles of India. These ships, you must know, are of fir timber. They have but one deck, though each of them contains some 50 or 60 cabins, wherein the merchants abide greatly at their ease, every man having one to himself. The ship hath but one rudder, but it hath four masts; and sometimes they have two additional masts, which they ship and unship at pleasure. . . . Each of their great ships requires at least 200 mariners [some of them 300]. They are indeed of great size, for one ship shall carry 5000 to 6000 baskets of pepper.

Chipangu [Japan] is an Island towards the east in the high seas 1500 miles distant from the Conti-

nent; and a very great Island it is. The people are white, civilized, and well-favoured. They are Idolaters, and are dependent on nobody. And I can tell you the quantity of gold they have is endless.

When you sail from Chamba [Indochina], 1500 miles in a course between south and south-east, you come to a great Island called Java. And the experienced mariners of those Islands who know the matter well, say that it is the greatest Island in the world, and has a compass of more than 3000 miles. It is subject to a great King and tributary to no one else in the world. The people are Idolaters. The Island is of surpassing wealth, producing black pepper, nutmegs, spikenard, galingale, cubebs, cloves, and all other kinds of spices. . . .

When you leave the Island of Seilan [Ceylon] and sail westward about 60 miles, you come to the great province of Maabar which is styled India the Greater; it is best of all the Indies and is on the mainland. . . . The people are Idolaters, and many of them worship the ox [sacred cow], because it is a creature of such excellence. They would not eat beef for anything in the world, nor would they on any account kill an ox.

*H. Yule, ed. and trans., *The Book of Ser Marco Polo* (Scribner's, 1903), vol. 1, pp. 423–426; vol. 2, pp. 249–250, 253–254.

We know of Chinese trading colonies in Moscow, Tabriz, and Novgorod during this period. Chinese engineers were employed on irrigation projects in Mesopotamia. Also there are records of Chinese bureaucrats who accompanied Genghis Khan on his campaigns and inspection tours from one end of Eurasia to the other. In addition there was the Christian Nestorian monk Rabban Bar Sauma, who was born in Peking and who traveled in 1278 to the Moslem

court in Baghdad. From there he was sent by the Mongols to Europe to seek Christian help against Islam. Starting out in 1287, he traveled to Constantinople, Naples, Rome, Paris, and London, meeting en route both Philip IV of France and Edward I of England. The most wide-ranging of these medieval travelers was the Moslem Ibn Battuta (1304–1378). Starting from his native Morocco, he made the pilgrimage to Mecca and journeyed on through Samarkand to

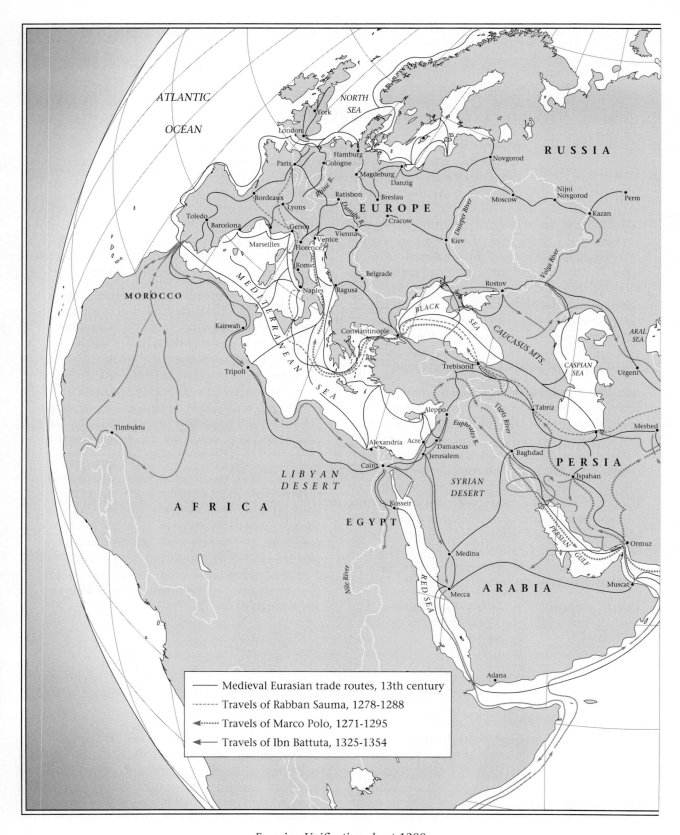

Eurasian Unification about 1300

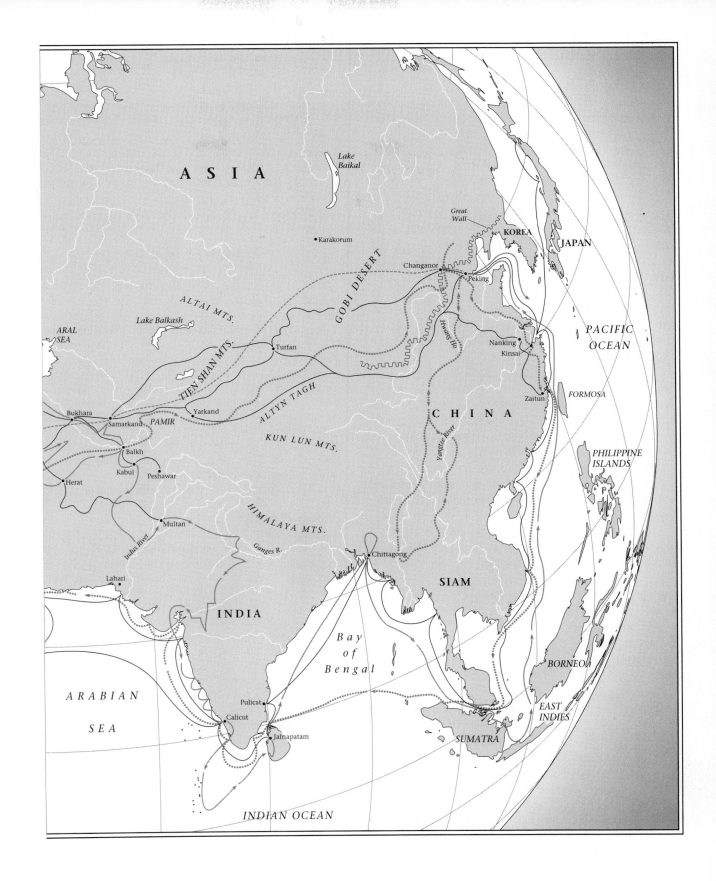

India, where he served as judge and also as ambassador to China. Returning later to Morocco, he resumed his travels, crossing north to Spain and then south to the interior of Africa, where he reached Timbuktu. When he finally returned to Morocco and settled down, he had traveled no fewer than 75,000 miles.

By all odds the most important traveler for the Western world was the famous Marco Polo. Accompanying his father and his uncle on their second journey to China, he arrived at Kublai Khan's court in 1275. He favorably impressed the khan and served him for seventeen years in various ways that required him to travel throughout the country. As an official he carefully observed the inhabitants and resources of the lands through which he journeyed, noting such things as "a kind of black stone, which is dug out of the mountains like any other kind of stone and burns like wood." In 1292 he escorted a Mongol princess on a voyage around Southeast Asia and across the Indian Ocean to Persia where she was to be the bride of the Moslem ruler. Marco Polo then continued westward to his native Venice, arriving there in 1295 after an absence of twenty-five years. Shortly afterward he was captured in a battle with the Genoese, and while in prison he dictated his account of his travels.

He told of the grand khan's palace with its gardens and artificial lakes and its elephants with harnesses of silver and precious stones. He told also of roads that were paved and raised above the surrounding ground so that they might drain easily; of the Grand Canal through which merchant vessels passed each year; of ports with ships larger than any known in Europe; and of lands that produced spices, silk, ginger, sugar, camphor, cotton, salt, saffron, sandalwood, and porcelain. Marco also described all the fabulous countries he visited and heard about while escorting the Chinese princess to Persia—Singapore, Java, Sumatra, Ceylon, India, Socotra, Madagascar, Arabia, Zanzibar, and Abyssinia.

It all seemed so fantastic and exaggerated that he was dubbed Il millione, "the man who talks in millions." Actually he had provided Europeans with the most comprehensive and authoritative account of China available until the mid-sixteenth century. The title of his book is significant—*The Description of the World*. In fact this work had suddenly doubled the size of the known world for Westerners (as shown in the map of Eurasian Unification about 1300, pp. 174–75.) Marco Polo opened up new vistas for his contemporaries fully as much as Columbus was to do two centuries later. Indeed it was his tantalizing picture of Cathay and the Spice Islands that beckoned the great explorers onward as they sought a direct sea passage after the Moslems had blocked the overland routes.

SUGGESTED READINGS

The most important works dealing with all types of interaction within Eurasia are the first volume of J. Needham, *Science and Civilisation in China* (Cambridge University, 1954); J. H. Bentley, *Old World Encounters* (Oxford University, 1993); and J. L. Abu-Lughod, *Before European Hegemony: The World System, A.D. 1250-1350* (Oxford University, 1989). The maritime trade is described by G. F. Hourani, *Arab Seafaring in the Indian Ocean in Ancient and Early Medieval Times* (Princeton University, 1951); P. D. Curtin, *Cross-Cultural Trade in World History* (Cambridge University, 1984); K. N. Chaudhuri, *Trade and Civilization in the Indian Ocean* (Cambridge University, 1985); and Vol. 4, Part III of the Needham study, which deals with Chinese maritime enterprise, including the Ming voyages. The overland trade is analyzed by G. F. Hudson, *Europe and China: A Survey of Their Relations from the Earliest Times to 1800* (Beacon, 1961); and by P. Yung, *The Silk Road: Islam's Overland Route to China* (Oxford University, 1986). An analysis of Eurasian trade in general is given in C. G. F. Simkin, *The Traditional Trade of Asia* (Oxford University, 1969). For technological exchange, the basic work is the multivolume study by Needham, just listed.

For the experiences of Marco Polo and other travelers, see *The Travels of Marco Polo*, trans. R. E. Latham (Penguin, 1958); L. Olschki, *Marco Polo's Precursors* (Johns Hopkins Press, 1943); I. de Rachewiltz, *Papal Envoys to the Great Khans* (Stanford University, 1971); and R. Dunn, *The Adventures of Ibn Battuta: A Muslim Traveller of the Fourteenth Century* (University of California, 1986), which provides a fascinating panorama of the entire Moslem world.

NOTES

1. H. Yule, ed., *Cathay and the Way Thither*, Hakluyt Society, Series 2, XXXVIII (London, 1914), pp. 152, 154.
2. Francis Bacon, *Novum Organum*, Book I, aphorism, p. 129.

10

Rise of Islam

The burden of the desert of the sea. As whirlwinds in the south pass through; so it cometh from the desert, from a terrible land.

Isaiah 21:1

We have revealed to thee an Arabic Koran, that thou mayest warn Mecca, the Mother of Cities, and those who are about her; that thou mayest give warning of the Day of Judgement, of which is no doubt—when part shall be in Paradise and part in the flame.

Koran, Sura XLII

The centuries between 600 and 1000 saw the emergence of Islam, a major turning point in Eurasian and world history. The spectacular conquests of the Moslem warriors united the entire Middle East as Alexander the Great had done almost a millennium earlier. The Islamic conquests of the seventh and eighth centuries united under the star and crescent all the territories from the Pyrenees to India and from Morocco to central Asia.

More remarkable than these military exploits were the cultural achievements of Islam. Although the conquered territories were the centers of humanity's most ancient civilizations, nevertheless, by the eleventh century, the Arabs had affected both their languages and their cultures. Arabic became the language of everyday use from Persia to the Atlantic. And a new Islamic civilization emerged that was an original synthesis of the preceding Judaic, Perso-Mesopotamian, and Greco-Roman civilizations. This transformation has lasted to the present day, so that Iraqis and Moroccans now have linguistic and cultural ties as strong as those of the English and the Australians.

I. MOHAMMED

Mohammed, the most influential historical personality of the Medieval Age, was born in 569. Since his father died before he was born, and his mother when he was six, Mohammed was brought up first by his grandmother and subsequently by his uncle. Little is known of his youth, though tradition has it that at the age of twelve he was taken by his uncle on a caravan to Syria. In the course of that journey he may have picked up some Jewish and Christian lore. At the age of twenty-five he married a wealthy widow, who bore him several daughters and two sons who died in infancy.

About his fortieth year Mohammed went through a period of intense spiritual tension, in the course of which he became convinced that God had chosen him to be a prophet, a successor to Abraham, Moses, and Jesus. Asked to describe the process of revelation, he answered that the entire text of the Koran existed in Heaven and that one fragment at a time was communicated to him, usually by the archangel Gabriel, who made him repeat every word. Mohammed now believed that he had received a divine call to teach of the unity and supreme power of Allah, to warn his people of the Day of Judgment, and to tell them of the rewards for the faithful in Paradise and the punishment of the wicked in Hell.

His teachings were written down soon after his death and became the sacred scripture of the new religion known as Islam, meaning "submission to God's will." Mohammed did not establish an organized priesthood nor did he prescribe specific sacraments essential for salvation. But he did call on his followers to perform certain rituals known as the Five Pillars of Islam:

1. Once in their lives believers must say with full understanding and absolute acceptance, "There is no God but Allah; Mohammed is the Messenger of Allah."
2. Five times daily they must pray—at dawn, at noon, in midafternoon, at dusk, and after it has become dark. Facing in the direction of Mecca, worshipers pray on a carpet, with their shoes removed and heads covered.
3. Moslems must give alms generously, as an offering to Allah and an act of piety.
4. Moslems must fast from daybreak to sunset during the whole month of Ramadan.
5. Once in their lives Moslems, if they can, must make the pilgrimage, or Hadj, to Mecca.

These rituals provided the believers with an extraordinarily powerful social cement. They prayed and fasted together, they assumed responsibility for their less fortunate fellow believers, and they journeyed to Mecca together—rich and poor, yellow, white, brown, and black. Furthermore, the Koran provided guidance for all phases of the life of the faithful—for manners and hygiene, marriage and divorce, commerce and politics, crime and punishment,

Page from an eighth- or ninth-century Qur'an in Kufic script (23.8 x 35.5 cm). Because of the Muslim aversion to images, calligraphy early became a major Islamic art form. The Arabic script developed primarily to render the Qur'anic text as exactly as possible, and the calligraphic art developed along with it. The horizontally elongated Kufic script was the earliest and dominated Qur'anic calligraphy for three centuries.

peace and war. Thus Islam was not only a religion but also a social code and a political system. It offered to its followers both religious commandments and specific guidance for private and public life. There was no split between the secular life and the religious, between the temporal and the spiritual, as there was in the Christian world. What is Caesar's, in Islam, is God's, and what is God's is also Caesar's. The Shari'a, or Holy Law, was until recently the law of the land throughout the Moslem world, and it is still the basic law in individual countries.

Mohammed slowly won converts to these teachings. The first were members of his immediate family and personal friends, who later enjoyed great prestige as "Companions of the Prophet." As the little band of converts grew, the wealthy merchants of Mecca became alarmed for fear that Mohammed's teachings would undermine the older religious beliefs and discourage pilgrims from coming to worship at the shrine of the Black Stone in their city. Because of the growing opposition, Mohammed accepted an invitation to go to Medina, an oasis town on the trade route nearly three hundred miles north of Mecca. There was a mixed population of Arab and Jewish tribes, so Mohammed was welcomed as an arbitrator. His emigration to Medina, known as the hegira, took place in 622, and the Moslem calendar is dated from the beginning of that year.

Since his teachings were based largely on Judaic doctrines, tales, and themes, Mohammed expected the Medina Jews to welcome him as the successor of their own prophets. Instead they ridiculed his claims, so Mohammed turned against them, eventually driving them out of the town and dividing their property among his followers. Gradually Mohammed persuaded the Medina Arabs to accept his religion, and he organized a theocratic state based on his teachings.

From his base in Medina, Mohammed organized attacks on the Mecca caravans. Such raiding was an accepted and popular economic activity among Arab nomads, who now flocked to the banner of the Prophet in the hope of winning booty, and incidentally salvation. By 630 the Moslems were strong enough to capture Mecca, whereupon Mohammed made the Black Stone, housed in the Ka'ba, the chief shrine of his religion. Thus he effected a compromise by which he preserved the basic tenets of his faith and yet rooted it in traditional Arab custom. By the time of his death in 632, most—though by no means all—of the Arab tribes had recognized his overlordship and paid him tribute.

Mohammed had found his native land divided with many local idolatrous practices. He left it with a religion and a book of revelation, and with a community and a state sufficiently well organized and armed to dominate the entire peninsula. Within a century his followers were to march from victory to victory, building an imposing empire across the breadth of Eurasia and spreading his creed, which today boasts half a billion followers, throughout the world.

II. AGE OF CONQUESTS

Precisely because the Moslem community was the product of Mohammed's genius, it now seemed likely with his death to break up into its component elements. The tribal sheikhs, who considered their submission to him ended with his death, stopped their tribute and resumed their freedom of action. This withdrawal, known in Islamic history as the Ridda, or apostasy, was answered with a series of well-planned campaigns that overwhelmed the "apostate" tribes and forced them back into the community of Islam. But the subdued tribes, sullen and resentful, obviously were ready to seize the first opportunity to break away again. The ideal distraction from this disaffection, the Moslem leaders knew, would be to initiate some foreign raids that would promise the booty beloved by every Bedouin. The resultant raids, then, did not begin as religious crusades to propagate the faith. Mohammed did not think of Islam as a universal faith and did not believe that God had chosen him to preach to any other people than his own Arabs. So the Arab raids grew out of the need to keep the turbulent Bedouins preoccupied and loyal to Medina.

The leader of the raids was the caliph, or deputy, who was chosen to represent the Prophet in his secular role. There was no possibility, of course, of a successor to Mohammed as Prophet, but a secular chief of the community was essential. Thus when Abu Bakr, Mohammed's father-in-law, was selected as caliph, it meant that he

The ritual worship, or prayer. These illustrations show the sequence of movement prescribed for the ritual prayers that each Muslim should perform five times a day. Various words of praise, prayer, and recitation from the Qur'an accompany each position and movement. The ritual symbolizes the Muslim's complete obedience to God and recognition of God as the one, eternal, omnipotent Lord of the universe.

was the defender of the faith rather than religious leader. It was under Abu Bakr that the apostate tribes were forced back to the fold and the earliest foreign raids begun.

Under Caliph Omar, who succeeded Abu Bakr in 634, the early raids blossomed into full-fledged campaigns of conquest. They did so because the outwardly powerful Byzantine and Persian empires were soon found to be hollow shells. They had been weakened by the series of wars between them, and their subjects were highly dissatisfied because of heavy taxation and religious persecution. Furthermore the Moslem forces now were growing from raiding parties into large-scale armies as entire tribes from all Arabia migrated northward, attracted by reports of dazzling riches. Any attempt to turn them back to their barren homeland would have provoked a new and possibly fatal Ridda, so the Moslem leaders crossed over into Syria at the head of their Bedouin forces. Thus the great conquests that followed represented the expansion not of Islam but of the Arab tribes, who on many occasions in earlier centuries had pushed northward into the Fertile Crescent. The unprecedented magnitude of the expansion at this time can be explained by the exceptional

weakness of the two empires and by unity and élan engendered by the new Islamic faith.

Once the invasions were under way the Arabs made good use of their experience in desert warfare. Mounted on camels, instead of horses like the Byzantines and Persians, they were able to attack at will and, if necessary, to retreat back to the safety of the desert. Just as the Vikings later were capable of ravaging the coasts of Europe because of their command of the sea, so now the Arabs used their "ships of the desert" to attack the wealthy empires. It was not accidental that in the provinces they conquered, the Arabs established their main bases in towns on the edge of the desert. They used existing cities like Damascus when they were suitably located and when necessary created new ones. These garrison towns met the same need for the emerging Arab Empire that Gibraltar, Malta, and Singapore later did for the British sea empire.

In 636 the Arabs won a decisive victory over the Byzantines in the ravines of the Yarmuk River, a tributary of the Jordan. Attacking in the midst of a blinding sandstorm they almost annihilated a mixed force of Greek, Armenian, and Syrian Christians. Emperor Heraclius fled to Constantinople, abandoning all of Syria to the

CHRISTIAN-MOSLEM MUTUAL SLANDER

Christians and Moslems were mortal enemies in the Middle Ages, fighting on battlefields in Europe, the Middle East, and overseas. They also had a low opinion of each other, as evident in the following two statements. The first is by a Moslem judge of Toledo, Spain, who placed northern Europeans at the bottom of his category of nations.* The second is by a Christian bishop who expressed the common Western belief in Moslem moral degeneracy.**

Judge Sa'id al-Andalusi: . . . As for the rest of this category which cultivated no sciences, they are more like animals than human beings. Those of them who live deep in the north have been so affected by the extreme distance from the sun from the Zenith above their heads, resulting in cold climate and thick atmosphere, that their temperaments have become chilly and their humors rude. Consequently their bodies are huge, their color pale and their hair long. For the same reason they lack keenness in intelligence and perspicacity, are characterized by ignorance and stupidity. Folly and mental blindness prevail among them as among Slavs, Bulgars and other neighboring peoples.

William of Adam, Bishop of Sultaniyah: In the Muslim sect any sexual act at all is not only not forbidden, but allowed and praised. So, as well as the innumerable prostitutes that there are among them, there are many effeminate men who shave the beard, paint their own face, put on women's dress, wear bracelets on the arms and feet. . . . The Muslims, therefore, forgetful of human dignity, are shamelessly attracted by those effeminates, and live together with them as with us husband and wife live together publicly.

*From Islam and the West by P. K. Hitti © 1962 by Litton Educational Publishing Inc.

**N. Daniel, Islam and the West (Edinburgh University Press, 1960), p. 144.

victors. Caliph Omar now turned against the neighboring rich province of Iraq. Its Semitic, partly Christian, population was alienated from its Persian and Zoroastrian masters. This split contributed to the great victory won by the Arabs in the summer of 637 at Qadisiya. The Persian emperor hastily evacuated his nearby capital, Ctesiphon, and fled eastward.

The astonishing triumphs at Yarmuk and Qadisiya left the Moslems with unheard-of riches, which further swelled the flood of Bedouin tribes from the southwestern deserts. Their pressure on the frontiers was irresistible, and the Arab armies rolled onward, westward into Egypt and eastward into Persia. Omar's successors in the caliphate bore the banners of Islam still further afield, driven on by the momentum of victory, of religious enthusiasm, and of nomadic greed. In North Africa the Arab forces, supplemented by native Berber converts, fought their way clear across to Morocco and then crossed the Straits of Gibraltar into Spain. In 711 they defeated Roderick, the last Visigothic king of Spain, and advanced to the Pyrenees and on into France. There, however, they were defeated by Charles Martel at Tours in 732.

At the same time other Moslem forces were expanding eastward into the province of Sind in northwest India. Then they turned northward, advancing as far as Talas in central Asia. Thus what had started out as a simple desert religion had grown quickly into a great Eurasian empire. By 750 Islam ruled over the vast territories stretching from the Pyrenees to Sind, and from Morocco to central Asia. (See map, Expansion of Islam to 1500, p. 182.)

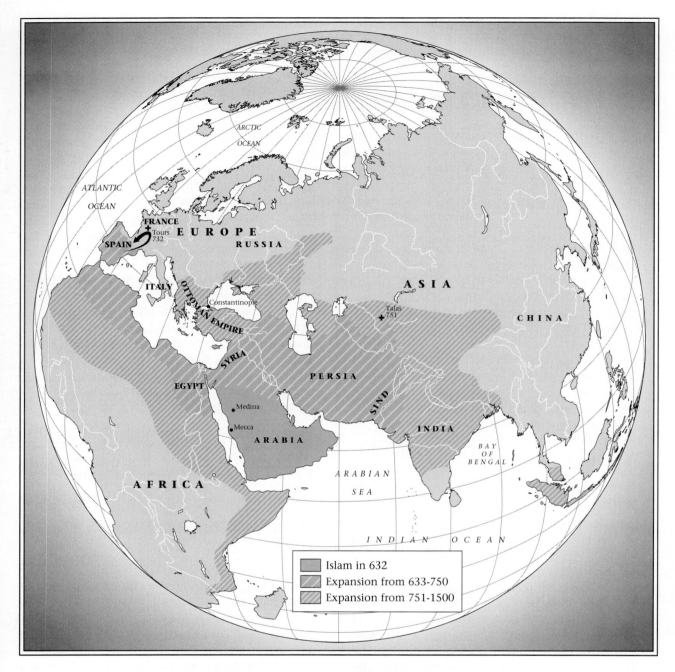

Expansion of Islam to 1500

III. ARAB KINGDOM TO ISLAMIC EMPIRE

With the first phase of expansion completed, the Arabs now settled down to enjoy the fruits of victory. Virtually an army of occupation in their subject lands, they lived mostly in strategically located camp cities, from where they controlled the surrounding countryside. Since Caliph Omar had decided at the outset that his followers should not be given fiefs in the conquered provinces, they now were supported by government pensions. The funds for these pensions were obtained from lands confiscated by the Islamic state and from taxes that were levied at a higher rate on non-Moslems than on Moslems. Apart from this discriminatory taxation, the non-Moslems were left virtually undisturbed. No effort was made to convert them;

indeed conversion was not at all welcomed for it involved, under the circumstances, a decline in revenue. Thus Islam was in effect a privilege of the Arab warrior-aristocracy who ruled over the much more numerous subject peoples.

This arrangement was soon disturbed by the appearance in increasing numbers of the Mawali, or non-Arab Moslems. These converts flocked to the cities, where they served the needs of the Arab aristocracy as servants, artisans, shopkeepers, and merchants. Being Moslems they claimed equality with the Arabs, but it was not granted. Although the Mawali fought in the armies of Islam, they were usually restricted to the infantry, which received a lower rate of pay and less booty than the Arab cavalry.

As the empire expanded and wealth poured into the cities from the subject provinces, the Mawali increased in numbers and wealth. But they were still excluded from the ruling circles, so they became a disaffected urban element, determined to gain status equal to their economic power. Thus the Arab Umayyad dynasty of caliphs, which had moved the capital from Medina to Damascus in 661, came to be regarded with much justification as a parasitic clique that had outlived its usefulness once the conquests were completed. The opposition to the Arab aristocracy, therefore, was both a national and a social movement of protest.

A disputed accession to the throne set off a decade of civil strife that ended in the accession of the Abbasid Caliphate in 750. This represented much more than a mere change of dynasty. The Mawali, and particularly the Persians, now replaced the old aristocracy. The Arabs no longer were a privileged salaried soldiery but were replaced by a royal standing army that was at first largely Persian. The former garrison cities became great commercial centers under Mawali control. Some of the Arabs became absorbed into the mass of townspeople and peasants, whereas others reverted to nomadism.

The imperial structure also changed radically, especially with the shift of the capital from Damascus eastward to Baghdad in 762. In effect this meant that the Abbasid caliphate was turning its back on the Mediterranean and looking to Persia for traditions and support. The caliph no longer was an Arab sheikh but a divinely ordained autocrat—the 'Shadow of God upon Earth." His authority rested not on tribal support but on the salaried bureaucracy and standing army. Thus the caliphate became an oriental monarchy similar to the many that had preceded it in Ctesiphon and Perespolis and Babylon. Under the order and security imposed by this monarchy, a syncretic civilization that was a mixture of Judaic, Greco-Roman, and Perso-Mesopotamian traditions evolved during the following centuries. Islam ceased to be merely the creed of a ruling warrior-aristocracy and became instead a new and distinctive civilization.

IV. ISLAMIC CIVILIZATION

Caliph Mansur, who selected Baghdad as the site for the Abbasid capital, foresaw a glorious future for his choice:

This island between the Tigris in the East and the Euphrates in the West is a market place for the world. All the ships that come up the Tigris . . . will go up and anchor here; wares brought on ships down the Tigris and along the Euphrates will be brought and unloaded here. It will be the highway for the people of the Jabal, Isfahan and the districts of Khurasan. Praise be to God who preserved it for me and caused all those who came before me to neglect it. By God, I shall build it. Then I shall dwell in it as long as I live and my descendants shall dwell in it after me. It will surely be the most flourishing city in the world.[1]

Mansur's expectations were quickly realized. Within a century Baghdad numbered about a million people. In the center was a citadel some two miles in diameter in which were the caliph's residence and the quarters of his officials and guards. Beyond the citadel walls a great commercial metropolis sprang up, supported by the plentiful produce of the fertile Mesopotamian valley. The main crops were wheat, barley, rice, dates, and olives. The provinces contributed rich supplies of metals— silver from the Hindu Kush; gold from Nubia and the Sudan; copper from Isfahan; and iron from Persia, central Asia, and Sicily. Precious stones came from many regions of the empire, while the waters of the Persian Gulf yielded pearls. Industry also flourished, textiles being the most important in the number of workers employed and the value of the output. The art of paper making, learned from Chinese prisoners, spread rapidly across the Islamic world, reaching Spain by 900.

Such a rich economy, stretching across the breadth of the far-flung Abbasid Empire, greatly increased interregional trade. Moslem merchants, as noted in the preceding chapter, traded overland through central Asia and overseas with India, Ceylon, Southeast Asia, and China. A flourishing trade was carried on also with Africa, whence were obtained gold, ivory, ebony, and slaves. We know about commerce with the northern countries from the discovery in Scandinavia of large hoards of Moslem coins dating from the seventh to the eleventh centuries. Such large-scale trade stimulated a highly developed banking system with branches in all leading cities, so that a check could be drawn in Baghdad and cashed in Morocco.

With this solid economic base, the Abbasid caliphs were able to enjoy themselves in their dazzlingly luxurious palaces. *The Thousand and One Nights* describes Harun al-Rashid (786–809), the best known of these caliphs, as a cultured ruler surrounded by poets, musicians, singers, dancers, scholars, and wits. Among the popular indoor games were chess, dice, and backgammon, and outdoor sports included hunting, falconry, hawking, polo, archery, fencing, javelin throwing, and horse racing. Harun was contemporary with Charlemagne, but their respective capitals, Baghdad and Aix-la-Chapelle, were quite incomparable—as incomparable as Baghdad and Paris today, but in the reverse sense.

The Abbasid Caliphate was noted not only for its affluence and splendor but also for its relative tolerance in religious matters in an age when this quality was markedly absent in the West. The explanation is to be found partly in the religious law of Islam. The sacred law recognized the Christians and Jews as being, like the Moslems, People of the Book. Both had a scripture—a written word of revelation. Their faith was accepted as true, though incomplete, since Mohammed had superseded Moses and Jesus Christ. Islam therefore tolerated the Christians and Jews. It permitted them to practice their faith, with certain restrictions and penalties.

The Abbasid Caliphate also was noteworthy for its achievements in the field of science, although the tendency here was to preserve and to pass on rather than to create something new. One of its greatest scientists, al-Biruni (973–

The Dome of the Rock in Jerusalem. An early example of Islamic architecture (but not a mosque), it dates from the seventh century and the first wave of Arab expansion. It is built on the rock from which Muslims believe Muhammad ascended into heaven and on which Jews believe Abraham prepared to sacrifice Isaac.

1048), stated, "We ought to confine ourselves to what the Ancients have dealt with and to perfect what can be perfected."[2] On the other hand, the sheer size of the empire, its contacts with literally all regions of Eurasia, and its rich legacy from the several great centers of civilization that it encompassed all contributed to the very real achievements of Islamic science. Baghdad, for example, boasted a "House of Wisdom" consisting of a school of translators, a library, an observatory, and an academy. The scholars associated with it translated and studied the works of Greek scientists and philosophers, as well as scientific treatises from Persia and India.

In astronomy the Moslems generally accepted the basic tenets of their Greek predecessors and made no significant advances in theory. But they did continue without interruption the astronomical observations of the ancients, so that the later Renaissance astronomers had available some nine hundred years of records, which provided the basis for their crucial discoveries.

In geography, as in astronomy, the Moslems made little theoretical progress, but the extent of their empire and of their commerce enabled them to accumulate reliable and systematic data concerning the Eurasian land mass. Al-Biruni's famous book on India, for example, described not only the physical features of the country but also the social system, religious beliefs, and scientific attainments of the Hindus in a manner that was not to be equaled until the eighteenth century. The Moslems also prepared charts and maps in which they naturally located Mecca in the center, as the contemporary Christian cartographers did for Jerusalem.

In addition to their own original achievements, the Moslems made an invaluable contribution in translating and transmitting ancient works. The Umayyad caliphs had distrusted all non-Arabs and were uninterested in their civilizations. The Abbasids, by contrast, had been strongly supported by Christians, Jews, and Zoroastrian Persians and were much more tolerant and broadminded. The "House of Wisdom" in Baghdad included a large staff of translators, one of the outstanding ones being a Christian, Hunain ibn-Ishaq (809–873). He visited Greek-speaking lands to collect manuscripts, and with his assistants he translated a large number of them, including works of Hippocrates, Galen,

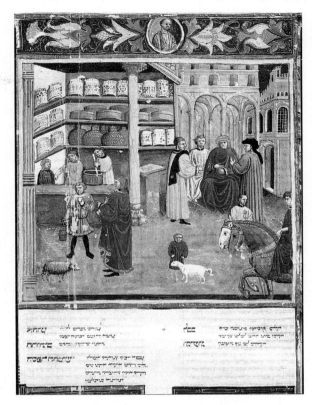

Fourteenth-century manuscript showing Avicenna and scholars. This page is taken from "The Canon" of Avicenna and is in the collection of the Bologna University Library.

Euclid, Ptolemy, Plato, and Aristotle. Another great translation center was in the city of Toledo in Moslem Spain, where the translators during the twelfth and thirteenth centuries included Jews, Spaniards, and foreign scholars from all over Europe. This activity was of utmost significance, for western Europeans had lost direct acquaintance with Greek learning and for long were unaware even of its existence. Thus Moslem scholarship preserved the Greek works until western Europe was ready once more to resume its study.

In conclusion, it should be emphasized that two basic bonds held together the diverse peoples of the sprawling caliphate: the Arabic language and the Islamic religion. Much more remarkable than the Arab conquests was the diffusion of the Arabic language. By the eleventh century Arabic had superseded the old Greek, Latin, Coptic, and Aramaic languages and prevailed from Morocco to Persia, as it does to the

Leaf from the manuscript of Dioscorides: a recipe for cough medicine and a doctor preparing it. Arab conributions to the field of medicine were substantial, and drugs in great quantities were carried to Europe in Italian ships.

lization evolved during the centuries following the conquests as a fusion of Christian, Jewish, Zoroastrian, and Arab religious elements, and Greco-Roman and Perso-Mesopotamian administrative, cultural, and scientific elements. The end product was not a mere mosaic or agglomeration of previous cultures but rather a fusion that represented a new and original civilization. It was diverse in its origins and strands yet uniquely molded by the distinctive imprint of Arabic Islam.

To the present day, Islam remains a major force, being the world's second-largest religion. It has nearly 1 billion followers, or about 18 percent of the world's population. By contrast, Christianity has about 1.7 billion, or 33 percent of the world's population. Moslems (literally, "submitters" to the will of God) range from the Atlantic coast of Africa, across North Africa, through the Middle East and south Asia, to Indonesia. Consequently many ethnic groups fill the ranks of the faithful; Arabs, the originators of Islam, now are a minority in their religion.

V. DECLINE OF THE CALIPHATE

The Abbasid Caliphate reached its height during the reign of Harun al-Rashid and then declined in much the same way as did the Roman Empire. There was first the matter of sheer size—a very real problem in an age when communications were dependent on horse and sail. The outlying provinces were 3,000 miles distant from the capital, so it is unsurprising that they should have been the first to break away: Spain in 756, Morocco in 788, and Tunisia in 800.

Further, as in the case of Rome, there was the problem of imperial expenditures, which were excessive and unsupportable by the prevailing economy and technology. The rampant luxury of the Baghdad court and the heavy weight of the inflated bureaucracy were not matched by technological progress. The resulting financial crisis forced the caliphs to appoint provincial governors as tax farmers in the areas they administered. With the revenues they collected, these governors maintained the local soldiery and officials and remitted an agreed sum to the central treasury. This arrangement left the governors-farmers the real rulers of the prov-

present day. This common language explains the feeling of common identity prevailing in this region, even though it includes Negroid Sudanese as well as the prevailing Semites, and Christian Lebanese and Coptic Egyptians as well as the prevailing Moslems. Even beyond this vast area that was permanently Arabized, Arabic exerted a profound influence on other Moslem languages. Arabic words are as common in these other languages as Greek and Latin words in English, and some of these languages (Urdu, Malay, Swahili, and Turkish until World War I) are written in Arabic script.

The Islamic religion also is a powerful bond—much more powerful than Christianity in this respect because it is not only a religion but also a social and political system and a general way of life. Religion thus provides the basis for Islamic civilization as language does for the Arabic world. We have seen that the Islamic civi-

inces, together with the army commanders with whom they soon reached working agreements. By the mid-ninth century the caliphs were losing both military and administrative control and were being appointed and deposed at will by Turkish mercenaries.

Imperial weakness, as usual, invited barbarian attacks. Just as the Roman Empire had been invaded across the Rhine and the Danube, so the caliphate now was assaulted from the north, south, and east. From the north came the Crusaders who overran Spain, Sicily, and Syria, aided by Moslem discord in all three areas. In Sicily the end of the local dynasty in 1040 was followed by civil war, which facilitated the invasion of the island by the Normans from southern Italy. By 1091 the whole of Sicily had been conquered, and the mixed Christian-Moslem population came under the rule of Norman kings.

Likewise in Spain the Umayyad dynasty was deposed in 1031 and the country was split up into numerous petty states ruled by "parties" or factions reflecting diverse ethnic groups. These included the Arabs, the Berbers, the indigenous pre-Moslem Iberian stock, and the "Slavs," or European slaves. This fragmentation of Moslem Spain enabled the Christian states of the north to expand southward. By 1085 they captured the important city of Toledo, and by the end of the thirteenth century only Granada on the southern tip of the peninsula was left to the Moslems.

The loss of Sicily and Spain to Christendom proved permanent, but such was not the case with Syria. Here also the warring of the several Moslem states enabled the Crusaders from 1096 onward to advance rapidly down the Syrian coast into Palestine. They established four states—Edessa (1098), Antioch (1098), Jerusalem (1099), and Tripoli (1109)—all organized along Western feudal lines. But these states lacked roots. They never assimilated their Moslem Arab subjects. Their existence depended on the sporadic arrival of recruits from Europe. Also they were all confined to the coastal areas and hence vulnerable to resistance movements organized in the interior. These states could exist only as long as the surrounding Moslem world remained divided. The disunity was ended by Salah ad-Din, better known in the West as Saladin. By uniting Moslem Syria and Egypt he sur-

rounded the Crusader principalities and began the counterattack in 1187. By the time of his death in 1193 he had recaptured Jerusalem and expelled the westerners from all but a narrow coastal strip. During the following century this also was overrun and the Moslem reconquest was completed.

In addition to these Crusader onslaughts from the north, the caliphate was attacked by Berbers from southern Morocco and the Senegal-Niger area and by the two Arab Bedouin tribes of Hilal and Sulaim from Upper Egypt. These tribes swept across Libya and Tunisia, wreaking havoc and devastation. It was this attack rather than the earlier seventh-century Arab invasion that ruined civilization in North Africa.

Finally, the third group of invaders were the Turks and Mongols from the East. Their incursions, lasting for several centuries and taking in virtually the entire Eurasian landmass, constitute a major chapter of world history. The Turco-Mongol invasions are comparable to the Arab-Islamic conquests in scope and impact. Indeed the two are intimately related, for many of the Turco-Mongols were converted to Islam, and they then extended the frontiers of their faith into distant new regions. The course and significance of these Turco-Mongol invasions is the subject of the following chapter.

SUGGESTED READINGS

For Mohammed and his teachings, see T. Andrae, *Mohammed* (Scribner's, 1936); E. Dermenghem, *The Life of Mahomet* (Dial, 1930); H. A. R. Gibb, *Mohammedanism: An Historical Survey* (Oxford University, 1953); and the convenient edition of the translation of the Koran by M. M. Pickthall (New American Library, 1953).

The Arabs and their general history are described authoritatively by A. Hourani, *A History of the Arab Peoples* (Harvard University, 1991); by P. Hitti, *History of the Arabs from the Earliest Times to the Present*, 5th ed. (St. Martin's, 1951); and B. Lewis, *The Arabs in History* (Home University Library, 1966). For the Arab conquests and early Islamic history, see M. A. Shaban, *Islamic History A.D. 600–750* (Cambridge University, 1972); and F. M. Donner, *The Early Islamic Conquests* (Princeton University, 1981). After the initial conquests, Islam continued to expand through quiet missionary work, as described by T. W. Arnold,

The Preaching of Islam: A History of the Propagation of the Muslim Faith (Constable, 1913).

Various aspects of Islamic civilization are considered by T. Arnold and A. Guillaume, eds., *The Legacy of Islam* (Clarendon, 1931); W. Montgomery Watt and P. Cachia, *A History of Islamic Spain* (Doubleday, 1967); A. G. Chejne, *The Arabic Language: Its Role in History* (University of Minnesota, 1969); R. A. Nicholson, *A Literary History of the Arabs* (Cambridge University, 1969); and A. Lewis, ed., *The Islamic World and the West, 622–1492 A.D.* (Wiley, 1970).

NOTES

1. Cited by B. Lewis, *The Arabs in History* (Hutchinson's University Library, 1950), p. 82.
2. Cited by A. Mieli, *La Science Arabe* (Brill, 1939), p. 376.

CHAPTER
11

Turco-Mongol Invasions

Nay, it is unlikely that mankind will see the like of this calamity, until the world comes to an end and perishes. . . . These [Tartars] spared none, slaying women and men and children, ripping open pregnant women and killing unborn babes.

Ibn al-Athir (Moslem historian, 1160–1233)

By all odds the most spectacular development during the half-millennium from 1000 to 1500 C.E. was the great eruption of Turco-Mongol peoples from the vast racial hive of central Asia. The historic achievement of the Turco-Mongols was that they jointly altered the traditional relationship between nomads and civilizations. For millennia the nomads had been on the outside, eyeing covetously the riches of civilized peoples. But with the Turco-Mongol conquests the balance shifted dramatically. The nomads became the unifiers and masters of most of the Eurasian landmass, rather than mere tenders of steppe animals.

During their centuries of glory the Turco-Mongols overran all Eurasia except for distant extremities such as Japan, Southeast Asia, southern India, and western Europe. These stunning conquests occurred in three stages. The first (1000–1200) marked the emergence of the Turks,

initially as mercenaries and then as masters of the Abbasid Caliphate. They infused vigor and aggressiveness into the now sickly world of Islam, extending its frontiers into Asia Minor at the expense of Byzantium and into northern India at the expense of Hindustan. The second stage, during the thirteenth century, saw the Mongols overrun not only central Asia, east Asia, and Russia, but also the Moslem Middle East, thereby halting the expansion of the Moslem Turks. The final stage (1300–1500) involved the disintegration of the Mongol Empire, which cleared the way for the resurgence of the Turks and the resumption of the Turkish-Islamic advance into Christian Europe and Hindustan.

This chapter will consider in turn each of these stages and their implications for general world history.

I. TURKISH INVASIONS

The Turks are a linguistic rather than an ethnic group. Their common bond is that they all speak one form or another of a Turkish family of languages. Although an ethnically mixed people, they are generally Caucasoid in appearance rather than Mongoloid. By the mid-sixth century they dominated the extensive steppe lands from Mongolia to the Oxus, or Amu Darya. From the eighth century onward they came increasingly under Islamic influence as a result of the Arab conquest of Persia and defeat of the Chinese at Talas (751).

The response of the Turkish tribes to the brilliant Abbasid Caliphate across the Oxus River was very similar to that of the Germans to the Roman Empire across the Rhine. First there was the cultural impact, as the primitive Turkish pagans succumbed to the teachings of Islam and to the lures of a sophisticated civilization. At the same time the tribes' warriors were entering the military service of the caliphate, as the Germans earlier had entered that of Rome. As mounted archers of great mobility, they soon demonstrated their superior military qualities and increasingly replaced the Arabs and Persians in the caliph's armed forces.

As the caliphs became weaker, the Turkish mercenaries, like their German counterparts, became masters rather than servants. They made and unmade successive caliphs in Baghdad. About 970 a branch of the Turkish people known as the Seljuks were crossing over unhindered into Moslem territory and soon had gathered power into their hands. This was formally recognized in 1055, when the caliph proclaimed the Seljuk leader, Tughril Beg, the "sultan," or "he who had authority." Although the caliphs remained the nominal heads of the empire, the real rulers henceforth were the Turkish sultans. Under their aggressive leadership, the frontiers of Islam now were further extended into two regions.

One was Asia Minor, which had remained for centuries a center of Christian Byzantine power against repeated attacks by Arabic Islam. But in 1071 the Seljuks won a crushing victory at Manzikert in eastern Asia Minor, taking prisoner the Byzantine Emperor Romanus IV. This proved to be a turning point in Middle Eastern history. The Asia Minor peasants, who had been exploited by corrupt Byzantine officials, now welcomed the Turks with relief. Thus between the eleventh and the thirteenth centuries the larger part of Asia Minor was transformed from a Greek and Christian to a Turkish and Moslem region, and it remains so to the present day. Furthermore, Byzantium was gutted by the loss of Asia Minor, a province that hitherto had provided the bulk of the imperial revenue and army manpower. Constantinople now was like a huge head atop a shriveled body. Thus the roots of the fall of Constantinople in 1453 extend back to 1071.

While the Seljuks had been pushing westward into Asia Minor, other Turks had been fighting their way southward toward the vast treasure house of India. Outstanding was a certain Mahmud (997–1030), who from his base at Ghazni in Afghanistan raided the Indian lands almost annually and finally annexed the Punjab, which has ever since remained Moslem. Mahmud's zeal in destroying Hindu temples and smashing their idols, a zeal that was based on the Islamic tenet that any visible representation of the deity was sinful, earned him the epithet "the image breaker." Fired by the fierce monotheism of Islam, Mahmud and his followers came to India not only in search of plunder but also to convert the infidels, or to exterminate them. There was also a social conflict involved—the clash between two different societies, one believing that all men are brothers and the other based on caste, which presupposes inequality. It was at this time, then, that the struggle of two fundamentally different cultures began. After World War II this struggle ended in the division of the peninsula into Hindu India and Moslem Pakistan.

Mahmud was followed by other Turkish invaders from Afghanistan. They advanced southward to Gujarat and eastward into the Ganges valley. In 1192 they captured Delhi and made it the capital of the Turkish Sultanate in India. During these campaigns, Buddhist monasteries were destroyed and Buddhist monks were slaughtered on such a scale that Buddhism never recovered in its place of origin.

The relative ease with which the Turks conquered a land in which they were hopelessly outnumbered was due partly to the outdated Indian military tactics. They were the same as those that had proven inadequate against

Alexander 1,500 years earlier. The infantry was usually an undisciplined rabble, and their vaunted elephants were useless against the Moslem cavalry. Equally damaging, and a more fundamental weakness, was the Hindu caste system, which left the fighting to only the Kshatriya, or warrior caste. The rest of the population was untrained and largely indifferent, particularly because class differentiation separated oppressive landlords from their peasants and so added to the fragmentation of the caste system. Thus the masses either remained neutral or else welcomed the invaders and embraced their faith. This pattern was to be repeated frequently in the future and explains why in modern times the British were able to rule from Delhi just as the Turkish sultans had before.

II. GENGHIS KHAN'S CONQUESTS

While the Turks were becoming the masters of the Moslem world, an obscure chieftain in far-off Mongolia was beginning his career of conquest that was to culminate in the greatest empire of history. Genghis Khan (spelled also Chinggis, Chingis, Jenghiz, etc.), whose personal name was Temujin, was born about 1167, the son of a minor clan leader. When Temujin was twelve years old his father was poisoned, and as a result the future Khan spent a childhood of misery. He was able to overcome these humble beginnings by mastering the complicated art of tribal politics, which called for a mixture of loyalty, cunning, and ruthless treachery, as well as physical prowess. After turning against his overlord and eliminating various rivals, he finally was able to combine the various Mongol-speaking tribes into a single unit. An assembly of Mongol chieftains, held in 1206, proclaimed him the supreme head of his people with the title Genghis Khan, signifying "ruler of the universe."

He was now in a position to satisfy his nomadic impulse for conquest and booty. "Man's highest joy," he reportedly said, "is in victory: to conquer one's enemies, to pursue them, to deprive them of their possessions, to make their beloved weep, to ride on their horses, and to embrace their wives and daughters." In this respect Genghis Khan was no different from the long line of steppe conquerors who had gone before him. Why then was he alone destined to become the master of the greater part of Eurasia? This question is particularly intriguing

Fifteenth-century Chinese painting showing Genghis Khan hunting.

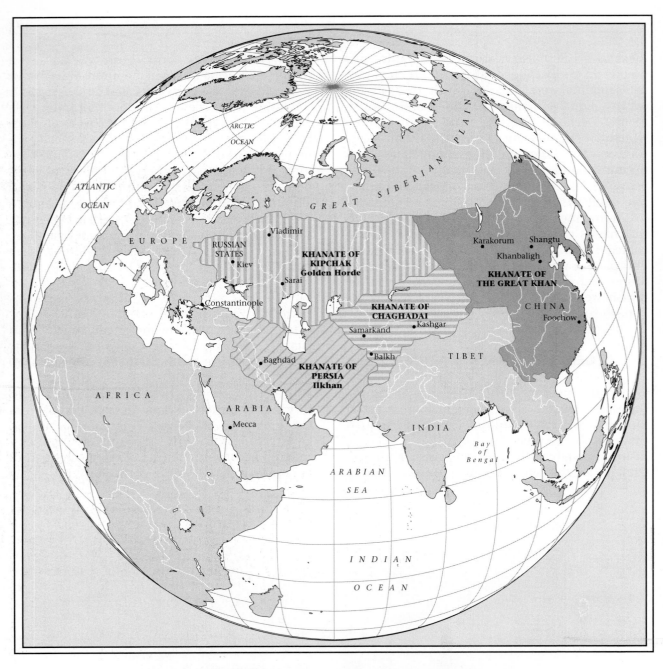

Mongol Empire at the Death of Kublai Khan, 1294

because, as a Mongol, Genghis Khan did not have the manpower resources of other nomad conquerors, who were almost invariably Turks. All the Mongol tribes together numbered about 1 million men, women, and children, which gave Genghis Khan a maximum of 125,000 warriors. With such limited resources, how was he able to come so close to becoming literally the "ruler of the universe"?

Genghis Khan began with the built-in advantage enjoyed by all nomad warriors—the fact that their daily life was a continuous rehearsal of campaign operations. Clad in leather and furs, leading extra horses as remounts, and capable of riding several days and nights in succession with a minimum of rest and food, these warriors introduced blitzkrieg into the world of the thirteenth century. During their campaigning on the plains of Hungary, they are said to have covered 270 miles in three days. They carried leather bags for water, which when empty could be inflated for swimming across rivers. Normally they lived off the countryside, but if necessary they drank the blood of their horses and the milk of their mares. Their skills in the hunt, acquired from boyhood, enabled them to coordinate the operations of flying horse columns over long distances. Their favorite tactic was feigned flight, during which the enemy might pursue the fleeing Mongols for days, only to be lured to ambush and destruction. Other tactical maneuvers included the tying of branches to the tails of horses to stir up dust in order to give the impression of large forces on the march, and also the mounting of dummies on spare horses for the same purpose.

The basic Mongol weapon was the compound large bow, more powerful than the English longbow and capable of killing at 600 feet with its armor-piercing arrows. This was a fearful weapon in the hands of Mongol horsemen, who were able to carry a supply of thirty arrows and shoot them all at full gallop. Other equipment included a steel helmet, light body armor made of hide, a saber, and sometimes a lance with a hook and a mace. The Mongol horses grazed only on the open range, with no shelter during the long, bitter winter and no hay or grain for supplementary feed. This made them somewhat stunted in size but very tough and adaptable. Genghis Khan further strengthened his forces by adding new skills and equipment learned mostly from the Chinese. Thus Genghis Khan supplemented his incomparable mounted archers with the siege weapons necessary for capturing fortified cities.

The Mongols were also masters of espionage and psychological warfare. Before undertaking a campaign they collected all possible intelligence regarding the enemy's roads, rivers, fortifications, and political and economic conditions. They also used agents to spread demoralizing stories about the size of the Mongol forces and the uselessness of resistance. In the course of the campaigning they used terror tactics to undermine enemy morale. Prisoners of war were forced to lead the assault against their own people, and entire populations were put to the sword when any resistance was offered.

Even with his military genius and superb fighting machine, Genghis Khan could not have become a world conqueror had he not appeared at the right historical moment. A strong and united China, such as had existed under the Han and the T'ang, could have stopped him with ease. So also could the Moslem Arabs have done so at the height of their power. But the Eurasian balance of power was quite different in the early thirteenth century. China was divided then into three fragments: the Ch'in dynasty ruling the north, the Sung the south, and the Tibetan Tanguts controlling the northwest with their kingdom of Hsi Hsia. To the west was the state of Kara-Khitai based on oasis cities such as Bokhara and Samarkand. Beyond that, on the Oxus River, was the Moslem kingdom of Khorezm, and still further west the Abbasid Caliphate at Baghdad, both far past their prime.

Genghis Khan first subjugated the Hsi Hsia state between 1205 and 1209 and forced it into a tributary status. In 1211 he attacked north China, first overrunning the region north of the Great Wall and then in 1213 piercing the wall and penetrating to the Yellow River plain. By 1215 he had captured and pillaged Peking and also gained the services of Chinese who knew how to besiege cities and others who knew how to administer and exploit agricultural societies. In accordance with his overall strategy, Genghis Khan now turned to the surrounding nomadic territories. Manchuria fell in 1216, Korea in 1218, Kara-Khitai in the following year. These conquests brought him to the frontiers of Khorezm, which he overran between 1219 and 1221. Rich and ancient cities such as Bokhara, Samarkand, and Balkh were pillaged and their inhabitants massacred. The only exceptions were the skilled artisans, who were sent to Mongolia.

Meanwhile, Genghis Khan had returned to Mongolia to direct another victorious campaign against the Hsi Hsia kingdom, which had revolted against his rule. This was his final exploit, for he died soon after in 1227. In accordance with his expressed wish, he was buried in his homeland beneath a large tree he had selected. The escort that had brought the corpse to the site were all slaughtered to ensure that the location of the grave should remain secret. (See map of Mongol Empire at the Death of Kublai Khan, 1294, p. 192.)

III. MONGOL EMPIRE

After a two-year interval, Genghis Khan's son Ogodai was selected as successor. During his reign from 1229 to 1241 the campaigning was resumed in the two extremities of Eurasia—China and Europe—some 5,000 miles apart. In China the remnants of the Ch'in state in the north were liquidated by 1234, and then the Sung in the south were immediately attacked. They resisted stoutly, but the war, which lasted forty-five years, ended in their complete destruction. At the same time Genghis Khan's grandson Batu was sent with a force of 150,000 Mongols and Turks to the European West. Crossing the middle Volga in the fall of 1237 he fell upon the principalities of central Russia. Town after town was captured, including the then comparatively unimportant town of Moscow. By March 1238 Batu was approaching Novgorod near the Baltic Sea, but fearing that the spring thaw would mire his horsemen in mud, he withdrew suddenly to the south.

Two years later, in the summer of 1240, the Mongols attacked southern Russia again, this time from their bases in the Caucasus. By December they had captured the ancient Russian capital of Kiev. Such was Mongol frightfulness that a contemporary monk recorded that the few survivors "envied the dead." The following year the Mongols pressed on into Poland and Hungary, defeated a German army of 30,000 at Liegnitz in Silesia, crossed the frozen Danube, captured Zagreb, and reached the Adriatic coast. Thus Mongol armies now were operating across the breadth of Eurasia from the Adriatic to the Sea of Japan. In the spring of 1242 came news of the death of Ogodai Khan in Mongolia, so Batu withdrew through the Balkans to the lower Volga valley, where he laid the foundations of the khanate known as the Golden Horde, a name derived from the golden tent of its khan.

Ogodai's successors decided to complete the conquest of south China and to take over the Abbasid Caliphate of Baghdad. In China, the Mongols were bogged down in decades of fighting before finally capturing the great southern port of Canton in 1277. The new khan, Kublai, moved his capital from Karakorum to Peking in north China. Kublai then launched new cam-

This illustration from a thirteenth-century Persian history of the Mongols shows the court of Genghis Khan. The Khan himself is seated on his throne, and his three sons stand at the left. One of these sons, Ogodai, succeeded his father in 1229.

paigns: on land against Indochina and Burma, and overseas against Java and Japan.

Meanwhile, other Mongol armies had been rampaging through the Middle East, capturing in 1258 the Abbasid capital, Baghdad. Most of its 800,000 inhabitants are reported to have been massacred, with the exception of a few skilled artisans who were sent to Kublai's court. It seemed that nothing could prevent the Mongols from advancing on Egypt and North Africa and from completing the conquest of the entire Moslem world. In 1260, however, the Egyptian Mamelukes unexpectedly defeated the advancing Mongols in Palestine. The defeat marked the high-water mark of the Mongol Empire in the Middle East, just as similar defeats in Japan and

Java marked its high point in the Far East. Unable to expand further, the Mongol Empire fell apart almost as rapidly as it had been built up.

IV. MONGOL DECLINE

The basic reason for the decline of the Mongols was that they were too few in number and too primitive in relation to their subject peoples. The Mongols, as Pushkin put it, were "Arabs without Aristotle and algebra." This left them vulnerable to assimilation as soon as they dismounted from their horses and settled down to enjoy their conquests. In this respect they differed fundamentally from the Arabs, who had both a language and a religion that their subjects were willing to adopt and which served as strong bonds for imperial unity. The Mongols, being less advanced than the Arabs, enjoyed no such advantage. Rather, the opposite was the case with them, for they adopted the languages, religions, and cultures of their more-advanced subjects and thereby lost their identity. This was the root reason why their empire dissolved so soon after its creation.

Indicative of the assimilation process was Kublai Khan's decision to move the Mongol capital from Karakorum to Peking. Inevitably he became a Chinese-style emperor, ruling from a palace of Chinese design, conducting elaborate Confucian ceremonies, and building new Confucian temples. As the Grand Khan, he was nominally the suzerain of all the Mongol khanates. Actually his authority did not extend beyond China. His brother Arikboga had contested his election as Grand Khan. Kublai Khan had prevailed only after a four-year struggle. Then he was challenged by his cousin, Kaidu, who controlled Turkestan, and the ensuing forty-year civil war ended in stalemate. Thus the Mongol Empire was shattered by internal dynastic rivalries as well as by cultural assimilation.

While Kublai Khan was becoming a Chinese emperor, Hulagu was becoming a Persian ruler. With Tabriz as his capital he established the so-called Ilkhanate. (The term *Ilkhan* means "subject Khan" and was applied to the Mongol rulers of Persia as subordinates to the Grand Khan.) His successor's adoption of Islam in 1295 as the official religion both reflected and accelerated the Mongols' assimilation into their Iranian-Islamic milieu. Likewise the Golden Horde across the Caucasus went its own way, influenced by the native Christian Orthodox culture and by the official Islamic creed. Before long the only remaining pure Mongols were those in ancestral Mongolia, where they came under the influence of Buddhism and sank into impotent obscurity.

It is a tribute to Marco Polo's keen insight that he foresaw Mongol decline even when he was serving under the great Kublai Khan. In his account of his travels, Marco Polo made the following significant analysis of the assimilation of the Mongols by the people they conquered.

All this that I have been telling you is true of the manners and customs of the genuine Tatars [Mongols]. But I must add also that in these days they are greatly degenerated; for those who are settled in Cathay have taken up the practices of the Idolaters of the country, and have abandoned their own institutions; whilst those who have settled in the Levant have adopted the customs of the Saracens.[1]

V. TURKISH REVIVAL

Since the Mongols were so few in number, they had taken an ever-increasing proportion of Turks into their armies. Then with the breakup of the empire these Moslem Turks quickly came to the fore, as they had earlier in the caliphate before the Mongol onslaught. A succession of military adventurers now rose and fell in the struggle for control of the central Eurasian steppes. The most remarkable of these was Timur, known to Europe as Tamerlane. He seized Samarkand in 1369, and from there he struck out in all directions. First he destroyed the Ilkhanate in Persia and Mesopotamia, then defeated the Golden Horde in Russia and the Ottoman Turks in Asia Minor, and he even invaded India and sacked Delhi. He was determined to make his capital, Samarkand, the finest city in the world, and after each campaign he sent back caravans loaded with booty, together with craftmakers, artists, astrologers, and scholars. At its height, his empire extended from the Mediterranean to China, and Timur was preparing to invade the latter country when he died in 1405. His empire then disintegrated even more rapidly than that of the Mongols.

After Timur, the outstanding development was the extension of Moslem Turkish power in India and in Byzantium. During the thirteenth century the Turkish sultans of Delhi, under the pressure of the Mongol threat, had confined themselves to strengthening their position in north India. In the fourteenth century, with the threat removed, they expanded two-thirds of the way down the peninsula to the Kistna River. Then in the aftermath of Timur's raid, north and central India were reduced to a few small Turkish-ruled states, with none strong enough to revive the Delhi sultanate. Meanwhile the expansion of Islamic power over a large part of India had provoked a reaction from the Hindus. They set up the large Hindu state of Vijanagar, comprising the whole of India south of the Kistna River. Such was the fragmented condition of the Indian peninsula when unity was imposed from without during the sixteenth century by another Moslem Turkish dynasty, the Mughal.

Meanwhile in the Middle East the frontiers of Islam were being extended at the expense of Byzantium by the Ottoman Turks. These newcomers from central Asia had entered the Seljuk Empire in its decline and settled in the northwest corner of Asia Minor, less than fifty miles from the strategic straits separating Asia from Europe. In 1299 the leader of these Turks, Uthman, declared his independence from his Seljuk overlord, and from these humble beginnings grew the great Ottoman Empire, named after the obscure Uthman.

The first step was the conquest of the remaining Byzantine portion of Asia Minor. This was accomplished by 1340, thanks to the disaffection of the Christian peasantry and the plentiful supply of ghazis, or warriors of the faith, who flocked in from all parts of the Middle East to battle against the Christian infidels. Next the Turks crossed the straits, winning their first foothold in Europe by building a fort at Gallipoli in 1354. They hardly could have selected a more favorable moment for their advance into Europe. The Balkan peninsula was divided by the strife of rival Christian churches and by the rivalries of the Byzantine, Serbian, and Bulgarian states, all past their prime. Also the Christian peasants of the Balkans were as disaffected as

their counterparts in Asia Minor. And Western Christendom was too divided to go to the aid of the Balkans even if there was the will to do so, which there was not, because of the ancient antipathy between Catholic and Orthodox Christians. Thus the way was clear for the Ottoman Turks, and they took full advantage of the opportunity.

They surrounded Constantinople by taking Adrianople in 1362 and Sofia in 1384. Then they were diverted for some decades when their sultan was defeated and captured by Timur in 1402. But Timur was a flash in the pan, and his death in 1405 left the Ottomans free to rebuild and to resume their advance. Finally, in 1453 they took Constantinople by assault, and the Ottomans were the masters of the entire Balkan peninsula to the Danube River, with the exception of a few Venetian-held coastal fortresses. (For details, see Chapter 12, Section IV.)

VI. SIGNIFICANCE OF TURCO-MONGOL INVASIONS

One result of the Turco-Mongol invasions between 1000 and 1500 was the emergence of a new Eurasian balance of power in which Islam was the central and decisive force. When the West began its overseas expansion in the late fifteenth century, Islam already was expanding overland in all directions. The Ottomans were crossing the Danube into central Europe; central Asia was completely won over, with the exception of the eastern fringes; and the Mughals were about to begin their conquest of virtually the entire Indian peninsula. Beyond Eurasia, Islam was spreading steadily into the interior of the continent of Africa from two centers. From the North African coast it advanced across the Sahara to West Africa, where a succession of large Negro Moslem kingdoms flourished. Likewise from the Arab colonies on the East African coast, Islam spread inward over lands that included the Christian kingdom of Nubia, which was conquered and converted.

Islam was also carried by Arab and Indian merchants to Southeast Asia. Here, as in Africa and other regions, conversion was easy because of the simplicity and adaptability of the new faith. All one had to do to become a Moslem

The Alhambra, palace of the Moorish kings at Granada, built between 1248 and 1354. Masterpieces of Islamic architecture throughout Eurasia are indications of the vast diffusion of the Moselm faith between 1000 and 1500.

was to repeat the words "I bear witness that there is no God but Allah and that Mohammed is the Messenger of Allah." Local practices and traditions usually were accepted and made holy simply by the addition of Islamic ritual. Thus the faith was spread, not by the sword, but by the unobtrusive work of traders who won over the populace by learning their language, adopting their customs, marrying their women, and converting their new relatives and business associates. By the end of the fifteenth century, Islam had spread as far east as Mindanao in the Philippines. Taking Southeast Asia as a whole, the main Moslem centers, as might be expected, were those areas with the most active trade contacts: the Malay peninsula and the Indonesian archipelago.

This diffusion of Islam throughout Eurasia during these five centuries almost tripled the area that accepted the Moslem faith, with important repercussions on the course of world history. The initial stage of Islamic expansion in the seventh and eighth centuries had made the Mediterranean a Moslem lake; this later stage of expansion made the entire Indian Ocean a Moslem lake. This meant that virtually all the goods reaching Europe from Asia now were carried along Moslem-controlled land or sea routes, especially after the Persian Ilkhanate embraced Islam in 1295. Thus the several decades after 1240 during which the Mongol Empire permit-

ted safe travel and trade across Eurasia were only an interlude between earlier and later eras when Arab-Turkish control of central Asia and the Middle East raised a barrier between China and the West. The continued expansion of the Moslem faith also served to make Islam by 1500 a world force rather than simply a Middle Eastern power. This has affected profoundly the course of world affairs to the present day. It explains why today the Indian peninsula is divided into two parts, why Moslem political parties are so influential in Southeast Asia, why Islam is a powerful and rapidly growing force in Africa, and why it is now the faith of 18 percent of the people of the world.

The Turco-Mongol invasions are significant also because of the cross-fertilization that they stimulated within Eurasia. In the technological field, we have seen that Pax Mongolica was responsible for the transmission of a cluster of Chinese inventions, including gunpowder, silk, machinery, printing, and the blast furnace for cast iron. (See Chapter 9, Section II.) Another example of cross-fertilization is the case of Ilkhanid Persia, which by its location was exposed to influences from both East and West. We know of Chinese artillerymen who reached Persia in the service of the Mongol armies. We also know of one Fu Meng-chi, who spread the principles of Chinese astronomy; of Chinese physicians at the Ilkhan's court; and of Chinese artists who left an indelible impression on Persian miniature painting. From the opposite direction, European influence was mostly in the field of trade and diplomacy. A colony of Italian merchants flourished in the capital of Tabriz, and from their numbers the Ilkhans recruited the ambassadors and interpreters for their various missions to Europe. And then there was, of course, Marco Polo, who escorted from China to Persia a Mongol princess to be the Ilkhan's bride and then proceeded to Venice.

Thus the Turco-Mongol invasions served to integrate the Eurasian landmass more tightly than ever before. This was noted at the time by a Chinese observer, Wang Li (1314–1389), who left the following remarkable account of the unprecedented integration unfolding before his eyes:

. . . the land within the Four Seas had become the territory of one family, civilization had spread everywhere, and no more barriers existed. . . . many [newcomers to China] forgot the region of their birth, and took delight in living among our rivers and lakes. As they settled down in China for a long time, some became advanced in years, their families grew, and being far from home, they had no desire to be buried in their fatherland. Brotherhood among peoples has certainly reached a new plane.[2]

Finally, the opportunities offered by this cross-fertilization were fully exploited only by the new civilization developing in Europe—a profoundly significant fact that was to mold the course of world history to the present day. All the other Eurasian civilizations were too set in their ways. At first it seemed as though the Islamic world would have no difficulty in adapting and changing. Despite the primitive background of Arabia from which it had emerged, Islam had proven itself remarkably adept at borrowing from the great established civilizations and creating something new and impressive. But there was too great a gulf between the dogma of the Islamic faith and the rationalist philosophy and science of the Greeks. In the early years the Caliph al-Mamun (813–833) had generously supported the translation of the ancient classics and had accepted the rationalist doctrine that the Koran was created and not eternal. But his successors were quite different. They supported

conservative theologians who rejected all scientific and philosophical speculation as heresy and atheism.

This was the triumph of scholasticism, in the sense that seeking God was more important than understanding nature. Such scholasticism had prevailed also in the early medieval West following the barbarian invasions. The papacy had then dominated the intellectual life of the age, and theology was the accepted queen of the sciences. The same development occurred now in the Islamic world following its series of barbarian invasions—Crusaders, Berbers, Bedouins, Seljuks, and Mongols. Here, as in the West, people turned to religion for succor and consolation in the face of material disaster. But whereas in the West scholasticism eventually was challenged and replaced, in the Moslem world it remained dominant through the nineteenth century.

In his *Incoherence of Philosophy*, the outstanding theologian of Islam, al-Ghazzali (1058–1111), strongly attacked the whole secular school. He argued that the ultimate source of truth is divine revelation and that the intellect should be used to understand that self-trust must be destroyed and replaced by trust in the divine. The extent of orthodox reaction is reflected in the work of the great historian and father of sociology, Ibn Khaldun (1332–1406). He was the first to view history not as the conventional chronicling of events or episodes—the view in his time—but as the science of the origin and development of civilizations. And yet this learned and creative thinker rejected philosophy and science as useless and dangerous:

It should be known that the opinion the philosophers hold is wrong in all its aspects. . . . The problems of physics are of no more importance to us in our religious affairs or our livelihoods. Therefore we must leave them alone. . . . Whoever studies it [logic] should do so only after he is saturated with the religious law and has studied the interpretation of the Koran and jurisprudence. No one who has no knowledge of the Moslem religious sciences should apply himself to it. Without that knowledge, he can hardly be safe from its pernicious aspects.[3]

Thus intellectual growth and innovation in the Moslem world ceased, and at a time when

Europe's universities were in full ferment, the Islamic madrasas were content with rote memorization of authoritative texts. Whereas the Moslem world had been far ahead of the West between 800 and 1200, by the sixteenth century the gap had disappeared, and thereafter it was the West that boomed ahead while Islam stood still and even went backward.

A similar disparity developed between the West and the other Eurasian civilizations, for the simple reason that only the West made the fateful transition to modernism. Both India and Byzantium were conquered by Islam and affected by its stagnation. China, reacting against the Mongols, who were expelled in 1368, developed a strong ethnocentrism—an almost instinctive hostility and scorn for all things alien and hence barbarian. Russia also succeeded in 1480 in throwing off the Mongol yoke, but permanent scars remained. The country had been closed to fresh winds from the West for 250 years, and Mongol ideas and usages had paved the way for the absolutism of the Muscovite state and of the Orthodox church.

The West alone was the exception to this general pattern. Only there occurred the great mutation—the emergence of modern civilization with a new technological base that quickly proved its superiority and diffused throughout not only Eurasia but the entire globe. This uniqueness of the West stems, as noted earlier (Chapter 8, Section V), from the shattering impact of the barbarian invasions, which plowed under the classical civilizations and allowed new concepts and institutions to take root and flourish. The following chapters first will consider the traditional Byzantine and Confucian civilizations that flanked the Islamic world on each side, and then will analyze the contrasting revolutionary civilization of the West.

SUGGESTED READINGS

For the Turkish invasions in various regions, see T. T. Rice, *The Seljuks* (Thames & Hudson, 1961); C. Cahen, *Pre-Ottoman Turkey* (Sidgwick & Jackson, 1968); S. Vryonis, Jr., *The Decline of Medieval Hellenism in Asia Minor and the Process of Islamization from the Eleventh through the Fifteenth Century* (University of California, 1971); H. Inalcik, *The Ottoman Empire: The Classical Age 1300–1600* (Weidenfeld & Nicolson, 1972); *The Cambridge History of Iran*, Vol. 5, *The Seljuk and Mongol Periods*, ed. J. A. Boyle (Cambridge University, 1931); M. Nazim, *Life and Times of Sultan Mahmud of Ghazna* (Cambridge University, 1931), for a discussion of the Turks in India; and H. Lamb, *Tamberlane the Earth Shaker* (McBride, 1928). An excellent collection of readings is presented by J. J. Saunders, ed., *The Muslim World on the Eve of Europe's Expansion* (Prentice Hall, 1966).

For the dynamics of Mongol expansionism, see various essays in O. Lattimore, *Studies in Frontier History* (Mouton, 1962), and his article "Chingis Khan and the Mongol Conquests," *Scientific American*, August 1963, pp. 55–68. Several biographies of Genghis Khan are available, including a popular account by R. Grousset, *Conqueror of the World: The Life of Chingis-Khan* (Viking, 1972); a scholarly study by B. Y. Vladimirtsov, *The Life of Chingis-Khan* (Houghton Mifflin, 1930); and H. D. Martin, *The Rise of Chingis Khan and His Conquest of North China* (Johns Hopkins Press, 1950), which is strong on Mongol military organization. Broader studies of the Mongol Empire as a whole are available in J. J. Saunders, *The History of the Mongol Conquests* (Harper & Row, 1972); J. A. Boyle, *The Successors of Genghis Khan* (Columbia University, 1971); and the authoritative evaluation by B. Spuler, *The Mongol Period* (Princeton University, 1995).

NOTES

1. R. Latham, trans., *Travels of Marco Polo* (Penguin, 1958), p. 71.
2. Cited by J. H. Bentley, *Old World Encounters* (Oxford University, 1993), p. 145.
3. Ibn Khaldun, *Muqaddimah*, trans. F. Rosenthal (Pantheon, 1958), pp. 250–258.

12

Traditional Byzantine Civilization

A thousand years of Byzantium produced extinction; a thousand years of medieval effort [in the West] produced the Renaissance, the modern state, and ultimately the free world.

William Carroll Bark

Byzantium was one of the traditional Eurasian civilizations that survived the barbarian invasions and continued without interruption from the Classical Age to modern times. But this unbroken, 1,000-year sweep of history eventually meant *obsolescence* and extinction, especially in the political sense. Because it was the most vulnerable, the Byzantine civilization was the first to suffer this fate. China, for example, faced nomadic invasions only from the northwest and was so far out of the way on Eurasia's eastern tip that the aggressive West was not able to break in until the mid-nineteenth century. While Byzantium faced a succession of barbarian invasions from across the Danube, comparable to those menacing China, it also had to bear the onslaught of the expanding West in the form of Venetian mer-

chants and Norman knights. At the same time a resurgent East assaulted Byzantium. First came the Sassanian Persian attack and then the Moslem Arab and Turkish invasions. Thus, whereas the traditional Chinese civilization endured to 1912, the Byzantine collapsed first in 1204, was partially revived in 1261, and survived in a crippled state until the death blow in 1453. (See map of Decline of the Byzantine Empire, p. 201.)

I. EMERGENCE OF BYZANTIUM

No Western capital approaches the proud record of the Byzantine capital, Constantinople, either in continuity or in the scope of its imperial rule. It was already an old city when rebuilt by Con-

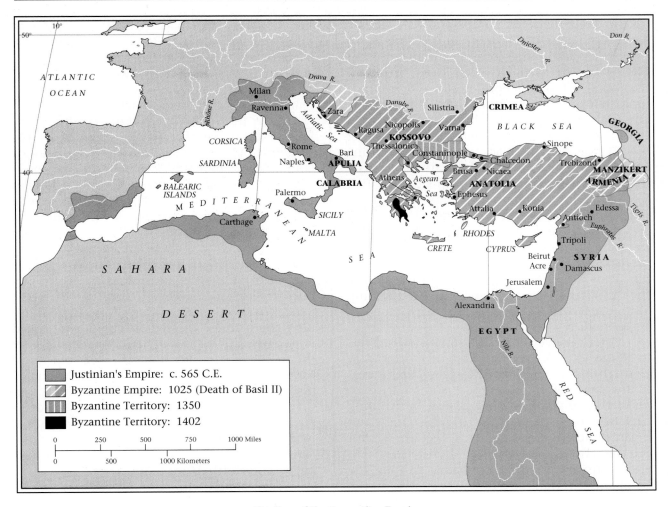

Decline of the Byzantine Empire

stantine in 330 C.E. to be the new Rome. Its origins go back to the seventh century B.C.E., when it was founded as the colony Byzantion by emigrants from the Greek city-state Megara. Despite its magnificent location, Byzantium, to use the common Latin form of its name, remained a second-class commercial city during the next thousand years. It was unable to rise to a rank worthy of its position as long as it was menaced and cut off from its hinterland by the barbarous Thracians. The conquests of Trajan and his successors brought the interior lands under Roman imperial control and ended this disadvantage. Thus when Byzantium became Constantinople, or the city of Constantine, it was secure by land as well as by sea, and in the following centuries it stood impregnable before

the barbarian assaults to which the first Rome succumbed.

For 1,000 years Constantinople was the capital of Byzantium, until it fell to the Ottoman Turks in 1453. Then it became the capital of a new empire. And as the Ottoman warriors pressed their conquests, the rule of Constantinople spread to new frontiers, reaching from Morocco to Persia and from Vienna to the Indian Ocean. Constantinople presided over this vast region up to modern times, when the Ottoman Empire gave way to the Turkish Republic. Then Kemal Ataturk moved his capital from Constantinople on the shores of the Bosphorus to the safety of Ankara on the Anatolian plateau.

The remarkable history of Constantinople is due in large part to its commanding position on the straits between Europe and Asia. To the south is the Sea of Marmora and to the north the bay of Bosphorus, forming the magnificent harbor known as the Golden Horn. Constantinople also has, on both north and south, a long, narrow, but navigable sea channel. The city is therefore protected by two marine gates that can be closed to hostile ships from either the Aegean or the Black sea. The Byzantine emperors supplemented these natural defenses with two great walls on the land side, the first four miles long, and the second—some thirty miles further west—forty miles long and twenty feet wide. These double ramparts, together with the natural bulwark of the Balkan Mountains, protected the land approaches to Constantinople. Thus the city was able to hold out during the thousand-year existence of Byzantium, although it was a besieged fortress for much of this period.

After the overthrow of Romulus Augustulus in Rome in 476 C.E., the Eastern emperors in Constantinople continued to regard themselves as the heirs of the Caesars. Justinian tried to make this imperial myth a reality by winning back from the barbarians North Africa, Italy, and a part of Spain. (See Chapter 8, Section IV.) But the revived empire proved short-lived. Soon after Justinian's death, a new barbarian tribe, the Lombards, overran most of Italy. Likewise on the Danube frontier, the Avars and Slavs were pouring southward into the Balkans, while in the East the Persians overran Syria, Palestine, and Egypt and camped on the shores of the Bosphorus opposite Constantinople.

Under the great Emperor Heraclius (610–641) Byzantium took the offensive against the surrounding enemies. In 627 Heraclius defeated the Persians and forced them to return all their conquests. Turning to the Danube frontier, Heraclius discovered that in the meantime the Slavs had occupied and sunk roots in large parts of the northern Balkans. Making a virtue of necessity, he assigned definite areas to them, and in return, they acknowledged his suzerainty and agreed to pay annual tribute. Thus the Slavic newcomers changed gradually from invaders into settlers. With the passing of a few centuries these widely scattered Balkan Slavs had developed along different lines and crystallized into four major groups: the Slovenes at the head of

the Adriatic; the Croatians between the Drave River and the Adriatic; the Serbs in the central Balkans between the Adriatic and the Danube; and the Slavs, who shortly were to adopt the name of their Bulgarian conquerors, in the remaining territory to the Black Sea.

Later in the seventh century the Byzantine Empire again was threatened, this time by the combination of Moslem sea raids and Bulgar land attacks. The Arabs developed a naval power with which they conquered Cyprus and Rhodes and then besieged Constantinople on several occasions, beginning in 669. At the same time Byzantium was threatened from the north by the Bulgars, who had occupied the territory between the Danube and the Balkan Mountains.

Once more Byzantium was saved by inspired imperial leadership, this time in the person of Leo III the Isaurian (717–741). A military commander of Syrian origin, he seized power when Constantinople was under siege by the Arabs. He not only lifted the siege but drove the Arabs back out of Asia Minor. By the end of his reign the imperial frontiers were secure, but they were drastically shrunken frontiers compared to those of Justinian. Italy had been lost to the Lombards; the northern Balkans to the Slavs and the Bulgars; and Syria, Palestine, Egypt, and North Africa to the Arabs.

This reduced empire, however, was a more homogeneous territory. It was strengthened rather than weakened by withdrawal to the Taurus Mountains, which separated Greek Asia Minor from what was now becoming the heartland of the Islamic world. This separation was reinforced by internal convulsions in the Moslem world that culminated in the accession of the Abbasid Caliphate (750). The Islamic capital was moved from Damascus to Baghdad so that the orientation of Islam now was to the East rather than toward the Mediterranean. In this way the Byzantine and Moslem empires were able to coexist peacefully until the appearance of the militant Turks in the eleventh century.

The emerging Byzantine Empire of the eighth century was much smaller than Justinian's short-lived creation but, as we have noted, was also much more homogeneous. It had shed the diverse racial, cultural, and religious elements of the eastern and western provinces, and the remaining core was basically, though not

Justinian and Retinue, *mosaic from San Vitale, Ravenna.*

exclusively, Greek. In this manner, then, the transition was made from the East Roman Empire of the sixth century to the Byzantine Empire of the eighth—an empire with a culture clearly distinct from both that of Islam to the east and that of the new Europe to the west.

II. BYZANTIUM'S GOLDEN AGE

The Byzantine Empire reached its height during the period between the early ninth and early eleventh centuries. Imperial administration was soundly based on the *themes*, or provinces, each headed by a *strategos*, or general. The general was in charge of both civil and military affairs. Heraclius had militarized the administration so that he could act quickly at a time of imminent foreign danger. Imperial lands in the themes were divided among the peasants in return for military service. Under strong emperors, this theme arrangement provided good administration, a reliable military reserve, and a well-filled treasury since the peasants assumed much of the tax burden.

Byzantium's economy also was solidly based on free peasant communities that functioned alongside the estates of the great landowners. In the urban centers that had survived since Greco-Roman classical times, craftmakers worked at a high level of competence. Arab writers described the quality of Byzantine handicrafts, especially the luxury products, as being equaled only by those of China. Equally important was the great volume of goods that passed through Constantinople from all regions of Eurasia—slaves and salt from the Black Sea lands; spices, perfumes, and precious stones

Fourteenth-century French illuminated manuscript depicting the papal coronation of Charlemagne in 800. This event caused Constantinople to recognize the political independence of the West in 812 with the granting of the title Basileus *to Charlemagne.*

from India; papyrus and foodstuffs from Egypt; silk and porcelain from China; and silver, wrought iron objects, and linen, cotton, and woolen fabrics from the West.

This political, economic, and military strength allowed the Byzantine emperors to launch reconquest campaigns that were more realistic than Justianian's, if not as ambitious. Crete and Cyprus were recovered, thereby curbing Arab naval raids in the Aegean waters. The imperial frontiers were extended also into northern Syria, Armenia, and Georgia. In the northern Balkans, where the Bulgars were a constant threat to the empire, Basil II won such a crushing victory in 1014 that he was known thereafter as *Bulgaroktonos,* or "the Bulgar-Slayer."

In cultural matters this was a period of stability and homogeneity. The Byzantines still called themselves *Romaioi,* or Romans, but Greek, in either its literary or popular forms, was the universal language of the empire. Religious homogeneity also had been promoted with the conversion of the Moslems on reconquered Crete and of the Slavs in the northern Balkans. In 865 the Bulgarian Khan Boris accepted Christianity from Constantinople in return for imperial recognition of his conquests. In the following years Byzantine missionaries provided the Bulgarians with an alphabet, translated the Scriptures into their language, and prepared a Slavonic liturgy. About the same time the Serbian tribes were converted to Orthodoxy, as were the Russians of the Kievan state.

Imperial stability was strengthened by the intimate, mutually supporting relationship between emperor and patriarch. The principle of a subservient state church was traditional and accepted. The emperor called himself not only *autokrator,* but also *isapostolos,* or the equal of the apostles. The tenth-century book of ceremony for the election of the patriarch of Constantinople spelled out the subservient relationship. The metropolitans of the church were to meet in the great Hagia Sophia church in Constantinople on the command of the emperor and submit to him three candidates for the patriarchate. The emperor was free to select any of the three or to reject all and to nominate his own candidate. The metropolitans then had to agree that the candidate was worthy of the post. In the installation ceremony the new head of the church was pronounced patriarch "by the will of God and Emperor."

In conclusion, Byzantium during these centuries was stable, powerful, wealthy, self-satisfied, and rather inward-looking now that a reasonable coexistence had evolved with both the Western and Moslem worlds. These characteristics are reminiscent of China under the Ming dynasty, as will be noted in the following chapter.

III. BYZANTIUM'S DECLINE

When Basil "the Bulgar-Slayer" died in 1025 the Byzantine Empire seemed secure and unchallenged in its splendid eminence. The northern frontier rested solidly on the Danube. Arabic Islam, now divided, was no longer a threat. And whatever was emerging in the West was patently primitive and insignificant in comparison to the second Rome on the Bosphorus. Yet within half a century after Basil's death the empire was in serious trouble, and less than two centuries later, in 1204, its capital had fallen to the despised Western barbarians.

LATIN CONQUEST OF CONSTANTINOPLE

A major event in the decline of Byzantium was the capture of Constantinople by the Latins of the Fourth Crusade in 1261. The following description by the contemporary Byzantine historian Nicetas Choniates reveals as much about Greek hatred for the Latins as it does about what actually happened.*

. . . How shall I begin to tell of the deeds wrought by these nefarious men! Alas, the images, which ought to have been adored, were trodden under foot! Alas, the relics of the holy martyrs were thrown into unclean places! Then was seen what one shudders to hear, namely, the divine body and blood of Christ was spilled upon the ground or thrown about. They snatched the precious reliquaries, thrust into their bosoms the ornaments which these contained, and used the broken remnants for pans and drinking cups. . . .

Nor can the violation of the Great Church [Santa Sophia] be listened to with equanimity. For the sacred altar, formed of all kinds of precious materials and admired by the whole world, was broken into bits and distributed among the soldiers, as was all the other sacred wealth of so great and infinite splendor.

When the sacred vases and utensils of unsurpassable art and grace and rare material, and the fine silver, wrought with gold, which encircled the screen of the tribunal and the ambo, of admirable workmanship, and the door and many other ornaments, were to be borne away as booty, mules and saddled horses were led to the very sanctuary of the temple. Some of these which were unable to keep their footing on the splendid and slippery pavement, were stabbed when they fell, so that the sacred pavement was polluted with blood and filth. . . .

Nothing was more difficult and laborious than to soften by prayers, to render benevolent, these wrathful barbarians, vomiting forth bile at every unpleasing word, so that nothing failed to inflame their fury. Whoever attempted it was derided as insane and a man of intemperate language. Often they drew their daggers against any one who opposed them at all or hindered their demands.

No one was without a share in the grief. In the alleys, in the streets, in the temples, complaints, weeping, lamentations, grief, the groaning of men, the shrieks of women, wounds, rape, captivity, the separation of those most closely united. Nobles wandered about ignominiously, those of venerable age in tears, the rich in poverty. Thus it was in the streets, on the corners, in the temple, in the dens, for no place remained unassailed or defended the suppliants. All places everywhere were filled full of all kinds of crime. Oh, immortal God, how great the afflictions of the men, how great the distress!

*D. C. Munro, trans., *Translations and Reprints from the Original Sources of European History*, rev. ed., series 1, vol. 1, number III (University of Pennsylvania Press, 1912), pp. 15, 16.

One reason for the dramatic reversal was the undermining of the imperial military system by the growing insubordination of the *strategoi*, or generals, in charge of the *themes*, or provinces. Basil II had been strong enough to keep the military in check, but his weak successors were unable to do so, especially when the *strategoi* joined forces with the great provincial landowners.

The empire was plagued also by serious economic ailments. The large private and monastic estates reduced imperial revenues, especially when Basil's successors relieved the large landowners of most taxes. At the same time imperial expenditures were rising because of court extravagances and the cost of the mercenary army. Equally serious were the mounting raids of Patzinaks and Seljuk Turks, which left

In the spring of 1204, Crusaders under the command of Baldwin of Flanders subjected the city of Constantinople to three days of looting and slaughter. The scene is illustrated here in a nineteenth-century painting by Eugène Delacroix.

certain regions devastated and unproductive. The Byzantine gold *solidus*, which had remained stable for seven centuries, now went through a series of devaluations.

In Byzantium, as in many other empires, internal weakness attracted external aggression. The Norman adventurers from the West, who originally had served as Byzantine mercenaries, now turned against the weakened empire and overran its possessions in southern Italy, which had survived since the time of Justinian's conquests. Likewise in the east were the Seljuk Turks who had infiltrated from their central Asian homeland into the Islamic Empire. There they were employed as mercenaries by the Baghdad caliphs. Gradually the mercenaries became masters, and in 1055 they captured Baghdad and founded the Seljuk Empire. These Turks brought new life into the moribund Islamic world, reuniting the lands between India and the Mediterranean and pressing on the Taurus

Mountain frontier that for centuries had separated the Byzantine and Islamic worlds.

This was the background of the two disasters that befell Byzantium in 1071, marking the beginning of centuries of decline. The first occurred at Bari in southern Italy, where the Normans conquered the sole surviving Byzantine foothold. The second and much more decisive setback was at Manzikert in Asia Minor. There the Seljuks defeated the Byzantine emperor in a fateful battle that began the transformation of Asia Minor from a Greek to a Turkish stronghold. Following this battle two rival emperors fought for the Byzantine throne, using Turkish forces against each other. Thus Turkish tribes were able to enter at will, gradually changing Asia Minor from the bedrock of Greek Byzantine power to the heartland of the Turkish nation.

The Byzantine Empire was saved from what appeared to be imminent dissolution by the shrewdness and tenacity of Emperor Comnenus (1081–1118). He granted valuable commercial concessions to the Venetians in return for their support against the Normans who were threatening to attack Constantinople. He also appealed to Western Christendom for assistance against the Moslem Seljuks. Instead of the few mercenaries he had hoped for, he received hordes of undisciplined Crusaders. Some were led by the Normans that Alexius had excellent reason to distrust. The contact between Eastern and Western Christendom resulted in mutual suspicion and open hostility. Greeks and Latins disliked each other's languages, religions, politics, and ways of life.

Such was the background of the Fourth Crusade, appropriately nicknamed the "businessmen's crusade." Characterized by the economic scheming of Venetian merchants, the quest for loot and lands by Western adventurers, the blandishments of a Byzantine pretender, and the long pent-up grievances harbored by Latins against what they considered to be the cunning, effeminate, grasping, and heretical Greeks, the Fourth Crusade was deflected by greed and revenge from its original goal of liberating Jerusalem. Instead the crusaders attacked Constantinople. A mixed force of French, Venetians, Flemings, and Germans stormed the capital in the spring of 1204 and subjected it to three days of merciless looting and slaughter. "Even the Saracens," observed a Byzantine chronicler, "would have been more merciful." Paradoxically, the end result of the Fourth Crusade was to pave the way for Islamic domination of the entire Middle East. Although the Byzantine Empire was restored in 1261, it never recovered from the traumatic shock of the Latin conquest, remaining in helpless impotence until the Ottoman capture of Constantinople in 1453.

IV. END OF BYZANTIUM

The victorious Latins set up their feudal states on the ruins of Byzantium. They established a Latin empire at Constantinople, a Latin kingdom at Thessaloniki, and several Latin states in Greece. The commercially minded Venetians occupied a whole quarter of Constantinople and annexed numerous islands and ports strategical-

ly located on their route to the Levant. These new states, however, were doomed from the outset. The native Greek Orthodox populations were bitterly hostile to the end. Furthermore, the Latin conquerors had won only a few isolated toeholds on the fringes of the Balkan peninsula and were surrounded on all sides by enemies. They faced not only the Serbian and Bulgarian kingdoms in the Balkan interior, but also three Greek succession states located at Arta in Epirus, at Trebizond on the southern shore of the Black Sea, and at Nicaea in western Asia Minor. The first of these Greek states was too poor to provide effective leadership, and the second was too isolated. So it was Nicaea, with its strategic location, adequate resources, and able leadership, that organized Greek resistance to Latin rule.

By skillful diplomacy and force of arms the Nicaean rulers steadily reduced the Latin Empire until only the city of Constantinople itself remained. Finally, in 1261 the Latin emperor and the Venetian settlers fled from Constantinople without offering resistance. The Nicaean emperor, Michael Palaeologus, then made his solemn entry into the capital and, amid popular acclamation, took up his residence in the imperial palace.

The final phase of Byzantine history took place in the period between 1261, when Michael Palaeologus recovered Constantinople, and 1453, when his successor, Constantinople Palaeologus, was killed at a gate of the capital fighting the Turks. During these two centuries the restored empire consisted merely of the cities of Constantinople and Thessaloniki, with small fluctuating areas around each, and two separate appendages: Mistra, in the Peloponnesus, and Trebizond, in northern Asia Minor.

The outlook for this pitiful remnant of empire was scarcely more promising than that of its Latin predecessors. In Asia it faced the formidable Turks, and in Europe it was surrounded by small Latin states that remained in Greece and by the Serbians and Bulgarians to the north. To these external dangers were added internal difficulties. Economically the empire was bankrupt. The Italian stranglehold on commerce continued unbroken, so that in the mid-fourteenth century the Genoese quarter in Constantinople was collecting seven times as much as the imperial government in customs revenues. The emperors were reduced to debasing their currency and pawning their crown jewels with Venetian bankers. Increased taxes commonly were avoided by the politically influential rich. The poor rose in revolt against the aristocracy of birth and wealth, so that cities were torn by social strife.

Between 1342 and 1349 the city Thessaloniki was ruled by revolutionary leaders known as the Zealots. They reduced taxes on the poor, canceled their debts, confiscated and distributed monastery lands, and introduced participatory democracy with mass rallies and popularly elected officials. Their political program appears to have been influenced by the example of the republican city-states in Italy. But a dying Byzantine Empire could not support the political and social innovations then emerging naturally in the vigorous and expanding West. With Serbian and Turkish aid the emperor suppressed the Zealots and ended their republic. The episode was symptomatic, however, of the deep and widespread discord, as is evident in the following contemporary account:

... the rising spread through the Empire like a terrible and cruel epidemic, attacking many who formerly were quiet and moderate. . . . And so all the cities rose against the aristocracy. . . . The whole empire was in the throes of the most cruel and desperate struggle. . . . The people were ready to rise in arms under the slightest provocation, and committed the most violent deeds because they hated the rich. . . .[1]

The empire was weakened also by religious dissension. Hoping to obtain Western aid against the approaching Turks, the emperors on three separate occasions had agreed to the submission of the Orthodox church to the papacy (Unions of Lyons, 1274; Rome, 1369; and Florence, 1439). These agreements proved meaningless, for the West gave insignificant aid, and Byzantium was further torn by the bitter popular opposition to granting any concessions to the hated Latins. "Better Islam than the pope" was the defiant popular response to the barbarities of the Fourth Crusade and to the exploitation by Italian merchants.

The cry of preference for the Turks had been heard frequently in the past, but in the mid-fifteenth century the situation was unique because the Turks then were in a position to accept the invitation. As noted in Chapter 11, Section V, the Ottoman Turks had taken over from the Seljuks, conquered the remaining Byzantine enclaves in Asia Minor, crossed the straits to Europe, defeated the Bulgars and Serbs, and finally by 1453 were ready to close in on the beleaguered Byzantine capital.

Constantinople's population by this time had shrunk to between 50,000 and 70,000. The total force available for the defense of the city, including a small number from the West, amounted to no more than 9,000. This was totally inadequate to man the extensive series of walls and to repair the breaches pounded by the enemy cannon. The Ottoman army, led by the capable Sultan Mohammed II, numbered at least 80,000. Yet the defenders, under the courageous leadership of Emperor Constantine, repulsed the attackers from April 2, when the siege began, to May 29, when the final assault prevailed. The city was then given over to the soldiery for the promised three-day sack. The contemporary Byzantine historian Ducas describes as follows this ending of a thousand years of Byzantium:

Three days after the fall of the city he [Mohammed] released the ships so that each might sail off to its own province and city, each carrying such a load that it seemed each would sink. And what sort of a cargo? Luxurious cloths and textiles, objects and vessels of gold, silver, bronze and brass, books beyond all counting and number, prisoners including priests and lay persons, nuns and monks. All the ships were full of cargos, and the tents of the army camps were full of captives and of the above enumerated items and goods.[2]

V. BYZANTIUM'S LEGACY

In retrospect Byzantium obviously made significant contributions in various fields. One was in its role as a protective shield behind which the West was left free to develop its own civilization. The full meaning of this advantage became clear when, after the fall of Constantinople in 1453, the Turks within barely half a century reached the heart of Europe and besieged Vienna. Equally important was Byzantium's stimulus to trade and general economic development. For centuries Byzantium was the economic dynamo for the entire Mediterranean basin, and its currency served as the standard international medium of exchange. Its merchants and its commodities did much to lift western Europe out of its feudalized self-sufficiency and to start the Italian city-states on the road to commercial domination of the Mediterranean. In the realm of culture, Byzantium salvaged the intellectual and artistic treasures of antiquity and transmitted them to posterity along with its own legacy. From Byzantium came Roman law codified by Justinian; a religious art that only recently has been properly understood and appreciated; and the literary and scholarly masterpieces of classical and Hellenistic times as compiled, annotated, and preserved by conscientious scholars.

Finally, Byzantium was for the eastern Slavs what Rome had been for the Germans—the great educator and the source of both religion and civilization. The early Russian principalities strung out along river routes carried on a flourishing commerce with Byzantium. Through Kiev were funneled raw materials gathered from the Russian countryside—furs, hides, grains, timber, and slaves—and in return the Byzantine traders delivered luxury goods such as fine cloths, glassware, spices, jewelry, and wine.

With Greek material goods came Greek cultural institutions. Most important to the eastern Slavs was *Orthodox Christianity*, adopted by Prince Vladimir about 988. This involved much more than a mere change of religion. An ecclesiastical hierarchy based on the Byzantine model was now organized. The head was the metropolitan of Kiev, appointed by and subject to the jurisdiction of the patriarch of Constantinople. Orthodox Christianity also brought with it a new religious and legal literature, including translations of the Bible, Byzantine collections of the writings of the church fathers, lives of saints, and law books. Byzantine art also was now introduced in the form of stone churches, mosaics, frescoes, paintings, and particularly icons, in which the Russians excelled and developed their distinctive Russo-Byzantine style. The Orthodox church also brought with it Byzantine ecclesiastical law and established ecclesiastical courts. As in western Europe, these courts had very wide jurisdiction, including all cases involv-

The Russian Orthodox cathedral of St. Basil in Red Square, Moscow.

ing morals, beliefs, inheritance, and matrimonial matters.

In the realm of politics the new church served to strengthen the authority of the prince. Just as in western Europe the papacy had transformed the Frankish kings from tribal chieftains to the Lord's anointed, so now Russian Orthodoxy transformed the heads of the principalities from mere leaders of bands of personal followers to "servants of the lord" and hence rulers by divine right. Furthermore, the Russian church, in accordance with Byzantine tradition, accepted secular authority and control. There was no counterpart in Moscow, as there had been none in Constantinople, of Gregory VII or Innocent III in Rome, demanding and exacting obedience from emperors and kings alike.

This tradition continued after the disappearance of Byzantium. The Russian Orthodox church transferred its loyalty and subservience to the Russian emperor, until the tsarist empire followed the Byzantine to extinction.

In conclusion, Byzantine civilization stands out for its historic role and achievements. Yet Byzantium did lack the freshness and luster of classical Athens, even though, by comparison, Athens was insignificant in size and in time. The reason is that the role of Byzantium was, in the proper sense of the word, conservative. This is not to say that Byzantium was static. From beginning to end it was adjusting itself to changing times and circumstances. But the fact remains that its destiny was to conserve rather than to create. It was born already an aged state within the Roman Empire. It lived in the shadow of past power and glory, which it sought to maintain or recover. It produced a remarkable succession of outstanding leaders—administrators, generals, scholars, and theologians—but because of the context in which they worked very few of them were genuinely creative.

The fact that the East Roman Empire survived that of the West by a full millennium constituted a great advantage at the outset. Between the fifth and eleventh centuries the West was primitive and insignificant in comparison to the second Rome on the Bosphorus. But these were centuries when the West, precisely because it had to start fresh, was laying the foundations for a new civilization, while Byzantium was living on its splendid but overpowering patrimony. This is why from the eleventh century onward the West was able to forge ahead with its booming economy, rising national monarchies, new intellectual horizons, and a dynamic expansionism that manifested itself first in local crusades and then in an overseas thrust that was to lead within a few centuries to global hegemony. And in pitiful contrast, during these later centuries Byzantium was incapable of breaking the bonds to the past and thus became an obsolete *anachronism* that fought a gallant but doomed holding action to the ignominious and inevitable end in 1453.

SUGGESTED READINGS

The best full-scale study is by G. Ostrogorsky, *History of the Byzantine State* (Rutgers University, 1957); and the best short study is by S. Vryonis, Jr., *Byzantium and Europe* (Harcourt, 1967). The latter author also has written an authoritative study of a decisive turning point in Byzantine history entitled *The Decline of Medieval Hellenism in Asia Minor and the Process of Islamization from the Eleventh through the Fifteenth Century* (University of California, 1971). One of the best sources of information on almost every aspect of Byzantium, the south Slavs, and relations with Kiev and Islam is the *Cambridge Medieval History*, Vol. 4 (Cambridge University, 1966). Another standard work that considers cultural as well as political matters is by A. A. Vasiliev, *History of the Byzantium Empire*, 2 vols. (University of Wisconsin, 1958). A short survey that concentrates on the state, on Christianity, and on the Byzantine mind is by D. A. Miller, *The Byzantine Tradition* (Harper & Row, 1966). For other phases of Byzantine culture, see D. T. Rice, *Byzantine Art* (Penguin, 1961) and A. Grabar, *Byzantine Painting* (World, 1953). Finally, a source for primary materials is provided by D. J. Geanakoplos, *Byzantium: Church, Society and Civilization, Seen Through Contemporary Eyes* (University of Chicago, 1985).

NOTES

1. Cited by G. L. Seidler, *The Emergence of the Eastern World* (Pergamon Press, 1968), pp. 116–117.
2. S. Vryonis, Jr., *Byzantium and Europe* (Harcourt Brace Jovanovich, 1967), pp. 190–192.

CHAPTER 13

Traditional Confucian Civilization

I am happy because I am a human and not an animal; a male, and not a female; a Chinese, and not a barbarian; and because I live in Loyang, the most wonderful city in all the world.

Shao Yung (Neo-Confucianist, 1011–1077)

The fact that the Han dynasty eventually was succeeded by the Sui and T'ang dynasties ensured that civilization in China was to continue along traditional lines. Hence the course of China's civilization contrasts sharply with the unique change that was taking form in the West following Rome's collapse. (See Chapter 8, Sections III–V.) The ensuing millennium was a great Golden Age for the Chinese people. During the Han period China had succeeded in catching up to the other Eurasian civilizations, but now, during the medieval period, China forged ahead. China remained the richest, most populous, and in many ways most culturally advanced country in the world.

The millennium between the sixth century, when the Sui dynasty restored imperial unity, and the sixteenth, when the Westerners began their intrusion by sea, was for China an era of unparalleled political, social, and cultural stability. But this stability paradoxically proved to be a curse as well as a blessing. It was a blessing because Chinese society during this millennium provided more material advantages and more psychological security for more people than any other society in the world. But the stability was also a curse because China was so successful and comfortable that it remained relatively unchanged, though not completely static. At the same time, however, as we shall see in the following chapter, the West was being transformed by its technological achievements, its economic vitality, and its social and political *pluralism*. All this engendered a dynamism that culminated in the West's domination of the entire globe. The end result, then, was the disruption of the beautifully balanced but conservative Chinese society by the irresistible expansionism of the West.

Despite this outcome, we should not overlook the fact that for a full millennium the civilization of China led the world by its sheer viability and by its contributions to the human heritage.

I. SUI AND T'ANG DYNASTIES

The Sui dynasty (589–618) played the same role in Chinese history as the Ch'in dynasty had some eight centuries earlier. Both dynasties reunited China after long periods of disorder, and both then proceeded to make fundamental contributions to the development of the country. But in doing so they drove their people so hard and antagonized so many vested interests that both scarcely survived their founders.

The great contribution of the Ch'in rulers was the imperial unity they forced on China through road and canal building; construction of the Great Wall; standardization of weights, measures, and script; and extension and strengthening of the frontiers. The efforts of the Sui emperors were very similar and equally exhausting. They reconstructed the Great Wall, parts of which had fallen into disrepair. They built the main sections of the gigantic canal system that came to be known as the Grand Canal. This met a pressing need by linking the Yangtze valley, which had become the economic center of the country, with the north, which remained the political center. But so heavy was the cost in treasure and lives that the Sui emperor responsible for the undertaking lost popular support and undermined his dynasty.

Equally exhausting were the series of campaigns that extended the imperial frontiers to include the island of Formosa (Taiwan), Annam and Champa in Indochina, and Kansu in the northwest. But the attempts to conquer the most northern of the three kingdoms into which Korea was then divided proved disastrous. Four successive invasions were repulsed by the resolute Korean defenders. The disaffected soldiers mutinied, and overtaxed Chinese peasants rose in rebellion in various parts of the country. The emperor fled to south China, where he was assassinated in 618. The victor in the ensuing struggle among several pretenders established the T'ang dynasty, regarded by many Chinese

and Western historians as the most outstanding of them all.

The most striking accomplishment of the T'ang dynasty was its expansion of the empire. In a series of great campaigns, it extended the frontiers even beyond those of the Han emperors. In central Asia it established Chinese *suzerainty* over the Tarim basin and beyond the Pamirs to the states of the Oxus valley and even to the headwaters of the Indus in modern Afghanistan. Other vast territories that now were forced to accept Chinese suzerainty were Tibet in the south, Mongolia in the northwest, and Korea and Manchuria in the northeast. The only other comparable empire in the world at the time was that of the Moslem Arabs in the Middle East.

China's foreign conquests were made possible by the reestablishment of strong central government at home. The Han dynasty had been undermined by powerful local families that had accumulated huge, self-sufficient, and tax-free estates. They built fortresslike manor houses on these estates and so could successfully defy central authority. Disintegration was also furthered by the appearance of Buddhist monasteries, which, with their extensive and growing landholdings, offered another challenge to the imperial government. The Sui and T'ang dynasties developed an antidote to this political fragmentation. It consisted of the *equal-field system* by which the central government assigned plots of about nineteen acres to all able-bodied peasants. This did not deprive the powerful families of their holdings, for the land assigned to the peasants was obtained from other sources, such as reclamation projects and fields that had been abandoned during the wars. Moreover, only the free peasants received the land grants, and in actual practice, by no means all of them got land. Nevertheless, the equal-field system did help somewhat to loosen the grip of the great families and to strengthen the T'ang regime. It halted for some time the growth of the large semifeudal estates. It increased government revenues, since the small peasants paid taxes whereas the politically powerful great landholders did not. Furthermore, the peasants were given military training and organized into a regular militia, thereby strengthening the military position of the imperial government.

The T'ang dynasty strengthened its authority also by developing a competent bureaucracy to administer the empire. The Sui earlier had reinstated the Han system of civil service based on competitive public examinations. The T'ang continued and expanded this system, following the basic Confucian tenet that matters of state are best resolved by recruiting people of talent. It rejected the typical Western practice of handling state affairs by changing laws and institutions. When fully developed, the Chinese system consisted of a series of examinations held amid elaborate ritual. The first, in the district and prefectural cities, occurred every two or three years, and approximately 2 percent of the candidates who passed these took the prefectural exams a few weeks later. Prefecture-examination survivors (about half the candidates) became eligible for appointment to minor posts and for further examinations held every three years in the provincial capitals. Success here entitled one to take the imperial examinations at the capital. Only 6 percent passed this hurdle and became eligible for appointment to high office; and only a third of these normally passed the final palace examination in the presence of the emperor himself. They were then admitted to membership in the most exalted fraternity of Chinese scholarship, the Hanlin Academy. Historiographers and other high literary officers were selected from the academy.

At first the examinations were fairly comprehensive, emphasizing the Confucian classics but including also subjects like law, mathematics, and political affairs. Gradually, however, they came to concentrate on literary style and Confucian orthodoxy. The net result was a system that theoretically opened offices to all talented males but in practice favored the classes with enough wealth to afford the years of study and preparation. This did not mean that a hereditary aristocracy ruled China; rather, it was a hierarchy of the learned, a "literocracy." On the one hand, it provided China with an efficient and stable administration that won the respect and admiration of Europeans. But on the other, it was a system that stifled originality and bred conformity. As long as China remained relatively isolated in east Asia, it made for stability and continuity. But with the intrusion of the dynamic West it prevented effective adjustment

A standing Buddha on a lotus pedestal from the early Sui dynasty (589–618). The work is carved from sandstone and has traces of pigment. (From Tianlongshan, Shanxi, China; 68.6 x 17.8 x 15.24 cm)

Sixth-century Chinese stoneware figure from the collection of the Victoria and Albert Museum, London.

and response. It was finally abolished altogether in 1905.

The capital of the T'ang Empire was Ch'ang-an, a magnificent city of probably over 1 million people. Its broad thoroughfares, crisscrossing in checkerboard fashion, often were crowded with Persians, Indians, Jews, Armenians, and assorted central Asians. They came as merchants, missionaries, and mercenary soldiers, for China under the T'ang was more open to foreigners than at any other time except for the short-lived Mongol Yüan interlude.

Freedom of thought was most apparent in matters of religion. The extension of imperial frontiers and the reopening of land and sea trade routes brought in many foreign religious ideas and missionaries. This was the case with Buddhism, which first entered China from India during the Han dynasty, and which began to seriously challenge the official Confucianism during the chaos following the collapse of the Han. In that time of trouble Confucianism was increasingly questioned because its emphasis on filial piety and family loyalty appeared to weaken an already weak state. Consequently Buddhism gained rapidly and reached the height of its influence during the early T'ang, which is sometimes called the "Buddhist period" of Chinese history.

Although Buddhism attained great wealth and influence in China, it became thoroughly sinicized in the process. It also contributed fundamentally to Neo-Confucianism. Since there was considerable religious toleration and freedom of thought in China, various Buddhist sects evolved, outstanding being Ch'an, which later appeared in Japan as Zen. This sect emphasized meditation and self-reliance and was the only one to continue a vigorous intellectual life after the T'ang. Another feature of *sinicization* was the government's attempt to control and even subsidize the monasteries and temples, following the typically Chinese concept that a religion should serve the interests of the state and function as its spiritual organ.

In the long run the attempts at control failed, and eventually the government resorted to outright persecution. The Buddhist emphasis on the salvation of the individual rather than on one's obligation to the family was too contrary to basic Chinese traditions. The complete with-

Seated Buddha from the T'ang Dynasty, dated 618–907 C.E.

drawal from society of monks and nuns not only was contrary to tradition but also was considered unnatural and antisocial. Most important, the government coveted the vast treasures and estates that the monasteries had accumulated through the centuries—hence the series of persecutions that crippled Buddhism in China, though it did not disappear altogether as it did in India. The persecution, restricted to the institutions and their clergy, did not include the rank-and-file believers, as happened in comparable situations in the West. The end result of this Buddhist interlude was minimal as far as the overall evolution of Chinese civilization was concerned. Buddhism made significant contributions to Chinese philosophy, metaphysics, art, and literature. But it did not remold Chinese society as a whole, as Christianity had remolded the European.

During the last century and a half of their reign, the T'ang rulers were faced with the usual problems of a dynasty in decline. Imperial expenses outstripped revenues. Population growth likewise outstripped land supply, so that peasant families no longer could be provided with individual plots. The equal-field system broke down, and the wealthy families once more enlarged their estates at the expense of the peasants. Since the revenue system was based on per-capita taxes, the burden of paying for the mounting imperial expenses fell on the peasants at a time when their holdings were shrinking.

The T'ang emperors managed to hang on for about another 150 years, but it was a period of steady deterioration. Incompetence and provocative luxury in the capital along with successive droughts and widespread famine provoked rebellions in many provinces. The dynasty enlisted the support of local military leaders and assorted "barbarian" border peoples. But these soon were out of control. They disregarded court orders and fought among themselves for the succession to the obviously doomed dynasty. The end came in 907, when one of the rebel leaders deposed the last T'ang ruler and sacked Ch'ang-an. The empire now broke into fragments, and the ensuing half-century is known as the period of the "Five Dynasties." An able general finally was able to restore unity and to found a new dynasty, the Sung, which, like its predecessor, endured for about three centuries (960–1279).

II. SUNG GOLDEN AGE

The Sung emperors were much more passive in their external relations than their Han and T'ang predecessors. Instead of beginning with great campaigns reestablishing imperial frontiers in the heart of Eurasia, the second Sung emperor merely tried to regain from nomad control the territory between Peking and the Great Wall. But he was disastrously defeated, and his successor gave up claim to this region. He even paid the nomads an annual "gift," which in fact was thinly veiled tribute. Thus the Sung never recovered the northeast territories in Manchuria, nor the northwest territories that provided access to the overland routes to the West.

This was a grave weakness for the Sung dynasty, leaving it vulnerable to nomadic invasions. The policy of paying "gifts" worked well for a century and a half, but disaster came when a Sung emperor made a rash attempt to recover the northeastern lands. Instead of easy victory he suffered a crushing defeat that was followed by massive invasion of north China. The Sung defenses crumbled, and the dynasty was left with only the Yangtze valley in central China and the lands to the south. Consequently the second half of the dynasty (1127–1279) is

Relief from the tomb of the T'ang Emperor T'ai Tsung (597–649) showing a chestnut bay battle charger.

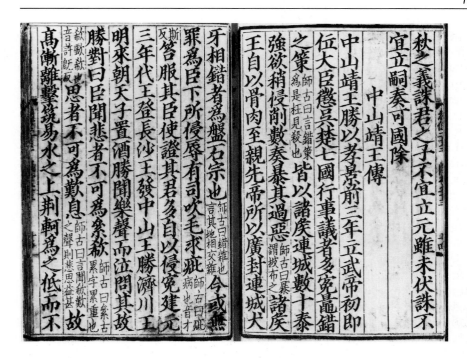

Blockprinted page from Han Shu *(History of the Han Dynasty). Printed between 1208 and 1224, this book is one of the finest examples of Sung printing.*

known as the Southern Sung, and the first half (960–1127) is called the Northern Sung.

The Southern Sung dynasty was much berated by later Chinese historians for failing at the outset to regain the outlying provinces and then suffering the loss of the entire northern half of the country. Although this criticism is undeniable, it is also true that in many respects Chinese civilization reached its height during the centuries of the T'ang and the Sung, particularly in the cultural fields. During these centuries the vast encyclopedias of Buddhist texts and Confucian classics appeared, as well as the comprehensive dynastic histories written by teams of scholars; this period also saw the appearance of the masterpieces of many great poets and artists; the art of calligraphy, depicted on scrolls prized as highly as paintings; the beautiful porcelain as thin as glass and almost as transparent; the priceless invention of printing, which was utilized for the mass duplication and distribution of Buddhist scriptures; and the extraordinary advances in science and technology that are only now being adequately understood. (See Chapter 9, Section II.)

In addition to its cultural attainments, the Sung period is noteworthy for a commercial revolution with much significance for all Eurasia. The roots are to be found in a marked increase in the productivity of China's economy. Steady technological improvements raised the output of the traditional industries. Agriculture likewise was stimulated by the introduction of a quickly maturing strain of rice that allowed two crops to be grown each season where only one had been possible before. Also new water-control projects undertaken by the Sung greatly expanded the acreage of irrigated paddy fields. Thus it is estimated that the rice crop doubled between the eleventh and twelfth centuries.

Increasing productivity made possible a corresponding increase in population, which in turn further stimulated production, in circular fashion. The volume of trade also rose with the quickening tempo of economic activity. For the first time there appeared in China large cities that were primarily commercial rather than administrative centers.

Even more marked than this spurt in domestic trade was the increase in foreign trade. Considerable overseas commerce had been carried on since Han times, but during the T'ang, and more especially during the Sung, the volume of foreign trade far surpassed all previous records. The basis for this burgeoning trade was, of course, the unprecedented productivity of China's economy. Important also were the improvements in maritime technology, including the use of the compass, of the adjustable centerboard keel, and of cotton sails in place of bamboo slats. Finally, overseas trade was stimulated by the initiative of Moslem merchants and mariners who were the great entrepreneurs in Asian seas at this period.

The end result was that for the first time the seaports rather than the old overland routes became China's principal contact with the outside world. Indicative of China's economic leadership at this time is the fact that its exports were mostly manufactured goods such as silk, porcelain, books, and paintings, whereas the imports were mostly raw materials such as spices, minerals, and horses. Finally, it should be noted that during the Sung the Chinese themselves for the first time engaged in overseas trade on a large scale. They no longer depended on foreign intermediaries. In conclusion, China during the Sung was well on its way to becoming a great maritime power. However, the all-important fact—for world history as well as for Chinese—is that this potentiality was never realized. And equally significant, this commercial revolution of the Sung era had none of the explosive repercussions on Chinese society that a corresponding commercial revolution had on Western society. (See Section IV, this chapter.)

III. YÜAN MONGOL RULE

The rule of the Southern Sung, though confined to only half the century, was exceptionally peaceful and prosperous. Meanwhile, north China was under the Ch'in, a people of Manchurian origin. About 1215 they appealed to the Southern Sung for help against the formidable Mongols, who had driven them out of Peking. The Sung, not aware of their deadly power, supported the Mongols instead by sending infantry skilled in siege warfare, and by 1234 the Ch'in were overwhelmed. Then the Sung emperor rashly attempted to secure north China for his own empire. The Mongols retaliated by promptly invading south China. Because the Mongols were preoccupied elsewhere, the war dragged on for decades, but the end came in 1279 when the last Sung ruler perished in a naval battle. A new Mongol dynasty that took

the name Yüan now began its rule, which was to last until 1368.

This was the first and only time that China was ruled by full nomads who had not already been partly sinicized by earlier contact with the empire. The first reaction of the rude conquerors was to level the cities and to incorporate their new subjects into the traditional Mongol tribal society. But they soon learned this was impossible and that a more lucrative alternative was feasible. A Chinese adviser described that alternative:

Now that you have conquered everywhere under Heaven and all the riches of the four seas, you can have everything you want, but you have not yet organized it. You should set up taxation on land and merchants, and should make profits on wine, salt, iron, and the produce of the mountains and marshes. In this way in a single year you will obtain 500,000 ounces of silver, 80,000 rolls of silk and 400,000 piculs of grain. How can you say that the Chinese people are of no use to you?[1]

The Mongols acted on this advice and established an administrative apparatus essentially similar to that of their Chinese predecessors. At the same time they were able to preserve their identity because their nomadic background separated them from their subjects in language, customs, and laws. They also took care to employ many foreigners in their service to counterbalance the Chinese majority, whom they did not trust. Marco Polo is the best known of these foreign-born bureaucrats, though most of them were central Asian Moslems.

Kublai Khan, who moved the Mongol capital from Karakorum to Peking and became essentially a Chinese emperor, dutifully performed the traditional Confucian imperial rites. He also sought to appease the Confucian literati by exempting them from taxation, but they remained largely alienated. They resented the large number of foreigners who had turned their civil service into an international bureaucracy. They also resented the Mongol toleration and patronage of various foreign religions, including Islam and Nestorian Christianity. (See Chapter 12, Section IV.)

Because of its nature and relatively short duration, Mongol rule in China did not leave a

Kublai Khan, wearing ermine coat, with Mongol warriors at the hunt. Note the camel caravan in the hills at rear.

duced by the Sung but developed further by the Mongols. Marco Polo repeatedly expressed his astonishment at the use of paper money, as did a fellow Italian merchant in the following words:

Whatever silver the merchants carry with them to Cathay the lord of Cathay takes from them and puts in his treasury and gives that paper money of theirs in exchange . . . and with this money you can readily buy silk and whatever other merchandise you desire to buy, and all of the people of the country are bound to receive it, and you shall not pay a higher price for your goods because your money is of paper.[2]

The able Kublai Khan died in 1294 at the age of eighty and was succeeded by his equally able grandson, Timur. But Timur died young, and the following khans were incompetent and debauched by palace life. Fratricidal conflicts broke out within the dynasty, and frequent flooding of the Yellow River produced widespread famine in north China. Rebellions broke out in most of the provinces, and only the rivalry among the rebel leaders enabled the Mongols to hold out as long as they did. Finally, the turmoil was ended by an able commoner who, like the founder of the Han, rose through sheer ability in time of crisis and opportunity to become the "Son of Heaven." Thus the Chinese Ming dynasty was established in 1368 and remained in power to 1644.

IV. MING ETHNOCENTRISM AND WITHDRAWAL

Two dynasties, the Ming (1368–1644) and the Ch'ing (1644–1912), ruled China during the more than half-millennium between the overthrow of the Mongols and the advent of the republic. These centuries comprise one of the great eras of orderly government and social stability in human history. A main reason for this unusual durability was the complete primacy of a new Confucian metaphysics known as *Neo-Confucianism*. This renaissance of Confucian thought took place mostly during the time of troubles following the collapse of the T'ang dynasty, when the needs of the age clearly called for something more than the mere memoriza-

deep imprint on the country. Perhaps the most lasting contribution was the selection of Peking (modern Beijing) as the capital. Situated in the north China plain on the routes leading westward to central Asia and eastward to Manchuria, (Beijing) has remained an important military, economic, and administrative center to the present day. Mongol rule also brought about a sharp rise in overland trade, since China now was part of a huge empire encompassing most of Eurasia. Commerce was facilitated by the widespread use of paper money, which was introtion of Confucian classics. Accordingly, a number of scholars undertook a searching reappraisal of the problems of humankind and of the universe.

A leader in this undertaking was Chu Hsi (1129–1200), who in his youth had studied both Buddhism and Taoism. Satisfied with neither, he turned to the Confucian classics, and with his remarkable talent for synthesis he worked out an interpretation that combined elements of Buddhism and Taoism with Confucianism and that was more satisfying and relevant for his time. His approach—essentially that of the empirical rationalist—taught that the universe is governed by natural law, which should be understood and respected. He also believed in the goodness of people and in their ability to become more perfect. He compared the individual to a mirror covered with dust, which if cleaned will be as bright as ever. Evil, therefore, was the result of neglect and of defective education, and hence could be corrected.

Chu Hsi's influence in the Confucian world was comparable to that of Thomas Aquinas in Western Christendom. Just as Aquinas soon was to weave Aristotle and St. Paul into the official scholastic philosophy, so Chu Hsi now integrated contemporary Chinese thought into Neo-Confucianism. And by his very comprehensive and persuasive ideas Chu Hsi, like Aquinas, discouraged further philosophical development. This was particularly true during the Ming period, when, as a reaction against the preceding foreign Mongol domination, there was a pronounced ethnocentrism and a looking backward to past traditions. In such an atmosphere, Chu Hsi came to be regarded as the absolute and final authority. "Ever since the time of the philosopher Chu," declared a Ming scholar, "the Truth has been made manifest to the world. No more writing is needed: what is left to us is practice."[3]

Since the Confucian classics, with Chu Hsi's commentaries, became the basis of the civil-service examinations, this Neo-Confucianism became the official orthodox view of the empire until the late nineteenth century. Its effect was to provide the growing social rigidity with an intellectual reason for its existence. It contributed fundamentally to the unique and long-lasting continuity of Chinese civilization, but the cost was stultifying conformity that quashed all originality or new ideas from the outside.

Chinese society owed its stability not only to Neo-Confucianism, but also to the entrenched power of the so-called gentry ruling class, whose power rested on their combined possession of land and office in an agrarian-based bureaucratic empire. As landlords and as money-lenders the gentry dominated the economic life of the villages and towns. Shortage of land and of capital enabled them to impose extortionate rents and interest rates. Frequent natural disasters bankrupted people with mortgages, who then virtually became serfs under contract to local gentry families. It was common for these families by late Ming times to have several thousand indentured peasant households of this sort.

The gentry also were degree holders; indeed, this is what the Chinese term for "gentry" literally means. Landowning was almost a necessity for financing the years of study necessary to become a degree holder, and hence to be eligible for a post in the bureaucracy. Thus the association between the local gentry and the imperial bureaucracy was intimate and mutually supporting. Frequently a government official arriving at a new provincial post found the native dialect quite incomprehensible and so was completely dependent on the local gentry for orientation and guidance.

Ming and Ch'ing China were ruled by the bureaucracy and the gentry together, if a meaningful distinction can be made between the two. Both the imperial establishment and the local gentry were interested in preserving the mutually beneficial status quo, and they cooperated to that end. Whereas earlier dynasties occasionally had attempted to force through land redistribution and other such reforms, the Ming and the Ch'ing carefully avoided any challenges to the gentry's control of the countryside.

By contrast, it is revealing and significant that the Ming government took the initiative in controlling and repressing the merchant class. This was a basic and most meaningful difference between the Western and Chinese societies. In the West, as will be noted in the following chapter, the bourgeoisie from the start enjoyed considerable autonomy and was able to increase it

ROOTS OF CHINESE STABILITY

Foreign observers invariably were impressed by the antiquity and stability of Chinese civilization. T. T. Meadows, a British consular officer who served in China in the mid-nineteenth century, gave the following explanation based on first-hand observation.*

The real causes of the unequalled duration and constant increase of the Chinese people, as one and the same nation . . . consists of three doctrines, together with an institution. . . . *The doctrines are*

I. That the nation must be governed by moral agency in preference to physical force.

II. That the services of the wisest and ablest men in the nation are indispensable to its good government.

III. That the people have the right to depose a sovereign who, either from active wickedness or vicious indulgence, gives cause to oppressive and tyrannical rule.

The institution is

The system of public service competitive examinations. . . .

The institution of Public Service Examinations (which have long been strictly competitive) is the cause of the continued duration of the Chinese nation: it is that which preserves the other causes and gives efficacy to their operation. By it all parents throughout the country, who can compass the means, are induced to impart to their sons an intimate knowledge of the literature which contains the three doctrines above cited, together with many others conducive to a high mental cultivation. By it all the ability of the country is enlisted on the side of that Government which takes care to preserve it in purity. By it, with its impartiality, the poorest man in the country is constrained to say, that if his lot in life is a low one it is so in virtue of the "will of Heaven," and that no unjust barriers created by his fellow men prevent him from elevating himself. . . .

The normal Chinese government is essentially based on moral force: it is not a despotism. A military and police is maintained sufficient to crush merely factious risings, but totally inadequate, both in numbers and in nature, to put down a disgusted and indignant people. But though no despotism, this same government is in form and machinery a pure autocracy. In his district the magistrate is absolute; in his province, the governor; in the empire, the Emperor. The Chinese people have no right of legislation, they have no right of self-taxation, they have not the power of voting out their rulers or of limiting or stopping supplies. They have therefore the right of rebellion. Rebellion is in China the old, often exercised, legitimate, and constitutional means of stopping arbitrary and vicious legislation and administration.

*T. T. Meadows, *The Chinese and Their Rebellions* (Smith, Elder, 1856), pp. 23, 24, 401–403.

with the passage of time. In China there was a corresponding merchant class, which during the Sung enjoyed a real commercial revolution. Furthermore, China made most of the basic technological inventions of medieval times. Yet the commercial revolution and the technological advances together were not enough to cause the revolutionary repercussions in China that completely transformed society in the West. The basic reason for this, as noted in Chapter 8, Section V, was the continuity of Chinese history—the fact that the Han dynasty was continued in essentials by the Sui, and the Sui in turn by the T'ang and the Sung, and so on in unbroken succession until the end of imperial history in 1912. Thus the traditional bureaucracy–gentry ruling establishment, propped up by the ideas of Neo-Confucianism, was able to absorb and blunt

Chinese general, one of the guardian figures along the road to the Ming tombs outside of Peking.

Chinese merchants and industrialists customarily organized themselves into local guilds headed by chiefs. But guild chiefs were certified by the government, which held them responsible for the conduct of individual members. Boat traders were organized under harbor chiefs who were also responsible to the government. More important were the government monopolies in the production and distribution of many commodities that the court and the administration consumed, including arms, textiles, pottery, leather goods, apparel, and wine. The government also completely controlled the production and distribution of basic commodities, such as salt and iron, that were necessities for the entire population. Such restraints deprived Chinese merchants of the opportunity for free enterprise and restricted economic growth. The restraints also promoted official corruption, for members of the imperial court used their privileged positions to manipulate the state monopolies for personal gain.

Another example of the restrictive, inward-looking policies of China's ruling establishment was its active opposition to overseas enterprise. Chinese emigrants had trickled down to Southeast Asia before the arrival of the Europeans. Probably at no time were there as many Spaniards as Chinese in the Philippines. In 1603, thirty-two years after the founding of Manila as a Spanish settlement, the Chinese population there was about 20,000 compared with perhaps 1,000 Spaniards. And these Chinese, who virtually controlled the economic life of the settlement, were extending their control to the other islands of the archipelago. When in that year, 1603, the Manila Chinese suffered one of the massacres that they and their compatriots in Southeast Asia have periodically endured to the present day, an official of the nearby mainland province of Fukien condoned the massacre and denounced all overseas Chinese as deserters of the tombs of their ancestors and people who were unworthy of the emperor's concern. Likewise an imperial edict of 1712 forbade Chinese to trade and reside in Southeast Asia. Five years later another edict allowed those already abroad to come home without fear of punishment, and in 1729 still another edict set a deadline after which those overseas could not be allowed to return. What a striking contrast between this

the effects of new technology and of economic growth. But in the West, Rome came to an end with no imperial successor. Instead, a new pluralistic civilization emerged in which gunpowder, the compass, the printing press, and the oceangoing ship were not muffled but rather exploited to their full potential with explosive consequences, first for Europe and then for the entire world, including China.

Explosive repercussions were impossible in China because the imperial establishment there was too enveloping and restricting. For example,

Chinese policy and that of the West. The Western states would soon be actively promoting overseas settlements and trading companies and would be ready to take up arms against any threats to these enterprises.

The bizarre history of the early fifteenth-century Ming voyages provides the most dramatic example of the negative official Chinese attitude toward overseas activities. These voyages had an astonishing range and showed a technological superiority that proved conclusively China's world leadership in maritime undertakings. Then came the imperial order forbidding further overseas expeditions and the immediate enforcement of that order. (See Chapter 9, Section I.)

Although the precise motives behind this edict are unknown, the significant fact is that it was possible to issue it only because Chinese merchants lacked the political power and social status of their Western counterparts. This fundamental difference in institutional structure and outward-thrusting dynamism deflected Chinese energies inward at this fateful turning point in world history and left the oceans of the globe open to Western enterprise. The inevitable result was the eclipse within a few centuries of the great "Celestial Kingdom." The barbarians of the West now came to the fore.

V. CHINESE CIVILIZATION IN JAPAN

Since the Chinese civilization and Chinese empires persisted in unbroken continuity to modern times, they have dominated east Asia in a way that no Western country has dominated the West. Consequently there did not develop in east Asia the political and cultural diversity that has characterized the West since the fall of Rome. The only exception has been in the steppes and deserts of the far north and west, where agriculture is climatically impossible and where the nomads accordingly developed a distinctive, non-Chinese, pastoral way of life. By contrast, in the neighboring Vietnamese, Korean, and Japanese lands, there was no climatic obstacle to the development of agriculture and hence to the spread of Chinese civilization. Of these three lands, Japan was able to remain the most independent of the Chinese colossus, both

politically and culturally, and hence played a correspondingly more significant role in both east Asian and world history. The remainder of this chapter, therefore, will concentrate on the evolution of Japan to the eve of the Western penetration.

Japanese history has been shaped to a considerable degree by the influence of geographic location. In this respect there is a close parallel with the British Isles at the other end of the Eurasian landmass. The Japanese islands, however, are more isolated than the British Isles; 115 miles separate them from the mainland, compared with the 21-mile width of the English Channel. Thus, before their defeat in World War

A clay statue of a warrior in armor from an ancient tomb.

II by the United States, the Japanese had been seriously threatened by foreign invasion only in the thirteenth century by the Mongols. The Japanese, therefore, have been close enough to the mainland to benefit from the great Chinese civilization but distant enough to be able to select and reject as they wished. In fact, the Japanese have been unusually sensitive and alert to what they have imported from abroad. Although popularly regarded as a nation of borrowers, they have independently evolved, because of their isolation, a larger proportion of their own culture than have any other people of comparable numbers and level of development.

The Japanese are basically a Mongoloid people who migrated from northeast Asia, but the hairy Caucasoid Ainu who originally inhabited their islands contributed to their racial composition. Malayan and Polynesian migrants from the south probably did also. Early Japan was organized into a large number of clans, each ruled by a hereditary priest-chieftain. Toward the end of the first century after Christ, the Yamato clan established a loose political and religious domination over the others. Its chief was the emperor, and its clan god was made the national god.

This clan organization was undermined by the importation of Chinese civilization, which began on a large scale in the sixth century. Buddhism, introduced from Korea, was the medium for cultural change, playing the same role here as Christianity did in Europe among the Germans and Slavs. Students, teachers, craftmakers, and monks crossed over from the mainland, bringing with them a new way of life as well as a new religion. More significant was the role of those Japanese who went to the "Celestial Kingdom" and returned as ardent converts. The forces for change produced the Taika Reform, which began in 645 and sought to change Japan into a centralized state on the model of T'ang dynasty China. In accordance with the Chinese model, the country was divided into provinces and districts ruled by governors and magistrates who received their power from the emperor and his council of state. Also, all land was nationalized in the name of the emperor and given to peasant households. The new owner-cultivators were responsible for paying to the central government a land tax in the form of rice and a labor tax that sometimes included military service.

These and other changes were designed to strengthen imperial authority, and they did so in comparison with the earlier clan structure. But in practice, the Japanese emperor was far from being the undisputed head of a highly centralized state. The powerful hereditary aristocracy forced certain changes in this Chinese-type administration that finally brought about its downfall. Although officials supposedly were appointed, as in China, on the basis of merit through examination, actually the old aristocracy succeeded in obtaining positions of status and power. Likewise, they kept many of their large landholdings, which were usually tax exempt and became manors outside the governmental administrative system. During this period the Fujiwara family perfected the *dyarchy*, or dual system of government. They did the actual work of ruling, furnishing the consorts for the emperor and filling the high civil and military posts. Meanwhile, the emperor passed his life in luxurious seclusion, not bothered by affairs of state or by contacts with commoners. His chief responsibility was to guarantee that his dynasty would continue forever. This dyarchical system of government, which had no parallel in China, remained the pattern in Japan until the country was opened up by the Europeans in the nineteenth century.

In cultural matters there was the same adaptation of Chinese models. The Japanese borrowed Chinese ideographs but developed their own system of writing. They borrowed Confucianism but modified its ethics and changed its political doctrines to suit their social structure. They accepted Buddhism but adapted it to satisfy their own spiritual needs, while keeping their native Shintoism. They built new imperial capitals, first at Nara and then at Kyoto, that were modeled after the T'ang capital, Ch'ang-an. But there was no mistaking the Japanese quality of the temples, pavilions, shrines, and gardens. The imperial court became the center of highly developed intellectual and artistic activity. Court life is delightfully described in Lady Murasaki's famous eleventh-century novel, *The Tale of Genji*. But this novel also reflects a society grown effeminate and devoted almost exclusively to aesthetic and sensual pleasures. This degeneration, which worsened in the next century, contributed to the coming of the new age of feudalism, when political power shifted from the imperial court to virile rural warriors.

VI. JAPANESE FEUDALISM

The Chinese system of imperial organization introduced by the Taika Reform of 645 worked effectively for a long period. By the twelfth century, however, it had been undermined and replaced by a Japanese variety of feudalism. One reason was the tendency of provincial governors, who were too fond of the entertainments of Kyoto, to give their powers and responsibilities to local subordinates. Another was that powerful local families and Buddhist communities were always hungry for land and often able to seize it by force. They were willing to bring new land under cultivation as long as the incentive of tax exemption was maintained. These trends reduced the amount of tax-paying land, which meant an increased tax load for the peasant owner-cultivators. They in turn either fled to the northern frontier areas, where the Ainu were being pushed back by force of arms, or else commended themselves and their lands to lords of manors. This freed them of taxes and provided them with protection, but at the cost of becoming serfs. The net result of this process was that by the end of the twelfth century, tax-paying land amounted to 10 percent or less of the total cultivated area, and local power had been taken over by the new rural aristocracy.

At the same time, the aristocracy had become the dominant military force because of the disintegration of the imperial armed forces. The Taika Reform had made all males between the ages of twenty and sixty subject to military service. But the conscripts were required to furnish their own weapons and food and were given no relief from the regular tax burden. This arrangement proved unworkable and was abandoned in 739. Government military posts usually were filled by effeminate court aristocrats. As a result, the campaigns against the Ainu were fought by the rural aristocrats. They became mounted warriors and gradually increased their military effectiveness until they completely overshadowed the imperial forces. A feudal relationship now developed between these rural lords and their retainers, or *samurai* (literally, "one who serves"). This relationship was based on an idealized ethic that was known as *bushido*, or "way of the warrior." The samurai enjoyed special legal and ceremonial rights, and in return were expected to give unquestioning service to their lords.

By the twelfth century, Japan was controlled by competing groups of feudal lords, who struggled to gain control of as much land as possible. The outcome was the rise of great territorial magnates known as *daimyo* ("great name"). At the beginning of the sixteenth century there were several hundred of these daimyo, each seeking to attain hegemony over all Japan.

One of the many lovely gardens of Kyoto, capital of the Ashikaga Shogunate.

VII. JAPAN'S WITHDRAWAL AND ISOLATION

The period of daimyo control was one of rapid economic growth, with important repercussions for Japanese society. Important technological advances were made in agriculture as well as in handicrafts. Production per acre apparently doubled or even tripled in some parts of the country. The increased productivity stimulated more trade and a shift from a barter to a money economy. Towns gradually developed in the fifteenth and sixteenth centuries at strategic crossroads or coastal harbors or major temples. In these towns appeared the Japanese guilds, or *za*, which, like their Western counterparts, sought to gain monopoly rights in the production or transportation of certain goods or in the exercise of certain trades or professions. They obtained these monopoly rights by paying fees to certain local authorities, thereby gaining greater freedom and higher status for their members.

Foreign and domestic trade quickened with the rising productivity of the Japanese economy. As early as the twelfth century enterprising Japanese had crossed overseas to Korea and then to China, prepared both for trade and for piracy. Gradually they extended their operations, so that by the late fourteenth century these pirate-traders were active throughout Southeast Asia. Japanese settlers and soldiers of fortune also were widely scattered, especially in Indochina, Siam, and the Philippines.

These socioeconomic developments began to undermine feudalism in Japan, as they had done earlier under similar circumstances in the West. If this trend had continued without interruption, Japan presumably would have followed the west European example and developed into a modern unified nation-state with an overseas empire. But Japan did not do so; instead it withdrew into seclusion.

A prime reason for this withdrawal appears to have been the penetration of the Western powers into the waters of Southeast and east Asia. This blocked the natural course of Japanese expansionism. If the Westerners had not appeared, the Japanese probably would have won footholds in Formosa and in various parts of Southeast Asia. But now the Japanese were alarmed by the obvious superiority of Western military technology on the seas, as well as by the surprising effectiveness of Western missionaries within Japan. The Japanese response was to withdraw into the almost complete seclusion adopted in the early seventeenth century by the Tokugawa Shogunate.

All missionaries were forced to leave and their converts required to renounce their faith. Eventually all foreigners had to depart, with the exception of a few Chinese and Dutch who were allowed to trade under restricted conditions on the Deshima islet in Nagasaki harbor. In addition, Japanese subjects were forbidden to go abroad on penalty of death. Thus began over two centuries of seclusion for Japan.

The end result, then, was not a modern expansionist nation-state. Rather, Japanese feudalism was preserved and shielded from outside influences by the Tokugawa walls of seclusion. In their search for stability, the Tokugawa imported Confucian ideas and institutions from China. They adopted the Confucian hierarchy of four classes—the warrior administrator, the peasant, the artisan, and the merchant. They also borrowed Confucian philosophy, with its emphasis on proper relationships between rulers and ruled. An influential school of Confucianism was established at Edo, and gradually the Japanese people were influenced by the ethical and moral standards of Chinese philosophy. Buddhism remained the dominant religion of the masses, but Confucianism slowly became the strongest intellectual force in Japan.

The cost for Japan, as for China, was institutional rigidity and obsolescence. Yet there was a fundamental difference between the two countries. Japan was not saddled with a monolithic, overpowering imperial structure, as was the case in China. Rather, the Tokugawas had merely papered over the cracks, so that when the West intruded in the nineteenth century, Japan, unlike China, was able to respond positively and creatively.

SUGGESTED READINGS

The basic works for China are listed in the bibliography for Chapter 8. To that list should be added the interpretative bibliographical essay published by the American Historical Association's Service Center for

Teachers of History: J. K. Fairbanks, *New Views of China's Tradition and Modernization* (Washington, 1968). This bibliography describes recent works on subjects such as the rise of the bureaucratic state, the role of the merchants, and class structure and mobility.

Some of the more important studies on the period from 220 to 1644 are W. Bingham, *The Founding of the T'ang Dynasty* (Waverly Press, 1941); E. A. Kracke, *Civil Service in Early Sung China, 960–1067* (Harvard University, 1953); J. T. C. Liu, *Reform in Sung China* (Harvard University, 1959); C. O. Hucker, *The Traditional Chinese State in Ming Times, 1368–1644* (University of Arizona, 1961); and E. Balazs, *Chinese Civilization and Bureaucracy: Variations on a Theme* (Yale University, 1964). Intellectual trends are analyzed in the following two volumes presenting assorted symposia papers: A. F. Wright, ed., *Studies in Chinese Thought* (University of Chicago, 1953); and J. K. Fairbank, ed., *Chinese Thought and Institutions* (University of Chicago, 1957). Another useful collection is by J. M. Menzel, ed., *The Chinese Civil Service: Career Open to Talent?* (Heath, 1963). Finally, there is M. Elvin, *The Pattern of the Chinese Past* (Stanford University, 1973), which analyzes why medieval China's flair for technology did not lead to an industrial revolution, as does also J. Needham, *The Grand Titration: Science and Society in East and West* (George Allen & Unwin, 1969). For those who find Needham's monumental volumes too massive, a more accessible yet reliable account is available in R. Temple, *The Genius of China: 3,000 Years of Science, Discovery and Invention* (Simon & Schuster, 1987). On a related subject, another readable work is by P. Snow, *The Star Raft: China's Encounter with Africa* (Weidenfeld & Nicolson, 1988). Finally, China's achievements during these centuries are analyzed in a global context by W. H. McNeill, *The Pursuit of Power* (University of Chicago, 1982).

On Japan, the American Historical Association's Service Center for Teachers of History has published a convenient general bibliography by J. W. Hall, *Japanese History: New Dimensions of Approach and Understanding*, 2nd ed. (Washington, 1961). The standard annotated bibliography is by B. Silberstein, *Japan and Korea: A Critical Bibliography* (University of Arizona, 1962). Invaluable source materials on Japanese political, moral, and philosophical thought are provided in R. Tsunoda et al., *Sources of the Japanese Tradition* (Columbia University, 1958). Standard general histories have been written by the British scholar G. B. Sansom, *Japan: A Short Cultural History*, rev. ed. (Appleton, 1944), and his definitive three-volume *A History of Japan* (Stanford University, 1958–64). The best introductory survey is by E. O. Reischauer, *Japan Past and Present*, rev. ed. (Knopf, 1953).

NOTES

1. Cited by J. Needham, *Science and Civilization in China* (Cambridge University, 1954), pp. 1, 140.
2. H. Yule, ed., *Cathay and the Way Thither*, Hakluyt Society, Series 2, XXXVII (London, 1914), p. 154.
3. Cited by L. C. Goodrich, *A Short History of the Chinese People* (Harper & Row, 1943), p. 200.

CHAPTER
14

Revolutionary Western Civilization

The chief glory of the later Middle Ages was not its cathedrals or its epics or its scholasticism: it was the building for the first time in history of a complex civilization which rested not on the backs of sweating slaves or coolies but primarily on non-human power.

Lynn White, Jr.

"We should note the force, effort, and consequences of inventions which are nowhere more conspicuous than in those three which were unknown to the ancients, namely, printing, gunpowder, and the compass. For these three have changed the appearance and state of the whole world."[1] This statement by the British philosopher-scientist Francis Bacon (1561–1626) is especially significant because all three of the inventions that he so wisely selected originated in China. Yet they had little effect on that country in comparison with their explosive repercussions in the West. Chinese civilization was too deeply rooted and Chinese imperial organization too all-embracing to allow such inventions to disrupt traditional institutions and practices. Thus print-ing was used to disseminate old ideas rather than new; gunpowder reinforced the position of the emperor rather than of emerging national monarchs; and the compass, despite the remarkable expeditions of Cheng Ho, was not used for world trade and exploration and empire building as in the West.

The root of this fateful difference is to be found in the unique characteristics of the new Western civilization—pluralistic, adaptable, and free of the shackles of tradition that bound all the other Eurasian civilizations. The new civilization brought about historic change not only for the West but also, as Bacon foresaw, for the entire globe as it came under the influence of the revolutionary new society.

I. PLURALISM IN THE WEST

"In order to escape the evils which they saw coming, the people divided themselves into three parts. One was to pray God; for trading and ploughing the second; and later, to guard these two parts from wrongs and injuries, knights were created."[2] This analysis by the secretary to Phillip VI of France describes simply but accurately the basic division of medieval Western society into priests, workers, and warriors. Although these three classes were to be found in all Eurasian civilizations, their status and interrelationships were unique in the West because of the disintegration of the Roman Empire and the failure to reconstruct it. Precisely how the classes functioned under these circumstances will be considered now in relation to the three institutions they represented: feudalism, manorialism, and the church.

Feudalism was a system of government in which those who possessed landed estates also possessed political power. State authority was replaced by contractual agreements between lords and vassals. Feudalism appeared when the German kings—who had taken over Roman imperial authority but lacked the funds to maintain a bureaucracy, a judiciary, and armed forces—found that their only alternative was to grant estates as reward for service. But the recipients, or vassals, tended to rule them as private realms. Charlemagne was strong enough to exact and enforce oaths of loyalty from his vassals. But under his weak successors political power shifted to the vassals, and their estates, or *fiefs*, became virtually private property. These powerful lords in turn subdivided their holdings into lesser fiefs, which they allocated to followers who were dependent on them rather than on the king. The feudal contract between these lords and vassals specified certain mutual obligations. The most important were that the lord should provide protection in addition to granting the estate, and the vassal rendered military service for as long a time each year as local custom required—usually about forty days.

This process of feudalization proceeded rapidly within each of the feudal kingdoms that took form following the disintegration of Charlemagne's empire. Since the legal justification for the fiefs of the great lords was supposed

The successor to feudalism, manorialism relied on the self-sufficiency of the serfs.

to come from royal authority, the lords were careful to select a suitable king even though they had no intention of respecting his sovereignty. But as western Europe settled down after 1000 and the foreign invasions ceased, the kings gradually were able to assert their feudal rights and to begin the building of strong monarchies. The ensuing struggle between kings and nobles was the essence of Western political history during the following centuries.

Just as feudalism emerged when large-scale political organization collapsed, so also manorialism emerged with the collapse of large-scale economic organization. Responding to this economic disintegration, the manor became a self-sufficient village worked by serfs who were not free to leave and who, by dint of their labor, supported a hierarchy of lay and clerical lords. The size of the manors varied considerably; inhabitants might number in the scores or the hundreds. Unlike slaves, serfs had recognized rights as well as responsibilities. They were entitled to protection, were assured a plot of land for the support of themselves and family, and enjoyed many religious holidays and harvest festivals that gave them relief from toil. In return they were required to till strips of land in the cultivated fields that were reserved for the lord, to perform other domestic and farm chores for the lord, and to give him a portion of any income from any source.

The *manor* had to fill almost all its own needs because of the virtual disappearance of long-distance trade, of centralized handicraft production, of imperial currencies, and the like. Despite, or perhaps because of, this self-sufficiency, manorial technology was not at all primitive compared to that of Roman times. When the economy of the empire disintegrated, there was a loss of luxury crafts, irrigation works, aqueducts, and road systems. But the self-sufficient villages, just because they were self-sufficient, had no need for imperial organization. They functioned—and with steadily improving efficiency—on a local, village-to-village basis. The manors kept and improved the mills and smithies and used more iron than ever before since it could be produced locally. Thus agricultural technology in the medieval West (as will be noted in Section III of this chapter) advanced substantially beyond Greco-Roman standards and had far-reaching effects on all aspects of life.

Turning to the Roman Catholic church, we find a similarly paradoxical development; that is, the pope emerged with more power precisely because of the fall of Rome. He did not have to fight against imperial domination, as did the bishops of Constantinople, Alexandria, and Antioch, who had to contend with the dictates of the Byzantine emperor. When one of these emperors sought to control the church in the West, Pope Gelasius (492–496) sent him a famous letter in which he asserted that "bishops, not the secular power, should be responsible for the administration of the church." Furthermore, the Byzantine emperors were distracted by the attacks of the Moslems and of other enemies. The popes were left free to strengthen their position in the West, and they did this in two ways. First, they made an alliance with the rising Franks, which culminated in the crowning of Charlemagne by Pope

Leo III in 800. Second, the papacy sent out missions to convert the pagans in northern Europe. They succeeded in organizing new churches that accepted the pope's authority—such as the English church in 597, the Lombard and Frisian in the seventh century, and the German in the eighth.

Such, then, were the components of the new pluralistic society emerging in the West: an independent church instead of one subject to dictation by the emperor; feudal kings and lords in place of imperial authority; autonomous manors working individually to tame the wilderness instead of the slave plantations of Roman times; and, before long, a rising merchant class operating effectively from its urban bases against nobles, prelates, and, ultimately, against monarchs. How this society, alone in all Eurasia, evolved and adapted during the half-millennium after 1000 and how it eventually developed the strength and dynamism for overseas expansion is the subject of the following sections.

II. GEOGRAPHIC BACKGROUND

Geographic considerations are a significant factor in Europe's thrust forward ahead of other regions during the medieval period. One of these considerations was an advantageous location. Being on the western tip of the Eurasian landmass, Europe escaped most of the great invasions after the year 1000. The importance of the remote location of western Europe is evident when we look at events in the rest of Eurasia—the disastrous Mongol conquest of Russia in the thirteenth century, the Ottoman Turkish conquest of the Balkan peninsula in the fifteenth and sixteenth centuries, and the repeated Berber assaults in North Africa. Spared such ravages, western Europe certainly had a substantial advantage over the more vulnerable regions to the east.

Equally important were Europe's exceptionally good natural resources. A large part of northern Europe is a great plain that begins at the western end of the Pyrenees and flares out to the north and east, becoming wider as it progresses until eventually it extends without interruption from the Black Sea to the Baltic. The prevailing westerly winds from the Atlantic sweep unhindered over these plains, across all Europe and deep into Russia. Hence Europe north of the Mediterranean basin enjoys a relatively moderate climate and constant rainfall, which along with fertile soils provide an ideal combination for productive agriculture. Rivers usually run ice-free and full-depth, providing convenient means of transportation and communication. The deeply indented coastline gives inland regions relatively easy access to coastal outlets.

These natural resources had always been available, of course, but they could not be effectively exploited until a certain level of technological competence had been reached. This need for adequate skills has existed everywhere and at all times. The United States, for example, has profited tremendously during the past century from the vast iron-ore deposits in the Mesabi Range of northern Minnesota. But for thousands of years Indians had fished and hunted in that area without exploiting the ore, or even being aware of its existence. The same is true currently of the rich oil fields now being tapped in the Middle East, in northern Alaska, and on various ocean floors. And so it was in medieval western Europe where, for the first time, advancing technology made it possible to exploit local resources effectively. The resulting increase in productivity had profound effects, including the shift of the economic and political center of Europe northward from its traditional site in the Mediterranean basin.

III. TECHNOLOGICAL PROGRESS

More technological progress was made during the period of medieval western Europe than had been made during the entire history of classical Greece and Rome. One reason for this was the absence of slavery, a practice that tended to inhibit new technology. Another was that the frontier conditions, which existed in many areas, called for labor-saving devices. The manorial system of the medieval West also contributed to technological progress. Under this system the social scale ranged not from a "divine" emperor to a subhuman slave but from a serf—with very definite rights and duties—to a manorial lord—who kept in touch with his serfs and had some real knowledge of the processes of production. Accordingly, manual labor acquired a status and respect that were unknown in the old slave-based civilizations.

Finally, technology in the West was stimulated by the humanitarian ethic of Christianity, which itself began as a revolt against the inhumanity of the old imperial society. The monks in the monasteries insisted that manual labor was part of spiritual life. Or, as they put it, "to work is to pray"—*laborare est orare*. These monks have gone down in history as the first intellectuals to get dirt under their fingernails. They were the first to combine brainpower and sweat, and in doing so they aided technological advance. In their monasteries they pushed the frontiers of settlement into the forests of northern and eastern Europe, and they also introduced advanced methods of agriculture.

The specific technological achievements of the West included basic inventions in the primary occupation of agriculture. One was the "three-field" rotation system of farming. Gradually adopted from the eighth century onward, this system raised productivity because only a third of the land lay fallow at any one time instead of the half left by the former "two-field" system. Another was the development of a heavy-wheeled plow with a sharp iron point that could cut under the sod six to eight inches or even more. Behind the plowshare was the mold board, so placed that it heaved over the cut sod. It was a very different implement from the primitive scratch-plow traditionally used in the light, thin soils of the Mediterranean basin. The new plow made it possible to cultivate the rich but heavy soils of central and northern Europe.

More effective use of horsepower also aided agriculture. In ancient times the horse had been of little use on the farm because the yoke then in use encircled the belly and neck of the animal. Consequently the horse strangled itself when it pulled too hard. By the tenth century, however, a harness had been developed that rested on the horse's shoulders. The horse could then pull without choking, increasing its pulling capacity four to five times. Hence the horse—fast and efficient compared to the ox, which had been used formerly—became an essential source of power in farming operations. The invention of horseshoes was also significant because it increased the usefulness of the horse for hauling as well as for plowing.

Finally, a brief look should be taken at the all-important water mill and windmill. Both of these were known in Greco-Roman times but were little used because of the abundance of slave labor and the scarcity of streams dependable the year around. These obstacles were absent in the northern lands, so the mill and the miller soon were to be found in almost every manor. And whereas the water wheel had been employed in the Mediterranean basin as a specialized device for grinding grain, in the course of the Middle Ages it was developed into a generalized prime mover. Thus water power came to be used for forge hammers and forge bellows; for sawmills and lathes; and for fulling mills making cloth, pulping mills making paper, and stamping mills crushing ore. Indeed, 5,000 mills were listed in England's *Domesday Book* of 1086. This represented one for every fifty households, certainly enough to affect living standards substantially.

IV. DEVELOPING ECONOMY

Technological advance was matched by corresponding economic advance. There was steady economic growth from 900 to 1300. Then came the fourteenth-century slump, brought on by a combination of factors: First there was a series of crop failures and famines, especially during 1315 and 1316; then came the Black Death, which carried off between one-third and two-thirds of the urban populations when it first struck in 1349, and which recurred periodically thereafter for generations; finally, there were the Hundred Years' War between England and France and other conflicts in Germany and Italy. Shortly after 1400, however, a revival set in, and the trend from then on was generally upward.

Europe's economic development was evident in all fields. New mining methods led to rising outputs of salt, silver, lead, zinc, copper, tin, and iron ore in central and northern Europe. Likewise, the rich timber and naval stores of Britain, Scandinavia, and the Baltic now were exploited more extensively than ever before. The same was true of the northern fisheries, particularly the cod of Iceland and Norway and the herring of the Baltic. Most important, of course, was the rise in the productivity of agriculture, in which most of the population was engaged. Peasants first began to cultivate the wastelands around their own villages. It is startling but true that in the twelfth century only about half the land in France, a third in Germany, and a fifth in England was under cultivation. The rest was forest, swamp, and waste. All around the edges of the small, tilled regions were larger, untilled areas open for colonization. Into these vacant spaces the European peasants streamed, preparing the way for the plow and hoe by clearing forests, burning brushwood, and draining swamps.

Peasants not only cultivated nearby unused lands but also with population growth emigrated to the vast underpopulated frontier regions. Just as the United States had its westward movement to the Pacific Ocean, so Europe had its eastward movement to the Russian border. By 1350 in Silesia, for example, there were 1,500 new settlements farmed by 150,000 to 200,000 colonists. Not only were there German colonists moving beyond the Elbe at the expense of the Slavic and Baltic peoples of eastern Europe, but also other colonists were pushing into Moslem Spain and Anglo-Saxon colonists were advancing into the Celtic lands of Wales, Scotland, and Ireland.

The combination of population increase and rising output in agriculture, mining, fishing, and forestry stimulated a corresponding growth of commerce and of cities. In the tenth century, merchants were to be found in Europe, but they traded mostly in luxuries. By the fourteenth century, however, commerce had advanced from the periphery to the center of everyday life. Goods exchanged included raw wool from England, woolen cloth from Flanders made from English wool, iron and timber from Germany, furs from Slavic areas, leather and steel from Spain, and luxury goods from the East. Although this commerce never engaged more than a small minority of the total population, nevertheless its great expansion in late medieval times had important repercussions for the whole society. Starting out as centers of local trade and local administration, towns slowly appeared. Urban progress came first in Italy, where the inhabitants of such centers as Venice, Amalfi, and Naples were cut off from their hinterland by the Lombard invaders and so took to the sea for a living. Later other cities appeared along inland

A fifteenth-century rendering of an eleventh- or twelfth-century marketplace. Medieval women were active in all trades, but especially in the food and clothing industries.

trade routes and the Baltic coast. The great fairs that developed along inland trade routes were also important for the distribution of goods. The most outstanding of the fairs were held in the county of Champagne, strategically located equidistant from Flanders, Italy, and Germany.

Western European cities were insignificant in medieval times compared to those of China, India, or the Middle East, both in population and in volume of trade. But they were quite unique because of their growing autonomy and political power. Precisely because they were starting fresh—and within the framework of a politically fragmented Europe rather than a monolithic empire—the burghers from the beginning exhibited a self-confidence and independence that had no parallel anywhere else in Eurasia.

As they acquired power and financial resources, the townspeople could usually get the king to give them a royal charter licensing them to unite in a single commune. The commune had the right to act as a corporation; to make agreements under its corporate seal; and to have its own town hall, court of law, and dependent territory outside the walls. The charter also permitted merchants and craftmakers to organize into guilds, which were voluntary associations designed for protection and mutual aid, including the regulation of manufacturing standards, prices, and working hours. Thus towns gradually came to be recognized as a new element in society, with inhabitants who were outside feudal law. For example, the custom was that if a serf escaped to a town and lived there for a year and a day without being apprehended, that person became free. A saying at that time was "Town air makes a man free."

In certain regions, groups of cities banded together to form leagues, which became powerful political as well as economic entities. When the Hohenstaufen emperors attempted to force the wealthy cities of northern Italy—Milan, Brescia, Parma, Verona, and others—to pay taxes and accept imperial administration, they organized themselves into the Lombard League. Aided by the pope, the league successfully waged war against the emperors. Likewise, various Baltic towns—Bremen, Lubeck, Stettin,

Italian bank at the end of the fourteenth century.

Danzig, and others comprising a total of ninety—organized themselves in 1350 into the Hanseatic League, which fought against pirates, pressed for trading privileges in foreign countries, and virtually monopolized the trade of northern Europe.

This evolution gave the European merchant status and power that were unique in Eurasia. Outside Europe, merchants had no chance to rise to positions of authority. In China, government was carried on by scholars; in Japan, by soldiers; in the Malay lands and in the Rajput states of India, by the local nobility; but nowhere by merchants. Nowhere, that is, except in Europe, where they were steadily gaining in political as well as economic power. There they were becoming lord mayors in London, senators in the German Imperial Free Cities, and grand pensioners in Holland. Such social status and political connections meant more consideration and more consistent state support for mercantile interests and, later on, for overseas ventures.

V. RISE OF NEW MONARCHIES

Western Europe by the tenth century had become a mosaic of petty feudal states that had gradually acquired the land and authority of the defunct Carolingian Empire. During the following centuries several traditions and interests operated at cross purposes. There were feudal kings engaged in continual conflict with their feudal vassals, who often held larger fiefs and wielded more power. There were city-states that sometimes combined in powerful organizations such as the Lombard and Hanseatic leagues. And in opposition to the particularist interests of these groups, there was the striving for a united Latin Christendom headed by the pope in Rome, or by a "Roman" emperor as the successor to Charlemagne and his predecessors. This complex of conflicting interests produced an infinite variety of constantly changing alliances and alignments at all levels of political life.

In very broad terms, the political evolution of western Europe after Charlemagne may be divided into three stages. Between the ninth and eleventh centuries, popes and emperors generally cooperated. The popes helped the emperors against the German secular lords, and in return they were supported in preference to the Byzantine opponents of papal authority. In 1073 a period of papal supremacy began with the accession of Pope Gregory VII. By the thirteenth century Pope Innocent III was involved in the affairs of virtually every European state, making and breaking kings and emperors. "Nothing in the world," he declared, "should escape the attention and control of the Sovereign Pontiff." For over two centuries, the papacy generally was recognized as the head of Latin Christendom.

The period of papal supremacy ended suddenly and dramatically when Pope Boniface VIII issued the bull *Unam sanctum* (1302), in which he set forth uncompromisingly the doctrine of papal authority: ". . . We declare, state, define and pronounce that it is altogether necessary to salvation for every human creature to be subject to the Roman pontiff." But what had been acceptable in previous centuries was no longer so. The monarchs and their councilors now were placing the welfare of their kingdoms ahead of the wishes of popes. Boniface was subjected to threats and mistreatment by an agent of the French king, and he died soon after his humiliation. In 1305 a French archbishop was elected pope as Clement V, and instead of going to Rome he took up residence at Avignon in southeastern France. During the next seventy years the Avignonese popes were the pawns of the French monarchy and lost their predecessors' commanding position in Latin Christendom.

The new power of the European kings was derived in large part from their informal alliance with the rising merchant class. The burghers provided financial support to the monarchs. They also supplied managerial talent in the form of chamberlains, overseers, keepers of the king's accounts, managers of the royal mint, and so forth. In return, the new monarchs provided the burghers with protection against the frequent wars and arbitrary demands of the feudal lords and bishops. They also served merchant interests by doing away with some of the crazy-quilt pattern of autonomous local authorities, each with its own customs, laws, weights, and currencies. With the removal of such encumbrances and the enforcement of royal law and order, the new monarchies emerged. By the fifteenth century, they encompassed roughly the territories of modern England, France, Portugal, and also, after the marriage of Ferdinand and Isabella, Spain.

These large new political entities proved to be essential for the mobilization of the human and material resources needed for overseas enterprise. Although most of the early explorers were Italian navigators, it was not accidental that their sponsors were the new national monarchies rather than their minuscule home city-states. The Spanish and Portuguese courts provided the backing for Columbus and da Gama, and the English and French courts quickly and eagerly followed up with backing for Cabot, Verrazano, and many others.

VI. RENAISSANCE FERMENT

The medieval West experienced cultural and intellectual developments that were as innovative and significant as the economic and political events. The centuries from the fall of Rome to about the year 1000 constituted a "Dark Age" in the sense that there was little cultural creativity. The weight of poverty, insecurity, and isola-

The University of Bologna in central Italy was distinguished as the center for the revival of Roman law. This carving on the tomb of a Bologna professor of law shows students attending one of his lectures.

tion was too great to permit the production of literary, artistic, or scholarly masterpieces. It is true that the monks in the monasteries did manage to preserve certain parts of classical culture, but they naturally concentrated on what conformed to their own religious convictions and ignored things that were more secular. The result was a "Christianized" or "clericized" culture that was supplementary to and dependent on the church.

In the eleventh century, cathedral schools were established by the bishops for the education of the priests of their dioceses. A century later the first universities evolved out of the cathedral schools. A distinctive feature of these universities was that they were self-governing corporations with a legal identity of their own. And rather than consisting simply of a liberal arts faculty, as did the cathedral schools, in addition they usually had faculties of canon law, civil law, medicine, and theology. The liberal arts curriculum was made up of the *trivium* (Latin grammar, logic, and rhetoric) and the *quadrivium* (geometry, arithmetic, music, and astronomy). The first universities appeared in the twelfth century at Bologna, Paris, and Oxford. In the following century others were founded at Padua, Naples, and Salamanca; and in the fourteenth century they spread to central Europe—to Prague, Cracow, and Vienna. All these universities were primarily institutions for training the clergy. This emphasis was natural and proper at a time when the clergy had a monopoly of literate occupations and administrative positions.

The educational and intellectual environment changed with the *Renaissance* ferment of the period from roughly 1350 to 1600. The Renaissance got under way first in Italy and hence reflected the conditions and values of contemporary Italian society. This was a bustling urban society based on flourishing industries and on the profitable commerce between western Europe and the wealthy Byzantine and Islamic empires. Prosperous cities such as Venice, Genoa, Florence, Milan, and Pisa were dominated by the great merchant families, who controlled politics as well as trade and crafts. It was these families that were the patrons of Renaissance artists and writers. Their needs, interests, and tastes colored the Renaissance cultural revival, even though the patrons included ducal families such as the Sforza of Milan, as well as popes such as Nicholas V, Pius II, Julius

THE RENAISSANCE GENIUS

The supremely talented Leonardo da Vinci was an outstanding Renaissance figure. He personified his age, not only because of his achievements in so many fields, but also because of his readiness to advertise his genius. At the age of thirty he wrote the following letter to the Duke of Milan, who was sufficiently impressed to hire the young man.

1. I have plans for bridges, very light and strong and suitable for carrying very easily, with which to pursue and at times defeat the enemy; and others solid and indestructible by fire or assault, easy and convenient to carry away and place in position. And plans for burning and destroying those of the enemy.

2. When a place is besieged I know how to cut off water from the trenches, and how to construct an infinite number of bridges, mantlets, scaling ladders, and other instruments which have to do with the same enterprise. . . .

4. I have also plans for making cannon, very convenient and easy of transport, with which to hurl small stones in the manner almost of hail, causing great terror to the enemy from their smoke, and great loss and confusion.

5. Also I have ways of arriving at a certain fixed spot by caverns and secret winding passages, made without any noise, even though it may be necessary to pass underneath trenches or a river.

6. Also I can make armored carts, safe and unassailable, which will enter the serried ranks of the enemy with their artillery, and there is no company of men at arms so great that they will not break it. And behind these infantry will be able to follow quite unharmed and without any opposition. . . .

9. And if it should happen that the engagement is at sea, I have plans for constructing many engines most suitable either for attack or defense, and ships which can resist the fire of all the heaviest cannon, and powder and smoke.

10. In time of peace I believe that I can give you as complete satisfaction as anyone else in architecture in the construction of buildings both pubic and private, and in conducting water from one place to another. . . .

And if any of the aforesaid things should seem impossible or impracticable to anyone, I offer myself as ready to make trial of them in your park or in whatever place shall please Your Excellency, to whom I commend myself with all possible humility.

*J. P. and I. A. Richter, eds. *The Literary Works of Leonardo da Vinci* (Oxford University Press, 1939), pp. 92, 93.

II, and Leo X; hence the secularism and humanism of the Renaissance—its concern with this world rather than the hereafter, and its focus on pagan classics rather than Christian theology.

The secularism and individualism of the Renaissance were reflected in its scholarship and education. The so-called father of Renaissance literature, Francesco Petrarca, or Petrarch (1304–1374), stressed the value of the classics as a means for self-improvement and a guide to social action. Likewise the new boarding schools of the Renaissance trained not priests but the sons of merchants. The curriculum emphasized classical studies and physical exercise and was designed to educate the students to live well and happily and to function as responsible citizens.

The Renaissance spirit is most strikingly expressed in its art. Since the church no longer was the sole patron of the arts, artists were encouraged to turn to subjects other than the traditional biblical themes. Religious themes continued to appear quite commonly, but in the

Commissioned in 1501, when the artist was 26, Michelangelo's David *became the symbol of the Florentine republic and was displayed in front of the Palazzo Vecchio. The detail shown here highlights the restrained emotion and dignity for which the statue is famous. [Michelangelo (1475–1564) David-p. (testa di profilo).]*

works of such masters as Leonardo da Vinci, Michelangeo, Raphael, and Titian, the emphasis shifted more and more to portraits designed to reveal the hidden mysteries of the soul, to paintings intended to delight the eye with striking colors and forms.

The Renaissance, not an exclusively Italian phenomenon, spread its innovations to northern Europe in the sixteenth century. Two factors responsible for this were the Italian diplomats and generals who were employed by northern monarchs and the printing press, which accelerated the circulation of books and ideas. Printing was particularly influential in northern Europe because literacy was more widespread there than in Europe's southern and eastern regions. The flood of printed matter fomented popular agita-

tion concerning political and religious issues and so contributed substantially to the Reformation and ensuing religious and dynastic wars.

In conclusion, what is the significance of the Renaissance in the perspective of world history? It is obvious that the new emphasis on human beings and on what they could accomplish was more conducive to overseas expansion than the preceding medieval outlook. The fact remains that there was an intellectual ferment in western Europe and that it had no counterpart in the rest of Eurasia. This is a fundamental difference of enormous import.

In China, Confucianism continued to dominate society. Its esteem for age over youth, for the past over the present, for established authority over innovation made it a perfect instrument for the preservation of the status quo in all its aspects. This atmosphere of conformity and orthodoxy prevented continued intellectual development and helps to explain why China fell behind the West in technology, despite its brilliant initial achievements in developing paper, printing, gunpowder, and the compass. These early inventions were not followed by the formulation of a body of scientific principles.

The situation was basically the same in the other Eurasian lands. In the Ottoman Empire, for example, the Moslem *medressehs*, or colleges, emphasized theology, jurisprudence, and rhetoric at the expense of astronomy, mathematics, and medicine. The graduates of these schools knew nothing about what was being done in the West and were not interested in finding out. No Moslem Turk believed that a Christian infidel could teach anything of value. Now and then, a rare, far-sighted individual warned of the dangers of this intellectual iron curtain separating the Ottoman Empire from neighboring Christendom. One of these voices was Katib Chelebi, the famous Turkish bibliographer, encyclopedist, and historian who lived in the first half of the seventeenth century. Coming from a poor family, he was unable to obtain a formal higher education. But this was a blessing in disguise. He was spared the superficial, hair-splitting concentration on Moslem sacred studies that was typical of Ottoman education at this time. The fact that he was self-taught explains in large part his open-mindedness toward Western learning.

One of Chelebi's works was a short naval handbook that he wrote following a disastrous defeat of the Ottoman fleet in 1656. In the preface of this work, Chelebi emphasized the need for mastering the science of geography and map making:

For men who are in charge of affairs of state, the science of geography is a matter of which knowledge is necessary. They may not be familiar with what the entire globe is like, but they ought at least to know the map of the Ottoman State and of those states adjoining it. Then, when they have to send forces on campaign, they can proceed on the basis of knowledge, and so the invasion of the enemy's land and also the protection and defense of the frontiers becomes an easier task. Taking counsel with individuals who are ignorant of that science is no satisfactory substitute, not even when such men are local veterans. Most such veterans are entirely unable to sketch the map of their own home region.

Sufficient and convincing proof of the necessity for learning this science is the fact that the heathen, by their application to and their esteem for those branches of learning, have discovered the New World and have overrun the markets of India.[3]

Chelebi saw the connection between Europe's intellectual advance and its overseas expansion. In his last work before his death in 1657, Chelebi warned his countrymen that if they did not abandon their dogmatism they would soon "be looking at the universe with the eyes of oxen." His prediction proved prophetic. The Turks continued to be steeped in their religious obscurantism, and like other non-Western peoples, they paid a high price. The Christian infidels with their new learning eventually became the masters not only of the New World but also of the ancient empires of Islam and of Confucianism.

VII. WESTERN EUROPE'S EXPANSIONISM

Between the fourth and tenth centuries Europe was invaded by Germans, Huns, Magyars, Vikings, and Moslems. But from the tenth to the fourteenth centuries this situation was dramatically reversed as Europe took the offensive on all fronts. (See map of Expansionism of the Medieval West, Eleventh to Fifteenth Centuries, p. 240.) Assorted crusaders pushed back the Moslems in Spain, southern Italy, Sicily, and the Holy Land, and even overran the Christian Byzantine Empire. Meanwhile in northeast Europe, German frontier lords were winning lands east of the Elbe. As German expansion continued east of the Oder it was carried on as a *Crusade* by the Teutonic Knights against the pagan Prussians. The Knights built strongholds and around them settled Germans, who provided the supplies and people for further expansion. German merchants soon appeared and founded towns at strategic points along the coasts and along river routes. Thus by the end of the fifteenth century large areas formerly occupied by Slavic and Baltic peoples had become thoroughly German from top to bottom: lords, bishops, townspeople, and peasants.

These Crusades were considered at one time to have been responsible for starting virtually every constructive development in the later Middle Ages, including the growth of trade and towns and the advances in culture. This interpretation is no longer accepted. Instead it is generally agreed that the Crusades were the consequence rather than the cause of this progress. Without the preceding technological advances, commercial revival, demographic upsurge, and general exuberance of spirit, the Crusades would have been quite impossible. This dynamism continued and picked up speed after the fourteenth-century slump. The result was to extend the expansionist drive of the crusaders to overseas territories.

A significant factor in the overseas drive was the Christian religion, with its belief that Christianity is universal, its zeal to make converts, and its crusading militancy. The early explorers and their backers were motivated partly by religious considerations. They wanted to reach the great countries of India and China, whose existence had been known to Europeans since the thirteenth-century travels of Marco Polo. These countries were known to be non-Moslem, and so it was hoped that they might join forces with the Christians. Also there was the enduring medieval legend of Prester (or Priest) John, reputed to be a powerful Christian ruler somewhere out in the vague East. For centuries, Christian leaders had dreamed of estab-

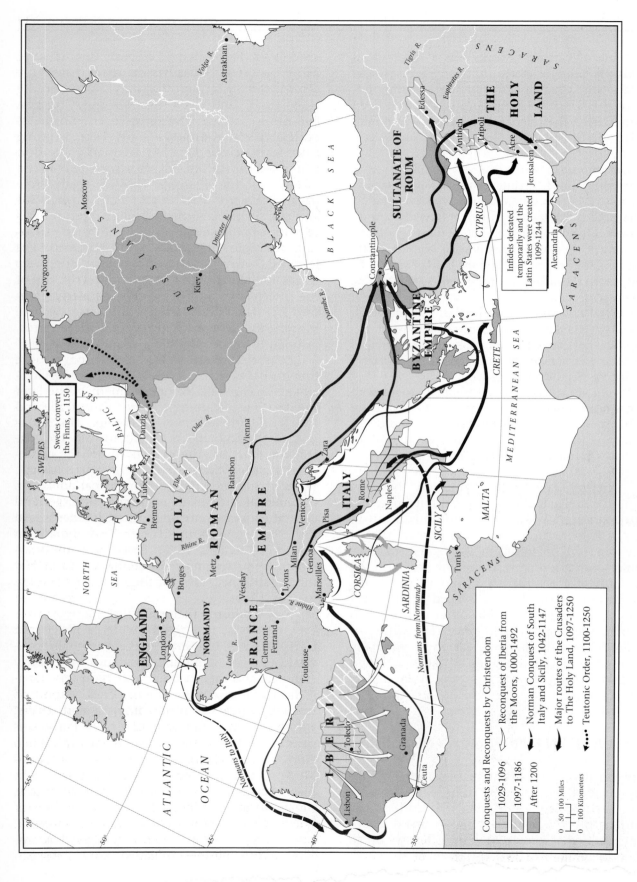

Expansionism of the Medieval West, Eleventh to Fifteenth Centuries

Conquests and Reconquests by Christendom

Reconquest of Iberia from the Moors, 1000–1492

Norman Conquest of South Italy and Sicily, 1042–1147

Major routes of the Crusaders to The Holy Land, 1097–1250

Teutonic Order, 1100–1250

1029–1096

1097–1186

After 1200

Infidels defeated temporarily and the Latin States were created 1099–1244

Swedes convert the Finns, c. 1150

50   100 Miles

0   100 Kilometers

lishing contact with him and launching a great assault on the Moslem world from both east and west. The Europeans did not find Prester John, but they did stumble on strange new peoples in Africa and the Americas—peoples who were barbarians and heathens and, therefore, fit subjects for conquest, conversion, and redemption.

God, along with gold, was perhaps the most compelling of the many motives that led Europeans to begin their overseas enterprises. Vasco da Gama explained to the surprised Indians that he had come to their land in search of Christians and spices. Likewise, the conquistador Bernal Diaz wrote in his memoirs that he and his comrades went to the New World "to serve God and His Majesty, to give light to those who were in darkness, and to grow rich, as all men desire to do."[4]

The continued technological advances of the West also contributed directly to overseas expansion. Particularly significant was the progress made in shipbuilding, in the instruments and techniques of navigation, and in naval armaments. Between 1200 and 1500 the

This Jesuit missionary, wearing his distinctive Catholic vestments, is baptizing an Indian in New France. French Jesuits proved to be more tolerant than most European missionaries in allowing Indian converts to retain at least some of their own customs.

tonnage of the average European ship doubled or trebled. Slender galleys with a burden of 150 to 200 tons gave way to round-hulled sailing ships of 600 to 800 tons. The stern rudder, adopted in the thirteenth century, rapidly displaced the older and less efficient lateral steering devices. Equally important was the Portuguese adaptation in the fourteenth century of the Arab lateen rig, which allowed vessels to sail more directly into the wind. Such advantages in the construction and rigging of ships represented a combining of innovations originally developed in northern Europe, in the Mediterranean, or in the Middle East. The result was a ship that was larger, speedier, and more maneuverable. It was also more economical because the elimination of 100 to 200 oarsmen with their food and equipment greatly increased the cargo space.

Hand in hand with these advances in shipbuilding went advances in the art of navigation. Particularly important were the increasingly effective use of the compass, the astrolabe, and the new maps now drawn with accurate compass bearings and explicit details concerning coastlines and harbors. At the same time the Europeans were taking a decisive and significant lead in naval armaments. Sea battles traditionally had consisted of boarding and hand-to-hand fighting on decks. This changed in the first two decades of the sixteenth century when Flemish and German metallurgists developed new techniques for casting guns. The new guns could shoot balls capable of damaging a hull at 300 yards. Naval tactics now shifted from boarding to broadside gunfire, enabling Europeans to seize and control the oceans of the world for four centuries. Their supremacy finally ended with the epochal Japanese naval victory over the Russians at Tsushima in 1905.

Along with advances in shipbuilding, navigation, and naval armaments came important new techniques for conducting business affairs. The invention in Italy of double-entry bookkeeping made it possible to see the financial state of a business at a glance. Also, the growing use of money and the minting of standard coins acceptable by everyone made it easier to conduct business. The development of banks and credit instruments, and the gradual ending of medieval Christianity's ban on interest charges or loans, also helped business. Finally, after European

Before Europeans could safely navigate the Atlantic, they needed larger and more maneuverable ships. This drawing illustrates the evolution of sailing vessels from the late Middle Ages to the fifteenth century. Technological improvements included larger hulls, more masts, and new arrangements of sails.

overseas expansion got under way, business was greatly strengthened by the development of *joint stock companies*. By providing a medium for investment with limited liability, these companies mobilized vast amounts of European capital for overseas enterprise. Eastern merchants, limited to their own resources or those of their partners, were unable to compete successfully in the long run with the several East India and Levant companies, the Muscovy Company, and the still extant Hudson's Bay Company.

In conclusion, the combination of all these factors imbued Europe with an impelling and unique dynamism. We can see how unique it was when we look at the variety of Eurasian responses to the expansion of the Moslem world in the fifteenth century. As noted in Chapter 11, Section V, Islam at that time was fanning out from the Middle East in all directions. The Turks, after capturing Constantinople, overran the Balkan peninsula and then crossed the Danube and pushed through Hungary to the walls of Vienna. Likewise in the East, the Turks under the colorful Babur were striking southward from Afghanistan, to begin the founding of the great Mogul Empire that would rule India until the British takeover in the nineteenth century. In Africa also, Islam was spreading steadily into the interior from its bases on the northern and eastern coasts of the continent. Finally, Moslem

merchants dominated the Eurasian sea routes running from the Red Sea and the Persian Gulf across the Indian Ocean and around Southeast Asia to the China seas.

With these advances by its soldiers, merchants, and preachers, the world of Islam had become the heartland of Eurasia. It occupied the strategic center of the great landmass, and the more it expanded, the more it isolated the Chinese at the eastern end of Eurasia and the Europeans at the western. The completely different responses of the Chinese and the Europeans to this encirclement have deeply influenced the course of world history from that time to the present.

The Chinese, as noted before, withdrew voluntarily, even though their earlier expeditions under Cheng Ho had clearly shown that they possessed both the technology and the resources to dominate the oceans. But during the Ming period, after the interlude of Mongol domination, the Chinese were turning their backs to the outside world. And their merchant class, which lacked the political power and social status of its Western counterpart, was unable to challenge imperial orders that banned overseas enterprise. Thus the Chinese turned their formidable talents and energies inward and deliberately relinquished a lead role in Eurasian and, ultimately, world affairs.

The response of Europeans was precisely the opposite. The geographic horizons and commercial ambitions of the Europeans had been broadened by *Pax Mongolica*, so that the sudden disintegration of the Mongol Empire left them with acute frustration and yearning. Likewise, the loss of the crusaders' outposts in the Levant, the Islamization of the Ilkhanate in Persia, and the Turkish conquest of the Balkans all served to deprive the Europeans of access to the Black Sea, the Persian Gulf, and the Indian Ocean. Thus the Europeans were effectively fenced in on the western tip of Eurasia. The all-important spice trade still flourished, as Italian merchants continued to meet Arab traders in the ports of the Levant and pick up cargoes for transshipment to the West. But though the arrangement was satisfactory for the Italians and the Arabs, who reaped the golden profits of the middleman, other Europeans were not so happy. They sought earnestly for some means to reach the Orient and to share the prize.

Their search was bound to succeed, given their technical skills, their economic strength, their intellectual exuberance, and the rivalry of their competing monarchies. There was no emperor in Europe to issue restraining orders; instead there were national monarchies competing strenuously in overseas enterprises. Also, there was in Europe a genuine need and strong demand for foreign products, and the merchants were sufficiently powerful to satisfy the need. Thus if Columbus had not discovered America and if da Gama had not rounded the Cape, assuredly others would have done so within the next few decades. In short, Western society had reached the takeoff point. It was ready to burst out. And when it did, it found the ocean ways clear, and it spread irresistibly over the entire globe.

VIII. WOMEN IN THE NEW WESTERN CIVILIZATION

In view of the current controversy about the status of women in various societies throughout the world, it is instructive to see how women were affected by the emergence of the new civilization in medieval Europe. We have seen that during the long millennia of the Paleolithic era, relations between the sexes were more equitable

Florentine women are shown doing needlework, spinning, and weaving. These activities took up much of a woman's time and contributed to the elegance of dress for which Florentine men and women were famed.

than at any time since. With the advent of agriculture and then of civilizations, women lost their equal status and became the subordinate and dependent sex. The degree of inequity varied from one region to another (as between the various Greek city-states) and from one period to another (as between republican and imperial Rome). But in all early civilizations, women definitely were the "second sex." They were restricted to the "inside" work, which was considered less important, whereas men were free to engage in the "outside" work, which was regarded as significant and creative.

This pattern continued during the thousand years of the medieval period, when a revolutionary new civilization gradually emerged in the West. But there were certain modifications that deserve attention and that are of some significance for women today.

The status of women in the new Western civilization was determined largely by two institutions—the Catholic church and feudalism. In theory the church championed equality in sex relations, as it did also in race and class. "For ye are all the children of God by faith in Christ Jesus," wrote Saint Paul. "There is neither Jew nor Greek, there is neither bond nor free, there is neither male nor female; for ye are all one in Christ Jesus."[5] In practice, however, the church was profoundly *ambivalent* on the sex issue. It viewed woman as Eve, the wife of Adam, and therefore the supreme temptress and the great obstacle in the way of salvation. But the church also viewed woman as the blessed Mary, the Holy Mother, the queen of virgins, and the mediator between God and humankind. Consequently the medieval woman found herself oscillating between the pit and the pedestal. Within the church itself she could not be ordained a priest and she was denied the right to preach.

The church did provide, however, one important institution designed specifically for the medieval woman, namely, the nunnery. This has been described as a "class institution,"[6] because would-be nuns were required, in practice though not in strict canon law, to bring with them a *dowry*. Though this dowry was not as much as a husband would expect, the nunneries nevertheless were open mostly to wealthy females from the nobility and, in the later Middle Ages, from the merchant families. Almost all medieval females married, and did so at a very young age. A small minority did not find a husband, either because of illegitimate birth or physical deformity or lack of adequate dowry, or because of a preference for a life as a bride of Christ rather than a bride of some man.

For these exceptional cases the nunnery offered an alternative to married life. Furthermore the cloister did provide certain advantages to life on the outside. The nuns usually could obtain a better education than was available to their secular brothers or sisters. If a nun was exceptionally ambitious and capable, she could rise to the office of abbess, managing large estates and assuming responsibility for as many as eighty nuns. Some of these nuns experienced the intense satisfaction of the contemplative life in the service of the Holy Father, and a few are remembered as great monastic saints. Others found in the cloisters self-respect and the respect of society, as well as the freedom from male authority that only the nunnery afforded. On the other hand, there were some who viewed themselves bitterly as the rejects of society: "I was not good enough for man and so am given to God."[7]

The second institution that most affected medieval women was feudalism. Since this was a system by which a lord granted land to a vassal in return for military service, feudalism created a male-dominated world. Feudal estates were passed on, with their military obligations, to a single male heir. A woman could inherit only in the absence of male heirs. Throughout her life the medieval woman was under the guardianship of a man—first her father and then her husband. If widowed, she became the *ward* of the feudal lord, who pocketed the income of the ward's estate until she remarried. The lord determined whom she should marry, so it was by no means uncommon for him to "sell" his ward's marriage to the highest bidder, or conversely, to exact payments from a widow who did not wish to marry or who wished to choose her own mate. Noblewomen also had to bear the cross of an idle and aimless existence. The management of their households and the care of their children were entrusted to stewards and nurses. Therefore there was little for them to do unless their husbands were absent on military service or court attendance. In essence, the unhappy lot of these noblewomen was to serve as pawns in the forging of political and economic alliances and then to produce heirs for the family into which they married.

This dependent and peripheral existence was escaped, to a large degree, by the working women in the villages and towns; hence the paradox that the status of medieval women "varied roughly in inverse ratio to wealth and social standing."[8] The great majority of village girls married and took their place beside their husbands in performing virtually every type of agricultural work. The few who did not marry were usually from the poorest families. So they supported themselves by leaving their village to work as serving girls in towns or as hired agricultural workers in neighboring villages. How laborious was the day-to-day life of peasant women is reflected in the following medieval proverb:

Some respite to husbands the weather may send,
But housewives' affairs have never an end.[9]

Likewise in the towns, women were active in almost all the trades. This is evident in the thirteenth-century *Book of Trades* (*Livre des Métiers*) by Etienne Boileau, which listed the rules of all the guilds in Paris. Of the 100 guilds enumerated, women were working in eighty-six. How important this female role was is evident in the use of the suffix *ess* or *ster* with medieval

English words to describe an occupation held by women.

Webster:	woman weaver
Brewster:	woman beer maker
Baxter:	woman baker
Laundress:	woman washer of clothes
Seamstress:	woman sewer
Spinster:	woman spinner
Governess:	woman teacher

Equal burdens and equal responsibilities did not win equal rights for medieval women. In the villages the housewives' labors never ended, yet they were excluded from all decision-making bodies. They could not serve as village notary or as parish priest or as scribe of the manorial court. The meetings of village landowners were attended only by men, except for unmarried or widowed female landowners. Married women who owned land were represented at all village meetings by their husbands. Likewise in towns, women enjoyed economic rights such as owning property, joining guilds, and engaging in commerce, but they had no corresponding political rights. Thus they could not elect or be elected to the governmental institutions of the towns.

The underlying inequity in sex relations is evident in various practices that were common in medieval Europe. One was the prevalence of wife beating. "A good woman and a bad one equally require the stick," ran a Florentine saying. A thirteenth-century French law code stated: "In a number of cases men may be excused for the injuries they inflict on their wives. . . . Provided he neither kills nor maims her, it is legal for a man to beat his wife when she wrongs him."[10] Sex inequity was manifest also in the persistence of the traditional double standard regarding adultery. Kings, noblemen, and merchants openly kept mistresses and spawned illegitimate children. But erring wives were disgraced and severely punished and their lovers castrated or killed. Also it was taken for granted that upper-class men should have access to lower-class women. A twelfth-century tract, *The Art of Courtly Love*, encouraged a knight who desired a peasant girl "not to hesitate to take what you seek and to embrace her by force."

Equally indicative of the pervasive sex inequity was the common assumption that women should be content with "little feminine trifles," while men occupied themselves with "high achievements." Leon Battista Alberti, a leading figure of the Italian Renaissance, wrote in the 1430s that men should "leave the care of minor matters" to their wives, so that the husbands could be free for "all manly and honorable concerns."[11]

All this harks back to the fateful shift in sex relations following the agricultural revolution, when women lost their equal status and a distinction began to be made between the unimportant "inside" work of females and the important "outside" work of males. Once this distinction was accepted, it became deeply rooted in civilizations throughout the world. What is significant here is that the distinction persisted not only in the successive ancient civilizations but also in the new civilization that emerged in western Europe. Despite the technological advances, the economic dynamism, and the political innovations, the customs of the past continued to weigh heavily on European women at the end of the Middle Ages. Built-in sex discrimination persisted even during centuries of technological, economic, and political transition. This triumph of the past over the present is noteworthy because the same pattern is discernible today, in our time, as is evident in the following "Rules of Conduct for Teachers," published in the Cabell County (West Virginia) Board of Education's school bulletin in 1915.

1. You will not marry during the term of your contract.
2. You are not to keep company with men.
3. You must be home between the hours of 8 P.M. and 6 A.M. unless attending a school function.
4. You may not loiter downtown in ice cream stores.
5. You may not travel beyond the city limits unless you have the permission of the chairman of the board.
6. You may not ride in a carriage or automobile with any man unless he is your father or brother.
7. You may not smoke cigarettes.
8. You may not dress in bright colors.
9. You may under no circumstances dye your hair.
10. You must wear at least two petticoats.

11. Your dresses must not be any shorter than two inches above the ankle.

12. To keep the schoolroom neat and clean, you must sweep the floor at least once daily; scrub the floor at once a week with hot, soapy water; clean the blackboards at least once a day, and start the fire at 7 A.M. so the room will be warm by 8 A.M.[12]

SUGGESTED READINGS

For works on the early medieval period following the invasions, see the bibliography for Chapter 12. A significant and stimulating study of medieval Europe in a global context is by R. L. Reynolds, *Europe Emerges: Transition Toward an Industrial World-Wide Society 600–1750* (University of Wisconsin, 1961). An excellent general history of the medieval West is by R. S. Lopez, *The Birth of Europe* (Lippincott, 1966).

The best introduction to feudal institutions is provided by J. R. Strayer, *Feudalism* (Van Nostrand, 1965); and by M. Bloch, *Feudal Society*, 2 vols. (University of Chicago, 1961). On social and economic developments there is J. LeGoff, *Your Money or Your Life: Economy and Religion in the Middle Ages* (MIT Press, 1988); R. H. Bautier, *The Economic Development of Medieval Europe* (Harcourt, 1971); R. S. Lopez, *The Commercial Revolution of the Middle Ages, 950–1350* (Prentice Hall, 1971); B. H. Slicher van Bath, *The Agrarian History of Western Europe, 500–1850* (Arnold, 1963); L. White, Jr., *Medieval Technology and Social Changes* (Clarendon, 1962). On the rise of the monarchies, see B. Guenée, *States and Rulers in Later Medieval Europe* (Blackwell, 1984). An excellent general introduction to the Renaissance is by W. K. Ferguson, *The Renaissance* (Torchbook, 1940). See also P. Kristeller, *Renaissance Thought*, 2 vols. (Torchbook, 1961–65); and W. Pater, *The Renaissance* (Meridian, 1961). Finally, the key question of why the West rather than some other region of Eurasia took the lead in overseas expansion is considered in J. R. Levenson, ed., *European Expansion and the Counter-Example of Asia, 1300–1600* (Prentice Hall, 1967); D. L. Jensen, ed., *The Expansion of Europe* (Heath, 1967); E. L. Jones, *The European Miracle: Environments, Economics and Geopolitics in the History of Europe and Asia* (Cambridge University, 1981). The latest analysis of why Europe bolted ahead of other continents is by A. W. Crosby, *The Measure of Reality: Quantification and Western Society, 1250–1600* (Cambridge University, 1996), which stresses the new technology and the new mentality viewing the universe in quantitative terms.

The pioneer study of medieval women is the still valuable survey by E. Power, "The Position of Women," in C. G. Crump and E. F. Jacob, eds., *The Legacy of the Middle Ages* (Clarendon, 1926), pp. 401–434. Important recent works are by S. Shahar, *The Fourth Estate: A History of Women in the Middle Ages* (Methuen, 1983); F. and J. Gies, *Women in the Middle Ages* (Crowell, 1978); S. M. Stuard, *Women in Medieval Society* (University of Pennsylvania, 1976); and S. H. Gross and M. W. Bingham, *Women in Medieval-Renaissance Europe* (Glenhurst, 1983).

NOTES

1. Francis Bacon, *Novum Organum*, aphorism, p. 129.
2. Cited by R. S. Lopez, *The Birth of Europe* (Lippincott, 1967), p. 146.
3. Cited in manuscript by L. V. Thomas, *Ottoman Awareness of Europe, 1629–1800*.
4. Cited by J. H. Parry, *The Age of Reconnaissance* (Weidenfeld & Nicolson, 1963), p. 19.
5. Galatians 3:28.
6. Eileen Power, "The Position of Women," in C. G. Crump and E. F. Jacob, eds., *The Legacy of the Middle Ages* (Clarendon, 1926), p. 413.
7. Eileen Power, *Medieval English Nunneries, c. 1275–1535* (Cambridge University, 1922), p. 31.
8. F. and J. Gies, *Women in the Middle Ages* (Crowell, 1978), p. 232.
9. S. H. Gross and M. W. Bingham, *Women in Medieval-Renaissance Europe* (Glenhurst, 1983), p. 84.
10. Ibid., p. 46.
11. Ibid., p. 228.
12. Republished in "Dear Abby" column by Abigail Van Buren, *Los Angeles Times*, June 17, 1979.

What It Means for Us Today

DEVELOPING SOCIETIES AND THE "RETARDING LEAD"

The most surprising and significant development during the thousand years of Eurasian medieval history was the rise of western Europe from poverty and obscurity. During most of this period from roughly 500 to 1500, the West was the underdeveloped region of Eurasia. We have seen that this underdevelopment proved an advantage in contrast to the development of China, which acted as a brake on that country. The Chinese enjoyed a sophisticated culture, advanced crafts, large-scale commerce, an efficient bureaucracy based on merit, and the creed of Confucianism that provided social cohesion and intellectual rationale. Very naturally, the Chinese considered their civilization to be superior to any other and regarded foreigners as "barbarians." When the first Westerners appeared on their coasts, the Chinese assumed there was nothing important they could learn from those peculiar "long-nosed barbarians."

This attitude, understandable though it was, left the Chinese unchanging during a time of great change. By contrast, the western Europeans, precisely because of their relative backwardness, were ready and eager to learn and to adapt. They took Chinese inventions, developed them to their full potential, and used them for overseas expansion. This expansion, in turn, triggered more technological advances and institutional changes. The end result was the transition from medieval to modern civilization, with the Europeans serving as the pioneers and the beneficiaries.

This was not the first time that a backward, peripheral region had led in the transition from one historical era to another. During the period of the ancient civilizations (3500–1000 B.C.E.), the Middle East had functioned as the developed core that made the basic innovations in agriculture, metallurgy, writing, and urban life. But this highly developed center fell behind during the transition from the ancient to the classical civilizations. It was the peripheral and comparatively backward regions of China, India, and Europe that pioneered in the creative innovations of the Classical Age, including effective exploitation of iron metallurgy, coinage, and the alphabet, as well as the new religions of Confucianism, Hinduism, and Christianity.

This pattern suggests that in history, nothing fails like success. Anthropologists refer to this as the *Law of Retarding Lead*, which holds that the best adapted and most successful societies have the most difficulty in changing and retaining their lead in a period of transition. And conversely, the backward and less successful societies are more likely to be able to adapt and to forge ahead.

The significance of this law is obvious for us today, when the West—the heir of medieval western Europe—no longer represents an underdeveloped region of Eurasia but rather the most highly developed part of the globe. Furthermore, we are living in an age of transition when the tempo of history has speeded up immensely in comparison with the Middle Ages. The speed-up is evident today in what has happened in the few years since World War II: the meteoric economic recovery of Japan and Germany since their devastation during the war, and the equally sudden political collapse of the Soviet Union from a superpower to a blank on the world map. In such a period of constantly accelerating change, adaptability is the key to personal and national success—or perhaps we should say, personal and national survival. President Lyndon B. Johnson summarized it best with this warning to his fellow Americans: "We must change to master change."

SUGGESTED READINGS

The full implications of the "retarding lead" concept are set forth in M. D. Sahlins and E. R. Service, eds., *Evolution and Culture* (University of Michigan, 1960); and E. R. Service, *Cultural Evolutionism: Theory in Practice* (Holt, Rinehart & Winston, 1971).

PART IV

Non-Eurasian World to 1500

Thus far we have dealt exclusively with Eurasian history. Now we turn to the history of the non-Eurasian part of the globe. The reason for this separate treatment is that the histories of the peoples involved were in fact largely separate. Before 1500, there was little interaction between the Eurasian and non-Eurasian segments of the world. Human history during those millennia was essentially regional, not global, in scope. Once human beings scattered to all the continents, they lost contact with each other and lived for thousands of years in isolation on their respective continents. Here we note the paradox that advances in human technology were responsible both for the early dispersal and isolation of human beings, and then for their later interaction and reunification.

We noted earlier (Chapter 1, Section III) that when our Paleolithic ancestors learned to use tools, to make clothing, and to control fire, they were able to leave what is commonly believed to be their original African homeland and to spread out and occupy all the continents except Antarctica. But once they settled down in their new homes, they did not keep contact with the relatives they had left behind because their technology was too primitive to allow voyages back and forth across the oceans separating the continents. This was especially true after the melting of the glaciers raised ocean levels and submerged the land bridge between Siberia and Alaska, and also the island stepping stones between Southeast Asia and Australia. For this reason, human settlements necessarily existed for millennia in regional isolation. They continued to do so until advances in shipbuilding and navigation technology enabled the Chinese to sail around Southeast Asia and across the Indian Ocean, and likewise the western Europeans to sail around the southern tips of Africa and South America and across the Atlantic, the Pacific, and the Indian oceans. In this way the peoples of the world reestablished direct contact with each other, thus beginning a new global phase of their history.

Because the Europeans took the lead in overseas exploration, history textbooks have focused on Columbus, da Gama, and Magellan, on their discoveries, and on the repercussions that followed. Such an approach is inadequate for global history. A global perspective requires consideration not only of the expanding West but also of the regions into which the West expanded. The peoples of these regions, after all, made up a considerable proportion of the human race, and their evolution must not be ignored. Moreover, the lands, peoples, and institutions of the non-Eurasian world were as significant in determining the outcome of Western expansionism as were the Westerners themselves. For these reasons, then, the following two chapters are devoted to Africa, to the Americas, and to Australia.

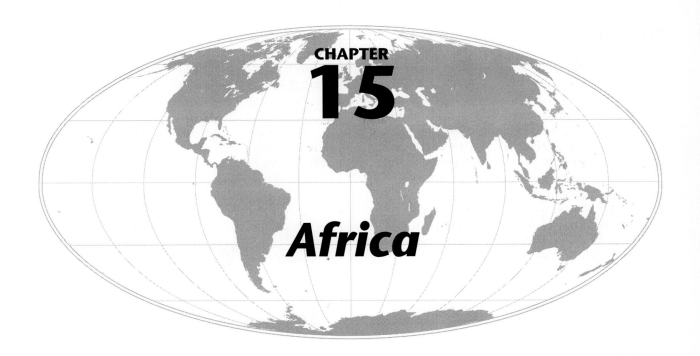

CHAPTER

15

Africa

On the woody vales of the Niger,
And the meandering plains of the Volta,
On the shoulders of Kilimanjaro
Carpeted with the icy sheen of snow,
There breathes the vast elusive Africa,
That Africa of long ago.

Michael Dei-Anang (Ghanaian poet)

A glance at a world map reveals that Africa is centrally located. To the north, Africa is separated from Europe by the Mediterranean Sea, a body of water that is narrow, is easy to cross, and historically has functioned as a highway. To the east the Sinai Peninsula provides a bridge to Asia, and the Red Sea is even narrower and easier to cross than the Mediterranean. Finally, the great expanses of the Indian Ocean are neutralized by the monsoon winds, which facilitate communication back and forth between East Africa and southern Asia.

Yet historically Africa was wrongly viewed as cut off from Eurasia and the rest of the world. Africa was viewed as isolated from other regions, and this perceived isolation affected the histori-

cal experiences of the continent. At the same time that historians emphasized the continent's isolation, they stressed the fact that Africa borrowed much from the outside world during this period; however, exchange is a two-way street that works only when there is meaningful contact and interaction. This chapter will examine the internal developments in Africa, and the continent's contacts with the outside world.

I. GEOGRAPHY

Viewed as a whole, the continent of Africa begins with small, fertile strips at its extreme northern and southern tips. These soon yield to the great desert expanses of the Kalahari in the south and the Sahara in the north. Next come the rolling grasslands, or savannas, known in the north as the Sudan, the Arab term meaning "the country of the black people." Then come the tropical rain forests, which in their densest parts are more difficult for outsiders to penetrate than the deserts.

The African continent is immense and diverse. Its geographical diversity has always posed a challenge to Africans, but it was never regarded as a barrier. What emerges clearly from historical developments is that even in the most geographically unfavored parts of Africa, the indigenous peoples created important civilizations and cultures.

Africa has often been artificially divided into North Africa and Africa south of the Sahara. But the Sahara Desert was never a divider or a barrier in the history of the continent. The perceived barriers provided a hindrance to outsiders and made Africa difficult to penetrate and conquer during the early period of the continent's history. Africa was not isolated from the rest of the world, however; it was criss-crossed with numerous trade routes that linked African communities, and trade routes also linked Africa with the outside world via the Red Sea, the Mediterranean Sea, and the Indian Ocean. Africa achieved at an early stage a high social, political, and economic organization, which effectively controlled trade, trade routes, and markets and for the most part kept potential invaders at bay.

In viewing political organizations on the continent, African historians have often given great emphasis to centralized kingdoms, states, and empires. Besides organized states, there were many African groups that remained decentralized but evolved appropriate structures of government that functioned and served them well. The Igbos of modern Nigeria, for example, who numbered in the millions, never developed centralized states.

II. AGRICULTURE AND IRON

Africa has often been seen as a borrower of technology and agriculture from Eurasia. Recent archeological research is changing our views of these developments in Africa, revealing that iron workings and knowledge existed in many parts

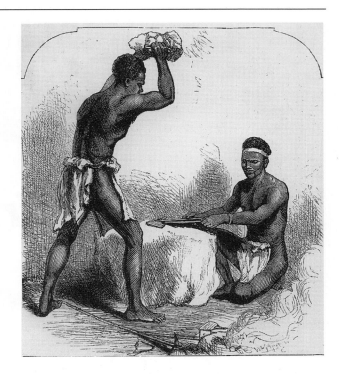

Iron tools were used in Africa long before the coming of the Europeans. This illustration, taken from David Livingstone's Last Journals, *shows Africans forging hoes.*

of Africa prior to the Christian era. There were iron workings in the lakeland regions of modern Tanzania by the seventh century B.C.E., in Meroe by the fifth century B.C.E., in Nok in West Africa by the fourth century B.C.E., and in the northern lake regions of East Africa by the third century B.C.E. What this suggests is that there were probably many areas that independently evolved the use of iron rather than importing it from the outside. These early users of iron probably kept their use of iron a secret. However, between the second and fifth centuries C.E. iron technology spread to most places in central, eastern, and southern Africa through Bantu farmers who had acquired the use of iron by this time.

The movement of the Bantu peoples from West Africa to central, eastern, and southern Africa has often been described as a migration, but it was a gradual movement of small numbers of peoples who often intermarried with the people in the areas they infiltrated. The Bantu were in the area of modern Zaire by the fifth century B.C.E., but the widespread use of iron between the second and fifth centuries C.E. allowed the Bantu to move more quickly to the rest of the southern portion of the continent.

The appearance of iron had repercussions in Africa as wide as those we noted in Eurasia. Iron-tipped hoes and iron-shod axes made it possible to extend agriculture into the forests of Africa, just as the earlier use of iron brought agriculture into the forests of central Europe and of the Ganges and Yangtze valleys. The resulting increase in agricultural output left a surplus available for trading purposes. As in Eurasia, this in turn led to social differentiation—to the division of peoples into rulers and ruled in place of simple kinship relationships; hence the appearance about the ninth century C.E. of definite state structures with military and administrative services and with the revenue sources necessary for their support.

Technological advances in Africa affected the ethnic composition of the continent. It was the accessible Negroes rather than the inaccessible Pygmies and San who adopted and profited from agriculture and iron metallurgy. Consequently, it was also they who increased disproportionately in number and who were able, with their iron tools and weapons, to push southward at the expense of the San and Pygmies. Their expansionism was particularly marked in the case of the Bantu, a predominantly Negroid linguistic group. Starting from their original center in the Cameroon highlands, the Bantu infiltrated in the early Christian era into the Congo basin, where they developed a symbiotic relationship with the sparse San hunters. From there they pushed southeast to the fertile, open Great Lakes country between 600 and 900 C.E. They then continued southward across the savanna at the expense of the San. These migrations explain why the Negroes were the predominant ethnic group by the time the Europeans arrived, whereas a millennium earlier they had shared the continent fairly evenly with the Caucasoids, San, and Pygmies.

African Agriculture

Before its desiccation 7,000 years ago, the Sahara supported a pastoral society that had flocks of sheep, goats, and cattle. These people also fished

Traditional African farming methods as painted by a modern African artist. The women in the left foreground are grinding grain in a large mortar, while the men beyond are hoeing and harvesting.

and herded flocks using sickles and blades which have been found in ruins.

It is not known precisely when these people began to grow food, but we do know that agricultural systems evolved in this area which supported extensive village populations with far-flung market and trading centers. These centers helped to give rise to African cultures such as the Nok, Benin, Ghana, Mali, and other Sudanic and East African kingdoms.

There was an intimate association between plants and African peoples, as was the case with other humans extending back to the roots of human origin. Although agriculture emerged in Egypt around 6500 B.C.E., tool kits associated with intensive gathering and the use of food crops go back as early as 18,000 years ago. The evidence indicates that these tool kits were African and not Near Eastern. The archeological evidence in Egypt suggests that the first farmers in that area 6,500 years ago also had sheep, goats, and cattle; cool seasons yielded crops such as barley, emmer, flax, lentil, and chickpea.

In the area of the West African forests there is also early evidence of the domestication of crops such as the oil palm, cowpea, and guinea yam. This domestication does not indicate borrowing from elsewhere. In the area of the savanna, for example, the rice cultivated is believed to be of savanna origin. Furthermore, in the area of Ethiopia most of the crops cultivated there are native to Africa, and there is no evidence that borrowing took place.

III. ISLAM

Africa was influenced by the impact of Moslem Arabs who overran all of North Africa in the seventh century C.E. and later extended their control down the east coast as merchants and colonists. From these coastal bases Islam had a profound influence on the African peoples. The impact of Islam was most obvious in the externals of life—names, dress, household equipment, architectural styles, festivals, and the like. It was evident also in the agricultural and technological progress that resulted from wider contact with the outside world; in East Africa, for example, the Arabs introduced rice and sugar cane from India.

Islam also stimulated commerce linking the African economy to the far-flung network of Eurasian trade routes controlled by Moslem merchants. From their bases in North Africa the Moslems used the camel much more than had the Romans, and they increased the number of trans-Saharan trade routes and the volume of trade. Southward they transported cloth, jewelry, cowrie beads, and, above all, salt, which was in urgent demand throughout the Sudan. In return the Africans provided ivory, slaves, ostrich feathers, civet for perfumes, and, most important, gold from the upper Niger, Senegal,

The Djinguereber mosque in Timbuktu. The mud and wood building is typical of western Sudanese mosques. The distinctive tower of the mosque was a symbol of the presence of Islam, which came to places like Timbuktu in central and West Africa by way of overland trade routes.

and Volta rivers. Much of this gold ultimately found its way to Europe—in such large quantities, in fact, that it became important for off-setting medieval Europe's unfavorable balance of trade with the East. The trade between the Sudan and North Africa was so profitable for both sides that by 1400 the whole of West Africa was criss-crossed with trading trails and dotted with market centers.

Meanwhile a similar trading pattern had been developing in East Africa. Moslem middle-men on the coast sent agents into the interior who brought ivory, slaves, gold from present-day Zimbabwe and copper from Katanga. These commodities then were exported through Indian Ocean trade channels, controlled at the time by Moslem merchants. In later centuries iron ore also was obtained from the interior, shipped to southern India, and made into the so-called Damascus blades. In return for these products, Africans received Chinese and Indian cloth and various luxury goods, especially Chinese porcelain, remains of which still can be found along the coast. This trade was the basis for the string of thriving ports and city-states along the East African coast. Thus we see that just as the Mediterranean Sea had made possible centuries-old interaction between North Africa and the peoples of Europe and the Middle East, so the Indian Ocean made possible similar interaction between East Africa and the peoples of the Middle East, India, Southeast Asia, and even the Far East.

To return to the role of Islam in Africa, it served also to stimulate the intellectual life of the Sudan. Literacy spread with the establishment of Koranic schools. Scholars could pursue higher learning at various Sudanese universities, of which the University of Sankore at Timbuktu was the most outstanding. This institution was modeled after other Moslem universities at Fez, Tunis, and Cairo. It was the custom for scholars to move about freely among these universities and others in the Moslem world in order to study at the feet of particular masters.

The adoption of Islam also strengthened the political organization of the Sudanic kingdoms. Traditionally Sudanic rulers could claim the allegiance only of their own kinship units or clans and of such other related kinship units that recognized descent from a great founding ancestor. But when the kingdoms were enlarged into great empires, the kinship relationship obviously became inadequate as the basis for imperial organization. The greater the extent of an empire, the more alien its emperor appeared to a large proportion of the subjects. Local chiefs could not be depended on to serve as faithful vassals; they tended instead to lead their own people in resistance to imperial rule. Islam helped to solve this institutional problem by strengthening the imperial administration. Moslem schools and colleges turned out a class of educated men who could organize an effective imperial bureaucracy. These men were not dominated by their kinship alliances; their own interests were tied to imperial authority, and they normally could be counted on to serve that authority loyally.

IV. TRADE AND SUDANESE EMPIRES

The Islamic conquest gave trans-Saharan trade new impetus and linked it to the Moslem world, whose monetary system depended upon gold. The earliest kingdom associated with the growth of trade across the Sahara is the Ghana Empire (400–1200). (See map of African Empires and Trade Routes, p. 256.) This empire was founded by Soninke-speaking Africans who lived in the area of the grassland south of the Sahara. Although we do not know the precise date for the founding of the kingdom, it was in existence by the fifth century C.E. Ghana's fame reached far beyond the Sahara and as far as Baghdad. The Arabic writer Al-Fazari, who lived at the court of the Abbasid caliph in that city, described Ghana as the "land of gold."

Moslems played a key role in trade and administration of the empire, but the king controlled the trade of the empire and administered justice in the kingdom. Despite the Moslem presence, the king clung to the religion of his ancestors.

The Ghana Empire reached its peak during the middle of the eleventh century and then began to decline. Religious conflict and destructive wars disrupted trading activities of the empire. Ghana also lost control of the gold-mining regions toward the end of the twelfth century. Furthermore, environmental factors such as desertification and overgrazing in the region

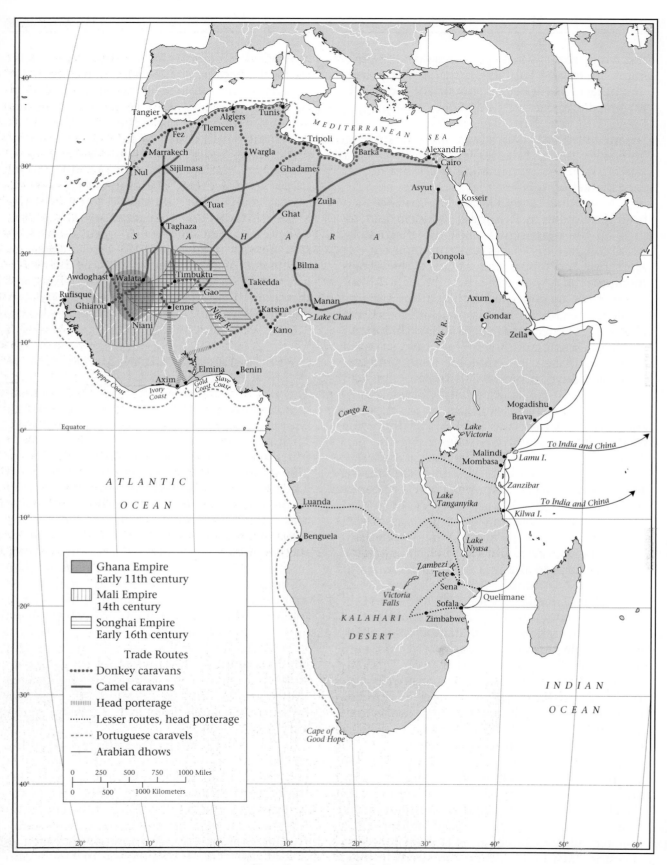

Legend

Ghana Empire
Early 11th century

Mali Empire
14th century

Songhai Empire
Early 16th century

Trade Routes

- ●●●● Donkey caravans
- ——— Camel caravans
- |||||||| Head porterage
- ······ Lesser routes, head porterage
- – – – Portuguese caravels
- ——— Arabian dhows

0   250   500   750   1000 Miles
0   500   1000 Kilometers

African Empires and Trade Routes

Map labels:

MEDITERRANEAN SEA

Tangier, Algiers, Tunis, Tlemcen, Fez, Marrakech, Nul, Sijilmasa, Wargla, Tripoli, Barka, Alexandria, Cairo, Ghadames, Tuat, Zuila, Ghat, Asyut, Kosseir, Taghaza, Dongola, Bilma, Awdoghast, Walata, Timbuktu, Takedda, Manan, Axum, Gondar, Rufisque, Gao, Ghiarou, Jenne, Katsina, Lake Chad, Zeila, Niani, Kano, Niger R.

S   A   H   A   R   A

Elmina, Benin, Axim, Gold Coast, Slave Coast, Ivory Coast, Pepper Coast

Equator

Congo R.

ATLANTIC OCEAN

Lake Victoria, Mogadishu, Brava, Malindi, Mombasa, Lamu I., Zanzibar, To India and China, Lake Tanganyika, Kilwa I., Luanda, Benguela, Lake Nyasa

Nile R.

Zambezi R., Tete, Sena, Victoria Falls, Sofala, Quelimane, Zimbabwe

KALAHARI DESERT

Cape of Good Hope

INDIAN OCEAN

forced farmers and traders to disperse and move to more favorable regions.

As the empire of Ghana declined, it gave way to the Mali Empire (1200–1500). The expansion and fame of Mali during this period depended on two able rulers: Mansa Musa (1312–1337) and Mansa Sulayaman (1341–1360). Islam became well established at Mansa Musa's court. The fame of Mali spread following Mansa Musa's pilgrimage to Mecca in 1324. Mansa Musa distributed gold and lavish gifts on his pilgrimage. In Egypt he distributed so much gold that his visit was noted by Arab historians as the most significant event in Egypt in 1324. On his return from his pilgrimage Mansa Musa brought back with him religious scholars and missionaries. The major commercial areas thus became major centers for education. Mansa Musa purified Islam on his return by stricter adherence to the Moslem religion.

Despite its commercial and political attainments, Mali began to decline as a result of internal political problems and outside attacks. The last of the great empires of the western Sudan was Songhay (1350–1600). Its origins go back to at least the eighth century. Trans-Saharan trade as well as its location in the fertile Sudan savanna area contributed to the rise of the kingdom. The location of the kingdom on the banks of the Niger River also afforded opportunities for fishing. When Songhay emerged as an empire, people were divided into three professional classes: the Sorko (mostly fishermen), the Do (mostly farmers), and the Gow or Gabibi (mostly hunters).

Songhay remained a small kingdom until it regained its independence from Mali in the late fourteenth century and began to expand. As an empire it enjoyed only about a century of brilliance, from the second half of the fifteenth century until the early decades of the sixteenth century.

The expansion of Songhay and the consolidation of the empire can be attributed to two monarchs: Sunni Ali (1464–1492) and Askia Mohammed (1492–1528). The latter exploited the strategic location of Timbuktu and revived the trade that was so vital to the empire. Realizing the importance of Islam, Askia reached out to the Moslem community. He made contact with notable Muslim scholars and encouraged education. In Timbuktu, his university in the mosque of Sankore produced many distinguished scholars. One of these has left us a description of the intellectual life of Timbuktu:

In those days Timbuktu did not have its equal . . .
from the province of Mali to the extreme limits of the

Examples of iron coins found in Equatorial Africa.

region of the Maghrib for the solidity of its institutions, its political liberties, the purity of its morals, the security of persons, its consideration and compassion towards foreigners, its courtesy towards students and men of learning.

Leo Africanus, the Moorish historian who traveled in the region, also wrote:

Here are great stores of doctors, judges, priests and other learned men that are bountifully maintained at the king's cost and charges, and hither are brought divers manuscripts or written books of Barbary, which are sold for more money than any other merchandise.

Despite its wealth and learning, the empire fell because of internal tensions and raids from Morocco. By the end of the sixteenth century Songhay was a shadow of its former self.

These empires had certain fundamental characteristics in common. They all were based primarily on trade, so that each extended its authority northward to control the import of salt and southward to control the purchase of gold. Each derived most of its revenues from levies on the buying and selling of these and other commodities. The revenues from these duties allowed for progressively greater sophistication in imperial administration. Thus the Songhay Empire was more complex than its two predecessors. It was divided into definite provinces, each with a governor on long-term appointment. It also boasted the beginnings of a professional army and even a number of ministries—for finance, justice, home affairs, agriculture, and forests, as well as for the Arabs and Berbers on the Saharan frontiers of the empire.

The Mali and Songhay empires owed much to Islam for furthering trade, providing a trained bureaucracy, and stimulating intellectual life. Islam also transformed the Sudan from an isolated African region to an integral part of the Moslem world. Thus the fourteenth-century Arab traveler Ibn Battuta included Mali in his journeys, which ranged as far east as China. Arriving at the Mali capital in June 1353, he was favorably impressed by the imperial administration and by the habits of the people:

The negroes possess some admirable qualities. They are seldom unjust, and have a greater abhorrence of

West African terra-cotta sculpture (36 cms high) from the Nok culture, which flourished in the Western Sudan from about 900 B.C.E. to about 200 C.E. The style of terra-cotta castings like this one suggests that they may have had wooden prototypes.

injustice than any other people. Their sultan shows no mercy to anyone who is guilty of the least act of it. There is complete security in their country. Neither traveler nor inhabitant in it has anything to fear from robbers or men of violence. They do not confiscate the property of any white man who dies in their country, even if it be uncounted wealth. On the contrary, they give it into the charge of some trustworthy person among the whites, until the rightful heir takes possession of it. They are careful to observe the hours of prayer, and assiduous in attending them in congregations, and in bringing up their children to them. On Fridays, if a man does not go early to the mosque, he cannot find a corner to pray in, on account of the crowd.[1]

Although Islam played a key role in the formation and functioning of the Sudanic empires, it should be noted that it was primarily an urban faith. It was the merchants and townspeople who became Moslems, whereas the country folk by and large remained loyal to their traditional pagan gods and beliefs. Thus the reliance of many of the emperors and of their imperial establishments on Islam was a source of weakness as well as strength. Islam, as we have seen, had much to contribute, but its base was narrower than it seemed to contemporary observers, who naturally visited urban centers and traveled along trade routes. Thus in times of crisis the town-centered empires proved unexpectedly fragile and quickly fell apart.

Another weakness of the Sudanic empires was their vulnerability to attack from the north by Berbers looking for the source of African gold or seeking to impose their particular version of the true faith. The fanatical Almarovids were responsible for the overthrow of Ghana in 1076, and likewise an invasion from Morocco destroyed Songhay in 1591. The latter catastrophe marked the end of the Sudanic imperial era. In the words of a seventeenth-century Timbuktu historian: "From that moment everything changed. Danger took the place of security; poverty of wealth. Peace gave way to distress, disasters, and violence. . . ."[2]

V. KINGDOMS AND STATES

The three empires noted above are the best-known African medieval political creations. In the rest of the continent, however, there existed a great variety of other political structures. In southeast Africa, for example, there were certain similarities to the situation in the Sudan. Just as the Sudan was famous for its gold exports, so southeast Africa was famous for the same reason in the Indian Ocean basin. And just as the Sudanic empires and North African states were nourished by the one trade pattern, so by the fifteenth century the Monomotapa Empire in the interior and the Kilwa city-state on the coast were supported by the other.

Monomotapa, a word adapted by the Portuguese from the royal title Mwenemutapa, included much of Zimbabwe and Mozambique. It controlled the sources of gold and the routes to the coast, after the fashion of the Sudanic empires. The monarchs of Monomotapa raised the Great Temple of Zimbabwe, a massive enclosure with walls thirty-two feet high, constructed to provide an appropriate setting for the conduct of royal ceremonial rites. On the coast, the merchant rulers of the port of Kilwa controlled the flow of goods from Monomotapa to the Moslem trading ships that ranged the Indian Ocean and even beyond to the China seas. "Kilwa is one of the most beautiful and well-constructed towns in the world. The whole of it is elegantly built," wrote Ibn Battuta—the same traveler impressed also by Mali.[3]

Just as the Sudanic kingdoms were ravaged by Berber invaders from the north, so Monomotapa and Kilwa were destroyed by Portuguese intruders from overseas. Within a decade after Vasco da Gama's rounding of the Cape of Good Hope in 1497, the Portuguese had plundered many of the coastal cities of southeast Africa and were carrying on in the Indian Ocean as though it were a Portuguese lake. Da Gama had missed Kilwa on his first voyage, but a Portuguese fleet was provided shelter there in 1500. Five years later another fleet responded to this

Benin King and Attendants, *from Nigeria, circa 1550–1680 B.C.E.*

9 *Copper crucifix of sixteenth or seventeenth century from the Kipangue Province of the Lower Congo*

10 *Head of Christ carved in wood in East Africa. The Arabic features and Assyrian beard are in sharp contrast with the Negro faces of the other side of the continent*

A sixteenth or seventeenth century copper crucifix from Kipangue Province, Lower Congo.

CONCLUSION

Contrary to popular belief, Africa during the period before European expansion was never isolated. External contact and internal relationships increased from the seventh century onwards with the dynamism brought by Islam. Interregional trade grew because of more effective means of communication. The camel was already in use in North Africa, but from the seventh century on its use became widespread. Cross-breeding of the two-humped camel of central Asia with the Arabian or one-humped dromedary produced two kinds of camels: One had a slow gait and was capable of carrying heavy loads for long distances; the other was faster and was used as a courier.

The increase in trade also gave impetus to navigation and allowed the Arabs to build up powerful fleets in the trade between East Africa and the countries of the Indian Ocean, the Red Sea, and the Mediterranean. There was also a spectacular growth of commercial towns all over the continent: Sidjimasa was a staging post for trans-Saharan trade; Cairo was central to the trade of the Moslem east and the Moslem west and the savanna area; and Awdaghust was the central market that linked North Africa with the savanna. On the East African coast, Moslem merchants settled in the commercial towns of Mogadishu, Malindi, Mombasa, Kilwa, and Sofala.

A variety of products were traded, including raw materials such as iron, flax, cotton, gum, and indigo; subsistence products such as sorghum, rice, shear-butter, millet, olive oil, salt, and fish; and also luxury goods such as gold and ivory.

The pre-1500 centuries saw significant economic, social and political developments. After 1500 other parts of the world would pull ahead of Africa in terms of development. The reasons for this divergence lie in Africa's internal developments and destructive external contacts after 1500, as we shall note in the next volume.

The British Africanist Thomas Hodgkin wrote that

Allowing for the difference between the Moslem and the Christian intellectual climates, a citizen of fourteenth-century Timbuktu would have found himself reasonably at home in fourteenth-century Oxford. In

hospitality with ruthless looting. A member of the expedition recounts that they captured this city of "many strong houses several stories high" without opposition from the surprised inhabitants. Then "the Vicar-General and some of the Franciscan fathers came ashore carrying two crosses in procession and singing the Te Deum. They went to the palace, and there the cross was put down and the Admiral prayed. Then everyone started to plunder the town of all its merchandise and provisions."[4]

Later the Portuguese made their way up the Zambezi River and similarly undermined the Monomotapa Empire. They settled in various strategic locations along the river and extended their influence in all directions until the inevitable showdown in 1628. With their firearms the Portuguese easily defeated two Monomotapa armies, but several substantial kingdoms survived on the ruins of the former empire.

the sixteenth century he would still have found many points in common between the two university cities. By the nineteenth century the gulf had grown very deep.[5]

Hodgkin's point describes a process that is certainly not unique to Africa. It is clear from the preceding chapters that divergence is a worldwide phenomenon for the simple reason that the West pioneered in modernization and consequently pulled ahead of all other societies. Yet the fact remains that the gap between the West and Africa opened much wider than that between the West and other Eurasian regions. Constantinople, Delhi, and Peking did decline in relation to London, Paris, and Berlin, but they did not decline to virtual extinction, as did Timbuktu.

SUGGESTED READINGS

A useful introduction to Africa is by J. F. A. Ajayi and M. Crowder, eds., *Historical Atlas of Africa* (Longman, 1985). On geography, see W. A. Hance, *The Geography of Modern Africa*, 2nd ed. (Columbia University, 1975); and G. W. Hartwig and K. D. Patterson, eds., *Disease in African History* (Duke University, 1978). Collections of source materials are provided by B. Davidson, *The African Past: Chronicles from Antiquity to Modern Times* (Little, Brown, 1964); and P. J. M. McEwan, ed., *Africa from Early Times to 1800* (Oxford University, 1968). The pre-Western history of Africa is presented as authoritatively as current knowledge permits by P. D.

Curtin, et al., *African History* (Little, Brown, 1978); J. D. Fage, *A History of Africa* (Knopf, 1978); and in more detail in R. Oliver and J. D. Fage, eds., *The Cambridge History of Africa*, 8 vols. (Cambridge University, 1975 ff.); *UNESCO General History of Africa* (University of California, 1981 ff.); and P. J. C. Dark, *An Introduction to Benin Art and Technology* (Oxford: Clarendon Press, 1973).

For African arts, see M. Posnansky, ed., *Prelude to East African History* (Oxford University, 1966); J. F. A. Ajayi and M. Crowder, eds., *History of West Africa*, vol. 1, 3rd ed. (Longman, 1985); B. Davidson, *The Prehistory of Africa* (Thames and Hudson, 1970); B. Davidson, *The African Genius* (Little, Brown, 1969); and B. H. Dietz and M. B. Olantunji, *Musical Instruments of Africa* (John Day, 1965). On the role of Islam in African history, see volumes II and III of *The Cambridge History of Africa* above; and N. Levtzion, *Ancient Ghana and Mali* (Methuen, 1973), a thorough study of what is known.

NOTES

1. Cited by C.M. Cipolla, *European Culture and Overseas Expansion* (Pelican, 1970), p. 105.
2. Ibn Battuta, *Travels in Asia and Africa, 1325–1354*, trans. H. A. R. Gibb (Routledge & Kegan Paul, 1929), pp. 329–330.
3. Cited by T. Hodgkin, "Kingdoms of the Western Sudan," in *The Dawn of African history*, ed. R. Oliver (Oxford University, 1961), p. 43.
4. Cited by B. Davidson, *Africa in History* (Macmillan, 1968), p. 63.
5. Ibid., p. 168.

CHAPTER
16

Americas and Australia

To the nations, however, both of the East and West Indies, all the commercial benefits which can have resulted from these events [the expansion of Europe] have been sunk and lost in the dreadful misfortunes which they have occasioned.

Adam Smith

The Vikings, who stumbled on North America in the eleventh century, tried for about one hundred years to maintain settlements there, but without success. In the fifteenth century Columbus likewise stumbled on the New World, but this time the sequel was altogether different. Instead of failure and withdrawal, Columbus's discovery was followed by massive and overwhelming penetration of both North and South America. The contrast shows how much European power and dynamism had increased during the intervening half-millennium.

Equally striking was the contrast between the rapid European penetration and exploitation of the Americas and the centuries that elapsed before the same could take place in Africa. One reason was geography; the New World was physically more accessible and inviting. The other reason was that the overall nature of the Indian cultures was such that effective resistance was impossible. And if this was true of the American Indians, it was much more so of the Australian aborigines who were still at the food-gathering stage. In this chapter we shall consider the physical setting and the cultural background of the fateful developments that followed the landing of Columbus in the West Indies and of Captain James Cook in New South Wales.

I. LAND AND PEOPLE

The Americas, in contrast to Africa, were exceptionally open to newcomers from Europe. No sandbars obstructed the approaches to the coasts. There were many more harbors available along the indented coastline of the Americas than along the unbroken coastline of Africa. Also, the Americas had a well-developed pattern of waterways that were relatively free of impediments and offered easy access to the interior. There is no counterpart in Africa to the majestic and smooth-flowing Amazon, Plata, Mississippi, and St. Lawrence rivers. The explorers soon learned the use of the native birchbark canoe, and they discovered that with comparatively few portages they could paddle from the Atlantic up the St. Lawrence, along the Great Lakes, and thence south down the Mississippi to the Gulf of Mexico. Or they could paddle north down the Mackenzie to the Arctic Ocean, or west down the Columbia or the Fraser to the Pacific Ocean.

The climate of the Americas, too, is generally more attractive than that of Africa. The Amazon basin, it is true, is hot and humid, and the polar extremities of both continents are bitterly cold. But the British and French settlers flourished in the lands they colonized north of the Rio Grande, and the Spaniards likewise felt at home in Mexico and Peru, which became their two principal centers. The climate there is not much different from that of Spain, and certainly a welcome contrast to the sweltering and disease-ridden Gold and Ivory coasts of Africa.

The Indians that the Europeans found in the Americas were the descendants of the bands that had crossed the Bering Sea from Siberia to Alaska. Until recently it was believed that the Indians first began crossing to the Americas about 10,000 years ago. New archeological findings, together with the use of carbon-14 dating, have forced a drastic revision of this estimate. It is now generally agreed that humans were in the New World roughly 30,000 years ago. The last major migration of Indians took place about 3,000 years ago. Then came the Eskimos, who continued to travel back and forth across the straits until modern political conditions forced them to remain on one side or the other. In any case, by this time the parts of America closest to Asia were densely enough populated to discourage further migration.

The actual crossing to the New World presented little difficulty to these early newcomers. The last Ice Age had locked up vast quantities of sea water, lowering the ocean level by 460 feet and thus exposing a 1,300-mile-wide land bridge connecting Siberia and Alaska. A "bridge" of such proportions was, in effect, a vast new subcontinent, which allowed ample scope for the transfer of plants and animals that now took place. Furthermore, this area, because of low rainfall, was covered not with ice but with lakes, mosses, grasses, and assorted shrubs typical of the tundra. This vegetation offered pasturage for the large mammals of the time: mastodon, mammoth, musk oxen, bison, moose, elk, mountain sheep and goats, camels, foxes, bears, wolves, and horses. As these herds of game crossed to the New World they were followed by the hunters who depended on them for food.

Even after rising temperatures lifted the sea level and submerged the connecting lands, the resulting narrow straits could easily have been crossed in crude boats without even losing sight of shore. Later and more advanced migrants probably traveled by boat from Asia to America and then continued along the northwest coast until they finally landed and settled in what is now British Columbia.

Most who crossed to Alaska moved on into the heart of North America through a gap in the ice sheet in the central Yukon plateau. They pressed forward because of the same forces that led them to migrate to Alaska—the search for new hunting grounds and the continual pressure of tribes from the rear. In this manner, both the continents were soon peopled by scattered tribes of hunters.

Regarding racial traits, all Indians may be classified as Mongoloids. They have the characteristic high cheekbones, straight black hair, but sparse hair on the face and body. Not all Indians, however, look alike. Those on North America's northwest coast have flatter faces and noses and narrower eyes (Mongolian fold) than do those of the southwest. The explanation for this difference is twofold: First, the earliest immigrants were much less Mongoloid in appearance because they left the East before the Asian Mongoloids—as we know them today—had fully evolved. Second, the immigrants at once spread out and settled in small, inbred groups in a variety of climates. This led to the evolution of a great variety of physical types, even though they are all of the same Mongoloid family.

II. CULTURES

The migrants to the New World brought little cultural baggage with them since they came from northeast Siberia, one of the least developed regions of Eurasia. They were, of course, all hunters, organized in small bands, possessing only crude stone tools, no pottery, and no domesticated animals, except perhaps the dog. Since they were entering an uninhabited continent, they were completely free to develop their own institutions without the influences from native populations that affected the Aryans when they migrated to the Indus valley, or the Achaeans and Dorians when they reached Greece.

During the ensuing millennia the American Indians did indeed develop an extraordinarily rich variety of cultures, which were adapted to one another as well as to the wide range of physical environments they encountered. Some remained at the hunting-band stage, whereas others developed kingdoms and empires. Their

Olmec Head. This colossal head, now in the Museo Nacional de Antropologia in Mexico City, was excavated at San Lorenzo. Carved of Basalt, it may be a portrait of an Olmec ruler. Olmec civilization thrived between 1500 and 800 B.C.E.

religions encompassed all known categories, including monotheism. They spoke perhaps 2,000 distinct languages, some as different from one another as Chinese and English. This number represents almost as much variation in speech as found in the entire Old World, where about 3,000 languages are known to have existed in 1500 C.E. Nor were these languages primitive, either in vocabulary or in any other respect. Whereas Shakespeare used about 24,000 words, and the King James Bible about 7,000, the Nahuatl of Mexico used 27,000 words, and the Yahgans of Tierra del Fuego, considered to be one of the world's most culturally retarded peoples, possess a vocabulary of at least 30,000 words.

Taking all types of institutions and practices into account, anthropologists have defined some twenty-two culture areas in the New World—the Great Plains area, the Eastern Woodlands, the Northwest Coast area, and so forth. A simpler classification, on the basis of how food was obtained, involves three categories: hunting, gathering, and fishing cultures; intermediate farming cultures; and advanced farming cultures. This scheme not only is simpler but is also meaningful from the viewpoint of world history, for it helps to explain the varied responses of the Indians to the European invaders.

The advanced farming cultures were located in Mesoamerica (central and southern Mexico, Guatemala, and Honduras) and the Andean highland area (Ecuador, Peru, Bolivia, and northern Chile). The intermediate farming cultures were generally in the adjacent regions, and the food-gathering cultures were in the more remote regions—the southern part of South America and the western and northern part of North America. It is significant that agriculture was first developed in the Americas in regions that were strikingly similar to the Middle East, where agriculture originated in Eurasia—that is, highland regions not requiring extensive clearing of forests to prepare the fields for crops, with enough rainfall to allow the crops to mature, and with a supply of potentially high-yielding native plants available for domestication.

The Indians domesticated over one hundred plants, or as many as were domesticated in all Eurasia, a truly extraordinary achievement. More than 50 percent of the farm products of the United States today are derived from crops grown by the Indians. Furthermore, we are realizing the superior food value of certain plants grown by the Indians but neglected by the European newcomers. One example is the grain amaranth, which had been as important as corn and beans to the Aztecs. They mixed the amaranth with human blood to form cakelike replicas of their gods and fed those replicas to the faithful. The Spaniards regarded this ritual as barbaric and as a mockery of Christian communion. Therefore, the Spaniards forbade the ritual by condemning to death anyone found growing or possessing amaranth. Yet this plant survives to the present day. A confection made of popped amaranth and honey is still popular in Mexico. Meanwhile, scientists are beginning to recognize the value of this grain, which can be ground into flour or popped like corn and can be used to make bread, crackers, cookies, soups, porridge, dumplings, and beverages. In addition to this versatility, a recent report of the National Academy of Sciences notes that amaranth is superior to other grains as a source of protein, vitamins, and minerals. Like the raised field agriculture noted above (Chapter 2, Section III), the current recognition of amaranth as "the grain of the future" points up the fact that lessons can be learned from our prehistoric ancestors, even in our age of "high technology."

Maize, which was the staple in almost all regions, was originally a weed with ears no larger than a person's thumbnail. The Indians bred it into a plant with rows of seeds on long cobs. So completely did they domesticate maize that it became completely dependent on humans for survival; it would become extinct if humans stopped planting it, for in its domesticated form it cannot disperse its seeds, the kernels. Also impressive was the skill of the Indians in utilizing large numbers of poisonous plants. One of these is manioc, known in the United States as tapioca. The Indians removed a deadly poison from manioc, leaving the starch. Other important plants grown by the Indians were squashes, potatoes, tomatoes, peanuts, chocolate, tobacco, and beans, a major source of protein. Among the medicinal plants bequeathed by the Indians were cascara, cocaine, arnica, ipecac, and quinine. The fact that none of the plants grown in America were cultivated in the Old World before its discovery of the New proves conclusively that the origins of agriculture were independent in the two hemispheres.

The regions where the Indians began agriculture were also the regions where they first developed it further and gradually evolved advanced farming cultures. This in turn profoundly changed the Indians' way of life. In general, the result was, as in Eurasia, a greatly increased sedentary population and the development of cultural activities not directly connected with bare subsistence. In other words, it was in these advanced farming cultures that it became possible to develop large empires and sophisticated civilizations comparable in certain respects to those in West Africa. Unfortunately, these indigenous American civilizations were suddenly overwhelmed by the Spaniards. Thus they left behind them little but their precious domesticated plants.

III. CIVILIZATIONS

The three major Amerindian civilizations were the Mayan, in present-day Yucatan, Guatemala, and Belize; the Aztec, in present-day Mexico; and the Inca, stretching for 3,000 miles from mid-Ecuador to mid-Chile. (See map of Amerindian Empires, p. 267.) The Mayas created the oldest civilization in the Americas and were outstanding for their remarkable development of the arts and sciences. They alone evolved an ideographic form of writing in which characters or signs were used as conventional symbols for ideas. They also studied the movements of the heavenly bodies in order to measure time, predict the future, and set favorable dates for sacrifices and major undertakings. So extensive was the astronomical knowledge compiled by highly trained priests that it is believed to have been at least equal to that of Europe at that time. The intricate sacred calendar of the Mayas was based on concurrent cycles merging into greater cycles as their multiples coincided in time. Some of their calendrical computations spanned millions of years, a particularly impressive concept of the dimension of time when we remember how recently in Europe the creation of the world was still fixed at 4004 B.C.E.

Mayan cities, if they may be so called, were ceremonial centers rather than fortresses, dwell-

Mayan figure of a dignitary or priest.

have been soil exhaustion or epidemic disease or peasant revolutions against the burden of supporting the religious centers and their priestly hierarchies. In any case, the great stone structures were abandoned to decay and were swallowed by the surrounding forest. They have been unearthed only in recent decades by archeological excavations.

The Aztecs were brusque and warlike compared to the artistic and intellectual Mayas—a contrast reminiscent of that between the Romans and the Greeks in the Old World. The Aztecs actually were latecomers to Mexico, where a series of highly developed societies had succeeded one another through the centuries. They were vulnerable to attacks by barbarians from the arid north who naturally moved down in response to the lure of fertile lands. The last of these invaders were the Aztecs, who had settled on some islands on Lake Texcoco, which then filled much of the floor of the valley of Anáhuac. As their numbers grew and the islands became overcrowded, the Aztecs increased their arable land by making chinampas—floating islands of matted weeds, covered with mud dredged from the lake floor, and anchored to the bottom by growing weeds. To the present day, this mode of cultivation is carried on in certain regions. Before each planting the farmers scoop up fresh mud and spread it over the chinampa, whose level steadily rises with the succession of crops. The farmers then excavate the top layers of mud, which they use to build a new chinampa, thus beginning a new cycle.

The chinampas enabled the Aztecs to boom in numbers and wealth. Early in the fifteenth century they made alliances with towns on the lake shore, and from that foothold they quickly extended their influence in all directions. Raiding expeditions went out regularly, forcing other peoples to pay tribute in kind and in services. By the time the Spaniards appeared on the scene, Aztec domination extended to the Pacific on the west, to the Gulf of Mexico on the east, almost to the Yucatan on the south, and to the Rio Grande on the north. The capital, Tenochtitlán, was by then a magnificent city of 200,000 to 300,000 people, linked to the shore by causeways. The conqueror Cortes compared the capital to Venice and judged it to be "the most beautiful city in the world."

ing places, or administrative capitals. This was so because the Mayas practiced slash-and-burn agriculture, which exhausted the soil within two or three years, requiring constant moving of the village settlements. To balance this transitory mode of life, the Maya cultivators expressed their social unity by erecting large stone buildings in centers that were devoted primarily to religious ceremonies. These buildings were large temple pyramids and also community houses in which the priests and novices probably lived. The architecture, produced entirely with stone tools, was decorated with sculpture that was unsurpassed in the Americas and that ranks as one of the world's great arts.

The Maya civilization flourished between the fourth and tenth centuries, but it then declined for reasons that remain obscure. It may

Aztec Empire (approximate area)

Inca Empire (approximate area)

Amerindian Empires on the Eve of the Spanish Conquest

A turquoise mosaic of a double-headed serpent of the Aztec culture.

Aztec power was based on constant war preparedness. All men were expected to bear arms, and state arsenals were always stocked and ready for immediate use. With their efficient military machine the Aztecs were able to extract a staggering amount of tribute from their subjects. According to their own records, they collected in one year 14 million pounds of maize, 8 million pounds each of beans and amaranth, and 2 million cotton cloaks in addition to assorted other items such as war costumes, shields, and precious stones.

The splendor of the capital and the volume of tribute pouring into it naturally led the Spaniards to conclude that Montezuma was the ruler of a great empire. Actually this was not so. The vassal states remained quite separate, practicing full self-government. Their only tie to Tenochtitlán was the tribute, which they paid out of fear of the Aztec expeditions. None of the Amerindian states, except for that of the Incas in Peru, was organized on any concept wider than that of the city-state. The Aztecs, in contrast to the Incas, made no attempt to adapt their subjects to the Aztec way of life in preparation for full citizenship.

The Spaniards were not only dazzled by the wealth and magnificence of the Aztec state but also horrified by the wholesale ritual massacre of a continual procession of human victims. These were slaughtered at the top of the ceremonial pyramids that abounded everywhere, and the Spaniards soon realized that the pyramids func-tioned as altars for human sacrifice. Sacrificial cults were common in Mesoamerica, but nowhere did they lead to the obsessive slaughtering practiced by the Aztecs. Indeed, the reasons for Aztec expeditions were not only to collect tribute for their capital but to take captives for sacrifice as well.

They considered the taking of captives as even more important than getting tribute, for their priests taught that the world was in constant danger of cataclysm, especially the extinguishing of the sun—hence the need for offering human victims to appease the heavenly deities. But this practice trapped the Aztecs in a truly vicious circle: Sacrificial victims were needed to forestall universal disaster; victims could be obtained only through war; successful war could be waged only by sacrificing victims, but these in turn could be secured only through war. Bernal Diaz was an eyewitness to the end result:

One certain spot in this township [Xocotlan] I shall never forget, situated near the temple. Here a vast number of human skulls were piled up in the best order imaginable,—there must have been more than 100,000; I repeat, more than 100,000. In like manner you saw the remaining human bones piled up in order in another corner of the square; these it would have been impossible to count. Besides these, there were human heads hanging suspended from beams on both sides. . . . Similar horrible sights we saw towards the interior of the country in every township. . . .[1]

Turning finally to the Incas of Peru, it should be noted that Inca was the title of their king of kings, so that it is technically incorrect, though common usage, to refer to them as the Inca Indians. Actually they were one of the numerous tribes of Quechua stock and language who raised llamas and grew potatoes. In the twelfth century they established themselves in the Cuzco valley, which they soon dominated. At this early stage they built up a dynasty made up of their war chiefs, with their tribespeople constituting an aristocracy among the other tribal peoples. The combination of a hereditary dynasty and an aristocracy was unique in the New World, and it was an effective empire-building instrument. Their empires were particularly strong because of the outstanding ability of the Incas, or heads of state, for generation after generation. The Inca's only legitimate wife was his own full sister, so that each Inca was the son of a sister and a brother. This full inbreeding had

continued for some eight generations, and the original stock must have been exceptionally sound because the royal princes, as the Spaniards observed, were all handsome and vigorous men.

From their imperial city of Cuzco in the Peruvian highlands, the Incas sent forth armies and ambassadors west to the coastal lands and north and south along the great mountain valleys. By the time of the Spanish intrusion they had extended their frontiers some 2,500 miles from Ecuador to central Chile. Thus they ruled much more territory than did the Aztecs, and furthermore they ruled it as a genuine empire.

This empire was held together physically by a road system, which can still be traced for hundreds of miles and which included cable bridges of plaited aloe fiber and floating bridges on pontoons of buoyant reeds. Equally important was an extensive irrigation system, parts of which are still in use and which made the Inca

The Inca city of Machu Picchu perches on a saddle between two peaks on the eastern slopes of the Andes.

Empire a flourishing agricultural unit. Communications were maintained by a comprehensive system of post stations and relays of runners who conveyed messages swiftly to all parts of the empire.

Imperial unity was furthered also by elaborate court ritual and by a state religion based on worship of the sun. The Inca was held to be a descendant of the sun; he played an essential role in its ceremonial worship. Other techniques of imperial rule included state ownership of land, mineral wealth, and herds; careful census compilations for tax and military purposes; the deposing of local hereditary chieftains; forced population resettlement in order to assimilate conquered peoples; and mass marriages under state auspices. Not surprisingly, the Inca Empire is considered to be one of the most successful totalitarian states the world has ever seen.

IV. AMERINDIANS IN HISTORY

Impressive as were these attainments of the American Indians, the fact remains that a handful of Spanish adventurers were able easily to overthrow and completely uproot all three of the great New World civilizations—and this despite the fact that these civilizations had dense populations numbering into the tens of millions. The explanation for the one-sided Spanish triumph is to be found ultimately in the isolation of the Americas. Not only were the American Indian civilizations cut off from stimulating interaction with civilizations on other continents, but also they were largely isolated from each other:

With respect to interrelations between Peru and Mesoamerica [reports an archeologist], it is sufficient to state that not a single object or record of influence or contact between these areas had been accepted as authentic from the long time span between the Formative period [about 1000 B.C.E.] and the coming of the Spaniards. . . .[2]

In other words, there is no reliable evidence of interaction between the Mesoamerican and Peruvian civilizations over a span of 2,500 years. And during those millennia, as we have seen, the various regions of Eurasia, and to a lesser extent sub-

Saharan Africa, were in continual contact. The end result was that the American Indians—even those of the Andes and Mesoamerica—lagged far behind the Eurasians and especially behind the technologically precocious Europeans. By 1500 C.E. the New World had reached the stage of civilization that Egypt and Mesopotamia had attained about 2500 B.C.E.

Precisely what did this mean when the Spaniards arrived and confrontation occurred? It meant, in the first place, that the Indians found themselves economically and technologically far behind the invader's civilization. The highly developed art, science, and religion of the Indians should not be allowed to obscure the fact that they lagged seriously in more material fields. The disparity was most extreme in Mesoamerica, but it also prevailed in the Andean area. In agriculture, the Indians were brilliantly successful in domesticating plants but much less effective in actual production. Their cultivation techniques never advanced beyond the bare minimum necessary to feed populations that rarely reached the numbers of those of the Old World. Their tools were made only of stone, wood, or bone. They were incapable of smelting ores, and though they did work with metal, it was almost exclusively for ornamental purposes. The only ships they constructed were canoes and seagoing rafts. For land transportation they made no use of the wheel, which they knew but used only as a toy. With the exception of the llama and the alpaca, which were used in the Andes but could not carry heavy loads, only the human back was available for transportation.

The immediate significance of this technological lag should not be exaggerated. The Indians obviously were at a grave disadvantage with their spears and arrows against the Spaniards' horses and guns. But after the initial shock, the Indians became accustomed to firearms and cavalry. Furthermore, the Spaniards soon discovered that the Indian weapons were sharp and durable, and they came to prefer the Indian armor of quilted cotton to their own. One of the conquistadors related that the Aztecs had

. . . two arsenals filled with arms of every description, of which many were ornamented with gold and precious stones. These arms consisted in shields of different sizes, sabres, and a species of broadsword,

The Pyramid of the Moon stands at the southern end of Teotihuacán's great central thoroughfare, the Avenue of the Dead.

which is wielded with both hands, the edge furnished with flint stones, so extremely sharp that they cut much better than our Spanish swords: further, lances of greater length than ours, with spikes at their end, full one fathom in length, likewise furnished with several sharp flint stones. The pikes are so very sharp and hard that they will pierce the strongest shield, and cut like a razor; so that the Mexicans even shave themselves with these stones. Then there were excellent bows and arrows, pikes with single and double points, and the proper thongs to throw them with; slings with round stones purposely made for them; also a species of large shield, so ingeniously constructed that it could be rolled up when not wanted; they are only unrolled on the field of battle, and completely cover the whole body from the head to the feet.[3]

This observation suggests that technological disparity was not the only factor that lay behind the Spanish victories. Another was the lack of unity among the Indian peoples. In both Mexico and Peru the Spaniards were able to use disaffected subject tribes who had been alienated by the oppressive rule of Cuzco and Tenochtitlán. The Indians were also weakened by over-regimentation and overdependency. They had been so indoctrinated and were so accustomed to carrying out orders without question that when their leaders were overthrown they were incapable of organizing resistance on their own. Once the kings Montezuma and Atahuallpa had fallen into Spanish hands, the Aztec and Inca empires became bodies without heads, and resistance was paralyzed.

This passivity was increased by religious inhibitions. The natives thought that both Cortes in Mexico and Pizzaro in Peru were gods returning in fulfillment of ancient prophecies. This explains the suicidal vacillations of Atahuallpa in Cuzco and of Montezuma in Tenochtitlán. To Atahuallpa the Spaniards were the creator-god Viracocha and his followers, and for this reason, the ruler waited meekly for Pizarro, who with his 180 men quickly seized control of the great empire. Likewise, to Montezuma, Cortes was the god Quetzalcoatl who was returning to claim his rightful throne, so that again the ruler waited listlessly for the Spaniards to ensconce themselves in his capital.

Equally disastrous for the Aztecs was their concept of war as a short-term ritual endeavor. Their main interest in war was to capture prisoners, whose hearts they offered to their gods. Accordingly their campaigns frequently were ceremonial contests during which prisoners were taken with minimal dislocation and destruction. This type of military tradition obviously was a serious handicap. The Spaniards killed to win; the Aztecs simply tried to take prisoners.

If the American Indians lacked the technology and the cohesion to repel the Europeans, even more serious was their lack of immunity against the diseases brought by the Europeans. Because the Indians had no contacts with peoples of other continents after crossing the Bering Sea tens of thousands of years earlier, they became biologically vulnerable to smallpox, measles, typhus, yellow fever, and other diseases carried by the Europeans and their African slaves.

Estimates of New World native populations before 1492 have been revised sharply upward in recent years. A total of 43 million to 72 million are now believed to have lived in North and South America. As might be expected, the large majority lived in the three great civilizations of Mesoamerica. Regardless of where they lived, all Indians died at an appalling rate on first contact with the Europeans. This is why the newcomers often found abandoned fields and deserted villages, which they simply took over. Mexico's population in 1492 is estimated at 25 million. By 1608, it had shrunk to about one million. The decline was equally precipitous in other

A sixteenth-century Aztec drawing depicts a battle in the Spanish conquest of Mexico.

regions. The island of Hispaniola (today Haiti and the Dominican Republic) had 60,000 Amerindians in 1508, 30,000 in 1554, and 500 in 1570. The magnitude and horror of this holocaust is evident in the following 1586 report from Peru:

Influenza does not shine like the steel sword, but no Indian can dodge it. Tetanus and typhus kill more people than a thousand greyhounds with fiery eyes and foaming jaws . . . smallpox annihilates more Indians than all the guns. The winds of pestilence are devastating these regions. Anyone they strike, they blow down: they devour the body, eat the eyes, close the throat. All smells of decay.[4]

Later, when the full flood of immigration from Europe was under way, the Indians were hopelessly overwhelmed. First came the traders, who penetrated throughout the Americas with little competition or resistance, for the Americas, unlike Africa, had no native merchant class. Then appeared the settlers who, attracted by the combination of healthful climate and fertile land, came in ever-increasing numbers and inundated the hapless Indians. When the latter occasionally took up arms in desperation, they were foredoomed to failure because they lacked both unity and the basic human and material resources. This was especially true north of the Rio Grande, where the Indian population had been sparse to begin with. Consequently there were few survivors, and these were herded into reservations. In the lands of the Aztecs, Incas, and Mayas, which had been more densely populated, a large number survived the European flood. Gradually these survivors staged a comeback as they developed immunity to the diseases of the Europeans and of the Africans. Today Indians comprise a majority of the population in countries such as Bolivia and Guatemala. In the United States, the U.S. Census Bureau reported in 1990 a total Indian population of 1.9 million, of which the largest number (308,132) are Cherokee, followed by Navajo (219,138), by Chippewa (103,826), and by Sioux (103,255).

It is apparent that the balance of forces was quite different in America than it was in Africa. Geography, relatively small population, and a comparatively low level of economic, political, and social organization all worked against the Indian and made it possible for the Europeans to take over the Americas at a time when they were still confined to a few toeholds on the coasts of Africa. Although the Amerindians were unable to offer much resistance against the European invaders, the fact remains that they made outstanding contributions to human development. By far the most significant of these contributions was their domestication of numerous plants that have become mainstays of daily diet throughout the world. Outstanding were maize, potatoes, beans (the major source of proteins), squashes, tomatoes, and chocolate. In all, about as many plants were domesticated in the Americas as in the entire Old World—a truly extraordinary achievement. More than 50 percent of the farm products of the United States today are derived from plants originally domesticated by the Indians. Since the United States is a major exporter of foodstuffs to the world markets, it follows that the world's total population would be substantially smaller today were it not for the Amerindian pioneers.

Finally it should be noted that ongoing archeological investigations necessitate constant revision of our understanding of Amerindian cultures. For example, recent excavations suggest that in addition to the Mayan, Aztec and Inca cultures, there may have been a fourth one in the Amazon jungle of South America. This finding is intriguing because hitherto it has been believed that early food gatherers lacked the skills and technology to survive in a tropical rain forest. Now, however, archeologists are finding and analyzing thousands of artifacts and charred food remains found in caves near the mouth of the Amazon that were occupied some 11,000 years ago. This was a distinctive culture because it was dependent primarily not upon big game hunting, as were the other Amerindian cultures, but rather on river and forest foraging—its people subsisting mostly on fish, mollusks, turtles and birds.

V. AUSTRALIA

Australia is the most isolated large landmass in the world. It is so isolated that archaic forms of life have survived to modern times, including plants such as the eucalyptus family, and mammals such as the monotremes and the marsupials. In Australia archaic human types also survived that were still in the Paleolithic stage when the first British settlers arrived in the late eighteenth century. As in the case of the American Indians, the date of the first aboriginal appearance in Australia has not been determined precisely. The latest findings indicate an arrival about 50,000 years ago. This means that the ancestors of the aborigines probably were the world's first mariners, since they had to cross about forty miles of open water at that time to reach the island continent from Southeast Asia.

Three different ethnic groups crossed to Australia, and they still can be detected in the present-day aboriginal population. The majority are slender, long-limbed people with brown skin, wavy to curly hair and beards, and little body hair. They have survived in substantial numbers because they live in desert areas that are of little use to the modern white settlers. In the cool and fertile southeastern corner of the continent, there are a few survivors of a very different native stock—thick set, with light brown skin, heavy body hair, and luxuriant beards. Along the northeastern coast, in the only part of Australia covered with dense tropical rain forest, lives the third ethnic group. Part of the Negroid family, they are small, of slight build, and with woolly hair and black skins.

The culture of these peoples was by no means uniform. The most advanced were those in the southeast, where rainfall was adequate for permanent settlements. But throughout the continent, the aborigines, thanks to their complete isolation, had remained Paleolithic food gatherers. Their retardation was particularly evident in their technology and in their political organization. They wore no clothing except for decorative purposes. Their housing consisted, in dry country, of simple, open windbreaks, and in wet country, of low, domed huts thrown together out of any available material. Their principal weapons were spears, spear throwers, and boomerangs, all made of wood. They were ignorant of pottery, their utensils consisting merely of a few twined bags and baskets and occasional bowls made of bark or wood. As food gatherers and hunters they were highly skilled and ingenious. They had a wide range of vegetable, as well as animal, foods and an intimate knowledge of the varieties, habits, and properties of these foods. They did all in their power to keep up the rate of reproduction of the plants and animals on which they depended. But since they were not food producers, their method of ensuring an adequate food supply was one of ritual rather than of cultivation. A typical ceremony was the mixing of blood with earth in places where the increase of game and plants were desired.

The poverty of Australian technology was matched by an almost equal poverty of political organization. Like most food-gathering peoples, the aborigines lived in bands, groups of families who normally camped together and roamed over a well-defined territory. They had no real tribes but only territorial divisions characterized by differences in language and culture. Consequently, they did not have chiefs, courts, or other formal agencies of government. Yet these same aborigines had an extraordinarily complex social organization and ceremonial life. The hunter who brought in game or the woman who returned from a day of root digging was required to divide his or her take with all kin according to strict regulations. Among the northern Queensland natives, when a person sneezed, all those within hearing slapped themselves on their bodies, the place varying according to their precise relationship to the sneezer.

So involved were these nonmaterial aspects of Australian society that they have been a delight to students of primitive institutions. But precociousness in these matters was of little help to the aborigines when the Europeans appeared in the late eighteenth century. If the American Indians with their flowering civilizations and widespread agricultural communities were unable to stand up to the whites, the Paleolithic Australians obviously had no chance. They were few in numbers, totaling about 300,000 when the Europeans arrived. This meant one or two persons per square mile in favorable coastal or river valley environments, and only one person every thirty to forty square miles in the arid interior. In addition to this numerical weakness, the aborigines lacked both the arms and the organization necessary for effective resistance. And unlike the American Indians and the African Negroes, they showed little inclination to secure and use the white man's "fire stick."

Thus the unfortunate aborigines were brutally decimated by the British immigrants, many of whom were lawless convicts shipped out from overcrowded jails. The combination of disease, alcoholism, outright slaughter, and wholesale land confiscation has reduced the native population to 45,000 today, together with some 80,000 mixed breeds. The treatment accorded to the Australians is suggested by the following typical observation of a Victorian settler in 1853: "The Australian aboriginal race seems doomed by Providence, like the Mohican and many other well known tribes, to disappear from their native soil before the progress of civilization."[5]

SUGGESTED READINGS

The most recent information on the peopling of the Americas is given in R. Shutler, Jr., ed., *Early Man in the New World* (Sage, 1973), which also contains a selection on the parallel peopling of Australia. A stimulating analysis of the European impact on the American Indians is given by F. Jennings, *The Invasion of America: Indians, Colonialism, and the Cant of Conquest* (University of North Carolina, 1975). The latest estimates on the numbers of American Indians are given in M. Denevan, ed., *The Native Population of the Americas in 1492* (University of Wisconsin, 1976). The lethal biological repercussions of European expansion are analyzed in A. W. Crosby, *Ecological Imperialism: The Biological Expansion of Europe, 900–1900* (Cambridge University, 1986).

A lavishly illustrated volume on the American Indians from their early migrations to the present day is *America's Fascinating Indian Heritage* (Reader's Digest Press, 1978). A stimulating interpretation is by P. Farb, *Man's Rise to Civilization as Shown by the Indians of North America . . .* (Dutton, 1968), which includes an analysis of the significance for modern people of the experiences of the Indians. Other noteworthy studies are by A. M. Josephy, Jr., *The Indian Heritage of America* (Knopf, 1968); C. Beals, *Nomads and Empire Builders: Native Peoples and Cultures of South America* (Chilton, 1961); and the excellent collection of readings by H. E. Driver, ed., *The Americas on the Eve of Discovery* (Prentice Hall, 1964). V. W. Von Hagen has readable accounts of all three of the leading American civilizations: *The Aztec: Man and Tribe* (New American Library, 1958), *The Incas: People of the Sun* (World, 1961), and *World of the Maya* (New American Library, 1960). The best general study of the Eskimos is by K. Birket-Smith, *The Eskimos* (Crown, 1971). Interesting details of recent archeological discoveries of early Indians in Chile, and how they got there, are given in *Science*, September 18, 1998, pp. 1775–76, 1830–35.

For the Australia aborigines the standard works are A. P. Elkins, *The Australia Aborigines*, 3rd ed. (Angus, 1954); W. E. Harney, *Life Among the Aborigines* (Hale, 1957); R. M. and C. H. Berndt, *The World of the First Australians: An Introduction to the Traditional Life of the Australia Aborigines* (University of Chicago, 1964); A. A. Abbie, *The Original Australians* (Muller, 1969); and G. Blainey, *Triumph of the Nomads: A History of Aboriginal Australia* (Overlook Press, 1976).

NOTES

1. J. J. Lockhart, trans., *The Memoirs of the Conquistador Bernal del Castillo* (London, 1844), I, 238.
2. R. M. Adams, "Early Civilizations, Subsistence and Environment," in *City Invincible*, eds., R. M. Adams and C. H. Kraeling (University of Chicago, 1960), p. 270.
3. Lockhart, *op. cit.*, I, 231–232.
4. Citd in E. Galeano, *Memory of Fire: Genesis* (Pantheon, 1985), p. 158.
5. Cited by A. G. Price, *White Settlers and Native Peoples* (Melbourne University, 1949), p. 121.

CHAPTER 7

The World on the Eve of Europe's Expansion

> . . . A technological revolution by which the West made its fortune, got the better of all the other living civilizations, and forcibly united them into a single society of literally worldwide range. The revolutionary Western invention was the substitution of the Ocean for the Steppe as the principal medium for world communication. This use of the Ocean, first by sailing ships and then by steamship, enabled the West to unify the whole inhabited and habitable world, including the Americas.
>
> *A. J. Toynbee*

During the medieval millennium between 500 and 1500 C.E., profound changes occurred in the world balance of power. At the outset the West was a turbulent outpost of Eurasia, wracked by the disintegration of empires and recurring invasions. As late as the twelfth century, the English chronicler William of Malmesbury voiced a sense of isolation and insecurity:

The world is not evenly divided. Of its three parts, our enemies hold Asia as their hereditary home—a part of the world which our forefathers rightly considered equal to the other two put together. Yet here formerly our Faith put out its branches; here all the Apostles save two met their deaths. But now the Christians of those parts, if there are any left, squeeze a bare subsis-

tence from the soil and pay tribute to their enemies, looking to us with silent longings for the liberty they have lost. Africa too, the second part of the world, has been held by our enemies by force of arms for two hundred years and more, a danger to Christendom all the greater because it formerly sustained the highest spirits—men whose works will keep the rust of age from Holy Writ as long as the Latin tongue survives. Thirdly, there is Europe, the remaining region of the world. Of this region we Christians inhabit only a part, for who will give the name of Christians to those barbarians who live in the remote islands and seek their living on the icy ocean as if they were whales? This little portion of the world which is ours is pressed upon by warlike Turks and Saracens: for three hundred years they have held Spain and the Balearic Islands, and they live in hope of devouring the rest.[1]

But already by the twelfth century the tide had begun to turn. The West was developing the internal resources and the dynamism that found expression first in the long-drawn-out and successful Crusades against Moslems and pagans and, later, in overseas expansion to all parts of the globe. By contrast, Ming China was withdrawing into seclusion, and the Ottoman Turks, after futile efforts to expel the Portuguese from the Indian Ocean, sadly concluded, "God has given the land to us, but the sea to the Christians." Equally revealing is the fact that in his famous Memoirs, Babur, the founder of the Mogul Empire, never once mentioned the Portuguese, nor did any Mogul navy ever attempt to restore Moslem primacy in the Indian Ocean. The seas of the world were thus left wide open for the Westerners, who took prompt advantage of the opportunity. The significance for world affairs is apparent in the following comment by an Ottoman observer in 1625:

Now the Europeans have learnt to know the whole world; they send their ships everywhere and seize important ports. Formerly, the goods of India, Sind, and China used to come to Suez, and were distributed by Muslims to all the world. But now these goods are carried on Portuguese, Dutch, and English ships to Frangistan [Western Christendom], and are spread all over the world from there. What they do not need themselves they bring to Istanbul and other Islamic lands, and sell it for five times the price, thus earning much money. For this reason gold and silver are becoming scarce in the lands of Islam. The Ottoman Empire must seize the shores of Yemen and the trade passing that way; otherwise before very long, the Europeans will rule over the lands of Islam.[2]

If this perceptive analysis is compared with that of William of Malmesbury half a millennium earlier, the basic change in the global balance of power becomes evident. Indeed, so basic was this change that it marked the beginning of the modern age of Western predominance.

Heralding the earlier classical and medieval ages had been land invasions by nomads who used their superior mobility to break into the centers of civilization when imperial weakness gave them the opportunity. Ushering in the Modern Age, by contrast, were sea invasions by the Westerners, who functioned with equal

This portrait of Katharina, by Albrecht Dürer, provides edvidence of African slavery in Europe during the sixteenth century. Katharina was in the service of João Bradao a Portuguese economic minister living in Antwerp, then the financial center of Europe. Dürer became friends with Bradao during a stay in the Low Countries in 1520–1521.

mobility on the world's oceans and thus were free to operate on a global scale.

In addition to their unchallenged maritime superiority, the Westerners had the more important advantage of overall technological superiority, which increased steadily during the following centuries. Thus whereas the sixteenth-century Europeans with their ocean-sailing ships and naval artillery enjoyed an advantage comparable to that of iron weapons over bronze, by the nineteenth century their steamships, factory industries, and machine guns gave them an advantage more like that of the agriculturist over the hunter. Thus the Europeans established their global domination as inexorably as the Bantu displaced the Bushmen. Hence the Europeans brought all continents into direct contact with each other, therby ending the Eurasian phase of world history and beginning the global. (See map of Culture Areas of the World About 1500, p. 278.)

NOTES

1. Cited by W. Clark, "New Europe and the New Nations," *Daedalus* (Winter 1964), p. 136.
2. Cited by B. Lewis, *The Emergence of Modern Turkey* (Oxford University, 1961), p. 28.

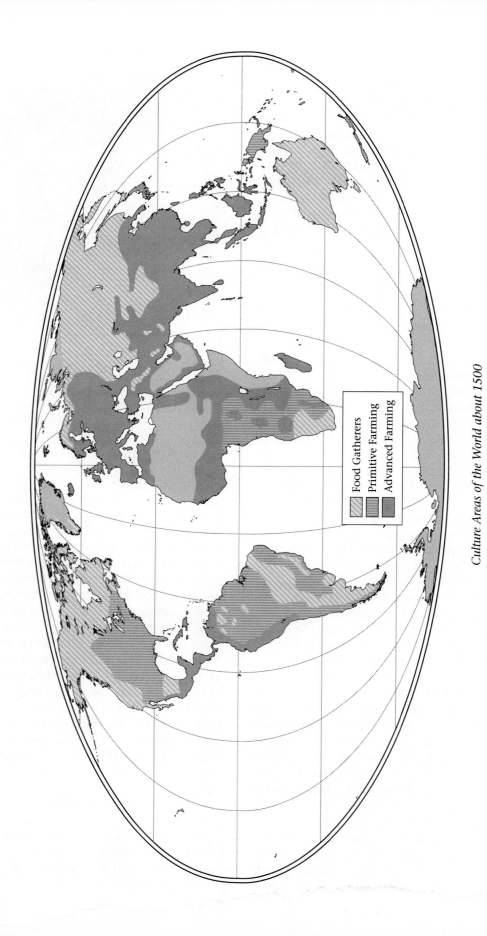

Culture Areas of the World about 1500

Food Gatherers
Primitive Farming
Advanced Farming

What It Means for Us Today

RACES IN HISTORY

When the western Europeans began their voyages of exploration, they found peoples scattered around the world and living at very different levels of development. The Chinese, for example, had a civilization that was so wealthy, sophisticated, and well governed that many of the early European visitors considered it superior to their own. Other overseas people were naked, nomadic food gatherers whom the Europeans looked down on as barely human. So they pushed them aside into deserts or jungles or enslaved them or hunted them down and exterminated them. In doing these things, the Europeans justified their actions on the ground that they were a superior people bringing the light of their superior civilization to the inferior (and therefore backward) peoples of the world.

This argument raises a question that is still a matter of dispute today. Are the various human races genetically equal, or are some inherently superior and others inferior? The great majority of scientists, though not all, agree that races are generally equal. Typical is the statement issued at an international conference of physical anthropologists and geneticists in September 1952:

> Available scientific knowledge provides no basis for believing that the groups of mankind differ in their innate capacity for intellectual and emotional development. . . . Genetic differences are of little significance in determining the social and cultural differences between different groups of men.[1]

If genes do not explain the great differences that European explorers found overseas, then what does? This is a burning question in today's world. It raises the controversial issue of racism, or belief in the biologically determined superiority of one race over another. Pope John II was sufficiently concerned about this issue to ask the Pontifical Commission, Iustitia et Pax, to "help and awaken consciences . . . about the reciprocal respect between ethnic and racial groups." The Commission reported in 1988 that racism is a modern phenomenon that did not exist in ancient times; Greeks and Romans were convinced of their cultural superiority over barbarians, but they did not consider the so-called barbarians to be inferior because of innate biological reasons. In premodern times, genetically based racism was not an urgent issue for the simple reason that the various races lived in regional isolation and therefore did not need to face this issue. But with Europe's overseas expansion and subsequent conquest and enslavement of Amerindians and Africans, racism became a convenient rationalization for justifying these actions. Pope Paul II denounced in 1537 those who held that "the inhabitants of the West Indies and the southern continents . . . should be treated like irrational animals and used exclusively for our profit and our service. . . . We hereby decide and declare that the said Indians, as well as any other peoples which Christianity will come to know in the future, must not be deprived of their freedom and their possessions . . . even if they are not Christians and that, on the contrary, they must be left to enjoy their freedom and their possessions. . . . The message she [the Church] proposes to everyone, and which she tries to live, is: 'Every person is my brother or sister.'"[2]

Returning to the above question about why European explorers found such extreme variations in the development of overseas peoples, the distinguished anthropologist Franz Boas has offered a theory that seems to mesh with actual historical experience:

> The history of mankind proves that advances of culture depend upon the opportunities presented to a social group to learn from the experience of their neighbors. The discoveries of the group spread to others and, the more varied the contacts, the greater the opportunities to learn. The tribes of simplest culture are on the whole those that have been isolated for very long periods and hence could not profit from the cultural achievements of their neighbors.[3]

In other words, the key to different levels of human development has been accessibility. Those with the most opportunity to interact with other people have been the most likely to forge ahead. Indeed, they were driven to do so, for there was selective pressure as well as opportunity. Accessibility involved the constant threat of assimilation or elimination if opportunity was not grasped. By contrast, those who were isolated received neither stimulus nor threat, were free from selective pressure, and thus could remain relatively unchanged through the millennia without jeopardizing their existence.

If this hypothesis is applied on a global scale, the remote Australian aborigines should have been the most culturally retarded of all major groups; next, the American Indians in the New World; then the Negroes of sub-Saharan Africa; and finally—the least retarded, or the most advanced—the various peoples of Eurasia, who were in constant and generally increasing contact with each other. This, of course, is precisely the gradation of culture levels found by the European discoverers after 1500. The Australian aborigines were still at the Paleolithic food-gathering stage; the American Indians varied from the Paleolithic tribes of California to the impressive civilizations of Mexico, Central America, and Peru; the African Negroes presented comparable diversity, though their overall level of development was higher; and finally, at quite another level, there were the highly advanced and sophisticated civilizations found in Eurasia—the Moslem in the Middle East, the Hindu in south Asia, and the Confucian in east Asia.

We may conclude, then, that the Western domination of the globe after 1500 did not mean Western genetic superiority. It meant only that, at that period of history, the western Europeans were in the right place at the right time. At other periods of history the situation was very different. For example, at the time of the classical civilizations it was the people of the Mediterranean who were in the center of things and who, therefore, were the most accessible and most developed. By contrast, the northern Europeans were then on the periphery, and were therefore isolated and underdeveloped. Thus we find Cicero writing to a friend in Athens in the first century B.C.E.: "Do not obtain your slaves from Britain because they are so stupid and so utterly incapable of being taught that they are not fit to form a part of the household of Athens."[4]

Likewise, during the period of the medieval civilizations, the Mediterranean was still the center, and northern Europe still an isolated region of backward peoples. Thus a Moslem in Toledo, Spain, wrote in the eleventh century: "Races north of the Pyrenees are of cold temperament and never reach maturity; they are of great stature and of a white color. But they lack all sharpness of wit and penetration of intellect."

Both Cicero and the Toledo Moslem seemed in their times to have been justified in looking down on northern Europeans as "stupid" and lacking in "wit" and "intellect." But Nordic "backwardness" in classical and medieval times had no more to do with genes than did the "backwardness" of Africans or American Indians or Australian aborigines in the times of the discoveries—or than does the "backwardness" of the underdeveloped peoples of the world today.

Regardless of the period, "backwardness" means vulnerability, because "backward" people lag behind others in numbers and in technology. This is especially true in today's world of six billion people and runaway technology. Consequently it is estimated that since 1500, at least one-third of the world's human cultures have disappeared—either overwhelmed or assimilated. Therefore the American Anthropological Association has established a "Committee for Human Rights," and likewise in 1972 a body entitled "Cultural Survival" was created. Seeking to protect existing cultures, it has spoken up, for example, in behalf of the Yanomami Indians imperilled by a gold rush in the Amazon basin, the Tibetan people pressured by the adjacent 1 billion Chinese, the Ogoni tribe in Nigeria disrupted by the operations of oil companies, and the Maya Indians harried by the Guatemalan army. Despite their precarious status, the "indigenous" peoples, as these members of endangered communities are commonly known, still comprise 5 percent of the world's population.[5]

SUGGESTED READINGS

The most useful book on the nature, significance, and results of race is by P. Mason, *Race Relations* (Oxford University, 1970). UNESCO has a collection of essays by an international group of scientists: *The Race Question in Modern Science* (Morrow, 1956). All these contributors agreed that race achievement is determined by historical and social backgrounds, not by genes. The opposite view has been set forth by A. R. Jensen, in *Genetics and Education* (Harper & Row, 1972), and in his *Bias in Mental Testing* (Free Press, 1980). Jensen's findings have been rejected by L. J. Kamin, *The Science and Politics of IQ* (John Wiley, 1974); and most entertainingly and authoritatively by S. J. Gould, *Ever Since Darwin* (Norton, 1981). An important analysis of the role of race during World War II in the Pacific is provided by J. Dower, *War Without Mercy* (Pantheon, 1986).

NOTES

1. Cited by UNESCO, *What Is Race?* (Paris, 1952), pp. 85, 86.
2. F. Boas, "Racial Purity," *Asia*, XL (May, 1940), p. 231.
3. Cited by R. Benedict, *Race: Science and Politics*, rev. ed. (Viking Press, 1943), p. 7.
4. Ibid., p. 8.
5. *New York Times*, March 19, 1996.

PART V

World of Isolated Regions, to 1500

Part V is concerned with two basic questions: Why should a study of world history begin with the year 1500, and why was it that Westerners took a primary role in carrying out the fantastic discoveries and explorations of the late fifteenth and early sixteenth centuries? The first question will be answered in Chapter 18; the second will be the subject of the remaining chapters of Part V.

We usually take it for granted that only Westerners could have made the historic discoveries that would change the course of humanity and begin a new era in world history. This assumption is quite unjustified, particularly in view of the great seafaring traditions of the Moslems in the Middle East and the Chinese in east Asia. Why then did the West take the initiative in overseas enterprise with repercussions that are still felt today? Chapters 18 and 19 will analyze the traditional societies in the Moslem and Confucian worlds, and Chapters 20 and 21 will offer an examination of the contrasting dynamism of Western society.

CHAPTER
18

Moslem World at the Time of the West's Expansion

He who would behold these times in their greatest glory, could not find a better scene than in Turkey.

H. Blount, 1634

To answer the question of why Columbus was not Chinese or Arabic, it is necessary to see what was going on in the Confucian and Moslem worlds at that time. In this chapter, and the following one, we shall analyze why China and the Middle East lacked the expansionism of western Europe, even though they were highly developed and wealthy regions. We shall see that paradoxically, it was their wealth and high level of development that left them smug and self-satisfied, and therefore unable to adapt to their changing world.

I. RISE OF MODERN MOSLEM EMPIRES

An observer on the moon looking at this globe about 1500 would have been more impressed by the Moslem than by the Christian world. The mythical observer would have been impressed first by the extent of the Moslem world and then by its unceasing expansion. The earliest Moslems were the Arabs of the Arabian peninsula who were united for the first time under their religious leader, Mohammed. Believing that he had received a divine call, Mohammed warned his people of the Day of Judgment and told them of the rewards for the faithful in Paradise and the punishment of the wicked in Hell. He called on his followers to perform certain rituals known as the Five Pillars of Islam (including daily prayers, alms giving, fasting, and a pilgrimage to Mecca). These rituals, together with the precepts in the Koran, provided not only a religion but also a social code and a political system. The converts felt a sense of brotherhood and common mission, which served to unite the hitherto scattered Arab peoples.

After the death of Mohammed in 632 C.E., the Arabs burst out of their peninsula and quickly overran the Byzantine and Sassanian empires in the Middle East. Then they expanded eastward toward China and westward across North Africa and into Spain. By 750, the end of this first phase of Islamic expansion, there existed a huge Moslem Empire that stretched from the Pyrenees to India and from Morocco to China (see map of Expansion of Islam to 1500, p. 287). The Moslems carried out the second phase of their expansion between 750 and 1500, during which time they penetrated westward to central Europe, northward to central Asia, eastward to India and Southeast Asia, and southward into the interior of Africa. Thus, the Moslem world doubled in size. It far surpassed in area both the Christian world on the western tip of Eurasia and the Confucian world on the eastern tip.

Not only was the Moslem world the most extensive about 1500, but it also continued to expand vigorously after that date. Contrary to common assumption, western Europe was not the only part of the world that was extending its frontiers at that time. The Moslem world was still expanding, but by overland routes, whereas the Christian world was reaching out overseas. The Portuguese in the early sixteenth century were gaining footholds in India and the East Indies, and the Spaniards were conquering an empire in the New World. But at the same time, the Ottoman Turks, a central Asian people who had converted to Islam, were pushing into central Europe. They overran Hungary, and in 1529 they besieged Vienna, the Hapsburg capital in the heart of Europe. Likewise, in India the great Mogul emperors were steadily extending their empire southward until they became the masters of almost the entire peninsula. Elsewhere the Moslem faith continued to spread into Africa, central Asia, and Southeast Asia.

The steady expansion of Islam was due partly to the forceful conversion of nonbelievers, though compulsion was not employed so commonly by Moslems as by Christians. But much more effective than these measures was the quiet missionary work of Moslem traders and preachers, who were particularly successful among the less civilized peoples. Frequently, the trader appeared first, combing proselytism with the sale of merchandise. His profession gave the trader close and constant contact with the people he wanted to convert. Also, there was no color bar, for if the trader were not of the same race as the villagers, he probably would marry a native woman. Such a marriage often led to the adoption of Islam by members of the woman's family. Soon religious instruction was needed for the children, so schools were established and frequented by pagan as well as Moslem children. The children were taught to read the Koran and were instructed in the doctrines and ceremonies of Islam. This explains why Islam, from the time of its appearance, was far more successful in gaining converts than any other religion. Even today, Islam is more than holding its own against Christianity in Africa, thanks to its unique adaptability to indigenous cultures as well as to the popular identification of Christianity with the foreign white master.

Apart from this ceaseless extension of frontiers, the Moslem world about 1500 was distinguished by its three great empires: the Ottoman in the Middle East, North Africa, and the Balkans; the Safavid in Persia; and the Mogul in India. These empires had all risen to prominence at this time and now dominated the heartland of Islam.

Their appearance was due in part to the invention of gunpowder and its use in firearms and cannon. The new weapons strengthened central power in the Moslem world, as they did at the same time in Christian Europe. Firearms, however, were by no means the only factor explaining the rise of the three Moslem empires. Equally significant were the appearance of capable leaders who founded dynasties and the existence of especially advantageous circumstances that enabled these leaders to conquer their empires. Let us consider now the particular combination of factors that made possible the growth of each of the three Moslem empires.

Ottoman Empire

The Ottoman Turks, who founded the empire named after them, were a branch of widely scattered Turkish people who came originally from central Asia (in contrast to the Semitic Arabs, who came originally from the Arabian peninsula). Over the centuries, successive waves of Turkish tribespeople had penetrated into the rich lands of the Middle East. They had appeared as

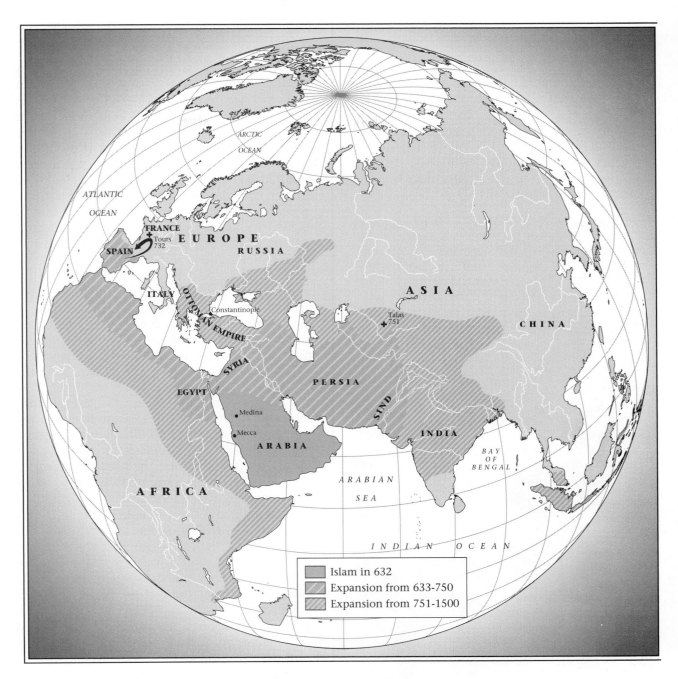

Expansion of Islam to 1500

early as the eighth century and infiltrated into the Islamic Empire, where they were employed first as mercenaries. In the tenth century, Mongol pressure from the rear forced more Turkish tribes, including a group known as the Seljuk Turks, to move into the Middle East. These newcomers broke the traditional frontier of Asia Minor along the Taurus Mountains—the frontier that had sheltered Rome and Byzantium for

1,400 years—by defeating the Byzantine army in the fateful battle of Manzikert in 1071. The victory made most of Asia Minor a part of the Seljuk Empire, leaving only the northwest corner to the Byzantines.

The Seljuk Empire, however, experienced a decline, disintegrating into a patchwork of independent principalities, or sultanates. In the late thirteenth century, the disorder was heightened by new bands of Turkish immigrants. One of these bands settled down on the extreme north-western fringe of Seljuk territory, fewer than fifty miles from the strategic straits separating Asia from Europe. In 1299 the leader of this band, a certain Uthman, declared his independence from his Seljuk overlord. From these humble beginnings grew the great Ottoman Empire, named after the obscure Uthman.

The Süleiman mosque, named after its founder, Süleiman the Lawgiver, is one of the finest mosques in Istanbul. Completed in 1557 by the architect Sinan, who is buried in the mosque, it rises above the Golden Horn on Istanbul's third hill. Sinan was a slave-soldier recruit who rose through the ranks to his high position.

The first step in this dazzling success story was the conquest of the remaining Byzantine portion of Asia minor. By 1340 all of Asia Minor had fallen to the star and crescent. In 1354 the Turks crossed the straits and won their first foothold in Europe by building a fortress at Gallipoli. They hardly could have selected a more advantageous moment for their assault on Europe. The whole of Christendom in that century was weakened and divided. The terrible plague, the Black Death, had carried off whole sections of the populations of many Christian nations. The ruinous Hundred Years' War immobilized England and France. (The dates of this conflict are significant. It began in 1338, when the Turks were rounding out their conquest of Asia Minor, and it ended in 1453, when they captured Constantinople.) The Italian states also could do little against the Turks because of the long feud between Venice and Genoa. And the Balkan peninsula was hopelessly divided by the religious strife of Catholic and Orthodox Christians and heretic Bogomils, as well as by the rivalries of the Byzantine, Serbian, and Bulgarian empires, all long past their prime. And in the Balkans, as in Asia Minor, the Christian peasants frequently were so discontented that they offered little or no resistance to the Turkish onslaught.

These circumstances explain the extraordinary success of the Ottomans as they spread out from their base in Asia Minor. In 1384 they captured Sofia, and soon after they had control of all Bulgaria. Five years later they destroyed a south Slav army at the historic battle of Kossovo, which spelled the end of the Serbian Empire. These victories left Constantinople surrounded on all sides by Turkish territory. In 1453 the beleaguered capital was taken by assault, ending a thousand years of imperial history.

The Turks next turned southward against the rich Moslem states of Syria and Egypt. In a whirlwind campaign, they overran Syria in 1516 and Egypt the following year. The final phase of Ottoman conquest took place in central Europe. Under their famous Sultan Suleiman the Magnificent, the Turks crossed the Danube River and in one stroke crushed the Hungarian state in the Mohacs Battle in 1526. Three years later, Suleiman laid siege to Vienna but was repulsed, partly because of torrential rains that prevented him from bringing up his heavy artillery. Despite this setback, the Turks continued to make minor gains: Cyprus in 1570, Crete in 1669, and the Polish Ukraine in the following decade.

At its height, the Ottoman Empire was indeed a great imperial structure. Its heartland was Turkish Asia Minor, but the majority of the population consisted of Moslem Arabs to the south and Balkan Christians to the west. The empire sprawled over three continents and comprised some 50 million people, compared to the 5 million of contemporary England. Little wonder that Christians of the time looked on the ever-expanding Ottoman Empire with awe and described it as "a daily increasing flame, catching hold of whatsoever comes next, still to proceed further."[1]

Safavid Empire

The second great Moslem empire of this period was the Safavid in Persia. That country had fallen under the Seljuk Turks, as had Asia Minor. But whereas Asia Minor had become Turkified, Persia remained Persian—or Iranian—in race and culture. Probably the explanation for this different outcome is that Persia had already become Moslem during the first stage of Islamic expansion in the seventh century, in contrast to Asia Minor, which had formerly been a part of the Christian Byzantine Empire. For this reason, Persia was not swamped by Moslem warriors as Asia Minor had been, and Persian society was left basically unchanged by the comparatively small ruling class of Turkish administrators and soldiers.

Persia remained under the Seljuk Turks from approximately 1000 C.E. to the Mongol invasion in 1258. The new Mongol rulers, known as the Il-Khans, were at first Buddhists or Christians, but about 1300 they became Moslems. Persia suffered considerable permanent damage from the Mongols, who destroyed many cities and irrigation systems, but this setback was overcome when the Il-Khan dynasty was replaced by the Safavid in 1500.

Shah Ismail I founded the new dynasty of Safavid monarchs, the first native Persian rulers in several centuries. In the twenty-four years of Ismail's reign, his military abilities and religious policy enabled him to unite the country. By his proclamation, the Shiite sect of Islam became the state religion, and through his ruthlessness,

The Sultan, Suleiman the Magnificent, battling the Hungarians.

the rival Sunnite sect was crushed. Persians identified themselves with Shiism, differentiating them from the Turks and other surrounding Moslem peoples who were mostly Sunnites.

The greatest of the Safavid rulers was Abbas I, the shah from 1587 to 1629. It was he who modernized the Persian army by building up its artillery units. Under his rule, Persia became an internationally recognized great power, as seen by the constant stream of envoys from European countries who sought an alliance with Persia against the Ottoman Empire. In fact, both these Moslem states figured prominently in European diplomacy during these years. Francis I of France, for example, cooperated with Suleiman the Magnificent in fighting against the Hapsburg Emperor Charles V. And the Hapsburgs, in turn, cooperated with the Persians against their two common foes. These relationships between Christian and Moslem states were denounced at the time as "impious" and "sacrilegious," but the fact was that the Ottoman and Safavid empires had become world powers that no European diplomat could afford to overlook.

Mogul Empire

Just as two outstanding Safavid rulers founded a "national" dynasty in Persia, so two outstanding Mogul rulers—Babur and Akbar—founded a "national" dynasty in India, a very remarkable achievement for Moslem rulers in a predominantly Hindu country.

The Moslems came to India in three waves, widely separated in time. The first consisted of Arab Moslems who invaded the Sind region near the mouth of the Indus in 712 C.E. These Arabs were unable to push far inland, so their influence on India was limited.

The second wave came in about 1000, when Turkish Moslems began raiding India from bases in Afghanistan. These raids continued intermittently for four centuries, with much loss of life and property. The net result was that numerous Moslem kingdoms were established in northern India, whereas southern India remained a conglomeration of Hindu states. But even in northern India the mass of the people continued to be Indians in race and Hindu in religion. They did not become Islamicized and Turkified, as did the people of Asia Minor. The explanation again is that Turks who came down from the north were an insignificant minority compared to India's teeming millions. They could fill only the top positions in the government and the armed forces. Their Hindu subjects were the ones who tilled the land, worked in the bazaars, and comprised most of the bureaucracy. In certain regions, it is true, large sections of the population did turn to Islam, especially some depressed castes who sought relief from their exploitation in the new religion. Yet the fact remains that India was an overwhelmingly Hindu country when the third Moslem wave struck in 1500 with the appearance of the Moguls.

The newcomers again were Turks, their leader being the colorful Babur, a direct descendent of the great Turkish conqueror Timur, or Tamerlane. In 1524 Babur, with a small force of 12,000 men armed with matchlock muskets and artillery, defeated an Indian army of 100,000. After his victory, Babur occupied Delhi, his new capital. Four years later he died, but his sons followed his path, and the empire grew rapidly. It reached its height during the reign of Babur's grandson, the famous Akbar, who ruled from 1556 to 1605.

Akbar was by far the most outstanding of the Mogul emperors. He rounded out his Indian possessions by conquering Rajputana and Gujarat in the west, Bengal in the east, and several small states in the Deccan peninsula in the south. Mogul rule now extended from Kabul and Kashmir to the Deccan, and later under Aurangzeb (1658–1707) it extended still further—almost to the southern tip of the peninsula. In addition to his military exploits, Akbar was a remarkable personality of great versatility and a wide range of interests. Although illiterate, he had a keen and inquiring mind that won the grudging admiration of Jesuits who knew him well. The astonishing range of his activities is reminiscent of Peter the Great. Like his Russian counterpart, Akbar had a strong mechanical bent, as evidenced in his metallurgical work and in his designs for a gun with increased firepower. He learned to draw, loved music, was an expert polo player, and played various instruments, the kettledrum being his favorite. Akbar even evolved an entirely new religion of his own, the Din Ilahi, or "Divine Faith." It was eclectic, with borrowings from many sources, especially from the Parsees, the Jains, and the Hindus. Akbar hoped that a common faith would unite his Hindu and Moslem subjects. But in practice, it had little impact on the country. It was too intellectual to appeal to the masses, and even at court there were few converts.

What Akbar failed to achieve by his synthetic faith, he did by ending discriminatory practices against Hindus and establishing their equality with Moslems. He abolished the pilgrim tax that Hindus had been required to pay when traveling to their sacred shrines. He ended the poll tax on Hindus, a standard levy on nonbelievers in all Moslem countries. Akbar also opened the top state positions to Hindus, who now ceased to look on the Mogul Empire as an

The Taj Mahal. Probably the most beautiful tomb in the world, the Taj was built from 1631 to 1653 by Shah Jahan for his beloved wife, Mumtaz Mahal. Located on the south bank of the Yamuna River at Agra, the Mughal capital, the Taj Mahal remains the jewel of Mughal architecture.

enemy organization. A new India was beginning to emerge, as Akbar had dreamed—a national state rather than a divided land of Moslem masters and a Hindu subject majority.

II. SPLENDOR OF MOSLEM EMPIRES

Military Strength

All three of the Moslem empires were first-class military powers. Eloquent proof is to be found in the appeal sent in December 1525 by the king of France, Francis I, to the Ottoman sultan, Suleiman the Magnificent. The appeal was for a Turkish attack on the Holy Roman emperor and head of the House of Hapsburg, Charles V. Suleiman responded in 1526 by crossing the Danube, overrunning Hungary, and easing the pressure on Francis. This was only one of many Ottoman expeditions that not only aided the French—and incidentally provided the Turks with additional territories and booty—but also saved the Lutheran heretics by distracting Hapsburg attention from Germany to the threatened Danubian frontiers. It is paradoxical that Moslem military power should have contributed substantially to the cause of Protestantism in its critical formative stage.

Moslem military forces generally lagged behind those of Europe in artillery equipment. They depended on the Europeans for the most advanced weapons and for the most experienced gunners. The discrepancy, however, was one of degree only. It was not a case of the Moslem

empires being defenseless because of lack of artillery. Plenty of equipment was available, though it was not as efficient and as well-manned as were the best contemporary European armies. The Moslems, and especially the Turks, were shrewd enough to pay for both Western artillery and artillerymen, but they lacked the technology and the industries to keep up with the rapid progress of Western armaments.

On the other hand, European observers were impressed by the vast military manpower of the Moslem world. It is estimated that the permanent regular forces of the whole of India at the time of Akbar totaled well over 1 million men, or more than double the size of the Indian armies in 1914. Furthermore, these huge military establishments were well trained and disciplined when the Moslem empires were at their height. For obvious geographic reasons, Europeans were most familiar with the Ottoman armed forces, with whom they had a good deal of firsthand experience. After this experience the Europeans were very impressed and respectful. Typical were the reports of Ogier Ghiselin de Busbecq, Hapsburg ambassador to Constantinople during the reign of Suleiman the Magnificent. After Busbecq inspected an Ottoman army camp in 1555, he wrote home as follows:

It makes me shudder to think of what the result of a struggle between such different systems [as the Hapsburg and the Ottoman] must be. . . . On their side is the vast wealth of their empire, unimpaired resources, experience and practice in arms, a veteran soldiery, an uninterrupted series of victories, readiness to endure hardships, union, order, discipline, thrift, and watchfulness. On ours are found an empty exchequer, luxurious habits, exhausted resources, broken spirits, a raw and insubordinate soldiery, and greedy generals; there is no regard for discipline, license runs riot, the men indulge in drunkenness and debauchery, and, worst of all, the enemy are accustomed to victory, we, to defeat. Can we doubt what the result must be? The only obstacle is Persia, whose position on his rear forces the invader to take precautions. The fear of Persia gives a respite, but it is only for a time.[2]

Administrative Efficiency

All heads of Moslem states had absolute power over their subjects. Accordingly, the quality of the administration depended on the quality of the imperial heads. In the sixteenth century, they were men of extraordinary abilities. Certainly Suleiman and Abbas and Akbar were the equals of any monarchs anywhere in the world. Akbar had a well-organized bureaucracy whose ranks were expressed in terms of cavalry commands. Excellent pay and the promise of rapid advance in the Mogul service attracted the best men in India and from abroad. It is estimated that 70 percent of the bureaucracy consisted of foreigners such as Persians and Afghans. The rest were Indian Moslems and Hindus. Upon the death of an official, his wealth was inherited by the emperor, and his rank became vacant. This practice lessened the evils of corruption and hereditary tenure that plagued Western countries at the time.

Since Akbar opened his bureaucracy to all his subjects, ability rather than religion became the criterion for appointment and advancement. Busbecq in Constantinople made precisely the same point about the Ottoman administrative system:

In making his appointments the Sultan pays no regard to any pretensions on the score of wealth or rank. . . . He considers each case on its own merits, and examines carefully into the character, ability, and disposition of the man whose promotion is in question. It is by merit than men rise in the service, a system which ensures that posts should only be assigned to the competent. . . . Among the Turks, therefore, honours, high posts, and judgeships are the rewards of great ability and good service. If a man be dishonest, or lazy, or careless, he remains at the bottom of the ladder, an object of contempt. . . . These are not our ideas, with us there is no opening left for merit; birth is the standard for everything; the prestige of birth is the sole key to advancement in the public service.[3]

Economic Development

As far as economic standards were concerned, the Moslem states in early modern times were, in current phraseology, developed lands. Certainly they were so regarded by western Europeans, who were ready to face any hardships or perils to reach fabled India and the Spice Islands beyond. Closer to home, the Ottoman Empire was an impressive economic unit. Its vast extent assured it of virtual self-sufficiency. For most Europeans, more dazzling than the Ottoman Empire was far-off, exotic India, the weaver of fabulous textiles, especially fine cotton fabrics unequaled anywhere in the world. India was the country that, since the early days of the Roman Empire, had drained gold and silver away from Europe.

As significant as the wealth of the Moslem empires was the control of south Asian commerce by Moslem merchants. Particularly important was the trade in spices, which were eagerly sought after in a world that knew so little of the art of conserving foodstuffs apart from salting. For centuries the spices, together with many other goods such as silk from China and cotton fabrics from India, were transported back and forth along two sets of trade routes. The northern land routes extended from the Far East through central Asia to ports on the Black Sea and Asia Minor; the southern sea routes, from the East Indies and India along the Indian Ocean and up the Persian Gulf or the Red Sea to ports in Syria and Egypt. With the collapse of the Mongol Empire, conditions in central Asia became so anarchical that the northern routes were virtually closed after 1340. Henceforth, most of the products were funneled along the southern sea routes, which by that time were dominated by Moslem merchants.

This commerce contributed substantially to the prosperity of the Moslem world. It provided not only government revenue in the form of customs duties but also a source of livelihood for thousands of merchants, clerks, sailors, shipbuilders, camel drivers, and stevedores, who were connected directly or indirectly with the trade. The extent of the profits is indicated by the fact that articles from India were sold to Italian middlemen in Alexandria at a markup of over 2,000 percent.

When the Portuguese broke into the Indian Ocean in 1498, they quickly gained control of much of this lucrative commerce. But they did so because their ships and guns, rather than their goods or business techniques, were superior. In fact, we shall find that the Portuguese at first were embarrassed because they had little to offer in return for the commodities they coveted. They were rescued from this predicament only by the flood of bullion that soon was to pour in from the mines of Mexico and Peru.

III. DECLINE OF MOSLEM EMPIRES

The Moslem world of the sixteenth century was most impressive. Suleiman, Akbar, and Abbas ruled empires that were at least the equals of those in other parts of the globe, and yet these empires began to go downhill during the seventeenth century. By the following century they were far behind western Europe, and they have remained behind to the present day.

One explanation is the deterioration of the ruling dynasties. Suleiman the Magnificent was succeeded in 1566 by Selim II, who was lazy, fat, dissipated, and so addicted to wine that he was known to his subjects as Selim the Sot. The same thing happened in Persia after Abbas, and in India after Akbar. Dynastic decline, however, was not the only factor responsible for the blight of the Moslem lands. All the European royal families had their share of incapable and irresponsible rulers, yet their countries did not go down with them.

A more basic explanation for the misfortunes of the Moslem world was that it lacked the dynamism of Europe. It did not have those far-reaching changes that were revolutionizing European society during these centuries (as we shall see in Chapters 22 and 23). In the Moslem economic field, for example, there were no basic changes in agriculture, in industry, in financial methods, or in commercial organization. A traveler in the Moslem lands in the seventeenth or eighteenth centuries would have observed essentially the same economic practices and institu-

The battle of Lepanto occurred off the coast of Greece on October 7, 1571. In the largest naval engagement of the sixteenth century, the Spanish and their Italian allies under Don John of Austria smashed the Turkish fleet and ended the Ottoman threat in the western Mediterranean.

OTTOMAN EMPIRE IN DECLINE

The British consul and merchant William Eton lived in the Ottoman Empire for many years at the end of the eighteenth century. His colorful report on Ottoman conditions and institutions reflects how far the empire had declined since its days of glory. *

General knowledge is, from these causes, little if at all cultivated; every man is supposed to know his own business or profession, with which it is esteemed foolish and improper for any other person to interfere. The man of general science, a character so frequent and so useful in Christian Europe, is unknown; and any one, but a mere artificer, who should concern himself with the founding of cannon, the building of ships, or the like, would be esteemed little better than a madman. The natural consequence of these narrow views is, that the professors of any art or science are themselves profoundly ignorant, and that the greatest absurdities are mixed with all their speculations. . . .

From the mufti to the peasant it is generally believed, that there are seven heavens, from which the earth is immovably suspended by a large chain; that the sun is an immense ball of fire, at least as big as the whole Ottoman province, formed for the sole purpose of giving light and heat to the earth; that eclipses of the moon are occasioned by a great dragon attempting to devour that luminary; that the fixed stars hang by chains from the highest heaven &c. &c. . . .

They distinguish different Christian states by different appellations of contempt. Epithets which the Turks apply to those who are not Osmanlis, and which they often use to denominate their nation:

Albanians	gut-sellers
Armenians	t-rd-eaters, dirt-eaters, also pack-carriers
Bosniaks and Bulgarians	vagabonds
Christians	idolaters
Dutch	cheese-mongers
English	atheists
Flemmings	panders
French	faithless
Georgians	louse-eaters
Germans	infidel blasphemers
Greeks of the islands	hares
Italians or Franks	many-coloured
Jews	mangy dogs
Moldavians	drones
Poles	insolent infidels
Russians	mad infidels
Spaniards	lazy
Tatars	carrion-eaters
Walachians	gypsies

It is a certain fact, that a few years ago a learned man of the law having lost an eye, and being informed that there was then at Constantinople an European who made false eyes, not to be distinguished from the natural, he immediately procured one; but when it was placed in the socket, he flew into a violent passion with the eye-maker, abusing him as an impostor, because he could not see with it. The man, fearing he should lose his pay, assured him that in time he would see as well with that eye as with the other. The effendi was appeased, and the artist liberally rewarded, who having soon disposed of the remainder of his eyes, left the Turks in expectation of seeing with them. . . .

*W. Eton, *A Survey of the Turkish Empire*, 4th ed. (London, 1809), pp. 190–93.

tions as the Crusaders had seen five hundred years earlier. As long as the rulers were strong and enlightened, the autocratic empires functioned smoothly and effectively, as Busbecq reported. But when central authority weakened, the courtiers, bureaucratic officials, and army officers all combined to fleece the productive classes of society, whether peasants or artisans or merchants. Their uncontrollable extortions stifled private enterprise and incentive. Any subject who showed signs of wealth was fair game for arbitrary confiscation. Consequently, merchants hid their wealth rather than openly invest it to expand their operations.

Another cause and symptom of decline was the blind superiority complex of the Moslems, with their attitude of invincibility vis-à-vis the West. It never occurred to them at this time that they might conceivably learn anything from giaours, or nonbelievers. Their attitude stemmed partly from religious prejudice and partly from the spectacular successes of Islam in the past. Islam had grown from an obscure sect to the world's largest and most rapidly growing religion. Consequently, Moslem officials and scholars looked down with arrogance on anything relating to Christian Europe. As late as 1756, when the French ambassador in Constantinople announced the alliance between France and Austria that marked a turning point in the diplomatic history of Europe, he was curtly informed that the Ottoman government did not concern itself "about the union of one hog with another."[4] This attitude was perhaps understandable in the sixteenth century; in the eighteenth it was suicidal.

One of the most damaging results of this self-centeredness was that it let down an intellectual iron curtain between the Moslem world and the West, especially in the increasingly important field of science. Moslem scholars knew virtually nothing of the epoch-making achievements of Paracelsus in medicine; Vesalius and Harvey in anatomy; and Copernicus, Kepler, and Galileo in astronomy. Not only were they ignorant of these scientific advances, but also Moslem science itself had stagnated, with little impetus for new discoveries in the future.

A final factor explaining Moslem decline is that the three great Moslem empires were all land empires. They were built by the Turks, the Persians, and the Moguls, all peoples with no seafaring traditions. Their empires faced inward toward central Asia rather than outward toward the oceans. The rulers of these empires were not vitally interested in overseas trade. Therefore they responded feebly, if at all, when Portugal seized control of the Indian Ocean trade routes.

This situation was significant, because it allowed the Europeans to become the masters of the world trade routes with little opposition from the Moslems, who hitherto had controlled most of the trade between Asia and Europe. The repercussions were far-reaching. The control of world trade enriched the Europeans tremendously and further stimulated their economic, social, and political development. Thus a vicious circle developed, with worldwide trade making western Europe increasingly wealthy, productive, dynamic, and expansionist, while the once-formidable Moslem empires, taking little part in the new world economy, remained static and fell further and further behind.

SUGGESTED READINGS

Directly relevant to this chapter is the excellent collection of sources by J. J. Saunders, ed., *The Moslem World on the Eve of Europe's Expansion* (Prentice Hall, 1966). The spread of Islam from the time of Mohammed to the end of the nineteenth century is well described by T. W. Arnold, *The Preaching of Islam*, rev. ed. (Constable, 1913).

For the various Islam empires, see H. A. R. Gibb and H. Bowen, *Islamic Society and the West*, Parts 1 and 2 (Oxford University, 1950, 1957); H. Inalcik, *The Ottoman Empire: The Classical Age, 1300–1600* (Weidenfeld and Nicolson, 1972); the multivolume *Cambridge History of Iran* (Cambridge, 1968ff.); N. Itkowitz, *Ottoman Empire and Islamic Tradition* (University of Chicago, 1980); the sprightly written S. Wolpert, *A New History of India* (Oxford University, 1977); and R. Dunn, *The Adventures of Ibn Battuta: A Muslim Traveller of the Fourteenth Century* (University of California, 1986), which presents a revealing overview of the Moslem world.

Finally, on the decline of the Moslem Empires, see J. J. Saunders, "The Problem of Islamic Decadence," *Journal of World History*, 7 (1963), 701–720; T. Stoianovich, "Factors in the Decline of Ottoman Society in the Balkans," *Slavic Review*, 21 (December 1962), 623–632; and B. Lewis, "Some Reflections on the Decline of the Ottoman Empire," in C. M. Cipolla, ed., *The Economic Decline of Empires* (Methuen, 1970), pp. 215–234.

NOTES

1. Mehmed Pasha, *Ottoman Statecraft: The Book of Counsel for Vezirs and Govenors*, W. L. Wright, ed. and trans. (Princeton University, 1935), p. 21.
2. C. T. Foster and F. H. B. Daniell, eds., *The Life and Letters of Ogier Ghiselin de Busbecq* (London, 1881), pp. 221, 222.
3. Ibid., pp. 154, 155.
4. Cited by W. Eton, *A Survey of the Turkish Empire* (London, 1809), p. 10.

CHAPTER
19
Confucian World at the Time of the West's Expansion

One need not be obsessed with the merits of the Chinese to recognize that the organization of their empire is in truth the best that the world has ever seen.

Voltaire, 1764

Corresponding to the Moslem world in the Middle East and south Asia was the Confucian world in east Asia. Just as the Moslem world was dominated by the Ottoman, Safavid, and Mogul empires, so the Confucian world was dominated by China, with Korea and Japan on the periphery. The two worlds were similar in one fundamental respect: They were both agrarian-based and inward-looking societies. Their tempo of change was slow and within the framework inherited from earlier times. On the other hand, the Confucian world differed substantially from the Moslem because of its much greater unity. China had no indigestible minority blocs comparable to the various Balkan Christians in the Ottoman Empire, and no religious divisions comparable to the Hindus and Moslems in the Mogul Empire. This cohesiveness of China was not a recent phe-

nomenon. It dated back for millennia to the beginnings of Chinese civilization and has persisted to the present day. Indeed, the Chinese civilization is the oldest continuous civilization in the world.

I. CONTINUITY OF CHINESE CIVILIZATION

One reason for the longevity of the Chinese civilization is geographic, for China is isolated from the world's other great civilizations to an unprecedented degree. China has nothing comparable to the Mediterranean, which linked Mesopotamia, Egypt, Greece, and Rome, or the Indian Ocean, which allowed India to interact with the Middle East, Africa, and south Asia. Instead, during most of its history, China was effectively cut off on all sides by mountains,

296

deserts, and the vast Pacific Ocean. The significance of this isolation is that it allowed the Chinese to develop their civilization with fewer intrusions from the outside than the peoples of the Middle East or India had to face. Consequently, their civilization was both more continuous and also more distinctive. It has more fundamental differences from the other great Eurasian civilizations than any of them have from each other.

The unique size of China's population has also contributed to the continuity of civilization. From the beginning China has been able to support a huge population because of a favorable combination of soil and climate. The monsoon rains come during the warm months of the year, so that two crops per year are possible in some areas south of the Yangtze River, in contrast to the average one-crop yields of the Middle East and Europe. Furthermore, rice produces a much larger yield per acre than the wheat or barley grown in most parts of Eurasia. Thus the census of 2 C.E. showed that Han China had a population of 59.5 million—more than that of the Roman Empire at its greatest extent. By the early sixteenth century, when the Portuguese first arrived, China's population was over 100 million, more than that of all Europe. By the mid-nineteenth century, when China was being forced open by Western gunboats, its population had spurted upward to over 400 million, partly because of the introduction of such New World food crops as peanuts, maize, and sweet potatoes.

Such an unequaled population made it possible for the Chinese to retain their identity regardless of the course of events. They had been conquered and ruled by the Mongols and Manchus, as well as battered and undermined by the West. But in the end their superiority in numbers together with their superiority in civilization always enabled them to assimilate or expel the intruders and to adapt selected aspects of foreign cultures to their traditional civilization. Never has wholesale transformation been imposed from the outside, as it was in Europe with the Germanic invasions, or in the Middle East and in India with the Moslem ones.

Another important factor in China's cohesiveness is the existence of a single written language that goes back several millennia to the earliest Shang dynasty. This written language is of special significance because it is understood by Chinese from all regions, speaking dialects as different from each other as Italian is from German or Swedish from Spanish. The reason it is understandable to all is that it consists of characters representing ideas or objects. These characters are pronounced in different ways in different parts of China, but the meaning of any character is the same no matter how it is pronounced. A Western parallel would be the arabic number system: For example, the word for the number 8 is pronounced differently in Italian, in Swedish, or in English, but the meaning of the symbol 8 remains the same in all three tongues. This common written language has been an important force in providing unity and historic continuity to China. In fact, it has done so to all of east Asia, for the Chinese method of writing has been adopted in whole or in part by most of the surrounding peoples, including the Japanese, Koreans, and some of the Southeast Asians.

Related to the common written language is the extraordinary system of public examinations which formed the basis of the merit system by which for nearly two millennia China staffed its civil service. "When the right men are available, government flourishes. When the right men are not available, government declines." This Confucian maxim expresses the fundamental Chinese doctrine that problems of state are better met by recruiting people of talent than by depending on laws and institutions, as was done in the West. When fully evolved, the Chinese system consisted of a series of examinations held, in ascending order, in district and prefectural cities, provincial capitals, and finally the imperial capital.

At first the examinations were fairly comprehensive, emphasizing the Confucian classics but including also subjects like law, mathematics, and political affairs. Gradually, however, they came to concentrate on literary style and Confucian orthodoxy. The net result was a system providing China with an efficient and stable administration that won the respect and admiration of Europeans. On the other hand, it was a system that stifled originality and bred conformity. As long as China remained relatively isolated in east Asia, it provided stability and continuity. But with the intrusion of the dynamic West the system prevented effective reaction and adjustment. It was finally abolished altogether in 1905.

Perhaps the most important factor contributing to the cohesiveness of Chinese civilization was the moral code and the literary and intellectual heritage known as Confucianism. This was made up of the teachings of Confucius (551–479 B.C.E.), the name being a Latinized form of K'ung-fu-tzu, or "Master Kung." Like most Chinese thinkers, Confucius was concerned primarily with the establishment of a happy and well-organized society in this world. His first principle was "every man in his place": "Let the ruler be a ruler and the subject a subject; let the father be a father and the son be a son."

Confucius also provided China with a philosophy of government. Just as the individual should be subordinate to the family, so the family should be subordinate to the emperor. But the emperor in turn should set an example of benevolent fatherhood, and this was to be done by following the ethics of Confucianism rather than a system of law. Confucius thus was the founder of a great ethical tradition in a civilization that, more than any other, came to concentrate on ethical values.

All these factors are necessary to explain the continuity of Chinese civilization since its beginnings about 1500 B.C.E. The history of the Middle East presents a sharp contrast: Alexander's conquests spread the new Hellenistic culture; the Moslem conquests brought radical

Confucius instructing his disciples in the precepts of living in a happy and organized society.

changes in race, language, and culture, as well as religion. India, likewise, was transformed fundamentally with the Aryan invasions about 1500 B.C.E. and the Moslem invasions after 1000 C.E. The historical evolution of China was never jarred by such violent upheavals. There were many invasions, and on two occasions foreign dynasties ruled the entire country, but these intrusions disturbed rather than transformed. Instead of massive breaks and new beginnings, China throughout its history experienced merely the rise and fall of dynasties within the traditional framework.

II. DYNASTIC CYCLES

The cyclical rise and fall of dynasties can be explained by certain recurring trends in Chinese history. Each new dynasty normally began by ruling the country efficiently and starting a period of comparative peace and prosperity. It stimulated intellectual and cultural life and protected the country by sending military expeditions against the nomads and extending the imperial frontiers. But gradually the dynasty was weakened by the personal degeneration of individual rulers and by court struggles between cliques of gentry and palace eunuchs. This deterioration and factionalism undermined central authority and promoted corruption in the bureaucracy. Together with the increasing luxuriousness of court life, the corruption meant heavier taxes on the peasantry, who ultimately had to produce the surplus that supported the entire imperial structure. Taxes tended to increase also because of the costly foreign wars and the practice of the emperors of granting tax exemption to many of the gentry and to Buddhist temples and monasteries. As the government became lax, the irrigation systems and other public works essential for agriculture tended to be neglected.

Thus an increasingly impoverished peasantry had to bear the burden of a mounting tax load. When the inevitable crop failures and famines were added to the burden, the explosion came, and revolts broke out against the government tax collectors and landlord rent agents. In time, local uprisings broadened into general insurrections. These in turn were an invitation to the nomads to invade, especially since the imperial armies by this stage were poorly maintained. The combination of internal rebellion and external invasion usually heralded the beginning of a new cycle—the approaching end of the old dynasty and the coming of a new one.

The first dynasty, the Shang (1523–1028 B.C.E.), arose in the north in the Yellow River valley. Already the Chinese had learned to make silk, had devised their distinctive writing system, had mastered the art of creating beautiful earthenware and bronze vessels, and had begun to make a clear distinction between "Chinese" and "barbarians" based on a sense of cultural rather than racial superiority.

The succeeding Zhou dynasty (1028–221 B.C.E.), although long lived, was unable to establish a stable central government. The Zhou political structure was somewhat similar to that of medieval Europe, with a large number of warring feudal states that disregarded the nominal Zhou overlord. But this troubled political scene led to anxious soul searching among Chinese intellectuals. Their speculations on the nature of humanity and society culminated in the great philosophical systems and literary classics of Chinese civilization. Both Confucianism and Taoism evolved, so that the Zhou centuries, spanning a period as long as the entire European Middle Ages, stand out as the era when the cultural foundations of China were laid.

The following Ch'in dynasty (221–206 B.C.E.), despite its short duration, was responsible for replacing Zhou feudalism with a tightly organized imperial structure that lasted, with occasional lapses, until the fall of the last dynasty in 1912. This structure included an all-powerful emperor, an efficient and disciplined bureaucracy, a network of military roads and the Great Wall in the north, all of which gave China the most stable and lasting government in the world.

The Ch'in dynasty was succeeded by the Han (206 B.C.E.–220 C.E.), which is noted for its expansion of China's frontiers in all directions—west into central Asia, north into Manchuria, and south into Indochina. The Han Empire was at least the equal of the contemporary Roman Empire in size, population, wealth, and cultural achievement. The Han dynasty was followed, after an intervening period of disorder, by the

T'ang and Sung dynasties (618–907 and 960–1279), which represented a continuation of the traditional civilization, although with certain refinements and modifications.

The Yüan dynasty that followed (1279–1368) was unique in that it was Mongol rather than Chinese. The Mongols, in fact, had overrun most of Eurasia, so that China was now part of a huge empire extending from the Pacific to the Black Sea. But these Mongol rulers were few in number compared to their millions of Chinese subjects, and they failed to win the support of the Chinese gentry and peasants. They ruled as conquerors, making few concessions to Chinese institutions or to the Chinese way of life. When their military power declined, their regime was swept away by rebellious peasants and hostile scholar-bureaucrats.

Following the expulsion of the Mongols, China was ruled by two more dynasties, the Chinese Ming (1368–1644) and Manchu Ch'ing (1644–1911). Although the Manchus were foreigners like the Mongols, they were successful in ruling China because they gave prestige and opportunity to Chinese scholar-bureaucrats while maintaining administrative control. The traditional institutions and practices continued smoothly and satisfyingly—the agricultural economy, the Confucian way of life, the examination system for the selection of public officials, and the revered rule of the Son of Heaven in Peking.

In ordinary times such order and permanence would be considered a blessing. But these were the centuries that witnessed the rise of a new and dynamic Europe—the centuries of the Renaissance, the Reformation, the commercial and industrial revolutions, the French Revolution, and the rise of powerful national states that quickly extended their domination over the entire globe. In such a period, stability became a curse rather than a blessing. China appeared, and in fact was, relatively static and backward. The idea of continual change and "progress," which now was taken for granted in the West, remained alien to the Chinese mind. The basic difference between Chinese and European attitudes toward the world about them was manifested in the Chinese decision to discontinue the spectacular overseas expeditions of the Ming dynasty (see Chapter 21, Section V).

III. EARLY RELATIONS WITH THE WEST

Relations between China and the West did not become continuous until the expansion of Europe following the voyages of Columbus and the Portuguese navigators. China began to feel the direct impact of the dynamic new Europe when Portuguese merchants opened trade with Canton in 1514 and established a permanent commercial base at Macao in 1557. The Portuguese purchased Chinese silks, wood carvings, porcelain, lacquerware, and gold, and in return they sold nutmeg, cloves, and mace from the East Indies; sandalwood from Timor; drugs and dyes from Java; and cinnamon, pepper, and ginger from India. No European goods were involved for the simple reason that there was no market for them in China. The Portuguese were functioning as carriers and middlemen for a purely intra-Asian trade.

The Dutch and the British arrived in the early seventeenth century to challenge Portugal's monopoly in the China trade. Neither was given official permission to trade, so for decades the Dutch and English preyed on Portuguese shipping and conducted an irregular trade along the south China coast. By the mid-eighteenth century the Chinese opened up the trade to all countries, though confining it to Canton and Macao. The English soon won the lion's share of this trade, partly because of their growing commercial and industrial superiority and also because of their convenient base of operations in India.

Meanwhile, the Russians in Siberia had been trying to open trade relations with China, and the Chinese had reacted by restricting and regulating the commerce closely. The treaties of Nerchinsk (1689) and Kiakhta (1727) allowed the Russians to trade at three border points and to send commercial caravans every three years to Peking. There they were permitted to build a church and maintain a priest and three curates, though their community in the Chinese capital was limited in numbers to 300. Under these terms a few goods were exchanged—Russian furs, leather goods, textiles, cattle, horses, and glassware for Chinese silks, tea, lacquerware, and porcelain.

Cultural interaction between China and the West during these early centuries was con-

Russians traveled through Siberia and set up forts along the Amur River, attempting to open trade relations with China. With Jesuit priests acting as interpreters and advisers, the treaty of Nerchinsk was signed in 1689.

fined to the efforts of the Jesuits to propagate their faith. The net result of centuries of Jesuit enterprise was negligible. Indeed, Europe had been much more impressed by China's examination system and Confucian ethics than China had been by Europe's science and mathematics. The Chinese remained supremely self-confident and self-contained. They had kept Western merchants confined to few seaports and frontier trading posts; they had accepted with a few exceptions only tributary relations in their conduct of international affairs; and they had shown only a passing interest in Jesuit teachings about science and theology. Rarely in history had a people faced the future with so much self-assurance and with so little understanding of the storms that awaited them.

IV. JAPAN ABSORBS CHINESE CIVILIZATION

Compared to China, Japan was on the periphery in the sixteenth century when the Europeans first appeared. This does not mean that the Japanese were primitive; indeed, they had evolved a complex and dynamic society. Although their first reaction to the appearance of the Europeans was positive—many of them embraced Christianity—soon they reacted against the "insolent barbarians" and severed virtually all ties with them. But the Japanese eventually came to realize that a policy of withdrawal was not realistic. They proceeded to study the ways of the West and adapt elements of Western culture to their needs. Thanks to their unique historical and cultural background, the Japanese were extraordinarily successful and quickly outdistanced the Chinese, who for so long had been their teachers.

The importance of geographic location is particularly apparent in the case of Japanese history. In this respect there is a close parallel with the British Isles at the other end of the Eurasian landmass. The Japanese islands, however, are more isolated than the British. One hundred and fifteen miles separate them from the mainland, compared to the twenty-one miles of the English Channel. Thus until their World War II defeat by the United States, the Japanese had only once before been seriously threatened by foreign invasion, and that was in the thirteenth century by the Mongols. The Japanese, therefore, have been close enough to the mainland to benefit from the great Chinese civilization, but distant enough to be able to select and reject as they wished.

The Japanese are basically a Mongoloid people who migrated from northeast Asia. But the hairy Caucasoid Ainu who originally inhabited the Japanese islands contributed to their racial composition, and Malayan and Polynesian migrants from the south probably did also. Early Japan was organized in a large number of clans, each ruled by a hereditary priest-chieftain. Toward the end of the first century C.E., the Yamato clan established a loose political and religious control over the others. Its chief was the emperor, and its clan goddess, the Sun Goddess, was made the national deity.

This clan organization was undermined by the importation of Chinese civilization, which began on a large scale in the sixth century. Buddhism, introduced from Korea, was the medium for cultural change, fulfilling the same function here as Christianity did among the Germans and Slavs in Europe. Students, teachers, craftsmen, and monks crossed over from the mainland, bringing with them a new way of life as well as a new religion. The impetus for change culminated in the Taika Reform, which began in 645 and

Yoritomo (1147–1198), first Minamoto Shogun of Japan and founder of the Kamakura Shogunate. He was the first founder of a long line of actual rulers of Japan.

sought to transform Japan into a centralized state on the model of the T'ang dynasty in China. In accordance with the Chinese model, the country was divided into provinces and districts ruled by governors and magistrates who derived their power from the emperor and his council of state.

These and other changes were designed to strengthen imperial authority, and they did so in comparison with the preceding clan structure. But in practice, the Japanese changed and adapted everything they borrowed from China. They limited the power of their emperor by allowing the hereditary aristocracy to keep their large landholdings. They borrowed Chinese ideographs but developed their own system of writing. They borrowed Confucianism, but modified its ethics and adjusted its political doctrines to satisfy their own spiritual needs, while retaining their native Shintoism. They built new imperial capitals, first at Nara and then at Kyoto, that were modeled after the T'ang capital, Ch'ang-an. But there was no mistaking the Japanese quality of the temples, pavilions, shrines, and gardens.

V. TOKUGAWA SHOGUNATE

The Chinese system of imperial organization introduced by the Taika Reform of 645 worked effectively for a long period. By the twelfth century, however, it had been undermined and replaced by a Japanese variety of feudalism. One reason for this was the tendency of provincial governors, who were too fond of the pleasures of Kyoto, to delegate their powers and responsibilities to local subordinates. Another was that powerful local families and Buddhist communities were always hungry for land and often able to seize it by force. These trends reduced the amount of taxpaying land, which meant an increased tax load for the peasant owner-cultivators. The latter in turn either fled to the northern frontier areas where the Ainu were being pushed back by force of arms, or else they commended themselves and their lands to lords of manors. This relieved them of taxes and provided them with protection, but at the cost of becoming serfs. The net result of this process was that by the end of the twelfth century, taxpaying land amounted to 10 percent or less of

the total cultivated area, and local power had been taken over by the new rural aristocracy.

At the same time, this aristocracy had become the dominant military force because of the disintegration of the imperial armed forces. The Taika Reform had made all males between the ages of twenty and sixty subject to military service. But the conscripts were required to furnish their own weapons and food and were given no relief from the regular tax burden. This arrangement proved unworkable and was abandoned in 739. Government military posts became sinecures generally filled by effeminate court aristocrats. As a result, the campaigns against the Ainu were conducted by the rural aristocrats. They became mounted warriors and gradually increased their military effectiveness until they completely overshadowed the imperial forces. A feudal relationship now developed between these rural lords and their retainers, or samurai (literally, "one who serves"). This relationship was based on an idealized ethic, known as bushido, or "way of the warrior." The samurai enjoyed special legal and ceremonial rights, and in return they were expected to give unquestioning service to their lords.

By the twelfth century, Japan was controlled by the competing groups of feudal lords. In the end, one of these lords emerged victorious, and he was appointed by the emperor to the position of Seii-Tai-Shogun (Barbarian-Subduing-Generalissimo), with the right to nominate his own successor. Henceforth Japan was controlled by a succession of shogun families, or shogunates. They commanded the military forces while the emperor lived in seclusion in Kyoto. The most important of these families was the Tokugawa Shogunate, founded by Tokugawa Ieyasu in 1603. It ruled the country until the restoration of imperial rule and the beginning of modernization in 1868. Ieyasu and his immediate successors formulated policies designed to perpetuate their family dominance. The material basis of their power lay in the Shogunal domain, which comprised between a fourth and a third of the total arable land and consisted of estates scattered strategically throughout the country. These estates provided control points against potentially hostile daimyo, or local landholding families. Top government posts were filled by members of the Tokugawa family or personal retainers. The emperor was provided with revenues for his own support as well as that of a small group of court nobles, but he had no political function or authority.

As part of their effort to prevent any change that might undermine their rule, the Tokugawa perpetuated a rigid, hereditary class structure. At the top was the aristocracy, comprising about 6 percent of the population. The vast majority of Japanese were farmers, the second-ranking class, which included landless tenants as well as landholders with plots ranging from an acre and a quarter to as many as eighty-five acres. Whatever their status, these peasants produced the rice that, in the final analysis, supported the aristocracy. The latter, in fact, measured their income in terms of rice.

The last two classes recognized by the Tokugawa were, in order of rank, the artisans and the merchants. The long period of peace and security during this shogunate allowed these townspeople to grow enormously in numbers and wealth. The Tokugawa created an ideological basis for their regime by sponsoring the Chu Hsi school of Confucianism, which stressed the virtues of filial piety and of loyalty to one's superior in any social grouping. Paternal power was absolute and unquestioned in the ideal Japanese family, and even more specifically spelled out than in China. Particularly appealing to the Tokugawa was the Confucian emphasis on the moral basis of political legitimacy and on all the conservative virtues. One effect of this ideology was that the Japanese family system, especially that of the samurai, was closely integrated into Tokugawan society because of its subordination to the interests of the shogun or the daimyo. This harmony between the family and the state, much stronger than in China, facilitated the modernization of Japan in the nineteenth century by providing a grass-roots basis for national unity and action.

VI. EARLY RELATIONS WITH THE WEST

For a while the Tokugawa policy of preserving the status quo was threatened by the intrusion of western Europeans. The first to appear were Portuguese traders in the mid-sixteenth century, who discovered that rich profits could be made in commerce between China and Japan. Because of raids by Japanese pirates, the Ming emperors had banned all trade with Japan. The Portuguese quickly stepped into the void and prospered handsomely, exchanging Chinese gold and silk for Japanese silver and copper. These merchants combined missionary enterprise with their commercial activities. Francis Xavier and other Jesuit fathers landed in 1549 and were allowed to preach among the masses of the people. They were unusually successful, apparently because their revivalist methods of proselytism satisfied the emotional needs of the downtrodden peasantry.

With the advent of the Tokugawa in 1603, Dutch traders, and a few British, were active in Japan alongside the Portuguese. The intense rivalry among these Europeans gave the Japanese a new freedom of action. They could now move against the missionaries without fear of losing the commerce. And they did want to curb the missionaries, whose success they feared was undermining the traditional Japanese society. Accordingly, Ieyasu decreed in 1614 that all missionaries must leave, and their converts, who by now numbered 300,000, must renounce their faith. This order was ruthlessly enforced. As a control measure, converts were forced to belong to a Buddhist temple, and many were executed for refusing. Missionaries also were martyred, but it was often difficult to distinguish between commercial and religious activities. The Japanese therefore went a step further and in 1624 banned all Spaniards, since they had been the most aggressive and defiant. In 1637 all Portuguese also were forced to depart, leaving only the Dutch, who had never shown any interest in propagating Christianity. Henceforth the Dutch were the only Europeans allowed to carry on trade, but only under severely restricted conditions on the Deshima islet in Nagasaki harbor. The isolationist policy was extended in 1636 to Japanese subjects, who were prohibited from going abroad on penalty of death. Over two centuries of seclusion had begun for Japan.

The policy of excluding all foreign influences and freezing the internal status quo was designed to perpetuate the Tokugawa dominance. In practice it proved extraordinarily effective. Japan was reunified and subjected to a centralized political control as thorough and as efficient as in any European state before the French Revolution. But a heavy price was paid for this security and stability. Japan did not have the transformation and rejuvenation of historical movements that western Europe did during this period. There was no ending of feudalism, no Renaissance or Reformation—or Counter-Reformation—and no overseas expansion. For the Japanese, as for the Chinese, the price of two centuries of comforting seclusion was institutional and technological backwardness. This became apparent, more quickly to the Japanese than to the Chinese, when the Europeans forcibly broke into the hermit world of east Asia in the mid-nineteenth century.

SUGGESTED READINGS

Useful annotated bibliographies are provided by the Service Center for Teachers of History of the American Historical Association: J. W. Hall, *Japanese History* (1961); C. O. Hucker, *Some Approaches to China's Past* (1973); and J. K. Fairbank, *New Views of China's Tradition and Modernization* (1968). Source materials on the culture of east Asia are available in W. T. de Bary et al., *Source of Chinese Tradition* (Columbia University, 1960); and R. Tsunoda et al., *Sources of the Japanese Tradition* (Columbia University, 1958).

An authoritative study of all east Asia is by E. O. Reischauer and J. K. Fairbank, *East Asia: Tradition and Civilization*, rev. ed. (Houghton Mifflin, 1978). Standard general histories of China are by W. Rodzinski, *The Walled Kingdom: A History of China from Antiquity to the Present* (Free Press, 1984); and C. O. Hucker, *China's Imperial Past: An Introduction to Chinese History and Culture* (Stanford University, 1975). Noteworthy is M. Elvin, *The Pattern of the Chinese Past* (Stanford University, 1973), which analyzes why medieval China's flair for technology did not lead to an industrial revolution. Comparable histories of Japan are by E. O. Reischauer, *Japan: The Story of a Nation*, rev. ed. (Knopf, 1970); G. B. Sansom, *Japan, A Short Cultural History*, rev. ed. (Prentice Hall, 1944), and the same author's definitive *A History of Japan*, 3 vols. (Stanford University, 1958–1964).

Finally, for the initial contact between east Asia and the West, see the multivolume work by D. F. Lach, *Asia in the Making of Europe* (University of Chicago, 1965 ff.); W. Franke, *China and the West* (Blackwell, 1967); G. F. Hudson, *Europe and China: A Study of Their Relations from Earliest Times to 1800* (Beacon, 1961); C. R. Boxer, *Fidalgos in the Far East, 1550–1770* (Martinus Nijhoff, 1948); C. R. Boxer, *The Christian Century in Japan, 1549–1650* (University of California, 1951); and J. D. Spence, *The Memory Palace of Matteo Ricci* (Viking, 1984), which provides a fascinating juxtaposition of two cultures, through the experiences of Ricci.

Expanding Civilization of the West: Renaissance and Reformation

Men can do all things if they will.

Leon Battista Alberti

For the work of God cannot be received and honored by any works, but by faith alone.

Martin Luther

. . . by an eternal and immutable counsel God has once and for all determined both whom He would admit to salvation, and whom He would condemn to destruction.

John Calvin

In the late Middle Ages, a curious and fateful development occurred in the Eurasian world. On the one hand, Islamic and Confucian empires were becoming increasingly ossified and were withdrawing into themselves. On the other hand, the western tip of Eurasia was experiencing an unprecedented and thoroughgoing transformation. Far-reaching changes were taking place in almost all phases of west European life. The end result was the emergence of a new type of dynamic, expansionist civilization—modern civilization, which was qualitatively different from the traditional agrarian-based civilizations of the rest of Eurasia and, for that matter, of the rest of the globe. Thus began what is now termed the process of modernization, which has persisted at an accelerating tempo to the present day and which has determined the course of modern world history.

I. MODERNIZATION

Economists define modernization as the process by which humans have increased their control over their physical environment as a means to increasing per capita output. Sociologists and anthropologists point out other features of modernization, including the awakening and activation of the masses, more interest in the present and the future than in the past, a tendency to view human affairs as understandable rather than as manipulated by supernatural forces, and, until recent years, a faith in the beneficence of science and technology.

From the viewpoint of world history the significance of this modernization process is that it led inexorably to European domination of the globe. The reason is that modernization provided the Europeans not only with superior economic and military power but also with superior sociopolitical cohesion and dynamism. For example, a handful of British merchants and soldiers were able to conquer and rule the great Indian subcontinent more because of its sociopolitical fragility than because of British military technology. Conversely, it is significant that there never has been any speculation about the possibility of a reverse course of events—the landing in England of Indian soldiers and merchants with the designs for trade and booty that had motivated the English nabobs. The notion that Indians might have been able to do in England what Robert Clive and Warren Hastings did in India seems so preposterous as never to be considered even as a remote possibility. But it is preposterous precisely because of the difference between English and Indian societies—the latter hopelessly fragmented, with an infinitely greater gulf between rulers and ruled than in the former. Whereas Clive and Hastings had been able to play off Moslems against Hindus, prince against prince, and local potentates against imperial officials, while the peasant masses remained inert in their villages, any Indian counterpart of Clive and Hastings doubtless would have encountered a united front of Protestants and Catholics and of government and citizens, including the gentry, the townspeople, and the peasants.

Such was the chasm, so fateful for world history, separating traditional societies from those that had undergone modernization. Furthermore, this modernization was not a one-shot affair. It continues to the present day and at an ever faster pace. In late medieval and early modern times, as we shall note in this chapter and the following one, modernization comprised the Renaissance and Reformation, economic expansion, emerging capitalism, state building, and overseas enterprise. These developments set off a chain reaction in the form of the great scientific, industrial, and successive political revolutions (Chapters 26 and 27) that have molded human history from the seventeenth century to the present.

II. RENAISSANCE

The term *Renaissance* is polemical. It means new birth or revival and was coined by fifteenth-century intellectuals who believed that their age represented the rebirth of classical culture following an intervening "age of darkness," as they termed the medieval period. This interpretation was accepted through the nineteenth century, but historians today no longer consider it to have been a case of medieval pitch darkness against Renaissance dazzling light. The fact is that interest in the classics was by no means completely absent during the Middles Ages, and conversely, certain characteristics associated with medievalism were very much in evidence during the Renaissance. So modern historians, although not discarding the familiar term, now define the Renaissance as connoting not a sharp break or turning point but rather an age of transition from medieval to modern civilization—roughly from 1350 to 1600.

The Renaissance began first in Italy and hence reflected the conditions and values of contemporary Italian society. This was a bustling urban society based on flourishing industries and on the profitable commerce between western Europe and the wealthy Byzantine and Islamic empires. The Italians were the middlemen in this commerce and prospered accordingly. By about 1400 the Venetian merchant fleet was made up of 300 "large ships," 3,000 ships of less than 100 tons, and 45 galleys, manned in all by some 28,000 men. Venetian shipyards employed an additional 6,000 carpenters and other workers. Comparable activity was to be found in other Italian cities such as Florence, Genoa, Pisa, and Rome. These cities were dominated by the great merchant families who controlled politics as well as trade and crafts. These families were the patrons of Renaissance artists and writers. Their needs, interests, and tastes colored the Renaissance cultural revival even though the patrons also included ducal families

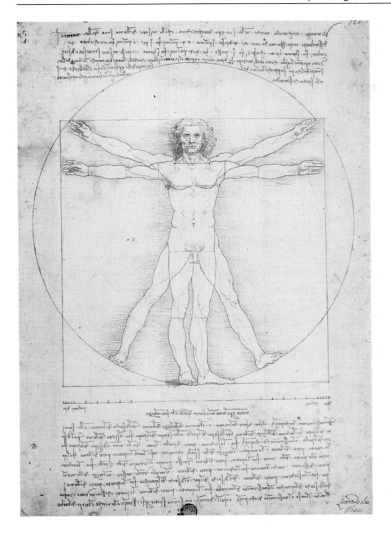

The true "Renaissance man"—Leonardo da Vinci. Painter, sculptor, inventor, Leonardo demonstrated how far ahead of his time he truly was with his Study of the Human Body, *1492.*

such as the Sforza of Milan, as well as popes such as Nicholas V, Pius II, Julius II, and Leo X. This explains the secularism and humanism of the Renaissance—its concern with this world rather than the hereafter and its focus on pagan classics rather than Christian theology.

At the center of most Renaissance art and literature was the person—the new Renaissance person who was the molder of his or her own destiny rather than the plaything of supernatural forces. People did not need to be preoccupied with supernatural forces; rather, the purpose of life was to develop one's innate potentialities. "Men can do all things if they will," wrote Leon Battista Alberti (1404–1472), and his own attainments abundantly validated this maxim. This Florentine patrician was an architect, mathematician, and archeologist, as well as playwright; poet; art critic; organist; singer; and, in his youth, a well-known runner, wrestler, and mountain climber.

The secularism and individualism of the Renaissance were reflected in its scholarship and education. The so-called father of Renaissance literature, Francesco Petrarca, or Petrarch (1304–1374), stressed the value of the classics as a means for self-improvement and a guide to social action. Likewise, the new boarding schools of the Renaissance trained not priests but the sons of merchants. The curriculum emphasized classical studies and physical exercise and was designed to educate the students to live well and happily and to function as responsible citizens.

The Renaissance spirit is most strikingly expressed in its art. Since the church no longer was the sole patron, artists were encouraged to turn to subjects other than the traditional biblical themes. Giotto (1276—1337) marked the transition in painting to naturalism. This trend was carried much further by Masaccio (1401–1428), who mastered the distinctive Renaissance invention of perspective. In contrast to medieval painting, that of the Renaissance projected light and shadow and gave the appearance of depth to figures and scenes.

By the mid-fifteenth century Italian Renaissance painting attained its maturity. In Florence, Masaccio was followed by Sandro Botticelli (1444–1510) and by the versatile genius Leonardo da Vinci (1452–1519), who was a sculptor, musician, architect, and engineer as well as painter. As such, da Vinci was the personification of the "new Renaissance person." His seventy-two-page notebook, known as the Codex Hammer, was sold in London on November 15, 1994, for $30.8 million. In this manuscript he speculated on why the sky is blue and why fossils are found on mountaintops. He also predicted the invention of the submarine and the steam engine.

About 1550, after two centuries of sparkling achievement, the Italian Renaissance began to wane. One reason for the decline was the French invasion of 1494, which precipitated decades of war that involved the various European powers and left the Italian peninsula devastated. More basic in the long run was the economic blow suffered when Vasco da Gama sailed into Calicut Harbor, India, on May 22, 1498. This ended the profitable monopoly that the Italians had enjoyed as the middlemen in the trade between western Europe and the East. In four years (1502–1505), the Venetians were able to obtain an average of only 1 million English pounds of spices a year at Alexandria, whereas in the last years of the fifteenth century they had averaged 3.5 million pounds. Conversely, Portuguese spice imports rose from 224,000 pounds in 1501 to an average of 2,300,000 in the four years from 1503 to 1506.

More serious than this commercial decline was the industrial. For centuries Italy had exported manufactured goods, especially textiles, to northern Europe and the Near East, and

also had derived substantial revenues from banking and shipping services. But by the late sixteenth century the British, French, and Dutch had surpassed the Italians, who were hampered by restricting guild regulations, high taxes and labor costs, and failure to adapt goods to changing tastes. Thus the average annual production of woolens in Florence was 30,000 cloths between 1560 and 1580, but only 13,000 between 1590 and 1600, and 6,000 by 1650. Likewise, Venice was producing an average of 20,000 to 30,000 cloths about 1600, but only 2,000 by 1700. This gap between Italy and the northern European countries was further widened by the growing importance of colonial trade, from which the Italian cities, lacking overseas possessions, were excluded.

To use modern terminology, Italy, which had been the developed part of Europe during the Middle Ages, now became the underdeveloped. It was Italy that henceforth exported raw materials (oil, wine, grain, wool, and raw silk) to northern Europe in return for manufactured goods. This meant that cities and their grandi no longer were dominant in Italy, their primacy being replaced by that of landed proprietors of a feudal character. Thus the economic foundations of the Renaissance crumbled.

III. RENAISSANCE LEGACY

The Renaissance was not an exclusively Italian phenomenon. Its innovations spread to northern Europe in the sixteenth century. The instruments of diffusion were Italian diplomats and generals employed by northern monarchs and the printing press, which speeded up the circulation of books and ideas. In the process of transmission northward the Renaissance changed somewhat in character. Whereas in Italy it had manifested itself primarily in art and literature, in the north it found expression more in religion and morals. But this was by no means exclusively so, as evident in the works of German painters such as Albrecht Dürer (1471–1528) and Hans Holbein the Younger (1497–1543), and of Flemish painters such as the Van Eycks and Peter Breughel. Breughel was the most unorthodox and socially conscious of the northern artists. Turning away from the tradi-

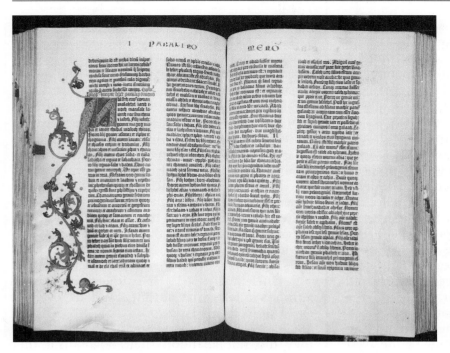

The printing press made possible the diffusion of Renaissance learning. But no book stimulated thought more at this time than did the Bible. With Gutenberg's publication of a printed Bible in 1454, scholars gained access to a dependable, standardized text, so that Scripture could be discussed and debated as never before.

tional themes of his predecessors—religious subjects and portraits of merchant families amid their luxurious surroundings—he focused on scenes from everyday peasant life. He also used his art to combat Spanish rule in the Netherlands, as in his painting *The Massacre of the Innocents*, depicting Spanish soldiers slaughtering women and children.

Printing was particularly influential in northern Europe because literacy was more widespread there than in the southern and eastern regions of Europe. The flood of printed matter certainly fomented popular agitation concerning political and religious issues, thereby contributing substantially to the Reformation and the ensuing religious and dynastic wars. Printing also stimulated the development of national schools of literature during this early modern period. Luther's translation of the Bible provided the basis for modern literary German. Likewise, the King James Bible and the plays of Shakespeare (1564–1616) laid the foundation for modern English literature. In Spain, Miguel de Cervantes (1547–1616) made the same contribution to the national language with his novel *Don Quixote*. And in France, this was the role of François Rabelais (c. 1490–1553) and Michel de Montaigne (1533–1592). The significance of

such literary endeavors was implicitly recognized in 1635 when the Académie Française was established for the purpose of officially defining the vocabulary and grammar of the national language.

In conclusion, what is the significance of the Renaissance in the perspective of world history? It is apparent that new emphasis on persons and on what they could accomplish obviously was more conducive to overseas expansion than the preceding medieval outlook. On the other hand, this point can easily be exaggerated and needs serious modification. The fact is that Renaissance Europe was not science-oriented. The leading figures tended to be more aesthetic and philosophical than objective and skeptical. They retained in various degrees certain medieval patterns of thought. They persisted in admiring and believing the incredible and the fantastic. They continued to seek the philosopher's stone that would convert other metals into gold. They still believed in astrology and confused it with astronomy.

The Iberian pioneers of overseas expansion definitely were not "Renaissance men." Prince Henry the Navigator, for example, was described by his contemporaries as a rigid, pious, and chivalrous ascetic rather than as a humanist.

Although a generous patron of sailors and cartographers, he was not interested in learning and the arts. The story of a school of astronomy and mathematics that he allegedly supported at Sagres is a myth. Thus the stimulation of rapidly widening "new intellectual horizons" explains less about the origins of European expansion before 1500 than it does about the impetus and irresistible power that that explosion of knowledge provided after 1600. Indeed, European expansion was vastly important in its own right. The fact remains that there was an intellectual ferment in western Europe and that it had no counterpart in the rest of Eurasia. This is a fundamental difference of enormous significance.

In the Ottoman Empire, for example, the Moslem medressehs, or colleges, emphasized theology, jurisprudence, and rhetoric at the expense of astronomy, mathematics, and medicine. The graduates of these schools were uninformed about what was being done in the West and quite uninterested in finding out. No Moslem Turk could believe that a Christian infidel could teach him anything of value. Now and then, a rare, far-sighted individual warned of the dangers of the intellectual iron curtain that separated the Ottoman Empire from neighboring Christendom. One of the voices was Katib Chelebi, the famous Turkish bibliographer, encyclopedist, and historian who lived in the first half of the seventeenth century. Coming from a poor family, he was unable to obtain a formal higher education. This was to be a blessing in disguise. He was spared the superficial, hairsplitting specialization on Moslem sacred studies that characterized Ottoman education at this time. The fact that he was self-taught explains in large part his open-mindedness toward Western learning.

One of Chelebi's works was a short naval handbook that he compiled following a disastrous defeat of the Ottoman fleet in 1656. In the preface of this work, Chelebi emphasized the need for mastering the science of geography and map making.

For men who are in charge of affairs of state, the science of geography is a matter of which knowledge is necessary. They may not be familiar with what the entire globe is like, but they ought at least to know the map of the Ottoman State and of those states adjoining it. Then, when they have to send forces on campaign, they can proceed on the basis of knowledge, and so the invasion of the enemy's land and also the protection and defense of the frontiers becomes an easier task. Taking counsel with individuals who are ignorant of that science is no satisfactory substitute, not even when such men are local veterans. Most such veterans are entirely unable to sketch the map of their own home regions.

Sufficient and convincing proof of the necessity for learning this science is the fact that the heathen, by their application to and their esteem for those branches of learning, have discovered the New World and have over-run the markets of India.[1]

Chelebi grasped the connection between Europe's intellectual advance and its overseas expansion. In his last work before his death in 1657, Chelebi warned his fellow citizens that if they did not abandon their dogmatism they would soon "be looking at the universe with the eyes of oxen." His prediction proved prophetic. The Turks remained steeped in their religious obscurantism, and like other non-Western peoples, they paid a high price. The Christian infidels with their new learning eventually became the masters not only of the New World but also of the ancient empires of Islam and Confucianism.

IV. REFORMATION IN GERMANY

The term *Reformation* is as misleading as the term *Renaissance*. Luther began as a reformer but ended as a revolutionary, driven by the logic of his basic convictions to challenge and reject the foundations of the Roman Church. Superficially, the Reformation can be interpreted as the reaction to certain abuses within the Church, including the illiteracy of many of the priests; the dissolute lives of some of the clergy, including popes; and the sale of religious offices, of dispensations (exemptions from church laws), and of indulgences (pardons for sins). Provocative as these abuses were, the fact is that they were more the pretext than the root cause of the Protestant Reformation. Indeed, at the time when the Reformation was getting under way, pious Catholics within the Church were beginning their own reform efforts to correct these conditions. To explain a basic upheaval that shattered the age-old unity of Western Christendom, it is necessary to go beyond abuses and to consider certain background historical forces that had been building up for centuries.

One was the undermining of the prestige of the papacy during the fourteenth-century "Babylonian Captivity," when soldiers of King Philip IV of France arrested Pope Boniface VIII. The arrest was followed by the transference of the papal capital to Avignon, where the popes perforce were subservient to French interests. Even more ruinous to papal prestige was the Great Schism at the end of the fourteenth century. Two popes, one in Rome and one in Avignon, each claimed to be the legitimate successor of St. Peter and excommunicated the other. Another factor behind the Reformation was the legacy of earlier heresies such as those of John Wycliffe in England and John Hus in Bohemia. The latter was burned at the stake at the Council of Constance in 1415, but his followers were still alive when Luther began preaching essentially similar doctrines a century later.

Political factors also were involved in the Reformation, namely the growth of national feeling in northern Europe and the related rise of the "New Monarchs" in various states. Both monarchs and subjects increasingly viewed the popes as foreigners with no right to meddle in national affairs or to raise revenues within national frontiers. This led to the final force behind the Reformation—the popular resentment against the taxes collected by the Church and against its great landed properties scattered throughout western Europe. The economic dispute, together with the preceding political factor, will be considered in more detail in the following chapter. Here it should be noted that the interests of the growing middle class and of the national monarchs led both to eye greedily the vast landholdings of the Church and its enormous movable wealth in the form of jewels, bullion, art objects, and luxurious furnishings.

A portrayal of Jan Hus as he was led to the stake at Constance. After his execution, his bones and ashes were scattered in the Rhine River to prevent his followers from claiming them as relics. This pen-and-ink drawing is from Ulrich von Richenthal's Chronicle of the Council of Constance *(ca. 1450).*

Martin Luther and the Wittenberg Reformers *with Elector John Frederick of Saxony (1532–1547), painted about 1543. Luther is on the far left, Philip Melanchthon in the front on the far right. [Lucas Cranach the Younger, German, 1515–1586, oil on panel, 27-5/8 x 15-5/8 in.]*

rulers were too weak to resist the powerful Church in cases of excessive exactions. One of these cases was the decision of the pope in 1517 to sell a large number of indulgences throughout Europe to pay for the repair of St. Peter's Church in Rome. The indulgence in Germany that triggered the Reformation promised absolution "from all thy sins, transgressions, and excesses, how enormous soever they may be . . . so that when you die the gates of punishment shall be shut, and the gates of the paradise of delight shall be opened. . . ." It was in protest against this "unbridled preaching of pardons" that Luther, then a priest at the University of Wittenburg, posted his ninety-five theses on the church door. Most of his propositions were not revolutionary, but he did argue that the "word of God" lay not in the doctrine of the Church but in the Bible, thereby undercutting Church authority.

Pope Leo X dismissed the incident as a "squabble among monks," but the theses were quickly translated into German and widely circulated in print. The enthusiastic popular response demonstrated that Luther had given voice to deeply felt national grievances. The ensuing public debate led Luther to spell out the revolutionary implications of his basic doctrine of justification by faith—that is, that the priestly offices and ministrations of the Church were unnecessary intermediaries between the individual and God. By the end of 1520 Luther had broken irrevocably with the Church and embraced the earlier heresies of Wycliffe and Hus as "most Christian." In October 1520 Luther burned a papal bull of excommunication, and the following year he was summoned to appear before the Imperial Diet meeting at Worms. Called on to recant, Luther refused "unless I am convinced by the testimony of the Scriptures or by clear reason." The emperor secured passage of an edict condemning the obstinate friar as a heretic, but the sympathetic Elector Fredrick of Saxony provided refuge in his castle and saved Luther from the fate of Hus.

In this place of exile Luther busied himself in the following years translating the Bible into German and building an independent German church. Emperor Charles V was unable to move decisively against the spreading heresy because he was involved in wars with the French and the

Equally coveted were the revenues flowing from the states to Rome in the form of the tithe; the funds from the sale of offices; and the innumerable fees for appeals, dispensations, and indulgences.

This combination of historical forces reached the explosion point first in Germany because that land was then a collection of over a hundred principalities—fiefs, ecclesiastical city-states, free cities, counties, and duchies—whose

Turks. By 1546 he was free of these distractions so he set out to crush the Lutheran princes and restore the unity of the church. He was encouraged in this by the pope, who provided money and troops. But the Lutherans banded together in the Schmalkaldic League and won support from the Catholic French king, who was more concerned with dynastic than religious considerations. The fighting dragged on inconclusively until the signing of the Peace of Augsburg (1555), which granted each German prince the right to select either the Catholic or Lutheran faith and to impose it on his subjects. Thus the end result of the Reformation in Germany was the roughly equal division of the country into Lutheran and Catholic states.

V. REFORMATION BEYOND GERMANY

The Peace of Augsburg opened the gates to the rising flood of heresy, or rather heresies. The settlement at Augsburg had recognized only Lutheranism as a possible alternative to the Catholic faith. But Protestantism by its very nature lent itself to a continual proliferation of new sects. Luther's fundamental doctrine of individual interpretation of the Scriptures led inevitably to different interpretations and hence to new varieties of Protestantism. In Switzerland, for example, John Calvin joined Luther in rejecting salvation by "works" but also rejected his doctrine of salvation by "faith." Instead Calvin preached predestination—each individual's fate was decreed by God before birth. "In conformity, therefore, to the clear doctrine of Scripture, we assert that by an eternal and immutable counsel God has once for all determined both whom He would admit to salvation, and whom He would condemn to destruction." Calvin differed from Luther also in requiring that the Church should actively intervene in community affairs to ensure the elimination of heresy, blasphemy, and wickedness. During his ascendancy in Geneva (1541–1564), his Consistory of Elders transformed that city into a Christian community whose austerity and holiness astonished visitors. Furthermore, the availability of printing presses enabled Calvin to make Geneva the headquarters of a proselytizing drive that profoundly affected such countries as

Bohemia, Hungary, the Netherlands, Scotland, England, and the thirteen American colonies overseas.

An entirely different form of Protestantism was that of the Anabaptists, whose religious and social radicalism earned them persecution by Catholics, Lutherans, and Calvinists alike. Carrying to its logical conclusion Luther's doctrine that every man should follow the dictates of his conscience, they demanded full religious liberty, including separation of church and state. Equally radical were their social teachings—their opposition to individual accumulation of wealth, to class or status differentiation, to military service, and to payment of taxes for war-making purposes. It is not surprising that these tenets, undermining the authority of all religious and political establishments, led to the persecution and wholesale massacre of Anabaptists throughout Europe. The Hutterites and Mennonites are their survivors who have managed to hold out to the present day.

The prevailing factor determining the religion of a state almost invariably was the decision of its prince. If he favored a break with Rome, the Reformation triumphed; if he opposed a break, the Reformation was doomed. Very substantial benefits awaited the prince who opted in favor of Protestantism. His political power increased for he became the head of his national church rather than having to accept the ecclesiastical suzerainty of the international papacy. His economic position also improved because he could confiscate Church lands and movable wealth and also check the flow of revenue to Rome. Despite these advantages of turning against the pope, as many princes remained loyal as chose to break away. One reason was the threat of attack by the imperial forces of Charles V supported by the pope. Also many princes found they could extract as many political and economic concessions from the papacy by remaining Catholic as they were likely to obtain as Protestant princes—hence the hodge-podge religious map of Europe that evolved after Luther's death.

This religious map eventually showed almost half the German states Lutheran, along with the Baltic lands of the Teutonic order and the Scandinavian kingdoms of Denmark-Norway and Sweden-Finland. In England, Henry VIII was a good Catholic in doctrinal matters and enjoyed as much control over the Catholic clergy as did the French king across the Channel. Yet Henry eventually established the independent Church of England (1534) because he was determined to divorce his wife, Catherine of Aragon. The pope could not oblige him because Catherine was the aunt of Emperor Charles V, whose army had sacked Rome a few years earlier. So Henry now became the head of the new Anglican church, and to ensure the support of his gentry, he gave them the expropriated monastery lands. But as long as he was alive, the new church remained staunchly Catholic in doctrine and ritual, the only innovation being the translation of the Bible into English. Henry's successors introduced changes in accord with their individual inclinations—Edward VI (1547–1553) moving far toward Protestantism, Mary (1553–1558) reverting to Catholicism, and Elizabeth (1558–1603) settling on a moderate Protestantism.

In the Netherlands (present-day Holland and Belgium), a combination of religious and political issues led to protracted war. The majority of the population in the northern Dutch provinces had become Calvinistic, which caused friction with the devout Catholic sovereign, Philip II of Spain. Political differences also were involved, the Netherlands challenging Philip's interference in what they considered to be their domestic affairs, and resenting also his heavy taxes and commercial restrictions. In 1566 Dutch resistance flared into what became the first modern revolution for national independence. The revolution in turn became an international war when Queen Elizabeth of England went to the aid of the Dutch rebels. Philip responded by sending his Invincible Armada of 132 ships northward in 1588. But the more maneuverable English ships forced the armada northward around Scotland and southward back to Spain—a defeated and battered remnant of the original expedition. The war continued its bloody course until a compromise settlement in 1609 recognized the independence of the northern provinces as the Dutch Republic, whereas the southern Belgian provinces remained under Spanish rule.

Meanwhile Calvinism had been spreading in France, where its adherents were known as Huguenots. The dynasty was not tempted to

The Saint Bartholemew's Day Massacre, as depicted by the contemporary Protestant painter François Dubois. In this notorious event, 3,000 Protestants were slaughtered in Paris and an estimated 20,000 others died throughout France. The massacre transformed the religious struggle in France from a contest for political power into a war for survival between Protestants and Catholics.

join its Protestant subjects because Francis I had obtained, by the Concordat of Bologna (1516), almost complete control over the Church offices and revenues in his realm. His successor, Henry II (1547–1559), severely persecuted the Huguenots. Mere ownership of a Bible was enough to condemn a subject as a heretic. Henry's death gave the Huguenots an opportunity, as neither the Queen Mother, Catherine de Medici nor her weak sons enjoyed the popular support that Elizabeth did in England. Despite Catherine's efforts for a compromise, the country was polarized between the growing, dynamic Huguenots and the large Catholic majority. The ensuing religious war culminated in the St. Bartholomew's Day Massacre (August 24, 1572), when thousands of Huguenots were massacred throughout the country. Even this slaughter did not subdue the new faith, the struggle dragging on with the Huguenots receiving help from Protestant groups in England, Holland, and Germany, whereas the Catholics received men and money from King Philip of Spain. Peace was not restored until 1598, when Henry IV issued the Edict of Nantes guaranteeing freedom of conscience to the Huguenots. By granting legal recognition and status to two religions in the same state, this settlement represented a turning point in European religious history comparable to the Augsburg Treaty that allowed a prince to choose between two religions.

VI. CATHOLIC REFORMATION

The Catholic Reformation formerly was known as the Counter-Reformation, but historians now recognize it as being more than simply an anti-Protestant movement. Its roots go back to pre-Luther times, so that the Catholic Reformation was a religious reform movement similar to the Protestant Reformation. In the late fifteenth and early sixteenth centuries, Catholic leaders in various countries had sought to correct abuses and regenerate spiritual values. In the process they organized new religious orders, such as the Capuchins, to revive Catholic piety and promote social service. But these early reformers, who tended to be contemplative and aristocratic, failed to arouse the masses or to win support in high Church circles in Rome. The Catholic

Reformation did not become a dynamic and effective movement until the seriousness of Luther's challenge in Germany became clear. The reformers within the Church had hesitated to launch a counter movement against the Protestants for fear of irrevocably splitting Western Christendom. And the popes for long ignored Luther, viewing him as another of the long line of critics and heretics who in the past had always been suppressed or won back to the fold. Not until Pope Paul III (1534–1549) and his three successors who presided in Rome until the end of the sixteenth century did the papacy appreciate the significance of Protestantism and take appropriate steps.

The two measures of Paul III that proved the most significant in shaping the course and character of the Catholic Reformation were his summoning of the Council of Trent, which met intermittently from 1545 to 1563, and his approval of the founding of the Jesuit order, the Society of Jesus, in 1540. The main achievements of the Council of Trent were the reaffirmation of traditional Catholic doctrine in firmly anti-Protestant terms and the adoption of practical measures to eliminate abuses and restore Church discipline. These measures included a ban on the sale of indulgences, the prohibition of any bishop from holding more than one benefice, the stipulation that every diocese should establish a seminary to train priests, and the publication of an *Index* of books that Catholics would be forbidden to read.

The Jesuit order was the creation of the Spanish Basque nobleman Ignatius Loyola (1491–1556). While convalescing from a serious war wound he read various religious tracts that induced a profound spiritual crisis. He resolved to turn his back on his past life of philandering and brawling and to devote himself to serving the Lord. With a group of like-minded young men he organized the Society of Jesus along military lines. Its members did not lead the contemplative lives of earlier Catholic reformers. Rather, they viewed themselves as soldiers of Christ, and they strictly followed Loyola's first rule in his Spiritual Exercises, requiring unquestioning obedience to the "Hierarchical Church."

It was the discipline and militancy of these Jesuits that ensured implementation of the reforms of the Council of Trent. Many members served as agents of the Inquisition, which had been founded in 1542 to root out heresy wherever it was discovered. Others established schools that trained a new generation of priests and laymen with the theological certainty and confidence that had made the Protestant heretics so formidable. Jesuit schoolmen and diplomats were largely responsible for the stamping out of Protestantism in countries such as Austria, Bavaria, and Poland, where it had gained many converts. In addition to combating Christian heretics in Europe, the Jesuits extended their operations all over the world to spread the gospel among the heathen in Asia, Africa, and the Americas. The nature and extent of their activities are indicated by the careers of such men as St. Francis Xavier in Japan, Matteo Ricci in China, Robert de Nobili in India, and Father Jacques Marquette in America.

VII. REFORMATION LEGACY

The legacy of the Reformation is ambiguous. It engendered doctrinal dissension and intolerance, which culminated in a succession of bloody religious wars. But the resulting fragmentation of Western Christendom compelled the contending sects to accept the fact that the hegemony of any universal church was not feasible—hence the gradual acceptance and implementation of religious toleration, a process so slow and contested that it is not yet fully complete. The Reformation was equally ambiguous concerning the status of the individual. Luther championed individual interpretation of the Scriptures, but when this led to the radicalism of the Anabaptists and to peasant revolts, he called on the civil authorities to destroy the "murdering, thieving hordes." Yet the emphasis on the reading of the Bible did lead to greater literacy, which opened doors to books and ideas other than religious.

The Reformation was ambiguous also in its effect on the status of women. In certain respects the Reformation enabled women to move forward. Protestant leaders rejected the medieval Catholic belief in the moral superiority of celibacy. Instead they considered married life desirable for three reasons: procreation of children, sexual satisfaction, and mutual help and comfort between partners. This attitude toward marriage and family encouraged the new idea of a single standard of morality for men and women, and also the equally novel idea of the right of a prospective bride or groom to veto a proposed marriage. Of course the transition from the old to the new was slow and erratic. Protestant theologians railed against adultery by men as well as women, but practice lagged far and long behind theory. Also young men were considered to be foolish "poor greenheads" if they did not select a wife who was not only compatible but "fit," a concept that encompassed the practical considerations usually emphasized by parents.

The principal Protestant leaders never considered or undertook a systematic reappraisal of the status of women. They stressed mutual love and respect between husband and wife, but they also took for granted the husband's primacy in the family. Luther made this quite clear: "Men have broad and large chests, and small narrow hips, and more understanding than the women, who have but small and narrow breasts, and broad hips, to the end they should remain at home, sit still, keep house, and bear and bring up children."[2]

Very different from mainline Protestantism were the radical sects such as the Lollards, Anabaptists, and Levellers. They favored free divorce and allowed women to participate in church government and to preach, and some even championed sexual freedom for both women and men. These sectarians were ahead of their time, for not only political but also technological reasons. The English Leveller leader, Gerrard Winstanley, conceded that sexual freedom outside the family left the mother and children vulnerable, "for the man will be gone and leave them, and regard them no more than other women . . . after he hath had his pleasure. Therefore you women beware. . . . By seeking their own freedom they embondage others."[3] Winstanley was acknowledging the fact that before the advent of effective birth control, sexual freedom amounted to freedom only for men.

Finally, as far as the immediate legacy of the Reformation was concerned, it shattered the universal medieval Church into a large number of local territorial churches—some national, some princely, some provincial, and some confined to a single city. The common feature of all these local churches was their control by secular rulers. Regardless of whether the church remained Catholic in doctrine or adhered to one of the Protestant faiths, it was the secular authority that controlled ecclesiastical appointments and church finances. The immediate and decisive legacy of the Reformation was the transfer of power from church to state. In this sense, the Reformation represents a stage in the evolution of the modern nation-state—the subject of the following chapter.

SUGGESTED READINGS

Standard general histories of this period are W. K. Ferguson, *Europe in Transition: 1300–1500* (Houghton Mifflin, 1962); E. Breisach, *Renaissance Europe 1300–1517* (Macmillan, 1973); and for a global perspective: J. L. Abu-Lughod, *Before European Hegemony: The World System A.D. 1250–1350* (Oxford University, 1989). E. Troeltsch, *Protestantism and Progress: A Historical Study of the Relation of Protestantism to the Modern World* (Beacon Press, 1966); and E. I. Eisentein, *The Printing Press as an Agent of Change: Communications and Cultural Transformations in Early Modern Europe*, 2 vols. (Columbia University, 1979).

The status of European women during these centuries is summarized in S. M. Wyntjes, "Women in the Reformation Era," in R. Bridenthal and C. Koonz, eds., *Becoming Visible: Women in European History* (Houghton Mifflin, 1977), pp. 165–191; and analyzed in detail in the two studies by R. Bainton, *Women of the Reformation in Germany and Italy* and *Women of the Reformation in France and England* (Augsburg Publishing House, 1971 and 1973).

NOTES

1. Cited in manuscript by L. V. Thomas, "Ottoman Awareness of Europe, 1650–1800."
2. Cited by S. M. Wyntjes, "Women in the Reformation Era," in R. Bridenthal and C. Koonz, eds., *Becoming Visible: Women in European History* (Houghton Mifflin, 1977), p. 174.
3. Cited by C. Hill, *The World Turned Upside Down* (Viking, 1972), p. 257.

CHAPTER
21

Expanding Civilization of the West: Economic Growth and State Building

> . . . the chief glory of the later Middle Ages was not its cathedrals or its epics or its scholasticism: it was the building for the first time in history of a complex civilization which rested not on the backs of sweating slaves or coolies but primarily on non-human power.
>
> *Lynn White, Jr.*

> Therefore it is necessary for a prince, who wishes to maintain himself, to learn how not to be good, and to use this knowledge and not use it, according to the necessity of the case.
>
> *Niccolo Machiavelli*

The Renaissance and Reformation, as we saw in the preceding chapter, contributed to the modernizing of western European civilization. During these times literacy increased and there was much intellectual ferment. There was a mass awakening and a degree of participation unequaled in other regions of Eurasia. A more direct contribution to the modernizing process was made by the concurrent economic expansion and state building. These provided Europe with the resources and dynamism necessary for the fateful expansion overseas. This expansion, which has molded world history to the present day, did not occur simply because Columbus sailed westward and stumbled on the new world. The Vikings also had stumbled on North America in the eleventh century and for about a hundred years had unsuccessfully tried to maintain settlements there. By contrast, Columbus was followed by people from all countries of Europe in a massive and overwhelming penetration of both North and South America. The difference in the reaction between the eleventh and fifteenth centuries suggests that certain developments had occurred in the intervening half-millennium that made Europe able and anxious to expand overseas. These developments included economic expansion and state building.

I. EXPANDING ECONOMY

Europe's economy did not grow uninterrupted during the medieval period. There was a steady rise from 900 to 1300, but then came the fourteenth-century slump, brought on by a combination of factors: a series of crop failures and famines, especially during 1315 and 1316; the Black Death, which carried off between one-third and two-thirds of the urban populations when it first struck in 1348 and 1349 and which recurred periodically thereafter for generations; and the Hundred Years' War between England and France and other conflicts in Germany and Italy. Shortly after 1400, however, a revival set in, and the trend from then on was generally upward.

Apart from the fourteenth-century decline, then, western Europe had fairly steady economic growth after the early medieval centuries. One reason for the advance was the cessation of invasions after 1000, with the ending of the Magyar and Viking attacks. Freedom from invasion was most significant, for it saved western Europe from the devastation suffered in eastern Europe from the series of onslaughts that lasted until the defeat of the Turks at the end of the seventeenth century. This also explains in part the marked increase of population in central and western Europe between the tenth and fourteenth centuries. Population in those regions grew about 50 percent, a rate of increase that seems insignificant today but that was unmatched at the time in any equivalent world area. The demographic spurt stimulated improvements in agriculture to support the growth of population, and the increased food supply in turn made possible further population increase.

Europe's rising agricultural output was obtained in two ways. One was through intensive development—through improved methods of cultivation. One outstanding improvement was the gradual adoption from the eighth century onward of the three-field system of farming. The three-field system raised productivity substantially, since only a third of the land was allowed to lie fallow instead of half. More effective use of horsepower also helped increase agricultural output. In antiquity the horse had been of little use on the farm because the yoke then

The three-field system of farming improved efficiency and increased production from the eighth century onward.

used strangled the horse if it pulled too hard. Moreover, without nailed shoes the horse often injured its hoofs and became useless. By the tenth century, however, Europe had developed the horse collar, which rests on the horse's shoulders and does not choke the neck. In addition, the horseshoe was invented and also the tandem harness, which allows more than one pair of horses to pull a load. The net result was that the horse, faster and more efficient compared to the ox, became an essential source of power in farming operations.

Europe's agricultural output was also raised through extensive development. Areas were opened up that had not been farmed before. It is startling but true that in the twelfth century only about half the land of France, a third of the land of Germany, and a fifth of the land of England were under cultivation. The rest was forest, swamp, waste. All around the edges of the small, tilled regions were larger, untilled areas open for settlement. Into these vacant spaces the European peasants streamed, preparing the way for the plow and hoe by clearing forests, burning brushwood, and draining swamps. The peasants not only cultivated the unused lands in their midst but also migrated eastward into the vast underpopulated areas of eastern and southern Europe. Just as the United States had its westward movement to the Pacific Ocean, so Europe had its eastward movement to the Russian border (see map of Expansionism of the Medieval West, p. 240.)

The growth of population and of agriculture stimulated a corresponding growth of commerce and cities. From new farm lands, surplus food was shipped back to more densely populated western areas, which in return provided the tools and the manufactured goods needed by frontier regions. Thus commerce flourished and towns grew up, especially along the Baltic coast. This economic growth is very important. It represents the beginning of the rise of northwestern Europe, a trend that later helped the British and the Dutch to overshadow the Spaniards and the Portuguese throughout the world.

Commerce was growing not only within Europe but also between Europe and the outside world. Here, again, growth began when the Viking raids stopped, ending the terror that had dominated European coasts from the Arctic to Sicily in the ninth and tenth centuries. Another impetus from the eleventh century onward was provided by the Crusades. The tens of thousands of Europeans who had participated in the expeditions returned with an appetite for the strange and luxurious commodities they had seen and enjoyed abroad. Also, the Crusades enabled the Europeans to snatch the Mediterranean from the Moslems and to make it a great trade route between East and West, as it had been in ancient times. A third reason for the growth of international trade was the establishment in the thirteenth century of the Mongol Empire, which imposed unity on most of the vast Eurasian landmass. European traders, especially the Ital-

ians, took advantage of the peace, security, and well-serviced routes, and traded almost directly with the Orient.

The extension and intensification of commercial relations had important repercussions. Europe's economy became much more geared to international trade than did the economies of the more self-sufficient empires of the East. Both the consumer and the producer in Europe became accustomed to, and dependent on, foreign commodities and foreign markets. As populations increased, the scale of operations also increased. The demographic pressure, together with the spur of competition between nations and city-states, drove merchants to seek new sources, new routes, new markets. Their competitive attitude was very different from that of the contemporary Chinese, who voyaged several thousand miles for completely noneconomic reasons (see Section V, this chapter). Since the Chinese were quite uninterested in trade, they brought back to their self-contained homeland such curiosities as giraffes for the pleasure of their emperor. For obvious geographic reasons, Europe was far from self-contained. It had urgent need for spices and other foreign products, which, together with the burgeoning economic activity and vitality, eventually put European ships on every ocean and European merchants in every port.

II. DEVELOPMENT OF TECHNOLOGY

While its economy expanded, Europe's technology also developed and provided the materials and techniques necessary for expansion. It would have been physically impossible for Europeans to reach India or the Americas without adequate ships and navigational instruments. The basis for their technological success in these areas is the steady, unspectacular, but immensely significant progress in improving tools and techniques that was made during the medieval period.

As Lynn White, Jr., has observed, the "chief glory of the later Middle Ages" was its unprecedented development of "non-human power." Examples were the water mills and windmills that were developed and used for grinding cereal, cutting wood, and draining swamps and

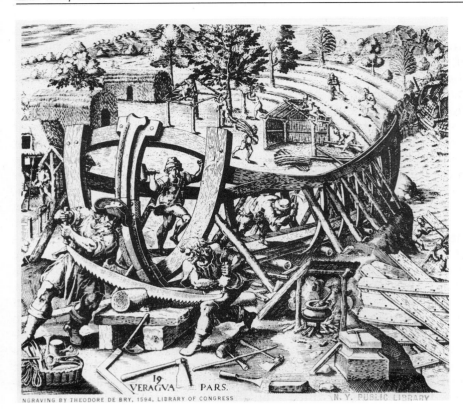

Shipbuilding in 1500—an example of the technological advances that increased European expansion.

mines. Other useful inventions included the carpenter's plane, the crank, the wheelbarrow, the spinning wheel, and the canal lock. Indeed, the Greeks and the Romans, despite their lofty achievements in philosophy and art, did less in a thousand years to relieve human toil through machine power than the medieval Europeans did in a few centuries.

An interesting illustration of the technological progress made by the western Europeans during the medieval period is found in a letter written in 1444 by a Greek scholar, Cardinal Bessarion. Bessarion, who had lived many years in Rome, was impressed by the advanced state of handicrafts in Italy. So he wrote to Constantine Paleologos, then ruler of the autonomous Byzantine province of Morea, and suggested that "four or eight young men" should be sent surreptitiously to Italy to learn Italian craft skills. They should also learn Italian "so as to be conversant with what is said." Bessarion was particularly impressed by the waterdriven sawmills that eliminated hand labor. He wrote about "wood cut by automatic saws, millwheels moved as

quickly and as neatly as can be." He referred to water-driven bellows when he mentioned that "in the smelting and separation of metals they have leather bellows which are distended and relaxed untouched by any hand, and separate the metal from the useless and earthy matter that may be present." Bessarion also reported that in Italy "one may easily acquire knowledge of the making of iron, which is so useful and necessary to Man." The significance of this testimony is obvious. The technological advances made by medieval western Europe had been of such magnitude that now, for the first time, an Easterner was recommending that pupils should be sent to the West to learn the "practical arts."[1]

As far as the overseas expansion of Europe was concerned, the most significant technological advances were those in shipbuilding, in the instruments and techniques of navigation, and in naval armaments. Hand in hand with these advances went advances in the art of navigation. The most important contributions in this field came from the Mediterranean. The Chinese appear to have possessed a magnetic compass, but it is not certain that the Europeans acquired it from them or from Arab intermediaries. In any case, the compass was the most useful single instrument for navigators, but it was supplemented by several others. The astrolabe, a graduated brass circle for estimating the altitude of heavenly bodies, was known before 800 but was first used in Western navigation by the Portuguese about 1485. It was an expensive instrument and was soon replaced by the simpler and cheaper quadrant. The determination of longitude presented more of a problem. A rough estimate could be gained by means of an hourglass, but precise reckoning had to await Galileo's discovery of the principles of the pendulum in the seventeenth century. Navigators were also aided by compilations of nautical information and by maps. The portolani of the Mediterranean seamen were the first true maps, furnished with accurate compass bearings and explicit details concerning coastlines and harbors.

When the Europeans reached the highly developed and militarily powerful countries of south and east Asia, their one decisive advantage was the superiority of their naval armament. In the first two decades of the sixteenth century the metallurgists of Flanders and Germany, and later of England, developed techniques for casting guns that were light enough to mount on ships and yet had great firing power. These new pieces, five to twelve feet long, could shoot round stones—and later cast-iron balls—that weighed five to sixty pounds and could damage a hull at a range of 300 yards. Naval tactics now shifted from boarding to broadside gunfire, and warships were redesigned so that soon they were able to carry an average of forty guns.

These developments gave the Europeans a decisive advantage and enabled them to seize and retain control of the oceans of the world. Eastern rulers hastened to arm their own ships, but their vessels were neither designed nor built for mounting guns. Before they could redesign their vessels, European naval armaments developed so rapidly that the designs of the Easterners were already obsolete. Hence the gap increased rather than narrowed, and the Westerners remained the unchallenged masters of the

Skilled workers were an integral component of the commerce of medieval towns. This scene shows the manufacture of cannons in a foundry in Florence.

seas until the epochal victory of the Japanese over the Russians at Tsushima in 1905.

As important as the European advances in marine technology was their discovery of the world wind systems. Thanks to Portuguese mariners, Columbus knew he could sail west with the trade winds, confident that further north he would find westerlies to bring him back home. Likewise, Vasco da Gama learned the basic pattern of Indian Ocean monsoons from local pilots. By 1522, when Magellan's ships returned to Spain after the first European voyage around the world, the wind system of the Pacific as well as of the Atlantic was known to the Europeans. Now they could sail all oceans with confidence.

Having made these advances in shipbuilding and in knowledge of world wind systems, the Europeans were able to exploit their advantages because of their favorable geographic location for crossing the Atlantic and reaching the treasures of the New World. Of course, West Africa also juts out into the Atlantic, as does the Iberian peninsula. But West African commerce for centuries had been directed northward across the Sahara to the Mediterranean. In East Africa the port of Sofala was engaged in overseas trade, but that trade naturally was conducted eastward across the adjacent Indian Ocean. Sofala is 3,000 miles farther away from the Americas than the Canary Islands (Columbus's jumping-off point), and China was still much more distant. So geographic location was an important factor, along with several others, in determining that Columbus should have been a European rather than an African or Asian.

III. EMERGENCE OF CAPITALISM

Because Columbus for various reasons turned out to be a European, it was Europe that experienced a powerful economic stimulus from the gold and silver that poured in from the Americas. The flow was so large that it tripled Europe's silver stock during the sixteenth century and increased the gold stock by 20 percent. In addition to this bullion windfall from the New World, Europe was further enriched by numerous overseas enterprises, so that profits poured in from the slave trade, from the spice trade, from exports to the colonies and imports from the colonies, and even from piracy. This external economic boost, combined with the internal commercial revival and technological progress noted above, led to greatly increased use of money in Europe's economy.

This monetarization undermined the feudal order that had developed after the fall of Rome. The bonds of serfdom could not be preserved indefinitely when it became known that freedom could be gained by flight to the growing towns or to the frontier lands opening eastward. The lords had to modify their demands or risk the loss of their labor supply. Serfs in western Europe increasingly paid for their land with money rather than labor, so that feudal lords became landlords and serfs became free peasants. The weakening of serfdom was a prerequisite to the expansion of Europe. It created a more fluid society that could accumulate the capital; provide the organization; and free the population needed for the work of exploration, conquest, and settlement. It is not accidental that among the European nations the degree of success in overseas enterprise was in direct ratio to the degree of liberation from the bonds of feudalism.

Likewise, use of money undermined the feudal craft and merchant guilds in the towns. The guilds, with their strict regulation of workmanship and of pricing and trading practices, were geared not to making profit but to preserving a traditional way of life. Guild members were committed to the concept of a "just price," and profiteering at the expense of a neighbor was considered unethical and definitely un-Christian. But these concepts and practices broke down with the appearance of entrepreneurs. They avoided the guilds by purchasing raw material and taking it to underemployed artisans in the countryside, who labored on a piece-work basis. The rationale of this "putting-out" system was profit rather than "just price." The entrepreneurs paid as little as possible for the material and labor, and they sold the finished product as dearly as possible to secure the maximum return on their capital investment.

Europe's economy was changed not only by the growing use of money but also by the minting of standardized coins that were acceptable everywhere and by the development of

Cosimo dé Medici (1389–1464), Florentine banker and statesman, in his lifetime the city's wealthiest man and most successful politician. This portrait is by Pontormo.

banks and of credit instruments. Florence led the way in 1252 with the gold florin, and other cities and states soon followed. Simple bills of exchange also appeared in Italy as early as the twelfth century. Gradually, mighty banking families appeared, first in Italy and later in northern Europe.

What was happening to Europe, then, was a historic shift to a fundamentally different type of economic system, the type known today as capitalism. Capitalism has been defined as "... [a] system in which the desire for profits is the driving motive and in which large accumulations of capital are employed to make profits by various elaborate and often indirect methods."[2]

The emergence of capitalism was epoch making. It affected not merely the economy but all aspects of life. Whereas in the early Middle Ages money had been peripheral and little used, by the late Middle Ages it provided energy that was responsible for Europe's future meteoric rise. No earlier societies or economic systems had been based on the notion of growth. Their aim had been only to maintain the material well-being of the past rather than to enhance it. But henceforth, with capitalism, the precise opposite was the case. Profits now were plowed back to increase the quantity of capital available for production. "Capitalizing" of profits, in the sense that surplus was converted into more capital, is the rationale behind the term *capitalism*. The new "capitalists" were not content with making a living but were driven by the urge to enlarge their assets. They did not cease their efforts when their needs for consumption were satisfied. The new "capitalist spirit" is epitomized by the statement of Jacob Fugger, the wealthiest banker of the sixteenth century, who said, "Let me earn as long as I am able."

In order to "earn," Fugger and his fellow bankers needed to be free to charge interest on money they loaned. But the medieval Church for long had denounced interest as constituting usury, a mortal sin and "a vice most odious and detestable in the sight of God." By 1548, however, some Church members were pleading for the acceptance of "moderate and acceptable usury." This modification soon gave way to the cynical attitude: "He who takes usury goes to hell; he who does not goes to the poorhouse." Given the choice of hell in afterlife, or poorhouse in the present, it is not surprising that usury won out. So it was the affluent European bankers who organized the numerous joint stock companies that won control of commerce on all oceans, garnering the ensuing profits.

These joint stock companies were the counterpart in early modern times of the multinational corporations of today. These new organizations were most effective instruments for economic mobilization and penetration. Anyone who wished to speculate with a little money could do so without risking one's whole future. The individual risked only the amount invested in company shares, and that person could not be held further liable for whatever losses the company might incur. Furthermore, there was no need for the individual investors to know or trust each other or to concern themselves with the specific conditions of the market and the policies of the company. These details of management were entrusted to directors selected for their responsibility and experience, and these directors in turn could choose dependable individuals to manage company affairs in the field. This arrangement made it attractive for all sorts of scattered individuals—a London wool merchant, a Paris storekeeper, a Harlem herring fisher, an Antwerp banker, or a Yorkshire landowner—to invest their savings in individual ventures. In this way it was possible to mobilize European capital easily and simply, and vast amounts were invested in various overseas undertakings. No Eastern merchants, limited to their own resources or those of their partners, and choosing their managers from their family

or circle of acquaintances, could hope to compete with the powerful and impersonal joint stock company. It became the instrument for the operation of European capitalism on a global scale. World commerce fell under the control of the various East India and Levant companies, the Muscovy Company, and the still-operating Hudson's Bay Company.

Thus we can see why an American historian has concluded that the most important figures in Europe's overseas expansion were not Columbus and da Gama and Magellan. Rather, they were the new entrepreneurs with capital. They were the merchants who stayed in the home ports but who were "responsible for the foundation of many of the colonies . . . who kept the colonies supplied . . . who opened new markets, sought new lands, and enriched all of Europe. . . ."[3]

The new capitalist economic system not only dominated the world economy in early modern times but it also continues to do so to the present day. The basic reason is to be found in its ruling principle: profit or perish. To avoid perishing, capitalist entrepreneurs through the centuries have maximized profit in two ways: by reducing the wages they pay their workers or by increasing their workers' productivity through improved technology. The first strategy has been much used but it can be carried only so far because workers obviously have to be paid a certain minimum amount if they are to be kept alive, healthy, and productive. The second strategy—improving technology—can be continued indefinitely. In fact, this is precisely what happened, as indicated by the constantly accelerating pace of technological innovation, strikingly evident in today's high technology. This built-in technological dynamism explains why Europe's capitalist entrepreneurs in early modern times won control of the global economy with their unceasing technological innovations and their joint stock companies, and also why today's capitalists continue to control the world economy with their biotechnology, their computers, and their multinational corporations. Just as Europe's joint stock companies a few centuries ago planted colonies in the Americas and penetrated irresistibly the markets of the Middle East and the Far East, so today the same inherent dynamism drives multinational corporations to move factories from continent to continent, to erect golden arches in scores of countries, and even to establish a 500-seat Kentucky Fried Chicken in Beijing's historic Tienanmen Square with a view of the Gate of Heavenly Peace and of Mao Tse-tung's mausoleum. The new enterprise retains its familiar slogan in Chinese—*Haodao shun shouzhi* ("So good you suck your fingers").

IV. RISE OF THE NEW MONARCHS

The emergence of capitalists in Europe was paralleled by the concurrent emergence of the "New Monarchs" who were building cohesive political structures. By the end of the fifteenth century, the trend toward national monarchies was apparent in the powerful political structures presided over by Ferdinand and Isabella in Spain (1479–1516), by Henry VIII in England (1509–-1547), and by Francis I in France (1515–1547). One reason for the success of these rulers was the revolution in military technology that came with the advent of artillery. Feudal lords no longer could defy royal authority from behind their castle walls. Only national monarchs possessed the financial resources and administrative organization necessary to purchase the guns, powder, and shot and to provide the required logistical support.

Another source of power for the new monarchs was their informal alliance with the growing merchant class. From this class the monarchs obtained essential financial support and also competent and subservient officials to staff the growing state bureaucracies. In return, the consolidation of royal power aided the burghers by ending the incessant feudal wars and doing away with the crazyquilt pattern of local feudal authorities, in which each had had its own customs, laws, weights, and currencies. As late as the end of the fourteenth century there were thirty-five toll stations on the Elbe, over sixty on the Rhine, and so many on the Seine that the cost of shipping grain 200 miles down the river was half its selling price. The elimination of such domestic barriers obviously was a great boon to entrepreneurs. So was the patronage of

the increasingly elaborate royal courts, which supported craftspeople and sometimes whole industries, as in the case of Gobelin tapestry and Sévres porcelain in France.

The new monarchs naturally had their own defenders and rationalizers, as do all political establishments. The best known of these was Niccolo Machiavelli (1459–1527). A product of the ruthless struggle for survival among the competing city-states of Renaissance Italy, Machiavelli viewed politics as a struggle for power in which the end justifies the means. In his book, *The Prince*, he set forth guidelines for the ruler who aspired to unite the fragmented Italian peninsula and to rid it of the French and Spanish invaders. With cool and relentless realism he rejected moral restraints and spelled out the difference between politics and religion or philosophy.

Niccolo Machiavelli

National monarchs pursuing strategies based on the precepts of *The Prince* were bound to clash with the two universal institutions of Europe, the papacy and the empire. The conflict was sharpened by the sensational rise of the Spanish dynasty through marriage ties. Ferdinand and Isabella married their daughter Joanna to Philip of Hapsburg. Charles, the offspring of this union, inherited the united Spanish kingdom together with the Spanish possessions in the New World and in Italy (Sardinia, Sicily, Naples). He also held the hereditary Hapsburg lands in central Europe (the duchies of Austria, Styria, Carinthia, Carniola, and the county of Tirol). In addition, Charles's grandmother, Mary of Burgundy, left him Burgundian territories, Franche-Comté, Luxembourg, and the wealthy Netherlands. And to crown this imposing edifice, Charles was elected in 1519 Holy Roman Emperor in spite of the opposition of the French and English monarchs, Francis I and Henry VIII, respectively. Thus Charles V, at the age of nineteen, became the ruler of a larger territory than had been collected under one monarch since the breakup of Charlemagne's empire seven centuries earlier.

For a time it appeared that western Europe would be united once more in a vast international organization. But the other European dynasties, and especially the Valois of France, were determined to prevent Hapsburg hegemony. The result was the long series of wars, partly religious, partly dynastic. This violence was followed by the even more disastrous Thirty Years' War (1618–1648) — a struggle between the Bourbon and Hapsburg dynasties for control of the continent of Europe. The principal victims of the three decades of fighting were the civilians who suffered at the hands of undisciplined mercenaries, especially when their pay was not forthcoming, as often happened. About a third of the population of Germany and Bohemia perished, and wholesale devastation ensued in the cities and the countryside.

The territorial provisions of the Treaty of Westphalia (1648) did not last, but their overall significance is clear. Henceforth the individual sovereign state was recognized as the basic unit in European politics, and relations between the states were conducted according to generally accepted tenets of diplomatic practice. Thus began the international anarchy of a world composed of states with unlimited sovereignty—a world that has persisted from the Westphalia conference to the present day.

V. WESTERN EUROPE ON THE EVE OF EXPANSION

Modern world history had been dominated by European expansion overseas and then by the disintegration of European empires during the twentieth century. The fateful expansion of Europe was largely the product of the historical forces analyzed in this chapter: the technological progress, the population increase, the resulting growth in economic productivity and resources, the emergence of dynamic capitalism, and the rise of the new monarchs. It was the European monarchs who issued charters to joint stock companies and backed them up, if necessary, with their royal navies. The Spanish and Portuguese courts, for example, provided the backing necessary for the achievements of Columbus and da Gama.

The significance of the unique western European complex of interests, institutions, and traditions is pointed up by the remarkable history of the famous maritime expeditions sent out from China during the Ming period (see map of Early Fifteenth-Century Chinese and Portuguese Voyages, p. 329). Between 1405 and 1433, seven ventures were made under the superintendency of the chief court eunuch, a certain Cheng Ho. The expeditions were startling in their magnitude and in their achievements. The first, comprised of sixty-two ships, carried 28,000 men. The average ship had a beam of 150 feet and a length of 370 feet, but the largest were 180 feet wide and 444 feet long. They were veritable floating palaces compared to Columbus's little flagship, the *Santa Maria*, which was 120 feet long and 25 feet wide. And the Santa Maria was twice as large as Columbus's two other ships, the Pinta and the Niña. The Chinese expeditions were impressive in performance as well as in size. They sailed around Southeast Asia to India; some went on to Aden and the head of the Persian Gulf; and individual ships entered ports on the east coast of Africa. During this time, it should be recalled, the Portuguese were only

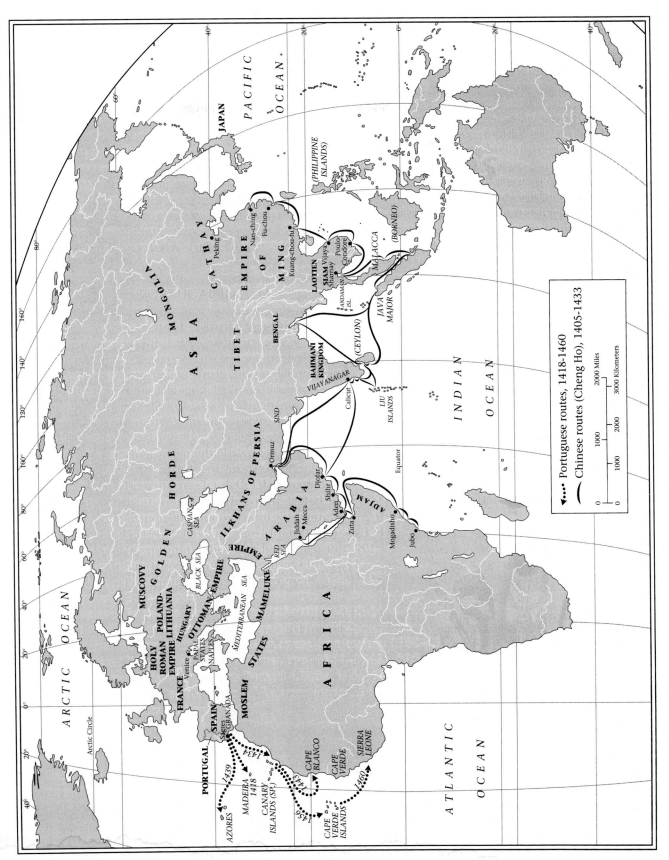

Early Fifteenth-Century Chinese and Portuguese Voyages

329

beginning to feel their way down the coast of Africa, and they did not reach Cape Verde until 1445.

Yet these remarkable Chinese expeditions were suddenly halted by imperial order in 1433. Why they were halted remains as much a mystery as why they were started in the first place. But the significant point here is that an order to stop would have been utterly inconceivable in Europe. There was no European counterpart to the Chinese emperor, who could and did issue orders binding on his entire realm. Instead, there were rival national monarchies that were competing in overseas ventures, and no imperial authority existed to prevent them from doing so. The political power and social prestige of the merchants in northwestern Europe, in contrast to the merchants' inferior position in China, made it quite impossible to enforce any decree banning overseas enterprise. Furthermore, Europe had a tradition of trade with the outside world. Its genuine need and strong demand for foreign products was altogether lacking in China.

In short, there was an impelling dynamism in Europe—a lust and an opportunity for profit. The uniqueness of western Europe is reflected in contemporary European and Chinese writings. "Coming into contact with barbarian peoples," wrote Chang Hsieh in 1618, "you have nothing more to fear than touching the left horn of a snail. The only things one should really be anxious about are the means to mastery of the waves of the seas—and, worst of all dangers, the minds of those avid for profit and greedy of gain."[4] By contrast, the Portuguese Captain João Ribeiro boasted in 1685, "From the Cape of Good Hope onwards we were unwilling to leave anything outside of our control; we were anxious to lay hands on everything in that huge stretch of over 5,000 leagues from Sofala to Japan . . . there was not a corner which we did not occupy or desire to have subject to ourselves."[5]

During the Middle Ages, a combination of developments isolated and fenced in the western Europeans, and so further stimulated their natural tendency to look overseas. The loss of the Crusaders' outposts in the Levant, the breakup of the Mongol Empire, and the expansion of the Ottoman Turks into central Europe up to the walls of Vienna served to restrict the Europeans. European merchants could no longer penetrate into central Asia, because chaos reigned where once the Mongols had enforced order. The Black Sea also became closed to Christian merchants when the Turks transformed it into a Moslem preserve. The all-important spice trade was little affected. Italian merchants continued to meet Arab traders in various ports in the Levant to pick up the commodities demanded by the European public. But though this arrangement was satisfactory for the Italians and Arabs, who reaped the golden profits of the middleman, other Europeans were not so happy. They sought earnestly for some means to reach the Orient directly, in order to share the prize. This explains why there were numerous plans in late medieval times for breaking through or getting around the Moslem barrier that confined Europeans to the Mediterranean. Europe at this time, as one author has put it, was like a "giant fed through the chinks of a wall."[6] But the giant was growing in strength and in knowledge, and the prison walls were not to contain him for long.

SUGGESTED READINGS

General interpretations of why European society became expansionist are given by E. L. Jones, *The European Miracle* (Cambridge University, 1981); E. R. Wolf, *Europe and the People Without History* (University of California, 1982); M. Beaud, *A History of Capitalism, 1500–1980* (Monthly Review Press, 1983); L. S. Stavrianos, *Global Rift: The Third World Comes of Age* (William Morrow, 1981); J. Baechlev, J. A. Hall, and M. Mann, eds., *Europe and the Rise of Capitalism* (Basil Blackwell, 1987); and the important three-volume study of F. Braudel, *Civilization and Capitalism, 15th–18th Century* (Harper and Row, 1981–84).

The development of Europe's economy in early modern times is analyzed in the first three volumes of the *Cambridge Economic History* (Cambridge University, 1941–1963); B. H. S. van Bath, *The Agrarian History of Western Europe, 500–1850* (Edward Arnold, 1963); F. Braudel, *Capitalism and Material Life, 1400–1800* (Harper & Row, 1973); and H. I. Miskimin, *The Economy of Early Renaissance Europe, 1300–1460* (Prentice Hall, 1969). European technological progress of this period is analyzed in the studies by L. White, Jr., *Medieval Technology and Social Change* (Oxford University, 1962), *and Machina Ex Deo: Essays in the Dynamism of Western Culture* (MIT, 1968); and also in the works of C. M. Cipolla, *Literacy and Development in the West* (Pelican, 1969), and *European Culture and Overseas Expansion* (Pelican, 1970), the latter dealing with guns, sails, and clocks. Provocative interpretations of the economic and technological changes in Europe are presented in the classics by R. H. Tawney, *Religion and the Rise of Capitalism* (Mentor, 1926); M. Weber, *The Protestant Ethic and the Spirit of Capitalism* (Scribner's, 1948); and, more recently, A. O. Hirschman, *The Passions and the Interests: Political Arguments for Capitalism Before Its Triumph* (Princeton University, 1977).

The question of why the West rather than some other region of Eurasia took the lead in overseas expansion is considered by J. Needham, *Science and Civilization in China* (Cambridge University, 1956ff.), especially Vol. 4, Part 3, which deals with Chinese nautical technology, including the Ming voyages. Other works on this subject are by C. G. F. Simkin, *The Traditional Trade of Asia* (Oxford University, 1968); J. R. Levenson, ed., *European Expansion and the Counter-Example of Asia, 1300–1600* (Prentice Hall, 1967); and J. M. Blaut, *The Colonizer's Model of the World* (Guilford Press, 1993). The latter book is unique in challenging the concept of a "European miracle," and emphasizing the role of overseas lands in stimulating Europe to global primacy.

NOTES

1. A. G. Keller, "A Byzantine Admirer of 'Western' Progress: Cardinal Bessarion," *Cambridge Historical Journal*, XI (1955), pp. 343–348.
2. S. B. Clough and C. W. Cole, *Economic History of Europe* (D. C. Heath, 1952), p. 66.
3. T. K. Rabb, "The Expansion of Europe and the Spirit of Capitalism," *Historical Journal*, XVII (1974), p. 676.
4. Cited by J. Needham, *Science and Civilization in China: IV, Civil Engineering and Nautics* (Cambridge University, 1971), p. 533.
5. Ibid., p. 534.
6. R. H. Tawney, *Religion and the Growth of Capitalism* (Murray, 1925), p. 68.

What It Means for Us Today

HISTORY AND FADS

Five centuries ago, Christopher Columbus set foot on San Salvador, a tiny island in the Bahamas. He assumed he had reached Southeast Asia, so he referred to the native islanders as Indians—a name that has stuck ever since. Soon after Columbus died, his assumption was proven wrong when Balboa reached the Pacific Ocean in 1513 and when Magellan's expedition sailed around the world from 1519 to 1522.

The realization that the Americas were a "new world" led to speculation about the origins of the Indians. Either they had originated in the New World, or they had arrived there from somewhere else. The idea of independent origin in the Americas was unthinkable heresy, for that would imply a dual creation—a duplicate Adam and Eve in a transatlantic Garden of Eden—a belief that clashed too much with the teachings of the Old Testament. So it was agreed that the Indians must be the descendants of Adam and Eve. A new question now arose: How did these descendants make their way from the Old World to the New? A great debate has raged over this question, with dozens of theories being advanced during the past four centuries and new ones still popping up in the present day.

Most of the theories are false, based more on faith than on reason. Various fads have gone through popularity cycles, each reflecting the knowledge and prejudices of their times. One of the earliest was the Lost Tribes of Israel hypothesis, for in those days, ancient Hebrew ethnology as described in the Old Testament was almost the only known example of the "primitive" way of life. So the early theorists were convinced that the Indians were the descendants of the Hebrew tribes conquered and carried away from Samaria by the king of Assyria in 721 B.C.E. Some supporters of the Lost Tribes theory believed that the Hebrews reached the New World by crossing the mythical continent of Atlantis, but most preferred a route across Persia and China to the Bering Strait.

In the eighteenth century Europeans were impressed by the achievements of the ancient Mediterranean peoples, and especially the Phoenicians, who were famous for their seafaring skills. The Phoenicians were believed to have rounded Africa's Cape of Good Hope and also to have crossed the Atlantic to the Americas. However, with the advent of nineteenth-century archeological discoveries in Egypt, that country came to be considered the origin of American Indian civilizations. This theory was widely accepted as fact because of the existence of pyramids in Mesoamerica that seemed similar to those of Egypt. Many other fads about the origins of the American Indians have come and gone. Thus our "redskins" have been traced back to Greeks, Trojans, Romans, Etruscans, Scythians, Mongols, Chinese Buddhists, Mandingoes or other Africans, early Irish, Welsh, Norse, Basques, Portuguese, French, Spaniards, and even survivors of the "lost continents" of Mu and Atlantis, which allegedly sank 11,000 years ago beneath the Pacific and Atlantic oceans, respectively.

All of these claims have been disproven, or at least found to be questionable, with a single exception: A late tenth-century Norse settlement in Newfoundland has been scientifically confirmed. One reason why so many believed, and still believe, in so many groundless theories is that they wrongly assume that common customs mean a common origin. On the contrary, one can go to the human relations area files in any major university and ask for an inventory of all the peoples of the world who practice some particular custom—say, preferred-cousin marriage. One will quickly be given dozens of examples from peoples all over the world who could not possibly have borrowed that marriage practice from one common source. But early writers, unfamiliar with modern anthropological science, very naturally assumed historical connection between similar customs in the distant past.

Also, apparently similar institutions or structures have proven on close examination to be quite different. Pyramids have been found in both Egypt and Mesoamerica, but those of Mesoamerica were primarily centers of religious ritual, whereas those of Egypt were vast tombs. Equally important is the fact that recent excavations reveal the gradual evolution of Mesoamerican pyramids over thousands of years. This long development period demolishes the theory that the technique of pyramid building had been transplanted full-blown across the Atlantic. Likewise, in the native California language known as Yuki, the word *ko* means "go," and *kom* means "come," yet no one could conclude from this example that Yuki and English are historically related.

Even if small numbers of ancient Old World seafarers had reached the New World, the claim that their cultures would have instantly dominated New World customs is highly questionable. Those who assume that small groups of Hebrews, Greeks, Romans, Phoenicians, or others could have arrived in the New World and spread their culture among natives over vast areas should consider the experience of eighteen Spaniards (sixteen men and two women) who were shipwrecked on the coast of Yucatan six years before

Cortes arrived. All were sacrificed and ritually eaten, except for two men who were enslaved by local chieftains. One of these survivors went so completely native that he wore the elaborate nose plug and earrings of his adopted tribe and refused to give up his new life to rejoin Cortes. Likewise, the Vikings, who we know did actually land in Newfoundland, were forced to give up their attempt to establish a colony because of the hostility of the local Indians. Thus until the appearance of modern repeating rifles and machine guns, small landing parties were either wiped out or assimilated into the local culture.

These are some of the reasons why a 1968 symposium held in Santa Fe, New Mexico, concluded that "there are to date—excluding the Viking contacts (that is, Newfoundland)—no verified archaeological finds of artifacts from one hemisphere in pre-Columbian context to the other." The symposium likewise agreed that "there is no hard and fast evidence for any pre-Columbian human introduction of any single plant or animal across the ocean from the Old World to the New World or vice-versa. This is emphatically not to say that it could not have occurred."[1]

What is the significance of this discussion for the student of history? In the first place, it points up the basic question of how human civilizations have developed—whether by diffusion from one or a few early centers or by independent inventions in various parts of the world. This question probes not only the origins of the American Indian civilizations but also the origins of civilizations throughout the globe. Did civilization spread from the Middle East to northwest Europe, North Africa, south Asia, and east Asia, or was it independently developed in these various regions? The controversy between the diffusionists and the independent inventionists has been long standing.

Increasingly we are realizing that it is not a case of either/or but rather of varying degrees of diffusion and independent invention. These varying degrees can be determined not by romantic speculations based on preconceived notions but rather by painstaking research and objective evaluation of the results. The more archeologists unearth human prehistory, the more they are realizing that all branches of the human race have been inventive in responding to their environments. The nature and the extent of their responses and achievements have varied greatly, depending on their historical and geographical backgrounds, especially the degree of accessibility to outside stimulation, as has been noted before.

Equally significant for students of history is the fact that many laypersons still cherish the vision of assorted Europeans, Asians, or Africans landing on the shores of the pre-Columbian New World, bearing aloft the torch of civilization. The fact is that humans today, as in earliest Paleolithic times, are mesmerized by the cult of the mysterious. They cling to romantic and simplistic explanations, even when they do not square with known facts. Our food-gathering ancestors depended on their totems and shamans or medicine men. Modern humans have similar faith in UFOs, numerology, tarot cards, intelligent plants, and astrology. Readers of this text will appreciate the significance of the following report by George Abell, professor of astronomy at the University of California, Los Angeles:

I have polled the general university students taking my survey astronomy courses and find that about a third have an interest and belief in astrology.

From discussions with my colleagues in other parts of the country I gather that about the same ratio holds everywhere and that it probably fairly well represents the fraction of Americans who believe in astrology. It is estimated that there are more than 5,000 astrologers making a living in the subject in the United States. More than 1,200 daily newspapers carry astrology columns.[2]

Professor Abell's report was made in 1975. Polls since that date indicate that faith in astrology is steadily increasing. Between 1980 and 1985 the proportion of American teenagers who believe in astrology has grown from 40 to 55 percent.[3] This resurgence of astrology today is especially noteworthy in view of the fact that it largely disappeared when modern astronomy began in the sixteenth century.

Similarly a 1996 *Newsweek* poll disclosed that 48 percent of Americans believe UFOs (Unidentified Foreign Objects) are real, and 29 percent think we've made contact with aliens, while another 48 percent believe there is a government plot to cover it all up. More specifically, some stargazers claim to have seen Elvis eating fried chicken on Uranus. Nor are Americans unique in this respect. In France, nearly 50,000 taxpayers in 1995 declared income from their work as stargazers, healers, mediums, and similar occupations. By contrast, France has 36,000 Roman Catholic priests and 6,000 psychiatrists.[4]

SUGGESTED READINGS

An interesting analysis of science and irrationality is given by M. Gardner, *Fads and Fallacies in the Name of Science* (Dover, 1957). A recent and fascinating survey of this subject is by the late space scientist, Carl Sagan, *The Demon-Haunted World: Science as a Candle in the Dark* (Random House, 1997). A similar survey focused on the United States, is by J. Gilbert, *Redeeming Culture: American Religion in an Age of Science* (University of Chicago Press, 1997).

NOTES

1. C. L. Riley et al., *Man Across the Sea: Problems in Pre-Columbian Contacts* (University of Texas, 1975), pp. 448, 452–53.
2. *Los Angeles Times*, September 14, 1975.
3. Ibid., April 21, 1985.
4. *Newsweek*, July 8, 1996, p. 50; *New York Times*, April 30, 1996.

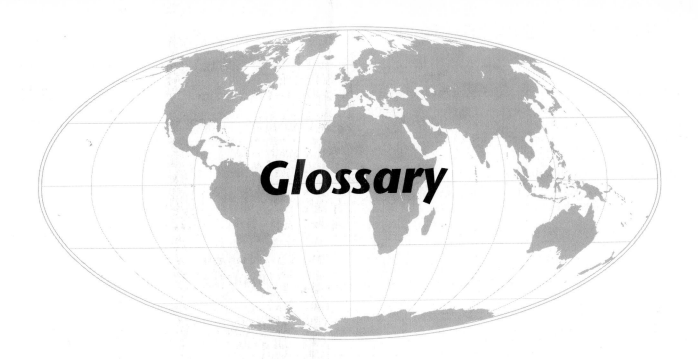

Glossary

agriculture   cultivating the soil, producing crops, and sometimes raising livestock

ahisma   nonviolence, a concept of India

Ainus   Caucasoid people who originally inhabited the Japanese islands

alienation   estrangement or withdrawal where good relationships formerly existed

ambivalent   being both attracted and repelled by a person or action

Anabaptists   members of a radical Protestant sect that arose in Zurich in 1524; it required adult as opposed to infant baptism, as well as nonresistance, mutual help, and separation of church and state

anachronism   a person or thing that is chronologically out of place

anarchy   lawlessness or disorder due to lack of governmental authority

apartheid   South African policy that excludes all nonwhites from any share in political life and confines Africans to separate areas known as Bantustands (preserves for the "Bantu" Africans)

archeologist   a person who determines the nature of past cultures by digging up and studying the things they have left behind

archeology   the science that determines the nature of past cultures from the study of things they have left behind

arts: liberal vs. servile   in the Middle Ages, liberal arts were done with the mind; servile arts involved a change in matter; e.g., a physician didn't change matter so his work was considered liberal, whereas a surgeon changed matter so his work was servile

asceticism   practice of self-denial

astrologers   those who study the stars and their imagined influence on human affairs

astronomy   science of the heavenly bodies and of their movements

audiencas   courts into which the huge vice-royalties of New Spain were divided

autarchic unit   self-sufficient, independent economic unit

Bantu   Negroid linguistic group originating in the Cameroon Highlands and later infiltrating the Congo Basin at the expense of the Bushmen and Pygmies; predominant ethnic group when the Europeans arrived in sub-Saharan Africa

benevolent despots   rulers such as Frederick the Great of Prussia (1740–1781), Catherine the Great of Russia (1762–1796), and Joseph II of the Hapsburg

Empire (1765–1790) who used their governmental authority for the benefit of the people

Bhopal city in India where a chemical accident in a Union Carbide Corporation pesticide plant in December 1984 resulted in over 2,000 deaths

biology the science that deals with living organisms

blitzkrieg new type of "lightning war" used by the Germans in World War II; first came dive bombers, then armored tank divisions called Panzers, and finally the lighter motorized divisions and infantry

Boers inhabitants of South Africa of Dutch descent

Bolsheviks literally "majority" in Russian; Lenin's followers

bourgeoisie the middle class, e.g., merchants, industrialists, professionals, etc.

boyars large landowners in tsarist Russia

Brahmins one of the highest Hindu castes; theoretically their occupation was that of priest or teacher; see *caste*

Buddhism a movement that was begun by Guatama Buddha in India in the fifth century B.C.E.; became full-fledged religion throughout Asia

bureaucracy a body of nonelected workers in any unit of government; first appeared in China

burghers middle-class townspeople

capitalism a system in which the desire for profits is the driving motive and capital is accumulated and used to make profits in a variety of ways

caste one of many hereditary groups in India that were originally based on color and occupation; there are four broad divisions with thousands of subdivisions; still in existence in rural India despite efforts to abolish them

Chernobyl town in the Soviet Union where a damaged nuclear reactor resulted, in April 1986, in radiation contamination of air, soil, water, and food supplies in the Soviet Union and in surrounding countries

city-state independent cities that were leaders of a particular region

civilization a stage of development in which people have achieved all or most of the following: writing, arts and sciences, cities, formal political organization, social classes, taxation

class differentiation the development from a homogeneous to heterogeneous society in which there is an increasing gap between rich and poor classes of people; opposite of egalitarian society

classical liberalism program by which the growing middle class proposed to get the benefits and control in government that it wanted; see also *democratic liberalism*

class struggle Marx's proposition that it is through conflict between opposing interests of classes that humankind has passed from one type of social organization to another

cold war name given to the series of crises after World War II that resulted from bad relations between the Communist and Western worlds

colonization establishment of settlements that are ruled by foreign countries

commercial agriculture agriculture in which most of the crops produced are sold for money rather than consumed by the family

commercial bonds ties based on the interchange of material goods; trade

Common Market an economic association with six original members: Italy, West Germany, Belgium, Netherlands, Luxembourg, and France; then in 1973 Britain, Ireland, and Denmark joined

concubine a mistress, or woman who lives with a man without marriage

Confucianism name given to the teachings of Confucius and his followers; mainly a practical moral system concerned with problems of everyday life and emphasizing conformity, propriety, and social responsibility

conquistadors New World soldiers of fortune from Spain; Cortes, conqueror of the Aztec Empire, is one of the best known

contemporary happening or existing in the same period of time

corvée compulsory labor, on projects such as building roads and fortifications

Cossacks Russian frontiersmen, mostly former serfs, who fled to the wild steppe country and became hunters, fishermen, and pastoralists

Crusaders people from Christian Europe who went on expeditions during the eleventh, twelfth, and thirteenth centuries seeking to capture the Holy Land from the Moslems

Crusades expeditions from Christian Europe during the eleventh, twelfth, and thirteenth centuries seeking to capture the Holy Land from the Moslems

cultural assimilation absorption into the cultural tradition of another group and the loss of one's own cultural identity

culture the way of life of a society; the ideas, habits, arts, and institutions that are passed on from generation to generation

cuneiform pictograph writings of ancient Mesopotamia; such writing is based not on the letters of an alphabet but on symbols that represent words or ideas; see *ideographic writing*

Cynicism Greek doctrine that held that virtue is the only good; everything else—riches, honor, freedom, even life itself—is contemptible

daimyo local lords in sixteenth-century Japan who fought each other to extend their domains

democratic centralism principle adopted by Lenin for the operation of the Social Democratic party; major issues were discussed freely, and decision reached by democratic vote; once a vote was taken every party member had to support the "party line" or be expelled

democratic liberalism doctrine that holds that the state is responsible for all its citizens; reforms of democratic liberalism were the prelude to the welfare state; see also *classical liberalism*

demographic pattern pattern of human population

dharma a Hindu and Buddhist term that means morality, obligations to family and society, and religious law

diadem headband worn as a badge of royalty

dialectics a science evolved by Socrates in which provisional definitions were tested by questions until universally recognized absolute truths were reached

diffusionists people who believe that human civilization developed by diffusion from the Middle East to northwest Europe, north Africa, south Asia, and east Asia

diviner one who prophesies or foresees

Domesday Book the record of a general survey of England ordered by William the Conqueror in 1086; it listed all the economic resources of the country

dowry the property that a wife brings to her husband in marriage

Duma Russian elective national assembly created after the Russian Revolution of 1905 and swept away by the Bolshevik Revolution of 1917

dyarchy dual system of government, as in Japan, where one family did the actual work of ruling while the emperor lived in luxurious seclusion and was responsible only for ensuring that his dynasty would continue forever

dynasty a succession of rulers of the same family

ecological pertaining to ecology, the science dealing with the relations between organisms and their natural environment

Economic and Social Council UN Council whose task was fighting hunger and disease; set up such agencies as the ILO; Food and Agriculture Organization; UN Education, Scientific and Cultural Organization; World Health Organization; and International Monetary Fund

ecosystem the complex of human community and natural environment, forming a functional whole

egalitarianism belief in human equality in all fields: economic, political, and social

empire a large area, usually including several countries or peoples, all under a single political authority

enclosures land closed off in England in the fifteenth to nineteenth centuries; left yeomen without grazing land or land for wood cutting; between 1714 and 1820 over 6 million acres were enclosed

enlightened despots see *Enlightenment* and *benevolent despots*

Enlightenment movement dating from the century prior to the French Revolution of 1789; leaders believed they lived in an enlightened age of reason and progress in contrast to the previous times of superstition and ignorance

Epicureanism Greek doctrine that defined philosophy as the art of making life happy, with pleasure (defined as serenity and avoidance of pain rather than indulgence) as the highest and only good

"equal-field system" during the Sun and T'ang dynasties in China, the central government gave plots of about nineteen acres each to all able-bodied peasants; in practice, only free peasants, and not even all of these, were given land

ethnic group a group that retains its own national characteristics, language, religion, customs, and institutions

ethnocentrism regarding one's own cultural group as superior and scorning all things alien

Europeanization term used to include political domination and cultural penetration by Europe as well as actual biological replacement of one people by another, as in the relatively empty territories of the Western Hemisphere and South Pacific that were inundated by European emigrants

evolution theory that all animals and plants have their origins in preexisting types and differences gradually evolved because of modifications in successive generations

extended family two or more married couples and their children

extraterritoriality right of foreigners to be exempt from the laws of a nation in which they are living; e.g., most ambassadors and diplomats are not subject to the laws of the nation in which they live but only to the laws of their own country

fecundity to be fruitful or fertile

feudalism political system that flourished in Europe from about the ninth to fifteenth centuries; a lord gave land to vassals, who in return, gave the lord military service

fiefs feudal estates granted by kings or lords as reward for military service; see *feudalism*

fluyt flyboat; a large, cheap Dutch merchant ship that was unarmed and had great capacity for carrying goods

food gatherer a person who collects foods, e.g., picks fruits, nuts, and plants; digs up roots and shellfish; catches fish

food-gathering culture culture in which people collect food as distinct from cultures in which people grow their food

food producer a peasant or farmer who grows food instead of gathering it

footbinding the practice of wrapping tightly the feet of young girls until the arch was broken and the toes were turned under—a procedure that stunted the feet to half normal size, crippled the girls for life, and made them dependent on men

foreclosure seizing of mortgaged property after failure to repay the mortgage or loan money

Fourteen Points Wilson's specific, detailed aims including open diplomacy, freedom of the seas, removal of international trade barriers, armament reduction, and application of the principle of self-determination to subject minorities in central and eastern Europe

franchise right to vote

fresco the art of painting on a surface of plaster

geocentric based on the earth as the center of perspective in contrast to heliocentric, or sun-centered

geology the science that studies the structure of the earth and the development of this structure in the past

giaours nonbelievers; derogatory term used by the Moslems to refer to their Christian subjects

Gosplan Soviet State Planning Commission, which prepared plans on the basis of general directions from the government and statistical data received from all parts of the country

gross national product (GNP) total output of goods and services of a country

habitat one's physical environment where one normally lives and grows up

hegemony influence of authority, economic or political, of one nation or people over another

Hellenism Greek culture that spread throughout the Middle East with the conquests of Alexander the Great

helot member of the lowest social class of ancient Sparta

hidalgos Spanish aristocrats who had most of the territorial wealth, were exempt from taxes, and looked down on people engaged in commerce and industry

hierarchy organization into a series of orders or ranks with each one subordinate to the one above it

hieroglyphics picture-writing system of ancient Egypt

high culture "upper-class" culture found in schools, temples, and palaces of the cities and passed on by philosophers, theologians, and literary men

Hinduism major religion of India

hominids humanlike ancestors of modern human beings who had a brain smaller and less developed than that of humans

homogeneity of similar or uniform structure throughout

Homo sapiens "thinking" humans; includes all members of the human race

hybrid vigor the superior qualities produced by interbreeding

ideographic script writing in which symbols represent ideas or objects; found in early China, Mesopotamia, and Egypt

imperialism the rule or control, political or economic, direct or indirect, of one state, nation, or people over similar groups; see also *new imperialism*

incipient agriculture the long gradual phase during which people made the shift from partial to full dependence on agriculture

independent inventionists people who believe that civilizations developed independently in the various regions of the globe

indigenous produced, growing, or existing naturally in a particular region

infanticide killing of infants; from Latin *cide* or kill, as in regicide, or killing of a king, and genocide, or killing of an entire people

injunction an order prohibiting a specified act

Islam the religion of the Moslems, based on the monotheistic teachings of the prophet Mohammed and spread by the Arabs; not only a religion but also a political system and social code

janissaries Ottoman infantrymen

joint stock companies sold stock or shares to investors who risked only the amount invested in the shares, regardless of what losses a company might have—a characteristic that encouraged investors to risk their money, and thus mobilized the large sums necessary for European economic expansion throughout the globe

jus gentium "law of the peoples"; a new body of law accepted by the Romans and applied to all peoples

jus naturale Roman legal concept that held that natural law was above that of mere custom

Koran bible of the Islamic faith; provided guidance for all phases of life—manners, hygiene, marriage and divorce, commerce and politics, crime and punishment, peace and war

kulaks well-to-do Russian peasants who were hostile to the Soviet regime; finally eliminated when agriculture was collectivized

Kuomintang Chinese National People's party founded by Sun Yat-sen

lactation taboo birth-control practice that forbade sexual intercourse while a woman was nursing a baby

latifundai large plantations that grew up in Italy in the second century B.C.E.; worked by slaves and owned by absentee landlords

Law of Retarding Lead the best adapted and most successful societies have the most difficulty in adapting during a period of transition and change

League of Nations created by the Versailles Treaty; its two basic objectives were (1) to preserve the peace and (2) to concern itself with health, social, economic, and humanitarian problems of international scope; failed in its first objective but succeeded in its second

Legalists adherents of a Chinese doctrine very different from Confucianism or Taoism; practicing statesmen interested in strengthening the princes they served so that they could wage war and unite the country by force; all aspects of life were regulated in detail by laws that would promote the state's economic and military power

Levellers group drawn mainly from the English lower-middle-class agricultural tenants who favored a democratic government and social reform

literocracy hierarchy of learned people such as those who ruled China before the intrusion of the West

low culture "lower-class" culture found in the villages and passed on by word of mouth among illiterate peasants

mandates people of the colonies taken from the Central Powers after World War I were regarded as unable to stand on their own feet; their tutelage was entrusted to "advanced nations" that were to exercise their tutelage on behalf of the League of Nations; this tutelage was not extended to the colonies of the victorious allies

manor a self-sufficient village worked by feudal serfs who had certain rights and responsibilities but were not free to move away

materialist interpretation of history Marx's theory that in every historical epoch the mode of economic production and exchange gives rise to a particular social organization and is the basic foundation for the political and intellectual history of that epoch

Mau Mau secret East African terrorist organization made up of members of the Kikuyu tribe

Mawali non-Arab Moslems

median situated at the midpoint between the two extremes, so that when nine incomes are arranged in order, the median income is the fifth from the top and from the bottom, whereas the average income is the sum of the nine incomes divided by nine

megalopolis very large urban unit; a big city

Mensheviks literally "minority" in Russian; Lenin's opponents within the Russian Social Democratic Party

mercantile activities see *commercial bonds*

mercantilism early modern rigid regulation of economic life in contrast to no regulation or "laissez-faire" policy

Mesoamerica central and south Mexico, Guatemala, and Honduras

mestizo person in Spanish America of mixed European and Indian origin

metallurgy the technique of extracting metals from ores

millennium period of 1,000 years; plural, millennia

modernization economists define modernization as the process by which humans have gained control over their physical environment by increasing output; sociologists and anthropologists term such features as the awakening and activation of the masses; more interest in the present and future than in the past; belief that human affairs are understandable rather than the result of supernatural manipulation; and until recently, faith in the beneficence of science and technology

monasticism life centered around the monastery, or dwelling place of persons under religious vows

monoculture cultivation of a single crop

multinational corporations business corporations that conduct commercial, industrial, or banking activities in many countries, and which are today's counterpart of the earlier *joint stock companies*

muzhik a Russian peasant

nationalism allegiance to the cause of the nation rather than to the church and region as before the nineteenth century

natural geopolitical center a natural central area whose location and physical features gave it regional leadership

natural selection an important part of the process of evolution; in the struggle for existence, the organisms whose genes are best adapted to the environment are selected and will survive and reproduce; the less well adapted will die out

Neo-Confucianism a combination of Buddhism and Taoism with Confucianism; believes humankind is good and capable of becoming more perfect, and evil is the result of neglect and defective education and can be corrected

Neolithic new stone age characterized by use of smooth, ground stone implements, and dependence on agriculture or food producing rather than food gathering

New Economic Policy (NEP) plan adopted by the Soviet government in 1921 that made some concessions; e.g., peasants were allowed to sell their produce on the open market, private individuals could operate small stores and factories and keep the profits

new imperialism the great European expansion of the late nineteenth century; differed from the old imperialist control of a state over another because it did not simply demand tribute but completely transformed the conquered countries

Nirvana the goal of Buddhism, which is to end sorrow by stopping desire; done by following the "eightfold path"

North Atlantic Treaty Organization (NATO) a mutual defense organization consisting of the United States, Canada, and several western European countries who agreed that "an attack on one or more of the signers is an attack upon all"

nuclear family married couple and their children

obsolescence the condition of being obsolete or out of date or out of fashion

oligarchy government controlled by a small group

Orthodox Christianity Greek Christian religion, which rejected leadership of the pope and instead was under the patriarch of Constantinople

orthodoxy belief in accepted standards and established doctrine

ostracism a form of punishment involving isolation or exclusion from a social group

ostrogs fortified posts or blockhouses built by the Cossacks as they advanced eastward

Paleolithic old stone age, characterized by use of rough, chipped stone implements and by dependence on food gathering

paleontology the science dealing with the life of past geological periods, as known from fossil remains

Palestine Liberation Organization (PLO) an organization consisting of several Palestinian nationalist groups; all are opposed to Israel but disagree about how an independent Palestinian state should be created

Panchayat elected council of five or more, usually caste leaders and village elders, who governed the traditional Indian village

paradox something absurd, false, and self-contradicting

parochialism being narrow or restricted—literally, confined to a parish

pastoral nomads people who make a living by domesticating animals and herding them from place to place in search of pastures

patrician aristocrat, or person of high birth

Pax Mongolica literally "Mongol Peace"; during the short period of Mongol peace, overland trade flourished from the Baltic to the Pacific because the Mongols ruled the entire area and kept the peace

Pax Romana literally "Roman Peace"; period brought about by Augustus and lasting for two centuries

peripheral located away from the center

philosophes a group who believed in the existence of natural laws that regulated the universe and human society

philosophical system system of ideas, beliefs, and attitudes

photosynthesis the process by which green plants utilize the energy of sunlight to manufacture carbohydrates from carbon dioxide and water—a process on which all plant and animal life on the planet depends

pictographs early cuneiform writing consisting of conventionalized pictures representing objects

plebians common people

Pleistocene epoch a period of glacial and interglacial stages during which animals adapted to changing environmental conditions

pluralism diversity or consisting of more than one

polis see *city-state*

praetorian a soldier of the imperial bodyguard of the Roman Caesars

productivity the conversion of resources into goods and services needed by humans; increased by using better seeds and tools, moving to better land, improving economic organization, etc.

proletariat the working class in industrial societies, e.g., workers in factories, mines, the docks, etc.

Quisling a Norwegian who collaborated with Hitler and whose name became a synonym for the self-serving traitor

rationalism a way of thinking based on logical thought and reason rather than on myths or traditional religion

Reformation basic upheaval that shattered the unity of Western Christendom; Martin Luther triggered the Protestant Reformation when he reacted against abuses in the Roman church

religious sanctions rewards and punishments to enforce rules of the religious elite

Renaissance intellectual and cultural awakening in Europe during the fifteenth to seventeenth centuries; emphasis was on the human being, and the purpose of life was to develop one's potentialities

revisionism a movement among twentieth-century socialists to adopt a "revised" strategy that depends on gradual reform instead of revolution to bring about a socialist society

sans culottes literally "those who lacked the knee breeches of genteel society"; French revolutionaries who wanted a more egalitarian state with equitable division of land; government regulation of prices and wages; and a social security system

savannas tropical or subtropical grasslands; treeless plains

Scholasticism a philosophy that taught that seeking God was more important than understanding nature, theology was the queen of the sciences, and one should turn to religion for succor and consolation in the face of material disaster

secession withdrawal from an organization such as a religious community or a political party

secular states states controlled by nonreligious leaders (layperson), as opposed to states controlled by religious leaders

Security Council UN Council made up of five permanent members, the United States, USSR, Britain, France, and China, and six two-year members elected by the General Assembly whose task is to maintain peace

self-determination the principle that all peoples should have the right to self-rule

shamans medicine men or women or sorcerers; individuals in early cultures who were part-time specialists and who used magical arts for the common good

sheikhs Arabian elective tribval chiefs who were leaders in the time of war

Shiite sect a Moslem sect that repudiated the first three successors of Mohammed; Persians (Iranians) identified with this sect

shogun generalissimo; a general who commanded military forces for the Japanese emperor

Silk Road overland route from China to the Middle East along which caravans transported Chinese silk, which was in demand throughout Eurasia

sinicization becoming modified by Chinese influence

Skepticism Greek doctrine that challenged the supremacy of reason and rationalism and adopted a questioning attitude

social homogeneity social equality that was a distinctive feature of Neolithic villages; all people shared equally in the ownership of land and other natural resources

socialism ideology calling for social and economic change and political reform; the government owns and operates the means of production and the main parts of the economy, e.g., banks, mines, factories, railroads, foreign trade, etc.; emphasizes community and collective welfare rather than the individual

soviets workers' elected councils that originated in the Russian Revolution of 1905 and reappeared in the 1917 revolution; soviets supplied the government with close rapport with the masses

steppe open, treeless plains with fertile black earth

stimulus diffusion a process that occurs when two different peoples first come in contact—they don't adopt one another's specific techniques or institutions completely but instead borrow underlying ideas or principles and adapt them to their specific needs; early civilizations often developed by this means

Stoicism Greek doctrine that accepted virtue as the highest good in life; people must put aside passion, unjust thoughts, and self-indulgence and perform their duties rationally and selflessly

strategos general in charge of both civil and military affairs in the Byzantine *themes*

subsistence agricultures type of agriculture that provides only the necessities of life, leaving little surplus for selling and buying; opposite of *commercial agriculture*

subsistence security multiple-crop agriculture providing a dependable food supply; if one crop failed peasants could depend on other crops for subsistence

suffragist one who favors extending suffrage, or the right to vote, to women

Sunnite sect a Moslem sect to which Turks and other surrounding peoples belonged and which set them apart from the Persian Shiites

surplus production of more goods and services than needed

surplus value Marxist theory that workers who provided the labor receive substantially less in wages than the price charged the consumer; hence the workers cannot buy what they produce; this leads to overproduction, unemployment, and finally, depression

suzerainty authority or rule or overlordship

taiga forest belt or zone

Taoism Chinese doctrine that stressed the importance of living naturally, conforming to nature's pattern; ambition was abandoned and honors and responsibilities rejected in favor of a meditative return to nature

tax farmer financier who paid a fixed sum to the central government for the privilege of collecting taxes in a given district and then kept for personal profit as much as could be collected above that sum

technology body of knowledge and skills evolved by humans to produce goods and services

thalassocracy civilization based on sea power, such as that of the Minoan civilization of Crete

themes provinces in the Byzantine empire

theocratic states states controlled by priests or other religious leaders

totem emblem or symbol of a particular group that stood for it or imposed rules on it; rules had to be observed to assure the well-being of the group

transformation to change very much the outward appearance or the internal structure

tribes inhabitants of villages of a given region identified and distinguished from others by their distinctive language and customs

tundra barren, frozen land along the Arctic coast

United Nations (UN) organization of nations set up in 1945 to carry out two basic tasks: (1) preserve peace and security and (2) set up international economic, social, and cultural programs; originally fifty charter members, with membership doubling by 1980

UNRRA UN organization set up to provide relief of all kinds to liberated countries; originated in the spring of 1944 and was to continue until the new national administrations could assume responsibility

urbanization shift from living in the countryside to the cities; development of characteristics typical to cities

utilitarian placing practical purpose above other considerations such as beauty

Utopian Socialists school of social reformers who produced blueprints for the operation of their projected model communities but did not indicate how these principles could be put into practice in the larger society

Vedas old and sacred Hindu texts consisting of hymns, prayers, and doctrines of Hindu divinities; similar to the Bible for Christians; *Veda* means knowledge

Versailles Treaty treaty with Germany, signed on June 28, 1919, that ended World War I; this treaty, together with separate treaties with the other Central Powers, are significant for world history because they applied the principle of self-determination to Europe but failed to apply it in overseas colonies

ward a person who is in the charge of or under the guardianship of another

Warsaw Pact formal military alliance concluded in May 1955 between Russia and the east European countries

white man's burden theory that Europeans were a superior race who had the duty to direct the labor and guide the development of inferior races; allowed Europeans to cloak their imperialism with a mantle of idealistic devotion to duty

World Zionist Organization nationalist Jewish movement established in Basel in 1897; wanted a Jewish commonwealth in Palestine after the end of the Ottoman Empire

Young Turks pioneer group of Turkish nationalists who wanted a new modern government in place of the Ottoman Sultanate

Zaibatsu literally "wealth-clique"; general name given to four giant family corporations that by World War II controlled three-fourths of the combined capital of all Japanese firms, three-fourths of all trust deposits, and one-fifth of all life insurance policies

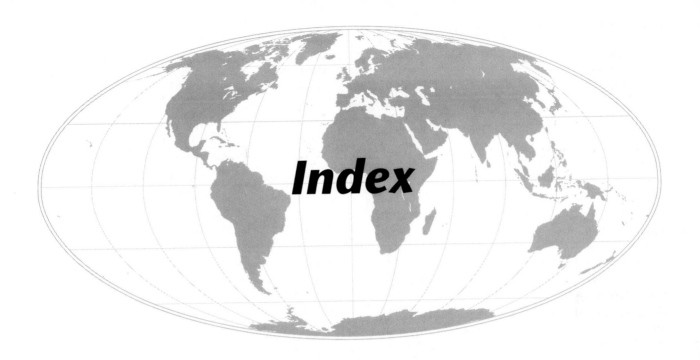

Index